Seventh Edition

YOUR GUIDE TO
COLLEGE SUCCESS

Strategies for Achieving Your Goals

Jane S. Halonen

John W. Santrock

WADSWORTH
CENGAGE Learning

Australia • Brazil • Japan • Korea • Mexico • Singapore • Spain • United Kingdom • United States

Your Guide to College Success: Strategies for Achieving Your Goals, Seventh Edition
Jane Halonen and John Santrock

Senior Publisher: Lyn Uhl

Executive Editor: Shani Fisher

Development Editor: Beth Kaufman

Assistant Editor: Joanna Hassel

Editorial Assistant: Sarah Turner

Media Editor: Amy Gibbons

Marketing Director: Jason Sakos

Marketing Coordinator: Brittany Blais

Senior Marketing Communications Manager:
   Linda Yip

Content Project Manager: Jill Quinn

Senior Art Director: Pam Galbreath

Manufacturing Planner: Sandee Milewski

Rights Acquisition Specialist:
   Shalice Shah-Caldwell

Production Service: Cenveo Publisher Services

Text and Cover Designer: Lisa Buckley

Cover Images: Students Studying on Steps:
   © John Giustina/Getty Images; Teenagers
   working on laptops in library: © Anderson
   Ross/Getty Images; Student planner:
   © Cengage Learning

Compositor: Cenveo Publisher Services

For product information and technology assistance, contact us at
Cengage Learning Customer & Sales Support, 1-800-354-9706

For permission to use material from this text or product,
submit all requests online at **www.cengage.com/permissions**

Further permissions questions can be emailed to
permissionrequest@cengage.com

Library of Congress Control Number: 2011942001

Student Edition:
ISBN-13: 978-1-111-83433-3
ISBN-10: 1-111-83433-4

Wadsworth
20 Channel Center Street
Boston, MA 02210
USA

Cengage Learning is a leading provider of customized learning solutions with office locations around the globe, including Singapore, the United Kingdom, Australia, Mexico, Brazil and Japan. Locate your local office at **international.cengage.com/region**

Cengage Learning products are represented in Canada by Nelson Education, Ltd.

For your course and learning solutions, visit **www.cengagebrain.com**

Purchase any of our products at your local college store or at our preferred online store **www.cengagebrain.com**

Instructors: Please visit **login.cengage.com** and log in to access instructor-specific resources.

Printed in the United States of America
1 2 3 4 5 6 7 15 14 13 12 11

Brief Contents

Contents

Carlos E. Santa Maria /Shutterstock.com

CHAPTER 4   Master Communication Skills and Build Relationships   97

CHAPTER 5   Navigate Differences   129

©Sonda Dawes / The Image Works

lightpoet/Shutterstock.com

CHAPTER 9 Succeed on Tests 289

CHAPTER 10 Express Yourself 327

GoGo Images/Superstock

Andresr/Shutterstock.com

CHAPTER 11   Take Charge of Your Physical and Mental Health   365

CHAPTER 12   Manage Money Intelligently   401

CHAPTER 13 Explore Careers   435

© Amy Etra/Photo Edit

Preface

Welcome to the 7th edition of *Your Guide to College Success*. We have written this textbook to support the unique adventure that lies ahead of you as you adjust to and learn to thrive in college. As psychology professors, we have some specific goals in mind that we think sets this book apart from other college success books.

We strive to be *encouraging*. It wasn't too long ago that first-year students typically encountered a long-winded speech during their orientation experience from a college official that went something like this: "Look to your left. Look to your right. Only *one* of you will *survive* to graduation…Will it be YOU?" We strongly disagree with this "motivational" strategy. We believe that by designing your life to incorporate a college education, you are making one of the wisest choices you can make. We want to do everything we can, working in concert with your talented instructors, to make this a meaningful and valuable experience that will give you a great foundation for college and for life.

We strive to be *personal*. We write with the full range of students in mind who will be taking this course. We draw examples from traditional-aged, "Millennial" students in face-to-face classes, from students who are starting college later in life, and from those whose college experience will be purely digital. Our backgrounds in psychology make us particularly attuned to the special stressors involved in managing college and living life. We know what it takes, not just to adjust in college, but to thrive in this new environment.

We strive to be *practical*. Throughout the text, we emphasize specific helpful strategies that will expand your options about how to handle the variety of challenges that college will impose. We wrote the book from the standpoint of creating the book we wish we had been able to use when we were just starting out. We emphasize helping you to become a reflective learner who knows how to solve problems effectively. Your experiences with this book should help you become a better critical and creative thinker.

We strive to be *engaging*. We take pride in generating writing that should be both informative and fun to read. By using real examples, vivid illustrations, and approachable language, we hope you look forward to your reading assignments in this course.

The College Success Learning Model

We use a unique six-part learning model to provide the basic infrastructure for the book. This easy-to-navigate model should help you master your college experience by focusing on achievable strategies that involve the following areas:

Know Yourself Each chapter opens with an opportunity to assess yourself in order to prepare you for what the chapter has to offer. Embedded in the chapter will be short self-assessments that give you an opportunity to pause and reflect about what the content means to you. Each chapter ends with several more detailed self-assessments to help you make the most of your learning gains in the chapter.

Clarify Values College offers a great opportunity to challenge the beliefs and values you currently hold. As a consequence, you may change your beliefs or develop new rationales to hold even tighter to your original values. Along the way, you will learn to clarify expectations that affect your performance—from the faculty, from your family, and from yourself.

Develop Competence No matter what your incoming level of skill might be, college will assist you to develop and refine in many arenas of life. Not only will your academic abilities improve, but you should develop skill sets that will have great appeal to employers following graduation.

Manage Life College won't be stress free. However, you can learn some specific strategies that can help you cope with both the predictable and unpredictable stresses college has to offer.

Connect and Communicate You are not in this alone! This dimension encourages you to explore and exploit all of the resources that college and your potential social networks can provide to help you achieve your goals.

Build a Bright Future Chances are that you see a college diploma as the key to success in life after college. We encourage you to think about how even your early experiences can set the stage for a bright future indeed.

Other Features of the Text

We have organized each chapter around the central themes that will help you achieve success in college. Your instructor may choose a different order than we have presented. However, if you know that there are some particular areas where you may need more immediate help, by all means, read ahead! For example, if you aren't very confident about the best way to take notes in college, take a look at Chapter 7, "Take Winning Notes," to help you address your concerns now.

In addition to the six-part learning model, we offer other features throughout the book:

- Chapter opening "spotlights" that describe real accomplishments of other students who have gracefully managed first-year challenges
- Additional "spotlights" embedded in the chapters, also drawn from real life, that illustrate central ideas
- Chapter outlines that help you anticipate the nature of topics that can be found in each chapter
- Boxed features that offer highlights or stories to drive home important principles
- Vivid photos that make chapter situations come to life
- Some of our favorite cartoons that can bring a smile to your face and help you not take life quite so seriously
- Review questions to help you assess how much you have learned and to promote mastery

Bryan Mauk

Spotlight On...

Helping the Homeless

Bryan Mauk was a college student at John Carroll University in Cleveland, Ohio, when he cofounded the Labre Project, named for the patron saint of the homeless. Bryan played a major role during his college years in providing food and personal contact to the homeless in Cleveland; the Labre Project reached 200 people a week. During his junior year, he was talking to five individuals who were living downtown in an alley dumpster when one man named Mike said, "Look around, remember us, graduate, and do something." For his community efforts, Bryan was one of four recipients of the Howard R. Swearer Student Humanitarian Award in 2007, and he recalls proudly that Mike was among the many friends who cheered him at graduation. With the aid of a subsequent grant from the Intercollegiate Studies Institute Simon Fellowship, Bryan

Photo Courtesy of Bryan Mauk

Your Journal

Your Journal

👥 Clarify Expectations

1. A Shared Path to Success

Form a small group in your college success class to compare your expectations for taking notes in this course. If you have another course in common, compare your approaches to that content area as well. See whether as a group you can determine which approaches are most effective in capturing the critical ideas in these contexts. How does the type of course influence note-taking strategies?

_____

_____

_____

2. Show and Tell

Carefully look over the notes that you have taken in a course where your learning isn't coming easily. Think about what clues to your struggle may be present in how you take notes. For example,

- Are you staying tuned in throughout the class?
- Are you writing down words that you don't understand?
- Do the lecture notes fit with the big picture?

Then follow up on your reflection by visiting your instructor during posted office hours. Take your notes and your observations with you. Ask the instructor to review your approach to see if other suggestions might improve your gains from note taking.

👤 Develop Competence

3. Note Taking Now

Spend the next 10 minutes skimming the next chapter in this text and creating an outline of its content. After you are done, compare your outline with the one the authors provide on the first page of the chapter. How was your outline similar or different? Did you miss any main ideas or capture any additional points? Think about how your presentation of content might differ if you had made a concept map or summary. Which strategy do you think works best for you?

_____

_____

_____

4. Primary versus Secondary Accounts

Read a newspaper account (a secondary source) of a recent scientific achievement or issue and list it below. Then ask a librarian to help you track down the original work (the primary source) in a scientific journal at the library or online. Compare the length of the reports, the language level difficulty, the order of importance of ideas, and any other contrasting features. Based on your observations, how would you say that primary and secondary sources differ?

Scientific achievement or issue: _____

Focus of secondary source: _____

Focus of primary source: _____

How do they differ? _____

📁 Manage Life

5. Daydream Believer

One of the biggest obstacles to successful listening in class is the tendency to daydream. Monitor your listening in your current courses for 1 week. In which class did you daydream the most? Why do you think this is happening? Perhaps the room is too hot or the lecture falls right after lunch. List some possible reasons below. Now list some strategies for conquering your daydreams and implement these strategies next week.

Daydreaming in class: _____

Possible reasons: _____

Strategies: _____

6. Word for Word

You notice that a friend who sits next to you in a particularly tough class exhausts himself by trying to take down every word the professor utters. Since the professor is a particularly speedy lecturer, it is no wonder your friend is worn out by the time class is over. What arguments would you mount to help your friend adopt a more strategic and less exhausting style?

_____

_____

_____

- Journal activities that take learning a step further and promote stronger reflection and writing skills
- Self-assessments that help you personalize your learning and set appropriate individual goals

New to This Edition

The 7th edition is a comprehensive revision in terms of both content and physical design. We listened carefully to our talented reviewers to make *Your Guide to College Success* an invaluable tool for college students of all kinds— new and returning, native-born and international. Our choices for updated student profiles carefully reflect a broad range of examples that include, among others, the oldest college graduate in America, a Rhodes scholar, a hockey star, and a first-generation student who happily graduated without debt.

Because it is never too early to begin thinking about what happens after graduation, we have expanded the content of each chapter's closing section, "Build a Bright Future." Your careful consideration of these components will provide you with the skill sets and focus necessary to achieve career success beyond your diploma.

We have added hundreds of new references to make each chapter more current and satisfying. Some highlights of those additions include choosing to live a more purpose-driven life (Chapter 1); expanded treatment of high-risk behavior in college (Chapter 2); the advantages of the pursuit of excellence (Chapter 3); rebounding from heartbreak (Chapter 4); recognizing and overcoming tendencies to stereotype (Chapter 5); growth opportunities through service learning (Chapter 6); the link between good reading habits and job success (Chapter 7); strategies for thriving in online learning environments (Chapter 8); developing test resilience (Chapter 9); building a professional portfolio (Chapter 10); interpreting health warning signs to reduce negative consequences (Chapter 11); strategies to overcome excess spending (Chapter 12); and the importance of developing flexibility to face an uncertain future (Chapter 13).

Our textbook is well-known for its well-tailored learning activities included at the end of each chapter to help you develop your critical thinking, problem-solving, and creative thinking skills. We kept the assignments that worked especially well, tweaked assignments that needed attention, and invented new approaches to foster those important learning outcomes.

For Instructors

An additional service available with the text is access to TeamUP, an unparalleled suite of services provided by Cengage Learning that offers you flexible and personalized assistance with using our programs and integrating them with your course materials. Whether online, on the phone, or on campus, TeamUP College Survival Consultants will strive to deliver high-quality service, training, and support. The team of consultants have a wide variety of experience in teaching and administering the first-year course. They can provide help in establishing or improving your student success program. They offer assistance in course design, instructor training, teaching strategies, annual conferences, and much more. Learn more about TeamUP today by calling 1-800-528-8323 or visiting http://www.cengage.com/teamup.

Instructor's Manual and Test Bank for *Your Guide to College Success: Strategies for Achieving Your Goals*, 7th Edition This guide for teaching the first-year seminar course includes sections on dealing with course challenges, using popular culture in the classroom, creatively applying the text features, and integrating technology resources. Each chapter also contains a convenient chapter overview, additional activities, collaborative learning suggestions, alternative teaching strategies, and quiz questions.

PowerLecture for *Your Guide to College Success: Strategies for Achieving your Goals*, 7th Edition This complete resource for instructors includes PowerPoint slides; ExamView, a premiere test-building program that allows instructors to quickly create tests and quizzes customized to individual courses; and additional resources to support your first-year experience course.

Custom Publishing Options Faculty can select chapters from this and other Wadsworth College Success titles to bind with your own materials into a fully customized book. For more information, contact your Cengage Learning sales representative or visit http://www.cengage.com/custom.

For Students

College Success CourseMate for *Your Guide to College Success: Strategies for Achieving your Goals*, 7th Edition The CourseMate includes an interactive eBook, interactive teaching and learning tools including quizzes, flashcards, videos, and more, as well as Engagement Tracker, a first-of-its-kind tool that monitors student engagement in the course. Go to www.cengagebrain.com for more information.

College Success Factors Index 2.0 College Success Factors Index (CSFI) 2.0 is an online survey that students complete to assess patterns of behavior and attitudes in areas that have been proven by research to affect student outcomes for success in higher education. A *Your Guide to College Success* specific CSFI course can be created to provide your students with specific remediation from the assessment to readings and exercises from the textbook. For more information, visit http://www.cengage.com/success/csfi2.

The College Success Academic Planner The College Success provides students with a spiral-bound calendar designed specifically for first-year college students. Featuring 18-month coverage, a unique design, and plenty of room for students to record their academic and personal commitments and schedule, the planner is a great way to encourage time management skills. For a minimal extra charge, the planner can be offered as a bundle with the textbook.

Acknowledgments

We consider ourselves to be among the luckiest of textbook writers.

We enjoy the process of making textbooks and have been blessed to be able to work with a Cengage team comprised of very talented people who share our passion for making books. We are most grateful to Shani Fisher, Executive Editor, Beth Kaufman, Developmental Editor, Sarah Turner, Editorial Assistant, and Jill Quinn, Content Product Manager for helping us realize the vision we had for this 7th edition of *Your Guide to College Success*. This particular edition was not only gratifying to develop, it was fun.

We are also lucky to have chosen spouses—Brian Halonen and Mary Jo Santrock—who have infinite patience with our long absences, who reflect enthusiasm about new ideas, and who help us to not take ourselves so seriously.

Our luck extends to the exceptional help we received from an extremely perceptive cadre of reviewers whose ideas helped us make this 7th edition into a much better book.

Rebecca Campbell, *Northern Arizona University*
Matthew McGraw, *Dabney S. Lancaster Community College (Virginia)*
Evelyn Peavy, *Copiah-Lincoln Community College (Mississippi)*
Anna Shiplee, *University of West Florida*
Theresa Wozencraft, *University of Louisiana at Lafayette*

Finally, we would be remiss if we did not thank reviewers who assisted us in previous editions. We are grateful for their contributions to the evolution of a book that we think justifies our pride.

Anne Aiken-Kush, *University of Nebraska, Omaha*

Alicia Andrade-Owens, *California State University, Fresno*

Frank Ardaiolo, *Winthrop University*

Diane D. Ashe, *Valencia Community College*

Clarence Balch, *Clemson University*

Marilyn Berrill, *Joliet Junior College*

Nate Bock, *University of Nebraska, Omaha*

Michelle Bowles, *University of North Dakota*

Phyllis Braxton, *Pierce College, Los Angeles*

Cynthia Bryant, *Tennessee Technical University*

Tricia Bugajski, *University of Northeast Oklahoma*

Bev Cavanaugh, *Joliet Junior College*

Diana Ciesko, *Valencia Community College*

Dorothy R. Clark, *Montgomery Community College*

Karen Clay, *Miami Dade College*

Rebecca Cole, *Northern Arizona University*

Carol A. Copenhefer, *Central Ohio Technical College*

Colleen Courtney, *Palm Beach Community College*

Dr. Kara Craig, *University of Southern Mississippi*

Anne Daly, *Cumberland County College*

Jan Daly, *Florida State University*

Susann B. Deason, *Aiken Community College*

Cynthia Desrochers, *California State University, Northridge*

Anthony R. Easley, *Valencia Community College*

Barbara Eddins, *Missouri Western State University*

Susan Epstein, *Drexel University*

Barbara Foltz, *Clemson University*

Stephen Ford, *Anne Arundel Community College*

Cheryl Fortner-Wood, *Winthrop University*

Yvonne Fry, *Community College of Denver*

D. Allen Goedeke, *High Point University*

Lewis Gray, *Middle Tennessee State University*

Lorraine Gregory, *Duquesne University*

Laurie Grimes, *Lorain Community College*

M. Katherine Grimes, *Ferrum College*

Erica Henningsen, *Colorado School of Mines*

Thomas N. Hollins, Jr., *J. Sargeant Reynolds Community College*

Hollace Hubbard, *Lander University*

Lucky Huber, *University of South Dakota*

Cynthia Jenkins, *University of Texas, Dallas*

Elvira Johnson, *Central Piedmont Community College*

Laura Kauffman, *Indian River Community College*

Elizabeth Kennedy, *Florida Atlantic University*

Susan Landgraf, *Highline Community College*

Christine Landrum, *Mineral Area College*

Alice Lanning, *University of Oklahoma*

Judy Lynch, *Kansas State University*

Jeannie Manning, *University of Nebraska, Kearney*

Sabrina Marschall, *University of Maryland, University College*

Maritza Martinez, *State University of New York, Albany*

Kathleen McGough, *Broward Community College*

Alison Murray, *Indiana University/Purdue University, Columbus*

Donna Musselman, *Santa Fe Community College*

Christina Norman, *University of Oklahoma*

Jean Oppel, *Oklahoma State University*

David M. Parry, *Pennsylvania State, Altoona*

Jori Beth Psencik, *University of Texas, Dallas*

Glen Ricci, *Lake Sumter Community College*

Ricardo Romero, *University of New Mexico*

Marti Rosen-Atherton, *University of Nebraska, Omaha*

Diane Savoca, *St. Louis Community College*

Regina C. Schmidt, *Texas Women's University*

Kimberly Shaw, *Boise State University*

Karen Siska, *Columbia State Community College*

Susan Sparling, *California Polytechnic State University*

Kathleen Speed, *Texas A&M University*

Sarah Spreda, *University of Texas, Dallas*

Lester Tanaka, *Community College of Southern Nevada*

Nancy Taylor, *Radford University*

Karen Valencia, *South Texas Community College*

Vivian Van Donk, *Joliet Junior College*

Kimberly Vitchkoski, *University of Massachusetts, Lowell*

Mary Walz-Chojnacki, *University of Wisconsin, Milwaukee*

Vicki White, *Emmanuel College*

Donald Williams, *Grand Valley State University*

Kathi Williams, *College of the Siskiyous*

Janie H. Wilson, *Georgia Southern University*

Brenda Winn, *Texas Technical University*

Kaye Young, *Jamestown Community College*

The College Success Model

Chapter 1

KNOW YOURSELF

CONGRATULATIONS! You have made one of the smartest decisions of your life by pursuing a college education. The goal of this book is to help you get the most out of your college experiences.

What is life like as you make this transition through your first year of college? To evaluate where you stand right now, place a check mark below in the appropriate space that applies to you, leaving the others blank.

Am I Ready for the Challenges of College?

	Very Much Like Me	Somewhere In Between	Not at All Like Me
I can describe my identity and values and how they will influence my success in college.			
I know what others will expect of my performance in college.			
I have positive expectations that I will succeed in college.			
I have effective thinking skills that will help me develop competence as I go through college.			
I manage my life effectively in many areas by being personally responsible, setting smart goals, and overcoming obstacles.			
I'm good at connecting and communicating with others.			
I am confident about my ability to create a positive future for myself following college.			
I know why building positive character is important.			

Spotlight On...

Malea Ritz
Making a Solid Transition

Malea Ritz knows about the frustrations, pressures, and joys of making a successful transition into college life. As a freshman journalism major at the University of Massachusetts, she met and conquered the challenges involved in starting college. What surprised Malea most about her first term in college?

Courtesy of Malea Ritz

Malea Ritz has a lot to smile about regarding her successful navigation of the challenges of her first term in college.

The Living Conditions. Residence hall life offers many adjustment challenges, especially those related to the serious loss of privacy. Walls are "paper thin," and bathroom and dressing space must be shared. Managing flimsy toilet paper and wearing flip flops in the shower fueled Malea's occasional questioning of the value of living at school until family and friends persuaded her that those stressors were normal and that she would adjust.

The Social Life. Malea described feeling some pressure to be extra friendly to her hallmates and to establish a social network quickly, but she concluded that finding new friends was easy to do. She followed some good advice from her resident assistant and left her door open during the first week of campus. It was strange operating "on display," but the practice may have broken down some barriers and given her a chance to get to know some people.

The Food. Malea pointed out a paradox of meal contracts. "Use all of your swipes, but don't get fat," she stated. Initially the all-you-can-eat option is attractive, but she knew that unrestrained eating can produce the "Freshman 15" (weight gain) consequence. She also acknowledged that the novelty of cafeteria dining quickly wears off, but most students don't have discretionary income to cover other options.

The Work. An honors student in high school, Malea tended to save up all her homework for Sundays, but she quickly discovered that this strategy wouldn't work in college. She claimed that she initially failed to recognize that college students must dedicate substantial time out of class to get a seemingly impossible workload under control. Although it may not be possible to get everything done, she proudly managed the academic demands to achieve a 3.6 GPA for her first term.

What was most critical to Malea's success in her first term? Malea stated that it wasn't until her second semester when she felt settled into her decision about college. She opted to move to a new residence hall closer to friends who shared her values. She also expanded her circle of friends through extracurricular activities on campus. She strongly recommended getting involved in campus life immediately to help identify the important relationships that will help you thrive in college.

(Source: Ritz, 2011)

The College Success Model

This book is organized around a model that maximizes your ability to succeed in college. As you will see, the College Success Model begins with the core dimension of understanding yourself better: *Know Yourself*. The model then provides five other key dimensions that highlight specific strategies for guiding your college success: *Clarify Expectations*, *Develop Competence*, *Manage Life*, *Connect and Communicate*, and *Build a Bright Future*. The model's six dimensions are portrayed in Figure 1.1.

In the following sections, you will become familiar with these six components of college success, and throughout the book you will learn about valuable strategies related to these components. We begin with the core dimension: Know yourself.

FIGURE 1.1

🖼 Know Yourself

In *Alice in Wonderland*, nineteenth-century author Lewis Carroll posed an intriguing question: "Who in the world am I? That is the great puzzle." College provides the perfect setting in which to answer that important question. Two of the important aspects of knowing yourself involve establishing or refining your identity and recognizing the values that influence your identity.

Establish Identity

Identity is a self-portrait that is composed of many pieces (Erikson, 1968). Think about the rich array of factors that contribute to defining who you are:

- The career and work path you want to follow (vocational/career identity)
- Your religious or spiritual beliefs (spiritual identity)
- Whether you are politically conservative, liberal, or middle of the road (political identity)
- Whether you are single, married, divorced, or cohabiting (relationship identity)
- The extent to which you are motivated to achieve and are intellectual (achievement identity)
- Whether you enjoy learning (intellectual identity)
- Whether you are heterosexual, gay or lesbian, or bisexual (sexual identity)
- Which part of the world or country you are from (national or regional identity)
- How intensely you identify with your cultural and ethnic heritage (cultural/ethnic identity)
- The things you like to do, such as sports, music, and hobbies (leisure interest identity)
- Your personality traits (such as whether you are introverted or extraverted, anxious or calm, friendly or hostile, and so on) (personality identity)
- Your body image (physical identity)

You probably recognized from the extensive list that developing an identity is a complex process. Your college experiences will challenge and likely change how you think about yourself.

Psychologist James Marcia (1994) concluded that people vary in the degree to which they are willing to explore and are able to commit to a specific identity. He proposed that each of us has one of four identity statuses based on exploration and commitment:

- *Identity diffusion* occurs when you haven't yet done much exploration or committed to an identity. You might have this status when you are just starting out in college and haven't yet explored or committed to a major. It's a good thing to claim proudly that you are "exploring" majors rather than feel uncomfortable about being "undeclared."
- *Identity foreclosure* consists of making a commitment without adequately exploring alternatives. For example, you may have arrived at college firmly committed to becoming an accountant "just like mom," and you have said you aren't going to consider any other pathway, even if an alternative could be a better match for your talents. Think about how a closed, too-early decision about a major or a career might deprive you of a more fulfilling experience.
- *Identity moratorium* involves being in the midst of exploring an identity, but having not made a clear commitment to an identity. In this example, you can be torn between majors or may experience multiple decisions about changing majors because none feels quite right. This pattern, too,

is normal, since you may change majors several times before settling into the one with the best fit.

- *Identity achievement* happens when commitment follows a healthy period of exploration. Ideally, college should facilitate this accomplishment by the time you graduate. There is some value in striving to declare a major by the time your general education requirements are over, since it will be more expensive and time-consuming to change your major if it means starting over on new requirements.

To evaluate your identity status in these different areas, complete Know Yourself: Self-Assessment 1.1, "What Is My Identity?," at the back of the chapter on page 22.

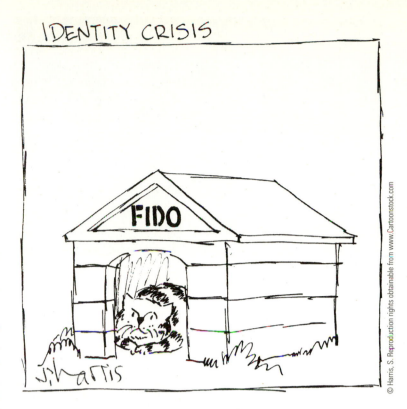

IDENTITY CRISIS

FIDO

© Harris, S. Reproduction rights obtainable from www.Cartoonstock.com

Your first identity is just that—your *first*. As you go through your college and adult years, many of you will change and change quite a bit. Based on the wealth of experiences college has to offer, you will reevaluate how satisfied you feel with aspects of your identity. You may embrace the identity you started with, revise your identity slightly, or abandon it in exchange for an identity you didn't know existed when you began your journey. In college, it is normal to ask ongoing questions about your identity development.

Some of you taking this course are traditional-age college students—18 to 21 years of age; for you, the college experience may produce a profound change in identity. Nontraditional or returning students have accumulated extensive life experiences before going to college and tend to be older than traditional-aged college students. If you are a nontraditional student, going back to college probably has prompted you to expect a less dramatic impact on your identity. Although both groups have "college student" as a common feature of identity, they also have distinctive features.

Emerging Adulthood If you are a traditional-age college student and have recently made the transition from high school to college, a new label likely describes you—*emerging adult* (Arnett, 2007, 2010). What does this term mean? Although emerging adults are 18 to 25 years of age, many feel in-between, considering themselves neither adolescents nor full-fledged adults yet. They experiment and explore, concentrating on what they want their identity to be and which career path and lifestyle they want to follow.

Most emerging adults also have a great deal of autonomy in directing their own lives. For many, the experience of self-direction is new and a little scary. Much like the student Malea Ritz, profiled at the beginning of this chapter, you may not even realize the degree to which your parents managed your time and addressed your needs before you started college. In college, nobody treats you like a kid anymore. You have more independence, choices, and responsibility. You are more on your own about how you use your time than you were in high school. For students who have experienced difficult times while growing up, emerging adulthood presents an opportunity to turn their lives in a more positive direction. In sum, emerging adults are at the "age of possibilities," a

Two main characteristics of Millennial students are their sophisticated use of technology and their ethnic diversity.

time when they have abundant opportunities to transform their lives.

The generation of traditional-age college students in college today have been labeled *millennials*, meaning individuals born after 1980, the first generation to come of age in the new millennium (Howe, Strauss, & Matson, 2000). A recent national survey revealed several features that make millennials stand out when compared to earlier generations (Pew Research Center, 2010). Millennials are more ethnically diverse and comfortable with individual differences. Social critics also describe this generation as being more confident, social, self-expressive, upbeat, and open to change, but less religious, than older adults.

A hallmark of millennials is their technological savvy. Called "digital natives" by Mark Prensky (2001, 2010), millennials have been described in the following way (Pew Research Center, 2010, p.1):

> They are history's first "always connected" generation. Steeped in digital technology and social media, they treat their multi-tasking hand-held gadgets almost like a body part—for better or worse. More than 8-in-10 say they sleep with a cell phone glowing by the bed, poised to disgorge texts, phone calls, e-mails, songs, news, videos, games, and wake-up jingles. But sometimes convenience yields to temptation. Nearly two-thirds admit to texting while driving.
>
> In some cases, millennials' confidence may be counterproductive. Research reveals that they don't fully recognize the dangers of driving while texting or the inadequate learning that often results from multitasking (O'Brien, Goodwin, & Foss, 2010).

Returning Students An increasing number of students start or finish college at an older age. Today, more than one out of five full-time students and two-thirds of part-time students are returning students. Some work full-time, are married, have children or grandchildren, are divorced, retired, or changing careers. Some have attended college before, while others have not.

If you have entered or returned to college at an older age, you may experience college differently than recent high school graduates. You may have to balance your classwork with prior commitments to a partner, children, a job, and community responsibilities. Juggling these multiple roles means you may have less flexibility than traditional college students about when you can attend classes. You may need childcare or have special transportation needs. As an older student, you may lack confidence in your skills and abilities or undervalue your knowledge and experience. As a "digital immigrant," you may even be a little intimidated by how technologically adept your younger counterparts' skills are compared to your own technology skills (Prensky, 2001, 2010).

Despite such challenges, take heart. As a returning student, you bring specific strengths to campus. These include a wide range of life experiences that you can apply to issues and problems in class. In light of your multiple commitments, you may be a better time manager than younger students. You may have greater maturity in work habits and more experience and confidence participating in discussions. You may also rebound from setbacks more easily. Failing a pop quiz, for instance, is not likely to feel as devastating for those who have experienced greater disappointments in life.

Regardless of your generation, the following strategies can help you get off to a good start in college:

- *Evaluate your support system.* A strong and varied support system can help you adapt to college. If you have a partner or family, their encouragement and understanding can provide crucial support. Your parents are just a phone call or e-mail away. Old friends also can lend support.
- *Make new friends.* As you seek out friends of different ages, focus on finding people who build your confidence and commitment to success. Evaluate whether new relationships are healthy and invest in the ones that provide the best feelings of mutual regard and respect.
- *Work hard.* Succeeding in college will entail some sacrifices as well as skill in stress management. Go to classes and do as much of the expected work as you can, but build in some time to take breaks and get refreshed.
- *Get involved in campus life.* The campus is not just for younger students. Check out the organizations and groups at your college. Join one or more that interest you. Being involved will foster a positive outlook and build your social network.
- *Don't be afraid to ask for help.* Learn about the services your college offers. Health, advising, and counseling services can help not just with routine adjustment challenges, but also with related concerns such as parenting and childcare, divorce, and time management. If you have any doubts about your academic skills, get some help from the study skills professionals on your campus.

What are some strengths of returning students?

Recognize Values

Exploring and choosing values that reflect who you are is an important aspect of knowing yourself. Just what are "values"? *Values* are our beliefs and attitudes about the way we think things should be. They involve what is important to us. We attach values to all sorts of things: politics, religion, money, sex, education, helping others, family, friends, self-discipline, career, cheating, taking risks, self-respect, and so on. As the contemporary U.S. columnist Ellen Goodman commented, "Values are not trendy items that can be traded in."

Connect Your Values with College Success One of the most important benefits of college is that it gives you the opportunity to explore and clarify your values. Why is this so critical? Our values represent what matters most to us, so they should guide our decisions. Without seriously reflecting on what your values are, you may spend too much time in your life on things that really aren't that important to you. Clarifying your values will help you determine which goals you really want to go after and where to direct your motivation.

Think Deeply about Your Values Sometimes we're not aware of our values until we find ourselves in situations that expose them. For example, you might be surprised to find yourself reacting strongly when you discuss religion or politics with other students. Spend some time thinking about and clarifying your values. This will help you determine what things in life are most important to you. Know Yourself: Self-Assessment 1.2, "What Are My Values?," toward the end of the chapter on page 23 will help you with this process.

Many students place family relationships high on their list of values. Positive, supportive family relationships can help you through difficult times as you go through college. In Chapter 4: Master Communication Skills and Build Relationships, you will read about some positive strategies for connecting with parents. One self-assessment that you can take to discover the extent of your family's involvement in your values is called the College Success Factors Index. Your instructor may assign you to complete this self-assessment online.

For some students, family relationships can actually interfere with their college success. Family members can introduce turmoil and undermine your ability to concentrate. They can also be neglectful, demonstrating little interest in your new life. Either condition can undermine your self-confidence. However, the intensity of college can provide a good opportunity to impose some distance and begin to develop some new, more nourishing relationships.

Stephen Covey, author of the best-selling book *The Seven Habits of Highly Effective People: Powerful Lessons in Personal Change* (1989), has helped many individuals clarify their values. He stresses that each of us needs to identify the underlying principles that are important in our lives and then evaluate whether we are living up to those standards. Covey asks you to imagine that you are attending your own funeral and are looking down at yourself in the casket. You then take a seat, and four speakers (a family member, a friend, someone from your work, and someone from your church or community organization) are about to give their impressions of you. What would you want them to say about your life? This reflective thinking exercise helps you to look into the social mirror and visualize how other people see you.

Stephen Covey's work provides lots of insights about recognizing values. At the end of this chapter, there is an activity in Your Journal that you can complete based on Covey's ideas. The activity is designed to help you recognize the values that are most important to you. Your Journal appears at the end of every chapter to help you develop your thinking and writing skills based on your college experiences. Similarly, you will have the opportunity to try out self-assessment strategies in the body of the chapter and at the end of the chapter.

The Path to Purpose *The Path to Purpose* is the title of a recent book written by Stanford professor William Damon (2008). He argues that many adolescents, emerging adults, and adults have become effective at finding short-term solutions to various tasks and problems to get through their lives. He says that although these short-term solutions (such as getting homework done, getting a good grade on a test tomorrow, and making a team) are often necessary adaptations to a situation, they can distract you from thinking about your life purpose. Questions such as "What kind of person do I want to be?," "What do I want to do with my life?," and "Why should I try to be successful?" can stimulate you to explore the big, long-term picture of what you want to do with your life. These interview questions that Damon (2008, p. 135) has used in his research are good springboards for reflecting on your purpose:

- What's most important to you in your life?
- Why do you care about those things?

- Do you have any long-term goals?
- Why are these goals important to you?
- What does it mean to have a good life?
- What does it mean to be a good person?
- If you were looking back on your life now, how would you like to be remembered?

A writing exercise related to these important questions appears in Your Journal at the end of the chapter.

Forge Academic Values Throughout college, you will frequently have opportunities to clarify your academic values. For example, when you make a choice to linger over a computer game rather than get to class on time, you make a statement about what really matters to you. The frivolous minutes you spend in short-term pleasures may cost you some points on the next exam. Your choices reflect your values. Deciding early to do your best, even if it requires sacrifice, will have the best long-term pay-off. Although your primary goal in seeking a college education may be learning about new ideas, your journey through college can also help to build your character.

What is the best way to demonstrate positive academic values?

Participate Fully College involves a higher level of personal responsibility than most students experienced in high school. This freedom can be alluring, even intoxicating. Especially when instructors do not require attendance, you may be tempted to skip classes. What's wrong with skipping class?

- It's expensive. See Figure 1.2 to calculate how much a skipped class will cost.
- It harms your learning.
- It hurts your grades.
- It annoys those who end up lending you their notes to copy. (If you must miss a class, be sure to borrow notes from someone who is doing well in the course!)

Participating fully in college involves academic engagement, such as not missing classes, taking good notes in class, reading assignments on time, and pursuing new learning experiences. Participating fully in college also includes becoming connected to others in effective and meaningful ways by making new friends, joining campus organizations, and attending campus events. Throughout this book, you will learn strategies for participating more fully in college, including in Chapter 2: Pursue Resources.

Participate with Integrity Most campuses publish in their college handbooks their expectations about appropriate academic conduct. Many colleges have adopted an honor code to promote academic integrity.

The code represents your formal agreement to abide by rules of conduct that promote trust and high ethical standards. Typically, codes address such problems as cheating, plagiarism (submitting someone else's work for your own), or other forms of dishonest performance. When a student violates the campus honor code, it dictates how severe the consequences might be. These may include something as mild as "censure," formal recognition of wrongdoing, to expulsion from school.

How much tuition did you pay for this term?
How many credits must you take on your campus to be considered full-time?
Divide the full-time hours into your tuition dollars (cost per credit hour):
How many credit hours does the course you're most tempted to avoid have?
Multiply the course credit hours by the cost per credit hour (cost of the course):
How many classes meet in this course over the term? Divide the cost of the course by the number of classes:
The final calculation represents the financial loss that happens every time you cut this class.

FIGURE 1.2 The Cost of Cutting Class

Why should you embrace academic integrity and commit to doing your best?

- Practicing academic integrity builds moral character. Doing the right thing often means doing the hard thing.
- Choosing moral actions builds others' trust in you.
- Making fraudulent grades keeps you from learning important things that will benefit you in the future.

By analyzing your values, you gain a better idea of how to develop competence and where to direct your energy and motivation.

As we leave the core dimension of "Know Yourself," we move into the structure that you can expect in each of the following chapters. As you read each dimension, you will notice that we provide some personal interest stories ("Spotlight On . . .") to draw your attention to students who have found unique and successful ways to master their college experience or who simply have important perspectives to share on the topics in the chapter. At the conclusion of the chapter, a summary of the key ideas of the chapter are presented along with review questions that give you an opportunity to assess what you've learned in the chapter. Finally, each chapter concludes with Your Journal, which consists of reflective and writing exercises, such as the one about Stephen Covey discussed earlier.

# Clarify Expectations

As you go through college, you will grapple with many expectations. You have to deal with the expectations others have related to your commitment and performance, specific expectations that influence the work you do on assignments, and your own expectations about whether you can live up to the ideals you have developed. Clarifying your expectations in all of these areas will help you to function at a level that challenges you but is not beyond your reach.

Understand Perspectives

Each of us has *personal expectations* about what we can achieve and how successful we will be in our academic pursuits in college. However, your instructors, your advisers, roommates, parents, partners, and even members of the community will all have expectations about what you will do in college as well. It may help to spend some time understanding their perspectives and developing strategies about how to meet their expectations or to deal with consequences if you choose not to do so.

College gives you an opportunity to become "people smart." In Chapter 4: Master Communication Skills and Build Relationships, you will learn some valuable strategies to help you develop interpersonal skills that can launch, sustain, or enrich relationships that may become lifelong sources of support for you. Nonacademic relationships will be important to develop and sustain as well. If you have a partner or spouse, you will have to meet his or her expectations while you are pursuing academic success if the relationship is going to survive your educational experience. Learning how to balance school, family, and work is the focus of Chapter 3: Manage Time Wisely.

Figuring out what instructors want from you may occupy significant portions of your academic life. Their expectations can be very high. The expectations may be stated clearly in course syllabi or they can be assumed, in which case the instructor expects you to know what is "standard" behavior in the college culture. If you have been around a college campus before, navigating is probably easy. If not, assumed expectations may be hard to identify. We provide some help in Chapter 5: Navigate Differences.

Yet another area in which you will benefit from fulfilling positive expectations is making contributions to your community. Effective ways to reach these positive expectations involve looking for opportunities to participate in community activities and seeking ways to help others in the community. Explore service learning opportunities to participate in worthy projects. Through such projects, you can get to know the community and its needs in new ways. Typically, such programs will lead you to embrace your civic responsibilities. The benefits of service learning are further discussed in Chapter 2: Pursue Resources.

Many college students find ways of applying course concepts in projects, such as Habitat for Humanity, that will benefit the community.

Stay Positive

It helps to approach the challenge ahead with a positive outlook. Set high personal expectations for yourself; establish realistic expectations that stretch your ability but aren't so grandiose that you can't meet them. Being optimistic rather than pessimistic will increase your motivation to tackle tough problems and persist until you can find a solution. Every chapter in this book addresses ways to handle difficult challenges. For example, in Chapter 3: Manage Time Wisely, you will learn lots of tips for reducing procrastination, and in Chapter 11: Take Charge of Your Physical and Mental Health, you will read about a number of strategies for effectively coping with stress and overcoming obstacles.

 # Develop Competence

Competence involves your skills and attitudes that demonstrate how effective and efficient you are. Developing competence in college involves improving your thinking skills.

Think and Learn

Building competence means putting a great deal of effort into thinking and learning, not just in the activities that instructors have in store for you, but also in the thinking and learning that can take place outside the college classroom.

To succeed academically in college, you need many high-level work skills. First, you have to figure out how to extract relevant information from lectures, readings, and other assignments in preparation for future requirements that will demonstrate what you have learned. In Chapter 7: Take Winning Notes, you will learn optimal strategies for becoming an effective reader and dealing with lectures that are hard to decode. In Chapter 8: Enhance Your Study Skills and Memory, you will learn valuable strategies for how to study and improve your memory skills, essential survival skills in college.

You may be required to take courses dedicated to speaking and writing. However, as you advance in your selected major, you likely will be obligated to complete complex projects that demonstrate your ability to integrate and present diverse sources of information. In Chapter 10: Express Yourself, you will learn how to give great speeches and write masterful papers.

Thinking reflectively, critically, and productively are key aspects of becoming a competent college student (Bonnie & Sternberg, 2011). Chapter 6: Expand Thinking Skills focuses on a number of strategies to improve your critical-thinking, reasoning, problem-solving, decision-making, and creative-thinking skills.

You know there are going to be quite a few tests in store for you in college. Chapter 9: Succeed on Tests provides a number of strategies for tackling test challenges ranging from pop quizzes to final exams.

Develop a Growth Mindset

Mindset is the cognitive view that individuals develop for themselves. You likely have one of two mindsets: (1) a *fixed mindset*, in which you believe that your qualities are carved in stone and cannot change; or (2) a *growth mindset*, in which you believe your qualities can change and improve through their effort (Dweck, 2006, 2012). Which mindset do you have? Complete Know Yourself: Self-Assessment 1.3, "Assessing Your Mindset," to find out.

Your mindset influences whether you will be optimistic or pessimistic, what your goals will be, how hard you will strive to reach those goals, and how successful you are in college and after. Carol Dweck (2006), a professor at Stanford University, who created the concept of mindset, studied first-year pre-med majors taking their first chemistry class. Students with a growth mindset got higher grades than those with a fixed mindset. Even when they did not do well on a test, the growth-mindset students bounced back on the next test. Fixed-mindset students typically read and reread the text and class notes or tried to memorize everything verbatim. The fixed-mindset students who did poorly on tests concluded that chemistry and maybe pre-med weren't for them. By contrast, growth-mindset students took charge of their motivation and learning, searching for themes and principles in the course and going over mistakes until they understood why they made them. In Dweck's analysis (2006, p. 61), "They were studying to learn, not just ace the test. And actually, this is why they got higher grades—not because they were smarter or had a better background in science."

Dweck (2006) recommends the following to develop a growth mindset:

- *Understand that your intelligence and thinking skills are not fixed, but can change.* Even if you are very bright, with effort you can increase your intelligence.
- *Become passionate about learning and stretch your mind in challenging situations.* It's easy to withdraw into a fixed mindset when the going gets tough, but as you bump up against obstacles during your first year of college, keep growing, work harder, stay the course, improve your strategies, and you will become a more successful college student.
- *Start now.* If you have a fixed mindset, commit to changing now. Think about when, where, and how you will begin using your new growth mindset.

To read about one college student who has a growth mindset, see "Spotlight On Marie Gay."

Manage Life

Successfully managing what life throws at you isn't easy. Mix in the demands of college and you are likely to find yourself being tested in ways you never anticipated. Everything seems to happen at once, and everyday life doesn't always respect the course planning you have in mind. The solution? Manage your life effectively during college by bringing it under control. Some strategies for doing so involve taking responsibility, choosing sound goals, achieving balance, and overcoming obstacles.

Take Responsibility

In college, you will be responsible whether you succeed or fail. If you take responsibility for your successes and failures, you have an *internal locus of control*. If you don't take such personal responsibility and let others—or luck—be responsible for what happens to you, you have an *external locus of control*. Being internally controlled means seeing yourself as responsible for your achievement, believing that your own effort will help you accomplish your goals. Being internally controlled is much more likely to help you succeed in college (Schunk, 2012).

In his book *The Road Less Traveled*, psychiatrist M. Scott Peck (1978, 1997) makes some insightful comments about why internal control may be hard to develop. He says that life is difficult and that each of us will experience pain and disappointment. Peck argues that we might be right that some of our problems are caused by other people, including our parents. However, you are not going to succeed in college and life thereafter by continually blaming others.

Some first-year college students lack motivation because they have not separated their parents' "shoulds" from their own, sometimes opposite, interests and motivations. Examine your motivations and interests. Are they yours, or are you currently acting as a clone to fulfill your parents' or someone else's motivations and interests? Your motivation will catch fire when you are doing what YOU want to do!

Choose Smart Goals

Setting appropriate goals usually is instrumental to achieving success. Commit yourself to setting goals and doing what you have to do to achieve them. A true commitment is a heartfelt promise to yourself that you will not back down. Your goals should engage you. If your goals do not move you, if they don't inspire you into action, then you need to reevaluate them and come up with ones that do challenge and excite you.

© John Lund/Jupiterimages.com

Make a Personal Plan A goal is nothing without a means of achieving it. Good planning means getting organized mentally, which often requires writing things down. It means getting your life in order and controlling your time and your life, instead of letting your world and time control you.

Persist until You Succeed Managing your life effectively also involves how hard you work and persist to finish challenging tasks. Getting through college is a marathon, not a hundred-yard dash. Studying a little here and a little there won't work. To be successful you have to study often, almost every day, for weeks and months at a time. You'll often need to make small sacrifices to gain long-term rewards. College is not all work and no play, but if you mainly play, you will pay for it by the end of the term.

Pace Yourself Setting reasonable completion dates to address the goals in your personal plan will require working out appropriate schedules to meet them. If you want to obtain a college degree, you might want to set a goal of 4 to 6 years from now as your completion date, depending on how much time each year you can devote to college. If your goal is to make one good friend, you might want to set a time of 6 weeks from now for achieving it. If you want to learn to be an expert Thai food chef, there's probably a reasonable timeframe for that goal as well.

Achieve Balance

Learning is greedy. If you waste too much time, you'll find yourself poorly prepared the night before an important exam, for instance. If you manage time well, you can relax before exams and other deadlines. Time management will help you to be more productive and less stressed, with a better balance between work and play. Chapter 3: Manage Time Wisely is all about getting your life under control. Among other things, it explains how to set goals and priorities, eliminate procrastination, and monitor your time.

Overcome Obstacles

M. Scott Peck also observed, "The truth is that our finest moments are most likely to occur when we are feeling deeply uncomfortable, unhappy, or unfulfilled. For it is only in such moments, propelled by our discomfort, that we are likely to step out of our ruts and start searching for different ways or truer answers." Peck's words remind us of the silver lining that often is embedded in life's turmoil. When you are in the thick of the turmoil, though, it can be hard to remember that important lesson.

Look at the setbacks you experience as opportunities to learn. Not only can you learn what you might have done wrong, but you can also learn what led you to choose the wrong path. This reflection can guide you in seeking the goals you truly want. In Chapter 11: Take Charge of Your Physical and Mental Health, you will learn a variety of strategies that can help you make sound choices to reduce your stress and build a healthier life.

Trouble with money is often the primary cause students must drop out or stop out of school (Pryor et al., 2009). Escalating tuition costs, the high price of textbooks, and the mounting expenses related to completing the work all add financial burden that may feel overwhelming. It is easy to make financial mistakes that have far-reaching implications for college success. Check out Chapter 12: Manage Money Intelligently to avoid those pitfalls.

Connect and Communicate

Taking responsibility for yourself does not mean doing everything in isolation. In this dimension of college success—connecting and communicating—you will learn how to expand your problem-solving abilities by reaching out to others and making the most of technology. Connecting and communicating are key aspects of college success. Nearly every performance can be improved by taking advantage of the rich resources that are available to you.

Thrive on Campus

To thrive on campus, you need to know what resources can help you and how best to use them. In Chapter 2: Pursue Resources, specific exercises will give you opportunities to learn more about campus resources that will support your college success. Don't hesitate to use these resources when you think that you need help. Your academic adviser will be especially useful in helping you meet your goals.

Benefit from Group Work

Learning how to connect with others by serving on a team will help you succeed in college and beyond. You may be surprised by how many times your instructor will assign you to group project work as a means of mastering the material. Sometimes these experiences will be exhilarating, but sometimes you'll have to function whether you enjoy the group or not. Chapter 5: Navigate Differences helps you understand how individual differences can influence performance. Chapter 4: Master Communication Skills and Build Relationships provides numerous communication strategies for being a good listener, resolving conflicts, getting along with instructors, improving relationships with your family, and other tips for getting along with diverse others. Increasingly, employers are looking for future employees who communicate effectively in group tasks and work together as a team. Engaging in these group activities during college will enhance your chances of being a positive candidate for a job and career after college.

Develop Digital Savvy

Technology can also expand your intellectual reach. Take every opportunity to use applications such as word processing, e-mail, spreadsheets, PowerPoint, and the Internet in your academic work and your broader college experience. If you don't have good technology skills, developing them will make your college life much easier and improve your chances of landing a good job later. And if you currently work and are looking for a new job (or pursuing a different career), technology expertise may help you achieve your dream position.

A surprising amount of academic work in college takes place in teams to promote work skills that will be highly valued by future employers.

At college, you will see why it is important to become "digitally savvy." Many instructors and institutions strive to reduce wasted paper. This means you will have to become expert in navigating electronic course support systems. Some professors allow students to take quizzes outside of class via computer but with time limitations. You may have to endure regular security measures to ensure you are submitting your own work. Research papers and other assignments may be submitted to an electronic drop box that "closes" at the deadline. You may opt to work collectively with others on a group report by producing a "google doc."

You may find that some (or all) of your courses are online. Although you gain significant control over how to manage the work in virtual environments, online courses require you to make important adaptations. For example, you may have to arrange for a proctor to oversee your test-taking to ensure academic integrity. Your tests may often be "open book." However, most of the time that is a signal that the test will be harder, forcing you to study ahead of time if you plan to do well. On the College Success CourseMate website for this book, you can connect with many other sites that have information to help you succeed in both online and traditional college courses.

 # Build a Bright Future

Philosopher Joseph Campbell offered some advice worth repeating when it comes to building a bright future: "Follow your bliss." This final dimension of the college success model highlights the importance of developing career-finding skills, striving to achieve high performance standards, taking pride in your integrity, and demonstrating resilience in the face of disappointment.

Discover Career Options

A main focus of college for many students is getting ready for the right career. Each of us wants to find a rewarding career and to enjoy the work we do. When you are well suited to the work, work doesn't feel like work. A successful career often depends on three factors:

1. Possessing a specialized knowledge base in a particular field (such as electrical engineering, nursing, or English)
2. Developing good work skills, especially for fields involving interpersonal communication and technology
3. Demonstrating a strong work ethic and integrity to promote trust from those who will work with you

If you're a typical first-year student, you may not yet have a clear idea of which particular career you would like to pursue. That's okay for right now, especially if you're currently taking a lot of general education courses. But as you move further along in college, it becomes more important to develop firmer ideas about your future.

College graduates can have careers that will earn them considerably more money in their lifetimes than the careers of those who do not go to college (*Occupational Outlook Handbook*, 2010–2011). In the United States, individuals with a bachelor's degree make, on average, over $1,000 a month more than those with only a high school diploma. Individuals with two years of college and an associate's degree make over $500 a month more than those who only graduated from high school. Over a lifetime, a college graduate will make, on average, approximately $600,000 more than a high school graduate will! College graduates also report being happier with their work and having more continuous work records than those who don't attend or don't finish college.

Exploring careers now will help you to link your short-term and overall college goals with some of your long-term life goals, and to be motivated by your long-term prospects. What do you plan to make your life's work? Is there a specific career or several careers that you want to pursue? If you have a career in mind, how certain are you that it is the best one for you? As discussed in Chapter 13: Explore Careers, college gives you time, resources, opportunity, and strategies to make a well-informed choice.

Strive for Excellence

Knowing you have done your best can feel rewarding regardless of whether your instructors concur that you have produced high-quality work. However, when you deliver a professionally engaging class presentation, figure out the chemistry "unknown," or capture a hard-won A, the feeling is hard to beat.

If you excel, scholarship donors may target you as a special individual worthy of additional financial support. You may be asked to join a variety of scholastic honor societies that can open up other kinds of opportunities, such as support for travel or participation in regional and national conventions. You might even be able to publish and present research findings with one of your professors. Such markers of excellence can make a real difference when it comes to the next step you take after graduation.

Another reason to work at capacity is the impact it will have on those who must vouch for your work in the future. Your faculty or internship supervisors will make glowing remarks about you if you have demonstrated your willingness to work hard to achieve high quality in what you do.

Develop Your Character

You have already developed some ideals that govern how you will negotiate the moral dilemmas that lie ahead. Now your ideals will be tested. For example, you will face some peer pressure to cut some inappropriate corners to get your work done. You might have to choose between being honest with a professor about failing a deadline or coming up with a lame and phony excuse. You might be confronted with watching a classmate steal glances at crib notes to earn an undeserved high grade. What will you do?

You obviously don't want to blight your record with the ugliness of an episode that suggests you have poor integrity. But it is more important to highlight the positive reasons to maintain high standards for character. President Thomas Jefferson recommended, "In matters of style, swim with the currents. In matters of principle, stand like a rock."

"Did you think the ladder of success would be straight up?"

Demonstrate Resilience

You won't be perfect in college. Don't even try. You are going to have disappointments, setbacks, and challenges that may make you reconsider the wisdom of capturing a college degree at all. However, every failure holds a lesson for those who pay attention. Get back on your feet and try again. What you have learned may make a crucial difference in your next project or challenge.

In all of the remaining chapters, the six-component College Success Model (Know Yourself, Clarify Expectations, Develop Competence, Manage Life, Connect and Communicate, and Build a Bright Future) you read about in this chapter will serve as the organizational theme. Use these important themes to guide your college success. We wish you all the best in your remaining journey through college.

The College Success Model

- The College Success Model begins with the core dimension of Know Yourself. The model then provides five other key dimensions that emphasize strategies for guiding your success in college: Clarify Expectations, Develop Competence, Manage Life, Connect and Communicate, and Build a Bright Future.

Know Yourself

- College provides the perfect setting for establishing an identity. Your identity is complex and can be evaluated in terms of identity statuses. Emerging adulthood—18 to 25 years of age—involves a transition between adolescence and adulthood, a time when many individuals explore and reevaluate his or her identity.
- Exploring and choosing values that reflect who you are is an important aspect of knowing yourself. Connect your values with college success and think deeply about your values, including developing a path to purpose.

Clarify Expectations

- Understand perspectives, including your own expectations and those of others, such as your instructors, advisers, roommates, parents, and partners.
- Stay positive by setting high personal expectations for yourself and being optimistic.

Develop Competence

- Think and learn. Develop high-level work skills.
- Develop a growth mindset rather than a fixed mindset.

Manage Life

- Take responsibility for whether you succeed or fail.
- Choose smart goals.

- Achieve balance, especially by managing your time wisely.
- Overcome obstacles. Look at setbacks as opportunities to learn.

Connect and Communicate

- Thrive on campus, especially by pursuing effective resources.
- Benefit from group work. Learn how to connect with others on a team.
- Develop digital savvy, using technology to expand your intellectual reach.

Build a Bright Future

- Discover career options and seek to find a rewarding career.
- Strive for excellence. Excelling in college will help to open career doors for you.
- Develop your character to enhance your future.
- Demonstrate resilience.

 Visit the College Success CourseMate for *Your Guide to College Success* for interactive resources at login.cengagebrain.com

Review Questions

1. What are the six components of the College Success Model?

   _____

   _____

   _____

   _____

   _____

2. Describe the four statuses of identity.

   _____

   _____

   _____

   _____

   _____

3. What characterizes millenials?

   _____

   _____

   _____

   _____

   _____

4. Discuss strategies that will benefit returning students.

   _____

   _____

   _____

   _____

   _____

5. What are some ways that values can enhance your college success?

   _____

   _____

   _____

   _____

   _____

6. What are some good questions to ask yourself in seeking to develop a path to purpose during college?

_____

_____

_____

_____

_____

7. What is meant by mindset? Describe how mindset can improve your academic success.

_____

_____

_____

_____

_____

8. What are some strategies for managing your life effectively in college?

_____

_____

_____

_____

_____

9. How can connecting and communicating benefit you during college?

_____

_____

_____

_____

_____

10. What are some good strategies for building a bright future?

_____

_____

_____

_____

_____

SELF-ASSESSMENT 1.1

What Is My Identity?

Your identity is composed of many different dimensions. To gain a better sense of your identity, for each item place a check mark in one of the four boxes that best reflects your identity in that domain of your life. Recall from earlier in this chapter these descriptions of the four identity statuses: diffusion—have neither explored alternatives adequately nor made a commitment; foreclosure—have made a commitment but have not adequately explored alternatives; moratorium—am in the process of exploring alternatives but have not yet made a commitment; achievement—have explored alternatives adequately and have made a commitment.

IDENTITY DIMENSION	IDENTITY STATUS			
	Diffusion	Foreclosure	Moratorium	Achievement
Vocational identity				
Spiritual and religious identity				
Achievement/intellectual identity				
Political identity				
Sexual identity				
Relationship/lifestyle identity				
Cultural and ethnic identity				
Personal characteristics				
Interests				
Values				

Interpretation. If you checked "diffused" or "foreclosed" for any areas, take some time to reflect about what you need to do to move to a "moratorium" status in those areas. If you checked "moratorium" for any areas, what aspects of this dimension are you exploring? A good exercise is to write about your identity statuses for each of the dimensions and think critically about whether you want to explore new aspects of the dimensions.

SELF-ASSESSMENT 1.2

What Are My Values?

This list presents a wide variety of values. Place a check mark in the spaces next to the ten values that are the most important to you. Then go back over these ten values and rank the top five.

_____ Having good friendships and getting along well with people
_____ Having a positive relationship with a spouse or a romantic partner
_____ Self-respect
_____ Being well-off financially
_____ Having a good spiritual life
_____ Being competent at my work
_____ Having the respect of others
_____ Making an important contribution to humankind
_____ Being a moral person
_____ Feeling secure
_____ Being a great athlete
_____ Being physically attractive
_____ Being creative
_____ Having freedom and independence
_____ Being well educated
_____ Contributing to the welfare of others
_____ Having peace of mind
_____ Getting recognition or becoming famous
_____ Being happy
_____ Enjoying leisure time
_____ Being a good citizen and showing loyalty to my country
_____ Living a healthy lifestyle
_____ Being intelligent
_____ Having good family relationships
_____ Honesty and integrity
_____ Dedication and commitment
_____ Having personal responsibility
_____ Other values

My five most important personal values are:

1. _____
2. _____
3. _____
4. _____
5. _____

As you review your selections, think about how you got these values. Did you learn them from your parents, teachers, or friends? Did you gain them from personal experiences? How deeply have you thought about each of these values and what they mean to you? Think about whether your actions support your values. Are you truly living up to them? Do they truly reflect who you are?

Assessing Your Mindset

Read each statement and place a check mark in the box next to each item to indicate whether you mostly agree with it or mostly disagree with it.

ITEM	Mostly Agree	Mostly Disagree
1. Your intelligence is something very basic about you that you can't change very much.		
2. You can learn new things, but you can't really change how intelligent you are.		
3. No matter how much intelligence you have, you can always change it quite a bit.		
4. You can always substantially change how intelligent you are.		

Scoring and Interpretation. Items 1 and 2 are fixed mindset questions; items 3 and 4 are growth mindset questions. Which mindset did you agree with more? You can be a mixture, but most people lean one way or the other. What did you learn about yourself? You could also substitute other skills and abilities (such as speaking skills, writing skills, math skills, athletic skills, and so on) for intelligence to discover whether you have a fixed or growth mindset in those areas.

Source: C. Dweck, Your Mindset from Dweck, C. (2006). Mindset. New York: Random House.

Know Yourself

1. Dreaming

Stephen Covey and his colleagues (1994) recommend the following activity to help you clarify your values (use your watch to go through the timed exercises):

a. Take one minute and answer this question: If I had unlimited time and resources, what would I do? It's okay to dream. Write down everything that comes into your mind.

b. Return to Know Yourself: Self-Assessment 1.2 on page 24 and review the list of five values that are the most important to you.

c. Take several minutes to compare this list with your dreams. You may be living with unconscious dreams that don't mesh with your values. If you don't get your dreams out in the open, you may spend years living with illusions and the feeling that you somehow are settling for second best. Work on the two lists until you feel that your dreams match up with your values.

d. Take one minute to see how your values relate to four fundamental areas of human fulfillment: physical needs, social needs, mental needs, and spiritual needs. Do your values reflect these four needs? Work on your list until they do.

Clarify Expectations

2. My Path to Purpose

In this chapter, you read about William Damon's view that too few college students have not adequately thought about their life purposes. Think deeply about each of the following questions posed by Damon (2008, p.135) and then write about your thoughts.

1. What's most important in your life?

2. Why do you care about those things?

3. What are your long-term goals?

4. Why are these long-term goals important to you?

5. What does it mean to have a good life?

6. What does it mean to be a good person?

7. If you were to look back on your life now, how would you like to be remembered?

Build a Bright Future

3. Mindsets of Mentors

Think about the growth mindsets of people you admire. Perhaps you have a hero, someone who has achieved something extraordinary. You may have thought his or her accomplishments came easily because he or she is so talented. But dig deeper. Learn more about how the person works and thinks. Chances are, if you find out more about the person, you will discover how much hard work and effort over a long period of time were responsible for his or her achievements.

_____

_____

_____

_____

Pursue Resources

Chapter 2

KNOW YOURSELF

YOU WANT TO BE INDEPENDENT, but even the most successful college students don't do it all on their own. They get connected to find the resources that will help them master college. They are as comfortable on campus as they are in cyberspace. They navigate skillfully in the community to pursue experiences that will enhance their learning. And they see the critical connection between their ability to learn about and use resources during college and their success in future work contexts. To evaluate your skill in making connections, place a check mark in the appropriate category for each characteristic below.

How Well Do I Know My Campus's Resources?

	Very Much Like Me	Somewhere In Between	Not at All Like Me
I know what campus resources are available to meet my needs.			
I know how to use library services efficiently.			
I plan to participate in one or more extracurricular activities.			
I have spent adequate time with my academic adviser.			
I have studied my college catalog and know how to use it as a resource.			
I know what I want my major to be.			
I have made a coursework plan toward a degree or certificate.			
I have selected a mentor.			
I can describe how contributing to the community can enhance my learning.			
I use the Internet appropriately to search for information and stay connected.			
I use a word-processing program for most of what I write.			
I use social-networking sites responsibly.			

© M.L. Harris/Getty Images

Spotlight On...

Brian Long
A Mentoring Success Story

As a teenager, Brian Long wasn't thinking about going to college. His world then was the street life of gangs. When he was seventeen, he and other gang members were arrested for an armed robbery they committed, and he served four years in prison. While in prison, he reflected on what he needed to do to change his life and decided to make some big changes.

When he got out of prison, Brian enrolled in Mitchell Community College in Statesville, North Carolina, to pursue a degree in counseling. At Mitchell, he signed up for the Minority Male Mentoring program, benefiting considerably from the coaching and advice he received from his mentors. Subsequently, Brian began to mentor other "at-risk" male college students. He believed that if the students he was mentoring could see how much he had struggled and all the trouble he'd had, and yet was resilient and succeeded in college, then they could be driven to succeed too.

In addition to taking courses and participating in the mentoring program at Mitchell, Brian started a basketball program at the college because he thought it might help some students stay in college. He commented, "Guys in college are staying in college so they can be on the basketball team." Brian graduated with an associate of arts (AA) degree with honors from Mitchell College in 2008. In 2010, he graduated again with honors for a human services degree from Gardner Webb University.

Brian continues to give back in a variety of ways. In 2008, Brian's compassion and caring were exemplified in his donation of bone marrow to help extend the life of a terminally ill 26-year-old individual. Currently he works at Appropriate Punishment Options, which helps unemployed adults find jobs. He does motivational speaking to gangs and prisoners and has written two books: *Set Free* and *Making a Difference*. From prison to successful graduate and author, Brian Long's experience provides powerful evidence of the importance of mentoring.

Photo Courtesy of Brian Long

Mentoring has powerfully and positively shaped Brian Long's college experience.

Mentoring has played a key role in Brian Long's adjustment to college and in his college success. As you read about Brian Long, think about the importance of finding the right resources and personnel for helping you succeed in college. Examine the chapter outline and predict how important it will be for you to pursue the resources that will enhance your college success.

(Source: Smith, 2007)

Clarify Expectations

Whether you are taking a full academic load of face-to-face courses or you plan to conquer your courses online, the college campus can be an intimidating place. The more quickly you can learn what to expect from the resources the college has to offer, the sooner you can get down to the business of succeeding.

Get to Know Your Campus

It costs you nothing to connect with your campus, yet nothing will help you to be more successful in college than knowing and wisely using your campus resources. You probably have visited some of them already—the bookstore for textbooks and supplies, the student center to check out bulletin boards, and the business office to make financial arrangements. However, most college campuses are very complex places that may take some time to get to know.

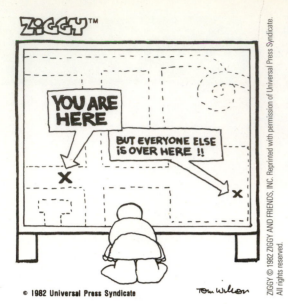

Begin exploring your campus by scanning the college website for relevant information. Most college websites are organized so you can explore academic programs, student activities, cultural calendars, campus maps, or other key information sources by pointing and clicking. You may be surprised at the diverse options available to you. Usually, contact information is available for those in charge of the areas that interest you. There may be opportunities to purchase navigational smartphone applications to help you find your way around campus and even to pinpoint what's for lunch. Many colleges provide a full-blown "e-campus," in which case you don't need to come to campus to explore resources; they can come to your aid through cyberspace.

You can also flip through the campus telephone directory. Most directories have compact listings of campus offices and services. For example, the campus childcare center might provide you with some alternatives for helping with family obligations. The tutoring center may be just the right spot to visit during downtime between morning and afternoon classes on Wednesday. Perhaps a service exists to assist you in identifying carpooling partners. A Spanish club might help you sharpen your language skills and give you the opportunity to meet other students with interests similar to yours.

An important goal in college is learning how to solve your personal problems and to have your needs met. Before you get oriented to the variety of services at the college, complete Know Yourself: Self-Assessment 2.1, "Campus Resources to Meet My Needs," at the back of the chapter on page 55 to get started.

Get the Help You Need

You can expect that most people on campus will be eager to help you in your quest to master college. You can learn a great deal about the best campus resources to contact for assistance if you make this an important goal and aren't afraid to ask questions. Whether you want information, advice, or training, here are some things you can do to get the help you need (Canfield & Hansen, 1995):

Your campus has many resources to assist students who are struggling academically.

- *Ask as though you expect to get help*. Your tuition dollars pay for assistance in the classroom, the library, and even the cafeteria line. Most campus employees—whether faculty or staff—strive to provide good customer service to their students. Act confidently to mobilize that assistance.
- *Ask someone who is in a position to help you.* You may have to do some homework to find out who can help you best. If someone you approach can't deliver, ask whether that person knows of someone else who might be able to help you. Form a network of resources.
- *Ask clear and specific questions.* Even those who enjoy helping students don't like to have their time wasted. Think ahead about what you need and what level of detail will satisfy you. Take notes so you won't have to ask twice.
- *Ask with passion, civility, humor, and creativity.* Enthusiasm goes a long way toward engaging others to want to help you. A polite request is easier to accommodate than a loud, demanding, or whiny one. Sometimes problems yield more readily to a playful question. A clever request is just plain hard to turn down. But size up whether a humorous approach is likely to be well received. If not, your good intentions and creativity may backfire.

Exploit Library Resources

Libraries may not seem to be a likely site for adventure. But in fact, each visit to the library can be a treasure hunt. The treasure might be a bit of information, an opportunity to go online, or a chance to check out a new book by your favorite author. The sooner you know what to expect about the library's operations, the more useful it will be to you.

One of your classes may involve a library tour. If not, ask a librarian for help in getting oriented. Librarians can give you a schedule of library tours or provide you with maps or pamphlets to help you search independently. Although librarians may look busy when you approach them, step up and ask for help. They expect to be interrupted. Most of them enjoy teaching others how to use the library. If you find an especially friendly librarian, cultivate the relationship. A librarian friend can be a lifesaver.

What must you know to use the library effectively? The following questions may help you organize your first tour:

- How can I check out materials?
- What are the penalties for late returns?
- Do instructors place materials on reserve? How does this work?
- What interesting or helpful journals does the library have? Are they available online?
- Can I access the library's resources electronically?
- How long does it take to get something through interlibrary loan?
- What kinds of reference materials are available?
- What technological resources does the library have that will help me succeed in college?

 ## Develop Competence

Succeeding in college means navigating academic requirements, but going at it alone is not a good idea. In this section, you will read about the types of requirements you may face and how important it will be to have an academically— your adviser.

Trust Your Adviser

Confer with your adviser regularly, especially when you have any questions about your academic life. Your adviser has important information about your course requirements that can help you realize your plans. Advisers can explain why certain courses are required and can identify instructors who will offer the right level of challenge. When it's time to register for next term's courses, schedule a meeting with your adviser early in the registration period and collaborate to develop a longer-term plan.

Bring a tentative plan of the courses that you think will satisfy your requirements, but be open to suggestions if your adviser offers you compelling reasons for taking other courses. For example, he or she may suggest that by taking some harder courses than you had planned to take, you can prepare yourself better for the career you have chosen.

You need an adviser you can trust. If the chemistry between you and your academic adviser isn't good, confront that problem by discussing what behaviors make you feel uncomfortable. Recognize that your own actions may have something to do with the problem. If you can't work out a compromise, request a change to find someone who is right for you.

Get to Know Your College Catalog

The college catalog is a valuable resource. Many colleges have moved the college catalog online, where it can be easily updated and downloaded, but you may be able to secure a print copy through your adviser or admissions office. College catalogs are regularly revised every one or two years. Requirements for specific programs sometimes change, and you usually will be held to the degree plan that was in place when you enrolled. However, an original requirement may be waived or modified if your argument for doing so is sound. You can plan more efficiently if you familiarize yourself with the curriculum terminology in the college catalog.

General Education Courses Especially in your first several semesters, you'll probably have to take a number of general education courses. Typically, you will select a set of courses that distribute your study across the social and natural sciences, humanities, and the arts. Some colleges include special requirements to develop writing and math skills or knowledge about diversity.

Many students are so eager to get to the specialized courses in their major that they resent liberal arts requirements, particularly when they must take courses in areas that strain their comfort levels. However, exposure to a broad liberal arts base not only provides a strong foundation but can also lead to experiences that prompt students to rethink their original majors. Do not postpone general education requirements in favor of courses in your major, because you will feel out of sync if you are taking introductory courses just prior to graduation.

Core Courses The catalog should tell you what the core requirements are for the degree program you are considering. Core courses may include *prerequisites* (courses you must take first to be prepared properly for other harder courses) and *corequisites* (courses you must take simultaneously, such as a lecture and a corresponding lab). Other requirements may specify a course sequence to fulfill requirements. Some courses have special registration requirements, such as "consent of instructor," "enrollment limited to majors," "seniors only," "honor students," and so on. You may be tempted to ask for a waiver of prerequisites, but it is usually not in your best interest to do so. Prerequisite courses provide building blocks that will facilitate your learning in the next course.

Electives In addition to core courses, you will be able to take *electives*, courses that are not required but count toward the total credits needed for graduation. You likely will take some of these in your major; others, outside your major. Electives provide you with an opportunity to explore your interests and expand your education. In some cases, students take an elective that interests them so much that it becomes a springboard for taking more courses in the area, establishing a major, or sometimes even changing majors.

Herald Carl Bakken/The Estate of Herald Carl Bakken

"Well, we've finally done it. We've listed two courses, each of which is a prerequisite for taking the other."

Forge an Academic Plan

Academic planning involves multiple stages. Short-term planning helps you make wise selections about how to register for the next term's courses. Long-term planning helps you maximize your ability to complete requirements for your targeted degree. Effective long-term planning can save you substantial time and money. Let's examine how to develop an academic plan.

Select the Right Courses With a little effort, you can learn how to select courses that both fulfill your requirements and are enjoyable. Here are some strategies for making sound selections:

- *List your constraints.* You might have childcare responsibilities, an inflexible work schedule, or commuting issues. If so, block out the times you can't take classes before you begin your selection.
- *Examine your interests.* In many ways, college provides an almost endless array of interests that you can explore by taking electives, participating in extracurricular activities, and signing up for internship experiences. You may find that your interests fluctuate a great deal over the course of your college experience. That's okay, but keep monitoring what interests you the most. To evaluate your interests, complete Know Yourself: Self-Assessment 2.2, "What Are My Interests?," at the back of the chapter on page 56.
- *Study your options.* Colleges have lists of the classes required for various specialty diplomas or majors. Examine the college catalog to determine courses that fulfill general education requirements and specific courses in the specialty or major that you want to pursue.
- *Register for a reasonable course load.* Many colleges do not charge for additional courses beyond those needed for full-time status. If you have that option, you might be tempted to pile on extra courses to save time and money, but think again. If you take too many courses, you may spread yourself too thin.
- *Take the right mix of courses.* Don't load up with too many really tough courses in the same term. Check into the amount of reading time and other time that specific courses require. If you can't find anyone else who can tell you this information, make appointments with instructors. Ask them what the course requirements are, how much reading they expect, and so on.
- *Ask the pros.* The pros in this case are students who are already in your preferred program. Ask their advice about which courses and instructors to take. On many campuses, academic departments have undergraduate organizations that you can join. If you want to be a biology major, consider joining a group such as the Student Biology Association. These associations are good places to get connected with students more advanced than you are in a major.

Choose Your Major One of the most frequent questions that you will be asked on campus is: "What's your major?" A college major, or field of concentration, is a series of courses that provides a foundation of learning in a specific academic discipline. Majors vary in the number of courses required, which makes a strong case for building your plan with your academic adviser. For example, engineering typically requires more major courses than does history and psychology, which allow you to choose more electives. If you want to be an English teacher in a public school setting, you need to get good advice about the blend of English and education courses you must take to satisfy certification in your state.

Before choosing a major, realistically assess your interests, skills, and abilities. If you get Cs and Ds in biology and chemistry even though you've honestly put your full effort into those courses, then pre-med or a science area probably won't be the best major for you. On the other hand, if you love the math or computer science class you're taking, a career related to those courses might be your best choice.

But be patient. The first year of college, especially the first term, is a time of exploration and learning how to succeed. Many first-year students who don't initially do well in courses related to a possible major are able to adapt, meet the challenge, and go on to achieve success in that area. After a year or two into your college experience, you should have a good idea of whether the major you've chosen is a good fit. At that point, you will have had enough courses and opportunities to know whether you're in the right place. Seek out students who are more advanced in the field you're considering. Ask them what it's like to specialize in that particular area, and ask them about various courses and instructors.

Unfortunately, too many students choose majors for the wrong reasons: to please their parents, to follow their friends, or to have a light course load. Resist these temptations. Instead, ask yourself what really interests you and what you really want to achieve. You have the right to choose what you want to do with your life. Reconsider your values and think about your long-term goals in life. You should be enthusiastic about the major and motivated to learn more about the field. To examine some possible links between majors, skills, and careers, see Figure 2.1.

Change Your Major If you're not sure what you want to pursue, you're not alone. More than two-thirds of first-year college students change their intended majors in the first year. The average number of times students change their majors over the course of their education hovers around three times. Don't panic. When college administrators have you fill out forms during your first year, most let you write "undecided" or "exploring" in the column for a college major. It is perfectly appropriate not to decide on a major before you do some exploring. In fact, some colleges won't let you declare a major until you have sampled many disciplines through general education requirements. However, if you're in a four-year program and aren't sure about a major after two years, you may end up taking extra courses that you don't need for graduation, and you might have trouble fitting in all the classes you do need to complete your major.

Some institutions offer more creative degree options through interdisciplinary combinations or individualized majors in which you will have greater latitude in designing your academic path. Even individualized majors, though, usually require one or two concentrations of courses to keep the coursework at least somewhat unified.

Double Your Major When two fields are equally appealing, some students choose to double their major. However, if you pursue this option, you must plan even more carefully if you expect to graduate in the same timeframe as that for a single major. In addition, you can expect the workload to be more intense because you will have to develop advanced skills in two disciplines simultaneously to complete the double major.

Complete Your Degree You have several options for completing your degree. For example, if you are a community college student, your goal may be a

SKILLS	MAJOR	POTENTIAL OCCUPATIONS/CAREERS
Research information Analyze numerical options Perform mathematical functions and apply formulas Communicate information through written and oral presentations	Accounting	Accountant Commercial/Consumer Loan Officer Compensation & Benefits Specialist Investment Analyst
Make three-dimensional models from plans and drawings Use computer-aided design and drafting software Research codes, laws, and regulations Prepare and give presentations	Architecture	Architect Building Construction Inspector Drafter Estimator
Use lab equipment and instruments to test materials Write articles, papers, and reports describing research Evaluate written and statistical data Develop and conduct scientific experiments	Biology	Epidemiologist Quality Control Soil Conservationist Pharmaceutical Sales
Enjoy working in team environments Focus on goals and results Analyze numerical data Lead and facilitate discussions	Business Administration	Retail Store Buyer Advertising Account Executive Production Manager Logistics Coordinator
Interpret systems analyst's program specifications Plan program logic for software applications Collaborate with teams of programmers, analysts, and end users Program, test, and correct errors	Business Computer Information Systems	Programmer Systems Analyst Database Administrator Website Specialist
Evaluate written and statistical data Develop and conduct scientific experiments Use sensitive lab equipment to test materials Read journals and articles	Chemistry	Science Lab Scientist Chemist Toxicologist Forensic Scientist
Design integrated hardware/software systems Prepare engineering specifications for performance and design Conduct research regarding various materials and components Prepare schematics of components for a computer	Computer Engineer	Computer Programmer Systems Analyst Operations Research Analyst Computer Network Analyst
Coordinate movements and choreography with others Listen to and follow director's/producer's instructions Create and develop character roles Practice complex dance patterns	Dance	Choreographer Dance Instructor Dance Therapist Arts Manager
Prepare and write reports Analyze statistical and numerical information Construct mathematical models Explain, interpret, and present information	Economics	Economist Underwriter Financial Analyst International Trade Specialist
Use computers to research databases for information Develop graphics using creative software Meet with other writers, editors, photographers, and graphic artists Pay attention to detail and style while writing	English	Continuity Writer Editor Journalist Screenwriter
Perform mathematical functions and apply formulas Analyze numerical data Use computer software to track information Present information to supervisor and committees	Finance	Treasury Management Specialist Financial Analyst Trust Officer International Trade Specialist
Use computer software to simulate three-dimensional models Analyze minerals using lab equipment Describe results in written reports and presentations Compile data from logs, articles, and research	Geology	Parks and Natural Resources Manager Hydrogeologist Park Ranger Oil Drilling Analyst

FIGURE 2.1 Choose the Best Major and Career for Your Skills

SKILLS	MAJOR	POTENTIAL OCCUPATIONS/CAREERS
Use a variety of resources and databases to research information Collaborate with various departments and people Research and prepare reports summarizing plans and projects Use computer software to develop models for projects	Government	Congressional Aide Public Administrator Urban/Regional Planner Lobbyist
Apply investigative and research skills to solving problems Synthesize data from a variety of resources Analyze and interpret data Write and present reports	History	Curator Lobbyist Paralegal Public Administrator
Coordinate with editors, graphics artists, and photographers Establish rapport with people as a part of the interview process Write and review articles Use computer databases to assist with research	Journalism	Public Relations Specialist Newspaper/Magazine Journalist Proofreader Editorial Assistant
Analyze statistical information Present information to groups of people Write papers to reinforce ideas Coordinate plans with team	Marketing	Advertising Copywriter Advertising Account Executive Distribution Manager Merchandiser
Design computer simulation models Analyze, interpret, and evaluate data Formulate and solve equations in order to explain concepts Compute and calculate applied mathematical formulas	Math	Actuary Inventory Control Specialist Investment Analyst Statistician
Make drawings using computer-aided design software Write reports outlining results of tests performed Conduct research and study effects Compare options and make recommendations to committees	Mechanical Engineering	Manufacturing Engineer Field Service Engineer Sales Engineer Industrial Designer
Follow director's instructions and composer's notations Concentrate on quality of sound during rehearsals and practices Develop new interpretation of musical compositions Collaborate with other musicians, directors, and producers	Music	Music Instructor Music Therapist Artist and Repertoire Manager Booking Manager
Observe, analyze, and interpret Resolve or mediate conflicts Listen effectively and establish rapport with people Evaluate various programs	Psychology	Human Resources Interviewer Case Worker Psychological Assistant Job Development Specialist
Interact well with diverse cultures Have insight into group dynamics Understand and improve relationships	Sociology	Demographer Market Research Analyst Nonprofit Administrator Case Worker
Establish rapport easily with people Assist people with the identification of appropriate services Consult with interdisciplinary treatment team Prepare and present reports	Social Work	Probation/Parole Officer Medical Social Worker Community Worker Training Specialist
Collaborate with directors, producers, and other actors Perform before audiences Research customs, social attitudes, and time periods Develop new ways to express character's emotions	Theatre	Set Designer Theatre Manager Television/Film Producer Stage Director

FIGURE 2.1 Choose the Best Major and Career for Your Skills (Continued)

certificate, a two-year degree, or a planned transfer to a four-year institution for a baccalaureate. If you are in a four-year college, you may not want to stop there but move ahead to graduate school. Let's look at these options in more detail.

A Certificate or an AA Degree Some students enter a community college with a clear idea of what they want to major or specialize in, but many others do not. The associate of arts (AA) degree includes general academic courses that facilitate transfer to a four-year institution.

In addition to a core of general education courses, obtaining an AA degree means either taking a concentration of courses in a major (or an area of emphasis) such as history, English, or psychology or taking a required number of electives. In most community colleges, a minimum of 60 or more credit hours is required for an AA degree. A typical breakdown might be 45 credits in general education and 15 in your major, area of emphasis, or electives. Some community colleges also offer an associate of science (AS) degree that requires a heavy science concentration.

If you plan to transfer to a four-year college, you'll need to select a college and study its degree requirements as soon as possible. You should consult regularly with an adviser at your community college and the four-year institution to ensure that you're enrolling in courses appropriate to your major at the new institution.

In addition to the AA option, many community colleges offer certificate programs designed to help people reenter the job market or upgrade their skills. There are many specializations: food and hospitality, graphic design, press operation, medical record coding, word processing, property management, travel management, vocational nursing, and others. Unlike AA and AS programs, certificate programs do not include general education requirements. Certificate programs focus specifically on the job skills needed in a particular occupation. The number of required credits varies but is usually fewer than the number required for an associate's degree.

The Baccalaureate Degree The ballpark for completion of a college degree is four years. However, depending on the major selected, summer classes, efficient planning, and good fortune, it is possible to complete the work in less time. Even with good planning and follow-through, however, it may take longer than four years, depending on the availability of courses in your selected major.

Although many first-year college students don't know what to major in or find themselves changing majors in their first year, it's still a good idea to map out a four- or five-year plan for your intended major that lists each of your courses every term until graduation. In this way, you can take control of your academic planning and give yourself the most flexibility toward the end of your four or five years of college. The risk in not doing so is that you'll end up in your junior or senior year with too many courses in one area and not enough in another. This predicament will extend the time needed to get your bachelor's degree. The four- or five-year plan also lets you see which terms will be light and which will be heavy, as well as whether you'll need to take summer courses. Of course, it's unlikely that you'll carry out your plan exactly. As you make changes, the plan will allow you to see the consequences of your moves and what you have to do to stay on track to complete your degree.

The four- or five-year plan is an excellent starting point for sessions with your academic adviser. The plan can be a springboard for questions you might have about which courses to take this term, next term, and so on. If you're considering several different majors, make a four- or five-year plan for each one and use the plans to help you decide which courses to take and when. If you're in a four-year institution, begin your planning with Know Yourself: Self-Assessment 2.3, "A Four- or Five-Year Academic Plan," at the back of the chapter on page 57.

The Graduate Degree If you hope to pursue graduate education, know that graduate programs vary in their expectations for your undergraduate preparation. For example, law schools admit students from many different undergraduate majors. In contrast, graduate schools in physics usually require a physics undergraduate degree or a large concentration of physics classes. Your adviser can help you pace your preparation for the process of applying to graduate school, including scheduling specialized testing and pursuing strong letters of recommendation.

Some universities also offer hybrid programs that combine baccalaureate and master's requirements in programs that are called "3+2" or "4+1." The formulas communicate how the university frames the years assigned to undergraduate and graduate courses to finish with a master's degree. To achieve an accelerated master's degree at the end of five years requires choosing a major early and sticking to the rigorous requirements throughout the plan.

Manage Life

Most campuses provide an array of services to help you feel supported throughout your college career. These resources can provide a lifeline in times of trouble.

Stay Healthy

Many campuses have fully equipped medical centers for students. Healthcare services may offer blood testing, health screenings, pregnancy tests, flu shots, and educational programs, as well as regular physicians' care. Smaller campuses may offer access to a nurse or health specialists trained in emergency care. Look up the phone numbers for these services and store them in your smartphone. When health emergencies arise, contact an employee of the campus or call the campus switchboard to explain the situation and request urgent help. Call 911 for serious emergencies.

Practice Safety

Personal safety is an important concern on all campuses. Security personnel monitor the campus for outsiders and sometimes provide escorts after dark. If you feel unsafe or spot activities that you think may threaten the well-being or property of others, do not hesitate to call the main campus telephone line or the campus security department to report your suspicions or concerns.

Most campuses teem with activity. Unfortunately, that level of activity also attracts people who know that a campus is an opportune environment for stealing. No matter what the size of your campus, possessions that can be converted to cash can disappear. Keep your personal belongings locked up when you are not around. Consider insuring valuable property.

Exercise good judgment about the risks you take. You'll be meeting many people who will enrich your life, but some may try to take advantage of you. Be careful about lending money or equipment, especially to people whom you have just met. Exercise your street smarts on campus to avoid potential exploitation.

You may sometimes feel pressured by friends to take safety risks, such as drinking inappropriately, taking drugs, or hanging out in places that don't feel safe. Don't succumb to peer pressure to do things that make you uncomfortable or place you at risk. True friends have your best interests at heart. If you feel pressure to take risks, it's time to reevaluate your friendships.

Unfortunately, you can also end up in the wrong place at the wrong time. Big parties, fueled by alcohol, can sometimes get out of hand. If a melee erupts, assess your risk and strive to keep your distance from the trouble. If the disruption is serious enough that security shows up to investigate, move rapidly out of the area. Don't stick around to see what happens, since you can quickly get drawn into actions that could be reflected on your record.

One final safety concern you may have in the aftermath of the 2007 massacre at Virginia Tech is the possibility that gun violence may erupt on campus. Despite the harrowing prospect of being involved in such an event, gun violence on campus is an extremely rare occurrence. However, most campuses have put in place "lockdown" procedures involving mass e-mail notifications and locking classroom doors until conditions are substantiated as safe. Here are some steps you can take to enhance your safety regarding disruption by an armed intruder on the campus:

- Register for emergency e-mail, Twitter, or text blasts to keep you informed about conditions.
- Do not strike out on your own to verify the origins of noises that could be coming from violence; leave heroics to armed campus security forces.
- Size up possible escape routes or hiding places in case an intruder might suddenly appear.
- If no escape is possible, lock or block the entrance and keep as quiet as you can.
- Disperse throughout the space to make it more challenging for the intruder to exert control over the room.
- Grab heavy items, such as textbooks, that could be lobbed at the intruder to disrupt or disorganize an impending assault.
- Cooperate fully with campus security to ensure the best outcomes possible, even if it means the temporary loss of your freedom to move about or leave the campus until the "all clear" sounds.

Maintain Balance

The crush of homework assignments and deadlines can sometimes threaten your sense of well-being. College life is often very challenging on a personal level, but two important resources—mental health and spiritual helpers—can come to your aid.

Mental Health Options Talking to a counselor or therapist may provide the relief you need. Large campuses have mental health departments or psychology clinics, but even small colleges are likely to provide access to mental health services. They may have on-site therapists and counselors who will give you support on a one-on-one or a group basis. The fee for such services will be on a sliding scale (meaning that the cost is proportional to your income), covered by your health insurance policy, or covered by your tuition.

Some student services offer topic-specific support groups, such as a group for single parents returning to college or for students struggling with English as a second language. In support groups, you can meet others who have problems similar to yours and who may have developed helpful solutions. Ask the counseling center personnel about support groups on campus.

If you do not find a group that addresses your concern, consider creating one. Most support groups start from the concerns of one or two students. The student services office can usually assist you with the advertising and the room arrangements to help your group get off the ground.

Spiritual Assistance Another path to balance is to draw strength from your spiritual beliefs. To address spiritual concerns, campus ministries usually coordinate religious activities for various denominations. These may be formal religious services or social groups where you can simply get together with others who share your faith. You not only can practice your faith, but you can also expand your network of friends with common values. Of course, religious services are also available off campus.

Exploring the religious practices of others also can be helpful. It may open your eyes to new perspectives or help you reaffirm the importance of the spiritual beliefs you had when you began college. Think through the following questions to chart your spiritual course: How important will it be for you to set aside time to explore your religious and spiritual concerns? If religion and spirituality figure significantly in your life, how will you find time for them? What kind of commitments should be in your schedule to help you keep up the practice of your faith?

Overcome Limitations

In the last decade, the number of college students with disabilities has increased dramatically. Today more than 10 percent of college students have some form of physical or mental impairment that substantially limits their major life activities. Students with disabilities include a number of injured veterans of wars in Afghanistan and Iraq who pursue a college education once they have returned to the United States. Federal regulations require colleges to make reasonable accommodations to allow students with a disability to perform up to their capacity. Accommodations can be made for motor and mobility impairments, visual and hearing deficits, physical and mental health problems, and learning disabilities (Hallahan, Kauffman, & Pullen, 2012).

If you discover you are struggling, study skills specialists can conduct diagnostic testing to determine the nature of your learning difficulties, if any, or they can refer you to specialists who provide this service. They can suggest compensating strategies for your assignments and may be able to give you some directions about taking courses with instructors who are more sympathetic to your struggle to learn. They also can set up and monitor additional study supports, including tutoring and study groups, to get you accustomed to the demands of college-level work.

If you have a disability, determine what level and kind of support you need to achieve college success. The level of service a college provides can be classified as follows:

Goodluz/Shutterstock.com

Many individuals overcome physical disabilities and other limitations to become successful college students. What are some services that colleges provide for individuals with physical limitations?

- *Minimal support.* Students generally adapt to the college and advocate for their own services and accommodations.
- *Moderate support.* The campus offers a service office or special staff to help students with advocacy and accommodations.
- *Intense support.* The campus provides specific programs and instructional services for students with disabilities.

Among the academic services that may be available for persons with disabilities are the following:

- *Referrals for testing, diagnosis, and rehabilitation.* Specialists who can help in this area may be located on or off campus.
- *Registration assistance.* Personnel typically provide guidance on such matters as the location of classrooms, scheduling, and in some cases waivers of course requirements.
- *Accommodations for taking tests.* Instructors may allow expanded or unlimited time to complete tests, and you may be able to use a word processor or other support resources during the exam.
- *Classroom assistance.* Someone may be assigned to take notes for you or to translate lectures into sign language. Instructors may allow their lectures to be taped for students with impaired vision or other disabilities.
- *Special services that address reading and visual disabilities.* Support services on campus are finding inventive new ways to help students overcome reading and visual limitations.

Connect and Communicate

Your college experiences will be enriched by the degree to which you reach out and build your own resources for the challenges that lie ahead. In this section, we discuss the importance of extracurricular involvement, cultural pursuits, contributions to the community, and skilled use of technology.

Pursue Extracurricular Activities

Participating in extracurricular activities does not just only improve your chances of meeting people who share your interests; research studies have demonstrated that such activities are also linked to higher self-esteem and academic success (Barber, Stone, & Eccles, 2010; Kort-Butler & Hagewen, 2011). Students who participate in extracurricular activities tend to have higher grade-point averages and higher rates of degree completion. Extracurricular activities can help you develop leadership skills, promote effective management of multiple commitments, and give you an opportunity to get to know your instructors informally. Students who participate are generally happier with their college experience than their counterparts who don't get involved.

Activities may be listed in the campus handbook or advertised in the student newspaper. Many majors sponsor clubs that allow you to explore careers through field trips or special speakers. If you're interested in journalism, you can work

Cheri Blauwet

Overcoming Limitations

2005 NYC Marathon
© Michael Krinke 2005

Cheri Blauwet is a remarkable person. As a student at the University of Arizona, she had a 4.0 GPA and earned degrees in cellular biology and music performance (in two instruments—piano and clarinet). As a college student, she singlehandedly convinced college officials to improve training facilities for students with disabilities, mentored children with disabilities, and did volunteer work for hospitals. Her athletic accomplishments include winning the Gold Medal in the 800-meter Athens Paralympics Games and being a two-time winner of the New York and Boston marathons in the wheelchair division (Blauwet, 2011). She graduated with a medical degree and is pursuing a degree from the Stanford University School of Medicine as part of her career path to becoming a physician in physical medicine and rehabilitation. She intends to specialize in the rehabilitation of individuals with disabilities in developing countries. In 2011, Cheri worked on completing her medical internship at Brigham and Women's Hospital in Boston. Reflecting on her college experience, Cheri says, "Coming to the University of Arizona and being a part of the Adaptive Athletics Program helped me to shape the development of my career and began to show me what was possible" (Thinkexist.com, 2008).

on the college newspaper or yearbook. Theater productions may not require a drama major before letting you get involved. Students interested in business can join an entrepreneurs' group to examine how businesspeople manage their lives and work. Intramural and campus sports also are available.

Of course, you can get too involved in campus life. Before you know it, you may have more commitments than you can manage and too little time to study. Have fun, but keep your larger goals in mind.

Involving Family Sometimes it may seem that your study life is too full to accommodate extracurricular activities, especially if you are a commuting student and have pressing responsibilities at home or in a job. However, enjoying leisure time and reconnecting with friends and family are both crucial for balance in your life. If campus participation creates too much strain at home, investigate activities that might welcome your partner, children, and friends who predated your college involvement. Concerts, fairs, and sports events can help you reconnect with your loved ones while you relax and have the fun that will help you manage your life. If your income is limited, look for activities that don't wipe out your cash.

Going Greek One decision that many first-year students face is whether to join a sorority or a fraternity, which are known as "Greek" organizations (after the Greek alphabet used to name most of them). They were originally established not only to enhance academic achievement but also to encourage social participation outside the classroom. Membership in a fraternity or sorority takes place through what is known as *recruitment* (formerly known as *rush*), a process of mutual selection that matches students interested in joining a Greek organization with the individual sorority or fraternity. Recruitment usually begins at the start of the fall or spring term. The organizations invite students to *pledge* when they think there is a good match between students' interests, values, and talents and those of the organization.

Joining a sorority or fraternity can have advantages and disadvantages. The advantages can include becoming closely connected with a group of people who share similar interests with you. You are a part of not only a sorority or fraternity at your particular college but also of a national organization with many chapters and a network of people. These contacts may be beneficial after college for social and business opportunities. Many sororities and fraternities also participate in worthwhile service activities, such as raising funds for children in foster care.

The disadvantages can include the extensive amount of time and money involved in pledging and membership. Costs can be substantial, from both direct membership expenses and indirect costs involved in preparing for and attending required social and civic events. Although many Greek organizations have embraced initiatives

Many students affiliate with a sorority or fraternity to enhance their satisfaction with social side of college.

AP Photo/April L. Brown

to reduce alcohol abuse and hazing, some have not. Consequently, affiliating with less responsible groups can be hazardous to your academic standing, physical health, and self-esteem.

Learning Communities A recent development on many campuses attempts to foster stronger academic performance by helping students meet others who share their interests and goals (Smith et al., 2004). *Learning communities* involve specialized course scheduling to enable groups of students to take sets of courses together. Students with the same interests may also live together on the same floor of a residence hall. The communities can be organized around honors status, interest in international issues, athletics, the arts, "green" issues, or any other concepts that produce sufficient interest. Learning communities appear to have a beneficial impact on how well students do academically and also provide a social network that promotes retention in college.

Enrich Your Cultural Life

Your campus and community may offer unique opportunities for cultural enrichment. Because most campuses are training grounds for artists and performers, they often operate an art gallery for display of student work or for work of invited artists. They also host live performances in music, dance, and theater to showcase student and faculty talent, as well as talent of outside professional performers. In the community, museums, galleries, theaters, the symphony, and political gatherings can all enrich your learning.

Invest in the Community

Some first-year programs create interesting ways to get to know the surrounding community through participation in "service learning" activities (Butin, 2005). Service learning opportunities may involve a commitment to build a Habitat for Humanity home, clean up litter on a stretch of highway, or distribute educational leaflets, among other worthy projects. Such projects have multiple goals. You can get to know the community and its needs in a new way as you exercise your leadership muscles and refine your teamwork skills. Typically, such programs are geared to help you embrace civic responsibilities.

Initially, students required to contribute time to a community project may feel some annoyance because they may not see clearly how the activity contributes to their personal learning goals; however, their objections will generally recede based on the success of the projects and the new connections and relationships such projects encourage. Service learning activities can provide a major boost to self-esteem and clarify the degree to which civic engagement could become a central personal value.

Connect through Technology

Computers are indispensable to college success. They support your efforts to think and learn, help you reach your college goals, provide a foundation for building essential career skills, and help you stay connected to the people who are important to you.

THE GREAT THING ABOUT THE INTERNET IS THAT NO ONE KNOWS YOU'RE A NERD!

COMIC BOOK CHAT ROOM

CHRIS MADDEN

Get Up to Speed Most instructors will assume that you have basic computer skills and will expect you to participate in class through e-mail, listservs, or electronic homework submissions. Check with your computer center for special classes, offered on campus or online, that will train you in using the best, most up-to-date computer programs. Most campuses provide free computer lab access. Still, early in your college experience, consider investing in a laptop to make your work portable and more efficient. Some campuses offer special-purchase or rental programs to allow you to expand your electronic resources.

Untangle the Web The Web (World Wide Web) is both the most exciting and the most frustrating aspect of the Internet. The excitement comes from the seemingly unlimited variety and scope of information presented in pictures, sounds, and dazzling graphics, available to anyone with a browser. With the simple click of a button on a site that interests you, you can navigate from one piece of information to other related information. When you find a site that you especially like and may want to revisit, you create a bookmark that lets you return there directly.

The Net can be invaluable in helping you solve academic problems (Howland et al., 2012). Googling a concept or topic on the Web is a great way to get inspiration for assignments. An enormous range and number of sites offer information that pertains to college subjects. For example, a class studying AIDS can find a wealth of facts about the disease, covering areas such as current research on medication, legal concerns, and support groups for HIV-positive individuals. Because many Web pages are updated frequently, this information may be among the most current professional research available.

However, Internet use can create certain problems (Smaldino, Lowther, & Russell, 2012).

First, students can experience frustration and feel overwhelmed as a result of the sheer quantity of information available on the Web. Searching using a key word via a browser may turn up thousands of possible hits. There may be no easy way to separate the treasure from the trash, and visiting every site takes too long. Some students report that they spend hours on the Web but still can't find answers to the questions that prompted their search.

Second, some websites are seriously out-of-date. The Web does not have the same quality control that the academic journals in your college library practice. Get in the habit of examining the information about the maintenance of the website. It will help you judge the currency and value of the information posted.

Third, it can be tempting to conduct research by using what is easy to access rather than identifying more appropriate sources. For example, when writing a paper, you may be disposed to cite a definition from Wikipedia, the communal electronic encyclopedia. Unfortunately, your instructors may judge that citation to be unacceptable. Instead, think about using the "wiki" as a starting point to conduct "preresearch," in which you get a general orientation to the topic before

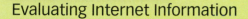

HIGHLIGHT

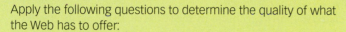

Evaluating Internet Information

Apply the following questions to determine the quality of what the Web has to offer:

- *How accurate is the information?* Do you have any way of checking the accuracy of the content?
- *How authoritative is the information?* What authority or expertise do the creators of the website have? How knowledgeable are they about the subject matter? For example, there is a big difference between the information about space launches that an armchair amateur posts and the facts that NASA sites provide.

- *How objective is the information?* Is the information presented with a minimum of bias? To what extent is the site trying to push a particular idea and sway opinions versus presenting facts?
- *How current is the information?* Is the content of the site up-to-date? When was the website last updated?
- *How thorough is the coverage?* Are topics covered in sufficient depth? What is the overall value of the content?

you get down to the serious work of scholarship from the legitimate sources you will cite in your project (Grathwohl, 2011).

Fourth, "canned" term papers can be downloaded and submitted for assignments. Not only does this practice short-circuit your learning, but instructors have developed a variety of electronic strategies to identify when your work is not original. Using canned term papers written by someone else can result in plagiarism charges and serious academic consequences if discovered by the instructor.

Finally, surfing the Web can steal too much time. Most users report that hours can slip away while they're online. Monitor your habits so you don't find yourself spending all your free time online.

Networking E-mail and instant messaging help you stay connected to people who are important to you. Many faculty members use these tools as well. For example, some of your instructors will incorporate electronic class participation through class listservs to help you practice using the concepts of the course. Some instructors welcome questions via e-mail because it's often more convenient than office hours for both parties. Many instructors are open to developing online relationships with their students, and some may prefer online chats to face-to-face discussions.

E-mail has its hazards, too (Lever-Duffy & McDonald, 2011). Install spam blockers and virus protection, or you can lose time and money in trying to manage your queue. Never send out personal data in response to requests over the Internet, especially your Social Security number. It is unlikely that you have won a lottery or a luxury cruise, or have a fortune waiting offshore, so don't fall for the scams that may infiltrate your screen.

Something you may already have done—and if not will likely do during college—is write an e-mail to a professor. Following are some tips on the best way to do this (Brandywine et al., 2011; Brandyon, 2011):

- *Use your college e-mail address if you have a choice.* For example, brsanchez@ucolorado.edu gives the professor better information about who sent the e-mail than brs@hotmail.com. This is especially important in large classes.
- *Offer an appropriate greeting.* Don't say something like "Hey Professor" or "Hi Doc." Start off this way: "Hello Professor Barker." Even if the professor

replies using his or her first name, continue to use Professor Barker's last name in subsequent e-mails unless given explicit permission to be more familiar.

- *Write a meaningful subject line.* Most professors get a lot of e-mails every day. Don't leave the subject line blank. Don't use a vague subject line such as "Hi" or "question." Write a clear, brief subject line, like "Question about the 1st test next Monday."
- *Be brief and write clearly.* Don't ramble—in most cases, don't write longer than what will fit on less than one screen. Use clear, grammatically correct complete sentences rather than abbreviations.
- *Sign the e-mail with your full name, course number, and meeting time.* This is especially important in large classes.
- *Review and proofread your e-mail.* Use spell-check to check for spelling errors. If the e-mail is about a sensitive, controversial issue, ask someone else to read the e-mail before you send it to be sure it won't offend the professor.

Use a Word-Processing Program Of all the tips for success in this book, one of the most important is to master a word-processing program and use it to write all your papers. Word-processing programs make the process of writing and rewriting papers easier because you can edit without having to retype most of your work (Newby et al., 2011). You also can select different print types (*fonts*) and use other features to highlight or underline key sections. With most word-processing programs, you can easily incorporate headers (standard headings at the top of each page), page numbers, and footnotes. Many programs will also develop your reference list, placing it in the conventional format for the discipline in which you're writing. Especially helpful are the features that allow you to check spelling, grammar, and word count when you complete your paper. Some applications can help you dress up projects with color features and graphics.

Word processing also involves some hazards. If you don't make a habit of saving your work often, you can end up with nothing to print or send. Also, spell-checkers do not substitute for good proofreading, because they identify words that are misspelled but not words that are misused. For example, most won't catch the difference between *there* and *their* or *to, too,* and *two*. The worst problem associated with word processing is that it might encourage you to procrastinate and therefore lose revision time, because your first draft can look very professional even if it isn't. Better papers are better because the writer allowed some time to think again and revise.

Consider Online Learning Technological advances have dramatically expanded the learning resources and opportunities available to students. Electronic texts, supplementary study and test-prep aids, online courses, and even online degree programs are in wide use.

Electronic Texts and Supplements Learning materials are commonly provided to students through a website or a CD-ROM. For example, this book has a companion website that can be accessed at www.cengagebrain.com. Electronic text supplements usually include review sections, practice tests with various types of items (such as multiple-choice and essay questions), and opportunities to expand your learning beyond the information found in the textbook. Take advantage of these electronic supplements to make learning more effective for you.

Online Courses and Virtual Colleges A key benefit of taking some of your courses online is convenience. This arrangement is especially helpful for students who travel or have other time or geographic constraints that make on-campus classes challenging to complete.

In a typical online course, you will find the syllabus posted and each week's assignments and activities fully explained. However, in some cases, online courses are self-paced, with all assignments due by the end of the term. You will probably be required to read a textbook and take quizzes or exams online, and, in some cases, to participate in online discussions. An instructor will monitor your work, and you will usually be able to contact him or her via e-mail.

Online education may not be for everybody. Many students want and need the personal interaction that a traditional classroom provides, and face-to-face contact might be especially important during your first year while you are settling in. Examine the Know Yourself: Self-Assessment 2.4, "Is Online Coursework for Me?," at the end of this chapter to evaluate whether this approach is a good match for your learning characteristics.

Many institutions offer complete degree programs online or host "blended" or "hybrid" programs that involve a mix of face-to-face and online activity. Such programs are often referred to as a *virtual college*. Some programs involve participation in a "cohort" of students. In this arrangement, a specific group of students commits to pursuing a degree together over a predetermined timeframe. Virtual colleges greatly increase one's opportunities to complete a degree and can especially benefit students who have to travel extensively or who can't always be present to attend classes on campus. For some students, virtual college solves the problem if there is no college nearby. However, if online degree programs attract you, be sure to evaluate the academic standing of the program carefully before you sign on the dotted line. Legitimate programs should be accredited by appropriate agencies. Also, before you make your decision, check the reputation of the program to find out how graduates with that specific degree fare in the job market. Find out what the completion rate is to help you gauge whether you can manage the challenge.

Expand Your Technology Tool Kit Developing expertise in using other technology tools—research databases, spreadsheets, and graphics and presentation software—can help you enormously if the particular task at hand is made easier by their use (Lever-Duffy & McDonald, 2011).

Research Databases Your campus library houses electronic databases that can be a big help with completing research assignments. Each database uses key words, years, or authors to direct you to specific articles in the professional literature. Table 2.1 lists some of the most frequently used academic databases.

You may encounter other databases as well. For example, business classes may explore how to keep track of inventory or potential customers. If you get a part-time job at the college, you may be working with databases of alumni addresses or bookstore inventories. Knowing how to navigate Excel or Access, popular database programs, may help you land a good job.

Database programs that allow you to perform calculations on numerical data are called *spreadsheets*. For example, you can enter data from a chemistry experiment into the columns of a spreadsheet and set up the spreadsheet program to calculate and summarize the results.

Graphics and Presentation Software graphics packages let you express yourself visually. They allow you to copy and design images, create animations, develop charts and graphs, and make impressive computer-driven presentations. Some of your courses may have graphics requirements. In other classes, graphics can improve the content and aesthetic appeal of your work.

TABLE 2.1 Helpful Library Research Databases

MULTIDISCIPLINARY	LITERATURE, ARTS, HUMANITIES
Academic Search Complete	Art Full Text
CREDO Reference	ArtSTOR
Expanded Academic ASAP	Humanities Full Text
Gale Virtual Reference Library	Literature Resource Center
JSTOR	
LexisNexis Academic	**SCIENCES**
	Biosis
BUSINESS	CINAHL
ABI/INFORM	Medline
Business Source Complete	ScienceDirect
Business and Company Resource Center	SpringerLink

SOCIAL AND BEHAVIORAL SCIENCES

ERIC

PsycINFO/PsycARTICLES

SocIndex with Full Text

Courtesy of Robert Dugan, Dean of Libraries, University of West Florida

When used properly, PowerPoint can be an especially powerful presentation software tool. If you have to prepare a class presentation, it can help you organize your content and put it in a dynamic, visually attractive format. PowerPoint is a staple of the business world, too. It simplifies the art of giving presentations and makes them much more professional, as well as more interesting for the audience. PowerPoint enables you to include a variety of visual elements that add impact to a presentation.

Used improperly, though, PowerPoint can be deadly. Flashy graphics are no substitute for a well-rehearsed presentation. Text presented on the screens should support material presented orally. It should be telegraphic or "bulleted" rather than consisting of massive paragraphs that will distract listeners from paying attention to what you are saying. Excessive use of animations and sound effects generally detracts from the quality of the thinking you are trying to showcase.

Avoid Computer Addiction Some users are so dedicated to their computers that they neglect their work or studies. How can a computer be so addictive? Here are some common attractions:

- *The compelling opportunity to explore the world.* Casual surfing of the Internet can take you in many directions. Anyone with a healthy curiosity can find it hard to stay away from the vast and varied sources of information that computers can reach.
- *The obsessive attraction of computer games.* The thrill of good performance is rewarding. It's easy to keep playing "just one more time" to see whether you can better your score. Hours slip by as you gradually refine your game skill and lose your real social connections.
- *The seduction of electronic relationships.* An electronic relationship between two people can feel profound because the absence of physical cues

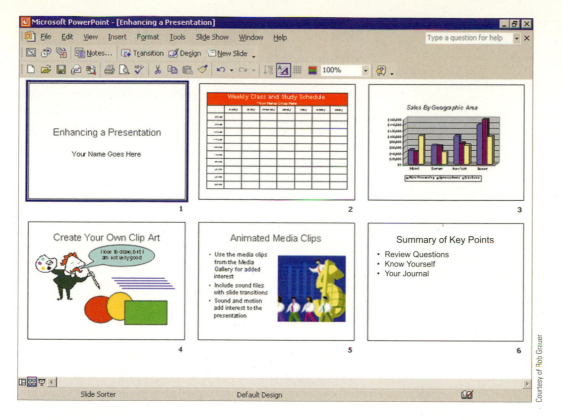

With PowerPoint, you can include a variety of visual elements that can add impact to a presentation.

may allow you to connect to another person in a novel way, unfettered by physical quirks or questionable hygiene. Without the other elements of real life intruding, such exchanges can lead to deeper emotional involvement and reward than a user may currently experience in face-to-face relationships. However, this sense of intimacy can be based on half-truths, or even lies, because you have no real way of knowing who the other person is. In any case, such relationships can be compelling and time-consuming. If you find yourself favoring e-friends over "real" friends, think twice!

- ***The overwhelming drive to stay connected.*** Although texting and e-mailing have added major convenience to our lives, they also pose dangers, both subtle and serious. The lure of messaging may prompt you to ignore the real people you are sitting beside, which can hurt feelings and alienate friends. Apart from that, texting while driving can be lethal.

Use Social-Networking Sites Responsibly The social environment of many college students includes the highly popular websites Facebook and MySpace, by which students can communicate with others who share their interests. Launched in 2004, Facebook has grown to the point where it surpassed Google in 2010 as the most visited Web portal on the Internet. Facebook links more than 600 million active users. The online directory lets students create profiles that can include their photographs, personal preferences, cell phone numbers, and college experiences. Also begun in 2004, MySpace provides a similar social networking opportunity.

Many college students who use Facebook and MySpace have apparently thought that the information they placed on the websites was private. Facebook has improved the security of its information recently; however, it still may be easy for anyone to access the information by including parents, college personnel, and employers. For example, all it takes to obtain the information you put on Facebook is an e-mail address. Thus, if you are a Facebook or MySpace user, you should never put your Social Security number, address, phone number, or date of birth information on the website. Another good strategy is to not post information on Facebook or MySpace that current or future employers might use against you in any way. A final strategy is to be aware that college administrators and personnel may be able to use the information you place on Facebook or MySpace to evaluate whether you have violated college policies (such as college drug use or language harassment policies).

A national survey revealed that 94 percent of first-year college students spent at least some time on social-networking sites such as Facebook and MySpace (Higher Education Research Institute, 2007). In this study, 21 percent (about one-fifth) of students spent six or more hours per week on the sites. These students said that they had slightly more difficulty in managing their time and using effective study skills than their counterparts who spent less than six hours on the sites. This study suggests that a good college success strategy is to limit the amount of time you devote to social-networking sites.

Build a Bright Future

Learning to use college resources expertly can help you build a strong foundation of academic and social skills for the future. In this section, you will explore how that foundation can help you in your future career, how it can be strengthened with the support of a professional mentor, and how it can contribute to problem solving if your first college choice doesn't live up to your expectations.

Link Resources to Careers

Becoming an expert in using the resources that college has to offer can help you succeed as you prepare for your career. Academic resources at your college, especially your academic adviser, will help you to get on the right track with courses and a major that match your skills and interests. Getting the right major will increase the likelihood that you will be prepared for working after college in a career that you enjoy and want to stay with.

Participating in extracurricular activities during college broadens your interests and helps to make you a well-rounded individual. When you interview for a job after college, you likely will be asked about your interests and activities. The breadth and depth of the extracurricular activities that you engage in during college will increase the positive profile you want to present to prospective employers.

Technology is at the cutting edge of so many jobs and careers today. Make every effort to become technology literate and proficient to increase your employment chances after college and advance in your career.

Select a Mentor

Imagine the course Brian Long's life might have taken if he had not gotten the benefits of experience with a gifted mentor as described in the chapter opener. There might be just such a person lurking in the college environment that could make a compelling difference in your own college experience and subsequent career.

Select a mentor to enhance your opportunities for college success. A *mentor* is an adviser, a coach, and a confidant who can help you become successful and master many of life's challenges. Mentors can advise you on career pursuits, suggest ways to cope with problems, and listen to what's on your mind. A mentor might be a student who has successfully navigated the first-year experience, a graduate student, an instructor, or a person from the community whom you respect and trust. As you read about in the chapter opener, Brian Long initially benefited from having a mentor and then, after several years, himself became a mentor to other students.

If you don't have a mentor, think about the people you've met in college so far. Are there people whom you admire whose advice might benefit you? If no one comes to mind, start looking around for someone who might fill this role. As you talk with various people and get to know them better, one person's competence and motivation can start to rub off on you. This is the type of person who can be a good mentor. Explicitly ask your preferred candidates to serve as your mentors. They will probably be flattered and will have a framework to understand why you want to capture some special time with them.

Consider a Transfer

Sometimes students start their education in a college that doesn't quite meet their expectations. If you decide to transfer to another college, you'll want to know whether the credits you've earned will transfer to the new school. Check the catalog of the new college and see how its requirements match up with those of your current college. The catalog will also describe transfer requirements. Next, be sure to talk with an adviser at the new college about which of your courses will transfer. Here are some questions you might ask the admissions adviser (Harbin, 1995):

- What are the minimum admission criteria that I have to meet to transfer to your college?
- Do I need a minimum grade-point average for admission? If so, what is it?
- What are the application deadlines for transfer admissions?
- Where can I get a transfer application?
- What else can you tell me about transferring to your college?

If you think you want to change colleges but aren't sure where you want to go, consult some general guides to colleges such as *Peterson's National College Data Bank* (www.petersons.com) or *Barron's Profiles of American Colleges* (www.barronseduc.com). Try to visit several campuses that might meet your needs. Talk with students there, as well as with an academic adviser. Walk around and get a feel for how you like the campus. Be clear about what aspects of your current life are unsatisfying and why the new school will be better.

Clarify Expectations

- Know which campus resources you need now or might need in the future.
- Investigate library resources and learn to use the library effectively.

Develop Competence

- Take extra steps to connect with your adviser if you aren't on campus during business hours.
- Get to know your college catalog.
- Get the right courses through such strategies as listing your constraints, examining your interests, and studying your options.
- Choose the right major for you. Realistically assessing your interests, skills, and abilities will help you.
- Target the right kind and level of program to meet your needs.

Manage Life

- Keep safe and healthy with support of on-campus resources.
- Find the right balance by addressing spiritual and mental health concerns.
- If you're a student with a physical limitation, learn about and use available campus resources.
- Think proactively about self-protective actions you can take if you feel under threat.

Connect and Communicate

- Participate in extracurricular and cultural activities to round out your experience.
- Consider service learning as a way of enriching your learning experience.
- Become expert at the use of digital strategies for word processing, social networking, and researching.

Build a Bright Future

- Link current resource uses to plans for succeeding in your career.
- Find a mentor to enhance your professional readiness.
- Consider transferring to another setting if your current experience proves too disappointing.

 Visit the College Success CourseMate for *Your Guide to College Success* for interactive resources at login.cengagebrain.com

Review Questions

1. What kinds of campus connections matter and why? Name at least three.

   a. Resource: _____

      Why is it important? _____

   b. Resource: _____

      Why is it important? _____

   c. Resource: _____

      Why is it important? _____

2. What is the best approach to engage people on campus so that they will want to help you solve your problems?

   _____

   _____

   _____

3. What are some key aspects of designing an academic career path? List three things you can do now to begin this process.

   a. _____

   b. _____

   c. _____

4. Why is your college catalog such a valuable resource? What are some of the most important facts you can learn from this guide?

   _____

   _____

   _____

5. What are some strategies for selecting the right courses?

   _____

   _____

   _____

6. What are some key considerations when selecting a major? How might you know whether you have made an inappropriate choice?

   _____

   _____

   _____

7. Name three college resources that can help you stay healthy and practice safety.

   a. _____

   b. _____

   c. _____

8. Why will participating in extracurricular activities improve the likelihood that you will stay in college?

   _____

   _____

   _____

9. List at least three important computer skills that will help you succeed in college. Which one do you think will have the greatest impact on your immediate success?

   a. _____

   b. _____

   c. _____

10. How can having a mentor help college students?

   _____

   _____

   _____

 **Know Yourself**

Campus Resources to Meet My Needs

First, cross off any items that you know you won't need. Add any other locations that you think you will need. Then answer "Yes" or "No" after the items that remain. Next, write down the location of the campus resource and any notes you want to make about it, such as its hours, phone number, and e-mail address.

Does My Campus Have	Yes or No	Location/Notes
Career services center?		
Student testing center?		
Math laboratory?		
Performing arts center?		
Campus security?		
Financial aid office?		
Resource center for students with disabilities?		
Childcare center?		
ROTC service?		
TV or radio station?		
Work-study program?		
Writing lab?		
Health center?		
Travel agency?		
Mental health services?		
Language lab?		
Intramural sports office?		
Student government office?		
Post office?		
Lost and found?		
Printing service?		
Banking center?		
Computer labs?		
Multimedia and graphics lab?		
International students' center?		
College newspaper office?		
Religious services?		
Campus cinema?		
Other		
Other		
Other		

Compare your information with that of others in the class. How are you doing in discovering resources on your campus? Put the information about resources in the planner that you carry with you on campus. Note: This list is also on the website for this book, where you can easily tailor it to meet your own needs and print out a copy.

© Cengage Learning 2013

Know Yourself

SELF-ASSESSMENT 2.2

What Are My Interests?

Answering these questions can help you pinpoint your interests.

What activities do you enjoy doing the most?

_____

_____

_____

When you are doing what you want, what are you doing?

_____

_____

_____

What do you do in your leisure time?

_____

_____

_____

What are your hobbies?

_____

_____

_____

Can you relate any of the activities, hobbies, or interests to possible academic majors? If so, which ones?

_____

_____

_____

Can you link any of the activities, hobbies, or interests to possible careers? If so, which ones?

_____

_____

_____

Source: Urbana-Champaign: Weston Exploration, U. of Illinois, *The Model for exploration*. Reprinted with permission.

SELF-ASSESSMENT 2.3

A Four- or Five-Year Academic Plan

Study your college catalog to find out what courses you need to graduate with a particular major. If you have not selected a major, examine the requirements for one you're considering. Then fill in the blanks with the courses you plan to take. Use this self-assessment to discuss your decisions with your academic adviser. The plan here is for schools on a semester schedule. If your school has a quarterly system, create your own plan by listing the quarters for each of the four or five years and then filling in the courses you plan to take.

Fall	Spring	Summer
	First Year	
	Second Year	
	Third Year	
	Fourth Year	
	Fifth Year	

© Cengage Learning 2013

SELF-ASSESSMENT 2.4

Is Online Coursework for Me?

Evaluating yourself on the following items should help you to determine whether online coursework would be a good idea for you.

Place a check mark next to the items that apply to you.

_____ I feel irritated by the amount of time I waste in commuting to classes.

_____ I have keyboarding skills that allow me to communicate with reasonable efficiency.

_____ I am intrigued with Internet resources and like to explore the Web in my spare time.

_____ I usually have good self-discipline about initiating and completing projects.

_____ I don't usually hesitate to express my opinion.

_____ I find it easier to write than to speak my opinions.

_____ I don't mind working on projects with others whom I have not met.

_____ I don't necessarily have to see people or be in their physical presence to develop a working relationship with them.

_____ I will be closer to some important career opportunities with each course I complete.

The more items you checked, the more success you are likely to have in online courses. If you have not developed good self-discipline, online coursework may not be for you.

Clarify Expectations

1. My Best Helpers

The names of the persons who have helped me the most on campus so far: _____

How they have helped me: _____

The aspect of college that I need the most help with right now is: _____

The person on campus who most likely could help me in this area is: _____

2. My Library Needs

Libraries provide many services that students are often unaware of. What service does your library provide that you might need to use in the next year? If you can't answer this question, obtain a library brochure of services or talk with a librarian about the services. Describe them below, linked with the need they will help fulfill.
Library service: How will I use it?

   a. _____

   b. _____

   c. _____

3. Only the Best

Ask students whom you trust, and who have been on campus longer than you, about where to locate at least five of the following:

- Best cheap, hot breakfast
- All-night food store
- Local businesses that give student discounts
- Best software
- Live music
- Best pizza
- Best coffee
- Free or cheap movies
- Best place for quiet conversation
- Best place to exercise
- Best bulletin board
- Best place to dance
- Discount bookstores
- Cheap photocopies
- Best place to view the stars

Your Journal

4. Your Cognitive College Map

You may have received a campus map as part of your orientation materials. Draw your own map as well. On it, emphasize the aspects of campus that are most important to you by drawing them larger and in a more stylized way. You might also try constructing the map using computer graphics.

 ## Develop Competence

5. Ask the Right Questions

Make an appointment to see your academic adviser. Create a set of questions to ask, such as:

- What classes should I take this term and next?
- What sequence of classes should I take?
- Am I taking too many difficult classes in one term?
- What electives do you recommend?
- What career opportunities are there if I study mainly ___ or ___?

Write about your conversation with your academic adviser.

_____

_____

_____

_____

6. Finding Your Bliss

List below three ways you will know that a college major is the right one for you:

a. _____

b. _____

c. _____

 **Manage Life**

7. Keeping Healthy

An Irish proverb states, "A good laugh and a long sleep are the best cures in the doctor's book." What resources on your campus can help you become healthier?

a. _____

b. _____

c. _____

8. Worst-Case Scenario

If in the unlikely situation you hear a gunshot on campus, describe three things you would do to enhance your safety.

a. _____

b. _____

c. _____

Connect and Communicate

9. Explore Extracurricular Activities

Locate or create a list of extracurricular events or meetings on your campus. Write down a few that appeal to you most, then attend one or two. Decide whether you want to make these activities a regular part of your college life by making a list of pros and cons for such involvement.

Interesting activities: _____

Pros for involvement: _____

Cons for involvement: _____

10. Dealing with Computers

What computer skills do you have? What computer skills don't you have? How would you go about using this strength and weakness to connect to another student who may have the opposite pattern so you can learn from each other? What other resources on campus can help you get proficient in computer use?

_____

_____

_____

Build a Bright Future

11. Explore Campus Jobs

Perhaps the fastest way to find work is to go to the financial aid office on campus. Ask for a list of available part-time jobs. Do any of these jobs appeal to you? Will any help you develop skills toward a future career? Write down at least three jobs that best link up with future careers that interest you. Include a strategy for exploring each opportunity.

a. JOB: _____

STRATEGY: _____

b. JOB: _____

STRATEGY: _____

c. JOB: _____

STRATEGY: _____

12. Linking College Resources with Jobs and Careers after College

Which college resources described in this chapter do you think will help you build a strong foundation for work and career advancement following college?

a. _____

b. _____

c. _____

Manage Time Wisely

Chapter 3

KNOW YOURSELF

WHAT YOU DO WITH YOUR TIME IS CRITICAL to your success in college and beyond. Highly successful scientists, businesspeople, and other professionals say that managing their time on a daily basis is crucial to reaching their goals. How you choose to spend your time can make all the difference between success and failure in college. How strong is your current ability to manage time effectively? For each item below, place a check mark in the box that best captures how effective you currently are with managing your time.

Do I Know How to Manage My Time?

	Very Much Like Me	Somewhere In Between	Not at All Like Me
I am good at spending time on activities that are related to my most important values and goals.			
I use a paper or an electronic planner to manage my time effectively.			
I have created a term planner and I monitor it.			
I regularly set priorities in managing my time.			
I make weekly plans, monitor how I use my time each week, and evaluate what I need to do or change in order to reach my goals.			
I complete daily to-do lists.			
I treat my academic commitment as a serious job.			
The time I spend on academics equals or exceeds the time I spend on leisure, play, recreation, sports, and watching TV or surfing the Internet.			
I don't procrastinate much.			
I'm good at balancing my academic life with other demands.			

© o44/o44/ZUMA Press/Newscom

63

Spotlight On…

Mark Polson

Creating a Personalized System for Effectively Managing Time

When Mark Polson was a college student at the University of Utah, he felt totally overwhelmed with all he had to do. He had a heavy class schedule, worked while going to school, and was having trouble finding enough time to study.

How did Mark solve his problem of having what seemed like too few hours for study time? His solution was simple. He started doing more planning ahead and more calculation of how much time to allot to the various tasks he faced. When the computer-based system he developed helped him to raise his grades, Mark got together with two of his friends from the University of Utah and created www.gradefix.com in 2006.

Mark Polson and his friends at University of Utah collaborated to turn time management troubles into a successful web-based solution to save time and raise students' grade-point averages.

The gradefix system helps college students by guiding them in finding the time necessary to do homework and to study on a regular basis so that they don't end up having to cram for an exam at the last minute. The website's creators say that college students who are natural procrastinators are likely to benefit the most from using their system. Gradefix users report achieving at least half of one grade letter improvement in their overall coursework. To use Mark Polson's gradefix system, go to www.gradefix.com.

After graduation, Mark moved into professional website design. He currently serves as the CEO of *Code Green*, a website design service that he manages out of Salt Lake City. Mark Polson exemplifies how a college student can turn a problem into a success. He learned not only how to raise his grades but also how to develop a successful business. Whether you use Mark Polson's time-management system, use another such product, or create your own system, you will see that effectively managing time is critical for success in college.

Mark Polson devised his own effective strategy for managing his time to succeed in college. Look at the chapter outline. Based on your profile of how you manage your time, which parts of the chapter should be most helpful to you?

Clarify Expectations

How often have you said or heard people say, "I just don't have enough time"? Tough luck! Each of us has the same amount of time—24 hours, or 1,440 minutes, a day—yet individuals vary enormously in how effectively they plan and use their hours and minutes. You can't really change the nature of time or buy more of it than you're given. What you can change is how you manage yourself in relation to time.

Orient to Time

People differ in how they relate to the importance of time in their lives. Many are scrupulous about meeting deadlines and being punctual for appointments; they would be completely lost without their watches or smartphones. Others tend to be lackadaisical about time; they usually show up late for appointments and struggle with schedules and deadlines. You will find a mix of both kinds of people in the college setting.

Most of your professors will expect you to arrive to class and turn projects in on the deadline. Not all professors rigidly observe those rules; some may arrive

"Before we begin our Time Management Seminar, did everyone get one of these 36-hour watches?"

©2000 by Randy Glasbergen. www.glasbergen.com

late and keep you past the formal end of the class; however, as the manager of the classroom, they call the shots. Some professors are sticklers about arrival; if you don't get to class punctually, you may find yourself locked out! Some will refuse to accept papers or projects that are even an hour late.

Many college students feel overwhelmed with all they have to do. Yet some of the busiest and most successful students get high grades and still find enough leisure time. How do they do it? They control their life by controlling how they spend their time (Sarafino, 2010). You alone control how you use your time. Once you've wasted time, it's gone and can't be replaced. Nevertheless, despite its importance, you may blanch at the concept of time management.

Challenge Myths about Time Management

See if any of the following misconceptions relate to your beliefs about time management (Mackenzie & Nickerson, 2009):

- *Time management is nothing but common sense.* Time management is simple, but it is not necessarily common sense. What is not simple is the self-discipline to use time-management strategies.
- *I do well in school and I'm happy, so I must be managing my time effectively*. It is more likely that you are successful in spite of the way you manage time. What if you could double your productivity with more effective time-management strategies? How much more successful do you think you could be?
- *I work better under pressure, and time management would take away my edge*. Hardly anyone really works best under substantial pressure. What really happens is that people do the best they can under stressful circumstances. Usually, this is nothing but a rationale for procrastinating. If you put off an important task until the last minute with the excuse that you work better under pressure, you leave yourself no time to carry out the planning that is necessary to produce outstanding results. You also leave no room for correcting mistakes or including better ideas that might come to you too late to be included. By not managing your time, you miss the opportunity to do your best.
- *Taking time management too seriously sucks all the fun out of life*. If suffering from constant stress, forgetting appointments, missing deadlines, and working feverishly through the night all sound like fun, perhaps you should reconsider. Think of effective time management this way: If you had two more hours a day (good time-management strategies can achieve this), could you think of some enjoyable ways to spend those hours?
- *Time-management strategies take a great deal of work*. Consider this: You don't have time *not* to use them. Once you learn how to apply effective time-management techniques, such as writing a daily plan and keeping a time log, they are not that time-consuming in themselves. A few minutes spent taking these steps can save you hours by keeping you on track.

Identify Your Core Values

In Chapter 1, you learned about the importance of knowing what your values are and creating goals that align with them. This is a good strategy to engage in before you develop plans for managing time effectively. You don't want to spend lots of time in activities that don't coincide with the values you admire the most or that don't mesh with your most important short-term and long-term goals. A key aspect of effective time management is to manage your time in keeping with your values (Tracy, 2010). In Chapter 1, Know Yourself: Self-Assessment 1.1, "What Are My Values?," on page 24, you evaluated what things in life are important to you. To what extent do those values link with your time-management skills?

If you claimed that education is one of your highest values, but you are spending the bulk of your time socializing with friends and participating in campus organizations, then something is wrong. Your energy should be oriented first toward your most important values, with other activities taking a back seat. When choosing how to spend your time, examine your values to help you make a smart decision. If education is not a high priority, then activities that express other values are likely to take precedence. Now complete Know Yourself: Self-Assessment 3.1, "My Five Most Important Personal Values: Round 2," at the end of the chapter on page 89, to see if this perspective prompts you to make any changes.

Embrace Efficiency

If you are open to possibilities, consider how your life might change if you begin to emphasize managing time more effectively to improve your efficiency. See Highlight: "Reap the Benefits of Good Time Management" to reflect on all the advantages that becoming an expert time manager would make possible.

HIGHLIGHT

Reap the Benefits of Good Time Management

Managing your time effectively brings a lot of benefits. You will:

- **Be more productive**. Using your time more effectively will increase your productivity in college. You'll have the hours you need to write that long term paper. Effectively managing your time will help you get better grades.
- **Reduce your stress**. Managing your time poorly will increase your stress. Imagine the day before an exam when you suddenly realize that you have a massive amount of studying to do. Panic! Tension builds and stress escalates. Effectively managing your time will help you reduce the stress in your life.
- **Improve your self-esteem**. Learning to manage time effectively will increase your self-esteem by making you feel successful and ahead of the curve. Wasting a lot of time will make you feel bad about yourself because you are constantly playing catch-up.
- **Achieve balance in your life**. Developing good time-management skills and actively using them will let you achieve a more balanced life. You'll miraculously have more time for school, work, home, family, and leisure.
- **Establish an important career skill**. College provides you with an opportunity to work on developing many skills that you can carry forward into a career. Being a great time manager is a crucial skill. In most careers, to be successful, you'll need not only to complete many different tasks but also to complete them quickly and by a deadline.

Develop Competence

In this section you will learn about various strategies and tools you can adopt for improving your time management.

Chart Your Course

Successful individuals differ in how they accomplish their plans, but they develop specific strategies that yield the best results for them. The act of setting goals and planning how to reach them will help you live the life you want to live. You need time to reach your goals, so the better you can manage time, the bigger you can dream.

Set SMART Goals Goals express your values. If education is a high-priority value, then your goal setting needs to concentrate on improving academically. Managing your time effectively will probably entail spending many more hours studying than socializing.

For every goal you set, you can apply SMART criteria that successful project managers use to keep themselves on course: Is your goal

- *Specific?*
- *Measurable?*
- *Attainable?*
- *Relevant?*
- *Timely?*

For example, the global and vaguely stated goal "I want to be successful" doesn't provide much direction or momentum. Instead, a SMART version that reflects a high-priority value related to education could be, "I want to achieve a 3.5 grade-point average this term by reviewing my notes every night for an hour." By specifying the timeframe, the arena of effort, and the method—assuming you are willing to put in the time—this goal is much more helpful in developing your internal controls.

In addition, you may want to distinguish short-term goals from those that will require effort over the long haul. Complex goals may require achieving subgoals along the way. Completion dates are another important feature. Great time managers also try to anticipate and overcome obstacles; they usually have a "Plan B" lurking just in case something goes wrong.

Make a Commitment Some college students benefit from writing a contract for themselves related to their goals and time-management action plan (Davis et al., 2008). In the contract, spell out your goals, how you are going to use your time to achieve them, and how you plan to reward yourself for your self-discipline and staying on track. Sign and date your contract. To ensure that you follow through on your self-contract, choose a support person to sit down with you every other week for the next three months to evaluate your progress. The figure on the left is a sample self-contract form.

SAMPLE SELF CONTRACT FORM

I, _____ am going to do
    (your name)

_____.
            (activity or goal)

for or by _____.
            (how long, how often, when)

I will monitor my progress by _____.
                    (the method that you will use)

I will evaluate my progress every _____.
                        (how often)

with my support person, _____.
                    (name)

If I stick with this plan and reach my goal, I will reward myself with _____.
            (something that will motivate you)

© Cengage Learning 2013

Plan for the Long Term This is a good time to think about linking your personal values with your goals. Write down one or more specific long-term goals (this term to more than a year) and short-term goals (from a week to a month) for each of your top five values, and fill in the blanks in Know Yourself: Self-Assessment 3.2, "Connect Your Values with Long- and Short-Term Goals," at the end of the chapter on page 90.

Develop an Action Plan Now that you have identified your most important values and related them to long- and short-term goals, the next step is to manage your time effectively so that you can reach these goals. Developing an action plan starts with evaluating how you spend your time. Let's see how this could change the way you live your life this term.

Plan for the Term, Week, and Day Break down your time by term, week, and day using the following term planner. As you create plans for coordinating within these three timeframes, always keep in mind the importance of breaking your goals down into subgoals and intermediate steps. For example, you might have a major paper in English due in 3 weeks that counts for one-third of your grade. This week, you could create the following subgoals related to the paper (Winston, 1995):

First Day: Go to library and survey topics.
Second Day: Narrow topics.
Third Day: Select topic.
Fourth Day: Construct outline.
Fifth Day: Write first two pages.

And so on.

Work Backward Many people find it helpful to work backward to reach a goal (Murphy, 2010). For example, decide on an important goal that you want to reach in one year. First, think about what you need to do each month between now and then to attain that goal. Then, think about what you need to do weekly to achieve it. Finally, think about what you can do in the next 24 hours to get started. In this way, you can focus on a goal and work backward to outline the steps that will enable you to reach it.

Choose the Right Planning Tools

There are two modes—paper-based or digital—of planning to help you develop and maintain your schedule. You may rely solely on electronic devices, on simple or complex paper tracking methods, or some combination of both.

Paper-and-Pencil Planning Simple paper-and-pencil strategies involve writing spontaneous "to do" lists and Post-it® notes in obvious places. Although that approach can work for many people, such methods tend to be a little haphazard.

Most people who rely on paper prefer strategies that are more systematic and structured. Among the most effective and popular of these are the Franklin and Franklin Covey planners. The Franklin Covey planner especially encourages you to think about your goals and values as you set up your time-management program. For example, it asks you to set a long-range goal, write down the value of that goal or what its role is in your life, and then list the intermediate steps and their deadlines for reaching the goal. The Franklin Covey planner comes in a college version called the Franklin Covey Collegiate Planner.

This Image illustrates the evolution of planning tools from simple Post-it® notes, to paper systems, to digital tools such as the iPhone and iPad.

Digital Planning People are increasingly using sophisticated cell phones and tablet computers (e.g., iPads) to manage their time. They include reminder functions, list makers, e-mail functions, music storage, and a staggering number of "apps" to provide diversion during boring wait times.

Advantages of electronic planners include the following:

- They are compact.
- They can sort, organize, and store information more efficiently.
- They can provide audible reminders of when to do things.
- They can easily exchange information between office and home computers.

Which should you use? Before you make an investment in an expensive digital device that may require a monthly communications fee, talk to owners of the device to find out their recommendations and regrets.

Schedule Your Time

The challenge of scheduling your time well involves blending multiple calendars into a workable whole. Your goals will be achieved most easily if you are operating from a single calendar that reflects all of your commitments, projects, and deadlines from coursework and extracurriculars. If you have family or job responsibilities, integrate those activities as well. Next, you will learn about schedules for different timeframes.

Create a Term Plan Whether you are a nontraditional or traditional college student, you will benefit enormously by mapping out a week-by-week plan for the entire term. Some colleges provide a term calendar that identifies breaks and holidays, or your college catalog may provide this information. A term planner that you can fill in is shown below.

First, write in your five most important values, then your five most important goals for the term.

Next, write in the weeks. After that, write in vacations and holidays.

Next, get out your course syllabi and write down dates and deadlines for exams, major homework assignments, and papers.

Consider coding your different courses by color. History might be in red, English in blue, biology in green, and so on. Using colored pencils allows you to revise schedules easily.

Highlight exam dates with a marker or write them in large letters.

Term Planner

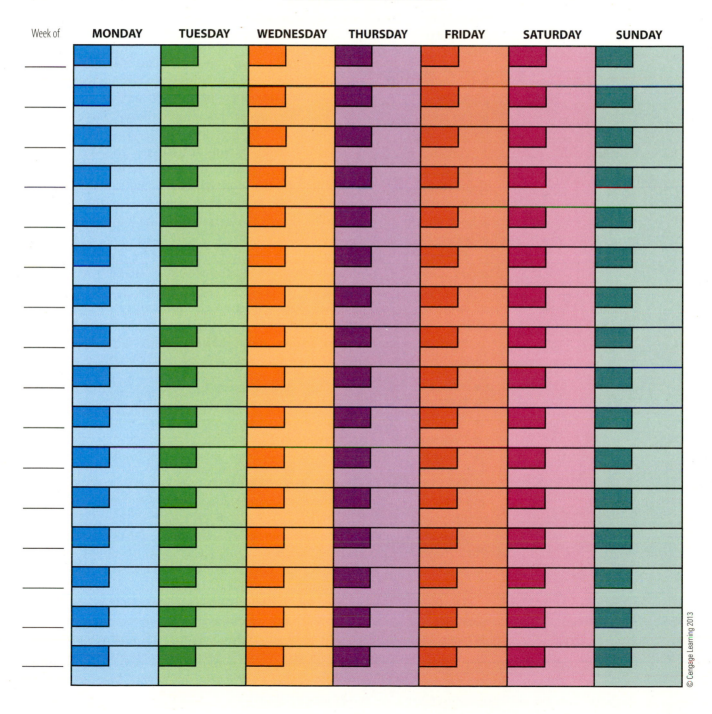

After you've written down your exam and other task dates on the calendar, look at the dates. Think about how many days or weeks you'll need to study for major exams and write major papers. Mark the days or weeks in which these tasks will be your main priorities. Keep in mind important nonacademic responsibilities such as employment, family commitments, commuting time, and volunteer work, and make sure to mark your calendar accordingly.

Keep a spare copy of your term planner in case you lose the original. You might want to carry a copy with you when you go to classes and place one on your bulletin board or in your desk. Consider posting an electronic version on your computer where you can access and edit it easily.

Your term calendar is not etched in stone. Check it regularly and decide when it needs modification. Your circumstances may change. An instructor might add another assignment or change a test date. You might find out that you need more study time than you originally predicted for a particular course, or your work schedule or family responsibilities may change during the term.

Manage a Weekly Plan In addition to your term plan, a weekly plan will help you maximize your time. Many corporate executives say that their weekly plans are critical for running their companies effectively. Even if your life goal is not to run a mammoth corporation, weekly planning skills will serve you well long after college.

As you construct your weekly plan, be sure to put enough time aside for doing assignments outside class. In a national survey, the more hours students spent studying or doing homework, the more they liked and stayed in college, improved their thinking skills, graduated with honors, and got into graduate school. Students who have higher grades and graduate with honors are less likely to watch TV or spend time partying.

On pages 72 and 73 is a grid on which to map out your weekly plan. You might want to make copies or create an electronic version so that you will have one for each week of the term. You can also use the weekly planning grids in a commercial paper-and-pencil planner or an electronic planner, as discussed earlier.

Next, ask yourself these questions about the next week:

- "What do I expect to accomplish?"
- "What will I have to do to reach these goals?"
- "What tasks are more important than others?"
- "How much time will each activity take?"
- "When will I do each activity?"
- "How flexible do I have to be to allow for unexpected things?"

Fill in your class hours, regular work commitments, family responsibilities, and other routine tasks in the *Plan* column. Then write in the remainder of the things you plan to do next week.

A good strategy is to fill in the *Plan* column at the end of the preceding week. Put it together on Friday afternoon or Sunday evening at the latest. The plan takes no more than a half hour to complete for most students, yet it can save you at least an hour a day that week!

During the week, monitor your schedule closely to see whether you carried out your plans. A good strategy is to sit down at the end of each day and write in the *Actual* column what you actually did that day compared with what you planned to do. Analyze the comparison for problems, and plan some changes to solve them.

Weekly Plan

		MONDAY		TUESDAY		WEDNESDAY	
		Plan	Actual	Plan	Actual	Plan	Actual
AM	6:00						
	7:00						
	8:00						
	9:00						
	10:00						
	11:00						
	12:00						
PM	1:00						
	2:00						
	3:00						
	4:00						
	5:00						
	6:00						
	7:00						
	8:00						
	9:00						
	10:00						
	11:00						
	12:00						
AM	1:00						
	2:00						
	3:00						
	4:00						
	5:00						

© Cengage Learning 2013

Use the weekly planner in concert with your term planner each week of the term.

Every weekend, pull out your term planner and see what your most important priorities are for the following week. Make any changes that are needed and then do the same thing with your weekly planner to stay focused.

THURSDAY		FRIDAY		SATURDAY		SUNDAY	
Plan	Actual	Plan	Actual	Plan	Actual	Plan	Actual

Apply the 80–20 Principle You might think that all your responsibilities are so important that you can't drop any of them completely or reduce the time they take (Davis et al., 2008). Vilfredo Pareto, an Italian economist, conceived of the *80–20 principle*. He observed that about 80 percent of what people do yields about 20 percent of the results they achieve, while about 20 percent of what people do produces about 80 percent of the results. For example, approximately 20 percent of a newspaper is worth your while to read. It is a good idea to skim the rest. At least 80 percent of people's mail (both e-mail and postal mail) is junk and best not read at all.

Many people spend their time in a frenzy of activity but achieve little because they are not concentrating on the things that will produce positive results for them. Separating the important communications from the junk will help you become a better time manager (Brown, 2010).

Make Swiss Cheese Time-management expert Alan Lakein (1973) developed the *Swiss cheese* approach of poking holes in a bigger task by working on it in small bursts of time or at odd times. For example, if you have ten to fifteen minutes several times a day, you can work on a math problem or jot down some thoughts for an English paper. You'll be surprised at how much you can accomplish in a few minutes.

Impose Set Times If you're not a cheese lover, the set-time approach, also developed by Alan Lakein, may suit you better. In this method, you set aside a fixed amount of time to work on a task. In mapping out your weekly plans, you may decide that you need to spend six hours a week reading your biology text and doing biology homework. You could then set aside 4–6 P.M. Monday, Wednesday, and Saturday for this work.

A Week Later: How Did You Do? After you have planned what you will do with your time for a week and monitored yourself, a very helpful exercise is to complete Know Yourself: Self-Assessment 3.3, "Evaluating My Week of Time Management," at the end of the chapter on page 91, to evaluate how effectively you stayed with your plan and to think about how you could better use your time.

Execute a Daily Plan Great time managers figure out what the most important things are for each day and allocate enough time to get them done. Figuring out the most important things to do involves setting priorities (Steel, 2010).

An effective way to do this is to create a manageable to-do list. Your goal is at least to complete all the priority items on your list. A no-miss day is one on which you can cross off every item, having completed them all. If that turns out to be impossible, make sure you finish the most important tasks.

The ABC Method A to-do list identifies and sets priorities for daily tasks and activities. It can help you to stay focused on what is important for you to accomplish that particular day and generally does not include your classes, which should be in your weekly plan. Time-management expert Stephen Covey (1989) recommends prioritizing tasks by A, B, and C and determining whether they are:

A   *Vital*. Extremely important tasks that affect your weekly goals and must be done today.
B   *Important*. Tasks that need to be done soon, such as projects, class preparation, buying a birthday gift for a friend, and other time-driven activities or personal priorities.
C   *Optional*. These also could be labeled "trivial." Examples include getting a haircut, going to a shopping mall, or rearranging your room. Do these activities when you have extra time, and consider practicing the Swiss cheese method here.

TO DO

A. The Most Vital:

1. Study for Biology Test

B. Next Two Most Important:

2. Go to English and History Classes
3. Make Appointment to See Adviser

C. Task	Time	Done
Study for biology test	Early morning, night	
Call home	Morning	
Buy test book	Morning	
Call Ann about test	Morning	
Make adviser appt.	Afternoon	
Do exercise workout	Afternoon	

© Cengage Learning 2013

FIGURE 3.1 Sample To-Do List

Figure 3.1 shows one student's to-do list. Notice that this student has chosen one A-level vital task and is planning to devote the most time to it. The student also has allotted time for two B-level important tasks.

Commercial planning tools—especially electronic planners—often are good for making to-do lists. Or you might just take a notepad and create a to-do list to be updated each day.

The Time Matrix Stephen Covey (1989) created a time matrix, another way you can set and monitor priorities. This time matrix of four quadrants helps prioritize your most important and most urgent activities. Important activities include those linked to your goals and values. Urgent activities require immediate attention but might not reflect those things most important to you. Following are some examples of activities that might be placed in the four quadrants.

1. IMPORTANT, URGENT	2. IMPORTANT, NOT URGENT
—Math test tomorrow	—Date with friend
—Make bank deposit today	—English paper due in thirty days
—Science project due today	—Call home
—Take back library book due today	—Visit with academic adviser today
3. NOT IMPORTANT	**4. NOT IMPORTANT, NOT URGENT**
—Ringing phone	—Hanging out at the student union
—Unnecessary work	—Watching TV
—Trivial questions	—Playing computer games
—Interruptions	—Reading comic strips

© Cengage Learning 2013

Guidelines for using this matrix to manage your time include (*College Success Planner*, 2000):

1. Spending time on important, nonurgent things (quadrant 2) before they become urgent (quadrant 1).
2. Not letting yourself be ruled by urgency.
3. Never avoiding important work because of tasks that are just urgent.
4. Doing important activities early. If you wait until they are urgent, you will just increase your stress level.
5. Identifying the most important work that needs to be completed after each class.
6. Setting priorities for your tasks and completing them in order.

Get in the habit of using the time matrix on a regular basis. It is a great organizing tool for setting priorities.

Do successful people really use strategies like the time matrix and to-do lists in their everyday lives? For the most part, yes. These strategies help them keep track of the tasks they want to complete and let them monitor their progress.

🗂️ Manage Life

Juggling the multiple commitments of college won't be easy, but there are some steps you can take to ensure your success.

Tune in to Your Biological Rhythms

It has been said that people will accept an idea better if they're told that Benjamin Franklin said it first. Indeed, Franklin did say, "Early to bed, early to rise, makes a man healthy, wealthy, and wise."

Some of us are "morning people." Others are "night people." That is, some students work more effectively in the morning, while others are at their best in the afternoon or evening. Evaluate yourself. What time of day are you the most alert and focused? For example, do you have trouble getting up in the morning for early classes? Do you love getting up early but feel drowsy in the afternoon or evening?

Many traditional-age college students in their late teens and twenties are "evening people," while nontraditional students in their 40s and older are often "morning people." One study assessed the memory of traditional-age college students and older adults in the

Bob Vitas

Master Time Juggler

Bogdan "Bob" Vitas beat some hefty competition when he won the title, *American University's Busiest Student* in 2009. Bob managed to stay on top of the demands of his

© 2011 Kelly Barrett/The Eagle

Bob Vitas concentrated on urgent tasks to avoid feeling overwhelmed in college.

double major in International Relations and Literature despite an impressive spread of other activities, including a job, promotion of a campus project to improve accessibility for disabled students, leadership in his fraternity, and volunteer time at the Center for Global Peace. How did he manage such an intensive schedule? Besides his commitment to a daily plan, he read on the Metro, exercised regularly first thing in the morning, and interjected 15-minute periods of calm self-reflection to restore his energy and motivation. He rewarded himself on the weekend by watching *House*, staying in touch with his family, and catching up on his sleep. Rather than feeling overwhelmed, Bob claimed to feel blessed. "It's almost dazzling that you have all of these opportunities in front of you and you just have to latch on to one and pursue it," Bob said. He added, "Always be doing what needs to be done, but leave enough time for yourself" (Parnassus, 2009). Following graduation, Bob became an international relations analyst for the U.S. Department of Labor and volunteers as an English teacher in the D.C. public school system.

Bob Vitas's Monday Schedule

6:30 A.M. — Morning Run
7:00 A.M. — Shower and rush to work
9:00 A.M.–1:00 P.M. — Meeting at USAID
1:30 P.M. — Dash back to AU
2:10 P.M.–4:50 P.M. — Class
5:00 P.M. — Meeting with independent study professor
9:00 P.M. — Go over tomorrow's meetings, e-mails
10:00 P.M. — Readings and homework
12:00 A.M. — Call family in Europe
1:00 A.M. — Bed

Are you a morning person or a night person? Knowing your biological rhythms might help you plan classes for the time when you are most alert.

morning and in the late afternoon (Hasher et al., 2001). The results: The memory of the traditional-age college students was better in the evening; the memory of the older adults was better in the morning.

If you're a night person, take afternoon classes. Conduct your study sessions at night. If you're a morning person, choose morning classes. Get most of your studying done by early evening.

What can you do if you hate getting up early but are stuck with early morning classes? Start your day off properly. Many students begin their day with too little sleep and a junk food breakfast, or less. Does this description fit you? Try getting a good night's sleep and eating a good breakfast before you tackle your morning classes. Exercise is also a great way to get some energy and to be more alert when you need to be—and is often more effective than caffeine.

Tackle Time Wasters

THE SECRET OF TIME MANAGEMENT

"No"

So many temptations can lure you from your plan, such as surfing the Web, texting, daydreaming, socializing, worrying, or procrastinating (Knaus, 2010). Many students don't say no to a request for their time because of their desire for approval, fear of offending, or false sense of obligation. Their reluctance can lead to wasting a lot of time in low-priority rather than high-priority activities. For example, you change your plan to go to the library to study when a friend says, "Come on with us and shoot some pool. You can afford a couple of hours with your friends." Decide what you need to do and what you can realistically do. Say no to everything else. If this is difficult for you, write "NO" in large letters on a card and place it next to the phone, at the computer, or on your desk (Yager, 1999). You might suggest someone else who could do what is asked, or offer to do it when you have more time.

Letting the telephone or e-mail interrupt you is another time waster. Instead of letting callers or instant messages control your time, try some of these strategies:

- Use an answering machine or voicemail to screen incoming calls, and return the calls at your convenience.
- Learn to say, "I can't talk right now. Can I call you back?" Set aside a time to return calls.
- When you leave a message, try to give a specific time for someone to return your call so that you avoid playing phone tag.
- Set a specific window to check your e-mail every day or two rather than responding to each message as it is received.
- Resist the impulse to stay in constant contact with friends through text messaging. Although text messages produce brief interruptions, the constant stream of social demands can compromise your best intentions. Shut it off!
- Consider changing your computer settings so messages don't pop up in the middle of an important project such as writing a paper or doing homework online.

Conquer Procrastination

Procrastination can take many forms (University of Illinois Counseling Center, 1994). Procrastination hurts many students' efforts to become good time managers (Ferrari, 2010).

Do you tend to put off until tomorrow what you need to do today?

Recognize Avoidance   It isn't as simple as you might think. For example, review Danger Zone: "Self-Defeating Time-Management Excuses" to see how a student can creatively avoid doing work with the use of twelve different excuses.

Of course, it isn't just distorting the realistic pressures that get in the way of good performance. What other problematic actions lead to fumbles in good performance?

- *Ignore the task and hope it will go away*. A midterm test in math is not going to evaporate, no matter how much you ignore it.
- *Underestimate the work involved in the task or overestimate your abilities and resources.* Do you tell yourself that you're such a great writer that you can grind out a twenty-page paper overnight?
- *Deceive yourself into believing that a mediocre or bad performance is acceptable*. You may tell yourself that a 2.8 GPA will get you into graduate school or a great job after graduation. This mindset may prevent you from working hard enough to achieve the GPA you need to succeed after college.

DANGER ZONE

Self-Defeating Time-Management Excuses

Here are a dozen predictable excuses for procrastinating and putting off studying until later:

1. *I work best under time pressure so I'm going to wait and study later.*
2. *I'll study better after I take a nap.*
3. *It's morning and I'm a night person—my body clock is out of sync.*
4. *My horoscope says it's a bad day. Maybe tomorrow would work better.*
5. *It's too nice outside to be studying in here.*
6. *Why study when I can play "Lord of the Rings" online?*
7. *This is going to give me a headache. I'm going to do something else.*
8. *Even if I do it, it probably won't be good enough, so why do it?*
9. *Ten years from now, will it really matter if I don't do this right now?*
10. *I think I'll wait until later when I'm more motivated.*
11. *I really have to update my Facebook page.*
12. *My instructor doesn't like anything I do, so what's the point?*

These statements demonstrate how easy it is for rationalizations and less important priorities to bump your good intentions and undermine your chances for success. Do any sound familiar?

"And then after high school, I spent twelve years in college and majored in procrastination."

- *Substitute a worthy but lower-priority, nonacademic activity*. You might clean your room instead of studying for a test. Some people say, "Cleanliness is next to godliness," but if it becomes important only when you need to study for a test, you are procrastinating.
- *Believe that repeated "minor" delays won't hurt you*. You might put off writing a paper so you can watch *Glee* or a *WrestleMania* webcast. Once a TV show or webcast has grabbed your attention, you may not be able to escape its clutches.
- *Dramatize a commitment to a task rather than doing it*. You take your books along on a weekend trip but never open them.
- *Persevere on only one part of the task.* You write and rewrite the first paragraph of a paper, but you never get to the body of it.
- *Become paralyzed when having to choose between two alternatives*. You sweat over whether to do your math or English homework first and you end up doing neither.

To evaluate whether or not you are a procrastinator, complete Know Yourself: Self-Assessment 3.4, "Are You a Procrastinator?," at the end of the chapter on page 92.

Overcome Delays Now that you understand what may be fueling your avoidance problems, here are some good strategies for overcoming procrastination:

- *Put a deadline on your calendar*. This action creates a sense of urgency. You might also stick deadline Post-it® notes on the mirror and in other places where you can see them at strategic times during the day. Think about other ways that you might create urgent reminders for yourself.
- *Get organized*. Some procrastinators don't organize things effectively. Develop an organized strategy for tackling the work you need to do. Your term planner, weekly planner, and to-do list will come in handy.
- *Divide the task into smaller jobs*. Sometimes we procrastinate because the task seems so complex and overwhelming. Divide a larger task into smaller parts. Set subgoals of finishing one part at a time. This strategy often makes what seemed a completely unmanageable task into an achievable one. For example, imagine that it's Thursday and you have fifteen math problems due on Monday. Set subgoals of doing five by Friday evening, five more by Saturday evening, and the final five by Sunday evening. Reward yourself for completion.
- *Take a stand*. Commit yourself to doing the task. One of the best ways is to write yourself a "contract" and sign it, like the self-contract we discussed earlier in the chapter. Or, tell a friend or partner about your plans.
- *Use positive self-statements*. Pump yourself up. Motivate yourself with thoughts such as the following (Keller & Heyman, 1987): "There is no time like the present." "The sooner I get done, the sooner I can play." "It's less painful if I do it right now. If I wait, it will get worse."
- *Dispute mental diversions* (Watson & Tharp, 2007). For example, tell yourself, "I really don't have much time left, and other things are sure to come up later," "If I get this done, I'll be able to better enjoy my time," or "Maybe if I just go ahead and get going on this, it won't be so bad."

- *Build in a reward for yourself.* A reward gives you an incentive to complete all or part of the task. For example, if you get all your math problems done, treat yourself tonight to a movie you've wanted to see. What other types of rewards can you give yourself for completing an important task?

Consider Plan B (or C)

At some point in the term, you may have to face the fact that your time-management skills are just not working. If you are feeling worn out and your test results demonstrate that you are not cutting it, those may be signals that it is time to adopt an alternative plan.

Evaluate Your Course Load Carefully consider how many classes you are taking and how much work each one requires. Consider taking a reduced class load to give yourself more time for studying and work. If you find yourself starting to go under, drop the course that produces the least chance of success. Don't shortchange your learning by spreading yourself way too thin.

Seek Expert Intervention Organizational consultants are emerging as new business professionals. Check your local yellow pages to see if there are any individuals whose skills are so strong that that they have launched a business in your area. Then check the website to see if you can determine the cost of getting a consultation to help you reorganize. Their coaching can be concentrated and invaluable. If none exists in your area, do a wider Web search, as many consultants may be able to coach you digitally into more successful practices. But don't forget that your campus may have lots of organizational experts who will help you change course for free.

Connect and Communicate

Time management is especially challenging for college students who have a partner or children, or commute. It can be especially daunting for individuals who have more than one of these responsibilities. If you face any of these challenges, you should schedule your classes for the next term at the earliest possible time during registration. Being proactive will get you the classes you want at the times you want. You can also talk with other students who share similar challenges. Here are some additional time-management strategies for students with these special needs.

Save Time for Relationships

Time is especially precious if you have a spouse, partner, or children. Communicating and planning are important assets in balancing your family time and academic time. You don't have to reach your goals all by yourself. In many instances, it helps to have one or more support persons around you.

Talk with Your Partner Communicate with your partner about his or her importance in your life. Set aside time for your partner. Plan ahead for tasks that require extra study time. Inform your partner about test dates and other deadlines. After you've created your weekly and term calendars, let your partner see how you plan to use your time, and consider posting a copy of your calendars on the refrigerator or in another prominent place. If your partner is also a student, you may be able to coordinate your schedules so you can spend free time together. If one person works and another is in school, perhaps work-related activities can be coordinated with school/study time, and vice versa.

Lori Scardino

Courtesy of UW-Eau Claire News Bureau

Lori Scardino managed college, kids, and a Girl Scout troop before heading to graduate school.

A Single Mother's Time-Management Strategies

While a student at the University of Wisconsin, Eau Claire, Lori Scardino found her time-management skills taxed. Yet Lori, a single mother, would later successfully complete a double major in biology and chemistry. In fact, Lori became so successful at managing her time that she also would serve as an officer in three college honor societies, coauthor published research, and be named to *USA Today's* 2007 National Academic All-Star team.

Lori wanted to return to college after a divorce, but she had been turned down initially because her grade-point average was too low. (Her GPA had dropped because earlier, during stressful times, she had left college without officially withdrawing, and consequently her class grades that term all turned into Fs.) So Lori attended a technical college, raised her GPA, subsequently reapplied to UW Eau Claire, and was admitted. When she resumed classes there, she was working full-time. As she adjusted to her return to college and her new routine, Lori also participated in various campus and community activities. She tutored other students in chemistry, volunteered at an elementary school, and led a Girl Scout troop.

How did she do it all? Lori creates an hour-by-hour schedule that she prints out for every day of the week. "Time management is crucial," she said. "I try to put my children—the time we have together—as my first priority. I don't do my own homework or things like that until they're in bed." Lori also commented that she stays organized by prioritizing her activities and being very selective about the campus

Build in Study Time at School If you have a partner or child, try to do some studying while you're still at school. Use time between classes, for example. Perhaps you can arrive at school thirty minutes before your first class and stay thirty minutes after your last class to squeeze in uninterrupted study time.

Creatively Manage Time with Children If your child has homework, do yours at the same time. Take a break for ten minutes or so for each hour you study at home, and play or talk with your child. Then go back to your studying. If your children are old enough to understand, tell them what your study routine is and ask for their cooperation. Consider having your children play with neighboring children during your study hours. If your children are young, this activity might be arranged under another parent's supervision. Or try to swap childcare with other student parents. Also check into childcare and community agencies that may provide service and activities for your children in the before-school and after-school hours.

Put Commuting Time to Good Use

If you commute to class, you already know how much time disappears on the road. Commuting students also tend to have family and work commitments that cut into study time. Courses may be available only at inconvenient times. Conflicts in schedules can make it difficult for commuters to take part in study sessions and other learning opportunities. Solving such scheduling problems requires good time management.

Following are some effective time-management strategies related to commuting:

- Save time by consistently using to-do lists and weekly plans.
- Electronically record your instructors' lectures if allowed. Listen to them on the way home or on the way to school.
- Rehearse what you learned in class each day on your way to work, school, or home.
- If you carpool with classmates, use the commuting time to discuss course material with them.
- Use a backpack or briefcase to carry books and papers that you use each day. Organize these materials the night before to make sure you have everything you need.
- Exchange phone numbers and e-mail addresses with other students in your classes early in the semester. Call them if you need to discuss course issues or their notes for a class you missed.

- Create a personal commuter telephone and/or e-mail directory. Important phone numbers and addresses might include your instructors and their secretaries or teaching assistants, the library, student services, study partners, and other campus resources.

Save Time for Yourself

Meditation specialist Jack Kornfield observed, "When we get too caught up in the busyness of the world, we lose connection with one another—and ourselves." His insight suggests the importance of building in leisure activity to replenish your reserves.

You can achieve short-term relief by engaging in short bursts of preferred activity. You can go online and play scrabble or poker. You can linger over a fresh squeezed glass of orange juice. You can listen to Coldplay's latest CD. You can challenge a hall-mate or a neighbor to some Frisbee. The point is that you need not sacrifice all things that provide pleasure while you pursue your degree. Think about the kinds of activities that would make you smile and keep a running list to remind yourself when you badly need a diversion.

You can also think about long-term goals. If education enhances your ability to do what you want to do, what fabulous activities do you want to pursue when the time is right and your resources can support the plan? Climb the Eiffel Tower? Camp at Yosemite? Do a week on Broadway? Wiggle your toes in the sand on Maui? Having serious long-term goals can sometimes sustain you when the going gets rough.

Build a Bright Future

Managing your time effectively will be one of the most important skills to enhance your chances of succeeding in work and a career.

Balance College and Work

Managing time can be hard if you must work to pay for college. Students who work full-time are less likely to complete college than those working part-time or not at all. Students with a full-time job also are less likely to have high grade-point averages, to graduate with honors, or to go on to graduate school. If you need to work, consider the following options.

Limit Work If Possible It's best not to work more than ten to twenty hours in a week. Full-time students who work more than twenty hours a week get lower grades than students who work fewer hours. Working long hours and going to college at the same time also limits your class choices and increases the chances that you will drop out of college.

Spotlight On... (Cont.)

organizations she joins, participating only in those that she is passionate about.

For her accomplishments, Lori received a fellowship to attend graduate school at the University of Wisconsin, Madison. She moved there with her daughters and is studying for her doctoral degree, with the goal of eventually becoming a college professor.

(Source: Good News Blog, 2007)

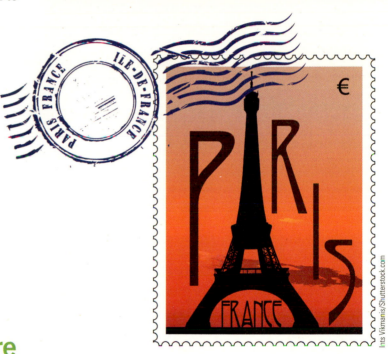

Ints Vikmanis/Shutterstock.com

Think about how success in college can help you climb the Eiffel Tower and other long-term goals.

Explore Financial Aid You may qualify for state or federal financial aid to help you afford tuition while working fewer hours. Visit your campus financial aid office or ask your adviser for more information. They will be able to guide you skillfully through the financial maze to determine if you have any solid leads for additional support.

Work on Campus If Possible Whether part-time work is positive or negative for college students depends on where they work. In general, a part-time job off campus is an academic minus, but a part-time job on campus is an academic plus. Why does it matter where you work? The answer has to do with involvement. Students who work part-time on campus will likely be connected with other students and faculty. These connections more than compensate for the time they devote to the part-time job.

Investigate Work-Study Options Work-study options are ideal in many ways. The work tends not to be grueling, such as receptionist duties or data tracking, and typically allows for quite a bit of down time in which you can study without guilt. Your employer will want you to succeed in college and can often show great flexibility about scheduling your hours flexibly to help when exams pile up. For example, you may be able to work extra hours when time is more plentiful in exchange for reduced hours during midterms or exams.

Groom Yourself for the Future Some jobs can help you develop your skills for future careers. Others are good just for the money. If you have some choices, select the one that corresponds most closely to the skill sets that can transfer to your desired occupational goal.

Find a College-Friendly Boss If you must work off campus, you probably will discover that college-friendly bosses work in the surrounding area. When you interview, don't forget to ask about flexible scheduling in relation to your academic demands. Be careful not to take advantage of that flexibility for anything but serious emergencies and academic work. In addition, some companies pay for the courses of their student employees.

Develop Winning Work Strategies

From part-time workers to corporate executives, managing time is critical to being successful at the work you do. Some case studies can illustrate the connection between juggling studies and developing winning strategies at work.

Consider Theo. He never thought his part-time job as a waiter at Pizza Hut would be such a challenge to his time-management skills. In just one shift, he had to take and deliver drink orders, make sure food arrived promptly from the kitchen, clear tables, and deliver dessert and the check, all while juggling similar needs for multiple tables and squeezing in some study time in the back when things were slow. He also had to make sure his shifts fit into his weekly schedule of classes and study time. Falling behind in his service meant lost tips. Falling behind in his tips compromised his ability to pay for college. His long-term goal of graduating on time depended on juggling all these competing demands.

Consider also Nancy, whose job as an advertising executive involves client presentations that are planned up to a month in advance. She has to balance all aspects of the presentation and make sure the art, slogan, and visual aids are developed simultaneously by different teams, all completed on time, without procrastination. She finds that working backward from the due date helps her create a good time-management plan, as well as prioritize and monitor tasks on a daily basis. While her business management major had helped her land the job, it is her time-management skills that now help her get the job done.

Describe Your Project-Management Skills

Your cumulative experiences in completing assignments across your courses should transform you into an effective project manager, a skill that employers find particularly valuable. Think about it! When you write a position paper for government, it is a project. When you publish a poem, it is a project. When you learn to administer flu shots, it is a project, too.

What do these projects—and other assignments—have in common? Many features parallel the kinds of project needs that constitute professional jobs after graduation. These may include:

- Following instructions accurately
- Working within the available resources and time constraints
- Designing a strategy to accomplish the objective
- Collaborating effectively with others
- Communicating accurately about the process and outcomes
- Overcoming problems
- Seeking and integrating feedback to improve the outcomes
- Devising an implementation strategy
- Determining the next step if all goes well
- Refining the approach if all doesn't go well

Remember to emphasize these refined skills when you build your resume and apply for positions. Your project-management skills can set you apart.

Set Excellence as Your Standard

A manager's secret when assigning an important task is to look for the person who is busiest if you want to get the work accomplished. That strategy sounds counterintuitive, but think about it. Genuinely busy people have figured out the time-management art and know how to move things around to accommodate the next challenge. In fact, they relish it.

Good time-management skills are essential for any job and will help make you a more valuable and successful employee now and in the future. Managing your time effectively will increase your efficiency and make you more productive as a worker. Just as in college, using your time in an optimum way means increasing the likelihood that you will complete your work tasks on time. Being a great time manager at work will give you an advantage over colleagues who don't manage their time well. As a result, you are likely to be assigned more important work tasks in the future.

Managing your time effectively at work will also give you more time to spend with friends, family, and leisure pursuits. Not only will managing your time inefficiently at work give you less time for these enjoyable aspects of your life, but it also is likely to increase your stress. Just as you might panic if it's the day before a test in college and you haven't studied for it, the tension will build as you approach a deadline for a project at work and you haven't managed your time effectively to get the work done to meet the deadline.

Being a good time manager at work will greatly improve your chances of reaching your work and career goals. These goals will unfold over many years, and how you manage your time daily, weekly, monthly, and yearly will help determine whether you achieve them.

- Know what it means to procrastinate and develop good strategies to conquer procrastination.
- Consider changing the weight of the load if your strategies are not working.

Connect and Communicate

- Balance college and time with partners and children by practicing good communication and coordinating your commitments.
- Use commuting time effectively.
- Schedule leisure activities to help restore your energy.

Build a Bright Future

- Balance college and work by limiting work and working on campus if possible.
- Locate work opportunities that allow you to learn about the jobs you aspire to in the future.
- Recognize the value of becoming expert in time management for your future occupational success.

Clarify Expectations

- Recognize how misunderstanding causes people to avoid being good time managers.
- Own the importance of developing efficient work patterns.
- Analyze how your core values intersect with effective time management.

Develop Competence

- Learn to set long- and short-term goals to achieve the outcomes you want.
- Experiment with different kinds of scheduling tools—either paper or digital or a combination—to find the best fit.
- Purposefully schedule your time by term, week, and day to reach your goals.

Manage Life

- Factor in when you are at your best during the day to shape your study plan.
- Identify the things that waste time without replenishing your spirit.

 Visit the College Success CourseMate for *Your Guide to College Success* for interactive resources at login.cengagebrain.com

Review Questions

1. What are some myths about managing time?

   _____

   _____

   _____

   _____

2. How can becoming a great time manager help you control your life?

   _____

   _____

   _____

   _____

3. What benefits does someone who effectively manages time enjoy?

   a. _____

   b. _____

   c. _____

4. What are some time wasters that you need to eliminate to give more time to productively pursue your success in college?

   _____

   _____

   _____

5. What does the 80–20 principle involve in managing time effectively?

   _____

   _____

   _____

6. What are some good strategies for staying on time to reach your goals?

   a. _____

   b. _____

   c. _____

   d. _____

7. What advice would you give someone who wants to create a term planner? A weekly planner?

a. _____

b. _____

c. _____

d. _____

8. What are some good strategies for creating to-do lists?

_____

_____

_____

9. What are some good strategies for tackling procrastination?

a. _____

b. _____

c. _____

d. _____

10. Describe ways to balance your academic responsibilities with all of the other demands in your life.

a. _____

b. _____

11. How can managing your time more effectively in college enhance your chances of being successful in your work and career after college?

_____

_____

_____

SELF-ASSESSMENT 3.1

My Five Most Important Personal Values: Round 2

After revisiting your values in this chapter, are the five you wrote down in Chapter 1 still the Big Five Values for you? Write down below the five values that are most important to you now:

1. _____

2. _____

3. _____

4. _____

5. _____

© Cengage Learning 2013

SELF-ASSESSMENT 3.2

Connect Your Values with Long- and Short-Term Goals

VALUE	LONG-TERM GOAL	SHORT-TERM GOAL
1. _____	_____	_____
2. _____	_____	_____
3. _____	_____	_____
4. _____	_____	_____
5. _____	_____	_____

SELF-ASSESSMENT 3.3

Evaluating My Week of Time Management

Earlier in this chapter, you planned how to use your time for a week and then monitored what you actually did during that time period. After one week of monitoring your time, what did you learn?

I spent too much time on:

1. _____
2. _____
3. _____

I spent too little time on:

1. _____
2. _____
3. _____

Next week, I will spend more time on:

1. _____
2. _____
3. _____

Next week, I will spend less time on:

1. _____
2. _____
3. _____

After a week of managing, monitoring, and evaluating my use of time, these are the most important things I have to work on to be a great time manager:

1. _____
2. _____
3. _____

Are You a Procrastinator?

	Strongly Agree	Mildly Agree	Mildly Disagree	Strongly Disagree
1. I usually find reasons for not acting immediately on a difficult assignment.				
2. I know what I have to do but frequently find that I have done something else.				
3. I carry my books/work assignments with me to various places but do not open them.				
4. I work best at the last minute, when the pressure is really on.				
5. There are too many interruptions that interfere with my accomplishing my top priorities.				
6. I avoid forthright answers when pressed for an unpleasant or difficult decision.				
7. I take half measures which will avoid or delay unpleasant or difficult action.				
8. I have been too tired, nervous, or upset to do the difficult task that faces me.				
9. I like to get my room in order before starting a difficult task.				
10. I find myself waiting for inspiration before becoming involved in important study/work tasks.				

Give yourself four points for each item you checked Strongly Agree, three points for each item you checked Mildly Agree, two points for each item you checked Mildly Disagree, and one point for each item you checked Strongly Disagree. Total your points: If you scored above 30, you likely are a severe procrastinator; 21 to 30, a chronic procrastinator; and 20 or below, an occasional procrastinator. If your score is 21 or above, seriously consider going to the college counseling center for some guidance in conquering your procrastination.

Source: University of Texas at Austin Learning Center

Your Journal

 ## Clarify Expectations

1. Watching Your Clock

You probably have a good sense about the degree to which you strive to be on time and meet deadlines. Are you usually early, on time, or late for appointments, classes, turning in assignments, meeting friends, and other activities in your life? How would you say that your friends would describe your ability to be on time or late?

_____

_____

_____

2. The Bad Rap

How did time management end up getting such a bad rap? Identify three reasons that people cite to justify not using time-management strategies to become more efficient.

1. _____

2. _____

3. _____

 ## Develop Competence

3. Make SMART Goals

The following are some vague plans. Make them more specific by applying the SMART principles that you read about in this chapter.

Vague: I'm going to start getting to school on time.

SMART: _____

_____

Vague: I plan to watch TV less and study more.

SMART: _____

_____

Vague: I'm going to quit wasting my time.

SMART: _____

_____

4. Put Swiss Cheese into Action

The Swiss cheese approach involves poking holes in bigger tasks by working on them in small bursts or at odd times. List your biggest task for next week. You should have some set time to work on it. However, also try to work on it in small bursts when you have a little time here, a little time there. At the end of next week, come back to this activity and write down how much more time you were able to sneak in on the big task by taking the Swiss cheese approach.

_____

_____

_____

📁 Manage Life

5. Change a Habit

Select a bad habit that is hurting your ability to effectively manage time. The bad habit I'm going to get rid of is:

_____

_____

_____

Many people find that in managing time, it helps to replace a bad habit with a new, more positive habit. Instead of spending time on my old bad habit, I will commit to spending more time on this good habit:

_____

_____

_____

6. Jump Start

In this chapter, we described some strategies for reducing procrastination. Get together with some other students and brainstorm about strategies for reducing procrastination. Summarize these strategies below.

_____

_____

_____

Connect and Communicate

7. Taking It to the Net

Go on the Internet and type in these words on your browser: Effective Time Management Skills. Spend some time looking at different sites and write down the three below that you think could help you manage your time more effectively:

1. _____

2. _____

3. _____

8. Build Your Future Vision

Take a pause and identify five very big lifetime goals you would like to achieve. Pick goals that will be facilitated because of the advantages you will have from completing your college education.

1. _____

2. _____

3. _____

4. _____

5. _____

Build a Bright Future

9. Time Management and My Future Career

The career I most likely will pursue at this time:

_____

_____

Write below on how developing effective time-management skills while you are in college will enhance your chances of advancing in this career:

_____

_____

10. The Deadline

Regardless of the career you enter, there will be deadlines when you have a limited amount of time to get a project completed, such as a report due on a specific date, sometimes even a few days in the future. Write below some positive things you are doing in college that are preparing you to be able to meet deadlines when they arise in your career:

1. _____

2. _____

3. _____

Write below some things you are doing in college that you will need to change if you are going to practice good time-management strategies for your future career:

1. _____

2. _____

3. _____

Master Communication Skills and Build Relationships

Chapter 4

KNOW YOURSELF

SUCCESS IN COLLEGE ISN'T JUST ABOUT GRADES. Total college success includes mastering communication and developing positive relationships with many different kinds of people. Being skilled in these areas will make your college years more enjoyable and productive. If you master these skills, you are likely to make relationships that will sustain you well beyond college. To see where you stand right now, place a check mark in one of three boxes below for each item that best characterizes you.

How Effectively Do I Handle My Relationships?

	Very Much Like Me	Somewhere In Between	Not at All Like Me
I am satisfied with how deep my relationships are with others.			
I am a good listener.			
I express myself precisely and effectively.			
I have strategies for resolving conflicts.			
If I get lonely, I can usually find ways to reduce those feelings.			
I know how to bounce back from being heartbroken.			
I avoid taking risks that might lead to sexual threat.			
I know how to maintain good relationships with my family.			
I get along well with people whose heritage differs from mine.			
I know how to build professional networks to support my career goals.			

© 2011 John Giustina/Jupiterimages Corporation

Spotlight On...

Michelle Morris
Citizen of the World

CHAPTER OUTLINE

- **Clarify Expectations**
  Assess Your Social Environment
  Recognize Attachment Styles

- **Develop Competence**
  Develop Good Listening Skills
  Express Yourself Effectively
  Tune in to Nonverbal Messages
  Resolve Conflict

- **Manage Life**
  Deal with Loneliness
  Rebound from Heartbreak
  Avoid Sexual Threats

- **Connect and Communicate**
  Connect with Parents at the
    Right Level
  Make Room for Partners
    and Family
  Get Along with Roommates
  Show Intercultural Competence

- **Build a Bright Future**
  Develop Professional Networks
  Look and Act the Part
  Link Communication Skills with
    Your Career

Michelle Morris has her eyes on the world. Her first trip outside America occurred when she was just 14, when she went with her family to Nicaragua, where she worked with a medical team to distribute medicines to poor people living in barrios. That experience had a profound impact on Michelle and initiated a wanderlust that ultimately shaped her career goals. At Gallaudet College, Michelle is majoring in international studies with a minor in government. Her objective is to have a career in political diplomacy, international development, or foreign services.

Michelle seems fearless about interacting in any human context. At age 16 she traveled to Russia to teach English and visit with children in orphanages. By the time she entered Gallaudet's Honors Program, she had captured three more passport stamps for trips to other cultures. In the First Year Study program, she signed up to study Costa Rican sign language through an immersion experience in that country. By the end of her first semester, she was off to India during winter break on a study tour with faculty. Her interpersonal skills allowed her to engage easily with both deaf and hearing locals, some of whom remain active Facebook friends.

Michelle's eagerness to learn prompted her selection for a weeklong seminar in the nation's capital, sponsored by the prestigious Washington Center. In this internship, as the only hearing-impaired participant, she interacted with college students from all parts of the country and had rich opportunities to explore matters of national security. She also began serious study of Hangui, the national language of Korea, at the Korean Embassy's Culture Center in Washington. She plans to parlay her experience into a 2-month internship in South Korea, but that trip will have to wait until she completes her study abroad trip to Spain.

Interacting with others can range from exhilarating to painful. Examine the chapter outline and think about how the information will be helpful to you in building a strong social foundation for college success.

(Source: Trudo, 2011)

Clarify Expectations

It's hard to do much in life without communicating. We communicate when we ask an instructor a question or listen to another student give an explanation of a concept. We communicate in the warmth of an intimate exchange, the heat of an intense conflict, even the chill of a faded relationship.

Communication skills are powerful. For example, asking good questions and listening carefully can stimulate thinking and advance learning. When you ask questions, you prompt others to go to a deeper level in their consideration. When others ask you questions, you may be surprised by how much more satisfying your ideas can become because you have been prompted to review, reflect, or defend your position. Good communication skills tend to inspire trust and promote genuine positive regard.

Good communication skills can also help you reach your goals and attain career success. Employers rate communication skills as the most important type of skill they look for in potential employees. In fact, when things turn foul in a job situation, chances are that poor communication skills will be at the heart of the trouble.

Assess Your Social Environment

College will provide many opportunities for you to design a satisfying social life. Hanging out and finding special people in your college life can lead to wonderful, fulfilling times. Unfortunately, poor social choices can also lead to unhappiness, anxiety, and even violence.

From the outset, mixers, student orientation sessions, and other social events at college will give you the chance to find and develop or expand your social circles.

© 2004 by Randy Glasbergen.
www.glasbergen.com

"Of course I can accept you for who you are. You are someone I need to change."

Many students prefer the security of navigating "in the pack." Others show some eagerness to date or spend their time with a significant other rather than hanging out with the group. Students without partners may view dating as a way to find a spouse. Others see it as an important part of fitting into the social scene. Some students date for romantic reasons; others date for friendship or companionship. Still other students, especially those who are attempting to combine work and school, may have very little discretionary time to take advantage of the social opportunities that college has to offer.

The quality of your social life can detract from or enhance your college success. For example, falling head over heels in passionate love so that all you can think about is your romantic partner can be disastrous. If that happens to you, you'll probably spend too little time studying. And nothing is harder on your GPA than a serious case of heartbreak. On the other hand, some people who date someone regularly or live with a partner feel more settled down and have greater freedom to work. Also, individuals who strike the right balance between socializing and studying may be more effective in their academic work because they feel relaxed and socially fulfilled.

Some first-year students without partners get hung up on wanting to date an ideal rather than a real person. They may search for the stereotypical campus all-star or the student with fashion-model looks. Some first-year students also look at every date as a potential girlfriend or boyfriend or even as someone they eventually might marry. College counselors say that such students would probably be better adjusted and happier if they broadened their perspective. Don't look at every date as a potential spouse. Dates can lead to new friends as well as to romantic partners.

It's not unusual for many first-year students to have a serious relationship with someone back home. Also, many commuting students have a romantic partner who does not go to college or attends college somewhere else. If one of these profiles fits you, you do not necessarily have to give up this romance. In fact, many preexisting relationships successfully weather this kind of challenge. However, the college experience may bring changes in personality, careers, and goals that may make it hard for old romances and relationships to survive.

Recognize Attachment Styles

Relationships play a powerful role in college. College students who have positive, close relationships are much happier than those who do not. One study found that very happy college students rated their relationships with their friends, family, and romantic partners more positively than college students who were average in happiness or very unhappy (Diener & Seligman, 2002). In this study, the very happy college students were more likely than the other two groups to spend more time with family, friends, and a romantic partner and considerably less time alone (see Figure 4.1, "Very Happy College Students").

Note: The daily activity scores reflect means, with 1 representing no time and 10 reflecting 8 hours per day.

After data presented by Ed Diener & Martin E.P. Seligman, "Very Happy People," *Psychological Science*, 13, 81–84. Copyright © 2002 by Blackwell Publishing. Reprinted by permission of the publisher.

© Cengage Learning 2013

FIGURE 4.1 Very Happy College Students

As social creatures, human beings seek to bond or to be attached to others and do so in different ways. These attachment styles affect the ease with which you make and maintain relationships with significant others in all settings, not just college. To learn more about your own attachment style, complete Know Yourself: Self-Assessment 4.1, "What Is My Attachment Style?," located at the end of this chapter on page 122.

Develop Competence

Effective communication can be hard work. Communication specialists often discuss the process as an exchange between a sender and receiver. The sender must formulate a message and deliver the message clearly. The receiver must decode the message accurately. This sounds simple enough, but in the back-and-forth exchanges of communication, messages can easily become garbled and misunderstood (Stewart, 2012). In this section, you will examine listening skills, nonverbal behavior, assertive expression, and conflict resolution.

Develop Good Listening Skills

In the third century BCE, the Greek philosopher Zeno of Citum said that the reason people have two ears and one mouth is so they can listen more and talk less. Listening is essential for building relationships, but many people fall into the bad habit of *pseudolistening*, in which a person goes through the motions of listening but doesn't really process any meaningful information. As one college student put it, "My friends *listen* but my parents only *hear* me talk."

Bad listeners can also hog conversations. They talk to, rather than with, others. They show greater investment in what they plan to say next than in their conversation partners. Their behavior initially frustrates and eventually alienates their respective partners, taking a huge toll on the quality of their interpersonal relationships.

Good listening skills provide a lot of interpersonal traction. By listening actively, rather than passively absorbing information, you will draw others to you. Following are some positive ways to be an active, competent listener:

- *Give complete attention to the speaker.* This focus shows you're interested in what the speaker has to say. Don't tend to your e-mail or try to keep an eye on a television. Make eye contact and lean forward to signal your full attention.
- *Paraphrase.* State in your own words what someone just said, such as "Let me see, what I hear you saying is . . ." or "Do you mean . . . ?" Paraphrasing is particularly useful when someone says something important or complex. A good paraphrase communicates that you cared enough to listen carefully and you understood the most critical elements.
- *Summarize central ideas.* Conversations can become strewn with bits and pieces of disconnected information. Active listeners pay attention to the key points covered by the speaker and may recount them ("Let's review the ground we've been covering so far"). Summarizing is especially helpful when the communication is complex or unfocused.
- *Synthesize themes and patterns.* A slightly more challenging listening skill is synthesizing what you hear into the most prominent themes or patterns. At times the speaker may not be aware that a central idea undergirds complex, messy, or emotionally charged communication. Reflecting an integration of those ideas (for example, "One theme you seem to be coming back to is . . . ") may produce important insights and increases your value as the listener.

- *Give accurate feedback.* Verbal or nonverbal feedback gives speakers an idea of how well they are getting their points across. Positive nonverbal feedback can include smiling and nodding, whereas a furrowed brow or a frown communicates disagreement. Effective listeners give honest feedback quickly, clearly, and informatively ("I understand what you mean" or "That was awesome"). Most helpful is feedback that details specifics of what was pleasing or upsetting.
- *Use extra care when offering negative feedback.* If constructive feedback is necessary, good critics try to find some positive aspects to comment on before moving to the developmental ideas that will be harder for the speaker to hear ("It is clear to me that you have great passion for this topic, but . . ."). Some good listeners ease into constructive suggestions by reporting their confusion about what the speaker intended ("I am confused by what you are trying to say. Would it be clearer if . . . ").

Express Yourself Effectively

Think of all the different kinds of messages you communicate in the course of a day: facts, beliefs, theories, preferences, thoughts, opinions, criticism, gossip, and feelings, among others. Regardless of the content of the message (the *what*), good communicators are strategic about the who, where, and when as well. They also know why they are communicating and what they hope to gain from the exchange. They pick and choose what they say, avoiding self-disclosure in some situations rather than blabbing everything to everyone.

You convey messages more effectively when you speak in a simple rather than a complex way, a concrete rather than an abstract way, and a specific rather than a general way. When you do need to convey ideas that are complex, abstract, or general, use appropriate examples to illustrate the ideas. Often the best examples are those that listeners can relate to their own personal experiences.

Good communicators also make their verbal and nonverbal messages consistent (Hybels & Weaver, 2012). If you say one thing and nonverbally communicate the opposite, you are likely to create confusion and distrust. For example, if you are trying to explain to an instructor why you didn't turn a paper in on time, and you look down at the floor rather than maintaining eye contact, the teacher may be less likely to believe you, even if your excuse is legitimate.

Decode Feelings Feelings can be especially tricky to communicate because you aren't always in tune with your feelings. Sometimes you can miscommunicate thoughts as feelings. For example, you could self-disclose the following statement: "I feel that the instructor is too harsh in grading." It isn't really a feeling. Lurking beneath that statement might be the unidentified emotion of disappointment or anger. A more precise and in-tune expression would be "I feel disappointed by the instructor's feedback." When you pinpoint and choose to share your true emotional state, it is much harder for the listener to object or argue.

Feelings are fairly transient; you can be outraged one moment and calm down fairly rapidly the next moment. Unfortunately, sometimes you can get swept away when in the grip of irrational feelings and go far beyond what you would really want to say if you were in better control. This fact suggests an important strategy for staying out of trouble on e-mail: Never blast a friend or colleague with a hot, angry e-mail message. You may regret the extreme statements you make, and unfortunately your communication can live on through forwarding and posting.

Monitor Codeswitching *Codeswitching* is the process by which individuals adapt their speech for different social circumstances or subcultures (Duvernoy, 2010). For example, when you talk to friends, you may incorporate slang and references that only your inner circle could easily interpret. Text-messaging language provides another example. Nontexters would be bewildered by the following sentence: "PCM B4 DNR," whereas texters know they need to plan to make a phone call (PCM = please call me) before (B4) dinner (DNR).

You'll fare better in college if you recognize that the college setting is geared to teach you how to communicate using professional "code." Think about the challenge as learning about the academic subculture. Exchanges in the academic setting tend to be more formal. The more progress you make in an academic program, the more your professors will expect professional "code" in your communications, complete with disciplinary jargon. Strive to practice professional code in classroom settings, and by all means switch back to informal "friendspeak" to reconnect and build relationships with your friends.

Some researchers believe that men and women talk in different codes. See Highlight: "Report vs Rapport" for an explanation.

Barriers to Effective Expression Good communicators avoid barriers to effective communication (Pearson et al., 2011). Consider Ethan's dilemma. Ethan's lab partner, Brian, is not getting his share of the work done on time and thus is jeopardizing Ethan's grade in the course. The following (based on Gordon, 1970) demonstrates many negative ways that Ethan's response could make the situation even worse:

- *Criticizing* (making negative evaluations): "You act like you don't know what you're doing in the lab."

HIGHLIGHT

Report vs. Rapport

Sociologist Deborah Tannen (2007) supports the idea that men and women often communicate as though they were from different subcultures. What seem to be the key differences?

- **Status vs. Support.** Men tend to see conversation as an opportunity to jockey for position or gain the upper hand. Women pursue talking as means of confirming their value or extending their influence through affirming others.
- **Independence vs. Intimacy.** Women invest their communication efforts to achieve close relationships with others. In contrast, men may want to confirm their separateness. The more women agitate for closeness, the more men may want to push away.
- **Advice vs. Understanding.** When men are presented with a problem, they listen to figure out how to fix it. On the other hand, women may talk about problems merely to get confirmation that someone cares about their circumstances. They become annoyed when men leap to "report talk" when what women want is "rapport talk."
- **Information vs. Feelings.** Men use conversation as a means of capturing attention and showing how much they know. The priority for women in conversations is more about communicating emotional states and seeking affirmation.
- **Orders vs. Proposals.** Women may make weak suggestions, such as "let's study at the library"; however, men may hear a "let's" statement as a command and blanch at that level of control. In turn, women get upset for being thought of as manipulative.
- **Control vs. Compromise.** Men tend to relish conflict, whereas women prefer compromise to avoid conflict. As a consequence, women end up yielding to the wishes of others with chronic feelings of not getting what they want, while men may be unaware that a compromise has even transpired.

Although it would be a mistake to expect that these contrasts characterize all men and women, Tannen's views have been widely accepted as validating the frustrations that happen when men and women can't understand what the other gender really wants. However, researchers have verified many of these patterns (Newman et al., 2008).

Threatening expressions increase defensiveness and make it more difficult to resolve problems because the climate becomes so tense.

- **Name calling** (putting down the other person): "You're such an idiot for not planning better."
- **Advising** (talking down to the other person while giving a solution to a problem): "You should really do a better job of time management."
- **Ordering** (commanding the other person to do what you want): "You have to make this your number-one priority!"
- **Threatening** (trying to control the other person): "If you don't listen to me, I'm going to ask the professor to let me change partners."
- **Moralizing** (preaching to the other person what he should do): "You know you shouldn't have gone out last night. You ought to be sorry."
- **One-upping** (pushing the other person's problems aside): "You think you have it bad? Let me tell you about how tough my schedule is."
- **Logical arguing** (trying to convince the other person with logical facts without considering the person's feelings): "Here are all the things you've done wrong that hurt our grade on our last lab report. You *know* I'm right." It's good to use logic to try to persuade, but if you lose sight of the person's feelings, no matter how right you are, the other person won't be persuaded and may be hurt.

Ethan would be better off stating simply that he thinks he and Brian need to talk about strategies for making their lab partnership work more effectively. He then should get ready to do some listening so that he and Brian can find a mutually satisfying solution. Good communicators strive not to trigger defensiveness so that the climate can promote the best, most face-saving outcomes.

Tune in to Nonverbal Messages

Communications experts believe you send or augment a message by the way you fold your arms, cast your eyes, move your mouth, cross your legs, or touch someone. Think about the following common examples. You might:

- lift an eyebrow for disbelief
- clasp your arms to isolate or protect yourself
- shrug your shoulders for indifference
- wink one eye for intimacy
- tap your fingers for impatience
- slap your forehead for forgetfulness

What messages does the body language of these graduates convey?

These are conscious, deliberate gestures people make in the course of communicating.

Are there also unconscious, nonverbal behaviors that offer clues about what a person is feeling? Hard-to-control facial muscles especially tend to reveal emotions that people are trying to conceal. Lifting only the inner part of your eyebrow may reveal stress and worry. Eyebrows raised together may signal fear. Fidgeting may reveal anxiety or boredom.

Many communications experts believe that most interpersonal communication is nonverbal (Knapp & Hall, 2010). Even if you're sitting in a corner silently reading a book, your nonverbal behavior communicates something—perhaps that you want to be left alone. It might also communicate that you're intellectually oriented.

You'll have a hard time trying to mask or control your nonverbal messages. True feelings usually express themselves, no matter how hard we try to conceal them, so it's good to recognize the power of nonverbal behavior (Verderber, Verdeber, & Sellnow, 2011).

Resolve Conflict

Conflicts are inevitable in our everyday interactions, especially in the intensely competitive college environment. Developing skills to resolve these conflicts can make your life calmer and more enjoyable (Wilmot & Hocker, 2011). Conflict can involve minor irritations and disappointment or can produce gut-wrenching turmoil. Conflict can lead to some serious consequences if handled badly, including broken relationships, heartbreak, reduced self-esteem, lousy grades, and even pressures to withdraw from school.

Conflict Styles Individuals deal with conflict in four main ways:

- *Aggression.* People who respond aggressively to conflict run roughshod over others. They communicate in demanding, abrasive, and hostile ways, often characterized by anger or entitlement. Aggressive people often are insensitive to the rights and feelings of others. As a consequence, they tend to alienate others by their bullying or obnoxious approach to solving problems.

- *Manipulation.* Manipulative people try to get what they want by making others feel guilty or sorry for them. They don't take responsibility for meeting their own needs. Instead, manipulative people play the role of the victim or martyr to get others to do things for them, working indirectly to get their needs met. Manipulators also alienate others who resent not being able to deal directly and honestly with the issues.

- *Passivity*. Passive people act in nonassertive, submissive ways. They let others run roughshod over them. Passive people don't express their feelings or let others know what they want or need. Extreme dependence drives away most other people unless they see the passive person as easy to exploit for their own purposes.

- *Assertiveness.* Of the four styles of dealing with conflict, acting assertively is clearly the most appropriate and the most helpful for building long-term solid relationships (Alberti & Emmons, 1995). Assertive people act in their own best interests without violating the rights of others. They stand up for their legitimate rights and express their views openly and directly. Be assertive in any situation in which you need to express your feelings, ask for what you want, or say no to something you don't want.

To evaluate your communication style in various situations, complete Know Yourself: Self-Assessment 4.2, "What Is My Communication Style?," at the end of the chapter on page 123.

Become Conflict Sturdy Many individuals shy away from conflict because they find such situations intolerable. This is unfortunate, since a conflict that reaches resolution can often improve the situation for both parties. What are some pointers that can help move conflict resolution toward positive outcomes and help individuals become less avoidant of conflict situations?

- *Accept the likelihood of conflict.* Most people function from good intentions. However, personal priorities, emergencies, misunderstandings, and human error can all divert good intentions from producing positive outcomes. Assume that benign causes, rather than nasty motives, are responsible for the conflict to reduce your emotional turbulence. Be vigilant for unjustified conclusions you may have drawn based on your reliance on stereotypes.

- *Prepare for confrontation.* Rather than fly off the handle, take a breath. Think through what you want to say and present your point of view in a manner that avoids attacking. Phrases like "I feel" or "It could be" signal your willingness to process issues in a rational and sensitive fashion. Never try to handle a serious conflict on e-mail. This mode simply won't allow you to convey your perspective effectively.

- *Intervene sooner rather than later.* Holding off on a confrontation actually makes matters worse. The longer you wait to fix a problem, the bigger the problem can grow and the angrier you are likely to be. Taking faster action preempts worse trouble down the road.

- *Listen to the opposition.* Leave room for others involved in the conflict to express their points of view. You may not be aware of actions you have taken that have inadvertently contributed to the problem. Try to put what you are hearing in your own words to confirm that you understand others' issues. Owning your share of the troubles demonstrates both empathy and humility. Apologize if you really have screwed up.

- *Avoid generating defensiveness.* When individuals are under attack, it is natural to respond defensively. In an attempt to "save face," you might counterattack, use sarcasm, blame others, or adopt other strategies that don't own up. Conflict is likely to resolve with the best outcomes when the climate allows for both parties to save face (Adler & Proctor, 2011). Present your position as your best guess rather than present an absolute conclusion about the wrongs committed by the other person. It may even help to provide some plausible hypotheses and invite discussion about the problem instead of presenting a final conclusion about who's to blame.

- *Converge on a plan.* Forge an action plan to resolve the conflict even if you jointly "agree to disagree" on the conflict issue. Formulate a strategy for evaluating whether those involved completed their commitments, including fair consequences for those who may not follow through.

Negotiate Effectively Everybody negotiates. You negotiate when you apply for a job, dispute a grade with an instructor, buy a car, ask your landlord to paint your apartment, or try to get your roommate or partner to do something. Whenever you want something from someone whose interests are at odds with your own, you can choose to negotiate.

Some negotiation strategies are better than others. Negotiating effectively helps you to get what you want from others without alienating them. Negotiation experts often describe three main ways of solving problems with others: win–lose, lose–lose, and win–win.

- *Win–lose strategy.* In this type of negotiating, one party prevails and the other comes up short, such as: "Either I get my way or you get your way." For example, roommates may have pooled their resources for a spring break trip but totally disagree about where to go. Eventually one of the roommates gives in. Most of the time a win–lose strategy is not wise. Why? Because the loser may harbor bad feelings and always feel dissatisfied with the outcome.

- *Lose–lose strategy.* This situation usually unfolds when both parties initially try a win–lose strategy that does not work. As a result of the struggle, both end up unsatisfied with the outcome. For example, after several frustrating sessions of being unable to develop a satisfying spring break plan, both roommates may just give up rather than suffer protracted turmoil.

- *Win–win strategy.* The goal in this strategy is to find a solution that satisfies both parties and to avoid winning at the other person's expense. By working together, the parties can find a solution that satisfies everyone. For example, after considerable discussion and negotiation, each roommate agrees to some concessions and they arrive at an agreeable vacation plan.

Some compromises are often necessary in the win–win ideal. You and the seller settle on a price for a used car. The price is between what the seller was asking and what you wanted to pay. Neither of you got exactly what you wanted, but the outcome left each of you happy. Similarly, you and your companion each want to see a different movie. To spend the evening together, you might choose another movie that you both agree on.

The best solutions of all, though, are not compromises. Rather, they are solutions in which all parties get what they want. For example, Andrea and Carmen are roommates with different study habits. Andrea likes to study in the evening. This leaves most of her day free for other activities. Carmen thinks that evenings should be for relaxation and fun. They arrived at the following solution. On Monday through Wednesday, Andrea studies at her boyfriend's; Carmen does anything she wants. On Thursday and Sunday, Carmen agrees to keep things quiet where she and Andrea live. On Friday and Saturday they both have fun together.

The win–win strategy gives you a creative way of finding the best solution for a problem between two or more parties. You can use it to solve conflicts with others and make everyone involved feel better.

Manage Life

Communication challenges can sometimes lead to some of the most difficult moments you will have in college. Reduce some of the stress of your first year in college by being prepared to deal with loneliness, to recover from getting your heart broken, and to manage unwanted sexual pressures.

Deal with Loneliness

Although college campuses teem with people, first-year students—whether residents or commuters—still report feeling lonely at times. Loneliness can be a dark cloud over your everyday life.

Especially when students attend college away from home, they face the challenge of forming new social relationships. Many first-year students feel anxious about meeting new people and developing new social lives; first-year students rarely carry their high school popularity and social standing into college. In one study, 2 weeks after the college year began, 75 percent of the first-year students felt lonely at least part of the time after arriving on campus (Cutrona, 1982).

Loneliness is not reserved for first-year students just out of high school. Older first-year students can be lonely as well. The demands of school, work, and family may leave little time to feel replenished through contacts with friends. Also, it is common for divorced adults and widows/widowers to return to college to further their education and develop new skills. Because of the dissolution of their marital relationship, loneliness may penetrate their lives.

Anonymous

Alone on Saturday Night

Posted on Saturday, May 9, 2009, 9:46 P.M.

I'm 20 years old and in college. I should be having the time of my life, right? I should be out mingling and partying and meeting new people daily . . . right? I'm not. I'm really not. It's Saturday night, 10:30 to be exact, and I've been sitting here just trying my darndest to convince myself that I'm a normal 20-year-old college student. But I'm not, I'm really not. I'm 5'6, 135 lbs, blonde haired and dark brown eyed. I'm pretty, maybe not beautiful but I'm pretty. So why can't I meet a God-damned person? Why can't I have friends and boyfriends and people who call me to hang out? Why? I stay cooped up in my stupid apartment, going out only for class and food. I stay hidden here, away from the world because I'm scared to go out. Why? I really couldn't tell you. I'm scared of uncomfortable situations and awkward silences. I'm scared of bad conversation and sounding stupid. And you know what? I'm incredibly . . . incredibly lonely. But you know what? As scared as I am of being alone forever, I'm even more scared of not being alone. What's wrong with me? Who thinks like that? I keep people at an arm's length because any closer and they could hurt me. But, keep enough people far enough away and soon enough those people are going to go and find people who will embrace them. And soon enough I stop keeping people at even an arm's length because even they walk away. Please, please if anybody can in any way (and hopefully a major way) understand this and connect to this, please contact me. I honestly think that I'm alone in doing this, acting like this. It's so abnormal and crazy that I feel like the only person in the entire world that feels this way. Am I?

From The Experience Project. Used with permission.

Are You Lonely? Time spent alone can be meaningful and satisfying. However, when you feel isolated and long to be with others, you need to do something to become more connected. If you think that you aren't in tune with the people around you and can't find companionship when you want it, you're probably lonely. If you've recently left an important relationship, you'll likely feel lonely until you rebuild your social network.

To evaluate the extent to which you are lonely, complete Know Yourself: Self-Assessment 4.3, "Loneliness," at the end of the chapter on page 124.

Strategies for Reducing Loneliness How can you become better connected with others? Whether you are a traditional or nontraditional student, here are some good strategies:

- *Get involved.* Explore activities with others through college, work, community announcements, or religious organizations. Join and volunteer time with an organization you believe in. You'll probably meet others who share your views. One social gathering can lead to new social contacts, especially if you introduce yourself to others and start conversations.
- *Stretch yourself.* Join a new group at dinner, sit with new people in class, or find a study mate or an exercise partner. Meeting new people and developing new social ties always involve risk, but the benefits are worth it.
- *Break the ice.* When you enter situations where you will be dealing with people you don't know, give some thought to possible topics of conversation that you can introduce to spark an exchange. You can ask:
  What's your favorite class so far?
  Where do you see yourself in 5 years?
  What's the best thing you've ever tasted?
  If you could walk onto any airplane, where would you want it to take you?
  What extracurriculars do you wish you had time for?
  Any topic that prompts self-disclosure can typically get the conversation moving forward.
- *Practice positive character.* Listen with complete attention. Be upbeat and constructive. Make a point to comment on something special about the other person. Be the kind of friend you would like to have.
- *Be smart about cyberspace relationships.* Although social websites, such as Facebook, have made it easier to find friends who share your interests, it's crucial to be scrupulously careful about posting personal details. You don't want to fall victim to financial or sexual predators. Don't substitute cyber distractions for face-to-face relationships.

- *Recognize the warning signs of loneliness.* People often become bored or alienated before loneliness sinks in. Take action to head it off. Planning new activities is easier than struggling to escape loneliness once it has set in.
- *Ask for help.* If you can't shed your loneliness and make friends on your own, contact the student counseling center at your college or a mental health professional in your community. A counselor or mental health professional can show you ways to connect with others and reduce your loneliness.

Rebound from Heartbreak

Loneliness tends to produce feelings of emptiness and sadness. Throw in gut-wrenching pain when you feel suddenly and permanently deprived from someone you love and you have an age-old formulate for heartbreak. Now put that anguish in the close quarters of the college environment and your plans for college success could easily be derailed (Gibson, 2010). How can you make a clean break?

1. *Maximize your distance.* Purge the phone number and don't give in to the old rituals that helped you stay in touch. Avoid monitoring your ex's behavior on Facebook and remove or block him or her from "friend" status. Change your routine to reduce awkward encounters.
2. *Reconnect with friends.* Especially if you let other relationships wane while your romance was hot, it is time to rekindle the relationships that were once important. Be careful not to focus solely on your pain so you don't wear out your welcome.
3. *Seek novel extracurriculars.* Try something new. Your campus will have a host of new social circles you can voluntarily pursue to fill your time and perhaps make some new and interesting friends.
4. *Don't even think about being "friends."* In the aftermath of a breakup, you will have to surrender whatever plans you once had during the romance. You simply will need time apart rather than trying to endure a forced friendship.

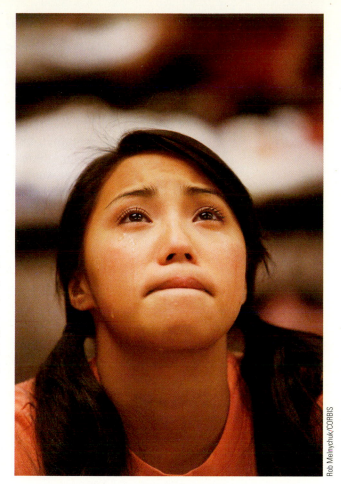

Rob Melnychuk/CORBIS

What strategies can lonely students use to become more connected with others?

DOONESBURY ©2011 G. B. Trudeau. Reprinted with permission of UNIVERSAL

Avoid Sexual Threats

Certain social choices can put students at risk of rape or other unwanted sexual acts. For example, some people engage in unwanted sexual acts even though they are not physically forced to do so. Why do they make such choices? There are several possible reasons:

- They might be turned on by their partner's actions, although they later regret their behavior.
- They might fear that the relationship will end if they don't do what their partner wants.
- They might be intoxicated or high on drugs at the time.
- They might feel obligated because of the time and money the partner spends on them.

Many college students participate in "hooking up," casual sexual relationships with partners selected from a group of their friends. Although such activity may not feel coercive because individuals participate of their own free will, there may be some not-so-subtle pressures to join in. Many students report substantial regret about participating, because it can negatively affect the relationship and even result in a pregnancy or a sexually transmitted infection.

A special concern is date rape, or acquaintance rape: forced sexual intercourse with someone who has at least a casual acquaintance with the victim. One-third to one-half of college men admit that they have forced sexual activity on women. Given this frequency, it pays to be vigilant about ways to avoid finding yourself in a compromising situation.

Rape is a violent crime. It traumatizes its victims, who initially feel shocked and numb (Kelly, 2011). Once the shock wears off, victims of rape typically feel shame of such magnitude that they do not report the crime and attempt to manage their trauma without appropriate intervention. Recovery is easier with the support of parents and friends, and professional counseling also can help. Reporting the crime and cooperating to secure appropriate punishment for the rapist can be an important part of recovery. In addition, successful prosecution reduces the likelihood that the acquaintance rapist will seek other victims.

In sum, monitor your sexual feelings and make wise sexual decisions. Act assertively to meet your social needs and to defend the kind of social life you genuinely wish to pursue. Sexual regret and academic achievement can be a difficult mix.

So far, we have explored ways to communicate more effectively and make solid social choices. It's also important to take special care to manage your life effectively by exploring, building, and protecting relationships that will facilitate your college success.

DANGER ZONE

Pregaming

Tad, a senior, and Angela, a first-year student, are on their way to an off-campus party before a football game at their college. It's their second date, and they are just getting to know each other. The party turns out to involve *pregaming*—drinking alcohol heavily before going out (Cameron et al., 2010). Tad begins drinking at the party and during the football game. After the game, he takes Angela, who also has had a few drinks, to his apartment, where he drinks more. He asks her to have sex with him and she says, "No, I'm just getting to know you." He persists in trying to have sex with her, but she fortunately is able to push him away and leaves the apartment. However, too often such circumstances lead to acquaintance rape.

Pregaming is a danger zone for alcohol and drug abuse, as well as acquaintance rape. Avoiding pregaming and limiting alcohol and drug intake in such situations are wise strategies.

Connect and Communicate

College can be a transforming experience. The personal changes that you will undergo may be a surprise not just to you but to your loved ones as well. Managing these important relationships effectively will help them stay vital even after you achieve your degree. Practicing good social strategies can also help you with the new relationships you may acquire during your college years.

Connect with Parents at the Right Level

Relationships between first-year college students and parents who provide financial and emotional support for them can vary considerably. Researchers have found a link between college success and the right level of involvement in student–parent relationships (Halberg, Halberg, & Sauer, 2000). When parents find it too challenging to let go, certain parent–child patterns may emerge that could impede the son's or daughter's development of independent decision making and his or her willingness to take on new experiences. For example, some parents believe that their college-age children are seriously in need of their guidance—a perspective that has given rise to the term *helicopter parents*. Such parents may become so overinvolved in a son's or daughter's academic decisions that the student remains dependent and avoids tackling new challenges. At the other extreme, some parents have little contact with, and provide little support for, first-year students who have left home, just as some students break off communication with their parents as soon as they no longer share living space. What can you do to connect with your parents at a level that is best for you—and them?

Let Your Parents Know You Haven't Fallen off the Planet No matter how much independence you want, it is not a good idea to break off communication with your parents, even if you felt stifled by them before you departed. You'll likely need them at some point, possibly for money, a place to live, or emotional support.

Maintaining communication with your parents doesn't mean you have to e-mail or call them daily. You don't have to tell them everything you do. However, if they don't hear from you for a couple of weeks, they may fear that something really bad has happened to you. In most cases parents want to know regularly how you are getting along.

What is regular contact? If you're away from home, a phone or text conversation or an informative e-mail once a week should do. E-mail is cheap, convenient, and easy—another great way to keep in touch.

If you're an emerging adult student in your first year, your parents are probably concerned about your increased independence. Without necessarily

JIM BORGMAN © 2006 Cincinnati Enquirer. Reprinted with permission of UNIVERSAL.

"Yes, Mother, I *told you*, I'm doing *fine* on my own at college... Hey, could you log on and find my schedule, order my books and call me when it's time for class?"

intending to crowd you, they may ask questions that seem intrusive: "How much are you studying?" "How come you didn't get an A on your English test?" "What's your roommate like?" "Are you dating anyone?" "Have you been going to religious services?" Try to listen politely to their questions. Realize that they probably have your best interests at heart. You don't have to tell them all the details of your life; they usually will accept your answers if you tell them a few general things and contact them on a predictable basis.

What Your Parents Can't Find Out without Your Approval Once you reach age 18, your parents should know only what you choose to tell them about your college experiences. According to the regulations described in the Family Education Responsibility and Privacy Act (FERPA), the college cannot release your records to anyone but you. Instructors are allowed to discuss your progress or problems only in your presence or with your written permission. During your orientation to college, you may be asked if you want to sign a waiver so the campus staff can contact your parents. You can sign the form and you can also rescind the form if you think that is in your best interest.

There are some important exceptions to this protection. If your parent presents tax records that indicate your dependent status, some colleges may honor the parent's request for information. In addition, if your behavior prompts concern for your physical or mental well-being, campus officials may contact your parents for help in solving the problem in your best interest.

Otherwise, this legal constraint encourages your family members to let you resolve your own problems. The regulation also should reinforce that you are responsible for your own circumstances. Don't ask your parents, or other spokespersons, to step in and resolve personal or academic problems when you can do it yourself. Use your control of personal information responsibly and wisely. Think about these situations as getting practice in advocating for your best interests.

Make Room for Partners and Family

Many nontraditional students face special challenges in their relationships as they attempt to succeed in college. Among these challenges are protecting relationships with a spouse or partner, and with children.

Relate to Your Spouse or Partner Following are some strategies for keeping relationships with a partner positive (Sternberg, 1988):

- *Don't take your relationship for granted.* The seeds of a relationship's destruction are planted when you or your partner take each other for granted. Nourish the relationship, giving it high priority along with your studies. Schedule time with your partner just as you do for classes and studying. Don't expect the other person to take over all of the household duties or pamper you.
- *Share your college life.* Let your partner know what you're doing in college. Discuss your schedule, what you're learning, and what your day is like. Look for campus activities or events—such as lectures, sporting events, and plays—that you can attend together. To avoid being too self-focused, remember to ask about your partner's activities.
- *Nurture positive esteem and confidence in the relationship.* Don't seek in your partner what you lack in yourself. Feel good about your pursuit of education—it will enhance your confidence. Actively look for opportunities that will build mutual good feeling. Test-drive your ideas with your partner

if your partner is willing. When both people have high self-esteem, their relationship benefits.

- **Be open with your partner.** Sometimes it seems easier in the short run to lie or hold back the painful truth. The problem is that once omissions, distortions, and flat-out lies start, they tend to spread and ultimately can destroy a relationship. Talk becomes empty because the relationship has lost its depth and trust.

- **See things from your partner's point of view.** Ask yourself how your partner perceives you. This technique helps you to develop the empathy and understanding that fuel a satisfying, successful relationship. Recognize that your intellectual changes may be taxing rather than exciting if your partner is not integrated into the process.

- **Be a friend.** Researchers have found that one of the top factors in a successful marriage is the extent to which the partners are good friends (Gottman & Gottman, 2009). Friendship acts as a powerful shield against conflict.

Care for Children If you're a parent as well as a student, you also face special challenges. Depending on their ages, your children may not be particularly patient with your sacrificing family time to meet obscure academic deadlines. How can you use parenting time to best advantage? Here are some helpful strategies:

- **Be authoritative.** Psychologists have found that the best parenting style is authoritative, which involves being nurturing, engaging in verbal give-and-take with the child, and exercising some control but not in a punishing way. That is, authoritative parents give children feedback to help them develop self-control but don't let them run wild. Children of authoritative parents tend to be well adjusted and competent. By contrast, being either permissive and uninvolved, or punitive and cold, is less effective as a parenting style. Children reared by these types of parents often have trouble controlling their behavior.

- **Communicate their value.** If your children are old enough, talk with them about how important they are to you as well as how important your education is. If possible, link your success in college with your hopes for a positive impact on your family. Set aside time each day to listen to your children, but be prepared to hear complaints about their perceptions that you are no longer as accessible as before.

- **Manage time effectively.** At times, you may feel overwhelmed with juggling a family and school. Planning is an important asset in your efforts to balance your academic and family time. Check into childcare facilities

Courtesy of Oklahoma State University

YOLANDA ODENKO   Spotlight On…

Dreaming Big and Working Hard

Family members matter. Take the case of soccer star Yolanda Odenyo, who won the 2009 Arthur Ashe Scholar and Athlete of the Year award. A human development major at Oklahoma State University, Yolanda broke all records at OSU while managing a 3.77 GPA. According to her college website (2009), she was

Award winning soccer forward Yolanda Odenko proved a strong connection to her family in adversity.

also a gifted and gracious collaborator in and out of the classroom. She conducted outreach for her campus ministry, taught Bible classes, and volunteered for blood drives, YMCA activities, and campus events. But she still found time to honor her sister who was killed in a car accident by establishing the "Score for Sasja" fund. Her fund-raising supports impoverished children in Kenya to attend high school. Odenyo attributes her success to being able to balance her life across her obligations. Following graduation, Yolanda headed into master's degree work in internal studies at OSU. For those just starting out in college, Yolanda recommends, "Utilize the services available to you. Everything you need to succeed is provided for you. Dream big and work hard."

What strategies can students who also are parents adopt to make their college experience successful?

and community agencies for services and activities for your children before and after school. Chapter 3 also offers a number of excellent time-management strategies that will help you strike a better balance between family and school obligations.

- **Set aside time for your children and yourself.** It's not going to be easy, but be sure to block out at least some time each week for activities you enjoy or for relaxation. You might have a hobby or enjoy cycling or going to movies. Set aside time every day for your children's interests as well.

Get Along with Roommates

If you live on campus, you will find that the quality of relationships with roommates varies. In many cases, a first-year student's roommate is a total stranger. You're asked to live in close quarters for 9 months with someone you know little or nothing about. That's enough to worry anyone. If you are lucky, you might become best friends. Or you might be mutually indifferent and simply live parallel lives in the same space. If you are unlucky, you might grow to hate each other.

Whenever two people live together, problems are bound to appear. You can learn a lot about the importance of give-and-take in key relationships by living with a roommate. What's the best way to build solid roommate relationships?

- **Address problems early.** Don't let problems fester. Detect and resolve them early.
- **Use good communication skills.** Listen actively and avoid barriers to communication whenever you can.
- **Show respect.** Be considerate of your roommate. For example, it's not a good idea to come in at 2 A.M., flip the lights on, and wake up your roommate. It's also not a good idea to switch on the CD or DVD player when your roommate is studying.
- **Be assertive.** If you think that you're doing more than your fair share of the giving in your roommate relationship, be more assertive. Stand up for your rights. Use the strategies for being assertive outlined earlier in the chapter.
- **Recognize your part.** Objectively review what aspects of your behavior might be challenging for your roommate. For example, you may have gotten into the habit of not keeping your room clean before you came to college. Old habits are hard to break. Keep your area clean and neat or at least try to match the level of neatness exercised by your roommate to avoid problems. Chances are good that your "roommate problem" involves some problem behaviors of your own.

But what if, after trying hard to reconcile problems, your roommate seems destined to ruin your adjustment to college life? What can you do?

If you live in a college dorm, you probably have a resident adviser (RA) with whom you can discuss your roommate problems. Take the initiative. Go to the RA and ask for advice. Try out the advice and give it a chance to work. Then, if things are still intolerable, go to the campus housing office. Courteously and clearly state your roommate problems and explore your options there. You are more likely to negotiate a different room assignment if your current situation is unacceptable to both you and your roommate.

Show Intercultural Competence

Regardless of the nature of the difference, how can you get along and communicate better with people who differ from you? Here are some helpful strategies:

Assess Your Attitudes One of the first steps is to understand your own attitudes better. Most of us sincerely think that we are not prejudiced. As a starting point, honestly evaluate your attitudes toward people who don't share your characteristics or background. You'll have an opportunity to learn more about managing prejudice in the next chapter.

Ethnic diversity is increasing in college populations. Take advantage of meeting diverse friends to expand your global awareness and understanding of diverse others.

Avoid Making Assumptions Do not assume that what works in American culture will work in other traditions. For example, the direct eye contact that communicates "respect" would be interpreted as hostile and disrespectful in other cultures. It helps to understand the norms that govern relationships in a specific culture or subculture.

Take the Perspective of Others You can improve your attitude toward others by clarifying your perspective and trying to better understand the views of others. Ask yourself:

- "What is the individual feeling and thinking?"
- "What is it about the person's background and experiences that makes the individual different from me?"
- "In what ways might we be similar?"
- "What kinds of stress and obstacles is she or he facing?"
- "Is the fact that the individual is different reason enough for me to not like the person or to be angry with him?"
- "How much do I really know about these other people? How can I learn more?"

Students can benefit from asking themselves these questions about gender, ethnic groups, and sexual orientation. They also can benefit by asking such questions about traditional and nontraditional students.

Seek Out Personal Contact The great civil rights leader Martin Luther King Jr. once said, "I have a dream that my four little children will one day live in a nation where they will not be judged by the color of their skin but by the content of their character." How can we reach the world Dr. King envisioned: a world beyond prejudice and discrimination? Mere contact with people from other ethnic groups won't do it. However, a particular type of contact—personal contact—often is effective in improving relations with others. *Personal contact* here means sharing one's worries, troubles, successes, failures, personal ambitions, and coping strategies. When we reveal information about ourselves, we are likely to be perceived more as individuals than as stereotyped members of a group. When we share personal information with people whom we used to regard as "them," we begin to see that they are more like "us" than we thought.

Tolerate Puzzles Avoid making judgments about what you cannot understand. It is natural to respond to novel behavior with confusion and perhaps even fear. However, recognize that behavior that seems nonsensical, offensive, or even bizarre is a puzzle that can be understood in cultural context. Communicate your eagerness to learn to solve the puzzle.

Respect Differences but Don't Overlook Similarities Think how boring our lives would be if we were all the same. Respecting others with different traditions, backgrounds, and abilities improves communication and cooperation. When we perceive people as different from us, we often do so on the basis of one or two limited characteristics such as skin color, gender, age, or a disability. When someone seems different, do you ever try to see how the two of you might be similar? Think about the many similarities between you and someone you regard as totally different:

- You might both be shy and anxious, fearful of speaking in public.
- You might both feel overwhelmed by all the demands you need to juggle.
- If you've both chosen the same campus to pursue your education, you might have similar achievement standards, such as making the dean's list.
- You may share an interest in a certain sport, type of movie, computer games, or food.

Broaden Your Knowledge In many instances, the more you know about people who are different from you, the better you can interact with them. Learn more about the customs, values, interests, and historical background of such people. Take a course on cultures around the world, for example.

Treat People as Individuals In our culture, we want to be treated as individuals. We each want to be unique. Your interactions with diverse others will improve if you keep in mind that they are individuals—if you avoid thinking of them as the members of a group. Talk with them about their concerns, interests, worries, hopes, and daily lives.

 Build a Bright Future

Your college years provide opportunities every day to practice your communication and relationship skills. Implementing the strategies recommended in this chapter not only will improve your communication skills and relationships in college, but will also provide the foundation for success in your work and career after college.

Develop Professional Networks

During her first year away at college, Martina discovered to her delight that there was a highly respected dentist, Dr. Denton, who attended her synagogue. During a social hour, she introduced herself and explained that she had been thinking about a career in dentistry. Dr. Denton invited her to visit him at his practice. He was happy to show Martina how he had built his business, and he became a special source of support for her as her undergraduate work unfolded.

Success in college is enhanced not only by good friendships but also by your ability to network effectively with people in general. Networking involves connecting with others to enhance your opportunities, but it is time well spent, particularly in building bonds that will help you professionally. Successful networking takes practice.

Following are some effective networking strategies (Mrosko, 2002):

- **Be patient and follow up.** In many instances, it takes time to develop a relationship. Effective networking doesn't happen overnight. Follow up with initial contacts. Consistent, focused contacts build relationships. Martina had to call Dr. Denton a few times before the relationship got rolling, but once he saw how serious her commitment was, he made time in his schedule to help her.
- **Encourage mutual gains.** Both sides need to receive a benefit, either now or in the future. Martina was able to gain insights into her chosen profession; Dr. Denton, by the assistance he provided, was able to experience once again the fun of preparing for a career.
- **Listen carefully.** Take notes and really hear what others are saying. Recording details shows that you place great value on the information and may reduce the embarrassing need to ask that details you can't remember be repeated.
- **Ask for help.** Be specific about what you need.
- **Become involved.** Become active in support groups and campus organizations. Volunteer to be on a committee. Identify specific interest groups that might help you realize your goals.

Look and Act the Part

College promotes learning how to adapt to different kinds of situations. Whether you like it or not, people are going to judge you based substantially on the nonverbal aspects of your communication. Just as you practice codeswitching in verbal language to adapt to the group you are in, you also need to practice adapting your clothing choices and other nonverbal aspects to promote the best impression.

If you get a job on campus, look around to see if there is an unspoken dress code at work. Although many business settings tolerate students who dress more casually and comfortably, other office settings may prohibit low-slung pants or exposed midriffs. Unless you have a clear vision about what you want to do professionally, consider holding off on that dragon tattoo.

Meeting a potential employer, or others in your professional network, usually requires a formal handshake. Don't present a limp or sweaty hand. Smile. State, "I'm pleased to meet you, Mr. X." Then try to match the pressure and rhythm of the hand clasp of the person whom you are meeting. When you take your leave, affirm that you enjoyed the meeting.

Getting involved with professional work settings as well as affiliating with fraternities or sororities will put you in formal dinner settings where you may be unfamiliar with how to navigate the array of utensils and the norms for dinner etiquette. If you find yourself anticipating this kind of event, check with Student Affairs officials on your campus to determine if they sponsor a "business etiquette" training session. In such situations, you will learn norms such as:

- which fork to use for the salad (go for the small one furthest to the left)
- which direction to pass the bread (counterclockwise)
- how to tell if the water glass is yours or your neighbor's to the right (bread plate on the left; drink on right)
- how to signal you do not wish to have coffee (place hand flat on top of the cup)

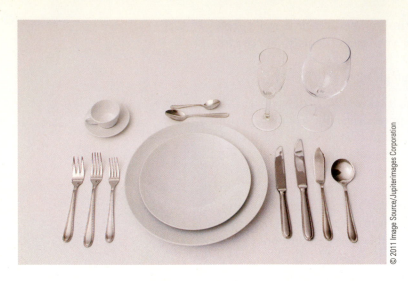

If a formal place setting makes you want to run away and order pizza, consider finding a short course on business etiquette to help you navigate which utensil to use for what kind of food.

© 2011 Image Source/Jupiterimages Corporation

With a little guidance and practice, you will learn the strategies necessary to dress properly and dine elegantly in case a formal dinner is part of your job interview or social circle.

Link Communication Skills with Your Career

Developing these communication skills as a college student will pave the way for you to be an outstanding communicator in your adult life at work and outside of work with family, friends, and others. Employers typically list good communication skills as the most important ability they look for in new employees.

Consider Antoine, who felt fortunate to land a part-time campus job working in the admissions office. Although he spent considerable time filing applications and doing data entry, he also answered phones and greeted parents and prospective students when they arrived on campus for interviews. He needed to listen closely to address their questions and communicate effectively about his college's strengths. The diverse student body in Antoine's campus gave him the opportunity to meet different types of people. He was motivated to act sensitively to prospective students from a variety of backgrounds to make them feel comfortable during their visits. Although he had always planned to be an accountant, the part-time campus job in the admissions office made him think more about ensuring that his future career included considerable interpersonal interaction. He was surprised by how much he enjoyed the interaction and how much his communication skills had already improved.

Cultivating good relationships with coworkers will benefit your career development and improve your chances of moving up the career ladder. Also, having good relationships with family members, a partner, and friends will help you add balance to your life after college. We live in an increasingly diverse world, and your relationship skills will help you interact with diverse others from backgrounds different from your own at work. Practicing these skills during college will make it much easier for you to engage in positive interaction with others at work after college.

Clarify Expectations

- Identify what kinds of opportunities exist in your social environment.
- Recognize how your personal attachment style may influence the development of healthy relationships.

Develop Competence

- Develop active-listening skills. Pay attention to the person who is talking. Paraphrase.
- Speak in simple, concrete, and specific ways. Make your verbal and nonverbal messages consistent.
- Fine-tune your ability to interpret nonverbal information, including facial expressions and clothing.
- Practice using professional quality standards in communication at college.
- Resolve conflicts with others by being assertive and negotiating effectively rather than relying on aggression, manipulation, or passivity.

Manage Life

- Determine the optimal balance between meeting your social and academic needs.
- Avoid the settings in which rape occurs most often, limit alcohol and drug use, and use good judgment. Make wise sexual decisions.
- Friends reduce loneliness, are a source of self-esteem, and provide emotional support.
- Recognize the potential hardships associated with falling in love and completing your academic work.

Connect and Communicate

- If you are a traditional student, keep in touch with your parents to ease any concerns about your independence.
- If you have a partner or spouse, use good communication skills to have a positive relationship with him or her during your college years.
- If you have children, be an authoritative parent, communicate well, and be a good time manager.
- If you have a roommate, address any problems early on, and use good communication skills.

Build a Bright Future

- Network to enhance your professional opportunities.
- Learn to adapt to professional dress and dining norms to prepare for job interviews.
- Cultivate good relationships with coworkers to enhance your chances of moving up the career ladder.

 Visit the College Success CourseMate for *Your Guide to College Success* for interactive resources at login.cengagebrain.com

1. Why is it important to be vigilant about interpreting social cues accurately?

_____

_____

_____

_____

2. Summarize the three styles of attachment, and describe the impact each style has in trying to develop new relationships.

_____

_____

_____

_____

3. List three basic strategies for improving your listening skills. Then list at least one situation in which you can practice each strategy.

1. Strategy: _____ Situation: _____

2. Strategy: _____ Situation: _____

3. Strategy: _____ Situation: _____

4. What are some ways you can enhance the likelihood of solving problems without creating a defensive climate?

_____

_____

_____

_____

5. Describe at least three strategies for combating loneliness.

1. _____

2. _____

3. _____

6. Discuss some approaches you can take to getting over a broken heart.

_____

_____

_____

_____

7. If you are a traditional student, list three common problems with relationships among roommates or other individuals with whom you might live. How can you solve these problems?

1._____

2._____

3._____

8. If you are a nontraditional student and have a partner or spouse and/or children, describe three issues that might arise involving your close relationships as you pursue a college degree. What are some positive ways of addressing these issues?

1._____

2._____

3._____

9. What are three ways that you can improve your social networking?

1._____

2._____

3._____

10. How does clothing selection and nonverbal communication influence the first impression you can make?

_____

_____

_____

_____

SELF-ASSESSMENT 4.1

What Is My Attachment Style?

To find out your attachment style, read each paragraph and then place a check mark next to the description that best describes you (Hazen & Shaver, 1987):

_____ I find it relatively easy to get close to others, and I am comfortable depending on them and having them depend on me. I don't worry about being abandoned or about someone getting too close to me.

_____ I am somewhat uncomfortable being close to others. I find it difficult to trust them completely and to allow myself to depend on them. I get nervous when anyone gets too close to me, and it bothers me when someone tries to be more intimate with me than I feel comfortable with.

_____ I find that others are reluctant to get as close as I would like. I often worry that my partner doesn't really love me or won't want to stay with me. I want to get very close to my partner, and this sometimes scares people away.

The three items correspond to three attachment styles—secure attachment (option 1 above) and two insecure attachment styles (avoidant—option 2 above, and anxious—option 3 above):

- *Secure attachment style.* Securely attached adults have positive views of relationships, find it easy to get close to others, and are not terribly concerned or stressed out about their romantic relationships. These adults tend to enjoy sexuality in the context of a committed relationship and are less likely than others to have one-night stands.
- *Avoidant attachment style.* Avoidant individuals are hesitant about getting involved in romantic relationships and once in a relationship tend to distance themselves from their partners.
- *Anxious attachment style.* These individuals demand closeness, are less trusting, and are more emotional, jealous, and possessive. They can present as "sticky fans" who can't tolerate any distance in the relationship.

The majority of adults (about 60–80 percent) describe themselves as securely attached, and not surprisingly, adults prefer having a securely attached partner (Shaver & Mikulincer, 2012).

If your attachments tend to be avoidant or anxious, you may find that your relationships with friends and romantic partners are difficult. This is an area that you can work to improve. However, even if your secure attachment style predicts healthy relationships, you will have to choose wisely to provide the right balance between meeting your social and academic needs.

Source: Hazan, C., & Shaver, P. (1987). Romantic love conceptualized as an attachment process. *Journal of Personality and Social Psychology, 52,* p. 515.

SELF-ASSESSMENT 4.2

What Is My Communication Style?

Think about each of the following situations. Check which style you tend to use in each.

	Assertive	Aggressive	Manipulative	Passive
You're being kept on the phone by a salesperson trying to sell you something.				
You want to break off a relationship that no longer works for you.				
You're sitting in a movie and the people behind you are talking.				
Your doctor keeps you waiting for more than 20 minutes.				
You're standing in line and someone moves in front of you.				
Your friend has owed you money for a long time and it's money you could use.				
You receive food at a restaurant that is over- or undercooked.				
You want to ask your friend, romantic partner, or roommate for a major favor.				
Your friend asks you to do something that you don't feel like doing.				
You're at a large lecture. The instructor is speaking too softly and you know other students are also having trouble hearing her.				
You want to start a conversation at a gathering, but you don't know anyone there.				
You're sitting next to someone who is smoking, and the smoke bothers you.				
You're talking to someone about something important to you, but he doesn't seem to be listening.				
You're speaking and someone interrupts you.				
You receive an unjust criticism from someone.				

Scoring and Interpretation

Total the number of your aggressive, manipulative, passive, and assertive marks. Whichever style has the most marks is your dominant personal style of interacting with others in conflicts. If you did not mark the assertive category 10 or more times, you would benefit from improving your assertive style of communicating. Use your responses to individual items to see the areas in which you could benefit from being assertive.

Source: The Anxiety & Phobia Workbook by BOURNE, EDMUND J. Copyright 2000 Reproduced with permission of NEW HARBINGER PUBLICATIONS in the format Textbook and Other book via Copyright Clearance Center.

Loneliness

Read each of the following statements and describe the extent to which they characterize you as:

1 = Never   2 = Rarely   3 = Sometimes   4 = Often

_____ 1. I feel in tune with the people around me.

_____ 2. I lack companionship.

_____ 3. There is no one I can turn to.

_____ 4. I do not feel alone.

_____ 5. I feel part of a group of friends.

_____ 6. I have a lot in common with the people around me.

_____ 7. I am no longer close to anyone.

_____ 8. My interests and ideas are not shared by those around me.

_____ 9. I am an outgoing person.

_____ 10. There are people I feel close to.

_____ 11. I feel left out.

_____ 12. My social relationships are superficial.

_____ 13. No one really knows me well.

_____ 14. I feel isolated from others.

_____ 15. I can find companionship when I want it.

_____ 16. There are people who really understand me.

_____ 17. I am unhappy being so withdrawn.

_____ 18. People are around me but not with me.

_____ 19. There are people I can talk to.

_____ 20 There are people I can turn to.

Total your score for these ten items: 1, 4, 5, 6, 9, 10, 15, 16, 19, 20. Next, reverse your score for items 2, 3, 7, 8, 11, 12, 13, 14, 17, and 18 (for example, if your score was a 1 on item 2, change it to a 4 for scoring purposes), and add up your total for these ten items. Add the two subtotals (subtotal 1 plus subtotal 2) to arrive at your overall loneliness score:

If you scored 70 or above, you likely have good social connections and experience little loneliness.

If you scored 60–69, you likely experience quite a bit of loneliness.

If you scored 59 or below, you likely experience a great deal of loneliness. If you are a lonely individual, a counselor at your college can likely help you develop some good strategies for reducing your loneliness and becoming more socially connected.

Source: From D. Russell et al., "The revised UCLA Loneliness Scale: Concurrent and discriminant validity evidence," Journal of Personality and Social Psychology, 39, 472–480. Copyright © 1980 by the American Psychological Association. Reproduced with permission. No further reproduction or distribution is permitted without written permission from the American Psychological Association.

Clarify Expectations

1. Are You Securely Attached?

According to Know Yourself: Self-Assessment 4.1, what is your attachment style? How do you think you developed this style—secure, anxious, or avoidant? Think about your experiences as you were growing up in your family, your relationships with your friends, and your relationship with romantic partners. Then write about your attachment history and how you came to have your current attachment style.

_____

_____

_____

2. Off Balance, Down, and Out

Think about a situation in which you totally misread the social situation. What important cues did you miss that could have given you a better direction in how to manage socially?

_____

_____

_____

 Develop Competence

3. Are Men Really from Mars and Women Really from Venus?

In the popular book *Men Are from Mars, Women Are from Venus* (Gray, 1992), the differences between men and women are described as being so extensive that the two sexes are from different planets. Get together with three or four male and three or four female college students and brainstorm about whether men and women are as different as this book suggests or whether they actually have more in common. Write down some of your conclusions here.

_____

_____

_____

4. What Does Touch Communicate?

Touch and posture can be important forms of communication. What are some different ways they can communicate information? How might the same touch or posture be interpreted differently depending on the identity of the person being touched—a friend, a romantic partner, an instructor, a person of a different age, or a stranger, for example?

_____

_____

_____

Manage Life

5. Combat Loneliness

Choose a club meeting or another social activity to attend. At this activity, strike up a conversation with one person in the room. Take some time to observe and listen, picking a person with whom you might like to have a relationship. Then come back to your room and write about the conversation. Write down other things that you would like to know about this person and make a plan for getting together again in the near future.

_____

_____

_____

6. Bar Smarts

You are at a bar or club when your best friend's longtime boyfriend or girlfriend, who has had one too many drinks, hits on you. How would you deflect the pass? What principles of good communication would you use to construct your response?

_____

_____

_____

Connect and Communicate

7. Improve Your Relationship with Your Parents

Write about your relationship with your parents. Describe ways that you could improve the relationship.

_____

_____

_____

8. Improving My Relationships beyond My Family

For one week, make a note of every situation in which you feel you could have communicated better with someone you have a relationship with outside your family. This could be a friend, a romantic partner, or someone else. At the end of the week, revisit this list and write down some strategies for improving similar conversations in the future. What barriers do you think you encountered, and how can you address them better next time?

_____

_____

_____

Build a Bright Future

9. Communication and Careers

Write about the communication skills you learned about in this chapter that you can improve during college so that you will be able to get a good job after college and advance in a career.

_____

_____

_____

10. Relationship Issues

Write about how the way you handle relationship issues might help or harm your success in college and in work and your career after college.

_____

_____

_____

Navigate Differences

Chapter 5

KNOW YOURSELF

YOUR SUCCESS IN COLLEGE will be influenced by how well you can deal with wide-ranging human differences. Some differences, such as gender, age, and other physical characteristics, are obvious. Other differences, such as first-generation status, religious tradition, political orientation, or occupation, may not be immediately apparent. Differences in learning styles, preferences, or disabilities also may not be easy to see but can have an impact on your success in college. To evaluate how effectively you can navigate individual differences in the college environment, select the category that best describes your characteristics below.

How Well Do I Interact with Others?

	Very Much Like Me	Somewhere in Between	Not at All Like Me
I recognize how expectations can help or hinder human interaction.			
I know how to overcome the effects of judgments based on stereotypes.			
I can describe types of learning experiences that are easiest for me.			
I know how my personality and background influence my classroom success.			
I know my greatest talents and weaknesses as a learner.			
I know how to make a good impression in academic settings.			
I can solve problems I may have with instructors.			
I recognize how background factors can influence learning.			
I know how to select and recruit a mentor.			
I can describe career options that fit with my learning style.			

© Sonda Dawes/The Image Works

Nola Ochs

It's Never Too Late

Imagine that you are about to meet a 95-year-old woman. If you are like most people, you probably will generate a set of expectations about your new acquaintance that involve fragility, limited mobility, declining cognitive skills, and perhaps even a rocking chair. When it comes to Nola Ochs, who holds the distinction in the *Guinness Book of Records* of being the oldest college graduate in the world, you'd be totally wrong.

Nola Ochs surpassed everyone's expectations when she trumped her record of being the oldest college graduate by earning her masters degree in 2010. She is pictured here with her granddaughter, Alexandra, when they shared the experience of graduating from Fort Hays State University in 2007.

A grandmother of 13, Nola completed her general studies degree from Fort Hays State University in 2007, the same year she was named *Kansas Woman Leader of the Year.* Ironically, her 21 year-old granddaughter Alexandra was also in the graduating class and witnessed the state governor personally awarding her grandmother's degree. The crowd recognized Nola's accomplishment with a standing ovation (Park, 2007).

Nola began her college education in 1930 but withdrew to raise a family of four sons on the family farm. Following her husband's death in 1972, she enrolled at Dodge City Community College to take a course in tennis. She enjoyed it so much that she just kept taking courses in everything that interested her. She was surprised to discover that she needed just 30 more credits to capture a college degree, so she moved from the family farm to reside in an apartment near FHSU to finish her degree. Her classmates benefited from Nola's firsthand knowledge of the 1930s Dust Bowl, World War II, the civil rights movements, and disco fever, among other historical events. Her success as a collaborator prompted her to express the desire to become a storyteller on a cruise ship during one of many interviews she granted near her famous graduation. Celebrity Cruises made that dream come true when they hired her for that job after graduation.

However, Nola was not content without academic challenge. She returned to FHSU and completed a master's degree in history in 2010. "She's one of the top graduate students we have," history professor

Raymond Wilson concluded. "And it's not like having a know-it-all in class or anything. As soon as she opens her mouth, everyone listens." Her professors weren't surprised to learn that she planned to compete for a graduate assistantship for the following fall semester.

Classmates will differ from you not just in ethnicity, interests, and traditions, but also in how they learn. Some will differ dramatically. Nola Och's story illustrates her unexpected success in college based on her active curiosity, her joy in collaboration, and her ability to overcome low expectations. Take a look at the chapter outline and anticipate what parts of this chapter might help you in your own navigation of individual differences and expectations.

(Source: Bauer, 2010)

Clarify Expectations

College represents a complex social hierarchy with fairly well defined roles. When you assume the role of the college student, you inherit significant expectations:

- Your parents or partner will want to be proud of your accomplishments and feel reassured that your tuition dollars have been well spent.
- Admissions officials expect you to live up to the potential in your competitive application.

- College administrators set forth formal expectations in the student handbook about following the rules and the consequences if they are not followed.
- Your professors will expect your best effort in the classes you take from them and probably will make their expectations explicit in the course syllabus.
- Informal expectations will also be a part of other roles you will play in college, such as roommate, study group colleague, or interest group member.

You will enact your student role in a unique fashion, bringing the distinctive learning history that has shaped your individual preferences for what and how you learn. Only recently has higher education started to examine how individual differences intersect with learning. These insights about your learning profile can help explain both what you have in common with your peers and how you differ from them.

Cognitive development is not the only goal in college. Most college mission statements claim that college will stimulate personal growth. By pursuing your education with classmates and professors who have diverse backgrounds, you have regular opportunities to benefit from collaborating with individuals whose background may be quite different from your own.

Understand Stereotypes

College abounds with stereotypes—the dumb jock, the science nerd, the "Gleek," the absent-minded professor, and the nightmare roommate—among others. Stereotypes represent positive or negative beliefs we maintain about individuals who share a particular characteristic with a group. We assume individuals with specific characteristics will act in a predictable way based on what we expect of the group.

These mental shortcuts are normal; we rely on them to make a complex world more manageable. We don't have to "start over" with every new person who enters our social sphere if we can make some predictions based on limited information (Macrae & Bodenhausen, 2000). For example, you probably maintain some stereotypes about the helpful nature of the college librarian that will make it easier to approach someone you don't know to ask for help.

On the other hand, when individuals behave differently than expected, stereotypes still tend to prevail and can then cause trouble. They are remarkably sturdy. Stereotypes can foster prejudice, which promotes jumping to conclusions without considering all the evidence (Lillienfeld et al., 2010). Positive stereotypes predispose us to have favorable prejudices and high expectations, while negative stereotypes foster low expectations, pessimistic predictions, and discriminatory treatment.

Despite the high ideals that members of the college environment typically strive for, you may not be immune to the adverse effects of stereotyping. See Know Yourself: Self-Assessment 5.1, "When Stereotypes Come Out to Play," at the end of the chapter on page 159 to evaluate your own vulnerability to typical stereotypes in the college setting.

Overcome Stereotypes

College will provide many opportunities to challenge the stereotypes you currently hold. Sometimes these can be modified or abandoned entirely when the opportunity arises to work alongside the individual whom we have prematurely and unfairly judged. Research (Aronson et al., 1978) has confirmed that the best means of overcoming misconceptions is to work with others on a common, unifying objective. As long as group members carry their fair share of the work, success can encourage you to modify the stereotyped way you previously thought.

Develop Competence

To become competent in navigating differences, we focus in this section on recognizing the variety of ways learning can be helped or hindered from the effects of native intelligence, learning styles, and personality patterns.

Estimate Your Intelligence

Perhaps at some point in your past, someone measured your intelligence. On the basis of your intelligence quotient (IQ) score, you may have been able to skip a grade or qualify for special help in school. But the idea of IQ is controversial: contemporary psychologists question the notion that we can capture individual intelligence with a single number.

Psychologist Howard Gardner (1989, 1999b) proposed that we would be wiser to consider several types of abilities rather than a single measure of intelligence. He formulated his theory of "multiple intelligences" based on patterns we observe in different sets of skills. Gardner suggested that these sorts of abilities cluster in nine different areas, or *domains:*

1. *Verbal-Linguistic Skills:* sensitivity to and appreciation of word meanings and the function of language
2. *Logical-Mathematical Skills:* orderly use of reasoning, logic, and mathematics to understand and explain abstract ideas
3. *Musical Abilities:* appreciating, performing, or creating music or the elements of music, such as rhythm and pitch
4. *Bodily-Kinesthetic Awareness:* coordinated and skilled use of objects in the environment, involving both gross and fine motor skills
5. *Spatial Skills:* accurate perception and reproduction of spatial images, including strong navigation and artistic skills
6. *Intrapersonal Abilities:* meaningful discrimination and interpretation of the behavior and moods of others
7. *Interpersonal Abilities:* accurate self-perception, including a refined capacity to identify and represent complex personal emotions and motives
8. *Naturalist Abilities:* understanding, relating to, classifying, and explaining aspects of the natural world
9. *Spiritual/Existential Abilities:* considering cosmic experiences that are not easily understood but are nonetheless important to understanding the deeper truths of human experience

Gardner argued that these domains are independent of one another, suggesting that humans can be highly developed in one area but not others. According to Gardner, most college courses tend to emphasize verbal-linguistic and logical-mathematic intelligences at the expense of other important skill areas.

You may be naturally more gifted in some areas than in others. Learning in those areas is simply easier for you. You may even resist taking courses typically required in general education (the first 2 years of college study) that don't fall within those easy areas. However, most college programs focus on developing a broad base of skills. So, for example, even if you don't have strengths in logical-mathematical skills, you'll probably have to take some basic courses that require those skills to earn your chosen degree.

Take a moment to complete Know Yourself: Self-Assessment 5.2, "Your Intelligence Profile," at the back of the chapter on page 160 to estimate your

"As smart as he was, Albert Einstein could not figure out how to handle those tricky bounces at third base."

intellectual strengths using Gardner's framework. This exercise also can help you predict which courses will be relatively easy or difficult for you. For example, if your strengths lie in spatial skills, then taking an art history course may be a surprisingly happy learning experience. If the area of interpersonal abilities is your main strength, then you'll likely do well in courses that focus on group work. By contrast, if algebra is "Greek" to you, you'll have to work much harder to grasp the concepts than will the mathematically gifted person seated next to you.

Consider getting help right away before you get too far behind in a course that doesn't match your preferred learning style. Find a study partner who demonstrates the intelligence that you need to develop, or work with your study skills center on campus to learn how to take advantage of your learning strengths and style.

If you cannot easily use campus resources to help you cope, conduct some research before registration to determine which instructors might provide a student-friendly approach that will give you a greater comfort zone when you tackle disciplines that are more challenging. Ask students who have been through the course before what to expect. Remember that your sources may have very different learning styles and may respond positively to instructors whom you could find unacceptable. Find students who seem to have the same learning preferences or values that you do to optimize your research time.

Learn about Learning Styles

People differ in how easily they learn, but describing these differences isn't easy. *Learning styles* generally represent different strategies or frameworks that may relate to more effective or efficient learning for specific individuals. Although not all frameworks have been substantiated as more than folklore (Lillienfeld et al., 2010), each of the perspectives may shed some light on why some contexts will seem easy and others will feel so challenging.

Psychologist Robert Bjork (1994, 2005) suggests that there is merit in working through "desirable difficulties" (cf. Bjork, 1994, 1995) because they can lead to personal growth. So it is not a good idea to pursue only learning contexts that are a good match for your learning style; greater long-term gains may occur in your flexibility as a learner when you are challenged in contexts that don't match your learning preferences.

Sensory Preferences Do you prefer to get input about the world through your ears, eyes, or sense of touch? The sensory mode you prefer may influence how easily you can learn in different academic situations. We explore the three sensory preferences as well as what you can do when your preferences and your professors' plans don't align.

Auditory Learning Some lucky people are good *auditory learners.* They absorb a lecture without much effort. They may not even need to take careful notes but learn just by listening. Auditory learners may avoid making eye contact with anyone in the class so that they can concentrate on catching every word and nuance.

If you are an auditory learner, your best match may be instructors who rely most on lecture to deliver the course content. When your instructor doesn't lecture, one of the following approaches may be useful:

- Concentrate on the spoken words.
- Rehearse key ideas in your head.
- Identify key concepts in your notes.
- Summarize the key themes of the class out loud to a study partner.
- Pay less attention to visual supports that may distract you.

Visual Learning Many of us have an easier time learning from lectures that use pictures, diagrams, cartoons, or demonstrations. Visual learners like to make images of words and concepts. Then they capture these images on paper for a quick review. Thus, they benefit from the use of charts, maps, notes, and flash cards when they study.

Visual learners may become distracted when instructors provide no visual anchors in their lectures. They typically get overwhelmed when instructors use slides with dense terminology and lecture at the same time. In this situation, visual learners need to tune out the auditory information and focus on what they can see for the most efficient processing.

If you are a visual learner, your best match may be with instructors who lecture but use extensive imagery to make the content memorable. When your instructor doesn't provide the visual supports that are more compelling, try the following strategies:

- Draw your own related pictures and graphs in your notes.
- Use arrows in your notes to highlight connections.
- Seek out related media that support or review key concepts.
- Try to visualize imagery that will help you remember.
- Create two or three images that capture the essence of the class.

Tactile or Kinesthetic Learning Some people are tactile or kinesthetic learners. They prefer touch as their primary mode for taking in information. Unfortunately, very few college classes provide an opportunity for tactile learners to use their preferred sensory mode. Art, recreation, and technical classes related to careers involving manual procedures are among the most prominent examples.

Tactile learners faced with auditory learning situations should write out important facts and perhaps trace the words that they have written with their fingers to give them extra sensory feedback. They can make up study sheets that connect to vivid examples. In some cases, role playing can help tactile learners learn and remember important ideas.

If you are a tactile learner, your best match may be with instructors who use active learning strategies, sometimes called an experiential approach. When your instructor doesn't use this approach, the following may be helpful:

- Make notes that highlight how the content is connected to you.
- Form a study group to give yourself a chance to discuss key ideas.

- Imagine how the information will have practical value for you.
- Record class information on index cards that you can handle.
- Select the two or three cards that represent the key ideas for each session.

Know Yourself: Self-Assessment 5.3, "Sensory Preference Inventory," at the end of the chapter on page 161 provides an opportunity to identify your preferred sensory mode for learning.

Experiential Learning Preferences Besides differing in intelligence domains and sensory preferences, people also differ in how they like to experience new ideas. Here are four distinct ways, mostly drawn from David Kolb's (1984) work on experiential learning. We will also explore how your experiential preferences relate to your intelligence profile and sensory preferences.

Learn by Doing Although some people can learn passively simply by listening, watching, or reading, those with active learning preferences fare better when they "learn by doing" through such things as problems or games and simulations. They like to apply principles through fieldwork, lab activities, projects, or discussions.

Many kinds of classes are ideal for learning by doing. These include science and math classes as well as career-oriented classes such as business and nursing. Visual and tactile learners benefit from active learning strategies. Active learning approaches also tend to appeal to people with refined intelligence in spatial skills and bodily awareness.

Learn by Reflecting Reflecting means having an opportunity to compare incoming information to personal experience. Reflective learners prefer classes such as the humanities, which tend to be rich in emotional content. Reflective learners often show preferences for learning through auditory sensory channels, because these situations provide a manageable mode of sensory input that can then be made more memorable through the personal examples the learner produces through reflection.

Reflective learners often demonstrate strengths in intrapersonal and spiritual/existential intelligences as well. Because they look carefully at a situation and think about its meaning, they often set reasonable goals and achieve them. Reflective students take time to respond to and reflect on the quality and accuracy of their answers (Kagan, 1965). Because they're good at problem solving and decision making, they like to set their own goals for learning (Jonassen & Grabowski, 1993). Whether or not you are primarily a reflective learner, you can probably improve your learning by noticing connections between what you're studying and your own experience, and by staying aware of your learning goals.

Reflective students tend to enjoy journal or blog writing, project logs, film critiques, and essay questions. They also prefer intimate discussions of content to group discussions. Learners who reflect carefully about ideas may not be the quickest to answer questions in class, because a question may provoke a great deal of thinking and remembering before the learner can arrive at a conclusion.

Learn by Critical Thinking Critical thinkers like learning situations that encourage them to grapple with ideas in ways that push beyond memorizing facts. They enjoy manipulating symbols, figuring out unknowns, and making predictions. They like to analyze relationships, create and defend arguments, and make judgments. Critical thinkers often are good with abstract ideas, even in the absence of concrete examples or applications. Classes that are theoretical in nature or that emphasize logical reasoning, model building, and well-organized ideas are especially appealing to critical thinkers.

Good critical thinkers perform especially well in courses that appeal to verbal-linguistic, logical-mathematical, and naturalist intelligences. They are comfortable in lecture-based classes that primarily rely on auditory sensory channels, although they also can exercise critical-thinking strategies in other learning situations to make course ideas more engaging. Debates and other opportunities to exchange ideas appeal to critical thinkers.

Learn by Creative Thinking In contrast, creative thinkers thrive in learning situations that offer opportunities for unique personal expression. Although humanities and arts classes in particular develop creative thinking, creative opportunities can be found in other courses, too. Creative thinkers prefer to write stories, brainstorm, solve problems in original ways, design research, and so forth. They think holistically, meaning that they try to consider a broad range of information in their problem solving. They may even enjoy violating the rules if it helps them come up with a unique solution or viewpoint.

Creative thinking is the hallmark of artists who demonstrate musical and spatial intelligence, respectively, relying on auditory and visual sensory processing. Creativity also underlies the development of new theories, research strategies, novels, and computer games. Creative thinking can be expressed in all domains of multiple intelligence.

What learning processes do you prefer? Complete Know Yourself: Self-Assessment 5.4, "Experiential Learning Preferences," at the back of the chapter on page 162 to identify your preferences among these experiential learning processes.

Put It All Together Now that you have examined native intelligence as well as a variety of learning styles and evaluated your own preferences, you may be wondering how all this relates and what it means for your success in college. See Table 5.1, "Linking Choice of Major with Learning Style Dimensions." First, go to Assessments 5.2, 5.3, and 5.4 to revisit your learning-style preferences and circle those preferences in the last three columns of Table 5.1. Then look in the first column to see which majors might be the best fit for you.

Target Personality Factors

Personality, the sum of an individual's enduring personal characteristics, also may influence learning effectiveness. Your personality style can facilitate or hinder your success in the classroom. We'll examine two popular approaches to understanding personality: the Five Factor Personality Model and the Myers-Briggs Type Inventory. At some point in your college career, you may end up taking a version of a personality test that uses either of these frameworks.

Five Factor Personality Model Many psychologists today believe that five basic personality dimensions are consistently demonstrated across cultures (Costa & McRae, 1995). Each dimension represents a continuum. The following list gives you an overview of these various dimensions and indicates how each

TABLE 5.1 Linking Choice of Major with Learning Style Dimensions

Are there some majors that seem to be a particularly good match for specific dimensions of the various learning styles? See how the following majors might logically be linked with learning style characteristics. Do your preferences relate to the majors that you think you would find most satisfying?

Major	Intelligence Profile	Sensory Preference	Experiential Learning
Anthropology	Naturalistic	Auditory	Reflecting/Critical thinking
Archaeology	Naturalistic	Tactile	Doing/Critical thinking
Art	Spatial	Visual	Doing/Creating
Biology	Naturalistic	Visual	Doing/Critical thinking
Business	Logical-math	Auditory	Doing/Creating
Chemistry	Naturalistic	Visual	Doing/Critical thinking
Criminal Justice	Intrapersonal	Auditory	Critical thinking/Doing
Dance	Bodily-kinesthetic	Tactile	Doing/Creating
Education	Interpersonal	Mixed	Reflecting/Doing
Engineering	Logical-math; Spatial	Tactile	Doing/Creating
English	Verbal-linguisitic	Auditory	Reflecting/Creating
Film Studies	Verbal-linguistic; Spatial	Visual	Creating/Doing
Foreign Languages	Verbal-linguistic	Auditory	Reflecting/Doing
Health Studies	Bodily-kinesthetic	Tactile	Reflecting/Doing
History	Verbal-linguistic	Auditory	Reflecting/Critical thinking
Journalism	Verbal-linguistic	Auditory	Doing/Reflecting
Mathematics	Logical-math	Visual	Critical thinking/Reflecting
Medical Technology	Logical-math	Tactile	Doing/Critical thinking
Music	Musical	Auditory	Doing/Creating
Nursing	Interpersonal	Tactile	Doing/Reflecting
Philosophy	Verbal-linguistic	Auditory	Reflecting/Critical thinking
Pharmacy	Interpersonal; Logical-math	Visual	Doing/Reflecting
Physics	Logical-math	Tactile	Doing/Critical thinking
Political Science	Verbal-linguistic	Auditory	Critical thinking/Reflecting
Pre-Law	Verbal-linguistic	Auditory	Critical thinking/Reflecting
Pre-Med/Pre-Vet	Naturalistic	Tactile	Doing/Critical thinking
Psychology	Intrapersonal; Naturalistic	Mixed	Doing/Critical thinking
Religion	Interpersonal	Auditory	Reflecting/Doing
Social Work	Interpersonal	Auditory	Reflecting/Doing
Sociology	Verbal-linguistic	Auditory	Critical thinking/Reflecting
Theater	Bodily-kinesthetic	Tactile	Doing/Creating

can affect your success in college. The mnemonic you can use to remember the five dimensions is OCEAN:

O = Open to experience

High O people are adventurous, imaginative, and unconventional. They tend to enjoy classes where they can experiment with new ideas.

Low O people are conventional, conservative, and rigid in their thinking, preferring more highly structured learning situations.

C = Conscientiousness

High C people are hardworking, ambitious, and driven. They tend to have developed work habits that score great grades (Noftle & Robins, 2007).

Low C people are pleasure-seeking, negligent, and irresponsible and so are more vulnerable to being placed on probation or being suspended.

E = Extraversion

High E individuals (extroverts) are high-spirited and energetic, thriving on the continuous opportunity that college provides to meet and work with different people.

Low E individuals (introverts) are reserved and passive, tending to seek less social stimulation to do their best work.

A = Agreeableness

High A people are good-natured, trusting, and helpful. They tend to be well liked and respected and may have an easier time negotiating positive outcomes to conflicts.

Low A people are irritable, suspicious, and vengeful. They are less likely to get any breaks when negotiating because they tend to approach conflict with a hostile attitude and low expectations of others.

N = Neuroticism

High N individuals suffer a variety of problems related to emotional instability, such as anger, depression, and impulsiveness, that can create constant chaotic conditions that can threaten academic survival.

Low N individuals adapt well, tolerate frustration, and maintain more realistic perspectives. They tend to have developed personal resources that can help them garner success and rebound from failure.

Robins and colleagues (2005) examined the impact of college on personality dimensions. They compared how personality changed from the onset of college through graduation and found that students' self-reports described increases in openness, agreeableness, extraversion, and conscientiousness as well as decreases in neuroticism. College changes not only your intellectual profile but your personality as well.

Myers-Briggs Type Inventory (MBTI) Another popular approach to understanding the role of personality in academic success is the Myers-Briggs Type Inventory (MBTI) (Myers, 1962). The MBTI assesses four dimensions of personality functioning by measuring responses to a series of questions that ask for a preference between two alternatives:

1. *Extraversion/Introversion (E/I)* measures social orientation. Extraverts (E) like talking with others and taking action. Introverts (I) prefer to have others do the talking. (This is similar to the "open to experience" dimension addressed in the Five Factor Model.)
2. *Sensing/Intuiting (S/N)* explores how students process information. Sensors (S) are most at home with facts and examples; they are drawn to realistic, practical applications. Intuiters (N) prefer concepts and theories, which can give greater play to imagination and inspiration.
3. *Thinking/Feeling (T/F)* emphasizes how students make decisions. Thinkers (T) like to take an objective approach and emphasize logic and

THIS STYLE . . .	PREFERS CLASSES THAT EMPHASIZE . . .	BUT CAN ADAPT BEST TO UNFAVORABLE CONDITIONS BY . . .
Extraverts	active learning, group projects	forming a study group to meet their social needs
Introverts	lectures, structured tasks	setting manageable social goals (for example, contribute to discussions once every two weeks)
Sensors	memorizable facts, concrete questions	identifying key abstract ideas and theories along with their practical implications
Intuiters	interpretation, imagination	identifying the most important facts and figures
Thinkers	objective feedback, pressure to succeed	seeking extra feedback from instructor to create feeling of external pressure
Feelers	positive feedback, individual recognition	seeking extra time from instructor to create personal connection
Judgers	orderliness, structure, and deadlines	setting own deadlines and structure
Perceivers	spontaneity, flexibility	assuming a temporary role of a student who must be rigidly organized to be successful

© Cengage Learning 2013

FIGURE 5.1 MBTI Styles in the Classroom

analysis in their decisions. Feelers (F) prefer emotion to logic; they give greater weight to the impact of relationships in their decisions.

4. ***Judging/Perceiving (J/P)*** taps how students achieve their goals. Judgers (J) prefer clearly defined strategies to achieve their goals and may jump to closure too quickly. Perceivers (P) like to consider all sides to a problem and may be at some risk for not completing their work. (This also taps characteristics similar to the "open to experience" dimension in the Five Factor Model.)

Your personality profile can be configured from your preferences on the four dimensions of the MBTI. The test captures your style using a four-letter code that communicates your preferences on each dimension. For example, the ENTJ code reveals an extrovert with a preference for an orderly pursuit of concrete details but a reliance on intuitive decision making. In contrast, the ISFP represents the style of someone who is drawn to solitary activities, relying on facts and emotions.

As you can imagine, students with these contrasting styles are unlikely to be equally happy in any class. For example, consider how students with different personality styles might relate to a highly structured classroom. Structure would be much more appealing to the introvert, who relies more on orderly process, than to the extrovert, who prefers spontaneity; the extrovert would have to do much more work to adapt to the highly structured classroom. See Figure 5.1, "MBTI Styles in the Classroom," for more examples.

You can find out about your MBTI profile from the campus counseling or career center, where trained MBTI examiners should administer and interpret the inventory. Alternatively, an online version, the Keirsey Temperament Sorter, is available at http://www.keirsey.com/sorter/instruments2.aspx?partid=0. However, beware of relying on the results of personality tests in a way that restricts your options or limits your horizons. Avoid turning personality test results into new stereotypes. Instead, use personality test results to help you avoid blind spots in your thinking and to increase your adaptability.

 **Manage Life**

You will have to deal with many different kinds of people in varying roles, but no relationship will be more important to your academic success than the ones you forge with faculty. You are likely to be inspired by and in awe of many of your professors, but you can expect some bumps and bruises along the way. What tips can help make your academic journey more satisfying?

Relate to Instructors

Many students never talk with an instructor in or out of class. One student remarked that he had no idea what kind of people his instructors were; for all he knew, they were all locked in a vault each evening and then unleashed on Monday to feed on poor students during the day. Of course, that's not so.

Instructors have personality styles and social relationships just as students do. Some are shy; others are gregarious. Some have strong, positive social relationships; others, miserable ones. For the most part, to get along with instructors, you are going to have to adjust to their styles because they are unlikely to adjust to yours.

Here are some good strategies for developing a positive relationship with an instructor (www.academictips.org).

Recognize Instructors' Humanity Like you, instructors are human. They have families and friends, likes and dislikes, and good and bad days. Understanding that they are human may help you to demystify beliefs that you won't be able to get along with them or get to know them no matter how hard you try.

Compare Your Styles You will probably like and get along better with an instructor whose learning and personality styles are similar to yours. But don't let differences between you and an instructor restrict your opportunity to get along with him or her. Just being aware of such differences may help you to think about ways to interact more positively.

Teaching styles are every bit as diverse as learning styles (Halonen, 2002). Instructors will vary not only in their disciplines but also in their enthusiasm, competence, warmth, eccentricities, and humor. Invest some time to maximize the match between their teaching styles and your learning needs.

Professors can be categorized as "student-centered," those who are interested in fostering intellectual growth, and "content-centered," those who focus on communicating the content. Professors design class experience to fit with their values. Student-centered instructors tend to prefer hands-on, interactive, and spontaneous designs. Content-centered instructors tend to lecture and to minimize the importance of class discussion.

Create a Good First Impression College instructors expect you to have academic common sense. Knowing how to develop relationships with your instructors is an important part of that common sense. These guidelines can help you get off on the right foot:

- *Buy the right stuff.* You won't look like a serious student if you don't have the required books.
- *Be prepared.* If you read assignments before class, you'll ask better questions and impress your instructors with your motivation to learn. You'll also get more out of the lecture or discussion.
- *Establish rapport.* By asking intelligent questions during class or visiting during office hours, you can stand out even in very large classes. Interviewing an instructor for this course can help you practice getting to know your instructors on an informal basis.

Just when you think you can speak in private conversation in the middle of class, you are likely to be wrong. This photograph illustrates why. Off-task students tend to stand out against the sea of faces paying attention.

The Fatal Question

When you can't attend a class, don't ask your instructor, "Did I miss anything important?" Although it may be innocent on your part, your question implies that your instructor regularly spends time on unimportant information. You can see how that interpretation might be offensive. Instead, ask, "Can I make up any of the work I missed?" Or you can talk with a classmate or borrow notes to help you get caught up.

Instructors joke about how regularly they must deal with this irritating *faux pas* or social error. Here is a sample of what they fantasize they would like to say in response:

- "No. When we saw you weren't here, we canceled class."
- "I was so heartbroken to note your absence, I became speechless with grief."
- "No, I *never* cover anything important."
- "Yes, we had the raffle for the Porsche and I drew your ticket but you had to be there to win."

Maintain the Connection Instructors respond most positively to students who show interest and enthusiasm for their courses. Later in the term, instructors have an easier time cutting some slack for students who have been responsive and responsible in the earlier weeks. When test scores fall between two grades, those students who seem to care about their work are often the ones who get bumped up instead of down.

For a specific example of an interaction that can get the relationship off track, see the nearby Danger Zone box: "The Fatal Question."

What additional strategies will help you develop a stronger connection with your instructors?

- **Stay on task.** As a student, it is easy for you to get distracted and disengage, but it is just as easy for the instructor to notice and take offense. Concentrate on keeping the connection between you and the instructor personal, positive, and lively.
- **Do the work on time.** College deadlines are not as flexible as high school due dates. If you miss a deadline, you may not be able to negotiate an extension. Most instructors do not extend deadlines to individuals without justification because they believe that doing so isn't fair to students who do their work on time.
- **Use the syllabus.** A course syllabus should describe how the instructor expects the course to proceed, including the course objectives, the reading list, grading policies, and other information that applies throughout the term. It may contain helpful hints on how to study for tests. Some instructors hold students responsible for reading all materials listed in the syllabus. This can be a surprise at test time if you thought that your class notes would be enough.
- **Stay straight.** Even when instructors don't explicitly mention their expectations about your ethical performance, they will assume that you have read and understood, and will abide by, the campus academic integrity code. Nothing ruins relationships with both your current and future professors more than the cloud of suspicion that develops around questionable integrity. Plan your work so that you aren't tempted to take shortcuts that could tarnish your reputation.
- **Stay cool.** The best classes run on respectful and civil behavior. Respect does not mean that you can't challenge or ask questions. In fact, many instructors (but not all) regard student questions as an essential part of classroom learning. However, all instructors expect participation to be civil (calm, polite, and efficient rather than prolonged, pointless, or profane). See the Highlight box: "How to Get on the Wrong Side of an Instructor," for other behaviors that can get in the way of a smoothly running class.

"Is the homework fresh?"

HIGHLIGHT

How to Get on the Wrong Side of an Instructor

BEHAVIORS THAT SHOW QUESTIONABLE MATURITY

Talking during lectures
Chewing gum, eating, or drinking noisily
Being late and leaving early
Creating disturbances
Wearing hats
Putting feet on desks or tables
Being insincere or "brownnosing"
Complaining about workload
Acting like a know-it-all
Wearing headphones
Making fun of others

BEHAVIORS THAT SHOW INATTENTION

Sleeping during class
Cutting class
Acting bored or apathetic
Multitasking
Being unprepared
Packing up books and materials before class is over
Asking already answered questions
Sitting in the back rows when there are empty seats in front
Yawning obviously
Slouching in seat

Not asking questions
Doing work for other classes in class
Reading the newspaper in class
Cruising the Internet
Text-messaging friends

MISCELLANEOUS IRRITATING BEHAVIORS

Cheating
Asking "Will this be on the test?"
Being more interested in grades than in learning
Pretending to understand
Blaming teachers for poor grades
Giving unbelievable excuses
Wearing tasteless T-shirts
Using foul language
Chatting off-task
Disclosing too much personal information
Answering every question

(Source: Based on Drew C. Appleby, "Faculty and staff perceptions of irritating behaviors in the college classroom," from JOURNAL OF STAFF PROGRAM AND ORGANIZATION DEVELOPMENT Copyright 1990 by NEW FORUMS PRESS INC. Reproduced with permission of NEW FORUMS PRESS INC in the format Textbook and Other book via Copyright Clearance Center.)

If you really want to stand out in a positive way among your peers, here is how to signal your intentions:

- *Sit in the front.* The most motivated, most interested students often sit close to the instructor to minimize distractions and to create the opportunity for informal discussion before or after class.
- *Bring articles or clippings related to the course to class.* Instructors like to see you make independent connections between the course content and your life outside the classroom. They may incorporate your ideas into the class and remember you for making the contribution.
- *Socialize informally.* On some campuses, faculty sponsor informal gatherings to help you network with others. You also can join student clubs with faculty sponsors. These are great opportunities to get to know the faculty as people.
- *Visit during your instructor's office hours.* Most instructors identify their office hours when the course begins. Check in with your instructor about something you found interesting or were confused about from class discussion. Ask the instructor to review your notes to see whether your note-taking skills are on target.
- *Use e-mail to connect.* Your e-mail represents you to the professor. Be polite, specific, and patient. Instructors don't respond well to overlong, whiny, or frivolous communications in their e-mail queues, and they may be unable to turn around a response quickly. Both your e-mail address and your sign-off should demonstrate maturity. Instructors may not get a favorable impression when they are responding to "hotbabe14." Be sure to provide sufficient lead time to get the help you need.

Solve Problems with Instructors

If you're lucky, you may not experience—and have to solve—any relationship problems with your instructors. However, several problems could prompt you to take action. It can be surprising when professors themselves are irresponsible or disrespectful, but it does happen. When such a situation arises and interferes with your learning, you should take responsibility to get the problem resolved.

Resolve a Mismatch Courses are unsatisfying when the instructor does not teach at a level the students can handle. In some of these courses, students feel overwhelmed by an instructor who talks over their heads. In other cases, instructors offer too little challenge and students feel cheated.

To resolve either problem, first talk with your classmates to verify that others are also struggling. Then, preferably with one or two other concerned students, request an appointment with the instructor and present your concerns directly. Many instructors will be pleased with your initiative and grateful for the feedback. Others will be less enthusiastic but can give you suggestions about how to cope with their demands. If you can't resolve the mismatch through talking with the instructor, consider withdrawing from the course. If necessary, you can take it again later with a different instructor.

Manage Boundaries Most instructors give clear signals about how and when they can be contacted. Instructors usually have office hours. They can and should respond to student questions or concerns during those periods as part of their professional responsibilities.

Instructors differ in their enthusiasm about being contacted outside class or office hours. Some provide home phone numbers and encourage you to call whenever you have questions. Others request not to be disturbed at home because they want to separate their professional and personal lives. It is easy to see you could get confused about how and when to contact their instructors. If your instructors have not specified that they can be reached at home, use memos, voicemail, e-mail, office-hour visits, or the time just after class to honor the boundaries drawn by your instructors.

Friendships between instructors and students pose an especially complex boundary problem. Many instructors don't think it is a good idea to be friends with students. They do not want to do anything that could compromise their objectivity. Other instructors believe that they can be objective in grading the work of a student-friend, so they aren't as rigorous about observing that boundary.

Keep Copies of Your Work When you and your instructor disagree about whether you have completed assigned work, you get stuck with the burden of proof. Get in the habit of making copies of your papers. Then, if a paper gets lost or misplaced, you can easily replace it. Keep returned projects in a safe place so that you can retrieve them if the instructor has failed to record them. It happens.

Know Your Rights As a student, you are guaranteed certain rights. The Family Educational Right to Privacy Act (FERPA), also known as the Buckley Amendment, ensures your right to privacy. How you perform in class should remain a private matter.

image100/CORBIS

If you have a complaint about a class, start by talking directly with your instructor. By describing the problem and offering your interpretation, you may be able to solve the problem quickly and fairly.

If you experience circumstances in which you believe your rights have been violated, you have several options. First, recognize that the instructor is the authority in the class. Weigh carefully how upset you are against the possible consequences of confronting an instructor who holds greater power and probably more credibility than you do.

If you decide to complain using formal channels, explain your concerns directly to the instructor. Ask for an appointment. Present your concerns and offer evidence to support it. If unsuccessful, appeal in writing to the instructor's immediate supervisor. In most cases, this supervisor is the department head or coordinator, who will hear you out and determine what steps to take. If you go directly to the supervisor without talking to the instructor, chances are good that the supervisor will refer you for a first discussion with the instructor, so you might as well begin your problem solving directly with the person causing you grief.

If the supervisor fails to take action and you still need further resolution, ask for an appointment with that person's supervisor, most likely the academic dean. At each stage of the chain of command, the person will review what attempts you have already made to resolve the problem before she does anything about it.

On a cautionary note, you're unlikely to have much luck appealing a final grade unless you can identify discriminatory treatment or a specific error in the instructor's judgment. Most college officials regard instructors as the final authority in grading and rarely overturn their grades.

Connect and Communicate

Many educators believe that elements in students' backgrounds beyond personality structure can strongly influence their learning. Ironically, that belief can also set the stage for promoting many of the stereotypes we introduced at the outset of this chapter. However, be aware that personal attributes—whether right or wrong—can influence what others may expect from you.

Recognize the Influence of Age

Your age can be a factor in your social and academic success, because how long you have been alive relates to how much you know and usually how comfortable you are with technology.

The Millennial Student Traditional-age or "millennial" students (between the ages of 18 and 22) may stand out in the classroom for their optimistic, laid-back, and heavily technological approaches to learning (Howe et al., 2000). Skilled use of technology can save time, expand your access to ideas, and open whole new worlds for you to explore from your keyboard, but it can also produce some disadvantages:

- *Multitasking.* Constant monitoring of cell phone messages and e-mail while watching television and doing homework is likely to lead to inefficient and shallow execution of academic work (Simpson, 2006).
- *Shopping rather than thinking.* You may find it easier to "shop" for information on the Web than to think things through for yourself. You can google your way and "cut and paste" to achieve completed projects, but you will be shortchanged if you don't wrestle with and think through concepts and projects yourself.

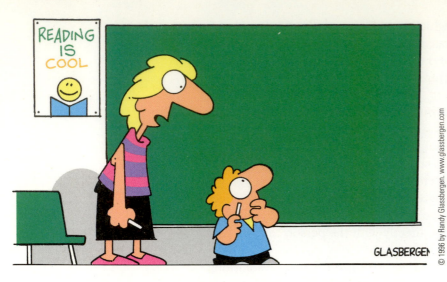

"There aren't any icons to click. It's a chalk board."

- ***Techno-Snobbery.*** Millennials often have a hard time imagining why some people fear technology. But techno-savvy millennials can be especially helpful to students and faculty who have less technical expertise.

The Nontraditional Student In contrast, nontraditional students often come off as more serious, driven, and intolerant of tangents in the classroom that they perceive may be wasting their valuable time. Nontraditional students are sometimes less inclined to use technology and can feel intimidated by the expertise so easily demonstrated by younger students. Rich in life experiences, they can sometimes dominate class discussions, generating some resentment from more traditional-age peers.

During their college experience, though, returning students are going to run into all kinds of challenges to their deeply held beliefs. Their personal convictions may encourage them to defend vigorously what they know to be true because they have lived it. Unfortunately, personal experience and depth of convictions do not guarantee that the principles will be valid for others. If you are a nontraditional student, practice *mindful* behavior. Become your own devil's advocate. Before committing to an obvious truth derived from experience, ask yourself:

- Does my personal experience lend itself to a bias in perception?
- Would my experience be true for everyone?
- What are some alternative explanations that could produce similar effects?
- Could I argue the opposing side?

Comprehend Gender and Sexual Orientation Effects

Higher education has evolved in dramatic ways in relation to gender and sexual orientation. Although tolerance and acceptance seem to be increasing, women and those with nontraditional sexual orientations still report that the campus is not always a safe place to pursue learning.

Gender *Gender* refers to the psychological characteristics of people as females and males. We live in a world in which gender roles are changing, and these changes have affected campus life (Matlin, 2008). Only a few generations back, women were either denied access to college or stereotyped as pursuing an "MRS" degree rather than being serious about an education.

According to the American Council on Education (Edmonds, 2010), women students are in the majority on most campuses. They earn more degrees at the bachelor's and master's levels than men and now achieve equivalent numbers of professional and doctoral degrees as men. At the master's level, women still predominate in education and nursing, and men earn the majority of degrees in engineering and business. Despite this progress, 20 percent of first-year college students have expressed the belief that a married woman should restrict her attention to home and family (Pryor et al., 2005).

Sexism Gender blueprints seem clear-cut. The well-adjusted man should be independent, assertive, and dominant. The well-adjusted woman should be dependent, nurturing, and submissive. These beliefs and stereotypes have led to *sexism*, prejudice or discrimination based on sex, especially discrimination against women.

In *The Mismeasure of Woman*, Carol Tavris (1992) observes that no matter how hard women try, they may not be able to measure up. They are criticized for being too female or not female enough. Tavris argues that women are judged by how well they "fit" in a man's world, a perspective that tends to fixate on the beauty of a woman's body.

In her study of women's lives, Jean Baker Miller (1986) concludes that a large part of what women do is active participation in the development of others. Women are inclined to help others emotionally, intellectually, and socially. College offers many opportunities for women to explore their lives and set out on a course to improve their opportunities while providing service to others. Women (and society) need to place a higher value on relationship skills. To be leaders, women do not need to stop caring for others but may be able to exercise distinctive leadership skills because of their relationship focus.

Sexual Harassment Sexual harassment in colleges and the workplace is also a major barrier to women's progress (Hyde & DeLamater, 2008). This includes:

- *Gender harassment.* Sexist remarks and behavior that insult and degrade women, a problem apart from harassment for sex.
- *Seductive behavior.* Unwanted, inappropriate, and offensive advances toward women.
- *Sexual extortion.* Harassment for sex, with the threat of punishment for refusal. For example, a woman might be threatened with a lower or failing grade if she does not go along with an instructor's advances or if she reports him to the school authorities.

Every college is required by law to take action against sexual harassment, and many have resources to protect people from this treatment. If you are sexually harassed, report it to your school's administration.

Sexual Orientation Dramatic change has also happened with regard to attitudes on campus toward sexual orientation. Historically, individuals felt pressure to maintain secrecy about sexuality (e.g., "Don't ask. Don't tell.") that didn't fit the heterosexual norm (Sanio, 1998). Surveys indicate that approximately 2–5 percent of U.S. adults have a same-sex sexual orientation (Kelly, 2008). About 1 percent of the population is bisexual (attracted to both men and women). Transsexuals account for an even smaller percentage.

Homophobia. In many ways, the college goals of lesbian, gay male, bisexual, and transsexual students are similar to those of heterosexual students. However, their minority status does bring some difficulties (Savin-Williams, 2008). Many heterosexual students still consider them abnormal rather than simply different. Lesbian, gay male, and bisexual students often encounter hostile comments and demeaning jokes. The prominence of bullying on campus leaped into the national spotlight when first-year student Trevor Clementi threw himself off New Jersey's George Washington Bridge following a Facebook harangue by his classmates (Guardado, 2010).

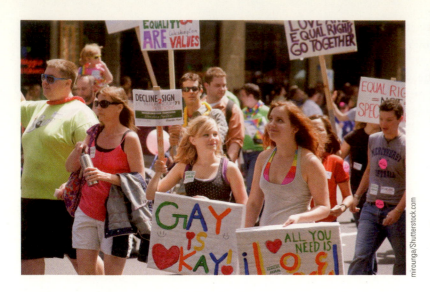

What are ways in which the college lives of gay, lesbian, and bisexual students can be improved?

Promote Sexual Tolerance How can lesbian, gay male, bisexual, and transsexual students have a better college experience? Below are some tips if you identify with these sexual orientations:

- *Learn more about sexuality.* Take a course on human sexuality. Researchers have found that college students who take such a course gain positive views of lesbian, gay male, and bisexual individuals (Walters, 1994).
- *Join organizations for alternative lifestyles.* Some of these organizations include friends and family members, as well as other students, regardless of sexual orientation. These groups provide a safe haven for students to voice their thoughts and feelings about sexual orientation.
- *If none exists, start one.* This action may require following procedures that your student activities office has established for creating a campus organization. If you feel uncomfortable on your own campus, consider joining an organization on a nearby campus or in the local community.
- *Take a stand.* Do not allow overt acts of discrimination and mistreatment go unreported or unchallenged. Object to demeaning humor and explain your position.

Protect Your Rights Neither your gender nor your sexual orientation should be an impediment to learning. Most campuses have embraced policies that reinforce respect for individual learners, regardless of their personal characteristics. They also have formal protocols for pursuing suspected discriminatory practices. These protections extend not just to gender and sexual orientation, but to all potential "protected" categories of religion, ethnicity, disability, and age.

Understand the Impact of Heritage

Family traditions and circumstances also can influence the quality of your experience in college.

First-Generation Students Students who are the first in their families to go to college may have a more complex challenge in navigating differences (Terenzini et al., 1996). The success of the individual student reflects on the family as a whole, and "first–generation" students keenly feel that "upward mobility" burden. However, their family members cannot share their experiences to help get them prepared. As a consequence, first-generation students are more vulnerable to "stopping out" or withdrawing. To reduce this disadvantage, many colleges have developed special support opportunities to retain first-generation students. For example, the University of Cincinnati sets up specialized housing called "Gen 1" and provides additional services to help first-generation students navigate college with fewer bumps (Tamsey & Peale, 2010).

If you are a first-generation student, your family members are likely very proud, perhaps even a bit envious, of the opportunity you have been able to realize. However, as your thinking and communication skills advance, you may discover that the new perspectives you express can produce some unanticipated challenges in your family life. Family members who were your chief supporters at the outset may now challenge you about acting superior to them. They may say that you ask too many questions, and they might even wish for a return to the good old days, when you were "nicer."

As your college experiences help you to examine issues more deeply and to express your positions more adroitly, you may enjoy trying to dazzle family members with your new skills. Recognize, though, that they are not used to your academic side and that they lack a point of reference in their own experience to help them understand the changes you are going through. Here are some strategies to keep the bond strong:

- *Recognize that your capacity to generate and express questions can upset family traditions.* Tread carefully when introducing potentially threatening observations.
- *Practice discretion in how much detail you provide.* Your family members may be turned off by long-winded analyses.
- *Attend to body language when you talk about your college experiences.* Glazed-over eyes, slumped posture, and nonresponsiveness signal that it might be time to change the conversation to a topic that can involve mutual participation.

Socioeconomic Status (SES) Socioeconomic status can also be a factor in academic success. If you are strapped for cash and must work multiple jobs to help pay for your degree, then your progress in achieving your degree is bound to be slower. Students without economic worries are much freer to pursue educational opportunities without employment distraction.

On the other hand, if attending college is not a particular hardship for you and your family, you may be able to justify not working at full capacity. Such actions reinforce stereotypes that college is not as much about learning as it is a holding pen for "rich kids" with limited vision.

Religious Beliefs College classes can sometimes put your religious beliefs to the test. You will encounter many people who have an entirely different

MIKE CLARKE/AFP/Getty Images/Newscom

If you're a student from the United States, respect the differences between yourself and international students. Value diversity. If you're from another country, create a support system and get involved in campus life. Be patient in adjusting to the new culture.

worldview. Their values may be hard to accept or even to tolerate. In some classes, you will find that your own religious expressions may be unwelcome or even derided. Your instructors won't appreciate your commandeering class discussions to proselytize. Think carefully before you offer religious justifications unless you get clear signals from your instructor that such ideas will be well received.

International Status Students from different cultures face even larger challenges. International students must not only navigate the unfamiliar cultural norms of the larger host country but must also master the language of the host culture. Although international students may pass language proficiency requirements, when they get in American college classrooms, their faculty and peers may routinely use idioms (e.g., It's "raining cats and dogs") that add another layer to their learning challenge. They may struggle with anxiety in and out of the classroom when they don't grasp the cultural significance of the communication surrounding them. In addition, their accents may hinder others from understanding what they are trying to communicate in English.

In American higher education, *implicit* (unspoken) values may subtly set certain kinds of expectations for student performance. Sometimes those values may not be consistent with how international students have been raised. If you are an international student, the following strategies may help you understand classroom dynamics in U.S. colleges:

- *Be patient.* Give yourself time to adapt to your new life. Things may not be easy at the beginning. Over time, your comfort with U.S. culture will grow. What seems odd or challenging right now may be easier to understand with a little more experience.
- *Create or join a support system.* Most campuses have international student clubs where you can meet and get to know other international students. If your campus has none, this represents a great opportunity to make a contribution to campus life by founding a support system.
- *Make new friends outside your comfort zone.* Get the most out of your international experience by reaching out to others to learn about their cultures. Reach beyond relationships with students from your home or host country and make connections with other international students who may share your struggles.
- *Be an ambassador.* Look for opportunities to share your background so your instructors and classmates can learn about your culture. Many

Spotlight On... Aisha Saad

Philanthropist to the World

Courtesy of the office of Undergraduate Admissions, University of North Carolina

Aisha Saad pursued many international experiences during her college years to contribute to her diversity skills.

During her undergraduate studies at the University of North Carolina, Aisha Saad interned during the summer at Cairo University's teaching hospitals in Egypt. Her international experience there included developing a health education program and conducting a workshop on the isolation of having a privileged life, which she later published in a *Health Affairs*, a policy journal. At her university, she has been the outreach coordinator for the Muslim Students Association. In a second international internship with a company that resurrects environmentally damaged areas, she went to Bhopal, India, to conduct research on an industrial disaster there. And in a third international internship, Aisha traveled to Peru to work with the country's Ministry of Health to participate in improving the diet and nutrition of Peruvians.

(Source: Marklein, 2009)

assignments or class projects lend themselves to your teaching others about your origins and culture.

- *Adopt a cultural mentor.* Identify someone who can provide social support and learning opportunities to make the most of your international adventure. Consider a faculty member or someone on the advising staff who seems especially interested in your background.

- *Understand individualism and autonomy.* In the United States, the primary emphasis in academic settings is on *individualism,* that is, individual performance rather than group achievement. Even when instructors assign group projects, grading practices tend to individualize achievement. This emphasis can be a trap if you come from a background that emphasizes *collectivism,* an orientation that places higher value on what is in the best interest of the group rather than the individual (Martin & Nakayama, 2011). Be sure that you establish your individual contributions even in group projects so that you are seen as doing your fair share.

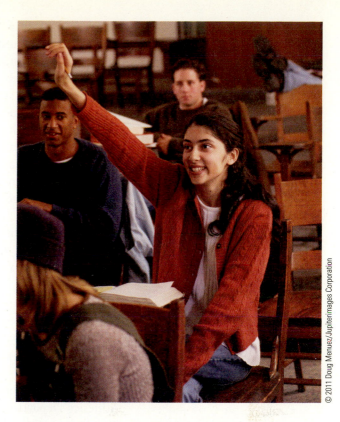

Honors students face some new and interesting challenges in navigating college.

Navigate Status Issues

Some students receive special treatment because of their distinctive performances or abilities, but aspects of their status can sometimes pose difficulties.

Honors Students If you are an honors student, you have likely worked very hard to get to where you are. However, many honors students are surprised by how hard they have to work to improve their thinking skills in college. Following are some adaptations that honors students often have to make:

- *Change strategies.* In high school, honors students may have gotten high grades by memorizing facts and concepts. However, once in college, many honors students report that they have to engage in higher-level thinking and reasoning to be successful. Make sure you understand the type of thinking demands you will need in your various courses rather than assuming your old strategies will always prevail. Be prepared to make some changes.

- *Don't dominate a class.* If you think your personal experience or keen insight somehow is essential in making a class work, you may try to dominate it. However, keep in mind that the class is larger than just you and the instructor. Once you have established your abilities, back off and let others in the class help, or you will be doing all of the work. Other students may find you *pedantic* (an intellectual show-off) rather than smart. If an instructor initially seemed enthusiastic about your contributions but now delays in calling on you, even if it means waiting for more reluctant performers to step in, take this behavior as a cue that you could be dominating the class.

Athletes Who gets less respect in an academic setting: blondes or jocks? Although the question may provoke a smile or frown, the fact is that college is not immune from reinforcing certain subcultural stereotypes about intelligence. Why does the stereotype of the "stupid jock" have such endurance?

Some athletes demonstrate misplaced priorities. Although they never miss a practice, they might be late for class. They invest themselves fully in training but somehow can't seem to get academic projects across the finish line. When individual athletes clearly fail to perform, it reinforces the generalized expectation that jocks don't care about their academic work.

Scandals related to academic integrity taint general beliefs about athletes' academic competence. For example, Florida State University recently had to substitute many players in a bowl game because officials discovered an extensive cheating network. Although academic integrity problems are not restricted to athletes, the glare of the spotlight makes such deviations very visible and even more damaging to the reputation of all athletes.

Hangovers caused by overindulgence—whether due to the celebration of a well-deserved victory or to solace for plans gone awry—interfere with the ability to think effectively, which can lead to chronic underperformance in academic areas. All college students, including athletes, need to monitor their alcohol intake.

If you are a college athlete, whether you like it or not, you represent the Athletics Department. Thus, your performance will reflect on the values of the department. Take your responsibility seriously. Effective academic preparation and participation are tools that can help defeat the stereotype. Wear your athletic identity proudly, but do the work that allows your coach to be proud of what you represent.

Extracurricular Interests Extracurricular activities and interests can exert a dramatic and positive influence on your success in college. Astin and colleagues (1993) identified that finding a way to connect to campus through organizations and clubs has a significant impact on students' staying in school. Therefore, pursuing a special-interest club or an activity that allows you to express your values can also provide emotional support by helping you connect with others who care about the things you do. Some college students find, though, that it is easy to get sucked into too many activities. Students who stretch themselves too thin face constant challenges as they sort out how they should allocate time to their overload of commitments.

 **Build a Bright Future**

A college degree can be a passport to a professional career, but a well-chosen major can also produce a great number of opportunities that are linked to your interests and skills. Although your professional destiny may be unclear at this point, you can use your strengths in navigating differences to help you prepare for the future.

Your learning style should influence which career you pursue and the major you choose to help you get there.

Target an Intelligent Career

One way to start planning your future is to link your natural intellectual talents to possible career options. Gardner's theory of multiple intelligences can help you explore the relationship between your intellectual ability and career choice. See Figure 5.2, "Intelligent Career Choices," for some typical and creative career choices based on the multiple intelligences model. Revisit your intelligence profile in Know Yourself: Self-Assessment 5.2, "Your Intelligence Profile," on page 160 and think about how well your profile matches up with these choices.

The theory of multiple intelligences suggests that intellectual strengths predict career choices. Review some traditional and less-conventional careers linked to different domains of intelligence.

INTELLIGENCE DOMAIN	TRADITIONAL CAREERS	LESS-CONVENTIONAL CAREERS	INTELLIGENCE DOMAIN	TRADITIONAL CAREERS	LESS-CONVENTIONAL CAREERS
Verbal-Linguistic	author reporter teacher librarian attorney advertising specialist politician	talk-show host poet children's book writer crossword puzzle maker campaign manager	Musical	performer singer music teacher	composer conductor sound effects specialist
			Spatial	engineer architect surgeon painter sailor Web designer fashion designer	mapmaker sculptor billboard designer
Logical-Mathematical	engineer scientist mathematician statistician insurance specialist computer expert claims adjuster	physicist astronomer astronaut	Bodily-Kinesthetic	artisan actor athlete dancer coach	professional juggler professional skater health writer
Intrapersonal	novelist psychologist philosopher	advice columnist feature writer	Naturalist	conservationist agricultural specialist floral designer museum curator librarian botanist	safari director antique specialist baseball card expert
Interpersonal	politician social worker sales manager psychologist public relations specialist nurse, doctor, or other health-care provider	religious leader			

FIGURE 5.2 Intelligent Career Choices

Find the Right Mix

Earlier in the chapter, you learned about the Myers-Briggs Type Indicator. Career counselors have used the MBTI to provide some direction to career selection. See Figure 5.3, "The Myers-Briggs Type Indicator and Potential Career Links," to learn how MBTI codes and personality factors predict professional styles that seem to be well suited to different occupational profiles.

Review the results of your self-assessments in this chapter one final time. What career directions and majors does your learning style suggest? If no

MYERS-BRIGGS CODE	DESCRIPTION	POSSIBLE CAREER MATCHES
ISTJ	Quiet, serious, responsible, sensible, patient, conservative, and loyal	Police and protective services, administrators and managers, engineers, military personnel, scientists, physicians
ISTP	Factual, sensible, logical, and reflective	Farming, mechanics, military personnel, engineering and science technicians, optometrists
ISFP	Quiet, practical, sensitive, and spontaneous	Nursing, secretarial, health service workers, clerical, technicians, forestry
ISFJ	Private, faithful, sensible, and sensitive	Nursing, clerical, teachers, librarians, physicians, health service workers
INFJ	Intuitive, caring, quiet, and peace-loving	Consultants, clergy, teachers, media specialists, physicians, social workers, marketing personnel, psychologists
INFP	Quiet, creative, sensitive, and perceptive	Physicians, editors and reporters, writers, journalists, psychologists
INTJ	Independent, innovative, logical, and driven by the inner world of ideas	Lawyers, scientists, research workers, engineers, computer systems analysts
INTP	Private, intellectual, impersonal, analytical, and reflective	Lawyers, scientists, research workers, engineers, computer programmers and analysts
ESTP	Outgoing, practical thinkers who are masters of experience and observation. They don't rely on their emotions to make decisions.	Marketing personnel, sales, police and detectives, public service and community workers, computer specialists and programmers
ESTJ	Assertive, practical, rational, loyal, opinionated, and decisive	Teachers, managerial and administration, sales, insurance and banking, military personnel, computer analysts, public relations
ESFP	Warm, outgoing, optimistic, and caring	Receptionists, hospitality and catering, designers, teachers, sales, artists and entertainers
ESFJ	Outgoing, sociable, practical, and organized	Receptionists, restaurant workers, sales, teachers, health service workers
ENFJ	Sociable, intuitive, sensitive, and organized	Teachers, actors, musicians, artists, counselors, writers, nurses, marketing personnel
ENTP	Enthusiastic, outgoing, analytical, multi-talented, independent	Marketing personnel, sales, journalists, actors, computer systems analysts, public relations
ENTJ	Outgoing, logical, decisive	Managerial and administrative, marketing personnel, sales
ENFP	Open-minded, imaginative, caring, and outgoing	Journalists, counselors, teachers, writers, social scientists

Note: The characteristics described and the occupations listed are provided to stimulate your thinking about your personality and possible links with careers. They are not intended as a formal testing of your personality and career interests.

Adapted from Looking at Type®: Your Career by Charles R. Martin. Used by permission of the Center for Applications of Psychological Type, Inc.

FIGURE 5.3 The Myers-Briggs Type Indicator and Potential Career Links

obvious directions appear, consider consulting with a career-counseling specialist on campus. Such a professional can help you make concrete links between your learning style and possible majors and careers.

You may be fortunate to have natural talents in many areas. You may discover many new abilities through your college experiences. Don't close off your options by locking yourself into a career path too soon. After you commit to a specific major, stay flexible about what the future may bring. The career you ultimately pursue may not even have emerged yet as a viable option. Versatility as a learner will give you more choices about where you want to go in your major and your career.

Find an Academic Mentor

It is never too early to start developing a professional network to help you realize your dreams about what can happen after graduation. A seasoned professional can be invaluable in providing feedback about the courses and other experiences that will prepare you best for the job market or graduate or professional applications. Think about the following candidates as possible mentors:

- *Your friendliest instructor.* You may want to stay in contact with the instructor who best fosters your enthusiasm for learning. Even if that instructor is not in your selected major, she may be able to offer some great general guidance about professional development.
- *The least popular instructor in your major.* This faculty member may have the most time available to devote to your cause and might appreciate some attention.
- *A willing alumnus.* Ask the head of the department in your major to connect you to someone who has already been through the major and has had some success after graduation. Alumni usually enjoy contact with undergraduates and may take special pains to help with sound advice.
- *A student leader.* Check with your adviser about identifying a student who really seems to have it all together, contact that student, and make a pitch that you are seeking expert mentorship. The student may be flattered and could have extensive social networks on campus to assist with nonacademic needs as well.
- *An experienced relative.* Sometimes your choice of major can overlap with the experience of a cherished relative. Don't overlook this helpful resource.
- *An adviser's nominee.* Clearly communicate your desire for a strong mentor to your academic adviser. Enlist some suggestions that link to your desired career goals. The adviser may have just the right off-campus supporter whose expertise can be invaluable.

Clarify Expectations

- Recognize that the role of college student entails both formal and informal expectations.
- Understand how stereotyped judgments can enhance or limit college success.

Develop Competence

- Identify your intellectual strengths and weaknesses.
- Understand how your sensory preferences shape your learning.
- Understand which courses and majors best fit your intellectual profile, background, sensory preferences, and learning processes.
- Link your personality style and background characteristics to your classroom success.

Manage Life

- Actively research instructor styles to find the right match for your interests, skills, and goals.
- Make a good first impression to establish yourself with your instructors.
- Maintain strong connections through conscientious and ethical behavior.
- Solve problems through effective interpersonal skills.

Connect and Communicate

- Recognize how age equips you for sharing experience in classes and using technology.
- Take into account how gender and sexual orientation can produce expectations that can limit learning experiences.
- Take active measures to strengthen family relationships as you change from your academic experience.
- Acknowledge how achieved status can influence how others respond to you.

Build a Bright Future

- Consider majors and career choices that match your learning style.
- Find a mentor who can help you shape your future plans.
- Stretch your ability to use different learning styles to have more career options later.
- Consider seeking career testing to help you decide on a direction.

 Visit the College Success CourseMate for *Your Guide to College Success* for interactive resources at login.cengagebrain.com

Review Questions

1. Discuss the relationship between expectations and stereotypes. Provide an example of a stereotyped judgment that led to positive outcomes in the college setting and an example of a judgment that led to a negative outcome.

   _____

   _____

   _____

2. List the nine types of intelligence that Gardner identified and circle the one that best represents you. How can you use this information to enhance your success in college?

   1. _____

   2. _____

   3. _____

   4. _____

   5. _____

   6. _____

   7. _____

   8. _____

   9. _____

3. List below the three types of sensory preferences for learning and circle the one that best represents you. How can you also use this to enhance your college success?

   1. _____

   2. _____

   3. _____

4. List below the four types of experiential learning preferences and circle the one that best represents you. Now consider the preferences you circled above. What does this imply about the types of courses in which you might be most successful?

   1. _____

   2. _____

   3. _____

   4. _____

5. What are some important things to do to get off on the right foot in class? List at least three strategies you can use now to make the best possible impression on your instructors.

   1. _____

   2. _____

   3. _____

   4. _____

   5. _____

6. Describe why boundaries between faculty and students can be hard to figure out, and discuss some consequences of that confusion.

_____

_____

_____

7. If you believe your rights have been violated, what corrective steps can you take?

_____

_____

_____

8. In what ways can the circumstances of your birth influence your learning?

_____

_____

_____

9. How have conditions changed in higher education in relation to gender and sexual orientation?

_____

_____

_____

10. How would you go about choosing a mentor?

_____

_____

_____

When Stereotypes Come Out to Play

Consider the following characteristics that might influence stereotyped judgments about performance in the college setting. On your first pass through the list, identify which of the factors might lead others to have expectations about how you will perform academically. On your second pass, identify where you are likely to engaged in stereotyped judgments about others based on each category.

First-time in college?	Height?
Ethnic Background?	Religion?
Political Affiliation?	Gender?
Sexual Orientation?	Sorority/Fraternity Affiliation?
Athletic Involvement?	IQ?
Hair Color?	Socioeconomic Status?
Physical Appearance?	Technological Savvy?

Your Intelligence Profile

Beginning courses in college will give you an opportunity to experiment with and improve different kinds of intelligence. See how different college courses promote specific kinds of intelligence. Then indicate your strengths by identifying all the characteristics that apply to you.

Mark the space using the following codes: 2, very much like me; 1, somewhat like me; 0, not like me.

Verbal-Linguistic (Great Books, Composition, History)

_____ I like to read.

_____ I enjoy finding out the meanings of new words.

_____ I appreciate humor involving wordplay.

_____ I enjoy telling or writing poems or stories.

_____ I recall written or verbal material well.

Logical-Mathematical (Algebra, Philosophy, Chemistry)

_____ I like working with symbols.

_____ Math comes fairly easily to me.

_____ I like to analyze and solve problems.

_____ I like to discover logical weaknesses in an argument.

_____ I enjoy listening to a good debate.

Musical (Music Appreciation, Orchestra)

_____ I enjoy singing or making rhythmic sounds.

_____ I like to listen to favorite CDs and downloads.

_____ I sometimes make up my own tunes.

_____ I would enjoy learning to play a new musical instrument.

_____ I enjoy music deeply even when it has no lyrics.

Bodily-Kinesthetic (Recreation Studies, Engineering)

_____ I enjoy working with my hands.

_____ It's hard for me to sit still for long periods of time.

_____ I am good in at least one sport.

_____ I enjoy a well-executed physical movement.

_____ I'm physically comfortable with my body.

Spatial (Geometry, Art, Computer Science)

_____ I can easily visualize objects.

_____ I tend to find beauty in things that others don't.

_____ I can usually get around without going the wrong way.

_____ I enjoy working on arts, crafts, or drawing.

_____ People often comment on my "good taste."

Interpersonal (Psychology, Sociology, Nursing)

_____ I like to be around people, and I make friends easily.

_____ I have a knack for remembering names and faces.

_____ I have demonstrated natural leadership tendencies.

_____ I notice subtle differences among people.

_____ I understand people better than many other people do.

Intrapersonal (Religious Studies, Film Studies)

_____ I prefer solitary activities to group work.

_____ I enjoy quiet time.

_____ I am very sensitive to emotional experiences.

_____ I know myself very well.

_____ I prefer to have a few deep friendships rather than lots of friends.

Naturalist (Biology, Evolution, Forensic Science)

_____ I have a strong curiosity about how nature works.

_____ I enjoy looking for patterns in things.

_____ I can learn more easily outdoors than indoors.

_____ Science classes tend to be easy for me.

_____ I have at least one collection that I keep in careful order.

Spiritual/Existential (Humanities, Philosophy, Religious Studies)

_____ I like learning about religious practices in other cultures.

_____ I wonder about life's absurdities and coincidences.

_____ I have lots of questions about the nature of the universe.

_____ I am not easily frustrated when big questions don't have easy answers.

_____ I think college students spend too little time thinking about issues with cosmic significance.

Add up your scores in each category. This inventory can reveal which multiple intelligence area is a relative strength and which is a relative weakness. In which dimensions did you score the highest? In which did you score the lowest?

 **Know Yourself**

SELF-ASSESSMENT 5.3

Sensory Preference Inventory

Using the scale below, enter the appropriate rating to each self-description in the open box.

Often = 5 points

Sometimes = 3 points

Seldom = 1 point

Then add the numbers in each column to find out your dominant sensory preference.

		VISUAL	AUDITORY	TACTILE
1.	I can remember best about a subject by listening to a lecture that includes information, explanations, and discussion.			
2.	I prefer to see information written on a chalkboard and supplemented by visual aids and assigned readings.			
3.	I like to write things down or take notes for visual review.			
4.	I prefer to use posters, models, or actual practice and do other activities in class.			
5.	I require explanations of diagrams, graphs, or visual directions.			
6.	I enjoy working with my hands or making things.			
7.	I am skillful with, and enjoy developing and making, graphs and charts.			
8.	I can tell if sounds match when presented with pairs of sounds.			
9.	I remember best by writing things down several times.			
10.	I can easily understand and follow directions on maps.			
11.	I do best in academic subjects by listening to lectures and tapes.			
12.	I play with coins or keys in my pockets.			
13.	I learn to spell better by repeating words out loud than by writing the words on paper.			
14.	I can understand a news article better by reading about it in the newspaper than by listening to a report about it on the radio.			
15.	I chew gum, smoke, or snack while studying.			
16.	I think the best way to remember something is to picture it in your head.			
17.	I learn the spelling of words by "finger spelling" them.			
18.	I would rather listen to a good lecture or speech than read about the same material in a textbook.			
19.	I am good at working and solving jigsaw puzzles and mazes.			
20.	I grip objects in my hands during learning periods.			
21.	I prefer listening to the news on the radio rather than reading about it in the newspaper.			
22.	I prefer obtaining information about an interesting subject by reading about it.			
23.	I feel very comfortable touching others, hugging, handshaking, etc.			
24.	I follow oral directions better than written ones.			
Total each column of numbers to find your stronger sensory preference.		Visual Total	Auditory Total	Tactile

Source: *The Barsch Learning Style Inventory* by Jeffrey R. Barsch, Ph.D. Copyright © 1996 by Academic Therapy Publications, Novato, CA. Reprinted with permission of the publisher. All rights reserved.

Experiential Learning Preferences

Each choice here captures an aspect of how people prefer to learn. Think about each choice in relation to yourself and circle the number in front of all of those items that apply to you.

When I have to learn how to operate a new piece of equipment, I

1. watch someone who knows how to operate the equipment.
2. carefully study the owner's manual.
3. fiddle with the dials until I produce a desired effect.
4. ignore the instructions and make the equipment suit my purposes.

What I like best about lectures is (are)

1. the chance to record the ideas of an expert.
2. a well-constructed argument about a controversial issue.
3. illustrations using real-life examples.
4. inspiration to come up with my own vision.

My class notes usually look like

1. faithful recordings of what the instructor said.
2. notes embellished with my own questions and evaluations.
3. outlines that capture key ideas.
4. notes with drawings, doodles, and other loosely related ideas or images.

I prefer assignments that involve

1. emotional expression.
2. analysis and evaluation.
3. solving practical problems.
4. creative expression.

In class discussion

1. I'm a watcher rather than a direct participant.
2. I'm an active, sometimes argumentative, participant.
3. I get involved, especially when we discuss real-life issues.
4. I like to contribute ideas that no one else thinks about.

I would rather work with

1. stories about individual lives.
2. abstract ideas.
3. practical problems.
4. creative ideas.

My learning motto is

1. "Tell me."
2. "Let me think this out for myself."
3. "Let me experiment."
4. "How can I do this uniquely?"

Interpretation: Look over your responses and add up the number of times you circled each number:

1. ____ (*learn by reflecting*)
2. ____ (*learn by critical thinking*)
3. ____ (*learn by doing*)
4. ____ (*learn by creative thinking*)

The alternative you circled the most is your preferred learning process. You may discover that you strongly favor a particular approach. Or you may find that your preferences are spread across several categories. Your experiences in college will help you develop your skills in all areas so you will become more flexible and more resourceful.

Your Journal

 ## Clarify Expectations

1. On a Mission

Go to your college website and find the mission statement. The campus community carefully constructed the mission statement to foster conditions that will best support your learning and personal growth. Are there any formal expectations identified in the mission statement that should help you navigate the social environment? Speculate about the informal expectations that may be implied by the statement. What is your part in helping the campus fulfill its mission?

2. Syllabus as Expectation

Consult the syllabus from the course you expect to be the most difficult for you. Examine it carefully and then try to predict how the class will proceed. What clues does the syllabus offer about how well the formal expectations fit with your willingness to meet those expectations? Ask yourself questions like these:

- "How labor-intensive will the course be?"
- "Where will the peak periods of effort occur?"
- "How should I pace my reading?"
- "Will there be an opportunity to develop my group work skills?"
- "How can I connect with the instructor if I run into a problem?"

 ## Develop Competence

3. A Matter of Style

You have had the opportunity to complete self-assessments designed to capture your strengths and style.

- List your strengths and weaknesses across the inventories.

_____

- What new insights do you have about your learning potential?

_____

- Did you learn anything that was distressing to you?

_____

- Considering your whole profile, what is one positive change you might make based on your knowledge that will enhance your success?

_____

4. Your Learning Metaphor

Think about what it feels like for you to learn in the college classroom. Do you feel like a sponge, soaking up every detail you can? Do you feel like a juggler? A prisoner? A butterfly? Are there other metaphors that describe your student experience? Describe or draw your metaphor and explain its significance. Go one step further and think about what your metaphor communicates regarding your personality style.

Manage Life

5. Develop Your Academic Integrity Pledge

Track down the rules that govern academic integrity on your campus. Read the rules carefully. Do you agree with the position taken by your campus regarding the consequences for academic dishonesty? In what ways do you think the rules could be improved? If possible, arrange to talk with a student who hears complaints regarding integrity violations. Compare that student's experience to your own speculations about the effectiveness of the rules. Then formulate your own personal pledge based on your study.

6. Connect with a Special Instructor

Make an appointment with the instructor who seems most approachable to you. Interview that instructor and see if you can find out the following information:

- How did your instructor's interest in the discipline begin?

_____

- What does your instructor remember from personal experience about being a first-year college student?

_____

- What advice would the instructor offer on how to get the most from college and how to avoid pitfalls?

_____

- How would your instructor describe his or her own learning style, and how does that influence course planning?

_____

- How good is the match between the instructor's intention and your learning style?

_____

Your Journal

 ## Connect and Communicate

7. Find Your Opposite

Pursue a conversation with someone in one of your classes who has expressed values that oppose your own. Identify five things you have in common. Did any commonality surprise you?

_____

_____

8. Take a Risk

Connect with a classmate and ask him to give you some feedback on what kind of student you appear to be. Are you giving off the impression you intend? What steps could you safely take to reflect your true interests and motivation about the class?

_____

_____

 ## Build a Bright Future

9. The Stylish Major

You have probably given some thought to the kind of major for which you would be best suited. Think about whether the major you've declared or to which you're most inclined is best suited to your learning style.

- What major are you considering?
- What intelligences fit best with this major?
- What sensory preferences might work best in this major?
- What learning process might be most emphasized in this major: reflection, active learning, critical thinking, or creative thinking?
- Does your personality style lend itself to the demands of the career?
- What is your conclusion about how well you might be suited to this major, based on your learning style?

10. Career Cruising on the Web

Instead of starting with the careers that you have been considering, go at it from another direction. Conduct a Web search to identify five career options that would fit well with your learning style. Be sure to include some unconventional career choices. Explain what you think the connection is between the career choice and your learning style.

Expand Thinking Skills

Chapter 6

KNOW YOURSELF

ONE OF YOUR PRIMARY PURPOSES in college is to become a better thinker. In this chapter, you'll explore ways to move beyond memorizing information to refine your thinking skills, including strategies for improving critical thinking, developing strong arguments, solving problems, making sound decisions, and becoming more creative. You'll also review the effects, both positive and negative, of relying on the Internet to expand your thinking capacity. To get a current picture of your thinking skills, place a check mark in the category that is most like you for each of the characteristics below.

Is My Thinking Optimal for College?

	Very Much Like Me	Somewhere In Between	Not at All Like Me
I accept that learning how to think better will involve hard work.			
I engage in cognitive control strategies to enhance my thinking skills.			
I can describe how critical-thinking styles differ.			
I know how to ask good questions.			
I argue effectively.			
I use systematic strategies to solve problems.			
I regularly make sound decisions.			
I can avoid ways of thinking about problems that prevent good decisions.			
I strive to be creative.			
I use the Internet strategically to enhance my thinking abilities.			
I make connections between thinking skills and effective career preparation.			

lightpoet/Shutterstock.com

Myron L. Rolle
A World Class Athlete and Scholar

During his freshman year, Myron L. Rolle was transformed by an encounter that changed the way he looked at the world and the way he thought about his place in it (Thompson, 2010). Myron was getting ready to play for the Florida State Noles in the Emerald Bowl in San Francisco. After walking around the city by himself, he stopped by a local restaurant and met a waitress who moved him beyond all understanding. Her tired face conveyed a life of suffering that penetrated his consciousness in a way he had never experienced before. Myron was so disturbed by the encounter and the overwhelming empathy he felt with her plight that he contacted his coach to help him cope with his concerns.

Rhodes Scholar Myron T. Rolle used his thinking skills to navigate the football field, pre-med training, and a wide variety of philanthropic activities.

© Jim McIsaac/Getty Images

Born in the Bahamas, Myron grew up and attended high school in New Jersey. He seemed to succeed in every activity he undertook. Besides being ranked as the number one high school prospect for college football in the country by ESPN, he edited the sports section of the school newspaper, acted and sang in the leading role in *Fiddler on the Roof*, and played sax in the school band. He later thrived at Florida State, where his high grade-point average in exercise science qualified him for medical school and helped him land a Rhodes Scholarship, an opportunity extended to only 32 exceptional people each year. He chose life at Oxford over completing his final year on the team at FSU and used the time to think through his future course, choosing between major league football and medicine.

Even before graduation, Myron's call to serve humanity prompted him to create a foundation that works on a variety of positive projects: founding a free clinic and sports complex in the Bahamas; launching an anti-obesity program serving Native American children in Florida; and designing a leadership academy for children in Florida's foster care system. When Princeton professor Cornel West met Myron during President Obama's inauguration, he bowed to the young man and commented, "You are the future of Black America."

In the summer of 2010, Rolle signed a 4-year contract with the Tennessee Titans. Although sports won over medicine in the first round, Myron's exemplary thinking skills, articulate presentation, and passion for public service ensure that his future options are wide open.

As shown in Myron L. Rolle's remarkable story, developing your thinking skills can lead to significant changes for you and others even before you graduate. Examine the chapter outline to help you focus on what aspects of thinking will be most helpful to you.

(Source: Thompson, 2010)

Clarify Expectations

Tom Brokaw, award-winning television journalist, may well have been addressing a commencement class when he delivered this widely quoted admonition: "You are educated. Your certification is in your degree. You may think of it as the ticket to the good life. Let me ask you to think of an alternative. Think of it as your ticket to change the world." We share his lofty sentiments. We hope this chapter will inspire you to think about how to use your thinking skills to make a difference.

Seek a Diploma for the Right Reasons

People attend college for many reasons. Some see college as a means to a very desirable end. They aspire to a job or a lifestyle that requires a college diploma and will do what they must to get the "paper," but they do not expect to be fundamentally changed by the experience.

Some people see college as a way to learn everything they can about a specific discipline. They find it satisfying to acquire each and every fact, thrilled with the expert knowledge they are accumulating, but again, they pay little attention to how they will be changed in the process.

Some recognize that the real power of college lies in its ability to transform. Regardless of your major, a good college education will not just produce disciplinary expertise and facilitate a career opportunity, but will also enrich your cognitive skills. It may even change your world.

Pursue Thinking Opportunities

Thinking is hard work. Unfortunately, some college classes may be set up in such a way that reasonable grades can be earned without much hard work. Although memorizing a list of facts or definitions requires time and energy, it isn't very hard to do. In fact, when instructors add rigor to their courses by requiring thinking activities, students sometimes balk:

- They worry that they won't be able to come up with satisfying work.
- They may feel emotionally upset if the conclusions challenge their values.
- They complain that test questions that require actual thought are "tricky."
- They prefer to economize on their efforts; if they don't have to think deeply, they can reallocate their time to other preferred (and less painful) activities.

It may help to think of your brain as a muscle that really gets a workout from the array of classes in store. If you go unchallenged, you go unchanged. To get the most from your education, you will need to embrace the sports mantra "No pain, no gain." See Know Yourself: Self-Assessment 6.1, "Seeking—or Avoiding—Rigor?," at the end of this chapter on page 197 to gain some insight into your stance about transformation.

 # Develop Competence

In this section, you will read about five important thinking skills that will give your brain a workout: cognitive control, critical thinking, questioning, offering criticism, and reasoning.

Engage in Cognitive Control

Cognitive control involves managing thinking processes to improve flexibility, control attention, and reduce interfering thoughts (Diamond, Casey, & Munakata, 2011). Cognitive control also has been referred to as *inhibitory control* or *effortful control* to emphasize the ability to overcome a strong inclination to do something less functional and instead do what is most effective (Diamond, 2010; Rothbart, 2011). Think about all of the times you have needed to (Galinsky, 2010):

- complete a task by resisting interfering thoughts or environmental distractions.
- suppress blurting out a response that would feel good at the time you said it but that you would later regret.
- persist working on boring or unrewarding tasks to achieve a long-term goal when there are so many other rewarding short-term activities.

Control Attention and Reduce Interfering Thoughts Controlling your attention is a key aspect of learning and thinking (Bjorklund, 2012). Periodically remind yourself to stay focused on what is important to learn and think about. Use a pet phrase like "Stay focused" or "Zero in" if you find yourself losing concentration.

Staying focused on reading this chapter from start to finish without interruption is an example of *sustained attention*. So is concentrating throughout a 50-minute lecture on what an instructor is saying. And so is sticking with something you are doing after you've initially not done well at it. Inhibiting our tendencies to give up is an important aspect of thinking (Galinsky, 2010).

Distractions that can interfere with your attention can come from the external environment (e.g., the "ding" of an incoming email message) or from competing thoughts in your mind. Self-oriented thoughts, such as worrying, self-doubt, and intense emotionally-laded thoughts may especially interfere with focusing attention on academic thinking.

Be Cognitively Flexible *Cognitive flexibility* involves being aware that options and alternatives are available and adapting to the situation. Before you can adapt, you need to be aware that a change may be useful, and also be motivated to change. Having confidence in your ability to adapt your thinking to a particular situation, an aspect of *self-efficacy*, or personal effectiveness, also is important in being cognitively flexible (Bandura, 2010). To evaluate how cognitively flexible you are, complete Know Yourself: Self-Assessment 6.2, "How Cognitively Flexible Are You?," on page 198 at the end of this chapter.

Think Critically

You have probably heard the term *critical thinking*, which involves thinking reflectively, thinking productively, and evaluating the evidence (Bonney & Sternberg, 2011).

Your critical thinking will improve when you increasingly ask not only "what" happened but "why" and "how"; when you examine supposed "facts" to determine whether there is evidence to support them; when you argue in a reasoned way rather than emotionally; when you recognize there sometimes is more than one good answer or explanation; and when you ask questions and think deeply about what we already know to create innovative ideas and new information. Among other benefits, when you think critically you improve your ability to learn and retain new information. Clearly, this advantage will benefit you in college and beyond.

The complexities of life in the 21st century underscore the need for critical-thinking skills (Magno, 2010). Preserving the environment, addressing poverty, and stabilizing the global economy are just a few of the challenges that require our best collective thinking. One aim of a liberal arts education is to help you develop broad critical-thinking skills by sampling the various ways of thinking required in different disciplines (Ratcliff et al., 2004).

Different disciplines tend to approach critical thinking in distinctive ways. For example, the natural sciences often emphasize critical-thinking skills related to problem solving. The humanities focus on the critical analysis of expressive works, including their cultural contributions. Exposure to various disciplines can help you develop a broad base of perspectives that will serve as the basis for becoming an expert at critical thinking.

Your own knack for critical thinking will depend on your learning style and the successes you've had in various thinking challenges. For example, your ability to be effective as a critical thinker will vary with the commitment you make to

© Carol Cable. Used with permission of the cartoonist.

study a discipline in depth. In some situations, your intrinsic interest in the topic will make it easy for you to grapple with the main ideas. In other situations, the content may seem hard to penetrate, so it may be more manageable to engage the material at a more shallow level.

Three general critical-thinking styles—*information avoiders*, *consumers*, and *strategists*—bring differing degrees of success in college (Potter, 2005):

- **Information avoiders** engage in very little critical thinking; they operate as though they are habitually on autopilot. They look for information that confirms what they already know and often feel overwhelmed by incoming data that doesn't fit with what they already believe.

- *Consumers* are good at gathering information but don't tend to fare as well when the thinking challenge goes beyond memorization. They prefer their knowledge already processed. Some college courses will be an ordeal because of the expectation about how much brainpower must be invested to be successful.

- *Strategists* like to engage information in effective and productive ways. They enjoy digging deep, playing with ideas, and developing fresh insights. They get bored in classes that merely transmit information. In contrast, they relish activities that allow them to display their cognitive skills.

Figure 6.1, "Three Types of Thinkers," provides more detail on how these knowledge styles differ. In addition, Know Yourself: Self-Assessment 6.3, "The Critical Difference," at the back of the chapter on page 199, gives you an opportunity to evaluate how well your characteristics match those of good strategic thinkers.

Ask Questions

One sign of a good critical thinker is the ability to ask on-target questions. When you were younger, you were probably constantly asking questions. But as you've gotten older, you may have acquired more passive learning habits. Unfortunately, if you haven't been asking questions often, these skills may be dormant.

Barriers to Good Questions One obstacle to asking questions can be fear of embarrassment. Good questions may occur to you, but you might choose not to ask them because you think asking questions might be a sign that you aren't particularly intelligent. If you were smart enough, you'd know the answer! You don't worry about what others think but worry about what others will think of *you*. Perhaps the instructor will think your question comes from left field. Or maybe other students will think you are showing off what you know.

The problem with worrying so much about what others think is that you sacrifice chances to improve your own thinking and speaking skills. It's *your* education. If you don't take risks, you won't develop your mind as much as you deserve.

Forming Good Questions Another problem students have is not being sure what kind of questions to ask. Your question type will depend on what kind of information you are trying to obtain (Strong et al., 2002). For example, your question can:

- **Read the lines.** These questions concentrate on identifying critical features or concepts. *What are the most important ideas being presented?*

INFORMATION AVOIDERS . . .	CONSUMERS . . .	STRATEGISTS . . .
• often miss the point	• struggle with identifying the most critical elements of a message	• can distinguish central ideas from nuances
• don't like to try new things	• memorize facts as "commodities"	• capable of memorizing and recalling detail for long periods of time
• rely on short-term memory strategies rather than more meaningful long-term learning	• rely heavily on expert opinion	• intrigued by the challenge of creative problemsolving
• don't check their intuitions against the facts	• prefer direction by others over self-direction	• adept at creating new categories of information
• avoid developing new ways to categorize information	• less adept at constructing new categories of information	• transform negative emotions into additional motivation to achieve goals
• feel overwhelmed by new information	• adept at managing emotions while coping with information	• energized by complexity and chaos
• reject uncertain or complex ideas	• concentrate on ways to reduce additional mental effort	• favor accuracy over efficiency, rarely jumping to conclusions
• make rapid decisions to escape cognitive discomfort	• favor efficiency over accuracy processing when the effort intensifies	

V. Ruggiero, "Three Types of Thinkers," from V. Ruggiero, Beyond Feelings: A Guide to Critical Thinking. 4th edition. Copyright © 1995 by The McGraw-Hill Companies, Inc. Used by permission.

FIGURE 6.1 Three Types of Thinkers

- **React to the lines.** These questions facilitate an emotional response to the content. *How does the issue or concept make you feel?*
- **Read between the lines.** These questions emphasize your ability to analyze the content into component parts. *What factors explain how the key ideas are developed?*
- **Read beyond the lines.** These questions prompt you to think about alternatives or future possibilities. *What difference will the ideas make in the long run?*

Suppose you are studying the history of cartooning in an arts appreciation course. What kinds of questions illustrate these distinctions?

- **Read the lines.** What role does cartooning play in modern culture?
- **React to the lines.** What range of emotions do cartoons stir?
- **Read between the lines.** What political agenda regarding conflict in the Middle East might be expressed by a particular editorial cartoon?
- **Read beyond the lines.** Would you anticipate that cartoons will become more or less powerful as agents of social change over the next decade?

Get your curiosity out in the open. If you recapture your enthusiasm for asking questions, your

A good critical thinker asks on-target questions.

You can improve your analytic skills by learning to ask some general questions that will help you break open the ideas you're studying (Browne & Keeley, 1990). Think of this set of questions as a starting point for helping you to move your analytic skills in the right direction:

- What are the issues and the conclusion?
- What are the reasons?
- What words or phrases are ambiguous?
- Are there value conflicts?
- What assumptions are being made?

- What is the evidence?
- Are there other ways to explain the results?
- Are there flaws in the reasoning?
- Is any information missing?
- Do the conclusions fit the reasons?
- How do the results fit with my own values?

From Browne, M. Neil & Keeley, Stuart M. *Asking the Right Questions: A Guide to Critical Thinking,* 7th edition. Copyright 2004, p. 13. Adapted by permission of Pearson Education, Inc., Upper Saddle River, NJ.

college years will be more interesting and fun. A special kind of thrill occurs when your thinking generates good questions. Have you ever gotten a warm glow when your question elicits a "Good question!" response from your instructor?

Although instructors may reassure you that "there's no such thing as a stupid question," there are definitely unwelcome questions. These include questions that detract from the momentum of the class, focus more on self-concerns than on the needs of the class, or demonstrate that the questioner has failed to pay attention. See Highlight: "Your Question Tool Kit" for some suggestions about appropriate question strategies.

Offer Criticism

When a teacher offers you a chance to practice the higher-order skills of thinking critically and judging the quality of ideas or of a performance, it's easy to feel intimidated. However, some strategies can help you:

1. *Decide whether you like what you're being asked to judge.* Your general reaction can set the stage for detailed analysis later on. For example, were you smiling or frowning during the State of the Union address?
2. *Look for both positive and negative attributes.* Some people unnecessarily limit their thinking by focusing only on the attributes that support their emotional responses. If you were very enthusiastic about the president's speech, try to find some weaknesses in the address. If you were dissatisfied, look also for positive features in what you heard.
3. *Use criteria to stimulate your thinking.* Evaluate to what degree the work you are evaluating is:

effective	sufficient	relevant
efficient	adequate	justifiable
reasonable	logical	comprehensive
beautiful	sensitive	understandable
practical	accurate	timely
thought-provoking	stimulating	original

Which of the criteria would apply to a presidential address? A work of art? A symphony? A public policy? A speech delivered by a fellow student?

4. *Use examples to support your judgment.* Expect to explain your judgment. Which phrases or examples in the State of the Union address stayed with you? What made the examples compelling?

Reason

Sometimes you may find that you don't have all the information you need to understand a phenomenon, make a prediction, or solve a problem. Through reasoning, you can derive the missing elements. Reasoning represents a special kind of critical thinking that you will often have to use as your course demands become more sophisticated.

Good reasoners effectively make inferences, use logic, and create and defend arguments. Good reasoning isn't always easy, but you can learn the basic principles and get better at it.

Make the Right Inferences As you head toward the library during finals week, suppose you come across an unfamiliar student who is out cold, sprawled between the bookshelves, her books scattered on the ground (Halonen & Gray, 2001). What do you think? Your observations might lead you to draw a variety of inferences. *Inferences* are interpretations that you derive from processing cues in a situation. For example, you could infer that your fallen campus colleague might be:

1. exhausted from studying for finals.
2. suffering from a serious health problem.
3. unconscious from drinking until the wee hours.
4. a psychology major doing an experiment.

All of these inferences are *plausible*, meaning that they are logical possibilities, potentially accurate ways to explain what you saw. However, it's likely that one explanation is better than the others because it seems to solve the puzzle. In such cases, the inference moves from being a plausible explanation to a compelling one in that it explains the situation more completely than alternative approaches.

You constantly make inferences, such as:

- Your roommate is scowling, so you infer that she failed a test.
- You find the dishes piled up, so you infer that you'll have to do them.
- You get an unsigned note asking you to go out for coffee, and you infer who was most likely to have written it.

Your interpretations of the events around you are based on your collected experiences. Therefore, your inferences will reflect that experience and sometimes produce biases in interpretation.

Go back to the example of the fallen colleague. If you inferred that the individual might be the victim of a world-class hangover, your past experiences may have created a predisposition or

What happened here? Your conclusions come from inferences you make from the clues in the scene.

Helder Almeida/Shutterstock.com

bias in how you make sense of what you see in this situation. You may have heard about a huge party off-campus the night before, where everyone got totally wasted. To test this proposition further, imagine that the fallen colleague is male, not male. Does changing the gender of the person change your interpretive bias? Are you more likely to assume that a male or female would drink too much? You can see how bias and previous knowledge can shape and possibly distort the reality that you experience.

Your ability to make accurate inferences is probably very good in most situations. However, inferences can be tricky. Notice, in the examples given, how easy it is to be wrong. In fact, think about a recent situation in which you jumped to the wrong conclusion. A faulty inference was probably to blame.

Sometimes inferences become *assumptions*—inferences that we accept as the truth, often without verifying their accuracy. An assumption is not based on fact or reason and may be false. You may not recognize that you're operating from a faulty assumption until you learn otherwise.

Learn How to Handle Claims Instructors may challenge you to sort fact from fiction. They may ask you to judge the *validity* (truthfulness) of a *claim* (a statement that can be either true or false but not both) (Epstein, 2000). Claims are different from *facts*, which are truths that can't be disputed.

> *Fact:* The moon is full at least once a month.
> *Claim:* The full moon makes people a little crazy.

Notice how the claim is debatable and requires evidence before we can determine its validity; the fact cannot be challenged.

When you evaluate a claim, you have three choices:

1. Accept the claim.
2. Reject the claim.
3. Suspend judgment until you have more information.

How will you rise to the challenge of determining whether the claims you hear are valid?

When to Accept a Claim There are three circumstances in which it's reasonable to accept a claim:

1. *Personal experience.* Trust your personal experience when your confidence level is high and there isn't a good contradictory explanation. For example, you may have been warned about the "freshman 15," the tendency for students to put on weight during the first year of college. Despite the warning, you notice the scale is starting to creep upward, a trend you attribute to increased snacking during study sessions. Your personal experience suggests that the claim that the first year can layer on pounds seems true, although it may not be true for every single first-year student.
2. *Trustworthy expert.* If someone with a trustworthy track record or other similar credential such as expertise makes a claim, it's reasonable in many cases to accept the claim as true. For example, claims about health risks from smoking that are reported in the *New England Journal of Medicine* are usually trustworthy. Claims by your next-door neighbor about the value of vitamin C in promoting longevity may not be as valid.
3. *Reliable media sources.* Unless the media source is going to profit from the claim presented, it may be reasonable to accept the claim. For example, local weather forecasters regularly make claims about future

weather patterns that generally are accurate. Some newscasters demonstrate their reliability with the accuracy of their predictions. However, just because someone is on the news doesn't make that person a reliable source.

When to Question a Claim Question claims that:

- *come from "unnamed sources."* If you can't verify the source, you shouldn't readily accept the claim.
- *confer an advantage.* Individuals sometimes make large profits by supporting certain claims. Be suspicious of claims that can be linked to payoffs. Jennifer Hudson may be an attractive actor, but her endorsement of a diet plan is likely to be more of an advantage to her than to you.
- *are used to sell a product.* Advertisements and commercials are always making claims and often repute these to be based on solid research. However, the research may be biased, or there may be contradictory findings that are not reported. For example, influenced by claims in advertising, millions of Americans take herbal supplements to enhance their memories. Scientific evidence has yet to substantiate these claims.
- *offer personal experience as "proof."* Human memory can sometimes introduce distortions that can lead you to endorse a claim that simply isn't true. For example, psychologist Elizabeth Loftus (1993) cleverly demonstrated that people can be tricked into recalling events in their childhood that never actually happened. After hearing family members describe the fictional experience (with Loftus supplying the script), the participants confidently recalled the scripted details of getting lost in a mall as though they had truly lived the experience. Loftus suggested that we may routinely "reconstruct" memories that represent a blend of the truth, perceptual distortions, and wishes.
- *appeal to common beliefs and practice.* Just because "everybody does it" doesn't make it right or truthful.
- *use language in misleading ways.* Politicians are often accused of putting a "spin" on their claims. For example, they might report that the "vast majority" of Americans believe in vouchers for private school, when the actual statistic in favor might be 51 percent at the time. Beware of overblown language that can disguise the truth.

Form Strong Arguments In formal reasoning, an *argument* is a set of claims. The argument begins with *premises*, initial claims that lead to a final claim called the *conclusion* of the argument (Epstein, 2000). A good argument is one in which the premises (1) are true and (2) lead logically to the truth of the conclusion. Good arguments are also called *strong* or *valid* arguments.

Here's an example of a good argument:

> *Premise:* All healthy dogs have fur.
> *Premise:* Spot is a healthy dog.
> *Conclusion:* Therefore, Spot has fur.

Some good arguments are reasonable because the premises and conclusion are sound, even though the conclusion may not be as absolute as the one in the prior example. In most cases, these plausible arguments deal with probable outcomes instead of definitive ones:

> *Premise:* Most dogs that live outside have fleas.
> *Premise:* Spot lives outside in a doghouse.
> *Conclusion:* Therefore, Spot probably has fleas.

Spot could be the rare exception, but the conclusion is logical if the first two premises are true.

These simple suggestions will help you develop the most persuasive arguments:

1. Be sure that the conclusion follows logically from the premises.
2. Challenge faulty or dubious premises.
3. Use precise language to pinpoint your claim. (Vague or ambiguous language makes your position easier to challenge.)
4. Avoid making claims you can't prove.

Form Counterarguments In many classes, you may be asked to find flaws in an argument. A counterargument challenges an argument by showing that:

1. a premise is false.
2. the conclusion is false.
3. the reasoning is weak or faulty.

In Figure 6.2, "Arguments: The Good, the Bad, and the Goofy," see whether you can determine exactly what weakens each argument.

Some counterargument strategies are ineffective. For example, ridicule is not a good way to counter argue. Ridicule or criticism of the person making the argument disrupts communication without improving anyone's understanding. See Danger Zone: "Offensive Defense" for an illustration of this problem behavior.

Another ineffective strategy is restating the original argument in a distorted way and then disproving the distortion. Suppose you are debating with a classmate the need for welfare reform to improve employment opportunities. Your classmate introduces a recent study suggesting that children on welfare perform poorly in school. He concludes that past welfare reform has been harmful to academic achievement and that there is no basis to believe that additional reform will enhance children's achievement. Note the drift and distortion in the argument. To be effective, a counterargument must accurately represent the original argument and defend against only that argument.

Refine Your Reasoning You can improve your reasoning skills in the following ways.

Be Willing to Argue Students can study reasoning as a formal science in logic classes, but you'll certainly have opportunities to create and defend arguments in many other formal and informal situations. You may have to present a position in a term paper, in a speech, or in answer to a complex question in class. Don't shrink from those opportunities to argue. Intellectual arguments can generate passion, too, but they need not have the same emotional intensity or feelings of personal risk as the arguments you have with loved ones.

Use Inductive and Deductive Reasoning There are two types of formal arguments: induction and deduction (Porter, 2002). *Induction* involves generalizing from specific instances to broad principles. For example, perhaps you really enjoyed your high school foreign language classes. Based on that experience,

DANGER ZONE

Offensive Defense

What began as a simple exchange about an application of supply-and-demand principles in your marketing class suddenly escalates. Tony is feeling pretty frustrated because you don't understand what he is saying. You keep asking for examples that provide convincing evidence for his point of view. In the heat of the moment, Tony loses his cool: "Well, who's doing better in this course, then? I got an A on the last exam. What did you get?"

Solution: Keep your cool. Tony is violating a fundamental principle in good argumentation: You attack the argument, not the arguer. How can you defend yourself? Try this: "Tony, our grades aren't relevant to the case you are making. Can you think of any other clear and on-target examples that could persuade me to see this situation your way?"

See if you can spot ways to challenge the following arguments.

"Logic: another thing that penguins aren't very good at."

Example 1
Premise: All birds have fur.
Premise: Tweetie is a bird.
Conclusion: Therefore, Tweetie has fur.
The first premise is false, so the conclusion is implausible.

Example 2
Premise: Penguins eat fish.
Premise: I eat fish.
Conclusion: Therefore, I am a penguin.
Although the premises are both true, the conclusion isn't supported.

Example 3
Premise: Penguins are the cutest birds.
Premise: The zoo has penguins.
Conclusion: Therefore, the zoo has the cutest birds.
Not necessarily. Although the conclusion follows logically, the first premise is debatable. What exactly is meant by "cutest?" There might be more attractive species or even more attractive penguins in some other locations.

FIGURE 6.2 Arguments: The Good, the Bad, and the Goofy

you might reason inductively that all language classes in college are bound to be great. Notice that your conclusion or rule—your induction—might be incorrect, because your first college language course may turn out to be disappointing. Inductive arguments are never 100 percent certain. They can be weak or strong.

In contrast, *deduction* moves from general situations or rules to specific predictions or applications. Deductive reasoning parallels the hypothesis-testing procedures used in the sciences. For example, your chemistry instructor may ask you to identify an unknown substance. By applying specific strategies of analysis, you narrow the possibilities until you know what the substance is. A deductive argument is 100 percent true if the premises are true and the reasoning is sound. When the premises are untrue or the logical connection between the premises and the conclusion is shaky, a deductive argument may be false. Look at the deductive examples in Figure 6.3, "Using Induction and Deduction." Is any one of these arguments completely convincing? Why or why not?

Check Your Assumptions It's easy to reach wrong conclusions from wrong assumptions. For example, the satirist Jonathan Swift caused a stir in the 18th century when he proposed one solution for two serious problems facing British society: too many orphaned children and not enough food. Swift proposed that both problems could be solved if the orphans were eaten! Those who *assumed*

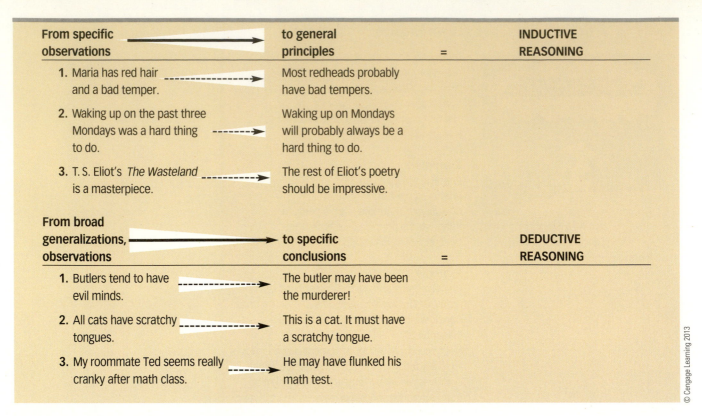

From specific observations	→	to general principles	=	INDUCTIVE REASONING
1. Maria has red hair and a bad temper.	--→	Most redheads probably have bad tempers.		
2. Waking up on the past three Mondays was a hard thing to do.	--→	Waking up on Mondays will probably always be a hard thing to do.		
3. T. S. Eliot's *The Wasteland* is a masterpiece.	--→	The rest of Eliot's poetry should be impressive.		

From broad generalizations, observations	→	to specific conclusions	=	DEDUCTIVE REASONING
1. Butlers tend to have evil minds.	--→	The butler may have been the murderer!		
2. All cats have scratchy tongues.	--→	This is a cat. It must have a scratchy tongue.		
3. My roommate Ted seems really cranky after math class.	--→	He may have flunked his math test.		

© Cengage Learning 2013

FIGURE 6.3 Using Induction and Deduction

Swift was putting forward a serious position were outraged. Those who carefully examined Swift's real purpose, and discovered that he meant to bring serious attention to these social problems, were amused by his wit and sensitized to the problem. Identify your assumptions and then do your best to verify them.

Know Your Own Bias We all have strong preferences and prejudices that may prevent us from evaluating an argument fairly. By acknowledging your own preferences and prejudices, you can increase the likelihood of coming up with more effective arguments. For example, if you know that you sympathize strongly with single parents, you can take this bias into account when you evaluate government policies that affect their lives. Good reasoners guard against their own "soft spots" to increase their objectivity.

Use a Protocol When considering an argument, Picciotto (2004) recommends the following framework to produce your best reasoning:

- What's the issue? Is it significant enough to warrant an investment of time?
- Do the claims have any foundation in fact?
- What is the nature of evidence that supports the claim—statistical, numerical, or anecdotal?
- How credible is the arguer? How credible are the sources used by the arguer?
- What assumptions—implicit or explicit—influence the claim?
- Does emotionally loaded language influence the argument's appeal?
- Does the argument contain any instances of problematic logic?
- Has the claim addressed elements comprehensively, or could something important be missing?

Know the Lingo Some specific phrases can help you launch the analysis of an argument (Missimer, 2005):

- I agree with the argument because . . .
- The argument is plausible but could have been stronger if . . .
- The reason supporting the argument is weak . . .
- The definition could be more precise . . .
- The author has not made assumptions explicit . . .

Take Time before Concluding Sometimes we short-circuit our reasoning. It's easy to get excited about a bright idea and stop the hard analytic work involved in thinking the problem through to the end. A premature judgment may work out, but it tends to make us even less exacting the next time we analyze a problem. Careful reasoners resist impulsive judgments. They thoroughly review an argument to make sure they have addressed all questions.

 # Manage Life

You might think that living a problem-free existence would feel terrific. Maybe it would—briefly. Problems add vigor and vibrancy to our lives; solid solutions and creative decisions bring a sense of accomplishment that makes the ordeal worthwhile. Failure also has a silver lining: The feedback from wobbly or ineffective solutions provides an opportunity to learn new and better ways for the future.

Solve Problems

Being in college will offer an array of problem-solving circumstances. The following represent problems that nearly all college students have in common: Where do I get the cheapest textbooks? What field should be my major? How will I make friends who will support my academic goals and future dreams? How will I ever complete three term papers at the same time? And the "Grand Problem" you will eventually want to solve: What's the next Big Step after graduation? We return to this question in the final section of this chapter.

In addition, your life circumstances may shape some distinctive problems you face and your decisions as to how to approach them (Hastie & Dawes, 2001). For example, if you are a millennial student, you might find yourself needing to strategize on how to get an overattentive parent to stop hovering. If you are a nontraditional student, you may need to figure out where you can park without getting a ticket. As an international student, you will fare best if you can express yourself clearly despite an accent that may challenge U.S.-born listeners. If you are a first-generation student, you will need to crack the code of what constitutes expected and acceptable behavior in the college setting—without the benefit of the socialization that happens more naturally in a family that has seen many members through a successful college experience. If you are an athlete, you must work out how to balance competing demands to protect both your competitive and your academic opportunities. And if you are an honors student, you must determine how to overcome stereotypes that might prematurely discourage friendships.

Find the IDEAL Solution Once a problem gets on your radar screen, it's tempting to hope that you can solve it without much thought. The fact is that good problem solving usually requires a great deal of thought, and a step-by-step approach often facilitates that thought process. Many people find it helpful to use a specific problem-solving system such as the five-step IDEAL method (Bransford & Stein, 1984). Let's see how that might apply to a common problem related to course scheduling.

1. *Identify the problem.* Bernita discovered when she arrived at her first art appreciation class that her instructor had already started. The instructor looked distinctly displeased as Bernita took a seat in the back of the class. When she looked at her watch, Bernita discovered that she was 2 minutes late. Obviously, she didn't want to annoy her instructor by arriving late to class each day. How could she avoid being late?

2. *Define the problem.* Be as specific and comprehensive as you can in defining a problem. Outline the contributing factors. There are two parts to this problem: The instructor is clearly a stickler for punctuality and Bernita is chronically late. Probably the main factor was the distance between the art class and the English class that Bernita had on the other side of the campus in the previous period. Even if she walked at top speed, she couldn't get to the art class on time.

3. *Explore alternative approaches*. Systematically gather and explore alternative solutions to isolate the best approach. What are some reasonable alternatives that Bernita can pursue? She can drop either class, or transfer into another section that prevents the conflict. She can talk to her art class instructor. He may be more understanding about her arriving a couple of minutes late if he sees that there is a legitimate reason. Or she can ask the instructor to wait until she gets there (maybe not). Or perhaps she can talk to the English instructor about leaving a couple of minutes early (maybe not).

4. *Act on the best strategy.* Take specific action to resolve the problem. Include more than one strategy. Bernita decided to explain to her art instructor why she would be a few minutes late to class, added that she would do her best to get there on time, and asked for her instructor's support. The instructor verified that Bernita would be late only by 2 minutes and asked that she sit near the door to minimize disruptions.

5. *Look back to evaluate the effects.* The final step is to evaluate whether or not your solution works. You might be pleased with how well it works and move on to your next challenge. Or you might discover that the solution is not working. In this instance, Bernita's problem solving was successful. Her solution not only saved her from the trouble and expense of dropping the class but also gave her a better personal connection with her instructor. Complete Know Yourself: Self-Assessment 6.4, "How Systematically Do I Solve Problems?," on page 201 at the end of this chapter to assess your own problem-solving strengths and weaknesses.

Acquire Problem-Solver Characteristics Problem solvers tend to approach complex situations with a questioning attitude that can clarify the situation. Five questions can help identify problems and get them resolved.

- **Who** is affected? With whom should I speak to find out more information?
- **What** are the issues? What are the resources?
- **Where** is the problem? Can I find additional information that will help me solve the problem?
- **When** can I expect a solution? At what point can I move ahead in the process?

- **Why** is this an important challenge? (based on Whimbey & Lochhead, 1991) What are some other ways you can maximize your problem-solving skills?

Observe Carefully Fictional detective Sherlock Holmes once commented to his partner, "You see, but you do not observe." Try to identify all the relevant factors in a problem from the outset. Careful observation involves analysis—identifying the relationships among the elements of the problem.

Generate Multiple Approaches to the Problem Think about the problem both logically and emotionally. Research what relevant experts might say. Ask opinions from those whose judgment you admire. Break the problem into smaller pieces. Work backward from your preferred outcome. Think through what would happen if you left the problem unattended.

Stay Positive and Persistent Don't be beaten by frustration. Search for ways to make the struggle invigorating rather than frustrating.

Show Concern for Accuracy Pay attention to detail. It's easy to let small errors occur in moments of inattention. Take care not to leave out crucial information. Proofread statements and recheck calculations before submitting your work for review.

Practice Mindfulness Developing the right frame of mind about possibilities is an essential ingredient in improving your ability to solve problems. There are many ways to practice *mindfulness*—the state of being fully alert and attuned to optimizing everyday experiences—to improve your problem-solving skills (Dweck, 2006, 2011; Langer, 1997). Here are several that are particularly helpful in a college setting:

- *Create new categories.* We often dismiss things by categorizing them in a global way. You might dismiss a "bad" instructor as not worthy of attention. However, if you look more closely at the various aspects of teaching, your perceptions will be richer. For example, perhaps the instructor's delivery is plodding but his choice of words is rich. Or his ideas are delivered without enthusiasm but his precise examples always make things easier to understand. A closer look can make us less judgmental and more tolerant.
- *Take control over context.* When you feel that your own options have been constrained, reexamine your circumstances to see whether you have overlooked some aspect of the situation that could make it more palatable or more rewarding. Myron Rolle's example in starting up an anti-obesity program for Native American students serves as a good illustration of what you can accomplish when you don't accept the status quo.
- *Welcome new information.* Humans tend to disregard information that does not fit with what we already know. This is an especially important tendency to overcome when you conduct research. Stay open to new information to maximize your pool of ideas. You may begin with one idea of what you want to prove but find that another possibility is actually more exciting.
- *Use technology.* The world is at your mouse's command through the Internet. The Web offers unlimited examples of good and bad problem solving.

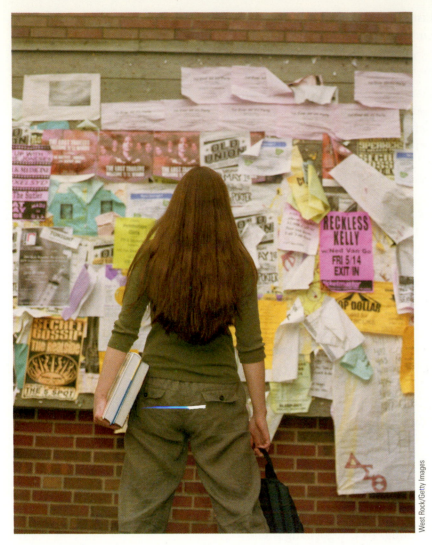

West Rock/Getty Images

Cultivate a growth mindset. Exploring new ideas and new opportunities leads to learning.

- *Maintain a growth mindset.* Be vigilant about the ways in which opportunities can lead to new learning. Even failure can provide powerful new insights that can help you more effectively in the long run.
- *Enjoy the process.* It's easy to become so single-minded about solving a problem that you forget to pay attention to the process of achieving it. Remember that the process is just as important as the outcome.

Make Good Decisions

Solving problems often requires making good decisions. Some decisions have far-reaching consequences. For example, you may have employed a distinctive process when you decided where to go to college, which may have included the use of systematic criteria. Perhaps you wanted a college close to home with low tuition costs, specific majors, and accessible classes. You might have examined the school's teaching reputation, whether the university featured a high-profile sports team, or if women could walk around safely on campus without escorts. On the other hand, sometimes decisions boil down to a gut feeling. For example, you may have decided to go to the campus you liked best when you visited. How satisfied you are now with your college experience may reflect how carefully you made that important decision. The more systematic you were in the process of making your decision, the more likely you are to be satisfied now with your choice.

Decide Systematically Making decisions systematically involves not only using higher-order thinking skills but also integrating those skills with your own values and self-knowledge. In contrast to going with a gut hunch to make a decision, systematic decision making requires many steps:

1. Recognize why a decision should be made, including what consequences might follow if no decision is forthcoming.
2. Identify relevant elements involved in the decision and reject distracters, elements that are not relevant or that may impede a good decision.
3. Assign relative weights to the elements, reflecting your values.
4. Generate as many options as possible, ruling out ideas that clearly will not contribute to a sound decision.
5. Speculate about the short-term and long-term consequences of proposed courses of action, including the potential for both positive and negative outcomes.
6. Choose the option that makes the most sense for you and your values.

Suppose, at this point in the term, you find yourself struggling with feelings of failure. You could alleviate the discomfort by dropping out (and perhaps open the door to whole new sets of discomforts), or you could systematically think through what factors might be contributing to your problem and might be fixable. Let's try out this strategy of midterm disillusionment.

1. *Why must you decide?* You may need to make an active decision to make some changes to secure greater success. A decision that addresses an appropriate course of action should free your energy. If you simply wallow in the mire and make no changes, your instructors could give you bad grades, probation, or other adverse consequences, which would diminish your sense of control over your own future.

2. *What elements contribute?* Are you taking too many credits? Is there an instructor whose style sets your teeth on edge and interferes with your learning? Maybe your roommate snores, so that sleep deprivation is taking a toll? Perhaps a breakup with a romantic partner is to blame? Do you have too little money to support your recreational interests? The latter can probably be ruled out as relevant to this decision.

3. *Which elements contribute the most?* Let's assume the problem rests with sleep deprivation from roommate snoring, based on your chronic sense of fatigue. Now your decision making can become more focused. The more specifically you can differentiate relevant factors, the more easily you can come up with a game plan that might address the issue.

4. *What options do you have?* Let's see: Earplugs! Change roommates. Get a prescription for sleep medications. Find a new university. Take regular naps.

5. *What are the consequences?* Earplugs are cheap. Roommate changes are not. Sleep medications may not protect you from the intrusiveness of world-class snoring and often come with unwelcome side effects. Changing settings is too extreme a course of action. It's unlikely that your schedule will allow for regular naps.

6. *Which course of action?* It seems reasonable to start with earplugs and perhaps work through other options if relief doesn't come.

Another strategy that can help with complex decisions is selecting a course of action that minimizes future regret. Can you envision how much turmoil you might feel if you do not take a particular path?

Accept Setbacks as Lessons No one looks forward to failing, but sometimes the impact of "blowing it" can have a profound effect on your learning and, consequently, your attitude about failure. In life, we often learn more from our setbacks and losses than we do from our gains and wins, especially if we are willing to analyze why things didn't go well for us.

Avoid Making Bad Choices All of us make bad decisions from time to time. We are likely to commit common judgment errors that we could avoid by knowing the traps (Halpern, 1997). These tips are especially helpful from the standpoint of managing life more effectively and smoothly.

- *Overconfidence.* Because we tend to be overconfident about the correctness of our past decisions, we usually neglect to notice that a path not taken might have been better than the one we chose. For example, you may be convinced that you chose exactly the right place to start or continue your college education. However, you can't be completely positive, because you won't have any way to compare how you might have felt had you opted for other campuses.

Solution: Be a little skeptical when you evaluate how wise your past decisions have been.

- *Confirmation bias.* We are inclined to look for evidence to support the outcome that we want rather than evaluating what is in our best interest. We also tend to ignore information that might change our minds. For example, you may be eager to avoid a particular course because you have heard that the instructor is lousy. You pay close attention to every report that supports the conclusion you have already drawn.

  Solution: Look actively for evidence that could prove you wrong so that your final conclusion will be well informed.

- *Overinvestment.* Once you've embarked on a course of action, especially if you've had to invest time or money, it may be hard to recognize a bad decision and to choose a different course. Shifting gears would mean losing what you have already invested. But if, for example, you've worked your hardest and just can't seem to do well in a particular class, don't stay there just because of the time you've already invested—unless you have a strategy in mind that could make things change positively.

  Solution: Be prepared to walk away when an investment sufficiently sours.

- *Hindsight bias.* It's easy to claim that we could have predicted something after it has already happened. Good decision makers don't waste time claiming they predicted what has become obvious. Also known as "armchair quarterbacking," coming up with explanations for the obvious can make you look foolish.

  Solution: Recognize that what you "knew all along" may just be a function of what you know right now.

Think Creatively

College abounds with opportunities for you to expand your creative abilities. Motivate yourself to exercise your creativity whenever you can. Seizing opportunities to develop your creative flair will go a long way toward building your self-confidence and self-esteem.

Creative people tend to have some common characteristics (Perkins, 1984): They

- *enjoy taking a unique approach to topics.* They choose new and exciting topics rather than going over more familiar territory as other students might do.
- *love the process of creating.* For example, creative students may feel as good when they are developing their work and when they turn it in as when they get back a successful grade.
- *are flexible and like to play with problems.* Although creativity is hard work, the work goes more smoothly when taken lightly; humor greases the wheels (Goleman, Kaufmann, & Ray, 1992).

Creative students thrive when they think of guidelines for assignments as a launching point for their imaginations. To evaluate your own creative style, complete Know Yourself: Self-Assessment 6.5, "My Creative Profile," at the back of the chapter on page 202.

Break the Locks Many people believe that they can't lead creative lives. You may be one of them. Despite childhoods filled with imaginative play, many of us surrender our sense of curiosity over time, reducing our capacity for creativity in the process (Beghetto & Kaufman, 2011; Fairweather & Cramond, 2011). A variety of "mental locks" can prevent us from pursuing creative responses, whereas a more flexible attitude sets the stage for creativity in school and throughout your life. Some of these locks and the "keys" for opening your mind include:

- I have to have the right answer.

  Sometimes the "right" answer isn't as much fun or as satisfying as an alternative.

- I must be logical.

  But I need to get in touch with my emotional side.

- I must follow the rules.

  But breaking the rules can be really liberating!

- I have to be practical.

  But not in every situation.

- Play is frivolous and wastes time.

  And I miss it! I want those feelings back!

- That's not my area.

  But it could be!

- I must avoid ambiguity.

  But ambiguity can open new doors.

- I can't appear to be foolish.

  But foolishness can be fun.

- To err is wrong.

  I'm designed to derail from time to time.

- I'm not creative.

  But I could be!

Spotlight On...

Nathan Segal

Advocate for the Elderly

Before starting at Yale, Nathan Segal took a year off to establish a badly needed service in Florida to assist the elderly in getting discounted prescriptions (Marklein, 2008). He first became aware of the problem when an elderly friend had trouble paying for her diabetes medication. After some research, Nathan discovered that many pharmaceutical companies provide discounting opportunities but don't advertise them effectively. The complexity of the application process also discouraged doctors from recommending this opportunity. Nathan organized a corps of volunteers to qualify seniors for the program and assist with their paperwork. He established a similar service when he began his history of science and medicine majors at Yale. *USA Today* honored his contributions with recognition as a member of All-USA College Academic First Team.

Foster Creativity Psychologists affirm that all people can be creative if they adopt the right attitudes and behaviors (Sternberg, 2011, 2012). The following basic steps can contribute to more creative and fulfilling lives:

1. *Don't accept other people's blueprints*. Question assumptions. Constantly look through and around problems to find a new approach. By moving away from how most people approach things, you may find yourself in the lead. For example, if everyone executes a PowerPoint presentation for a speaking assignment in a class, you will stand out by using chalk and the blackboard or markers on newsprint to support your key ideas. Think about how others will execute an assignment and, within reason, choose a course that makes your work stand out positively.

2. *Be vigilant about what others can't see.* Look for new and intriguing ways to redefine the problem. Use your unique past experiences to help you build a richer array of factors to consider in coming up with new insights.

3. ***When something sparks your interest, follow it*** (Csikszentmihalyi, 1995). When something sparks your interest, it often is short-lived, such as an idea, a flower, or a song. You may feel you are too busy to explore the idea, flower, or song further or that they are none of your business because you aren't an expert on them. Yet the world is your business, and you don't know which part of it is best suited to your interests until you make a serious effort to learn as much as possible about it.

4. ***Wake up in the morning with a specific goal*** (Csikszentmihalyi, 1995). Creative people wake up in the morning eager to begin their day. They do so not because they are necessarily cheerful, enthusiastic types, but because they know there is something meaningful to do each day and they can't wait to get started.

5. ***Be surprised by something every day*** (Csikszentmihalyi, 1995). Possibly something you see, hear, or read will surprise you. Absorb yourself in a lecture or a book. Be open to what the world is telling you. Life is a stream of experiences—swim widely and deeply in it and your life will be more enjoyable and productive.

6. ***Differentiate the good from the bad.*** Creative people generate many possibilities, but not all of them are appropriate. Don't linger on ideas that don't have strong potential.

7. ***Take the plunge before you are an expert.*** You don't really need to know absolutely everything about something before coming up with some new insights that could solve the problem. In fact, sometimes too much knowledge can reduce your willingness to "think outside the box."

8. ***Take sensible risks.*** All creative people face obstacles. Having courage and staying open to new experiences will contribute to selecting reasonable risks. Creative people take risks and learn from their mistakes. Picasso created more than twenty thousand paintings; not all of them are masterpieces. Your learning will be limited if you don't stick out your neck once in a while. If you're considering a particularly creative approach to an assignment, however, share your plan with your instructor ahead of time.

9. ***Motivate yourself.*** If you concentrate on the joy of the process rather than the prospect of rewards, your creative approaches are likely to feel much more rewarding and easier to sustain over time (Hennesey, 2011).

10. ***Spend time in contexts that will support your creativity.*** Find friends who will recognize your distinctiveness. Choose a major in which your individuality can shine. Avoid work environments that feel oppressive, mechanical, or uninspired.

11. ***Actively pursue the creative life.*** If you accept the proposition that you are not creative, then you won't be. If you open yourself to maximizing your creative potential, you begin the journey.

12. ***Go with your second impulse.*** Your first impulse is likely to represent an easier path, perhaps arising from routine ways that you

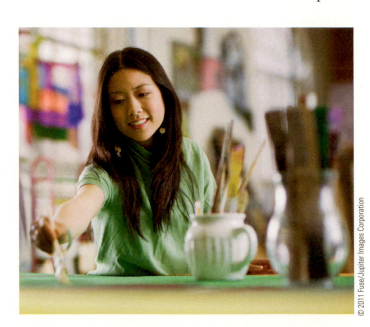

Creativity is a built-in demand for classes in the arts, but what will happen if you strive to take a creative approach in other classes as well?

approach problems. Go with an approach that is less characteristic of your style.

Change Your Environment If you accept the proposition that everyone has the potential to be creative, this means you, too! But you may need to rethink your environment to promote a more creative style. Here are some simple ideas to experience greater creativity on a day-to-day basis.

- Decorate your door or bathroom mirror. Find images, cartoons, headlines, and pictures that express who you are and put them up.
- Use a thesaurus. In writing projects, come up with new words that may have a stronger impact on your readers.
- Sit in a different place. Unless you are restricted by a seating chart, move around in classes or in the dining hall. Humans are creatures of habit. Breaking your habit can produce a new perspective and new friends.
- Think "connections." Explore how what you are learning in one context might inform what you are learning in another. These connections may provide you with some novel insights that you can share during class discussion.

 # Connect and Communicate

Although thinking is essentially a private activity, you will find many opportunities in college to expand the quality of your own thinking by reaching out.

Following are some strategies for improving your thinking skills by connecting and communicating.

Brainstorm Alternatives

One of the most popular strategies for enhancing creativity is to engage in *brainstorming* (Adair, 2010). The success of brainstorming rests on being able to overcome set ways of thinking about something.

Brainstorming is more productive when participants engage in the following (Adair, 2010; Prather, 2010):

- *Set free-wheeling expectations related to a particular topic.* Encourage all kinds of contributions, the goofier the better. However, it is important to stay focused on a topic; otherwise thinking can become too chaotic. It may help to invite others who are well known for their original thinking. You don't need a strong disciplinary background to make solid contributions.
- *Prepare individual ideas first.* Use Post-it notes or index cards to record individual responses before the group discussion begins. This strategy helps quieter members feel empowered about making contributions.
- *Suspend criticism, editing, and defending.* Accept all ideas without trying to judge them. The goal is lots of simple ideas rather than elaborate or complex proposals.
- *Focus on quantity.* Greater numbers of ideas encourage the likelihood that some great ideas will survive.
- *Connect and combine.* One person's contribution can stimulate other contributions. Build on prior contributions.
- *Establish quiet moments.* Reflection may encourage deeper, more remote connections.

- *Play devil's advocate.* When an idea meets the criteria, take a moment to consider the consequences if the idea is implemented and fails.

Brainstorming can come in handy when an instructor assigns you to an unspecified group project. Taking the time to play with the ideas on the front end of the project can make for a richer and more efficient experience in the long run.

Use the Internet as a Thinking Tool

The Internet has transformed nearly every aspect of our lives and offers extraordinary potential to enhance the way people think. With the universe of information just a few clicks away, the efficiency of solving problems that require assembling lots of data has improved dramatically. Now most projects can be managed from your laptop. However, the Internet also produces some threats.

Reliance on Wikipedia Established in 2001, Wikipedia represents collaborative digital scholarship that has become a natural first stop for finding out information quickly. However, many critics have suggested that the encyclopedia is not reliable because of biases of the contributors, vandalism, profanity, and the inclusion of irrelevant details. Founder Jimmy Wales (2011) posted a defense of the wiki that emphasized how quickly errors get corrected and said that the error rates in wiki are comparable to those of professionally written encyclopedias. Still, many professors will blanch if you attempt to build a paper on Wikipedia since it does not meet the academic standard of *professional* "peer review" by experts in a particular field.

Think Critically When Using the Internet Although it has dramatically expanded our access to information, surfing the Internet can lead the unwary user into a quagmire of data. An uncritical user can end up with too much, too little, or invalid information. This problem poses a special threat for students who like the convenience of doing research on the Internet but may lack the critical-thinking skills necessary to separate the valid and valuable from all the rest. Just because you can find an answer doesn't make it true. Thinking critically about the objectives and strategy of your search will make your surfing profitable.

"Are we thinking here, or is this just so much pointing and clicking?"

Locate What You Need Allow yourself a reasonable amount of time to play with different strategies to produce the best results. Identify and enter key concepts in a search engine. If you are operating in a particular discipline-based database, you may have the best luck by entering the basic concepts of the discipline to begin tracking down information. If you get an excess number of hits, refine your search by adding more parameters.

For example, you might limit your search to articles printed only in the last 5 years. Or you might conduct a search by combining two key terms. A search that specifies one term, then "OR," then another term will hit any article in which either term is present. "First ladies" or "foreign policy" will produce a broad search, identifying any online resource that addresses either term. By contrast, using "AND" instead of "OR" will narrow your hits to any resources that deal both with first ladies *and* foreign policy. You should be able to narrow down efficiently which first ladies had an influence on foreign policy.

What happens if there are too few hits to be helpful? Think about an overarching term in which the key concept you have already tried could be embedded. Suppose you need to find information about an obscure tree disease for a botany class. If you come up empty-handed by entering the name of the disease, enlarge your search to "tree disease." Usually, however, the problem is too much rather than too little information.

Find the Best Data Determining what information is sufficiently high quality is another challenge. Following are some strategies to increase the likelihood that your resources will be credible:

- *Avoid opinion pieces that can't be substantiated.* The Internet is the perfect vehicle for anyone with a point of view and a computer to try to capture and persuade an audience. The Internet does not police itself. Be vigilant about entries that appear to offer facts that can't be corroborated.
- *Identify the author and verify the author's expertise.* The most valuable websites are those that present information by experts in the specific discipline in which you are conducting your search. Individuals with scholarly degrees, affiliations with well-known institutions, or well-established reputations will be easier for you to claim as credible sources. If the author's name is present, you can do an additional search to identify the author's credentials if those are not available on the website. Web pages that do not credit an author are suspect. Similarly, blogs contain a distinctly personal perspective that probably won't earn a place in your harvest of sound data.
- *Check the date.* Information on older websites may be outdated enough that their inclusion will demonstrate that your search wasn't thorough. Trace information to its original source to strengthen your confidence. One of the best features of the Internet is that it can direct you toward original citations in published journals, many of which may be online.
- *Don't settle for the first data you find.* Although it may be easy to obtain information from Wikipedia, pursue higher-level, more respected material in relevant professional journals.
- *Don't be taken in by aesthetically pleasing websites.* Websites can be highly attractive and seductive, even when the information they contain isn't sound. Look for indicators that the scholarship is solid, such as well-defined concepts, charts and tables, and sponsorship by reputable organizations.

Although the Internet contains a bounty of useful information, it also is a playground for con artists and hoax perpetrators who may try to entice you through compelling graphics and offers that are truly too good to be true. Evaluate the potential gems you discover by going beyond the introductory website. Consider visiting http://www.snopes.com, where you can find some examples of unfounded claims that have been debunked.

App Nation Our lives are improved by a variety of "apps," mobile applications that facilitate solving personal research problems, from getting current weather reports to locating the closest Starbucks. To the extent that applications free us from the drudgery of solving problems the old-fashioned way, they are great. But you won't make progress in your thinking goals if you are so addicted to your "self phone" that you cannot function face-to-face.

Build a Bright Future

One serious test of the value of college for many students is whether it has prepared them well for the workplace. Whether you are looking ahead to a first job

Holley Frommel

Courtesy Holley Frommel

Transforming an Internship into a Future

Holley Frommel had no idea when she signed up for Professor Athena du Pre's Leadership and Communication class at the University of West Florida what kind of future would unfold from the fruits of a powerful course assignment. Each class

Holley Frommel's leadership skills during a service learning assignment at the Ronald McDonald House evolved into a paid internship and later a full-time job in public relations.

adopts a service learning project to provide direct benefits to the Pensacola community as it provides a backdrop against which to practice skills that will prepare students for different kinds of positions in media. After conducting a needs assessment at the Ronald McDonald House, a facility that provides housing and support for the families of seriously ill children, Holley's class chose the ambitious project of raising funds to buy a van for the Ronald McDonald House.

According to her peers, Holley's leadership made a significant difference in the outcome. Not only did the class raise $2,000 directly through more traditional methods, but they also sold sponsorships for the project to ensure that local companies would have their logo featured on the customized "wrap" on the RMH van. Holley noted, "A $2,000 sponsorship guaranteed an advertisement that associated each business with this great cause for the life of the van." The fundraising quickly mounted to a whopping total of $46,000 raised in the span of one semester. Holley's class bought not just the van but also insurance and gas for several years into the future.

Members of the staff at Ronald McDonald House were so impressed that they later selected Holley

or a better job, employers will be less interested in the bank of specific facts that you have accumulated than in what kind of a thinker you have become as a result of your college experience. The process of effective career planning provides a final avenue for discussing high-quality problem solving and decision making.

Improve Career Decisions

How might a failure to engage in effective thinking harm your own future career decisions? To increase your chances of making good decisions about future careers, avoid the following traps (Swartz, 2001).

Don't Make Snap Decisions People tend to make decisions too quickly, before they have had time to consider all of the options. Hasty decisions are much more likely when you are trying to solve short-term problems, leaving you vulnerable to long-term problems. An example of this failing is taking the first job offer you get. Although the offer might be a good match for your skills, such a quick decision precludes another alternative that might be even better.

Expand Narrow Thinking You may simplify choices in a way that overlooks a broader array of options. Your rush to choose from column A or B may keep you from turning the page to see many other options in columns C–F. Many students feel pressured to establish their careers. You might decide that advertising is the way to proceed and not consider any other options that might be more satisfying.

Contain Sprawling Thinking You may entertain too many options. By attending to too many possibilities, you may neglect the in-depth consideration that might make the best option stand out. If you find yourself making job interview appointments with more recruiters than you reasonably can prepare for, you may be suffering from thinking sprawl.

Clarify Fuzzy Thinking You may not think through a problem carefully to isolate the key factors that will lead to a solution. Sadly, many students complete their majors using fuzzy thinking. They may graduate without any distinct ideas about what they can legitimately pursue as employment options.

Add Power through Service

An effective way to prepare for the workplace is by getting experience as a leader and problem solver in service learning opportunities. Some instructors include projects that apply course concepts and principles to serve a larger civic purpose. See the nearby "Spotlight On Holley Frommel" to see how closely tied service learning can be to shaping your future.

Spotlight On... (Cont.)

for their first paid internship, where she completed training videotapes in English and Spanish that would assist clients who struggled with hospital forms printed in English. The internship evolved into the public relations administration job she originally thought would be fulfilling. However, after completing her master's degree in organizational communication, Holley has returned to get some science courses under her belt so that she can pursue a career in direct healthcare service.

Clarify Expectations

- Recognize the role that college plays in promoting better thinking.
- Pursue thinking opportunities in your courses.

Develop Competence

- Engage in cognitive control by controlling your attention, reducing interfering thoughts, and being cognitively flexible.
- Understand what critical thinking is and how it can benefit you now and in the future.
- Understand the different kinds of effective questions you can ask.
- Know how offering criticism can enhance critical thinking.
- Make accurate inferences by attending to the proper cues; evaluate arguments by looking at the logic of the premises and conclusion.

Manage Life

- Use a systematic approach to problem solving, including evaluating the consequences.
- Use skilled questioning to facilitate good solutions to problems.
- Engage in mindfulness by increasing attention and careful reflection.
- Practice decision-making skills that integrate your knowledge, values, and thinking skills.
- Go beyond the ordinary. Increase your creative thinking.

Connect and Communicate

- Improve brainstorming results by avoiding critical commentary.
- Be wary about information gathered from the Internet.

Build a Bright Future

- Avoid making snap decisions or applying narrow, sprawling, or fuzzy thinking that could limit your options.
- Recognize the importance of making the right match in your career search.
- Participate in service learning to develop leadership skills and give back to the community.

 Visit the College Success CourseMate for *Your Guide to College Success* for interactive resources at login.cengagebrain.com

Review Questions

1. Describe three reasons why students would rather not think if they had the choice.

   1. _____

   2. _____

   3. _____

2. What are some indications that a course will provide a rigorous experience?

   _____

   _____

   _____

3. List three things that distinguish good critical thinkers from bad ones. Do these characteristics apply to you? If not, how can you improve your critical-thinking skills?

   1. _____

   2. _____

   3. _____

4. Write down a question you have about something you are currently studying. Is it a "good" question based on what you have read in this chapter? Analyze why or why not.

   Your question: _____

   Your analysis: _____

   _____

   _____

5. What steps can you take to construct a good argument?

   _____

   _____

   _____

6. Describe the IDEAL problem-solving strategy below. What are some other strategies for successful problem solving?

   I: _____

   D: _____

   E: _____

   A: _____

   L: _____

   Additional Strategies: _____

7. What are some criteria you can use when offering critical feedback?

_____

_____

_____

8. List some steps you can take now to improve your creativity.

_____

_____

_____

9. Why are accumulated facts less important than thinking skills to potential employers?

_____

_____

_____

10. What thinking errors complicate job choice?

_____

_____

_____

_____

_____

_____

SELF-ASSESSMENT 6.1

Seeking—or Avoiding—Rigor?

When it is time to register for your next term's courses, which course characteristics will have the greatest priority for you? Rank-order the following characteristics from 1 (greatest priority) to lowest priority (9):

_____ Rigorous reputation of professor

_____ Cost of textbook

_____ Intensity of reading requirements

_____ Intensity of writing requirements

_____ Public speaking requirement

_____ Group work opportunity

_____ Convenient location

_____ Convenient time

_____ Specified learning outcomes

What do your choices say about your goals for personal change? Could you be avoiding some opportunities that might encourage you to stretch?

SELF-ASSESSMENT 6.2

How Cognitively Flexible Are You?

Circle the number that best reflects how you think for each of the four items:

	Exactly Like You	Very Much Like You	Somewhat Like You	Not Too Much Like You	Not At All Like You
1. When I try something that doesn't work, it's hard for me to give it up and try another solution.	1	2	3	4	5
2. I adapt to change pretty easily.	5	4	3	2	1
3. When I can't convince someone of my point of view, I can usually understand why not.	5	4	3	2	1
4. I am not very quick to take on new ideas.	1	2	3	4	5
Add your numbers for each of the four items: Total Score:_____					

If your overall score is between 20 and 15, then you rate high on cognitive flexibility. If you scored between 9 and 14, you are in the middle category, and if you scored 8 or below, you likely could improve your cognitive flexibility.

Source: Ellen Galinsky (2010). *Mind in the making*. New York: Harper Collins, p. 19.

SELF-ASSESSMENT 6.3

The Critical Difference

For each of the 30 items below, choose the number that most closely corresponds with your profile.

0 = Not at All Like Me 1 = A Bit Like Me 2 = Like Me 3 = Very Much Like Me

_____ 1. When I encounter a new idea in a course, I like to analyze it in depth.

_____ 2. The most important element in any course is a well-prepared instructor who can present the information clearly.

_____ 3. I don't like memorizing lots of material.

_____ 4. I like courses where we deal with a few topics but really analyze them in depth rather than courses where we cover many different topics but don't go into much depth on any one.

_____ 5. I dislike tests where you're supposed to guess what the instructor wants.

_____ 6. In many courses, I just can't get started.

_____ 7. While the instructors are lecturing, I often find myself thinking beyond the points they are trying to make.

_____ 8. It is important for instructors to hand out study guides before the test so I can know what I should study.

_____ 9. When I have a difficult problem, I like to "cut to the chase" and make a quick decision rather than doing a lot of work that might not amount to anything.

_____ 10. Not all ideas in a course are equally important; I like to decide for myself what is important more than I want my teacher to make that decision for me.

_____ 11. During class, I try to write down everything the instructor says.

_____ 12. My instructors usually lecture in a way that is hard to follow.

_____ 13. I get excited by challenges; the harder the challenge, the more excited I get.

_____ 14. I do not like the instructor to waste class time by getting off the track and telling irrelevant stories that won't be on the tests.

_____ 15. If I do not understand the course material, I try not to worry about it.

_____ 16. When I run into something that does not immediately make sense, I keep working with it and analyzing it until I really understand it.

_____ 17. I think test questions should be taken directly from the class notes. It's not fair when the instructor surprises me with a test question about material we did not cover in class.

_____ 18. I prefer that the instructor never call on me during class.

_____ 19. The learning challenge I like the most is the task of trying to make order out of chaos.

_____ 20. My confidence level in a course is highest when the course has a lot of well-organized facts that I can memorize easily.

_____ 21. It is the instructor's job to motivate me to do my best work.

_____ 22. I'm the kind of person who likes to set my own goals for learning, even if they are very different from the instructor's goals in the course.

_____ 23. When I am exposed to new information, I want my instructor to tell me what is most important.

_____ 24. No matter how hard I work, I never seem to do as well as I would like.

_____ 25. When my instructors give reading assignments, I like it when they don't tell me what to look for in the reading; I like to determine what is important for myself.

_____ 26. I hate courses where the instructor gives you lots of readings and you have to figure out what is important in those readings.

_____ 27. If I don't learn much in a course, it is usually because the material was too hard.

_____ 28. I am often frustrated in courses when we don't examine something in enough depth to find out what is really going on.

_____ 29. During the first class meeting, I want to get an accurate idea of how hard the course will be.

_____ 30. When I get a low grade on a test or an assignment, I feel frustrated and it is hard to shake that feeling.

The Critical Difference

Score sheet:

1. _____	2. _____	3. _____
4. _____	5. _____	6. _____
7. _____	8. _____	9. _____
10. _____	11. _____	12. _____
13. _____	14. _____	15. _____
16. _____	17. _____	18. _____
19. _____	20. _____	21. _____
22. _____	23. _____	24. _____
25. _____	26. _____	27. _____
28. _____	29. _____	30. _____
Total _____	Total _____	Total _____

Circle the largest number of the three totals. If that circled number is more than 25 and the other two totals are below 15 each, then the circled number indicates your dominant critical-thinking style. If no total is more than 20, and especially if all three totals are similar (within about 7 points of each other), then you have a mix of styles. The right column represents the information avoider style. The middle column represents the consumer style. The strategist style is represented in the left column.

How Systematically Do I Solve Problems?

Think about the problems you've faced in your academic and personal life in the last month. Review how regularly you went through each of the stages of the IDEAL model.

	Usually	Not Usually	Explain

Identification:
    I accurately identify when
    something needs attention.			

Definition:
    I describe problems comprehensively, including
    all factors that might influence the problem.			

Evaluation:
    I figure out different approaches to take
    and decide on the best alternative.			

Action: I put my plans into action.			

Looking back:
    I purposefully examine how effective
    my chosen solutions are.			

As you examine the results of your review, which aspects of problem solving are your strengths?
What elements do you need to practice to become more systematic in your problem solving?
What ideas do you have for incorporating these skills into your problem-solving style?

🖼 Know Yourself

SELF-ASSESSMENT 6.5

My Creative Profile

To get some measure of your creative potential, answer the following:

1. If you were managing a rock group, what original name would you give it?

2. You've been asked to plan a birthday party for your 5-year-old nephew. How would you make it different from other parties his friends have attended?

3. How many uses can you think of for a pencil?

4. What kind of musical instrument could you make out of the contents of the junk drawer in your family's kitchen?

5. You've just been invited to a costume party. What will you wear?

6. What theme would you propose for a sales campaign for your favorite shoe?

7. What business could you establish that would make the lives of your classmates easier? What would you call the business? How would you promote and develop it?

8. What is one strategy you could develop that would make people less afraid of failure?

9. You have to negotiate a late deadline for a paper with your instructor. How might you do that creatively?

10. How many creative uses can you think of for a remote control unit?

This assessment highlights flexible thinking. If you found yourself stumped by most of the items, then you may not have developed the flexible mindset that helps creative people. If you answered a few of the questions, then you can probably point to a few creative areas in your life. If you felt exhilarated by the questions, chances are good that you're often creative.

© Cengage Learning 2013

202 CHAPTER 6 Expand Thinking Skills

Your Journal

Clarify Expectations

1. No Pain, No Gain

Think about a specific situation you may have confronted already in which thinking caused your brain to hurt. List all the reasons that you found this task to be flummoxing. How does your list of avoidance behaviors compare to the list we provided? Did you come up with any new reasons why we sometimes want to run away from the challenge?

_____

_____

_____

2. Thinking as Transformational

Chances are good that you are at least halfway through your first semester in college. Although you may not feel transformed, you may be starting to feel different. Describe three ways in which your thinking skills may be changing. If you can, try to link those changes to some specific causes. Are there instructors, classes, or peers that are helping you develop your skills?

_____

_____

_____

Develop Competence

3. Claims Detector

Record the claims you hear in the media for one day. Commercials are especially good targets for this activity. Pick the claim that is most interesting to you and see if you can convert the commercial claims into premises and conclusions. Should you accept the claim, reject the claim, or suspend judgment based on the evidence offered?

CLAIM: _____

PREMISES: _____

_____

_____

CONCLUSION: _____

ACCEPT, REJECT, OR SUSPEND JUDGMENT: _____

4. A Question a Day

Sometimes it's hard to overcome the impression that if you ask questions, other people will think you don't know what's going on. Good questions show just the opposite—that you're alert, thoughtful, and invested. For at least 1 week, make a point to ask a good question in each of your classes. Bring it up in class, ask your instructor after class, or e-mail your question to the instructor. How did this experiment improve your ability to ask questions? How did you feel about becoming more actively involved in your learning?

_____

_____

_____

Manage Life

5. Your IDEAL

Consider an important issue in your life right now and apply the IDEAL problem-solving strategy listed below. Did this help you come up with some ideas for resolving this issue? Why or why not?

Identify the problem: _____

Define the problem: _____

Explore alternative approaches: _____

Act on the best strategy: _____

Look back to evaluate the effects: _____

6. "I Wonder ..."

Here is a simple exercise to increase your creative thinking. Each day for a week, take a few minutes to ask yourself a question that begins with "I wonder . . ." Ask this question about a particular aspect of your life. For example, "I wonder . . .

- . . . if there is a more efficient way to get ready for the day."
- . . . if I'd like four kinds of cereal mixed up together."
- . . . what outcomes would result if I visited during my professor's office hour."
- . . . how I could have behaved differently in the fight I had with my best friend."

   It's important not to censor yourself, no matter how impractical or outlandish the question sounds. If your exercise produces serious questions, you may want to pose them to your friends. Listen carefully to your friends' responses. You'll probably discover that your questions have some assumptions that deserve to be challenged or fine-tuned (Goleman et al., 1992).

Connect and Communicate

7. Creative Surfing

Find out what the Internet has to offer concerning problem solving. Enter "problem solving" into a search engine and visit at least three sites that address the issue. List the sites and their main premises below. What did you learn about problem solving? Why has the Internet become such a boon to problem solving?

Site #1: _____

Site #2: _____

Site #3: _____

8. Brainstorm Credentials

Think about the experiences you have already had as a brainstormer. Whether they were satisfying or not, evaluate which components you are good at and which could stand some improvement:

Being uninhibited about expressing ideas
Identifying the strengths in others' ideas
Suppressing criticism
Generating lots of ideas
Applying criteria to choose a solution
Playing devil's advocate

Build a Bright Future

9. Anticipating Troubles

Football coach Lou Holtz once said, "I think everyone should experience defeat at least once during their career. You learn a lot from it." As you consider a preferred scenario for how you want to create your career, brainstorm some of the kinds of mistakes that would be likely in that career. See if you can rank-order the mistakes in terms of their lethality. Are there any mistakes that you couldn't really bounce back from?

_____

_____

_____

_____

_____

10. Service Advantage

Unlike Holley Frommel, not everyone who does a service learning project can turn it into a full-time job. However, there are still many advantages to taking courses that require this kind of investment. See if you can identify the advantages of service learning to you, to your instructor, to the college, and to the group for whom the service is rendered. For practice, see if you can also identify some potential disadvantages.

_____

_____

_____

_____

_____

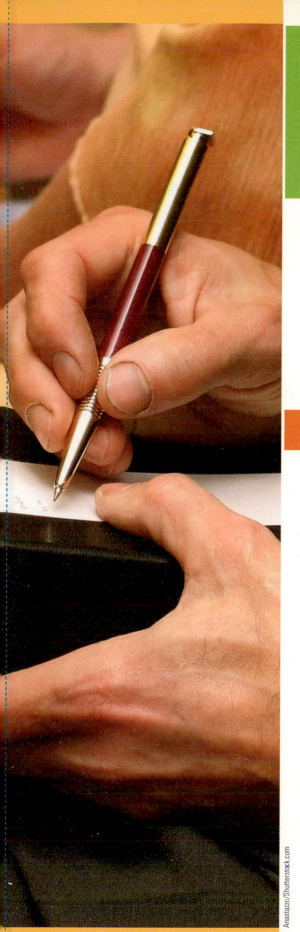

Take Winning Notes

Chapter 7

KNOW YOURSELF

TO SUCCEED IN COLLEGE, take charge of new ideas and make good judgments about their importance to your learning. Learning to use the best strategies for taking notes in class and reading effectively will contribute significantly to your academic success in college. To see where you are right now, place a check mark next to only those items that apply to you.

How Well Do I Process Information?

	Very Much Like Me	Somewhere In Between	Not at All Like Me
I absorb information from lectures, group work, and textbooks in an organized way.			
I read assignments before going to the class.			
I know how to stay focused during difficult lectures.			
I'm familiar with different note-taking methods.			
I know the difference in purpose and value when comparing primary and secondary research sources.			
I pace my reading according to my depth of understanding.			
I use various strategies to read more effectively and efficiently.			
I use my notes to improve my learning as well as my test performance.			
I can manage the stresses associated with taking notes in lecture and reading.			
I see the connection between effective note-taking and professional success.			

Anastazzo/Shutterstock.com

Spotlight On...

Rachelle Taylor
Improving the Quality of Life for People with Disabilities

When she was in high school, a trip to a ski resort with friends in 1999 changed Rachelle Taylor's life. She attempted a 360-degree jump but instead landed on her neck, snapping her back in half. Most people would have been daunted by such an unexpected turn, which left Rachelle as a paraplegic, but she decided to reclaim her life after a year of therapy and graduated with her high school class on time.

Courtesy of Rachelle Taylor

Rachelle Taylor's successful strategies for processing information helped her realize her goal of becoming an advocate for people with disabilities.

Rachelle pursued a major in political science with an emphasis in law and a goal of becoming an advocate for people with disabilities at San Diego State University. She offers inspirational talks to help people understand physical disability. She also consults with designers and architects to make the world more accessible. "I am a living advertisement for spinal cord injuries," Taylor says. "Everywhere I go, I end up talking about it with someone" (Christy, 2005).

Despite the adversity she faced, Rachelle attributed her success in keeping up with classes to two special strategies. First, she routinely rewrote lecture notes she took in class as a way to stay actively involved with material. On the second pass, she made stronger connections among the points, verified her understanding of difficult concepts, and created tidier notes. Developing and maintaining strong relationships with her teachers and professors was especially important in her college success. Following her accident, she discovered how much her teachers genuinely cared about her success. They actively pitched in to help her keep up and realize her goals.

Rachelle Taylor emphasized how important it was for her to develop her own individual strategies for coping with the mounds of information she needed to master in college. Examine the chapter outline to anticipate where you are likely to learn the most to deal with your own mounds of data.

Clarify Expectations

College demands enormous preparation, requiring you to sift through and master an extraordinary amount of information. Extracting what you need from academic resources is no small feat.

Strong academic performance depends on your ability to process information from lectures and texts effectively and efficiently (Beglar & Murray, 2010). This chapter describes a simple, easy-to-remember approach for sorting through information and making good decisions about what you need to learn and how to learn it—the "Five Cs":

- *Commit* yourself to do your best work.
- *Concentrate* to eliminate distractions and focus on the material.
- *Capture* critical information.
- *Connect* new ideas to what you already know.
- *Consolidate* new information with optimal strategies.

Whether you are learning from an instructor, a printed text, or the Internet, you can apply this approach to your classes and reading assignments to help you learn more effectively. Clarifying expectations can increase your commitment to the hard work ahead.

Commit to Preparation

Here's a surprising fact: Most college students don't do their assigned reading at the time that would be most useful to build their learning, if at all (Nilson, 2006). Many students sandwich their reading assignments between intense work and social obligations. Sleep-deprived college students find it easier to drift off than to follow through. Some students don't bother to buy course textbooks, expecting—sometimes disastrously—that all the important "stuff" will be covered in lectures. They hope to get by with merely course credit, rather than investing fully to maximize the impact of their tuition dollars.

To be successful, develop the expectation that academic work is your primary obligation while you are in college. Although class attendance and preparation tasks should be your first priority if you hope to succeed, circumstances can distract you from your good intentions. Think about how you will stand out among your peers and establish yourself as a genuine scholar if you prepare properly.

Read the course syllabus to determine the topics for discussion in class. Do the reading associated with these lecture topics *before* you get to class. Instructors expect that you will not just be present for class, but that you also will be prepared for class by using effective reading strategies and note-taking skills that will help you retain key information.

Successful students start fresh; they tend to buy new, rather than used, textbooks since others' marginal notes may be distracting and inaccurate (Bell & Limber, 2010).

Commit to Participation

It's easy to follow through on your commitment to learning when courses match your learning style or personal interest. When the content of the class or the style of the instructor is not such a good match, making a strong commitment to the class is even more important. This commitment involves more than just showing up, whether filling a seat in a traditional classroom or sitting in front of a monitor. Before each class, get ready to be in top form to learn while you are in the class.

Anticipate Any extra work you do to prepare for each class period will help you build a network of ideas about the course content and ultimately make it easier for you to demonstrate what you know at test time. Review your notes from the last class as well as your reading assignment. Identify areas that are difficult to understand. Think about questions that could clarify them, or search the Web to find other sources that might make these ideas clearer.

Think about the format for the class, and prepare accordingly. Will it be a lecture, lab, or seminar? Will it be face-to-face (F2F), blended, or fully online? In a seminar format, the instructor expects that your participation will be more active and visible than in a traditional lecture. Labs may entail careful rehearsal of directions before class begins so that you can allocate in-class time more profitably to the procedures. Online courses work best when you make thoughtful contributions to threaded discussions based on the information you have already learned. Anticipating how the class will flow and which ideas will be most important will help you learn more effectively, regardless of the class format.

Be Timely In F2F classes, get to class a few minutes early. Arriving early gives you a chance to review your notes and to be ready to go as soon as the instructor begins. Well-organized instructors may use the first few minutes of class to review the previous class, and they often develop favorable expectations of their own about hard workers who show up early. Reviewing allows you to rehearse what you've been learning and sets the stage for how the upcoming class will unfold.

Time is also critical in online course design. Although the course may permit some latitude about how you pace your work, you will probably find a rigorous set of deadlines.

Own the Responsibility You are in charge of your learning. From the outset of each course, expect to be present and participate to optimize your learning. Taking accurate, high-quality notes can improve your test performance (Peverly et al., 2007). In fact, studies that compare the impact of taking notes with not taking notes have shown significantly higher memory for note-takers (Larson, 2009).

Unfortunately, life will throw some curves at you to undermine this commitment. In some cases, you may need to miss a class because of health reasons or an unexpected emergency. Even though an instructor may excuse your class absence, the instructor may not have the information presented in the class available for students who did not attend the class. A very important point is to select a "study buddy" who can help you catch up if you must miss a class. But exercise good judgment. See Danger Zone: "Getting By with a Little Help from Your Friends" to explore threats to your best performance.

You also need to decide whether to lend your notes to others. If you genuinely want to help others in the class, by all means, say "yes." Lend only a copy of your notes rather than your originals to buffer yourself from accidents and losses.

Develop Competence in Taking Lecture Notes

You will learn best in a lecture if you concentrate on the task at hand and become a competent note-taker (Kisslinger, 2011).

Concentrate in Class

Many factors can influence how effectively you concentrate during class: distractions, your natural interest in the topic, your physical status, and possibly your learning style preferences. For example, if you're an auditory learner or have a natural interest in the topic, getting what you need from a lecture may not be difficult. Regardless of the quality of information the instructor provides, you will fare best if you can use strategies that will help you focus on the ideas being presented.

Choose a Quiet Space If you can't see or hear clearly in lecture, find a spot in the class where you can. The instructor may not realize how noisy the room is for you, so do what you need to ensure your best hearing. Close doors and windows to reduce unwanted noise. Move away from chatty neighbors.

Reduce Off-Task Pressures Get the sleep you need, and eat before class to quiet a growling stomach. If a specific worry keeps bothering you, write it down separately from your notes. Promise yourself that you'll worry about it later so that you can let it go for now.

Stay Tuned In during Lecture If something in the lecture distresses you—either content or delivery style—focus on hearing what you most likely will be tested on. Breathe deeply and use other stress-management techniques to stay in tune.

DANGER ZONE

Getting By with a Little Help from Your Friends

Hallie was feverish and decided to stay in bed rather than struggle through government class and possibly spread her illness to her classmates. She phoned her best friend Terry to let her know she wouldn't be there and asked Terry to make a copy of her notes. When Terry passed Hallie the notes a few days later, Hallie was startled to see just three lines on the page. The notes said, "There was a guest speaker, Mr. Johnson, or something like that. He was really boring. You were right to stay home in bed." Unfortunately for Hallie (and Terry), Mr. Johnson was a local city council member whose presentation served as the heart of the next exam.

When you miss a class, don't assume that any old notes will do. When life throws emergency conditions your way, borrow notes only from students who have demonstrated a good grasp of the course. Your best friend might not be the best person to ask.

Track Your Progress At the end of each class or study session, estimate what percentage of time you were on track and write it in the upper-right corner of your notes. Try to make regular improvements in your rate.

Listen Actively Many students expect that lectures provide an opportunity to relax while the instructor does the work. However, even when the class design emphasizes lecture, you should expect to do your part by listening actively (Lebauer, 2011).

On average, speakers say about 150 words per minute, and listeners can process about 500 words per minute, more than three times the speed of speech (Nichols, 1961). Put that extra time to its best use through active listening. Active listeners sort through the information they hear and figure out what's most important. They connect what they hear with things they already know. Although it's harder mental work, active listening is an efficient way to get the most from a lecture.

In contrast, passive listeners merely write down the instructor's words without necessarily understanding the ideas or making judgments about their importance. This approach shifts actual learning to a later time, when the ideas have already faded. Putting off learning until later not only makes ideas harder to learn but also steals time from preparations for the next assignment.

Adapt to Instructor Style Instructors differ in their lecture skill. Some make learning easy; others make it tough. And students can react differently to the same lecturer. For example, some students might find an instructor's personal anecdotes riveting, while others might think of the examples as an annoying waste of time.

Develop your listening skills so that you can compensate for any lack in speaking ability on the part of your instructors. See Highlight: "Tame the Tough Lecture" to help with the most challenging lecture styles.

Capture Key Ideas from Listening

Some instructors will help you spot their main ideas by starting with a preview, outline, or map of the material that a lecture will cover. Some may provide advance access to their PowerPoint slides and even provide full or partial notes to assist your learning. Others won't take special steps to help you develop effective notes, but they will still expect you to grasp their organization (even when it's obscure) (Lebauer, 2011). How can you experiment to find the right note-taking groove?

Identify Key Words, Themes, and Main Points Key words, themes, and main points are ideas that the instructor repeats, highlights, illustrates with examples, supports with related facts, or displays on a blackboard or screen. Many instructors organize courses around a central set of concepts or terms. Don't gloss over words you don't recognize. Any unfamiliar term or phrase is a new idea you need to learn. Identify emerging themes from the details of the lecture.

Recognize Organization Patterns in the Lecture Academic information comes in predictable patterns (Strong et al., 2002). Facts, stories, predictions, analogies, statistics, opinions, comparisons, and explanations provide the details to drive the main point home. Listen for some key words that will signal these patterns of how main points and supporting details relate to help you to grasp the flow of the lecture and minimize getting lost in details and digressions (Kisslinger, 2011). Some examples of such patterns include:

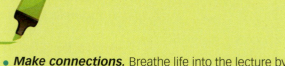

Tame the Tough Lecture

Here are some examples of the kinds of lecturers that you may experience during your college years, as well as strategies for working with them:

THE FAST-TALKING LECTURER

Enthusiastic instructors may talk too fast for you to catch what they're saying. When you're confronted with a fast talker:

- **Say, "Please slow down."** Most fast-talking instructors know that they talk too fast. Many appreciate a reminder to adjust their pace, but of course, make this request in a polite manner.
- **Encourage the instructor to write down the key terms.** Seeing them written down will help you understand them. Also, when the instructor writes on the board, you may be able to catch up.
- **Focus on the major thrust, not the detail.** Fast talkers are hardest for students who attempt to take notes word-for-word. Concentrate on the major ideas instead.

THE BEWILDERING LECTURER

Some instructors use more sophisticated language than you may be used to hearing. Some give boring lectures because they have lost interest in their work, have never learned how to teach information effectively, or simply suffer from stage fright. The following strategies can improve your learning when your instructor is hard to understand:

- **Prepare for class carefully.** If you do the assigned readings before class, you'll already be familiar with many key concepts.

- **Make connections.** Breathe life into the lecture by applying what you hear to what you already know.
- **Ask for restatements or examples.** If you persist in asking for interpretations when an instructor's language is too complex or too bland, the lecturer is likely to simplify to avoid losing the time it takes to reexplain.
- **Change your attitude.** Show active interest even in challenging courses. You may emerge from the class with an enriched vocabulary and more self-discipline in working with people who aren't quite your cup of tea.

THE DISORGANIZED LECTURER

Some instructors give poorly organized lectures. They may go off on tangents or don't teach from an organized plan. If you have a chaotic instructor:

- **Look at the big picture.** Concentrate on the larger themes so that you won't feel overwhelmed by disconnected details.
- **Rely on the textbook.** Use this important resource to fill in the blanks that a chaotic lecturer produces. The text publisher may offer other support features, such as a study guide or website, that can contribute to your understanding.
- **Form a study group.** Pool your resources to make sense of the teaching.
- **Impose organization.** Use note-taking strategies that will help you see the connections among the ideas. Try to organize the lecture materials to give them some structure; for example, create an outline.

- **Listing.** Instructors present all the relevant facts, concepts, and events using signal words such as *first, second, also, in addition, another, moreover, next,* and *furthermore.*
- **Comparison.** These patterns focus on similarities and differences, such as *on one hand, similarly, in contrast, but, then, either, or, compared to, opposite of,* and *like.*
- **Sequence.** Many times, instructors will incorporate timelines, chronologies, or stages. Signal words include *first, second, finally, while, now, then,* and *next.*
- **Problem-Solving.** The instructor identifies a problem, establishes conditions for solving the problem, explains the solution, and predicts the aftereffects. Signal words include *since, resulting, hypothesis, leading to, because, so, if . . . then,* and *solution.*
- **Cause-and-Effect.** These patterns involve showing causal connections between two event expressed as *prediction, effect, causation,* and *control.*

- *Examples.* These patterns involve defining a concept and then offering examples or illustrations to clarify the term. Signal words include *for example*, *for instance*, *other examples include*, and *such as*.

Relate Details to the Main Point Instructors usually intend their stories or analogies to do more than entertain. Check to make sure that you understand why the instructor chose a particular story or example. Pay attention to how much the instructor relies on important details at test time. Some instructors may expect you to be accountable for all the details. Others will pay less attention to your rote recall of minor details but will instead emphasize your ability to communicate your understanding of the main ideas with the most important details.

Listen for Clues Pay special attention to words that signal a change of direction or special emphasis. Transition speech, such as "in contrast to" or "let's move on to" or even "this will be on the next exam," signals the change of topics or emergence of new key points. Lists usually signify important material that is also easy to test. Instructors are most likely to test for ideas that they consider exciting, so listen for any special enthusiasm.

Work on Your "Sixth Sense" Some students just seem to have a knack for figuring out which aspects of an instructor's material will end up on the test. Actively categorize what your instructor is saying by asking yourself questions such as:

- "Is this statement central to my understanding of today's topic?"
- "Does this example help clarify the main ideas?"
- "Is this a tangent (an aside) that may not help me learn the central ideas?"

Save Your Energy Don't write down what you already know. If you have read your assignment, you should be able to recognize when the lecture overlaps the text. Open your text and follow along, making notes in the margins where the instructor stays close to the text. Pay closer attention when what you hear sounds unfamiliar.

Connect Ideas

The best listeners don't just check in with the lecturer from time to time. They work at listening by using strategies to create more enduring impressions of the lecture and to escape daydreaming (Kisslinger, 2011).

Paraphrase What You Hear If you can't translate the ideas from a lecture into your own words, you may need to do more reading or ask more questions until you are able to do so.

Relate Key Ideas to What You Already Know When you can see how the course ideas connect to other aspects of your life, the ideas will be easier to remember. For example, if you're studying in sociology how societies organize into different economic classes, apply those ideas to the neighborhood where you grew up.

Make a Note of Unknown Words Sometimes unknown words are a signal that you've missed something. Keep a running list of the words that gave you trouble. Your list becomes a natural tool for review before exams.

Get Involved When you determine the direction the class will take, you can come up with examples that make ideas more compelling. Suggest those examples to the instructor. Say, "Would this be an example of what you are talking about?" Ask questions. Answer questions when the instructor asks them. Participate in discussions that are prompted by the lecture. No matter what form your involvement takes, it will help you stay engaged with the ideas in the lecture.

Consolidate New Information

Taking great notes is your opportunity to think and learn actively during your time in class. With proper planning and monitoring, great notes will cut your review time and help consolidate your learning to enhance your test performance (Peverly et al., 2007).

Asking questions in class will help you stay connected with the ideas in the lecture and will create a dynamic learning environment that helps others learn, too.

Develop Your Style A successful note-taking style reflects not just the complexity of the course content and the lecturer's style but your own learning preferences as well. If you're a visual learner, use images, arrows, or other graphic organizers to help you remember the important material and relationships more easily. Color-code parts of your notes or draw sketches. If you're an auditory learner, you may thrive in lectures; however, you may be tempted to take down every word. It is critical to translate input from a lecture into your own voice, especially if English isn't your native language (Wilson, 1999).

The worst strategy students can adopt when taking lecture notes is trying to get down every word the instructor says. Transcribers reproduce the lecture word-for-word, an approach that pays off for medical records transcribers, but not for students.

Professional transcribers do well if they can get down 80 to 90 words per minute using shorthand. By contrast, students who transcribe an instructor's words without using shorthand may write at fewer than 20 words per minute (Kierwa, 1987). By concentrating on capturing individual words, they get only a portion of the message and certainly miss the big picture.

Sometimes students actually use note taking to dodge the harder work of paying careful attention and thinking. Their learning likely would be better served by devoting more attention to the lecture.

Exploit Technology Technology can also enhance your note-taking prowess. Many students like to bring laptops to class to capture information. Unless you have developed facility with a graphics program, you are more likely to rely on the word-processing program to help you with the verbal aspects of the class. However, many software programs convert written notes into typewritten text and graphics. Recognize that instructors may monitor your use of the laptop to ensure that you are paying attention rather than engaging in an off-task activity.

If you use digital note taking, experiment with the best way to manage your records. At a minimum, maintain a separate folder for each course on your hard drive or desktop to help you separate and sort your classes. A file for each class

© The New Yorker Collection 1996 Arnie Levin from cartoonbank.com. All Rights Reserved.

"As I get older, I find I rely more and more on these sticky notes to remind me."

experience, featuring a prominent date and housed in the appropriate folder, will help you keep the activities appropriately sequenced and make the class easier to review.

Choose the Best Method Choose the approach that suits your learning needs and preferences. Here are several popular note-taking methods.

Summary Method Monitor the lecture for critical ideas and pause at intervals to summarize what you think is most important. Summarizing appeals most to students with auditory learning preferences. They are comfortable in the world of words and have learned to trust that they can extract the key ideas after the fact. Translating the material into their own words provides great writing practice.

Writing summaries may be time-consuming, but it helps you take responsibility for judging what is crucial and relating that to other aspects of the course. It's also an effective way to handle a disorganized lecturer.

Outlining An outline summarizes key points and subpoints, as demonstrated in Figure 7.1, "Take It In." When you use an outline form, your results are neat and well organized. Naturally, outlines are easiest to create when the lecture itself is well organized. Some outliners don't use numbers and letters because the task is too distracting. They simply indent to signify subpoints. The distinctiveness of an outline appeals to students who are especially good at analysis and critical thinking.

Students who like to analyze enjoy outlines that clearly highlight the main points with supportive details tucked neatly under subheadings. The outline shows links among ideas and reduces extra verbiage that can distract from key points. If you are a visual learner, an outline can especially benefit your learning through its visual display of key headings.

It may not always be easy to impose a crisp outline on a messy presentation. That challenge can sometimes divert the outliner's attention from listening to the

This format organizes lecture coverage by main headings and subheadings.

Chapter 6
Target Information

I. Commit, Concentrate, Capture, Connect
    A. Identifying what you need is hard work
        1. From lecture
        2. From text
    B. 4-part approach can help make good decisions

II. Take Charge of Lectures
    A. Commit to the course
        1. Not hard to commit when interest is high
        2. When not a good match . . .
            a. Be present
            b. Be ready
            c. Be punctual

    B. Concentrate
        1. Overcome distractions
            a. Sit near front
            b. Reduce noise
            c. Reduce off-task pressures
            d. Stay tuned in
            e. Track your progress
        2. Adapt to Teaching Styles
            a. To cope with fast talkers
                 (1) Tell them "Slow down"
                 (2) Ask them to write down key words
                 (3) Focus on key ideas
            b. To cope with bewildering lecturers . . .

FIGURE 7.1 Take It In

content of the lecture to the process of creating an acceptable outline. However, outlining is a popular strategy if students choose to rewrite their class notes.

The Cornell Method Shown in Figure 7.2, "The Cornell Method," you draw lines to create functional areas on the page. Use the largest area on the right side of the page to take your notes during class. After class is over, use the blank left side of the page to write short headings or questions for each part of your notes. Use the bottom of the page for a summary or other comments and questions.

The Cornell method creates a great tool for reviewing. Cover up the right portion of the page and use the phrases or questions on the left side as prompts. As you read each prompt, practice recalling the details on the right. Choose the Cornell method if you demonstrate a preference for auditory learning and are conscientious about review. The format commits you to working actively with verbal representation of the notes, capturing themes, analyzing trends, and generating questions.

The Question Technique An adaptation of the Cornell system may be especially helpful in getting you ready to take exams (Pauk, 2000). Rather than highlighting key phrases or words in the left column, formulate specific questions that are answered by the material you have written on the right. For example, your class notes on photosynthesis on the right side might reflect the question "How do you define photosynthesis?" on the left.

Concept Maps A concept map provides visual cues about how ideas are related by creating information hubs related to the main topic (Novak & Cañas, 2008), as shown in Figure 7.3, "The Concept Map." Some students construct concept maps from lecture notes during class. Others may draw concept maps after class as a way to review the material.

Concept maps especially appeal to visual learners with a creative flair. They are more engaging to create and benefit your memory more than other formats for visual learners. A risk with this method, however, is that the concept mapper

The Cornell method separates running notes taken during class from summary phrases and an overall summary or comments added after class. To review, cover the material on the right and pratice recalling it from the cues on the left.

	Dr. King – – Psychology 21 Tues. 9 – 14 – 02
	Topic: Optimism & Pessimism – – Seligman's theory
Success:	Talent and desire, 2 keys to success. Is there a 3rd key – –
2 keys or 3?	"optimism"? (=expecting to succeed)? The real test = how you
	react when something bad happens. Give up or fight on?
	Psych lab experiments can teach dogs to be helpless. If dog is
Lab studies on	trained to think it has no control over when it will get shocked, it
learning/unlearning	starts acting helpless even when it could jump away & not get
helplessness	shocked. Same type thing happens to people in childhood. If they
	don't think they can change things, they act helpless: pessimistic.
	But you can also train a dog out of being helpless. All depends
	on expecting to be or not be in control.
	How optimists vs. pessimists explain bad events.
	Pessimist:
	1. Personal – – "Bad things are my fault."
"P P P"	2. Permanent – – "Can't get better."
	3. Pervasive – – "Affects everything I do."
	Optimist:
	1. Impersonal – – "Bad things not my fault."
	2. Momentary – – "Can change tomorrow."
	3. Particular – – "Doesn't affect the rest of me."
Pessimism ⟶	Everyone can get depressed, but pessimists stay depressed longer.
depression	Why? Because of how they explain things.
Therapy = Change	Cognitive therapy: Change the way pessimist explains things to cure
explanations	their depression. How? First get them to hear what they tell
	themselves when things go bad. Then get them to change what they
	say.

Seligman found that desire and talent don't always win. Optimism also important. Pessimists can become "helpless" in hard times. Optimists recover faster. Training pessimists to think more optimistically might reduce depression.
Q: But how does it work? Find out Thursday!

FIGURE 7.2 The Cornell Method

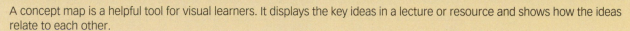

A concept map is a helpful tool for visual learners. It displays the key ideas in a lecture or resource and shows how the ideas relate to each other.

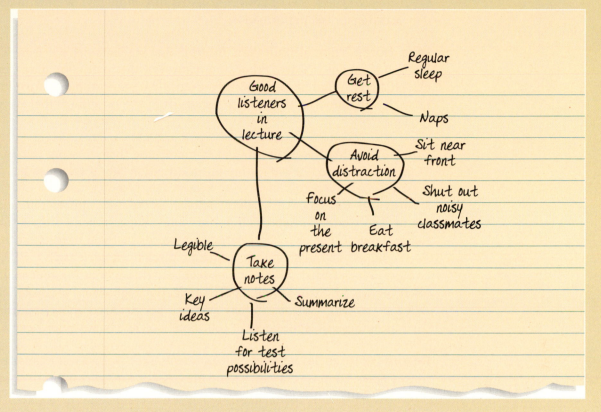

FIGURE 7.3 The Concept Map

can be more drawn to the creative process and committed to making an aesthetically pleasing map than to listening to the content of the lecture and correctly identifying the relationships being represented.

Master Note-Taking Strategies for Lectures Whichever format you choose, combine it with the following strategies for optimal learning.

Gather Notes Systematically Get in the habit of placing your notes in the same place, whether it is a folder on your Mac or a spiral-bound lined pad. Use this location only for the notes that belong to the topic. If you are using individual notebooks for each topic, be sure to include your name and e-mail address or phone number, in case you lend your notes to a classmate or they become lost. Three-ring binders allow you to rearrange and add pages. Write on only one side of the page to make your notes easy to arrange and review later. Some students, especially tactile learners, use index cards because they're easy to carry, organize, and review.

Clearly Identify the Context Include the topic or title of the lecture, if any, along with its date. This notation will make it easier to track down specific information in sequential order when it's time to review.

Go Long Psychologists have suggested that students who make comprehensive notes tend to do better on exams than those who take sketchy, cryptic notes (Williams & Eggert, 2002). Longer notes require more review time to consolidate learning for test performance.

Take Notes from All Relevant Input Some students believe that only the instructor's input is worth recording. However, the instructor may treat any class material as fair game for testing, even when other students introduce the ideas. Also summarize the relevant details from videos or films that are shown in class.

Don't Erase Mistakes Erasing takes more time than crossing out an error. Drawing a line also lets you restore the information later if you need it.

Abbreviate Use standard abbreviations to record information quickly. Figure 7.4, "Common Abbreviations for Notes," suggests some simple substitutions. Develop your own abbreviations for words that you need to write often. For example, you can abbreviate academic disciplines, such as *PSY*, *BIO*, *ENG*, and *LIT*. When instructors use terms regularly throughout the course, develop abbreviations for them as well. For example, *EV* might stand for *evolution*, and *A/R* for *accounts receivable*. When you use personalized abbreviations, write their meanings inside the cover of your notebook as a handy reference.

Record Lectures Selectively Some students like to record lectures as a backup for the notes, but it isn't always a good idea. Ask the instructor's permission and only record the lecture only if you:

- need the complete text of a lecture, as when the content is extremely difficult or tricky.
- have a learning disability that hinders listening carefully or accurately.
- are less efficient in the language in which the lecture is being presented because that language is not your primary language.
- have a plan for how to listen regularly to the recording.
- take advantage of commuting time to listen.
- must be absent but can get a classmate to record for you.

Without a plan or special need to justify recording, you may end up wasting time and energy to produce a stockpile of audio recordings that you never listen

---

Using your own abbreviations or the standard abbreviations in this list will save you time when you take notes.

i.e.	= that is (to clarify by restating a point)	<	= less than
e.g.	= for example (to clarify by adding a typical case)	>	= more than
vs.	= versus (to identify a contrasting point)	k	= 1,000 (as in 10 k for 10 thousand; k kilo)
∴	= therefore (to come to a conclusion)	~	= approximately
∵	= because	??	= I'm confused
w/	= with	*	= important, testable
w/o	= without	@	= at
→	= leads to		

© Cengage Learning 2013

FIGURE 7.4 Common Abbreviations for Notes

220   CHAPTER 7   Take Winning Notes

to. You also may be tempted not to listen as carefully as you might while the class is actually in progress.

Review Your Work The final details of becoming a competent note-taker during lectures involve steps that only the best students tend to pursue. However, each element can set you apart as a serious learner.

Review Your Notes Often Review your notes right after class whenever possible to consolidate your learning, and add whatever might be missing. Highlight certain phrases, identify the key points, and revise unclear notes. Review notes from the previous class just before the next meeting as a way to get back into the subject.

Don't record lectures unnecessarily, or you may end up with an unmanageable inventory of recordings that you probably will never listen to.

Request Feedback about Your Notes Especially in classes where you struggle with note taking, see your instructor during office hours and ask for help. Ask whether you are capturing the main ideas in your notes and get suggestions for how to improve.

Evaluate Your Note-Taking Strategy When you get a test back, examine the format of your notes to see what accounted for your success. Continue to practice only the strategies that served you well. Evaluate your own style of listening by completing Know Yourself: Self-Assessment 7.1, "Auditing Your Note-Taking Style for Lectures," on page 242 at the end of this chapter. The results will show where you can improve.

Develop Competence in Taking Notes from Reading

The five Cs—Commit, Concentrate, Capture, Connect, and Consolidate—work as well for reading as they do for lectures. A systematic approach to reading will help you to achieve your reading goals and make your learning more efficient and effective.

Concentrate during Reading

The scope and complexity of Rachelle Taylor's information-processing skills (discussed at the beginning of the chapter) highlight an important feature about the role of concentration during note taking. Some material must be studied for complete mastery and

Kristin Beniek

Spotlight On...

Helping Others Take Great Notes

Kristin Beniek made an unusual commitment to help others get the most from lectures by becoming a sign language interpreter for the University of Minnesota (Heilman, 2007). After obtaining a visual arts degree from St. Cloud State University, she entered the Peace Corps, and during her 3-year assignment to Ghana, she learned to sign. At age 31, she completed an associate's degree in American Sign Language. As a campus interpreter, she gets requests to go to all kinds of events where she helps hearing-impaired students "to take it all in." Kristin expects to keep refining her skills through ongoing professional development. "It's always different," she says. "There's always something developing, and you're always learning something new."

requires full concentration; other information requires merely a "drive by" in which concentration can be less intense.

If you're very interested in a topic and already know something about it, you may not need specific strategies to comprehend the reading. You can just dive in and take appropriate notes. But what if the reading is unfamiliar and difficult? In that case, read both selectively and systematically (Conley, 2012). The next section provides some specific pointers on making sound decisions when your workload becomes overwhelming.

Capture Key Ideas from Reading

Many of the note-taking strategies used in lecture can be imported to taking notes during reading. However, you also have the opportunity to exercise more control over what you do and learn in taking notes during reading. Use Know Yourself: Self-Assessment 7.2, "What's Your Reader Profile?," on page 243 at the end of this chapter to see how your reading skills stack up before you explore all the options.

Recognize the Purpose Speculate about how each individual reading assignment can contribute to the learning goals. Are there critical pieces of information that you must learn in the reading, or is this assignment one that serves to "enrich" learning ("It won't be on the test," for example)? In the latter case, the priority for reading won't be as intense.

Identify Key Words, Themes, and Main Points Texts, just like lectures, tend to be organized in predictable ways (Vacca, Vacca, & Mraz, 2011). Paragraphs usually contain thesis statements that provide the focus for what the writer is trying to say. Paragraphs in the beginning of texts orient the reader to their purpose. Paragraphs toward the end often summarize the most important ideas. In some texts, critical information is highlighted with bold or italicized fonts.

Read Strategically and Selectively Sometimes reading assignments can feel overwhelming, especially if they are long and complex. Efficient students recognize that they may not need to read every single word in an assignment, especially when pressed for time across different courses. Good students develop a reading system that addresses different levels at which they can read, depending on the difficulty and importance of the material as well as the time they have to devote to the task (Hippie, 2010). A good system includes some of the following types of reading: previewing, skimming, active reading, analytic reading, and reviewing. Figure 7.5, "Choose Your Reading Effort Level," demonstrates how these different strategies are related.

Previewing Preview all material before you sit down to read. Previewing helps you estimate how intense your reading effort will need to be and how much time it will take to complete the assignment.

For effective previewing, look at these factors:

- *The context for the assignment.* To see how the assignment fits into the course, think about the class activities that have led up to the assignment.
- *The length of the reading.* By applying your reading speed to the number of pages in the assignment, you can estimate how long it will take.
- *The structure and features of the reading.* A good time to take a reading break is at the end of a section. Also, textbook features such as summaries can help you rehearse your learning.
- *The difficulty of the reading.* Higher-level material may require more than one reading.

Approaching your reading assignments strategically means adopting different reading strategies. The type of reading you choose depends on your available time, the complexity of the material, and your motivation to master the ideas. As you go from the top to the bottom of the pyramid, the intensity of your effort increases: You become more involved with the material, and the reading task becomes more demanding. The consequences of your review may return you to the reading to skim, read actively, or read analytically.

For any given assignment, review after your most intense level of reading. Return to previous levels if review suggests that you need to do so.

INTENSITY OF EFFORT

Preview

Skim

Read Actively

REVIEW

Read Analytically

FIGURE 7.5 Choose Your Reading Effort Level

Skimming Whereas previewing helps you size up the reading, skimming covers the content at a general level. When you skim, you read at about twice your average rate.

Focus on introductory statements, topic sentences (usually the first sentence in the paragraph), and boldface terms. Slow down to examine summaries carefully. Skimming the text before you settle down to read more intensely can give you a good sense of the kind of information your assignment contains. You'll see where you'll have to read more carefully.

Sometimes you may simply run out of time to read assignments as thoroughly as you should. Rather than abandon your reading, skim some assignments. Reserve this strategy for easier courses so that you can concentrate more intensely on the tougher ones.

As you grow accustomed to how the readings relate to a course and how your instructor chooses test material, your ability to read selectively will improve (Frank, 1996). Skimming provides you with the surface structure of the ideas in the text when that is all you have time for. Successful skimmers can usually participate in class discussions with some confidence if they rehearse the main ideas and have read some key passages.

Active Reading It's easy to engage in empty reading. Your eyes track across the lines of text but your brain fails to register anything meaningful. Read texts actively to prevent the wasted time of empty reading or to avoid having to read the same material again (Conley, 2012; Marr, 2011). Immerse yourself in what the author is trying to say. Identify the main ideas and understand how the supporting points reinforce those ideas. Also, construct the meaning in what you read by linking the information to your own personal knowledge or experience. Use these questions as guidelines for active reading:

- Have I ever experienced anything similar to what is described in the reading?
- How does this relate to things I already know?
- How might this be useful for me to know?
- Do I like or agree with these ideas?
- How does the reading relate to current events?

Active readers form as many links as possible between their personal experience and knowledge and the material they're reading.

Analytic Reading Analytic readers break ideas open or dig underneath their surfaces. They spot flaws in the writer's logic and identify which elements are clear and which are confusing. Analytic reading involves comparing the quality of the work to other related works you have read. Good analytic readers question both the author and themselves as they dig their way through a reading. The following questions may help you become an analytic reader:

- What are the author's values and background? Do these influence the writing? How?
- Does the author's bias taint the truthfulness of what I'm reading?
- What implicit (unstated) assumptions does the author make?
- Do I believe the evidence?
- Is the author's position valid?
- Are the arguments logically developed?
- What predictions follow from the argument?
- What are the strengths and weaknesses of the argument?
- Is anything missing from the position?
- What questions would I want to ask the author?
- Is there a different way to look at the facts or ideas?
- Would these ideas apply to all people in all cultures or in all situations?

Reviewing The final step in a successful reading plan is to review the material after you have read it. Reviewing makes the main points stand out and makes them easier to remember.

Think of reviewing as an opportunity to test yourself on your own comprehension. Question yourself on details or write out summaries of what you've read. The quality of your notes can make all the difference when it's time to study for a test. With well-constructed notes that you have reviewed systematically after your classes, your final review should be a breeze.

Figure 7.6, "Reading Strategies for Different Situations," recommends some combinations for different reading tasks. Another strategy to address the level of reading effort is to think about the overall pace of reading required for the purpose (Schaffzin, 1998). In general, textbook reading requires a slow pace because your goal is mastery of the material. Since you must study and memorize the details to survive a test, it pays to go slowly. In contrast, you can grasp other reading matter, such as the kind you would find in newspapers, magazines, and memos, by using a medium reading speed. Your reading should strive to produce an overall grasp of the main themes and ideas with less attention to the details. Finally, some writing lends itself to a fast pace, such as fiction and other narrative forms.

When you want to develop understanding of the ideas:

Preview → **Active reading** → **Review**

When you want to practice critical thinking about your reading:

Preview → **Analytic reading** → **Review**

When you have trouble retaining what you read:

Preview → **Skim** → **Active reading** → **Review** → **Review**

When you don't have time to read for mastery:

Skim → **Review**

(Pay close attention to summaries and boldface terms.)

FIGURE 7.6 Reading Strategies for Different Situations

Now that you have had an opportunity to explore all the choices you can make regarding depth of reading, take a moment to evaluate what your typical pattern likely is by completing Know Yourself: Self-Assessment 7.3, "What Is Your Reading Pattern?," at the end of the chapter on page 244.

Distinguish between Primary and Secondary Sources There are two general types of readings for courses: primary sources and secondary sources. *Primary sources* refer to material written in some original form, such as autobiographies, speeches, research reports, scholarly articles, government documents, and historical journal articles. For example, you may read the U.S. Constitution as a primary source in your political science class.

Secondary sources summarize or interpret these primary sources. A magazine article that discusses politicians' interpretations of the Constitution generally would be considered a secondary source. Textbooks are secondary sources that try to give a comprehensive view of information from numerous primary works.

You have many more opportunities to read primary sources in college than you did in high school. Many people find reading original works exhilarating. For example, reading a speech by Frederick Douglass about the abolition of slavery will likely stimulate you more than reading interpretations of his speeches. However, primary sources may be more difficult to read than secondary sources. Primary source vocabulary may be more abstract; you may need a dictionary close by to help you decode the meaning. Secondary sources often summarize and interpret the meaning of the primary source. Although original works must be chewed and digested, the secondary source does some of the chewing and digesting for you.

Interpreting original ideas is also more challenging than accepting others' interpretations. When reading primary sources, learn as much as you can about the intentions of the authors and the historical context in which they were writing. Understanding a historical period will help you interpret texts written at that time.

Connect Ideas

Notes from your reading especially help you construct your experience from and shape your reflections about the reading. Following are some specific strategies to help you connect the ideas you read about.

Write Your Notes in Your Own Words Translating an author's words into your own "voice" increases your personal connections to the material and makes it easier to remember. This practice also helps you avoid plagiarism when you use the notes to write a paper. When you literally lift the words of an author from a text and later present these words as your own, you are stealing the thoughts and expressions of another. Instructors likely will view this practice as laziness or deceit and may penalize you.

Avoid Writing Down Things You Don't Understand You simply won't understand some ideas on a first reading. You may feel tempted to write down unclear ideas with the intention of returning to them later. Don't. Instead, mark the passage with a question mark and do what you can to clarify it before you record it and move on.

Think and Record in Images Turn information from the text into some other form, such as a list, table, graph, or picture, to make it easier for you to recall. Diagrams and tables also can be effective tools for summarizing.

Explain Yourself It's easy to read a complex mass of material and think that you understand what you've read when in fact you've missed one or more key ideas. Imagine that you have a study companion who struggles to understand the central ideas in assignments. Regularly explain the key ideas in the reading to your "friend," especially when the material is harder or less interesting for you than usual. When you can't explain the passage easily, you need to review it. Of course, if you use this strategy, you may want to tell your roommates or family about it so they won't think you're losing it!

Make the Author Your Companion As you read, imagine talking to the author as a way of energizing your reading. When you approach reading as one end of a conversation, it may be easier to make comments, to see relationships, and to be critical.

Relate Key Ideas to What You Already Know When you can see how the course ideas connect to other aspects of your life, including your experiences in other courses or contemporary events, the ideas will be easier to

remember. For example, if you're studying in sociology how societies organize into different economic classes, apply those ideas to the neighborhood where you grew up or to ideas from your business or economics class.

Consolidate New Information

What strategies can move the information you've just encountered into long-term retention? Three good strategies to help you retain information longer when you are taking reading notes are highlighting the text, personalizing it, and making external notes as you read.

Highlight the Text Ideally, highlighted topic sentences, key words, and conclusions should make up much less than one-quarter of a text. Although this strategy may keep you engaged with the reading, it presents several hazards. It's easy to slip into mindlessness when you highlight text, with the result that you think you are reading but you aren't absorbing the key ideas. Also, simply highlighting does not show why you thought that passage was important. When it's time to review, you still need to carry the complete text with you. Finally, if you sell your text after the course is over, the highlighting will reduce its value. Other strategies that promote deeper involvement are likely to be more helpful in the long run. See Figure 7.7, "Highlighted Notes from Reading," for a model of effective highlights.

JEFF SPICER/Alpha/Landov

Imagine what fun it would be to engage J. K. Rowling about Harry Potter's exploits. Imagine similar conversations with other authors to get the most from your reading.

Personalize the Text Use marginal notes to simulate an interaction with the author. Contemplate what questions you would like to ask. Identify areas that might not make sense to you. Jot down a personal example that illustrates a key point. Fill the margins with your good connections. To make your learning more vivid, you can draw arrows or thumbs-down signs when you disagree, and circle key terms. Draw symbols. Write summary notes (Fisher & Frey, 2012).

Take External Notes as You Read Earlier in the chapter, you learned about four techniques you can use to take notes from lecture: summarizing, outlining, the Cornell method (with its variant, the question method), and concept mapping. These techniques also work for notes that you take from reading. What are some advantages of applying these methods to taking notes from texts?

Summarizing This technique helps you extract the key ideas from passages and put them in your own words. Summarize after each major subdivision in your reading. If the text has no headings, summarize after you have read a small or sufficient number of pages.

Outlining Outlining imposes a systematic organization with predictable headings (I, A, 1, a . . .) to represent the complexity of the materials you read. Outlines distinguish main points (headings I and A) from supporting points (1 and a) and facilitate quick review for exams. Outlining tends to be a preferred note-taking mode for people who enjoy making explicit the nature of the relationship among concepts in the reading. Outlining from texts works best when the assigned

Minorities and Stardom

Stark, R. (1994). Sociology. 5th Edition.

NBA = African-American?

The majority of players on every team in the National Basketball Association are African American. White boxing champions are rare. A far greater proportion of professional football players are African American than would be expected based on the size of the African-American population. Furthermore, African Americans began to excel in sports long before the Civil Rights Movement broke down barriers excluding them from many other occupations. This has led ==many people, both== African American and white, to ==conclude that African Americans are born with a natural talent for athletics==. How else could they have ==come to dominate== the ranks of superstars?

main question →

The trouble with this biological explanation of African Americans in sports is that it ignores an obvious historical fact: It is typical for ==minorities in North America to make their first substantial progress in sports== (and, for similar reasons, in entertainment). Who today would suggest that Jews have a biological advantage in athletics? Yet at the turn of the century, the number of Jews who excelled in sports far exceeded their proportion in the population. And late in the 19th century, the Irish dominated sports to almost the same extent as African Americans have done in recent decades.

example: Jews showed same pattern 19th cent.

By examining an encyclopedia of boxing, for example, we can draw accurate conclusions about patterns of immigration and periods at which ethnic groups were on the bottom of the stratification system. The (Irish) ==domination of boxing in the latter half of== the 19th century is obvious from the names of heavy-weight champions, beginning with bareknuckle champ Ned O'Baldwin in 1867 and including Mike McCoole in 1869, Paddy Ryan in 1880, John L. Sullivan in 1889, and Jim Corbett in 1892. The list of champions in lower-weight divisions during the same era is dominated by fighters named Ryan, Murphy, Delaney, Lynch, O'Brien, and McCoy.

Early in the 20th century, Irish names became much less common among boxing champions, even though many fighters who were not Irish took Irish ring names. Suddenly, champions had names like Battling Levinsky, Maxie Rosenbloom, Benny Leonard, Abe Goldstein, Kid Kaplan, and Izzy Schwartz. This was the Jewish era in boxing.

Then (Jewish) ==names dropped out of== the lists, and (Italian) and eastern European names came to the fore: Canzoneri, Battalino, LaMotta, Graziano, and Basilio; Yarosz, Lesnevich, Zale, Risko, Hostak, and Servo. By the 1940s, fighters were disproportionately (African American). Today, African-American domination of boxing has already peaked, and Hispanic names have begun to prevail.

history of boxing:

Irish ↓
Jews ↓
Italians ↓
Af. Am.

The current overrepresentation of African Americans in sports reflects two things: first, a *lack of other avenues to wealth and fame,* and, second, the fact that minority groups can overcome discrimination most easily in occupations in which ==the quality of individual performance is most easily and accurately assessed== (Blalock, 1967). These same factors led to the overrepresentation of other ethnic groups in sports earlier in history.

1. ⟩ *key ideas*
2.

It often is difficult to know which applicants to a law school or a pilot training school are the most capable. But we can see who can box or hit a baseball. The ==demonstration of talent==, especially in sports and entertainment, tends to ==break down barriers of== discrimination. As these fall, opportunities in these areas for wealth and fame open up, while ==other opportunities remain closed.== Thus, minority groups will aspire to those areas in which the opportunities are open and will tend to overachieve in these areas.

this is why

FIGURE 7.7 Highlighted Notes from Reading

reading materials are logically organized. If they are not, less rigid strategies may be easier to implement.

The Cornell Method When applied to notes from texts, the Cornell method combines the best features of creating external notes with the personalization of making notes in the margin of your book. When you use this method, subdivide the note page into a main portion summarizing what you read and smaller sections for your responses, answers, questions, and connections, as discussed earlier. Figure 7.8, "The Cornell Method in Reading," provides good examples of note taking from reading.

Concept Mapping This strategy turns the content from the reading into a visual representation. Developing maps strongly appeals to visual learners. Concept maps can get messy if the text contains dense, interrelated content, but they also provide a great tool for review.

Other Note-Taking Strategies A few other tips can make the difference in producing effective and efficient note-taking practices during reading.

Pace Yourself According to the Difficulty Level You may need to read some difficult writing three or four times before it begins to make sense. When you have two or more kinds of reading to complete, read the harder or duller assignment first, while your concentration is strongest.

Work on Reading Faster Fast readers tend to be more effective learners than slow readers, not only because they remember more of what they read but also because they save valuable time (Armstrong & Lampe, 1990). Evaluate your reading speed by completing Know Yourself: Self-Assessment 7.4, "How Fast Do You Read?," at the end of the chapter on page 245. Improve your reading speed by concentrating on processing more words with each sweep of your eye across a line of text. For example, read the last line by dividing it into phrases as you read: Improve your reading speed • by concentrating • on processing more works • with each sweep of your eye • across a line of text.

As you work to take in larger units of meaningful text, both your speed and comprehension should increase. Don't mouth words as you read or trace words with your fingers. Both strategies will slow you down.

Manage Your Reading Session Take breaks at regular intervals throughout a reading session. How long you can read between breaks depends on how hard you have to work to grasp the ideas. Examine the material to see whether there are natural breaks that correspond to your attention span, such as the ends of sections. A fresh start may be required if you find yourself reading and rereading the same passage. Try writing a note on the reading. Take a break. Get something to drink. Call a classmate to confer about your struggle. Return to the passage with an intention to read more slowly until the clouds part. However, do not take a short break to engage in addictive activities. It's probably best to let Angry Birds stay angry and sudoku boxes go unfilled because it may just be too hard to return to work if you divert to activities that quickly become time sinks.

Periodically Evaluate the Quality of Your Notes Especially after an exam, review your reading notes to see how well they worked. What changes should you make to improve your effectiveness or efficiency?

Stark, R. (1994), _Sociology_. Belmont, CA: Wadsworth. p.333

"Natural talent" of A-A's in sports?	Minorities and sports
	Popular biological view: African-Americans born with natural athletic talent because so many pro athletes are A-A, compared with their percentage in U.S. pop.
But similar pattern for other minorities	But other minorities also made their first big progress in sports (& entertainment). See lists of boxing champions:
	* Irish dominate last half 19th century
	* Jews around 1900
	* Italians dominate after Jews
	* A-A dominate after Italians
	* Hispanic champions now (& future)?
	Proposed sociological reason for numbers of A-A in pro sports?
Real reasons for current number of A-A's in sports?	1. "Lack of other avenues to wealth and fame"
	2. "Quality of individual performance easily and accurately assessed" in sports.
	Importance of talent in sports & entertainment tends to break down discrimination barriers in these areas before other areas of life.

People say A-A's excel in pro sports now due just to "biology." But other minorities have gone though the same pattern of excellence in sports until they were accepted in other fields. In sports individual talents can be seen, so discrimination barriers not as bad as in other fields.

Q: What about other sports beside boxing? What about music? Same pattern? How much are opportunities changing for A-A's outside sports?

FIGURE 7.8 The Cornell Method in Reading

© Cengage Learning 2013

Manage Life

Whether you are studying print or media materials or attending class, many challenges await you. Following are some good strategies to help you stay the course so you can learn the information you need to be successful.

Stay Positive

Keep a positive attitude. Others have succeeded before you. Consider Rachelle Taylor's optimism despite the serious challenges she faces in the aftermath of her snowboarding accident. If Rachelle and others can manage their challenging lives effectively, so can you. If you approach your note taking with a feeling of defeat, it will be easier to give up.

Do the Work

The best way to be prepared is to attend all your classes. Even if you haven't done the assigned reading, the class will still be worthwhile. The lecture may be so fascinating that it is easier to sit down and do a double dose of reading in preparation for the next class. If you can't attend class, use good judgment about how to compensate.

Assignments aren't usually optional in college. Instructors design assignments to help students develop expertise in the content and skills that the course has to offer. If you decide not to submit an assignment, you don't just lose points; you also lose ground in your learning. From the outset of the class, plan how to complete all your assignments to get the most from your courses.

Successful students complete assigned readings before class to facilitate their understanding. Some students unwisely assume that reading assignments aren't all that important because the instructor will cover the material in class. Many instructors assign reading as a related but independent resource; they do not review the reading in class. You may be called on to report your impressions. It's embarrassing when you haven't got a clue about what to say.

Plan Time and Space to Read

College reading takes concentration. Schedule blocks of time for reading in a place where you won't be interrupted. On your main schedule, set aside times for study. Clear other concerns from your mind so that you can concentrate. You might want to review the time-management scheduling you completed in Chapter 3: Manage Time Wisely to see if you are including enough time for the reading assignments in your courses.

Students differ about where they prefer to read. Many like the library; others find the library environment too quiet or, conversely, too distracting because of all the people around. Try out a few settings to find out which ones work best for you.

If you can spend only a little time on campus, you may face particular challenges in securing quiet space and uninterrupted time. Some commuters who take public transportation can read and review with ease while they travel. If you're stuck with reading an assignment in a noisy environment, you may want to wear headphones with familiar instrumental music just loud enough to block the distractions. If you have a long drive to school, you can listen to taped classes in the car.

If you have to read in distracting environments, minimize the distraction. For example, on a crowded bus, you might want to read while listening to music played at a low level through headphones.

If you must combine reading with childcare:

- Plan to read during children's nap times, after they have gone to bed, or before they get up.
- Set a timer for 15 minutes and provide activities that your children can do at the table with you. Let them know that at the end of 15 minutes—when the timer goes off—everyone will take a play break.
- Find other students with similar childcare needs. Pool your resources to hire a regular babysitter, or trade babysitting services to free up more time for reading.

Own Your Confusion

It's inevitable: Sometimes you are going to be confused. The instructor may use terms you don't understand or link concepts in ways that may be too subtle to grasp the first time you hear them. If English is your second language, there may be other reasons why you lose your way. The instructor may speak too fast for you to process the information or may use jargon in a way that you haven't previously heard. Clearly mark your notes with a question mark or other code, identifying the problem. Make a point to confer with classmates, check on the Internet, explore your text for backup support, or talk with the instructor after class until you get back on the right path. However, it is unlikely that the confusion will clear without some effort on your part.

Monitor Your Zoning Out Your brain operates at a speed that is not always compatible with the reading. It is normal to find yourself losing focus and getting off task, especially when the material or the lecturer doesn't grab you. If you think your rate of zoning out interferes with your learning, set up a consultation with your college's learning center to see whether some specific strategies will help keep you on task.

Seek Expertise You can ask to have your reading abilities tested formally by reading specialists at the college. They can help you identify specific problems and solutions.

Set Goals Make commitments that will help you feel more responsible for what you've read. Join a study group. Tutor another student who needs help. If you're shy or self-conscious, approach one of your instructors with a plan about how you want to contribute to class on a given day to help build your confidence about participating. Ask whether she could call on you in relation to material you have prepared especially well. Through this unusual but constructive approach, you're likely to gain your instructor's cooperation, because you are demonstrating your motivation while sensitizing the instructor to the fact that participation is hard for you.

 # Connect and Communicate

As you build your note-taking expertise in both lecture and reading, you will undoubtedly notice that the nature of various disciplines influences the kind of notes you take. You also may benefit by reaching out to find new resources that can shed light on the topics at hand. Along the way, your vocabulary will be expanding as well.

Connect to the Disciplines

Liberal arts programs almost always require reading about topics that don't come naturally. In some readings, technical terms may slow you down. Other readings may require more imagination. This section offers tips that will help you read more efficiently in a variety of disciplines, some of which will be more challenging for you than others.

Literature Literature courses include poetry, novels, plays, and short stories. Appreciation of these literature forms comes most easily to people who enjoy reflective learning and who like to think critically. For them, many great works of literature provide wonderful opportunities to learn and think more deeply. Following are some good strategies if you find reading literature to be challenging:

- *Use your imagination.* Visualize the action. Participate at the level the author intended: Use as many senses as the author used—taste, smell, sound—as you recreate the author's world in your imagination.
- *Look for connections.* Are any of the experiences like your own? Do the characters remind you of anyone you know?
- *Monitor theme development.* Most powerful literature concentrates on specific themes. Look for emerging themes and keep track of the manner in which the author pursues the theme. The work will hang together better as you read and as you later try to remember the elements for testing purposes.
- *Make the author real.* Search the Internet for a good biography or personal details about the author. You may gain insight into the author's motivation to create the work.
- *Create a character list.* If the reading is complex, make a list of key figures as they are introduced so you can easily review as the story progresses.
- *Predict what will happen.* Once you understand the direction the work is taking, see whether you can anticipate what happens next.
- *Read aloud.* Some great works are savored best when read aloud. Find a study partner and share the assignment. You will probably need more time, but the investment will be worthwhile, because you will generate more vivid memory cues by reading aloud.
- *Budget sufficient time.* Complex reading takes time. Be sure to set aside sufficient time not just for reading but for thinking, too.
- *Take reasonable short cuts* (Schaffzin 1998). When time escapes you, read the first and last chapter. Cruise shortened versions. If you have 2 hours, it is usually better to invest them in the text than watching a movie version. Film directors may not stick to the script, and you might be exposed for not having done your reading.

"Read the book!" "See the movie!"

History Good readers in history put conscientious effort into seeing how events, places, and people interconnect. Try these approaches to build your skill and enjoyment in reading history:

- *Put yourself in the picture.* As you read about events, think about how you might have reacted to them if you had been present when they were happening.

- *Change history.* Predict an alternative course of history by changing a critical event or two. How might the ripple effect have changed some element of your life?
- *Distinguish central ideas from supporting ideas.* You won't be tested on every detail you read. Practice identifying the most critical aspects of the story that seem more "testworthy."
- *Imagine or draw the timeline.* See whether you can determine how one event led to another. Impose pictures on the timeline that capture the flavor of the era or the action.
- *Make it into a movie.* Imagine a cast of film stars in the roles of the historical figures you're reading about. This technique might help you visualize the action better.
- *Reinforce what you know by watching relevant films critically.* If you have the chance to see a movie that depicts the historical time you are studying, watch carefully to spot mistakes that expose what the filmmaker didn't understand about the era.
- *Don't forget the big picture.* Keep in mind how each new event or person you encounter in your learning adds to your understanding of the grander historic scale.

Natural and Social Sciences The sciences can be especially challenging because of the level of abstraction in some scientific writing. The terminology presented in the sciences represents a kind of shorthand that allows scientists to communicate with each other. Learning these terms can be daunting without some helpful strategies, such as:

- *Keep a running glossary of terms.* Treat the sciences like a foreign language. Each new term stands for a concept. Study the meaning of each, and record the terms and ideas in a safe, reliable place. Some students, for example, write the terms inside the cover of the textbook or a notebook, create a "terms bookmark" that helps them track their progress in the text, or dedicate a computer file to rehearse important terms easily.
- *Accept the role of numbers.* If you aren't comfortable with numbers, you may be turned off by the practice of measurement and statistics that pervades most sciences. Don't be. When numbers accompany text, spend extra time understanding their significance.
- *Think practically.* See whether you can come up with a practical application of the scientific relationships you're reading about. For instance, imagine yourself as the head of a lab charged with exploiting a new scientific discovery for public benefit. You can even turn science into science fiction! For example, you might explore how the principles underlying the discovery might develop a great science fiction plot.
- *Look for links in the news.* Many publications and news magazines feature regular science columns that discuss applications of science and technology to daily life, health, and the environment. Get in the habit of looking for these columns and finding topics that relate to your class.
- *Search the Internet.* The Internet is another source of ideas that will help you with the vocabulary of science. Finding information about the scientists themselves will help make the enterprise feel more real to you.
- *Look for overlaps.* Where does your life intersect with the scientific ideas you're trying to learn? If the material doesn't have any relevance for you now, would it be relevant for your relatives or for you at a later time in your life?

Find New Resources

Sometimes the style of an author or a lecturer is hard to comprehend. You can go beyond assigned materials to achieve the level of information processing that will serve you best.

Get Help on Campus Consider talking to your instructor or a tutor about finding other sources. For nonfiction, find a clearer book on the same topic at the library or bookstore. Make sure that it covers things similar to your assigned text. Some bookstores sell guides to certain disciplines that may help to clarify basic ideas.

Your course textbook may provide either a published or an electronic study guide to help you practice the key ideas. You may be tempted to sell your introductory textbooks when the semester is over, but reconsider. If you keep your textbooks, you have a convenient reference on hand when you are challenged in later, tougher courses.

Take What You Need from the Internet The Internet is one of your best learning resources, but you have to use it properly to maximize your benefits (Vacca, Vacca, & Mraz, 2011).

Check before You Search You may plan to conduct your research process completely online, for convenience. Although there is a lot of valuable information on the Internet, many instructors have strict requirements about what may or may not be used in their assignments. Some may exclude Internet sources because of uncertainty about quality.

Navigate to the Right Spot If you are starting a cold search on the Internet, spend some time playing with the key word searches to find the most valuable resources. An ambiguous or poorly defined search can produce too many hits for you to review, especially if you are in a time crunch. Cut back on your harvest of information by adding some terms to the search, or more sharply define the key terms you are using.

Monitor the Quality of the Resource Not everything on the Internet is credible. Some sites are simply not appropriate for work you need to submit at the college level. Use information developed by recognized experts in the field. If you have questions about the suitability of a resource, ask your instructor.

Beware of Cut-and-Paste Shortcuts The information on the Internet is so easy to transport from one context to another that it may be tempting to capture the information by executing a cut-and-paste command from a Web page to your computer. When you intend to use the information in your own paper, be careful to paraphrase what you have captured. Many instructors use special programs to detect materials that have been downloaded from the Internet into student papers, and the penalty for evidence of plagiarism can be severe.

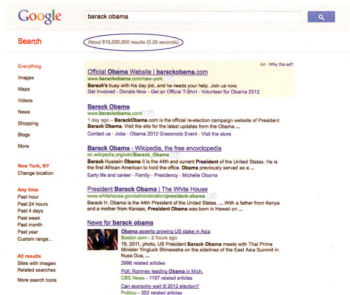

©2011 Google

Sifting through the vast array of information on the Internet to get what you need takes time, energy, and careful attention.

Garth Neustadter

Photo Courtesy of Garth Neustadter

A Five C Expert

As a superb demonstration of the five Cs, Garth Neustadter of Lawrence University took first-prize honors in the 2007 International Film Composing Competition sponsored by Turner Classic Movies. Garth repeatedly watched the 90-second clip from the 1924 classic film *Beau Brummel*. Then he recruited friends and faculty members from Lawrence to help him develop his composition, which prevailed over stiff competition.

"I felt that the material was something that I could work with. . . . The challenge of the clip was having to convey such a variety of contrasting emotions in such a short amount of time. Ninety seconds may seem like a relatively short amount of time for which to write music, but after deciding which musical cues will correspond to actions on screen, [and after] composing, orchestrating, and recording, I had invested close to 100 hours in the project."

(Source: Lawrence Unviersity, Shining Light, 2008)

Make Durable and Protective Records Create an electronic document for every research citation you produce (Rosen, 2006). The best strategy is to cut and paste the passage that you want to capture as the foundation of the note you wish to make—but don't stop there. Be sure to include the URL (Internet address of the Web page), and date the record to indicate when you retrieved the information. Write down the author and the date that the author originally submitted the information, if available. Finally, write down in your own words what you intend to do with the passage. This final step can help you avoid inadvertently cutting and pasting another person's work into your writing. Many libraries currently offer automated strategies to help you develop durable records. If you don't know how to navigate these services, confer with your local librarian.

Bookmark Important Resources Sometimes you get lucky. You may find a superb website that will continue to provide helpful information to you for the duration of a course. Enter the site into your list of favorites so you can easily refer to it again.

Enrich Your Vocabulary

In the process of learning the specialized languages in a discipline, you'll also expand your general vocabulary. Get a dictionary or use the electronic version on your computer to look up words you don't know. Once you look up a word, practice using it to help you remember it. Visualize some situation related to the word.

If you don't have a dictionary nearby when you need it, you may be able to use "word attack" skills to understand a word. That is, you can often divide a word into parts that give you hints about the meaning. Knowing common prefixes and suffixes (word beginnings and endings) can help. See Figure 7.9, "Word Attack Skills," for some common examples. You can also determine the meaning of a word from the context of the sentence.

Sometimes unknown words are a signal that you've missed something in a previous lecture. If you take notes on a laptop, you may be able to look up meanings in an electronic dictionary as you go.

Build a Bright Future

When you think about how much time you will spend over the course of your college career learning from texts and lectures, you may feel a bit resentful. Sometimes such systematic study can feel like busy work, especially if the process you go through doesn't quite translate into the grades that you want. But think again. This practice should transfer into solid work skills that will help you crack a variety of professional problems.

Prefixes (word beginnings) and suffixes (word endings) provide clues about word meanings. Here are some common examples from Latin and Greek.

Prefixes	Meaning	Example
a, ab	without or not	*a*theist: nonbeliever in God
ad	to	*ad*vocate: to speak for
ambi	both	*ambi*valent: uncommitted
con	together	*con*vention: formal gathering
de	from or down	*de*spicable: abhorrent
dis	not	*dis*interest: boredom
ex	over	*ex*aggerate: to magnify
hyper	above	*hyper*active: overactive
hypo	under	*hypo*dermic: under skin
mono	single	*mono*lingual: speaking one language
non	not	*non* responsive: not reacting
pro	forward	*pro*duction: process of making
re	back, again	*re*vert: return to former state
sub, sup	under	*sub*ordinate: in a lower position
trans	across	*trans*pose: to change places

Suffixes	Meaning	Example
-able, -ible (adjective)	capable of	respons*ible*: in charge
-ac, -al, -il (adjective)	pertaining to	natur*al*: related to nature
-ance, -ence (noun)	state or status	dalli*ance*: playful activity
-ant, -ent (noun)	one who does	serv*ant*: person who waits on others
-er, -or (noun)	one who does	contract*or*: one who builds
-ive (adjective)	state or status	fes*tive*: party like
-ish (adjective)	quality of	fool*ish*: like a fool
-less (adjective)	without	heart*less*: harsh, unfeeling
-ly (adjective/adverb)	like	miser*ly*: like a miser
-ness (noun)	state of	peaceful*ness*: state of peace

FIGURE 7.9 Word Attack Skills

Read for the Future

Professionals read and write in very specific forms. As a consequence, once you elect a major, you will begin an apprenticeship in learning how to read, as well as how to prepare, the preferred communication forms for the profession to which you aspire. For example, healthcare professionals must process medical reports and research studies. Business majors, once on the job, will be reading memos, announcements, annual reports, and performance reviews. Musicians will need to master reading musical notation, critiques, and perhaps even instruction manuals to keep instruments in tune.

Master Listening for Workplace Success

Any profession that you pursue will test you regularly on how well you can read and listen. The practice you received in detailed listening from taking notes in lectures will have some positive effects on how well you will process information as a professional. Get in the habit of extracting accurate and sufficiently detailed notes to help you get ready for the listening challenges your chosen profession will contain. For example, you may need to:

- record and implement a medical program for a client.
- absorb the key points from a proposal to increase sales, based on what you hear at a marketing meeting.
- identify, communicate accurately, and take action on the primary complaints of a dissatisfied customer.
- report the details of a community meeting about a current dilemma that influences social policy.

Think about the activities related to taking good notes as the way you become the architect of your learning. How your build your learning will develop in a manner that will be uniquely your own.

Clarify Expectations

- Make a commitment, concentrate, capture key ideas, make connections, and consolidate your learning if you want your learning strategies to be successful.
- Commit to careful preparation and full participation to get the most from your courses.

Develop Competence in Taking Lecture Notes

- Overcome distractions to improve your concentration.
- Adapt your listening skills to the demands of the course and the style of the instructor.
- Find a note-taking format that works well with your learning style.
- Use your notes strategically to improve your ability to recall information.

Develop Competence in Taking Notes from Reading

- Find the right time and space to make your reading effective and efficient.
- Tailor your reading intensity and speed to the course requirements.
- Experiment with note-taking strategies that will help you identify and retain the most important ideas.
- Use your own words to record ideas from texts in order to learn the material well and avoid plagiarism.

Manage Life

- Maintain a positive outlook to help you endure the hard work.

- Overcome the predictable difficulties associated with trying to do systematic preparation and participation in class.

Connect and Communicate

- Develop specialized ways of processing information within different disciplines.
- Use campus resources to help during the trouble spots.
- Harvest what you need from the Internet by using strategic search methods.

Build a Bright Future

- Be patient with the degree of effort you'll need to apply in processing information in your classes.
- Imagine how refined note-taking and reading skills will benefit you in your future work.

 Visit the College Success CourseMate for *Your Guide to College Success* for interactive resources at login.cengagebrain.com

Review Questions

1. How does clarifying your expectations influence your ability to commit to high-power performance in taking notes?

   _____

   _____

   _____

   _____

2. Write down the Five Cs of learning new information. Also include a few ways each can be applied to learning from lectures and reading assignments.

   1. C:_____

   2. C:_____

   3. C:_____

   4. C:_____

   5. C:_____

3. What are three tips for listening most effectively to challenging lectures? How can these tips also be applied to absorbing information from difficult readings?

   1. _____

   2. _____

   3. _____

4. What style of note taking makes the most sense for each of the classes you're currently taking? List your classes below, followed by the best method.

   1. _____

   2. _____

   3. _____

   4. _____

   5. _____

5. List the three ways to process information as you read. How can each style help you succeed in your various college courses? What type do you currently use most often and why?

   1. _____

   2. _____

   3. _____

6. What are some good strategies for taking notes on your readings? List a few pros and cons of each.

_____

_____

_____

_____

_____

7. Describe three typical threats that may compromise your intentions about being an effective and efficient note-taker.

1. _____

2. _____

3. _____

8. Pick two contrasting disciplines you are studying this semester. Discuss the central features of both that should influence how you take notes in each discipline.

1. _____

2. _____

9. In what ways can the Internet help or hurt your production of high-quality notes?

_____

_____

_____

_____

_____

10. Generate three examples of how the development of high-quality information-processing skills could influence your future professional success.

1. _____

2. _____

3. _____

Auditing Your Note-Taking Style for Lectures

	Always	Sometimes	Never
I approach listening actively.			
I select note-taking formats to suit the various courses I take.			
I organize my notes in one place.			
I label the lecture with title and date.			
I take notes from all participants in class.			
I concentrate during class.			
I work to build my vocabulary.			
I cross out errors instead of erasing them.			
I try not to write dense notes. I leave space for adding more later.			
I listen for directional cues or emphasis.			
I avoid shutting down when I have a negative reaction to what I hear.			
I highlight key ideas or themes.			
I use abbreviations to save time.			
I personalize my notes.			
I review my notes after class.			
I pay attention to the quality of my note-taking process as I go.			
I would consider asking the instructor for help in constructing better notes.			

Results: Look at the pattern of the responses that you made on this assessment. Your best note-taking strategies are reflected in checks in the Always column on the left. If the majority of your checks fall in the Always column, you are establishing a good foundation for study with your note-taking practices. Now look at the items marked Never. What would it take for you to add each of these items to your note-taking toolbox?

SELF-ASSESSMENT 7.2

What's Your Reader Profile?

Circle the alternative that best describes you as a reader.

1. When I have an assignment to read,
   a. I'm usually enthusiastic about what I'll learn.
   b. I like to wait to see whether what I have read will be valuable.
   c. I'm generally apprehensive about reading assignments because I'm afraid I won't understand them.

2. What is my attitude toward the authors of my college books?
   a. I think of them as human beings with an interesting story to tell.
   b. I haven't really given the writers much thought.
   c. I think of them as people who will probably talk over my head.

3. When I plan my reading,
   a. I think about how the assignment fits in with the objectives of the course.
   b. I review the prior assignment to set the stage for current work.
   c. I plunge in so I can get it done.

4. I take breaks
   a. to consolidate the information I read.
   b. to help me study longer and more productively.
   c. whenever I lose interest in my reading.

5. When I don't know a word,
   a. I look it up, write it down, and practice it.
   b. I try to figure it out from the context of the sentence.
   c. I usually skip over it and hope it won't make too much difference in the meaning of the passage.

6. When I can't understand a sentence,
   a. I reread the sentence more carefully.
   b. I try to figure out the sentence from the context of the paragraph.
   c. I skip the sentence, hoping it will make sense later.

7. When the whole assignment confuses me,
   a. I try to find more materials that will shed some light on my confusion.
   b. I ask the instructor or someone else for ideas about how to cope with the assignment.
   c. I tend to give up on it.

8. When I read,
   a. I try to read as fast as I can while still understanding the meaning.
   b. I try to sweep as many words as I can at a glance.
   c. I take it one word at a time—speed doesn't matter to me.

Results: Alternatives a and b of each question indicate successful reading habits. Revisit any c alternatives that you marked. Think about possible causes of these less successful patterns. You may benefit from a visit with a reading specialist on campus.

Source: Vincent Miholic, "What's Your Reader Profile?," from "An inventory to pique students' metacognitive awareness of reading strategies," *Journal of Reading* by International Reading Association. Copyright 1994. Reproduced with permission of the author and International Reading Association in the format Textbook and Other book via Copyright Clearance Center.

SELF-ASSESSMENT 7.3

What Is Your Reading Pattern?

Monitor how you read your assignments for 1 week. Then rate how regularly you engage in different kinds of reading:

	Regularly	Sometimes	Rarely
Previewing:	_____	_____	_____
Skimming:	_____	_____	_____
Active reading:	_____	_____	_____
Analytic reading:	_____	_____	_____
Reviewing:	_____	_____	_____

In what area are you the strongest? How might this strength impact your academic performance? In which area do you need the most practice?

SELF-ASSESSMENT 7.4

How Fast Do You Read?

Select a text from one of your courses. Set a timer for 5 minutes and start reading. When the timer goes off, stop reading. Count the number of lines you read in the 5-minute period. Pick several lines at random in the text and count the number of words in the lines. Multiply the number of lines you read by the average number of words per line. This will give you an approximation of the total words you read in the 5-minute period. Finally, divide by 5 to produce your reading speed in words per minute.

Content area: _____

Date of assessment: _____

Number of lines read: _____

× Number of words per line: _____

= Approximate total words: _____

Divided by 5 (minutes): _____

Approximate words per minute: _____

How does your reading speed compare with these average speeds for different kinds of reading (Skinner, 1997)?

Skimming	800 words per minute
Active reading	100 to 200 words per minute
Analytic reading	under 100 words per minute

Results: Use this estimate as a baseline for your reading speed. If the material was well suited to your interest areas, you were probably able to read within the range for effective active reading. If the material was very familiar, your rate was probably higher, approaching the rates found in skimming. If your reading rate was below 100 words per minute, this may be a cause for concern. Although that reading rate is acceptable for complex materials, a slower reading rate on routine materials predicts that you may have difficulty keeping up with your reading assignments.

Consider going for a more thorough evaluation of your reading strengths and weaknesses at the campus study skill center. Professional assistance can pinpoint any problem and make your future reading strategies much more successful.

Clarify Expectations

1. A Shared Path to Success

Form a small group in your college success class to compare your expectations for taking notes in this course. If you have another course in common, compare your approaches to that content area as well. See whether as a group you can determine which approaches are most effective in capturing the critical ideas in these contexts. How does the type of course influence note-taking strategies?

_____

_____

_____

2. Show and Tell

Carefully look over the notes that you have taken in a course where your learning isn't coming easily. Think about what clues to your struggle may be present in how you take notes. For example,

- Are you staying tuned in throughout the class?
- Are you writing down words that you don't understand?
- Do the lecture notes fit with the big picture?

Then follow up on your reflection by visiting your instructor during posted office hours. Take your notes and your observations with you. Ask the instructor to review your approach to see if other suggestions might improve your gains from note taking.

Develop Competence

3. Note Taking Now

Spend the next 10 minutes skimming the next chapter in this text and creating an outline of its content. After you are done, compare your outline with the one the authors provide on the first page of the chapter. How was your outline similar or different? Did you miss any main ideas or capture any additional points? Think about how your presentation of content might differ if you had made a concept map or summary. Which strategy do you think works best for you?

_____

_____

_____

_____

4. Primary versus Secondary Accounts

Read a newspaper account (a secondary source) of a recent scientific achievement or issue and list it below. Then ask a librarian to help you track down the original work (the primary source) in a scientific journal at the library or online. Compare the length of the reports, the language level difficulty, the order of importance of ideas, and any other contrasting features. Based on your observations, how would you say that primary and secondary sources differ?

Scientific achievement or issue: _____

Focus of secondary source: _____

Focus of primary source: _____

How do they differ? _____

📁 Manage Life

5. Daydream Believer

One of the biggest obstacles to successful listening in class is the tendency to daydream. Monitor your listening in your current courses for 1 week. In which class did you daydream the most? Why do you think this is happening? Perhaps the room is too hot or the lecture falls right after lunch. List some possible reasons below. Now list some strategies for conquering your daydreams and implement these strategies next week.

Daydreaming in class: _____

Possible reasons: _____

Strategies: _____

6. Word for Word

You notice that a friend who sits next to you in a particularly tough class exhausts himself by trying to take down every word the professor utters. Since the professor is a particularly speedy lecturer, it is no wonder your friend is worn out by the time class is over. What arguments would you mount to help your friend adopt a more strategic and less exhausting style?

_____

_____

Connect and Communicate

7. Analyze the Sixth Sense

Some students seem to have an uncanny ability to figure out which information given in class will show up on the tests. Think about what kinds of cues they're picking up on in their instructors' communication and apply the strategies to one of your courses.

- How do the instructor's vocal cues tell you what's important?

_____

_____

- What kind of words show an instructor's intent?

_____

_____

- What behaviors show excitement in the instructor's delivery?

_____

_____

- How does your instructor tend to stress important concepts?

_____

_____

8. Internet Hell

As terrific as the Internet is for gathering information, it can also pose hazards to your note taking and learning. Outline three problems that could result from improper use of the Internet. Then speculate about what adverse consequences each problem might produce.

1. Problem: _____

   Consequence: _____

2. Problem: _____

   Consequence: _____

3. Problem: _____

   Consequence: _____

Build a Bright Future

9. Taking Advantage

Based on the preferences in note-taking styles you have already demonstrated, speculate about what kinds of professions might be the best showcase for your particular style of processing information. See if you can identify at least three occupations in which your preferred note-taking strategies might serve well.

1. _____

2. _____

3. _____

10. Professors as Readers

Interview your favorite instructors in your major to identify the information formats they have mastered. If you haven't declared an interest, identify an instructor whom you'd like to get to know better. Ask about the kinds of things the instructor likes to read, both for the profession and for fun. Then make it a point to find some examples of the communication types the instructor describes, either in a visit to the library or in an Internet search. Who knows? You may get a recommendation for your new favorite novel in the bargain!

_____

_____

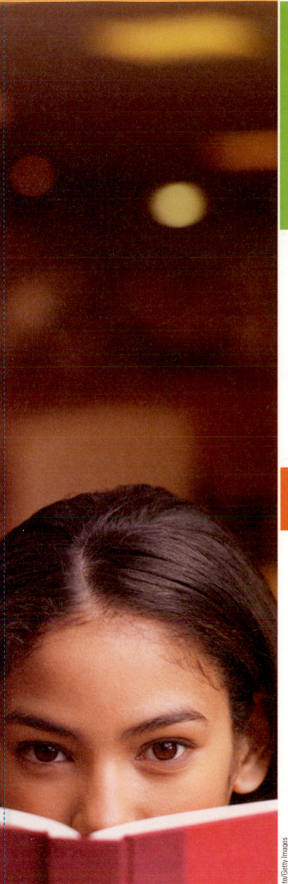

Enhance Your Study Skills and Memory

Chapter 8

KNOW YOURSELF

STUDYING WORKS BEST WHEN you know how to make good use of your study time. This chapter explores ways to bring your study habits under your control, improve your memory, and get the most from your study of various disciplines. You also will read about how to enrich your study by facing and overcoming predictable obstacles. To evaluate where you stand right now, place a check mark in the category that best applies to you for each of the skills below.

Are My Study Skills and Memory Strategies Up to Par?

	Very Much Like Me	Somewhere in Between	Not at All Like Me
I can estimate how much time I should be studying for each class.			
I choose appropriate places and times to study.			
I organize effective study and review sessions.			
I can describe how assignments vary in the depth of thinking required.			
I can explain how to improve memory.			
I adapt my study strategies to suit different disciplines.			
I know the impact of sleep deprivation on study quality.			
I know how physical limitations affect study success.			
I know how to connect with peers in online environments.			
I know how study skills prepare me for future employment.			

Stockbyte/Getty Images

Ryan Barbin
The 30-Minute Solution

Following 5 years of service in the Navy, during which time he served on the USS *Nimitz*, Ryan Barbin knew what he wanted to do with his veteran's benefits—capture a college education. He enrolled at Highline Community College in Washington to begin work on the next phase of his life. He was able to transfer his military discipline to good use when he achieved a respectable 3.54 average taking a full load of classes. His efficient study patterns still allow time for working at an electronics store, working out, and snowboarding.

Courtesy of Ryan Barbin

With sound study strategies, Ryan Barbin has managed a high grade point average while working full-time as a sales rep in an electronics store.

How does Ryan sandwich his academic work in with other obligations and leisure pursuits? He recommends simply going over notes once every day. Ryan makes a point to refer to the text for anything unclear or missing from his lecture notes. He also emphasizes pacing, studying in 30-minute blocks with 30-minute breaks. Reading is challenging, so the breaks allow optimal concentration. Memorizing is not difficult for Ryan. One of his favorite mnemonics, or memory tricks, is MINDS R CRUEL, which represents the first letter of each human body system to help master content in biology. He doesn't believe in cramming and says that systematic study helps avoid the last-minute panic that torments so many students.

"Trust me," Ryan stated. "You do not need to give up your life for school. You just have to prepare yourself for class and take your life goals one step at a time."

When he completes his work at Highline, Ryan is headed to Central Washington University and eventually hopes to pursue a master's degree in industrial psychology.

Success in college depends on your ability to optimize blocks of time for study despite the forces that seem to work against you. Look at the chapter outline and anticipate which areas might be most useful in managing your study.

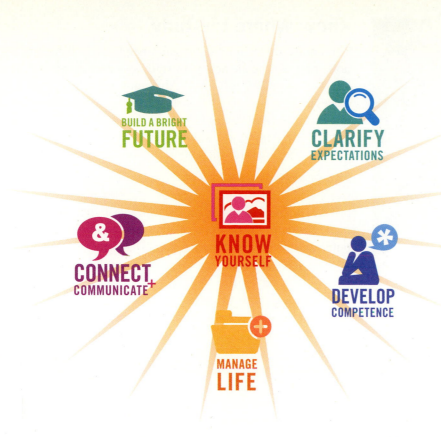

 Clarify Expectations

To do well in college, most students need concentrated study time with notes from readings and classes. A systematic study strategy will make your investment of time and effort pay off by helping you to:

- recall the core material of the course easier.
- develop richer insights.
- establish good work habits that will carry over into your career.

The amount of time students report doing assignments or studying relates to many aspects of college success (Astin, 1993). Students who study more hours are more satisfied with college than are students who study less. Also, those who invest more time studying report that college improves their cognitive skills and emotional life. But studying *more* is only one way to improve. Studying *more effectively* saves time so that you have more of it for social life and other interests.

Imagine the motivation that Ryan Barbin needed to organize his life so that he could earn his degree. Are you willing to make that investment? See Know Yourself: Self-Assessment 8.1, "What's the Right Ratio?," on page 281 at the end of the chapter to estimate your orientation toward making the commitment you need to succeed.

Visualizing success will make your goal easier to accomplish. Imagine yourself, after a good study session, coming to class and participating actively in a discussion. Imagine raising your hand to answer a question so effectively that the entire discussion ratchets up a notch. How about getting back a test with a big fat "A—Good Job" at the top? If you can't get motivated to study, just imagine the positive outcomes that can make you feel at the top of your game. That should help you manage the hard work in between.

Know Where to Study

The phone rings. Your downstairs neighbor is throwing a noisy party. Someone near your study space insists on watching *American Idol* full blast. And your relentless appetite craves nachos. At times the world is so full of distractions that it seems impossible to find the right time and place to study. But your success as a student depends on your conquering these distractions and sticking to a good study routine.

The Best Available Space Find the best place you can to work, and study there consistently. The best place is usually private, quiet, well lit, and a comfortable temperature. For many students, the best place will also offer access to a computer and an Internet connection. That way you can have Web resources available to support your work and still maintain a quick fix for the social deprivation that can happen during long periods of study. While you are connected, you will need to guard against allowing yourself to get distracted by the nonacademic temptations the internet has to offer.

Narrow your study sites to one of a few places that provide you with the working space, storage space, and electronic access that will make your work efficient. Finding a study space at home may be easiest, but you have other options as well. Colleges usually try to maintain other quiet spaces on campus, which include general-use computer labs, wireless hubs, or laptop hookups to facilitate both studying and maintaining your personal network. You may find just the setup you need in the library, in a dedicated lab, or even in the quiet but wired spaces of some campuses. Residence halls often set aside study spaces away from noisy roommates. Ask other seasoned students about good study places on campus to find the most promising and productive sites.

Commuters can use driving time to review audio recordings of complicated lectures. Some instructors make podcasts of their lectures more commonly available to facilitate review. Carpooling with someone in class also provides review time. Riding on a bus or train, especially if the commute is long, provides blocks of study time, if you can study well in this type of environment. You might even be able to use your laptop effectively if you take precautions regarding computer safety and power needs.

The Right Conditions Although some students can concentrate in strange places and odd postures, most find that sitting at a desk improves concentration. If you don't have a desk drawer for storage, use boxes or crates to contain and organize your supplies and books. Set up a simple filing system if you can.

Wherever you study, minimize noise. Many people study best when the CD player, radio, and television are off. Some people like music in the background to mask other sounds and give a sense of control over the environment. If you can't control the noise around you, use headphones and soft instrumental music to minimize distraction. Online courses provide great flexibility, but they require more self-discipline in managing time and space than regular classes. How can you pull together these ideas to develop the most supportive study environment?

Some students can study effectively in uncomfortable postures and distracting environments, but many prefer to study at a desk or a table. Have you figured out where you study best?

StockLite/Shutterstock.com

1. *Strategize about how to share study space if your resources are limited.* Hang a bulletin board near the space so that everyone sharing the space can see schedules—and perhaps the latest A paper.

By permission of Tony Cochran and Creators Syndicate, Inc.

2. ***Develop a schedule for access to the family computer if you rely on it for your coursework.*** Practice saving your work, and respect the privacy of others who share your equipment.
3. ***Defer maintenance on chores that can wait, or delegate them to another family member.*** Don't forget to show appreciation for their support of your dreams.
4. ***Consolidate tasks.*** By keeping a running to-do list, you might accomplish four or five tasks during your library visit instead of just one.
5. ***Consider working at atypical times.*** Getting up earlier or waiting for the family to head off to bed may provide the fewest interruptions.
6. ***Establish and defend your boundaries.*** It is inevitable that you will have to say "no" if you are going to meet your goals.
7. ***Be a digital study buddy.*** Find someone in the class whom you can connect with online who can provide mutual motivation for crossing the finish line.

Know When to Study

To succeed in college, you are going to have to invest some hours each week learning from your notes and reading assignments. How can you best use those hours wisely? How can you motivate yourself to orchestrate your time to maximize available hours for study?

When to Review Look over your notes immediately after class. This practice allows you to rehearse new ideas and identify unclear ones while they are fresh. You can then clarify them with your instructor or in your reading. Reviewing your class notes and notes on reading assignments before the class meets again adds another rehearsal session that prepares you to participate in the next class more effectively. It also reinforces your memory on those concepts.

Before you shift gears and disconnect from a specific class, consider one or more of the following to facilitate more enduring learning:

- ***Rewrite and reorganize your notes.*** This habit not only allows you to create a neater, clearer set of ideas for study but also provides an immediate review to help you take in and organize information.
- ***Highlight the most important ideas.*** Underline or color-code the ideas you think may appear on a test. Write notes in the margins that will make the material more meaningful to you.
- ***Write a summary paragraph capturing the main ideas.*** What were the main points covered in class? How did this class fit into the overall course?
- ***Identify any ideas that are still confusing.*** Make notes about what remains unclear so that you can look up the answer in your reading. You also can ask other students or the instructor.

Successful students often get to class about 10 minutes early to review their notes. Anticipating class events can save you time in the long run.

Schedule regular cumulative review sessions. Devote some time to seeing the big picture in each of your courses. Look at how each lecture fits the broader course objective. If you regularly review your notes during the term, you'll need less review time right before exams.

Know What to Study

Use the daily and weekly calendars you established in Chapter 3 to decide when your activities must intensify or when you can take a much-needed recreation break. Keep your long-term goals posted in your study area or use them as your screen saver so that you can have easy access to reminders about what your commitments will require.

Set subgoals for each study session. Plan how long your study session will be, as well as what specific tasks you want to accomplish and in what order. Following Ryan Barbin's lead, build in some break time to help your concentration stay fresh. Monitor how well you're achieving these subgoals and adapt your planning and resources accordingly.

 # Develop Competence

Successful studying requires a plan. You need to size up the complexity of learning that is required. You also need to memorize the important elements of content that drive the assignment. Finally, you need to consider any specific expectations from the professor who gave the assignment.

Learn Bloom's Taxonomy

College instructors sometimes rely on a classic framework, Bloom's Taxonomy, which clarifies different kinds of learning and organizes them according to complexity. Some instructors may explicitly identify their use of Bloom's Taxonomy in their syllabi. In other cases, instructors use the basic idea—the scaffolding of cognitive skills—implicitly in the design of their courses.

Benjamin Bloom and his colleagues (1956) developed their hierarchy of cognitive skills to describe the kind of work that college courses require. They originally distinguished lower-order thinking skills, such as *knowledge* and *comprehension*, from higher-order thinking skills, such as *application*, *analysis*, *synthesis*, and *evaluation*. Some instructors introduce Bloom's Taxonomy as a framework to help students understand how to delve more deeply into their studies.

The New Bloom's Taxonomy Recently, Bloom's colleagues (Anderson & Krathwohl, 2001) modernized the original taxonomy with the following, arranged from lower-order to higher-order cognitive skills:

- *Remember.* Retrieve pertinent facts from long-term memory (*recognize, recall*).
- *Understand.* Construct new meaning by mixing new material with existing ideas (*interpret, exemplify, classify, summarize, infer, compare, explain*).
- *Apply.* Use procedures to solve problems or complete tasks (*execute, implement*).
- *Analyze.* Subdivide content into meaningful parts and relate the parts (*differentiate, organize, attribute*).
- *Evaluate.* Come to a conclusion about something based on standards/ criteria (*check, critique, judge*).
- *Create.* Reorganize elements into a new pattern, structure, or purpose (*generate, plan, produce*).

(Source: From McKeachie. Teaching Tips: Strategies, Research and Theory. 11/E Student, 11E. © 2002 Wadsworth, a part of Cengage Learning, Inc. Reproduced by permission. www.cengage.com/permissions)

Beginning courses tend to emphasize the lower-order cognitive skill of remembering, which is usually assessed using multiple-choice tests. To study for tests that involve lower-order learning, rely on the effective memory strategies discussed later in this chapter.

Advanced courses emphasize higher-order cognitive skills. Application skills help you transfer your knowledge to novel examples. Practice in analysis contributes to your effectiveness in reasoning and asking questions. Evaluating requires making decisions or judgments. Creating involves the integration of ideas into a new creation or perspective. Higher-order tasks require you to show greater independence and creativity in your thinking.

You can follow the spirit of Bloom's Taxonomy in your own approach to studying. Challenge yourself to go one level above what the course requires. For example, if your instructor emphasizes the learning of facts and figures in assignments, practice applying course materials to new situations. This emphasis will promote learning that endures.

Improve Your Memory

No matter what your learning profile, you will spend a substantial amount of time in college committing important facts, ideas, and theories to memory. Memorizing is a fundamental skill that expands your knowledge base and lays a foundation for more sophisticated thinking skills as you learn about different disciplines. Especially in your early courses, your tests may depend entirely on memorization; for example, naming the levels of the phylogenetic scale in zoology or recognizing the musical instruments in a symphony requires memorization. Let's explore how memory works before we look at methods for improving your memory.

Understand How Memory Works The ability to absorb and use information depends on three processes: *encoding,* or taking in new information; *storing* the information for later use; and *retrieving* the information on command. Though encoding happens first, we discuss it last to relate it to later storage and retrieval.

Storage New phone numbers don't automatically go into your long-term memory for important contacts. You retain the number briefly, for 30 seconds or so, just long enough for you to punch in the number. Then it vanishes, unless you rehearse it or use other memory strategies to retain it longer. Besides being brief, "working" memory has other features:

- *It's fragile.* Unless you rehearse the information, it will disappear. If you're interrupted while rehearsing the information—suppose someone asks you a question after you have looked up a phone number—your memory will be disrupted and you'll probably lose the information.
- *It has limited capacity*. Working memory can hold approximately seven "chunks" of information before the system becomes overtaxed and information is dumped out of awareness (Miller, 1956).
- *It can be tricked*. You may be able to trick working memory into holding more detail through a process called "chunking": making each memory "chunk" represent more than one piece of information. This is the basis for the *mnemonics,* or memory aids, discussed later.

Long-term memory stores a mountain of facts and impressions from your education and life experience. Cognitive scientists describe long-term memory as partitioned into two special functions: procedural and declarative (see Figure 8.1, "Long-Term Memory").

- *Procedural memory* consists of the "how" of memory, the repository of directions for various activities that you have internalized. When you have to learn a new clinical procedure in nursing, you will be expanding procedural memory.

- *Declarative memory* consists of the "what" of memory, the great store of facts and ideas that constitute your personal encyclopedia. Declarative memory is further subdivided into two more functions (Tulving, 1972):
  - *Semantic memory* represents your recall of basic facts and ideas. What is the meaning of *prerequisite*? When did the Great Depression begin? What was Edgar Allan Poe's most famous poem? Expanding the content of semantic memory is one of the primary goals of a college education.
  - *Episodic memory* consists of your recall of personal details in your life. What was the best movie you ever saw? Where did you go on your last group date? When did you last see your car keys?

Long-term memory appears to have no limits; many long-term memories endure. For example, you may be able to recall the name of your first-grade teacher even though you haven't thought of her in a long time. You can also remember vivid information without much practice.

Long-term memory is built through association. The more you know about a topic, the easier it is to learn more, because you have more ways to make associations between new ideas and what you already know. For example, if you're a fan of old movies, you may devote a great deal of memory storage to retaining odd facts about directors, movie locations, and favorite actors. If you're not a sports fan, then you'll feel bewildered when your sports-focused friends discuss Brett Favre's career statistics. People easily store vast quantities of information in long-term memory on the topics that interest them most. If you don't know much about a subject, then your task is harder. You'll be building your concept base from the ground up.

Retrieval If material is learned well, retrieval from long-term memory is not a struggle. Unfortunately, no matter how hard you study, you're bound to forget some things you learn. There are two main reasons why you forget something you thought you learned: interference and decay.

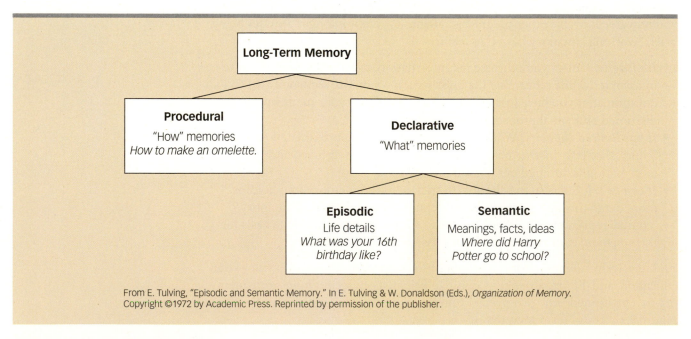

From E. Tulving, "Episodic and Semantic Memory." In E. Tulving & W. Donaldson (Eds.), *Organization of Memory.* Copyright ©1972 by Academic Press. Reprinted by permission of the publisher.

FIGURE 8.1 Long-Term Memory

- **Interference** can crowd out memories, making them difficult to retrieve. For example, when you take a full academic load, the sheer volume of the material may cause interference among the subjects, especially when courses use similar terms for different purposes.
- **Decay** is the disintegration of memory that occurs when the ideas are not kept active through use. If you do not regularly review material or do not practice retrieving information, it may be impossible to recall it when you want it, such as during a test. Thus it is important to regularly review what you have learned.

Memory research suggests that long-term memory can be remarkably creative . . . and deceptive. Elizabeth Loftus (2003) demonstrated in a series of clever experiments that people could report vividly recalling events that had never really happened to them. Once we are convinced that we know something, we may fill in the gaps without realizing how much we've invented.

Ideally, you'll gear your learning strategies toward building your long-term memory with important and meaningful information. Learn course information so that you can recall it not just for tests, but well beyond the end of the course.

Encoding The difference between great and mediocre results in memorizing can depend on the quality of encoding. Four general encoding strategies provide a foundation for effective long-term memory (Higbee, 2001):

1. **Pay attention.** Don't allow yourself to be distracted when you're processing information about things you must do or remember. Some absentmindedness is caused by failing to absorb the information in the first place.
2. **Create meaning.** Memorizing through rote rehearsal is one route to long-term memory, but it tends to lead to superficial learning. Digging deep to comprehend information will produce more enduring learning than investing time to commit meaningless information to memory.
3. **Impose organization.** Organize concepts in a tree diagram or concept map, as shown in Figure 8.2, "Tree Diagrams," to provide additional cues

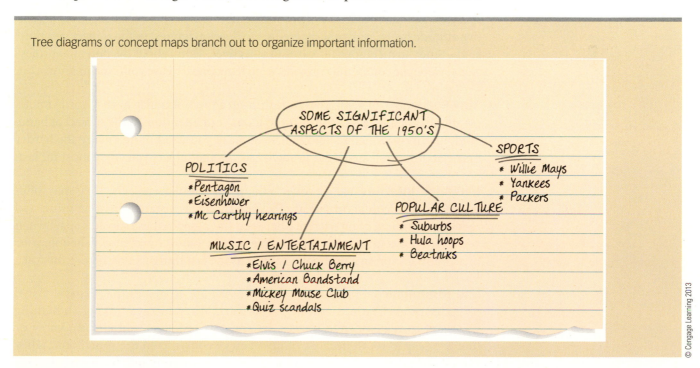

Tree diagrams or concept maps branch out to organize important information.

© Cengage Learning 2013

FIGURE 8.2 Tree Diagrams

for remembering ideas. For example, suppose you're studying important events in U.S. history in the 1950s. Construct a map that captures the important, related details of the period to make them easier to remember. You don't have to be artistic to draw pictures, make arrows, or create stars in the margins of books or notes.

4. *Expand associations*. Personal connections will make learning and recalling unfamiliar or abstract ideas easier (Matlin, 1998), especially if you're a visual learner. For example, in history you may have to learn about periods that seem quite remote to you. Think about how these periods might have involved your own ancestors. For example, would your great-grandmother have been a flapper during the Roaring Twenties, or would she have led a different kind of life? Make her the focal point of your learning about this era. If you don't know anything about her, imagine her.

Ask yourself questions about what you've read or what you've recorded about class activities. Expand the number of associations you make with the information. This strategy makes the ideas easier to recall. Add this activity to your rehearsal time. The following questions, and others like them, can help you create additional links to course concepts:

- Have I ever seen this concept before?
- Do I like or dislike the ideas?
- What are some practical examples of the concept?
- Are there other ways to explain the concept?

This practice will improve not only your memory for course concepts but also your ability to think critically about them.

Apply Additional Memory Strategies The following strategies provide additional help for memorizing different types of information.

Adopt the Right Attitude Memorizing new material is a challenge, but a positive attitude helps. Make a serious effort to develop interest in the subject you must study. Study to meet specific learning objectives. Think about the potential professional value the course may provide, even if you have to use your imagination a bit.

Stay Focused Concentrate on one thing at a time. You may have to study multiple subjects in one session. If so, try to focus your attention on the subject at hand. Study the most difficult subjects first because you need more energy for harder material. Reward yourself at the end by saving the subject you enjoy most for last.

Minimize Interference If you're taking two similar subjects, they may offer overlapping or conflicting ideas. To keep the ideas separate in your mind and reduce the amount of interference between them, space these subjects apart when you study. If you must study for multiple tests in a short timeframe, schedule your final study session in a particular subject as the last thing you do before the test.

Use Mnemonics Mnemonics (ne-MON-ix) are strategies that expand visual or auditory associations and help you learn. They involve linking something you want to remember to images, letters, or words that you already know or that are easy to recall because of how you've constructed the mnemonic. They can be visual or text based, logical or goofy, complex or simple. See Figure 8.3, "Examples of Mnemonics from Various Disciplines," for some common examples, including the one introduced by Ryan Barbin in the opening spotlight.

DISCIPLINE – BASED QUESTION	MNEMONIC	MEANING
Business: *What's a good strategy for analyzing problems?*	SWOT	Strengths, weaknesses, opportunities, threats (a technique for analyzing problems)
Physics: *What are the visible colors in the light spectrum?*	ROY G. BIV	Red, orange, yellow, green, blue, indigo, violet (the visible colors in the light spectrum)
Geography: *What are the names of the Great Lakes?*	HOMES	Huron, Ontario, Michigan, Erie, Superior (the Great Lakes)
Music: *What are the notes of the treble clef?*	Every Good Boy Does Fine	E G B D F
Astronomy: *What are the 8 planets in order from the sun?*	My Very Elegant Mother Just Serves Us Nachos	Mercury Venus Earth Mars Jupiter Saturn Uranus Neptune
Biology: *What are the systems in the human body?*	MINDS R CRUEL	Muscular, Integument (Skin), Nervous, Digestive, Skeletal, Respiratory, Circulatory, Reproductive, Urogential, Endocrine, and Lymphatic

FIGURE 8.3 Examples of Mnemonics from Various Disciplines

The following strategies provide additional help for memorizing different types of information:

- *Rhymes.* If you were raised in the United States, you most likely learned when Columbus came to America through rhyme: "In fourteen hundred ninety-two/Columbus sailed the ocean blue." The rhyme leaves an indelible impression. Eventually you don't have to repeat the rhyme to remember the date. Here's another example, from first aid: "When the face is red, raise the head. When the face is pale, raise the tail." Remembering the rhyme allows you to make a swift decision about appropriate treatment.

- *Songs.* Melodies also can produce enduring memories. Many children learn their phone numbers or addresses when parents sing the information to them using a familiar melody. A more complex example is represented by a song that helps chemistry students recall the names on the periodic table.

- *Acronyms.* Acronyms are special words (or sentences) that you construct using the first letter of each word in the list you wish to memorize. (See Figure 8.3 for some examples.) The acronym cues you not only to the items on the list but also to their proper order.

- *Method of loci (LOW-sigh).* In another mnemonic, you associate the parts of a list with a physical sequence of activities or a specific location that you know well. For example, the method of loci can be found in a creative pharmacy major's attempt to remember the path of a red blood cell by imagining an oversized body lying on a floor in a familiar room and walking his way through the heart, arteries, and veins.

- *Visualization.* Using your imagination to come up with provocative images can provide memory cues. Making visualizations ridiculous is the best way to make them memorable (Lorayne & Lucas, 1996). Substitute or combine objects, exaggerate their features, make them disproportionate, or involve action in an image to make it distinctive. Two good examples come from creating visualizations to learn Spanish (Schandillia, 2007). To learn the word *caballero* for "gentleman," picture an elegant old fellow sitting in a cab. To learn "to shave oneself"—*afietarse*—imagine shaving your "arse" while sitting in a Fiat!

- *Props.* Create a set of flash cards and carry them with you. Rehearse while you wait in grocery store lines, at the Laundromat, and at doctors' offices. Consider creating audio recordings of the ideas you want to memorize, and review those while driving or doing chores.

- *"Cram Cards."* Whenever you can't commit important information to long-term memory through regular study and rehearsal, write down the essential points on a small card (Frank, 1996). Don't overload it with detail. Study the card before your test, up to the point when your instructor says to put materials away. Then rehearse the information until you can write it down in the margins of your test booklet. In this way, your working memory can help you when your long-term memory cannot. Be sure to put the card away before the test begins. It could easily be mistaken for a cheat sheet.

- *Overlearning.* When you think that you really know your stuff, study just a bit longer to "overlearn" the material. Overlearning improves the integration and the endurance of your learning and helps you avoid partial memories.

Partial memory occurs when you remember something about a concept but not enough to help you. For example, you may recall where a concept appeared on the textbook page but fail to remember its meaning. Or you may be able to remember that a concept starts with *p*, but the rest of the word eludes you. Instances of partial memory suggest that your study strategies need more work.

When you partially recall important information, you may be able to retrieve the whole of what you stored in memory if you temporarily change the direction of your thinking. Focusing away from the problem gives your mental circuits more time to "warm up," sometimes causing a term or name to surface.

- *Situational Cues.* If you can, when you take an exam, sit in the seat you normally sit in for class. Being in the same place may help you dredge up memories that might be hard to remember without context cues.

Samuel Park

Marrying Music and Memory

John Blackie/The University of West Florida

Samuel Park memorizes thousands of notes embellished with just the right emotional expression to create winning violin performances.

As you watch his fingers fly over the strings, you can't help but wonder how violinist Samuel Park renders a perfect performance without benefit of sheet music. Memorizing not just thousands of notes in any given concerto, Sam also must memorize the links between passages and the emotional expression each passage should convey.

Born in Frankfurt, Germany, Sam attended college in both Germany and the United States. His superb musicianship was rewarded when he won numerous state and regional competitions. During his undergraduate years, he also squeezed in playing with local and regional symphonies and participated in prestigious international and national festivals. Sam currently is pursuing his doctoral degree at the renowned music school at the University of North Texas, where he serves as concertmaster of the UNT Concert and Baroque orchestras.

How does Sam manage to absorb so much detail to deliver flawless performances? He doesn't set out specifically to memorize but studies each piece—its structure, emotional tone, history, connections—in such depth that memorization results. He overlearns each note with concentrated practice so his fingers won't fail when performance time arrives.

Source: Massachusetts Institute of Technology

Evaluate Your Progress How skilled are you in using memory-enhancing strategies to achieve your goals? Complete Know Yourself: Self-Assessment 8.2, "Am I Ready to Learn and Remember?," at the end of the chapter on page 282, to identify strategies that you use now and ones that show promise for helping you study more effectively in the future. Another way to evaluate your progress involves examining your test results to determine whether your strategies worked. You may need to study for longer periods or to seek new, more efficient methods for learning new ideas.

If you prefer memorizing information to other kinds of academic work, you're in good company. Most beginning students prefer well-structured, simple learning tasks (Baxter Magolda, 1992). Memorizing basic facts feels like a manageable challenge in most courses. However, college courses will routinely challenge you to go beyond rote memory and learn more deeply. One reason to accept these challenges now is that they can build your confidence for upper-level courses that you'll take later on.

Master the Disciplines

If you're majoring in an area that will train you for a specific profession such as business or medicine, you may wonder why you need to take liberal arts courses at all. Each discipline represents a specialized way of thinking about human experience. Thus, exposure to a wide range of fields should help you develop a richer perspective on life and more ways to view and handle problems. Students must get beyond memorizing facts and concepts to understand how disciplines uniquely flavor the interpretation of fact (Gardner, 1999a).

Courses differ in how much they make you think. You may have already noticed that you have to adjust your study strategies to different disciplines, especially when a class isn't a great match for your learning style. Here is a four-part framework that we will apply to the major disciplines to help you adjust to these differences and maximize your results:

- *The Rules*. Although each discipline requires memorizing new content, each also has sophisticated frameworks and theories that require deeper levels of thinking and understanding.
- *The Risks*. Each discipline tends to have special challenges associated with developing mastery.
- *The Resources.* Your learning style will make some disciplines more successful than others for you. Which elements of your learning style facilitate that success?
- *The Remedy*. If you're studying a discipline that doesn't match your learning style, there are things you can do to improve your efficiency and effectiveness.

The Humanities Humanities courses develop your understanding of human experience. Most emphasize exploring your subjective experience as you read literature, examine specific periods in history, or evaluate the ideas of philosophers.

The Rules Typically each humanities course is built within a particular *framework*, or set of concepts or theories, that will help you develop a new perspective or richer appreciation for the human condition. For example, learning about literature will expose you to various frameworks of literary criticism, such as psychoanalytic or feminist theory. Each framework in turn is built on a distinct set of values and assumptions.

Applying the frameworks to literature will probably lead you to different kinds of conclusions. A psychoanalytic framework prompts you to look at unconscious motivations; a feminist framework sensitizes you to social forces that create different options for women and men. You can apply these frameworks to expand your personal insight. Humanities instructors look to your insights as evidence that you understand the frameworks.

The Risks You may assume that there is only one right answer and may be afraid that you'll look foolish if what you say is "wrong." However, the objective of most humanities courses is to encourage breadth of thinking. Take the risk of sharing your insights. You may end up offering ideas that your class members have never heard.

Notice that by using your imagination to think about your assignments, you also make new connections to the assigned material. The more connections you make, the easier it will be for you to recall information. This strategy also helps you anticipate and practice for essay tests.

The Resources Because of their learning styles, some students have a natural advantage in humanities courses. Those who will be drawn to humanities as a major tend to have the following characteristics:

- If you have verbal-linguistic intelligence, you bring a love of words and their meanings to complex humanities assignments.
- If you're skilled in auditory processing, you can track difficult lectures with ease.
- If you enjoy assignments that emphasize reflection and creative learning styles as well, humanities assignments offer you wide latitude for personal interpretation.
- If you like to think critically and creatively, you'll have many opportunities to create and defend your perspective.

The Remedy Not everyone has a learning style that makes learning in the humanities easy. What are some strategies you can use to enhance your success in humanities classes?

- *Keep a dictionary nearby.* You're bound to run into new terms that will slow down your reading.
- *Compare ideas.* Exploit any opportunity to discuss central ideas or identify challenging concepts.

HIGHLIGHT

Deep Study Strategies for the Humanities

Suppose you've enrolled in a film appreciation class. You've just read a chapter about the works of Steven Spielberg. Asking the following (or similar) questions during your review session will help you probe the material most deeply:

Remember. What are the names of Spielberg's past films? When did his first film debut?

Understand. Name the ways his films could be regarded as successful. What themes does he regularly present in his films?

Apply. What other filmmakers tend to borrow from Spielberg's methods? Think about how a different director might have directed the film *A.I. Artificial Intelligence*.

Analyze. Why are his films so financially successful? What role has technology played in his productions?

Evaluate. In what ways do you think his work is unique? Rank Spielberg's films from best to worst.

Create. Propose a story line that would be intriguing to Spielberg. How might his films have been different if he'd been born 20 years earlier?

- *Practice making conclusions.* Rehearse aloud or on paper the key ideas and principles you draw from the assignment.
- *Read to make connections.* The more you read about a topic, the more you'll have to reflect on.

The Natural Sciences and Math Natural science courses such as chemistry and physics explain the natural phenomena of the world, including everything from how fast an apple falls from a tree to the mysteries of the cell. Mathematics provides the tools to measure observations and assess change.

The Rules Natural science and math are loaded with theorems, laws, and formulas that you'll probably need to memorize, but comprehension should be your primary objective. Most of the activities that you undertake in science and math provide practice in application; you apply the rules to produce a specific outcome or solution. The more you practice applying the principles or formulas, the more enduring your learning will be.

The Risks Natural science and math often have an unappealing reputation. The stereotype is that only science and math "geeks" do well in these courses. It will help if you deflate your images about science slightly. For example, you regularly act as a scientist does when you figure out how things work, although you may not be as systematic or careful in your observations as scientists are. With some practice, you, too, can do real science.

The Resources The natural sciences and mathematics attract students who have particular strengths in the logical-mathematical and naturalist dimensions of intelligence. Although the stereotype suggests that scientists do their work alone, progress in science depends on collaboration. Therefore, interpersonal intelligence—knowing how to work well with others—also facilitates discovering and sharing new scientific knowledge.

Visual learners manage the challenges of mathematical formulas and also bring strong observational skills to science problems. Kinesthetic learners—those who learn best by doing, touching, and experiencing—function well in laboratory exercises or field applications. Solving problems in natural science and mathematics also offers opportunities to exercise critical and creative thinking, thoughtful reflection, and active learning.

The Remedy If you don't have natural abilities to support your learning in the natural sciences and mathematics, think about the following:

- *Talk about what you already believe.* Sometimes preexisting notions can interfere with learning new ideas in science. If you state what you really know or think about a scientific event, it may be easier for you to see where your explanation may not be adequate. Scientific explanations may then offer a clear improvement.
- *Make a total commitment.* Go to every class. Read every page of the text. Work every sample problem. Find other similar problems to solve. You may need to invest even more than the standard 2-to-1 ratio of out-of-class study to in-class time to get the basics.
- *Practice every day.* Committing to a little time each day will help you master the scientific terminology and formulas that facilitate scientific and mathematical competence.
- *Collaborate with others.* Most scientists do not work in isolation. Collaboration is a good model for beginners as well. By talking through

"All very well and good—but now we come to chart B."

problems with other students, you can improve your scientific problem solving.

- *Generate applied examples*. Identifying personal connections to the material will make abstract ideas more concrete.
- *Change the medium you are working in*. Some students find science and math too abstract. By changing the format of the problem, you may discover a clue about how to work with the ideas involved. For example, if a problem is presented in pictures or symbols, translate those to words. If you have a difficult word problem, try using pictures or symbols.
- *Know why you're studying*. Keep the big picture in mind. What will you accomplish by learning the skills involved in any given assignment? The long-range goal may help you stay motivated through the hard parts.
- *Be persistent and check your work*. Some problems don't yield a fast answer. Keep working, seeking, and persisting until you gain the insight you need to crack the problem. Be sure to check your answers so you don't lose credit because of carelessness. Scientists value precision and accuracy.
- *If you get confused, find another class section and sit in*. Sometimes it helps to sit through a class twice, as you may be able to do if your instructor teaches multiple sections.
- *Don't let anxiety overwhelm you*. Practice the skills and try to relax. If that doesn't work, seek counseling or tutoring.

The Social Sciences Because the social sciences use scientific methods to understand human experience, they often draw on both the sciences and the humanities.

The Rules The social sciences produce laws and theories to explain the behavior of individuals and groups. Concepts in the social sciences often serve as shorthand for complex patterns of behavior. For example, *social stratification,* a sociological concept, refers to how people in a society can be classified

Spotlight On...

Alia Whitney-Johnson

Engineering with a Twist

Alia Whitney-Johnson was hardly a typical engineering student. Even before she graduated with her degree in civil engineering from Massachusetts Institute of Technology, she distinguished herself in her expert and unusual engineering applications. In 2005, she founded Emerge Global, a nonprofit organization that focused on giving young sexually abused mothers in Sri Lanka a second chance. Alia introduced beading and launched a business enterprise that has already transformed the lives of over 170 Sri Lankan mothers. She established her jewelry-making business while studying the problem of protecting vegetation from the ravaging effects of tsunamis. Alia was designated a Truman Scholar, a Rhodes Scholar, and one of the "Top 10 College Women" by *Glamour Magazine* for her skills in civil and social engineering.

(Sources: Massachusetts Institute of Technology, 2011)

into groups according to how much money they make, what types of jobs they have, how much power they wield, and so forth. Much of what students need to memorize in social science courses comprises new terms—such as *stratification*—that explain human behavior.

The Risks Learning in the social sciences can be challenging because what you are expected to learn may conflict with what you previously believed. Say, for example, that you heard on television and from your Uncle Ernie that it's dangerous to wake up a sleepwalker. It made sense to you, so you believed it. In your psychology class, however, you discover that this knowledge is inaccurate and that it is more dangerous to allow a sleepwalker freedom to walk into trouble. You have to reject some things you thought were true—such as opinions from Uncle Ernie—to make room for new ideas derived from social science research.

Social scientists draw on multiple theories to explain the same thing. Social science is considered to be a "soft" science because it has to explain many deeply complex problems that depend on numerous circumstances.

The Resources Both interpersonal intelligence and intrapersonal intelligence— that is, self-understanding—can help you understand the social part of social science. Logical-mathematical intelligence and naturalistic intelligence support the science part of social science. Auditory and visual sensory styles help social scientists do what they do. The strong analytic requirements of social science tend to reward critical thinking, although other kinds of processing can also help.

The Remedy

- *Expect complexity*. You're less likely to be disappointed by the limits of social science if you understand that not all your questions will have exact answers. The most interesting topics are complex and do not present simple answers.
- *Use your own experience*. Most of the topics you'll study correspond to things you've already experienced. When you connect concepts to your experiences, you can create additional associations that will make them easier to learn. However, don't restrict yourself to understanding only what you've personally experienced.
- *Stay open to alternative explanations*. Recognize that your experience may not be typical of the systematic observations in science. You'll need to practice staying objective as you evaluate evidence, and you may need to reevaluate the firm conclusions you have drawn from your personal experience.

Foreign Languages Many colleges require students to study a foreign language to help them step outside their own culture and develop a broader perspective.

The Rules The study of a foreign language is loaded with rules. Proper grammar, verb tenses, and noun forms, such as feminine and masculine, all **represent**

"I'm a social scientist, Michael. That means I can't explain electricity or anything like that, but if you ever want to know about people, I'm your man."

rules that you must learn in order to acquire a new language. You may also learn the norms and practices of the culture in which the language is practiced.

The Risks Many foreign languages have new sounds that may not be natural to you. You may fear revealing any shortcomings in your "ear" for language. The amount of time you have to spend drilling can also be daunting. Overcoming the risks and succeeding in foreign language classes involve understanding and memorizing as much as you can.

The Resources If you're blessed with a good ear for language, chances are that you have a strong auditory sensory preference. Your fascination with words and meanings in another language points to verbal-linguistic intelligence. Because learning a new language requires a lot of memorization, the learning process of reflection may be the best tool available to help you in that process.

The Remedy
1. *Use color-coded materials.* Color-coded flash cards may give you additional cues about the kinds of words you're trying to learn. For example, use blue cards for verbs, yellow for nouns, and so on.
2. *Construct outrageous images.* Construct an image from the sounds of the language that will help you recall the vocabulary. For example, suppose you are trying to memorize the French word for "five." The word is *cinq* (pronounced "sank"). Picture the numeral 5 sinking below a water line to make it easier to recall.
3. *Talk out loud.* Label objects that you know. Rehearse routine conversations and stage practices with classmates when you can. Read your assignments aloud to improve your ear for the language.
4. *Don't get behind.* Keep up, because this type of class work will pile up fast.
5. *Distribute your practice sessions.* Although using shorter but frequent study sessions to memorize college material is good in general, it's essential when you're learning a foreign language. Regular practice sessions make your learning last longer.
6. *Immerse yourself.* Try to find some natural exposure to the language you're studying. For example, find a pen pal. Watch movies or television programs that feature the language you're studying.

 Manage Life

In this section we explore the biggest impediments to successful studying: sleep deprivation and learning differences. See what you can do to overcome these problems and promote a balanced lifestyle.

Secure Proper Sleep

Pay attention to your natural rhythms. Research suggests that many young adults undergo developmental changes that predispose them to being night people (Carskadon, 1999). They require more rest to cope with those changes and may not get in sync until later in the day. Sometimes that preference lingers so that even older students may feel more functional later in the day than early in the morning.

If you're a night person, review sessions may be most effective after supper and late into the evening. If you're a morning person, you need to study earlier in the day to maximize your attention and concentration.

If you aren't getting the proper amount of rest, you are in good company (Jensen, 2003). Experts say that the average number of sleep hours by college students dropped from 7.3 in 1978 to 6.65 by 2001, and a decade later, students seem even more worn out in class. Fewer students report that they get consistent hours of sleep. A recent study revealed that more than 60 percent of college students were not getting adequate sleep (Lund et al., 2010).

How Much Sleep Do You Need? You should be able to stay awake and alert if you have had sufficient sleep. Sleep experts suggest that traditional-age college students may need 10 hours of sleep per night because of the significant physiological changes that are unfolding (Maas, 1999). Experts suggest that young adults actually need at least 9.2 hours per night to function optimally (Carpenter, 2001). However, college students report that they sleep an average of only 6 hours of sleep per night—a 4-hour deficit that can take a toll on memory, mood, concentration, and other crucial ingredients of college success. Many may even experience a sleep disorder, a problem that is exacerbated by cramming strategies, trying to balance too many activities, and excessive video game playing and social networking. See Know Yourself: Self-Assessment 8.3, "Sleep Disorder Test," at the back of the chapter on page 283 to confirm whether your sleep problem is serious enough to need attention.

Combat Fatigue What if the demands of your schedule prevent you from getting all the sleep that you want or need?

- *Avoid getting too comfortable.* It is just an invitation to doze.
- *Use your desk only for studying.* When you drift to sleep at your desk, you learn to associate your desk with napping, a cue you may not be able to afford.
- *Set an alarm.* Buy a wristwatch that can signal you at reasonable intervals to keep you focused.
- *Make a commitment to others.* Study with others and use the social contact to keep you from dozing off.
- *Take a 5-minute fresh-air break.* A brisk walk can clear your mind so you can focus better when you return to your studies.
- *Stay involved in your reading.* The more invested you are, the less tempting it is to give in to sleepy feelings.
- *Get enough sleep to begin with.* You can manage a late night every once in a while, but a steady diet of all-nighters guarantees that you'll be fighting off the sandman.

Manage Learning Differences

Some college students suffer from an extra layer of challenge in college caused by the invisible problem of learning disabilities. However, in the words of entrepreneur Walt Disney, who was reported to have a learning disability, "If you can dream it, you can do it."

The Americans with Disabilities Act requires campuses to support the special needs of students with disabilities. Most campuses have offices dedicated to helping students figure out some strategies that can help them level the playing field. In addition, many instructors have developed their own strategies to assist students with short-term and long-term impairments that affect their ability to learn.

The Nature of Disabilities Students with learning disabilities represent a particular challenge for college success. Researchers have documented learning disabilities in all nations of the world (Lerner, 2006). Nearly 1 in 10 people in the United States experiences learning complications that interfere with incoming information by scrambling printed words, garbling spoken words, or causing confusion regarding numbers. As a result of chaotic encoding, people with disabilities can show problems in expression, including impaired short-term memory, problematic spelling, confusion about terminology, substandard grammar, and poor math skills.

Clearly, students with learning disabilities face daunting problems, including some unfounded prejudices of instructors and students who equate learning disability with low intelligence. This challenge is sufficiently problematic that some researchers (Levine, 2003) advocate using the term *learning difference* rather than *learning disability* to reduce the stigma associated with being "LD."

However, many individuals with learning disabilities find great success in school and afterward in their careers. In fact, a disproportionate number of successful CEOs of companies have dyslexia, one of the most common learning disabilities, which involves interference with a person's ability to read (West, 2003).

Learning disabilities do not prevent professional success. Businessman Charles Schwab and entertainers Patrick Dempsey, Jay Leno, and Whoopi Goldberg all have revealed their struggles with learning disabilities.

People with dyslexia report that words and sentences are hard to decode. Because they worry about performance and their slower rate of reading, students with dyslexia often feel singled out in classes for "not trying" or for "failing to live up to their potential," despite the fact that they try hard to keep up. West argues that such experiences appear to produce even greater motivation for individuals with learning disabilities to succeed and that they work hard to develop successful compensating strategies.

Students with learning disabilities who thrive in college demonstrate different characteristics than students with LD who fail to accomplish much (Mercer & Mercer, 2005). Successful LD students seek support systems to help them cope. They also stay positive, show strong verbal abilities, and find careers that play to their strengths as well as minimize their deficits. They persevere. In contrast, unsuccessful LD students don't take control of the situation and don't secure the emotional or academic support they need to help them weather the challenges. They often put themselves in situations that expose their weaknesses and may show higher rates of unemployment.

Evaluate Your Issues Given the crucial importance of getting support systems in place, students who suspect they might have a learning disability should seek a formal evaluation of their status. However, many students think they might have learning disabilities when they really don't. Sometimes they simply don't put in enough study time, or their anxiety sabotages them on tests. When you confer with your adviser about your academic struggles, prepare an honest estimate of how much work you're putting in on your studies. Your problems may lie in ineffective study strategies rather than a learning disability.

If you've experienced criticisms about your performance even though you're trying hard, you may find it helpful to complete Know Yourself: Self-Assessment 8.4, "Could I Have a Learning Disability?," at the end of the chapter on page 284, which identifies many characteristics of learning disabilities. This inventory will not tell you whether you have a learning disability; it merely provides a rough outline of concerns that you can raise with your academic adviser to sort out whether more diagnostic testing is in order.

Know Your Rights If you have a learning disability, your academic outlook can still be good. Students whose learning difference can be verified by a qualified examiner may apply for special education support through the Education for All Handicapped Children Act of 1975. In addition, campuses may offer assistance such as longer test periods for students with language-processing problems.

Learn to Cope You need to own the problem and understand the ways in which learning disabilities can influence your achievement. Traditional-age students have grown up in school systems that have been organized to detect learning disabilities and to help students deal with the consequences. However, seasoned students can sometimes discover upon returning to college that a learning disability explains their past academic struggles (Shapiro & Rich, 1999). It is understandable to be upset when college officials propose a learning disability, but recognize that this information will help you do the problem solving that should reduce your frustration over putting out lots of effort with too little achievement.

Your campus may have an office dedicated to getting some "accommodations" that will level the playing field with your peers. The process starts by talking with your instructors. If your limitation is a learning disability, you may have to secure formal documentation before you request an accommodation. Here are some questions you can use to open that conversation:

- Do you mind if I record your lecture?
- Have you worked with students who have had challenges like this?
- Do you have any advice for helping me succeed?
- May I use a spelling device to help me in exams that require me to write?
- May I arrange for extended time to finish exams?
- Is it possible to get assignments in advance?
- Do you know of any tutors who might help me?
- Would you like to have more specific information about my particular limitation?

Compensate If you do have a learning disability, you'll need to develop a set of strategies to compensate for the challenges your learning style presents. Among other things, you can:

- Set up a study group to discuss course material with others.
- Compare your notes with a friend's after each class to see whether you've missed any important details.
- Use audio versions of textbooks when available.
- Use a spell-checker.
- Get support from the campus study skills center.
- Ask friends to proofread your written work.
- Alert your instructors to your special needs.
- Restrict yourself to using just one calendar to minimize confusion.

If you work on compensating strategies for learning disabilities, the ideas you develop in college will continue to serve you throughout life.

 # Connect and Communicate

Your peers can be an invaluable resource in your study success. Whether you participate in a study group (face-to-face) or benefit from threaded discussions online, you may be able to glean the additional insight you need to own the course content.

Join a Study Group

Working in a study group adds a vital element to your education and expands your resources. Besides learning the course content better, you can improve your ability to communicate, develop your project skills, and deal better with conflict. How can you make group work most efficient and effective?

Don't wait for an instructor to convene a study group. Find interested, competent classmates to meet with regularly and talk with about a challenging course. Once you have made the commitment, stay the course. Some additional strategies include:

- Identify the hardest concepts or ideas you've encountered.
- Talk about the problems or ideas you especially like or dislike.
- Discuss which parts of the readings interest you the most.
- Help one another share and clarify everyone's understanding of the material.
- Discuss strategies for remembering course material.

- Generate questions to prepare for tests.
- Keep your commitments.

Make Your Study Group Work Whether the group is collaborating on a 10-minute discussion project in class or a challenge that spans several weeks, effective groups usually work in stages such as the following:

1. *Plan the task*. As the group convenes, lay the groundwork for working together efficiently by doing four things:
   a. Introduce group members: "Who are we?"
   b. Identify the purpose of meeting by agreeing on goals and objectives: "What tasks do we need to do?"
   c. Create a plan for working together productively: "How can we work together efficiently?"
   d. Set criteria for success: "How will we know we've succeeded in our task?"
2. *Come to a consensus*. Once the ground rules have been established, your group can address the specific task at hand. You don't have to choose a formal leader, although that might be helpful. Group members who ask questions and move the group along help through informal guidance.
3. *Evaluate the results*. In the final stage of the discussion, summarize what has been accomplished and evaluate how well the group has performed so that you can improve its efficiency. Then, plan your next meeting.

Promote Strong Group Performance Other suggestions for promoting productive study group time include the following (Fleming, 2010):

- Limit the size of the group to no more than five to promote full participation.
- Exchange contact details and have each member describe the contributions each can make.
- Give your group an official name to promote identification with the mission.
- Set a standard place and time to convene.
- Share moderator responsibilities for keeping the group on track. The moderator should recognize great ideas that contribute to group satisfaction and also identify when the process gets off track.

Eliminate Group-Work Obstacles Group work can provide some of your most exciting—and most frustrating—learning. When you join others to solve a problem or explore the meaning of a work of art, your pooled brainpower can result in insights you might never have had on your own. Effective groups tend to bring out the best in their members.

However, whether your group is face-to-face in the library or screen-to-screen in the digital world (Paloff & Pratt, 1999), people regularly have problems working in groups. Figure 8.4, "Common Problems and Sensible Solutions for Study Groups," describes some common group-work problems and what to do about them.

Thrive Online

Connecting with your peers is an essential part of good online course design. However, building relationships with people in the digital world adds another layer of complexity. You may have to learn to work effectively with others without

PROBLEM	SOLUTION
Failure to do groundwork	**Establish goals**
Group members may be so eager to get on with the task that they jump into a chaotic and unsatisfying discussion.	Your group will collaborate more efficiently if you have a clear picture of what the group wants to achieve and how you hope to achieve it.
Conflict avoidance	**Legitimize difference of opinion**
Some groups become disorganized as disagreements emerge. Conflict is valuable because differences of opinion can lead to a better discussion or well-considered solution.	When conflict emerges, ask group members to support their opinions with evidence. Let the quality of evidence persuade the group.
Unequal participation	**Specify useful roles**
When groups are large and some members take charge, shy or unprepared members may be less likely to participate.	Ask quiet members to serve the group by taking notes or summarizing the key ideas. Ask them directly about their opinions.
Domination by one member	**Ask for space and cooperation**
Sometimes leaders push too hard and end up alienating other group members. They may not recognize the value of involving all members to improve the quality of the group's conclusion.	When leaders get too pushy, suggest that other members need more time and space to express their ideas. If this gentle confrontation does not work, be more forceful. Point out what the group may lose when some don't participate.
Off-task behavior	**Ask for concentrated effort**
Less committed members may engage in behaviors (such as popping gum) that distract the group.	Suggest that the offending person change the behavior to help promote a more favorable, quiet working environment.
Members who coast	**Clarify expectations**
Some group members may not contribute once they sense that the group will succeed by the work of the more energetic or motivated members.	Express your disappointment and anger about the unfair distribution of work. Propose some consequences for those who aren't doing their fair share.

FIGURE 8.4 Common Problems and Sensible Solutions for Study Groups

the helpful cues that come from seeing body language and directly observing emotional expression. What are some strategies that will help you thrive in the digital learning environment (based on Evans, 2004)?

- *Anticipate trouble.* Although the digital environment has become more reliable, it is better to be safe than sorry. Incorporate more time in your study plan in case there are technological problems. Plan for more time than you may need to get things done on time. Instructors show little patience with last-minute computer problems that prevent completion of assigned work. Have a backup plan for securing an alternate computer or printer. Consider e-mailing yourself at the same time you e-mail assignments to create a digital trail of completion in case your instructor has technological problems on her end.
- *Read postings twice.* It is pretty easy for time-pressed students not to read comments accurately. Read everything twice, including online instructions from the professor, to maximize your ability to interpret the information on the post.
- *Add value in your posts.* Avoid bland responses that add little to the discussion. Ideally, your response should be the perfect stimulus to spur

others to comment. Introduce a related example, point out a flaw, develop a metaphor, provide a meaningful quotation, or ask other questions that can make peers think more deeply about the task. However, stay on point. Don't try to address more than one focus in any post.

- *Clearly label your contributions.* Identify what problem you are responding to and be consistent in how you present your identity so your peers and instructor won't be challenged by keeping track of multiple versions of your self-presentation.
- *Keep conversations public.* Asynchronous (work at your own pace) designs may mean that you will be posting your responses to class problems at all hours. Stay in specified channels so your instructor can track the progress you and your classmates are making on assignments. If you move out of specified channels, you may benefit from making copies of those conversations for instructor review.
- *Avoid posting in anger.* It is easy to get angry online from responding to a socially clumsy post. However, if you jump in with your own hot response, you will only aggravate the situation. Calm down before you react online. Draft your response and go have a soda. Then come back in a better frame of mind before you hit the "send" button.
- *WHATEVER YOU DO, DON'T USE CAPS.* Even if your goal is communicating something pleasant, most readers experience that kind of post as "yelling."

Build a Bright Future

Developing good study strategies and strong people skills will go a long way toward helping you secure the bright future you have in mind. You will be confronted with new things to learn well after graduation. By developing sturdy study strategies now and learning to work not just with your own abilities but also with the strengths and weaknesses of others, you become a valuable future employee.

Forge Professional Skill Sets

Employers are specific about the skills they look for in potential employees (Hansen & Hansen, 2011). Developing study skills, especially if you work with study groups to expand your learning, lays a great foundation for building a compelling resume.

What Professional Skills Can You Build on Your Own? There are several ways you can build your appeal to future employers in your solo study efforts:

- *Planning and organizing.* Getting your own study goals met is not that different from achieving the goals of an employer. Project-management skills (designing, planning, organizing, and implementing) are core to both endeavors.
- *Managing multiple priorities.* If you think about each course as a project, your ability to balance the demands of multiple courses means you must juggle multiple projects with different deadlines at the same time. Succeeding with your own courses can persuade employers that you will be adaptable and flexible in addressing the multiple projects they have in mind.
- *Using analytical and research skills.* Think about how your ability to size up and follow instructions and information, recognize key elements,

develop a research plan, and factor in multiple perspectives could make you an appealing candidate to a future employer.

- *Solving problems and being creative.* Think of devising an effective study strategy as solving a problem. The collective experience entailed in completing an undergraduate degree gives evidence that you can solve the problem handed to you by each of your instructors. To the extent that some of your solutions can be creative, those examples can set you apart from other candidates.

- *Having computer and technical literacy.* The ability to navigate computer hardware and software not only helps in supporting a strategic study plan, but it prepares you well for the digital challenges that lie ahead in most professional jobs.

What Skills Can You Build in Groups? Whether you are honing your group skills in study groups or class discussions, the results can inspire employers to want to work with you.

- *Communication skills.* What examples can you find about how well you can listen, express yourself orally, and communicate in writing from the work you do to prepare for tests in your courses? These skills are essential to effectiveness in the workplace.

- *Interpersonal skills.* You won't want just to get along in the workplace; you will want to thrive. You can prepare for interpersonal effectiveness by resolving conflicts, inspiring others, and building your trustworthiness.

- *Leadership abilities.* Those who fare best in the workplace are those who demonstrate their readiness for additional responsibility. Think about your group experiences as opportunities to develop a distinctive leadership style. Your employer may quickly recognize your ability not just to collaborate but also to motivate and manage the efforts of coworkers.

- *Teamwork skills.* As an employee you will probably serve on a variety of teams to accomplish the employer's goal. Think of each group project as an opportunity to get the whole team successfully across the finish line. The "high 5s" that you exchange when successful in college pave the way for success in professional team assignments.

- *Multicultural sensitivity and awareness.* It is rare that you will be in a group with people who are perfectly predictable. Seek all of the opportunities you can to gain experience with people whose backgrounds diverge from your own. College experiences provide a safety net for you to learn about others and how best to work with them as compared to the workplace, where insensitivity and blunders can cost you your job. Strive to build rapport with others even if you have little in common with them or don't particularly like them. Succeeding in group efforts will give you something in common and help you overcome negative first impressions.

Prove Expertise in Internships

Alan was almost supernaturally good in recalling obscure sports facts. He recognized that the more he knew about a team, the easier it was to attach additional, interesting details in declarative memory about sports. He was surprised and disappointed to discover that memorizing facts in college courses was not as easy. However, he made the most of his study skills to pursue a career in sports broadcasting. He chose a major in communication arts with an emphasis on broadcasting as the best preparation for his goal. His senior internship allowed him to live the life of a broadcaster for 10 hours a week. His knowledge and enthusiasm were so impressive that he received a job offer shortly after graduation. Within a few years, a radio station hired him as a sports reporter and Alan was well on his way to achieving his dream.

Julie had always wanted to be a music teacher. She thought it would be gratifying to teach children about the transforming power of music. She was profoundly disappointed when she took a course in music appreciation and the professor required her students to memorize long passages of music so that they could identify them at test time in as few bars as possible. Although Julie understood how recognizing great works could enhance appreciation, she doubted that it would help her produce the transforming effect she wanted for her future students. In her field placement, she began experimenting with ways to allow children to create music and to evaluate what worked and what didn't work. To no one's surprise, Julie easily captured her dream job after graduation and also went on to earn teaching awards that honored her creativity.

© moodboard/Corbis

Many students discover through college presentation projects that they have a knack for teaching.

Manage Life

- Secure appropriate sleep to manage study session strain.
- Undergo special testing if your results don't match your efforts.
- Develop compensating strategies to minimize the effects of a learning difference.

Connect and Communicate

- Assign roles, plan tasks, set criteria for success, and evaluate your progress to ensure an effective study group.
- Solve routine problems that compromise group progress.
- Take extra precautions to produce optimal results with online groups.

Build a Bright Future

- See the connection between effective studying and preparing for the workforce.
- Recognize how internships can showcase study skill expertise.

Clarify Expectations

- Find a quiet place and use it consistently.
- Schedule study times that fit with your energy level and course demands.
- Set goals for what you want to accomplish in a study session.

Develop Competence

- Consider Bloom's Taxonomy to maximize study gains at different depths of thinking.
- Understand the rules, risks, resources, and remedy for each discipline.
- Prepare to think more abstractly as coursework deepens.
- Attend, concentrate, and minimize interference to enhance memorization effectiveness.
- Use mnemonics to build personal connections to your coursework.

 Visit the College Success CourseMate for *Your Guide to College Success* for interactive resources at login.cengagebrain.com

1. List a few important issues to consider when deciding where to study, when to study, and what to study.

_____

_____

_____

2. What is the difference between lower-order and higher-order cognitive skills? Provide a few examples of each.

_____

_____

_____

3. Describe the difference between short-term memory and long-term memory. How can you use this information to improve your study strategies in the future?

_____

_____

_____

4. Why do students rely on mnemonics to jog their memories?

_____

_____

_____

5. How do the different disciplines encourage different kinds of study? List some specific strategies for success in the discipline area you are considering for your major.

_____

_____

_____

6. Describe the impact of sleep deprivation on the quality of your study time.

_____

_____

_____

7. How can learning disabilities influence study success? What can students do to address such disabilities?

_____

_____

_____

8. List three pros and three cons of working in study groups. Now write down a strategy for addressing each con.

Pro: _____   Con: _____

Pro: _____   Con: _____

Pro: _____   Con: _____

Strategy: _____

Strategy: _____

Strategy: _____

9. Describe some additional steps you can take to enhance the success of group work online.

_____

_____

_____

_____

_____

10. How does success in study translate to later success in the workplace?

_____

_____

_____

_____

_____

 **Know Yourself**

What's the Right Ratio?

Studying constantly is likely to produce an imbalanced life. Studying too little won't get you where you want to go either. Most instructors advocate studying at least 2 hours outside of class for every hour you spend in class. Harder subjects may demand even more study time. Which of the following represents your general orientation toward study?

_____ I study every minute I'm not committed to some other activity.

_____ I try to schedule systematically for 2 or more hours for each hour in class.

_____ I average about 1 hour outside of class for each hour in class.

_____ I'm lucky if I can squeeze in any study outside of class.

Am I Ready to Learn and Remember?

Review the elements of effective study strategies below and decide whether each statement is something you already do well or something you need to improve.

	I Do This Well	I Could Improve This
To take advantage of my best energy levels, I purposefully schedule when I will study certain subjects.	_____	_____
I select study environments that have few distractions.	_____	_____
I review course materials regularly to spread my learning out over time.	_____	_____
I try to find some angle in my assignments that will increase my interest.	_____	_____
To ensure my understanding and increase my personal involvement, I question what I read.	_____	_____
I look for ways to add meaning to course ideas during review sessions.	_____	_____
I rehearse key ideas to the point of overlearning.	_____	_____
I use mnemonic strategies for memorization. (List several specific strategies you use):	_____	_____

_____

_____

	I Do This Well	I Could Improve This
When I feel frustrated by partial recall, I divert my attention to recover more details.	_____	_____
I schedule an intensive review session before a test.	_____	_____
I avoid cramming whenever I can.	_____	_____
I use review tests to see whether I need to change my study strategies.	_____	_____

Look over your answers. Could the areas you need to improve mean the difference between a mediocre performance and honor-quality work? What would you need to do to improve? How could you reward yourself for adopting better strategies?

SELF-ASSESSMENT 8.3

Sleep Disorder Test

Nearly one-third of all Americans suffer from sleep problems that make both waking and sleeping less than ideal. Check whether the following characteristics apply to your sleep patterns to determine if professional assistance might help.

If you have experienced any of the listed symptoms in the last year, check-mark the corresponding line.

_____ I have difficulty falling asleep.
_____ Thoughts race through my mind, preventing me from sleeping.
_____ I am afraid to go to sleep.
_____ I wake up during the night and can't go back to sleep.
_____ I worry about things and have trouble relaxing.
_____ I wake up earlier than I would like to.
_____ I lie awake for half an hour or more before falling asleep.
_____ I feel sad and depressed.
_____ I've been told that I snore.
_____ I've been told that I stop breathing while I sleep, although I don't remember this when I wake up.
_____ I have high blood pressure.
_____ My friends and family say they have noticed changes in my personality.
_____ I am gaining weight.
_____ I sweat excessively at night.
_____ I have noticed my heart pounding or beating irregularly at night.
_____ I get morning headaches.
_____ I have trouble sleeping when I have a cold.
_____ I suddenly wake up gasping for air.
_____ I am overweight.
_____ I seem to be losing my sex drive.
_____ I feel sleepy during the day, even if I slept through the night.
_____ I have had trouble concentrating in school or at work.
_____ When I am angry or surprised, I feel as if I'm going limp.
_____ I have fallen asleep while driving.
_____ I feel as if I go around in a daze.
_____ I have experienced vivid dream-like scenes upon falling asleep or waking.
_____ I have fallen asleep during physical effort.
_____ I feel as if I am hallucinating when I fall asleep.
_____ I feel as if I have to cram a full day into every hour to get anything done.
_____ I have fallen asleep when laughing or crying.
_____ I have trouble at work because of sleepiness.
_____ I have vivid nightmares soon after falling asleep.
_____ I fall asleep during the day.
_____ No matter how hard I try to stay awake, I fall asleep.
_____ I feel unable to move when waking up or falling asleep.
_____ I wake up with heartburn.
_____ I have a chronic cough.
_____ I have to use antacids almost every week for stomach trouble.
_____ I have morning hoarseness.
_____ I wake up at night coughing or wheezing.
_____ I have frequent sore throats.
_____ Other than when exercising, I still have muscle tension in my legs.
_____ I have noticed (or others have commented) that parts of my body jerk during sleep.
_____ I have been told I kick at night.
_____ I have aching or "crawling" sensations in my legs.
_____ I have leg pain during the night.
_____ Sometimes I just have to move my legs at night—I can't keep them still.
_____ I wake up with sore or achy muscles.

Source: http://www.mountcarmelhealth.com/114.cfm

Could I Have a Learning Disability?

You may have a learning disability if you have the following difficulties. Check any that apply to you.

_____ Misunderstand simple printed materials
_____ Have a great deal of trouble working with basic math problems
_____ Have difficulty writing and speaking
_____ Approach studying in a haphazard manner
_____ Get easily distracted
_____ Confuse _left_ and _right_ or other spatial words
_____ Arrive late often (such as to class)
_____ Struggle with categories and comparisons
_____ Have trouble with fine motor skills or finger control
_____ Feel awkward in gross motor (body) movements
_____ Misinterpret subtle nonverbal cues
_____ Have difficulty following instructions
_____ Reverse letters in words or words in sentences
_____ Hear teachers complain that you "are not living up to your potential"

If you feel frustrated in any of these areas, you may want to see if you have a learning disability. First, talk with your adviser about the nature of your difficulties. Your adviser can recommend changes in your study strategy or refer you to a specialist on campus who can help you with diagnostic testing. On some campuses, this evaluation is expensive, but you're likely to get advice that makes the investment worthwhile.

Clarify Expectations

1. Call Waiting

You're assigned to a discussion group that will meet throughout the semester, but one of the group members brings her cell phone. The phone usually rings 5 minutes into the meeting. She excuses herself to take the call and usually misses more than half of each meeting. What strategies could you and your group use to address this challenge?

_____

_____

2. Creative Space Management

Identify a place where you have a hard time studying, such as a bus, a noisy dorm room, or a crowded kitchen table. List three strategies that would help you make this place better for studying.

1. _____

2. _____

3. _____

Now try each one. Did they work? Why or why not? What did this exercise teach you about your ideal study location?

_____

_____

_____

 ## Develop Competence

3. Deep Study

Pick a topic area from a subject you're currently studying. Develop a question based on each order level of Bloom's Taxonomy. Now come up with a tentative answer for each question. How much harder do you have to work to come up with a good answer to a higher-order question than a lower-order one? Think about the balance of lower-order and higher-order questions across the courses you are taking. What should this balance suggest about how you study in your courses?

Remember: _____

Understand: _____

Apply: _____

Analyze: _____

Evaluate: _____

Create: _____

How to Remember

What is something that you frequently forget? It could be an important concept from one of your classes, a particular type of appointment, or where you last left your keys. List a few strategies that might help you address this memory lapse. Try each one. Which strategy worked best and why?

Strategy 1: _____

Strategy 2: _____

Strategy 3: _____

5. Reduce Your Disciplinary Risks

Many people have fears related to disciplines they are required to study to complete their education. In what discipline are you least comfortable? Describe the source of your concern. What might you do to get more comfortable with this discipline? Can you identify any role models who can help you develop a more positive attitude?

Discipline: _____

Issues of concern: _____

Strategies for greater comfort: _____

Potential role models: _____

Manage Life

6. Sleep Doctor

Chances are good that you aren't getting the sleep you need. What should your goal be for sleep? What pressures keep you from getting the sleep that would be in your best interest? Which of those pressures are fixable?

_____

_____

_____

7. Thrive Even with Learning Differences

Who is the learning disabilities specialist on campus? Find out and write down the contact information below. If you suspect that you might have a problem, make an appointment with this individual to find out about further testing. If you don't think you have a learning disability, talk with a classmate who does. Find out what kinds of compensations seem to be most effective for him. Do some of the compensations seem as if they might also be useful to you? Which ones?

Learning disabilities specialist: _____

Phone number and e-mail address: _____

Information on testing: _____

Helpful compensation strategies: _____

Connect and Communicate

8. Study-Group Savvy

In which courses would you benefit from forming a study group?

_____

_____

_____

What special talents would you bring that would help the group succeed? Do you have any personality quirks or negative work habits that could adversely affect the group's outcomes? What can you do to address those problems in the study group?

Positive talents: _____

Negative traits: _____

9. Digital Monsters

Describe five different problems that students experience when they are not adept at maneuvering in online study groups. What steps can you take to ensure that you don't turn into a digital monster?

_____

_____

_____

 **Build a Bright Future**

10. Workplace Readiness

Are you better at reaping benefits from solo study or from working with groups? Review the specific skill sets that help prepare you for professional life. Identify the skills in which you excel and the ones where you could stand some polishing.

_____

_____

_____

11. Internship Detective

The prospect of an internship may feel quite remote at this point in your education. However, it is not too soon to begin thinking about ways to build your experiences and enhance your appeal to future employers. Identify five work settings that you might have some curiosity about that could give you a good idea about whether that workplace holds promise for your future. If you have identified a major, confer with your adviser to see if internship placements are currently used to help you apply your learning. How does your dream list match up to the reality?

_____

_____

_____

Succeed on Tests

KNOW YOURSELF

BY THIS POINT IN THE TERM, you've probably already faced one ongoing challenge that all college students encounter—tests! Happily, some tests match how well you've studied and what you've learned. Other tests, however, may have led you to think that you and the instructor weren't on the same planet, let alone in the same classroom. To evaluate where you stand right now with regard to test taking, estimate your likelihood of engaging in the following success behaviors. Place a check mark in the box that best captures how you currently approach test-taking challenges.

How Do I Approach Tests?

	Very Much Like Me	Somewhere In Between	Not at All Like Me
I pace myself effectively to get ready for a test.			
I figure out ahead of time what will be on the test.			
I control my nervousness about test performance.			
I read all directions carefully before I start.			
I know effective strategies for performing well on different kinds of tests.			
I regularly complete tests in the allotted time.			
I use test results to improve my learning and future test performances.			
I distinguish myself positively in test situations.			
I can describe the consequences of academic dishonesty at my college.			

Royalty-Free/CORBIS

289

Spotlight On...

VIVIANA ALCAZAR
From Mexico to Stanford

Viviana Alcazar credits the three closing lines of the poem "Digging" by Irish poet Sean Heaney as a powerful motivating force in her own academic goals and personal life:

> Between my finger and my thumb.
> The squat pen rests.
> I'll dig with it.

What resonated for her in this work was the recognition that Heaney represented the generation in his family that had made the leap from working with his hands in the field to pursuing

Viviana Alcazar fulfilled her dream of becoming the first person in her family to complete college when she graduated from Stanford in 2007.

higher education. As the daughter of parents who had completed only the third grade and also subsisted as farmers, Viviana longed to make that leap herself.

Viviana Alcazar's journey has not been easy (Freeman, 2007). Born in Mexico, Viviana immigrated with her family early in her life to the United States, only to return to Mexico when the family farm needed tending. She came back to the United States and entered Canada Community College to begin working on her dream. One year into her college work, her personal life became much more challenging. Her mother, who had made enormous sacrifices for her family, was diagnosed with stomach cancer. With her father still earning a living in Mexico, suddenly Viviana needed to become a caretaker, a house manager, and a special big sister who kept the family together stateside. Despite those challenges, she maintained a 4.0 average, worked as a teaching assistant, and nurtured her dream of getting her baccalaureate degree.

Awarded a Jack Kent Cooke Scholarship, Viviana's dream came true at Stanford University. Her track record of hard work and skilled use of mentoring culminated in a double major in English and Spanish literature, preparing for a career of teaching literature in a liberal arts setting.

Photo Courtesy of Viviana Alcazar

Take a look at the chapter outline. Based on your profile of test-taking characteristics, which parts of the chapter should be most helpful to you in becoming a better test-taker? What preliminary goals can help you achieve greater consistency in test-taking skills?

(Source: Freeman, S. G., 2007)

Clarify Expectations

By this point in the semester, you may have already gotten back some exam results. If you have been successful, you've met or exceeded your expectations. However, if not, you either need to adjust your performance expectations or embark on some strategies to improve your test scores.

Get in Gear

No matter what course of study you pursue in college, your professors will evaluate how well you are learning. Most students discover that there are important differences between tests in high school and those in college, Tests and quizzes take place more often in high school than they do in college. Although that arrangement may initially sound like you are catching a break, the down side of less frequent testing is that each college test performance carries substantially more weight in determining your grades. For example, in some classes your scores on merely a midterm and a final examination will determine your grade. Therefore, although you undergo fewer exams and quizzes, each experience is likely to be more intense since more is at stake.

As you can see in the graph, grades drifted downward from high school to college. This means that you have to study harder to maintain the same grade point average in college.

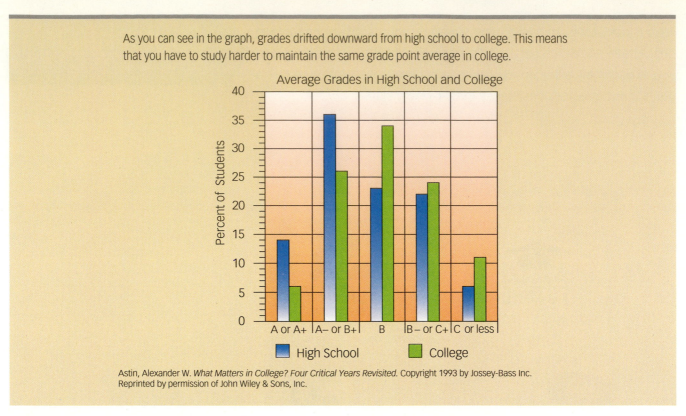

Average Grades in High School and College

FIGURE 9.1 How Grades Can Change

Even though you may have fared well in high school test situations, most students report that maintaining a good grade point average is more challenging in college. See Figure 9.1, "How Grades Can Change," to see how grades tend to drift downward as testing difficulties intensify.

Get On with It!

Believe it or not, tests can benefit you. They can help in the following ways:

- *Pace your reading.* College reading assignments can feel overwhelming, so it's easy to get behind. Tests throughout the term push you to do the work on time.
- *Consolidate your learning.* Tests encourage you to study the course material more intensively and retain the ideas longer. Your effort in preparing for tests can produce insights you might not have made without the pressure of the exam.
- *Improve your thinking.* Whether you're figuring out which multiple-choice alternative to eliminate or determining how to structure an essay, tests give you practice in careful observation, analysis, judgment, and other critical-thinking skills.
- *Give feedback.* Test results tell you whether your study strategies have worked. Good results confirm that you're on the right track. A string of poor scores suggests that you need to improve your motivation or study skills.
- *Confer special status.* Good results might qualify you for a scholarship or allow you to skip preliminary courses and move on to more advanced ones.

Size Up the Challenge

No two professors test alike. They choose specific test strategies that fit with the depth of learning that they hope to help you achieve.

Know What to Expect Most instructors describe the kinds of tests they are planning either during the class or in the syllabus. Some even make sample tests from prior semesters available for study purposes. Many welcome questions about how to prepare. For example, the following questions may help give you the direction you need to be successful:

- How long will the test be?
- What types of questions will be on it?
- Are there any particular aspects of the work we've been doing that you'll emphasize? (Note: This question is much better than "Will this be on the test?")
- Are there penalties for wrong guesses?
- Will this material also be covered on a cumulative exam at the end of the term?

Some instructors don't offer much direction or many clues about their tests. What if your instructor is inscrutable *and* unapproachable? You may know some students who have completed the course before you. Find out what they did to succeed or what strategies didn't work. Don't be afraid to research your instructor's testing practices.

Test conditions vary. In large lecture classes, security issues may be intense. For example, your instructor may require you to sit in alternate seats to reduce cheating. Proctors may roam the aisles and retrieve all materials after the test. Your instructor may not even be present, so you might want to get all your questions answered before the day of the test. In smaller classes with the instructor present, you may be able to clarify issues as they arise.

"Psych Out" the Teacher Some students seem psychic when guessing what will be on a test. How do they do it? They size up the instructor by identifying what concepts have been stressed enthusiastically during class lectures and discussions. Instructors often use specific cues to identify important and testable material (Appleby, 1997). They may be signaling probable test material when they:

- repeat or emphasize certain concepts.
- illustrate key ideas with examples.
- stop pacing back and forth behind the lectern.
- intensify eye contact.
- use gestures in more dramatic ways.
- change their tone of voice.
- say "in conclusion . . . " or "to summarize . . . "
- pause to allow you time to write your notes.
- write on the board or point to ideas on an overhead transparency.
- highlight ideas in their introductory remarks or conclusion.

Don't Skip the Prior Class Most instructors devote at least a few minutes of the last class before an exam to narrow down the most critical material or even to give hints about what the exam will contain (McWhorter, 2000). Pay close attention to the information that might telegraph what the instructor thinks is most important for testing purposes.

After each assignment	Write a summary paragraph of what you learned and how it relates to the course objectives.
After each class	Review your notes to consolidate your learning.

During the last class before the test	Find out about the test:
	    What will be and won't be on the test;
	    The format of the test;
	    The contribution of the test to your grade.
	Clarify any confused ideas from past classes.

After the last class before the test	Plan your final review session.

The night before the test	Organize your notes for systematic review.
	Study the test material exclusively—or last—to reduce interference.
	Practice the kind of thinking the test will require:
	    Rehearsal and recital for objective tests;
	    Critical analysis for subjective tests.
	Identify any fuzzy areas and confer with classmates to straighten out your confusion.
	Get a good night's sleep.

The day of the test	Organize your supplies. Eat a good breakfast/lunch/dinner. Review your notes, chapter summaries, and/or course glossary.
The hour before the test	Review your notes. Go to the classroom early and get settled. Practice relaxing and positive thinking.

© Cengage Learning 2013

FIGURE 9.2 Timetable for Sensible Study Strategies

Protect Your Study Time

Classmates may request your help at the last minute, especially if you live with them. You may happily accept. Helping others as a peer tutor can build your self-esteem and give you more opportunity to rehearse material (Karabenik & Newman, 2006). Or you may need to use the time alone to master the material yourself. If giving help does not work with your study schedule or your priorities, explain that you've planned out your study strategy and need every minute of quiet concentration to do your best.

What if a loved one makes demands on your time that interfere with your study schedule? Explain to partners or family members, including children, that you need extra help from them before a test to make it as easy as possible to study. Promise them that you will spend time with them after the test. Then keep your promise.

If you clarify expectations and plan accordingly, your work is much easier as the test gets closer. Figure 9.2, "A Timetable for Sensible Study Strategies," summarizes strategies for pacing yourself for the least stressful test preparation.

 # Develop Competence

Students who are good at taking tests rely on more than just intelligence. They recognize that specific test-taking skills can make all the difference, including preparation, attack skills specific to testing format, and review. Where can your skills stand some improvement?

Tailor Study Strategies to Test Format

Courses differ in the depth of knowledge that may need to be assessed. For example, beginning courses are much more likely to concentrate on shallower kinds of cognitive demands, such as memorization. On the other hand, advanced courses (or really tough professors) may intensify their demands to require analysis, synthesis, and even creative responses in a test situation. Let's explore how different kinds of test formats promote specific study strategies.

Objective Tests Memorizing facts is usually a good strategy for answering simple, objective test questions. These include tests with multiple-choice, matching, true/false, and fill-in-the-blank items. Successful memorizing strategies include using flash cards, making a concept vocabulary list, reviewing a text's study guide, and reorganizing your notes. Find the memorizing strategy that works best for the specific challenge.

At the college level, most instructors ask objective questions that require more than just rote memory. When you have to do more than recall facts, your study strategy will also be more complex. Draw organizational charts or diagrams to identify relationships. Design some practice questions that exercise your ability to reason.

Essay Tests Digesting a whole term's worth of material for an essay can be a challenge. If you know the specific topics ahead of time, scan the notes you've made and highlight all related ideas in a specific color. This strategy will let you concentrate on those ideas as you think about questions or practice answers. If you don't know the essay topics ahead of time, go back over your course and reading notes and write a paragraph for each text chapter or course lecture. These paragraphs should summarize the key ideas in the passage.

Procedural Tests Some types of tests ask you to demonstrate specific procedures, such as applying a formula to solve a math problem, conducting an interview in nursing, or solving for an unknown in chemistry. To prepare for procedural tests, perform the target skill until you're comfortable with it. If test time will be limited, build time limits into your practice.

To succeed on tests, you need to review your notes to think about how the ideas can be incorporated in designated test formats.

Set the Stage for Test-Taking Success

Inventor Henry Ford once said, "Before everything else, getting ready is the secret to success." Whether you're filled with dread or eager to show what you know, the following preparation can give you the best chance of doing well.

- *Get a good night's sleep.* Sleep deprivation produces substantial risk on academic performance (Trockel et al., 2000). You need at least 8 hours of sleep to stay alert and do your best thinking, problem solving, and communicating. If you deprive yourself of restorative sleep, you are at a disadvantage before you even begin.
- *Bring supplies for your comfort.* A bottle of water or cup of coffee may keep up your spirits (and your caffeine level). Instructors usually specify what comforts you can bring to class. Avoid causing distractions, such as unwrapping noisy candy wrappers; other students are likely to be as

nervous and distractible as you are. If you get stress headaches, don't forget to pack your pain reliever.

- *Bring required academic supplies—and spares.* You may need to bring a blue book (a standard lined essay book for handwritten responses). Bring a sharpened pencil or pen and a backup, a calculator, scratch paper, or whatever other supplies the instructor allows. Make sure you have a watch or can see a classroom clock so you can pace your work.

- *Organize your resources.* In some cases, instructors may let you bring a summary of notes to jog your memory during the test. They even may let you have open access to your books and notes (a sure sign that the test will be hard). Write your summaries clearly so that you don't lose time trying to decode your own writing. Attach some tabs, use marked index cards, or highlight your resources in other ways that will make them easy to navigate under pressure.

- *Bring permitted reference aids.* Expect that your cell phone or laptop will be prohibited as a security measure. However, if you struggle with writing and spelling, bring a dictionary or a spell-checker if it is permitted. Many instructors will let you use such an aid because it shows your desire to do good work. Ask first. Don't assume everything is fair game.

Use General Test-Taking Strategies

The following general strategies will help make the most of your studying to succeed on tests, regardless of their specific content:

- *Relax.* Take a deep breath. The calmer you stay during a test, the better you'll do. Take relaxing breaths at the start and continue breathing calmly throughout the test. Concentrate on breathing slowly from your diaphragm. When you do this right, your stomach will move out as you breathe in, and in as you breathe out. "Chest breathing" can make you feel more agitated.

- *Look at the entire test.* Examine the structure. Count the pages. Think about how to divide your time, given your strengths and weaknesses. If the test includes different types of questions (such as multiple-choice and short essay), begin with the type you do best on to build your confidence.

- *Plan your attack.* As you plan how to allot your time, leave more time for parts that require more effort or that make up more of your total score. Knowing how points will be distributed across the test will help you decide where to spend your time if it becomes clear you won't be able to finish. For example, the multiple-choice section may be worth 20 points and the essay section 50 points. Even though the multiple-choice questions come first, you may want to start with the essay, which counts for more. Find out whether there are penalties for guessing. Try to allow time at the end to review your work.

- *Read the instructions . . . twice!* You'll be very upset if you discover near the end of the exam time that you were supposed to answer only certain questions rather than all the questions on the test. Read the instructions carefully to make optimal use of your available time.

- *When you get stuck, identify the problem and move on.* You'll be taking most exams under time pressure, so you can't afford to spend too much time probing the depths of your memory. If time is left over after you've finished the parts of the exam that you could answer with confidence, return to the parts you skipped.

- *Concentrate despite distractions.* If you start daydreaming, circle the item that got you off task and come back to it later. Avoid getting caught up in competition with any students who complete the test early. You won't know if they are demon test-takers or have just given up. Do the test at your pace—don't worry about who gets done first.
- *Ask for clarification.* When you're confused, ask your instructor or proctor for help. Most instructors try to clarify a question if they can without giving away the answer. Some inquiries can prompt an instructor to throw out questions that generate too much confusion.
- *Learn from the test.* The test itself may jog your memory. One area of the test may hold clues that can help you with other areas.
- *Proofread your work.* Whether it's a series of math problems or an extended discussion on Japanese haiku, review your work. Under pressure, it's easy to misspell, miscalculate, and make other errors, even on things you know well. Using clear editing marks on your test paper demonstrates that you were being as careful as possible about your work.

Deploy Specific Test-Taking Strategies

Instructors choose different formats to assess different kinds of thinking skills. Multiple-choice and true/false tests tend to favor lower-level thinking skills such as memorizing and applying. Essay tests will be considerably more challenging. Learn how to approach each type to produce your best outcome.

Multiple-Choice Questions You'll probably face many tests that are mainly multiple choices. In multiple-choice tests, "question stems" or incomplete statements are followed by possible answers from which to choose. Figure 9.3, "Multiple-Choice Format," provides an example. The following strategies will help improve your scoring on multiple-choice questions:

- *Read the test items carefully and completely.* Cover up the alternatives and read just the stem. See whether you can answer the question in your head before you look at the alternatives. Then read *all* the alternatives before you identify the best one. This is especially important when your instructor includes "All of the above" or "A and C only" types of choices.
- *Strike out wrong answers.* When you can't easily identify the correct answer, eliminate the wrong choices so you can concentrate only on real contenders. Sometimes instructors include humorous distracters that can easily be dismissed. Don't dwell on their motives or allow yourself to get distracted. Strike those answers and move on.
- *Mark answers clearly and consistently.* Use the same method of marking your choices throughout the test. This practice may be important if questions arise later about an unclear mark. If your test is machine scored, avoid having extra marks on the answer sheet. They can be costly.
- *Change your answers cautiously.* Make sure you have a good reason before you change an answer. For example, change your answer if you mismarked your exam, initially misread the question, or clearly know you're moving to the correct alternative. If you aren't certain, it's best not to change. Your first impulse may be best.

The best way to succeed on multiple-choice tests is	*[question stem]*
A. Read the question carefully	*[contender]*
B. Check on the weather	*[distracter]*
C. Look for language cues to throw out choices	*[contender]*
D. Cry like a baby	*[distracter]*
E. A & C	*[correct answer]*

© Cengage Learning 2013

FIGURE 9.3 Multiple-Choice Format

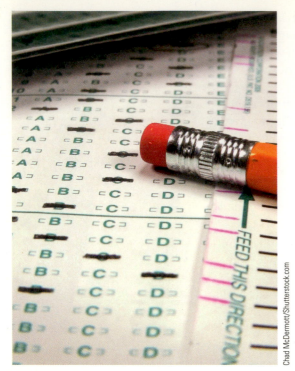

Professors often rely on scantron forms for evaluating answers to multiple-choice questions.

- **Guess.** Some instructors subtract points for incorrect answers. In such a case, answer only the questions that you know for certain. However, most multiple-choice tests give credit for correct answers without extra penalty for wrong answers. In this situation, guess. If the question has four alternatives, you have a 25 percent chance of being correct.
- **Look for structural clues.** When the item involves completing a sentence, look for answers that read well with the sentence stem. (See Figure 9.4 for examples.) Sometimes instructors don't pay close attention to how the wrong alternatives read. If a choice does not work grammatically with the stem, it's probably not the right choice. In complex questions, the longest alternative may be the best one. The instructor may simply require more words to express a complex answer.

True/False Questions True/false questions ask you to make judgments about whether propositions about the course content are valid or truthful. For example, consider this item: "True or False: It is always a bad idea to change your answer." This would be a good true/false question to assess your understanding of the last section on multiple-choice questions (the answer is "False"). To maximize your performance on true/false items:

- **Go with your hunch.** When you don't know the answer on a true/false question, you have a 50 percent chance of being right when you guess. Choose the alternative with the intuitive edge.
- **Don't look for answer patterns.** Instructors generally strive to make the order of true/false answers random. This means there is no particular pattern to the answers. Selecting "False" on question 35 should have no bearing on how you answer question 34 or 36. Focus your energy on the questions themselves rather than on trying to detect nonexistent patterns.
- **Honor exceptions to the rule.** If you can think of exceptions to the statement—even one exception—then the statement is probably false. In the earlier example, if you can think of even one circumstance in which changing your answer is a good idea, then the statement should be marked "False."
- **Analyze qualifying terms.** Pauk (2000) describes qualifying terms that suggest a question is true without exception as "100 percent words." Those terms suggest an unlikely or unwarranted generalization. In our example,

In this example, spot the grammar clue that can help you determine the correct answer. Don't change your multiple-choice answers unless you can find an

A. Error in how you marked your test booklet

B. Typo in the sentence stem

C. Justification from peeking at your lecture notes

D. Clues from cloud formation out the classroom window

A is the right answer because "an" links grammatically to "Error."

FIGURE 9.4 Using Grammar Tools to Find Multiple-Choice Answers

"It is always a bad idea to change your answer," the word *always* makes the statement invalid, because there are some times when changing your answer makes sense. Other 100 percent words include *never, none, every, all, entirely, only, invariably, best,* and *worst.*

Fill-in-the-Blank Questions Like multiple-choice questions, fill-in-the-blank questions test how well you recall information. An example of a fill-in-the-blank format is "Instructors try hard to make a ___ pattern of answers on true/false tests." (The answer is "random.") You either know or don't know the answers to these kinds of questions, but you may recover some answers that you don't know initially by skipping them and returning to them after you complete the rest of the test. This process may cue you to come up with just the right fill-in answer.

Short-Answer Questions Short-answer questions demonstrate how well you can explain concepts briefly. For example, a short-answer question might be "Describe some strategies for doing well on true/false questions." To maximize your score on short-answer questions, write clear, logical, and brief answers. Writing a great deal more than asked, or including information not asked for, suggests that you do not understand the concepts. When you skip a short-answer question because it stumps you, look for cues in the rest of the test that may help you to go back and answer it later.

Essay Questions Essay questions evaluate the scope of your knowledge and your ability to think and write. They tend to be much more demanding than objective test questions. What are some steps you can take to do your best on essays?

- *Anticipate possible questions.* If you were in your instructor's shoes, what questions would you ask? If you practice predicting and answering questions, your performance is likely to improve even if your predictions aren't on target. For example, an essay question that you could predict about the material in this section could be "Compare and contrast multiple-choice and essay-question strategies as a way of measuring your learning."
- *Read the question carefully.* A well-developed answer won't help you capture points if you don't answer the right question.
- *Highlight the requested action.* For example, in our earlier sample question, you could underline compare and contrast to keep you focused on the most successful approach. See Figure 9.5, "Decode Essay Questions," for help.
- *Outline the key ideas.* A systematic blueprint can help you capture the most important ideas in your answer (as shown in the following example):
  I. How are multiple-choice and essay questions alike?
      A. They're constructed from the same material.
      B. You start with remembering concepts.
      C. You demonstrate your mastery of material.
  II. How are multiple-choice and essay questions different?
      A. Multiple-choice questions usually rely more on rote memory—recognition or recall of terms. Essays usually involve higher-order thinking skills.
      B. Multiple-choice questions can be answered more quickly.
      C. Multiple-choice questions usually have precise right answers.
      D. Essay questions are usually harder to answer.

Look carefully at the verbs your instructor uses in essay questions. This chart offers some hints about how your instructor wants you to construct your answer.

When your instructor wants you to . . .	Your answer should . . .
ANALYZE	break into smaller parts and interpret importance
APPLY	extend a concept or principle to a new situation
COMPARE	identify similarities between two concepts
CONTRAST	distinguish important differences between two concepts
CRITICIZE	judge the positive and negative features of a concept
DEFINE	offer the essential idea behind a concept
DESCRIBE	provide sufficient details to establish key ideas in a concept
DESIGN	develop a new strategy to accomplish a goal
EVALUATE	make a well-reasoned judgment about value or worth
EXPLAIN	clarify the meaning of a concept through detail or example
GENERALIZE	apply a principle to make predictions about a new problem
HYPOTHESIZE	develop a specific prediction about a complex situation
IDENTIFY	designate the key elements involved
ILLUSTRATE	provide examples or details to clarify
INTERPRET	offer your distinctive point of view about a concept's meaning
LIST	identify factors in a systematic or comprehensive manner
PREDICT	offer your best guess about an outcome
PROVE	create your best argument using examples or reasoning
RECOMMEND	put forward a preferred course of action with a rationale
RELATE	draw connections among ideas
REVIEW	discuss the most important aspects of the concept
SUMMARIZE	briefly identify the most critical ideas

FIGURE 9.5 Decode Essay Questions

E. Essay questions are probably harder to grade.

F. Well-written essays require planning and outlining.

- *Represent the question in your opening sentence*. Don't waste time rewriting the question. Set the stage for the information that will follow, such as: "Instructors use multiple-choice and essay questions to evaluate how much you have learned from a course. These strategies share some similarities, but each offers some strategic advantages over the other."

- *Develop the main body of the essay.* Each paragraph should address an element required in the question: "The common characteristics of multiple-choice and essay questions include . . . . Multiple-choice and essay questions also differ in what information they impart about a student's learning . . . ."

- *Use organizing notations, headings, or subpoints to clarify your thinking*. If you run out of time, the organizers may help you capture some additional points.

- *Summarize only if you have time.* Write like a reporter; present key ideas first and follow with details. This practice increases the likelihood that you'll cover the most important and point-scoring information before you run out of time.

- **Write legibly using dark ink**. If your handwriting gets worse under stress—slow down. Carefully cross out parts that you don't want to count. Instructors can't give credit for what they can't decipher. Leave space between your answers so that you can add items if you have more time or your instructor can use the space for feedback.

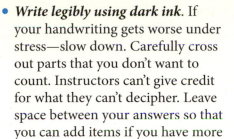

- **Proofread your work.** Under time pressure, your written language can easily escape your control. Go back over your work and make any corrections the instructor will need in order to understand you clearly. Don't worry about the mess. Your own editing marks show that you care about the quality of your thinking.
- **Don't bluff.** The longer you write and the more you ramble, the more you expose what you really don't know.
- **Use humor carefully**. Unless you have clear cues from your instructors that they would appreciate a light-hearted response, don't substitute humor for an effective answer.

Know Yourself: Self-Assessment 9.1, "How Well Do I Test?," at the end of the chapter on page 318 reviews many points that we've just covered. Use it to evaluate your current test-taking methods and to identify areas that need improvement.

Review Your Work

Some reviewing of your test results will help you do better on the next test. Review to achieve several solid outcomes:

- Consolidate your learning
- Analyze what worked and what didn't work in your study strategy
- Ensure that the grade was accurate

Review all items, not just ones on which you made mistakes. Review and rehearse one more time the material that your instructor thinks you need to learn in the course. This strategy can help you in the long run, especially if you have a cumulative exam at the end of the term or if the course is an important building block for courses that will follow.

Your test review should tell you whether your study strategy worked. Did you spend enough time studying for the test? Did you practice the right kinds of thinking to match the particular demands of this instructor? How can you use your study time more efficiently for the next test? Talk with the instructor about better ways to prepare.

What if your instructor doesn't allow extensive time for review of your exam during class—or worse, doesn't return the exams at all but only gives you a grade? Visit your instructor during office hours and ask for the chance to review your test results. This visit also allows you to clarify any questions you have about your instructor's testing or grading practices, and it shows that you are taking personal responsibility for your learning.

Manage Life

Especially around midterms and finals, you are likely to experience greater stress. If you haven't taken appropriate steps to prepare, chances are good that your stress level will be even more intense. This section provides some great survival tips to reduce the likelihood that test results will threaten your plans to complete your degree.

Adopt the Right Attitude

No doubt about it: Testing can be stressful. Nearly everyone feels some test anxiety, but some students are overwhelmed by it. Others view testing as doing battle. They cast the instructor as a villain out to bring them down by using "tricky" questions. These students get distracted into trying to "outfox" the instructor rather than learning the material.

It is easier to maintain a positive attitude about testing when you don't have to spend much time feeling regret for making bad choices. See Know Yourself: Self-Assessment 9.2, "Minimizing Regret," at the end of the chapter on page 319 to gauge how much time you spend feeling bad after exam performance.

Going boldly into a test, armed only with hopes of doing well rather than with solid preparation, will rarely achieve the outcome you want. Instead, facing the test with the confidence that comes from conscientious planning and systematic study is the best way to overcome unproductive attitudes and emotions.

Pace Yourself Don't count on cramming! Eleventh-hour learning is fragile. It may crumble under pressure. Distributing your learning means you won't have to go through a last-minute rush to learn.

- *Concentrate on the big picture.* Keep a master calendar for the term. Put all your scheduled tests on it. Post the calendar in your study area.
- *Design your test preparation across courses.* Plan how you'll read, study, and review assigned materials and class notes according to the test demands in all your courses. Wherever possible, distribute your study sessions over time to minimize interference among courses.
- *Keep up with your reading.* If you keep up with your reading, class experiences will reinforce your learning. Avoid massive catch-up reading the night before the test—there will probably be too much ground to cover, understand, and remember.
- *Reward yourself for staying on target.* Getting a shiny A grade would be a powerful reward for strong test-preparation habits. However, that reward may come too far in the future to help you sustain better test preparation. Instead, reward yourself on a regular basis for sticking to your study plan. For example, after you've studied hard each evening, watch a video of a favorite TV show, listen to some music that you really like, or talk with someone you enjoy.
- *Schedule a concentrated review session.* If you've kept up, a solid review session the night before your test should be adequate.
- *Don't skip a class to cram.* This strategy is a real problem in the weeks that lead up to final examinations, because all your instructors may use that time to give exam pointers or review essential material that may be critical to your success.
- *Avoid multitasking.* Concentrate on just one thing to maximize the benefit of any study session. (Yes, shut off your cell phone.)

You know cramming isn't an optimal strategy, but sometimes it just can't be avoided. You may have too many courses to manage any other way. What are some of the best ideas for last-minute, concentrated study?

- *Clear the decks.* Dedicate your last study session before the test to only that exam to reduce interference.

- *Use textbook study aids.* The chapter headings and chapter end matter can help you organize your last-minute study strategies by identifying key ideas before you begin reading. First, go through and look at the headings—in a good textbook, these will provide you with an outline of the key ideas in the chapter. This practice is especially appropriate in an introductory book. Then read the summary and look at the key terms and review questions. You will get a pretty good idea of the most important material in the chapter.

- *Skim for main ideas.* Once you know what to look for, skim the chapter with the key ideas in mind. You may even want to skim just to answer the review questions. Scan each paragraph in relevant readings for the key ideas. Topic sentences that capture the central idea of each paragraph are usually the first or the last sentences in the paragraph. Skim the entire assignment to improve your chances of remembering the material.

- *Divide and conquer.* Once you've skimmed the entire body of study materials, size up how much you have to learn in relation to your remaining time. Divide the information into reasonable sections and make your best guess about which will have the largest payoff. Master each section based on whatever time you have left. Even if you don't get to the lower-priority material, your test performance may not suffer much.

- *Stay focused and alert.* Study in good light away from the lure of your bed. Take regular breaks and exercise mildly to stay alert through your session. Caffeine in moderation and regular snacks also may help. Avoid sugary snacks because they can generate an energy slump after digestion.

- *Be cautious about professional summaries.* Use professional summaries of great works if you can't complete a full reading. If you rent a film version of a great work of literature, be aware that films and even professional summaries often depart from the original in ways that may reveal your shortcut.

- *Learn from your mistakes.* When you enter a test feeling underprepared, you've undermined your ability to succeed. Even if you luck out and do well, this strategy shortchanges what you think and learn over the long term. Consider the factors that left you in such desperate study circumstances. Do all you can to avoid getting stuck in a situation where you have to cram.

Address Your Social Style If you have an extroverted style, studying with others will motivate you to do your reading and help to identify trouble spots. Ask other students who seem to understand the course—at least as well as you do, if not better—to join a study group. Screening helps to ensure that the group will be productive and not slowed down by students who use the group for social purposes or don't reliably do their work. To improve testing success, study-group members can

Keep healthy supplies nearby to help you cope with stress during testing.

Jon Ramsey

Overcoming Disabilities

Doing well on tests may involve facing the fact that you have some test-taking deficiencies. Jon Ramsey graduated from the University of Oregon with a double major in Spanish and international studies and a 3.2 GPA. He had a long history of anguish related to test taking because of a reading disability (Sherman & Ramsey, 2006). From the beginning of his education, Jon could not make sense of print and would cry or throw tantrums. Jon's tendency to struggle with letters prompted his family to shorten his birth name of Jonathan to Jon to make things easier for him. His family jokingly referred to him as "Noj," reflecting his tendency to commit letter reversals—which later became diagnostic of the problem that would make academic learning so difficult for Jon.

For families challenged by such learning disabilities, Lewis and Clark College offers special support in a program called Reversals. With the help of the program, Jon invested a lot of time after school in listening and reading practice, supported by tutors and family members. His ultimate success in developing compensating strategies helped him accomplish his dream of entering the Peace Corps after graduation, when he will be working in Latin America. Jon has remained good-natured about his struggles and his triumph: "If you see my ninth-grade teacher, tell her what I'm doing."

compare notes to create the most comprehensive understanding, share hunches about likely test material, develop practice questions, and challenge fuzzy explanations.

On the other hand, if the stimulation of a study group is not compatible with your introverted style, find less socially intense support strategies. For example, identify another strong student with a similar style and make a commitment to connect via e-mail to clarify questions or try out test-taking strategies. Or fly solo. You may be most comfortable, productive, and confident without distraction.

Face Up to Weaknesses Many students have additional burdens in coping with the challenges of college tests. For students with learning disabilities, timed tests are especially difficult. They may have trouble interpreting instructions or actually understanding the exam questions themselves. As a consequence, they sometimes cannot use regular exam formats to demonstrate what they have learned. See "Spotlight On Jon Ramsey" to explore how this challenge can be overcome.

If you invest substantial time in getting ready for exams but are disappointed with the yield, consider seeking some assistance to evaluate whether learning disabilities could be the explanation. On the other hand, if you are doing poorly, consider whether your poor performance could simply be explained by insufficient study time and adjust your preparation accordingly.

Protect Your Health If you stay healthy throughout the term, you'll have fewer problems in managing your study schedule and fewer distractions at test time. You can't do your best if you're fighting off the urge to nap, feeling bad from a hangover, or coming down with a cold. Wash your hands often and stay well hydrated to give your immune system its best shot at keeping you on your feet.

Exploit Your Learning Style Adapt your preferred learning style to the kind of thinking measured by the test. Take responsibility for finding out as much as you can about what the test will cover and then plan a suitable study strategy. Keep track of your progress as you prepare for the test.

Many tests, especially in introductory-level courses, focus on memorization. Your most effective memorization strategy will use your preferred sensory mode effectively. For example:

- *Visual learners* should use visualization techniques or drawings and diagrams to memorize material.

- *Auditory learners* may prefer to rehearse key ideas aloud or make up songs or rhymes to fix facts in memory.
- *Tactile learners* may try role play or other hands-on strategies to add cues that help them recall information.

Control Your Test Anxiety

A few butterflies at test time are okay. A little anxiety even can be a good sign. It encourages you to prepare for the test and can motivate you to do your very best. Too many butterflies, though, can cripple your test performance. Nervousness and worry activate the emergency systems in your body. Your pulse increases. Your heart beats faster. Your hands perspire. These responses prepare you to freeze, flee, or fight, and none of these responses is helpful to the challenge at hand.

Test anxiety is surprisingly common (Cizek & Burg, 2006). In the last few years, "high-stakes" testing has become an inescapable part of making progress through the U.S. educational systems, but the relentlessness of being subjected to tests that direct your future can be unsettling. It is no wonder that negative attitudes and lowered expectations for success in test situations are a predictable result.

Know Yourself: Self-Assessment 9.3, "How Serious Is My Test Anxiety?," at the end of the chapter on page 320, will help you determine if your test anxiety is interfering with your performance.

Don't Sabotage Success Test-anxious students sabotage their own efforts because they focus on themselves in negative ways (Kaplan & Saccuzzo, 1993). Preoccupied with the certainty of their own failure, they can't free up the energy to perform well. This reaction increases their chances of failure. Text-anxious students interpret even neutral events as further proof of their own inadequacy. For example, if a test proctor looks troubled, test-anxious students may assume that their own behaviors somehow caused the troubled look. They are more likely to experience stress-related physical symptoms, such as an upset stomach or stiff neck, which further hinder performance.

If you have anxiety about tests, you need to do two things (Zeidner, 1995):

- Cope with your anxiety.
- Improve your study skills to build your competence and confidence.

If you learn to cope with anxiety but don't improve your study skills, you'll feel calmer and more in control but won't improve your performance. By contrast, if you improve your study skills but don't master your anxious feelings, your performance may still erode. It will take some effort to do both things, but consider the long-term rewards.

Master Anxiety What are some specific things you can do to master test anxiety?

- *Invest your time properly.* Think about it. If you haven't spent as much time preparing for a test as you should, it makes sense to be frightened about performing poorly. Test jitters may only mean that you need to invest more time. If the format your instructor will be using doesn't play to your strengths as a test-taker, allocate more time to compensate for this challenge.
- *Neutralize anxiety.* One simple strategy is to neutralize your anxious feelings by learning to breathe in a relaxed manner under stress. See Highlight: "Get a Grip" for pointers on how to achieve greater control.

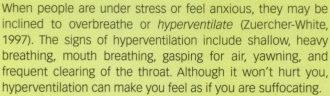
When people are under stress or feel anxious, they may be inclined to overbreathe or *hyperventilate* (Zuercher-White, 1997). The signs of hyperventilation include shallow, heavy breathing, mouth breathing, gasping for air, yawning, and frequent clearing of the throat. Although it won't hurt you, hyperventilation can make you feel as if you are suffocating.

Ironically, your sense of smothering is caused by taking in too much air. What can you do to get a grip and breathe more normally during exams?

- **Hold your breath.** If you can devote a minute or two to holding your breath in several 10- to 15-second spurts, carbon dioxide will build up and counter hyperventilation and feelings of panic.

- **Breathe into a paper bag.** You may look a little funny, but this trick works. Exhale carbon dioxide into a paper bag that covers your mouth and nose. Then rebreathe the carbon dioxide until you feel calmer.

- **Breathe from your diaphragm.** You may have to practice this technique ahead of time to deploy it in the classroom. To learn diaphragm breathing:

  1. Find a comfortable place to recline and place a pillow on your stomach. Breathe in slowly through your nose and watch the pillow rise. Breathe out slowly and watch the pillow lower.

  2. Once you get the hang of it, remove the pillow but place your hand on your stomach. You will be replacing visual cues with kinesthetic cues that will be helpful when you try breathing in different postures. Concentrate on your stomach as it moves up and down with your measured breathing.

  3. Practice diaphragm breathing in different postures, without your hand on your stomach. Emphasize rehearsal of the skill while sitting for greatest help during the exam.

  4. Slow down your breathing. Pause before inhaling. This practice will give you the greatest sense of control over your feelings of panic.

  5. Once you have achieved success, practice twice a day. Maximum success will occur when you can move easily into controlled breathing at the first hint of panic. Practice will facilitate your command.

- **Talk positively to yourself.** Test-anxious students often make their anxieties worse by predicting their own failure. Instead of tormenting yourself with criticism and dire predictions, substitute positive statements, such as "I will overcome this challenge" or "I feel confident I will do well." If you practice an optimistic outlook, more increased self-esteem will follow.

- **Exercise regularly.** Many students find relief from their anxieties by building a regular exercise program into their busy schedules. Exercise is a great stress reliever. It also promotes deeper, more restful sleep.

- **Avoid drugs.** Monitor your caffeine intake. Too much can compound agitated feelings. But this effect is minor compared with the problems that result from using harder drugs to ward off anxiety or to stay alert. Alcohol is not a good solution for reducing exam anxiety, although college students commonly cite worries about grades as a cause for drinking too much (Kiefferv, 2006).

- **Find support.** Most campuses offer support groups for test anxiety. These groups emphasize study strategies, anxiety management techniques, and moral support.

Handle Emergencies Honestly

What happens if you can't make it to the test? Most instructors have strict rules about taking scheduled tests on time to ensure fair treatment for all students. However, sick children, car accidents, and deaths in the family can interfere both physically and emotionally at test time.

If you can't report at the scheduled time, call your instructor *before* the test. Explain your situation. Ask whether you can take a makeup exam. Being courteous encourages your instructor's cooperation.

Keep in mind that experienced professors have heard a variety of excuses for failing to perform, and they develop radar about which excuses are bogus. Instructors may ask you to document your absence (for example, with a doctor's excuse) before they'll let you make up a test. Don't be surprised if an instructor asks you to produce an obituary for any funeral-related absence; the common occurrence of this excuse is the reason many professors joke about final exam week being a threat to grandparents everywhere. Do all you can to take tests on schedule to avoid complications of this type. See the Danger Zone: "The World's Toughest Test" to see what can happen when you fail to exercise personal responsibility about testing demands.

Recover Your Balance

At some point in your college career, you may not perform as well on a test as you hoped you would. Sometimes instructors don't design tests effectively. At other times, you simply may be pushed in too many directions to concentrate and do your best. Or the course may be a bad match for your natural skills and interests and consequently your study regimen may be uninspired.

Don't let yourself become undone by one failure. Frame this disappointment as an opportunity to do some good critical thinking to figure out the causes of poor performance and to craft some new strategies to improve your situation. This approach can start by a careful review of your test results.

 # Connect and Communicate

Grades don't change what you learned for the test, but they can affect your self-esteem and motivation to study in the future, two important keys to success. For example, good grades make you feel proud. They encourage you to stick with the study strategies that worked. Bad grades prompt you to make changes in order to succeed. But bad grades also can harm your self-esteem.

Understand Grading Systems

What systems of grading do most colleges use?

Traditional Grades Most schools use the traditional *A–F* grading system. Many also include plus (+) and minus (−) to make even finer distinctions in quality of work. Schools that use the traditional system convert grades into a *grade-point average*, or *GPA*. In this system, $A = 4$ points, $B = 3$ points, $C = 2$ points, and $D = 1$ point. The point values of grades in all your courses are added up and then averaged to create your GPA. For example:

American history	C	2 points
College algebra	A	4 points
Business	A	4 points
Sociology	B	3 points
	Total	13 points

Divided by 4 courses = 3.25 GPA

If your GPA falls below 2.0, you may be placed on academic restrictions or probation. On some campuses, probation limits the number of courses you can take in the next term and slows down your progress in your major. Because GPA is averaged across terms, a bad term's GPA will exert a heavy weight on your overall record, even if your performance improves in later terms. If your GPA remains low, you can flunk out.

Instructors sometimes assign test or course grades by using a curve. The overall results of the test for the class are tied to the strongest performance in the class. Other students' scores are judged in relation to that strongest score. For example, suppose that on a test with 100 points, the highest score was 85. An instructor who is grading on a curve might give A's to scores of 76–85, B's to scores 66–75, and so on. Instructors may do this when a test turns out to be much harder than originally intended. However, even when most of the class performs poorly, some instructors don't curve the grades.

Pass/Fail Systems Some schools determine progress on a pass/fail basis, giving only pass (*P*) and fail (*F*) grades. When this is the only grading system a college uses, students may get extensive feedback about how well they have met their learning objectives. Instead of a grade-point average, students graduate with other indicators of the quality of their work, such as a *narrative transcript*. In this document, their instructors describe their academic work and how well they achieved their goals.

Some colleges use both *A–F* and pass/fail grading. For example, students might get *A–F* grades in most of their courses but be allowed to take a certain number of credits outside their majors on a pass/fail basis. This dual system allows students to take some courses that they otherwise might avoid because of a potential mediocre grade.

The presence of grades appeals to externally motivated students who find that they can more easily settle down and do the work when they know feedback will help them stay the course. Other students with stronger intrinsic motivation think grades and the pressures that go with them are distracting. Which do you prefer?

Know When to Challenge

Check the grading. Instructors can easily make errors when applying test keys or counting up point totals. Also identify questions that were not clearly written. Even if your critique of a question does not persuade an instructor to change your grade, your review may give you insight into how the instructor constructs tests, which can help you on the next one. Instructors are unlikely to change a grade without good reason. Most construct tests carefully and grade them as fairly as possible. However, if you believe that the instructor misunderstood you or made an actual error in calculating your score that affects your grade, by all means ask for a grade change. Remember, though, that instructors can't give you extra points if it gives you an unfair advantage over others in the class.

If you view grades as a key to the future, you may want to fight for the grade you deserve. Some strategies for getting maximum consideration from your instructor include the following:

- *Ask for time after class to present your case.* Most instructors will not spend class time on the challenges of one student. They also don't like to be bugged just before classes begin while they are trying to get ready.
- *Develop your argument.* Point to evidence, such as an interpretation in the book that conflicts with something said in lecture, to support your request. If you misinterpreted the question, sometimes you can capture partial credit with a well-developed argument.
- *Avoid labeling the question as "bad."* Placing blame on instructors irritates and alienates them.
- *Be gracious, whether you win or lose.* Most instructors remember and admire students who effectively advocate for themselves.

Build Trust through Integrity

Every test gives you an opportunity to demonstrate your personal integrity—and integrity matters. Would you want to be cared for by a physician who cheated her way to a medical license? When the outcome of education involves life-and-death decisions, we clearly want to be cared for by someone with sound knowledge and skills.

Even if you don't plan to become a physician, you'll benefit from direct and accurate measurements of what you know. For example, survival in more difficult, advanced courses may depend on your learning from an earlier course. By cheating, you increase the likelihood of serious academic problems in the future.

In their mission statements, most colleges pledge to foster moral and ethical behavior. Some colleges have a stringent honor code. The principles of the code, usually described in the student handbook, recognize that students will have plenty of opportunities to cheat. When you exercise integrity instead of cheating, you demonstrate that you're a trustworthy, moral person—not only to your classmates but also to the instructors whom you will be asking for letters of reference after graduation.

How Bad Is the Problem of Cheating in College? In *The Cheating Culture*, David Callahan (2004) argues that moral values are in dramatic decline, and he suggests that widespread cheating in college is a reflection of the significantly larger cultural problem. In addition, new technologies offer students inventive ways to procure high grades by circumventing all of the hard work in the course (Glater, 2006). Students with integrity problems use cell phones, iPods, and Internet cruising to engineer favorable exam results just as they shop for term papers online rather than write them.

Unfortunately, cheating is widespread in college (Anderman & Anderman, 2010). The first multicampus survey on cheating (McCabe, Trevino, & Butterfield, 2001) examined more than 6,000 American undergraduates on more than 30 campuses and revealed that 78 percent of college students cheat at least once; over half of the respondents claimed that they cheated on tests. Another analysis (Athanasou & Olasehinde, 2002) compared results across many years of surveys on cheating and estimated that approximately 60 percent of both males and females cheated in college.

What Behaviors Constitute Cheating? Three distinctive categories of behavior reflect compromises in academic integrity (based on Cizek, 1999):

- Taking, giving, or receiving information illicitly from others (including copying from others' work with or without their permission, submitting purchased essays, or recycling papers from prior courses without permission)
- Using inappropriate information or material (including improper paraphrasing and copying of material without appropriate acknowledgment, fabricating data or references, or collaborating inappropriately when required to work individually)
- Evading standard assessment conditions (including substituting someone else's performance, giving untruthful excuses or engaging in other behavior such as offering sexual favors or threats to secure special treatment, destroying resource materials to handicap other students' performance, securing advance information about examinations, or smuggling restricted information into testing contexts)

Why Do Students Cheat? Cheating in college has many causes (Whitley & Keith-Spiegel, 2002). Often students who cheat feel pressure to succeed. They feel overwhelmed by the demands of so many deadlines and can't see any other way to get by. Successful cheating gives students better grades with less effort.

Many students and instructors simply expect people to cheat if they have the opportunity. Some students reason that because other students cheat, it's okay for them to cheat, too. Instructors sometimes make it easy to cheat by not monitoring tests closely.

Often students who cheat do not get caught or aren't punished when they are caught. Although most students recognize that cheating involves some risk, they report that they have seen students cheat and get away with it. Many instructors don't feel confident in challenging students who cheat, so they overlook suspicious acts. Inaction by the instructor encourages others to cheat.

Online students may feel tempted to take advantage of lax monitoring by their professors. For example, they collaborate when projects are supposed to be individual efforts. Against directions, they use the Internet to mine for answers that they haven't really learned. They may even fast-talk another student into taking an exam for them. The remote conditions of online learning encourage students who disregard the value of academic integrity to take advantage of the looser supervision.

Some students who cheat may not recognize when they are cheating (Keith-Spiegel, 1992). Some students "work together" and share answers either before or during a test. They believe that there is nothing objectionable about sharing answers as long as both parties agree to collaborate. These students don't recognize that how they arrive at answers is just as important as the answers themselves. This tendency can be a particular problem for international students who may have learned academic practices in a culture where work is more collaborative than it is in the individually oriented United States.

How Else Do Students Justify Cheating? Figure 9.6, "Excuses for Academic Dishonesty" (Whitley & Keith-Spiegel, 2002), summarizes explanations that students offer for their behavior.

Even if they get away with cheating, some students struggle with a nagging conscience. The relief they initially feel in escaping a bad grade can give way to

Denial of Injury:	*Cheating hurts no one.* *Cheating is only wrong in courses in your major.*
Denial of Personal Responsibility:	*I got the flu and couldn't read all the chapters.* *The course is too hard.*
Denial of Personal Risk:	*Professors won't do anything to you.* *No one ever gets caught.*
Selective Morality:	*Friends come first and my friend needed my help.* *I only did what was necessary at the time.*
Minimizing Seriousness:	*It's only busy work.* *Cheating is meaningless when it has little weight on my grade.*
A Necessary Act:	*If I don't do well, my parents will kill me.* *I'll lose my scholarship if I don't get all B's.*
Dishonesty as a Norm:	*Society's leaders do it, so why not me?* *Everyone does it.*

Adapted from Academic Dishonesty: An Educator's Guide by Whitley, Bernard E. Copyright © 2002 Reproduced with permission of Taylor & Francis Group LLC-Books in the format Textbook and Other book via Copyright Clearance Center.

FIGURE 9.6 Excuses for Academic Dishonesty

self-doubt, dissatisfaction, and guilt. These students suffer because they have fallen short of their own ideals, creating long-term harm for their self-esteem and self-confidence. Furthermore, once they cheat and get away with it, they may be tempted to do it again the next time they aren't as prepared as they should be.

What Happens When Cheaters Get Caught? Cheaters face multiple risks. Being accused of cheating in front of others is humiliating. Being found guilty of cheating means that the accused may have to explain this judgment to friends or parents. Worse, some instructors will turn those accused over to a student court for punishment, spreading their humiliation even further.

Penalties for cheating differ. An instructor may give cheaters a zero on the exam or an automatic F in the course. On campuses that practice a strict honor code, one episode of cheating leads to expulsion. On some occasions, cheating students have experienced surprising consequences. For example, Randy substituted his roommate's work from the prior semester in his French class, thinking that he would do it "just this once." The instructor recognized the work because it stood out the first time. Busted, Randy took a zero in the course and lost "face," tuition, time, and course credit. What he didn't expect was that his adviser refused to write letters of recommendation for graduate school. One impulsive act had a far-reaching impact on his future.

Why Do Other Students Tolerate Cheating? Most students won't report other students' cheating. In one survey, 3 out of 4 of the students witnessed cheating by others, but only 1 in 100 informed their instructors (Jendrick, 1992). Many of the students ignored the situation even though it made them angry or upset. One third of the students said that cheating didn't bother them. Some researchers (McCabe, Trevino, & Butterfield, 2002) have concluded that peer attitudes toward cheating have a stronger influence on individual student decisions to cheat than any other factors the researchers studied.

What's the Best Way to Avoid Getting Entangled in Cheating? Sometimes students can end up being confronted with accusations that are off-base. Lathrop and Foss (2007) recommended developing a strong sense of ownership by working on mastery of the course ideas. Avoid loaning your paper out, and be vigilant about not leaving copies on public computers where they can be downloaded and submitted by others. If your paper is stolen, report it immediately to the instructor. Show the documentation of the notes you took along the way. Another way to avoid false accusations is to talk regularly with your instructor so that your hard work and content mastery are easily apparent.

What Will You Do When Faced with an Opportunity to Cheat? If honesty is an important value for you, then you may have already committed yourself to making sure that you take no shortcuts to success. But what if you're not persuaded? Perhaps you've seen dishonest people get away with too much. After all, if 78 percent of students report that they have cheated, how wrong can it be?

Cheating is not a victimless crime. Students who cheat potentially rob themselves of learning that may be useful to them in the future. If you aspire to true excellence, you can't really do so by being a fraud. If you can't be a trustworthy student, how can you be a trustworthy partner or friend? To explore your own perspective about cheating, complete Know Yourself: Self-Assessment 9.4, "Your Personal Honor Code," at the end of the chapter on page 321.

How does testing produce the best options for what you want to do after graduation? Obviously, higher grades are more effective than lower ones in helping communicate to future employers that you are a hard worker. But in this closing section, we also explore other developments that can set you apart, including developing a "test-sturdy" approach if your future plans will involve graduate school or other activities with high-stakes testing.

Target Your GPA

Imagine yourself at the end of your college career. How important will your GPA be toward securing the future you have in mind? Not all opportunities following college require a 4.0.

However, especially if you decide to continue your studies in graduate school, you need to start right now building a GPA that gives you the widest options. Write down the GPA range that you think would be most desirable at the conclusion of your career. Be realistic. Keep in mind how willing you are to make the sacrifices that will be required to excel.

If you excel academically, you may become an *honor graduate*. Colleges that embrace the standard way of distinguishing academic quality use the following designations:

- Summa cum laude (with highest honor)
- Magna cum laude (with high honor)
- Cum laude (with honor)

In addition, your major department may confer special recognition for an academic job well done in the discipline.

High grade-point averages often figure in other forms of recognition. The "Dean's List" and "President's List" may provide recognition on a semester-by-semester basis when your work exceeds specific levels determined by the college.

Continuously high grade-point averages may qualify you for induction in national honor societies. The most widely recognized general academic societies include Phi Kappa Phi and Phi Beta Kappa. In addition, majors may offer their own honor societies for work achieved at a specific level. For example, nursing students can qualify for Sigma Eta Neu. Psychology students can be inducted into Psi Chi. Once you have settled on a major, find out if such opportunities exist in your home department. It will create another impressive line on your resume, particularly if you can exercise some leadership in helping the organization meet its goals.

If you excel academically, you may receive special recognition at the graduation ceremony.

Pursue Distinction

From the beginning of your college career, concentrate on making good choices that allow you to commit fully to a course of action that will help you distinguish yourself. When you ask for a letter of reference from your faculty, they will need to focus on various "hooks" that allow them to write about you in a positive or, even better, a glowing manner.

What strategies can help?

- *Pursue opportunities to work with a faculty member.* See if you can join a research team. To show that you are serious, learn all you can about the faculty member's work before you discuss the possibilities. Volunteering time can sometimes lead to paid opportunities. The more the faculty member has a chance to work with you, the more accurate the letter of support will be.

- *Get deeply involved in your major.* Most majors have student interest groups that not only help you plan for the future but also provide an opportunity for you to refine your leadership skills. Avoid getting committed to too many things. Constantly explaining your inability to get things done because you are "overcommitted" demonstrates that your judgment may be as poor as your time-management skills.

- *Set the bar high.* Strive to be the best you can be in your chosen field. If public speaking is your thing, join a mock trial society or other preprofessional speaking development groups, such as forensics. If science is your calling, set a goal to be involved in a project that could lead to a publication or presentation at a regional or national conference. It you come alive in the arts, compete in juried art shows or musical competitions. Nearly every major has special ways students can excel.

- *Then set the bar higher.* Students with spectacular college records may qualify for national recognition. For example, the Jack Kent Cooke Scholarship program that supported Viviana Alcazar makes scholarship support available to a select number of outstanding students. Similarly, *USA Today* elects 20 students every year to the All-Star Team, particularly highlighting high-achieving students who also make significant service contributions to others. Many recent winners have been profiled in this book. Your campus may have an office dedicated to helping students identify special opportunities for recognition. A comprehensive roster of national and international competitions for exemplary students can be found at the following website operated by Oklahoma State University: http://www.nchchonors.org/scholarships.htm.

Get Test Sturdy

You may have thought that once you got into college that would be the last of the high-stakes tests (for example, ACT and SAT) that you would ever have to take. However, contemporary educational and professional practice relies on testing, so chances are good that you will be facing a few more big tests in your professional life.

Some people appear to be naturally good at enduring high-stakes testing. For example, in 2009, about 300 students scored a perfect 2400 on their SAT tests. However, as shown in "Spotlight On Marissa Pan," success in high-stakes testing requires a blend of preparation, practice, and nerve management.

Virtually every profession relies on high-stakes national testing to make decisions about who is qualified. These tests serve a gatekeeping function for the professions. For example, admission to many graduate programs requires a strong performance

"You're kidding! You count SATs?"

Marissa Pan

High Stakes Testing Perfection

Courtesy of Marissa Pan

Marissa Pan of Alpharetta High School near Atlanta was one of the elite group in 2008 who scored perfectly when she took her SATs to qualify her for entrance into college. She attributed her success on the exam to her love of reading and the support of her parents, who reinforced the importance of education. Although she never made anything lower

Marissa Pan managed to score perfectly on her SATs.

than an A in her academic work, she still was nervous. She took the extra measure of participating in a 4-week examination practice course.

On the morning of the exam, she ate a good breakfast but also packed some cheese and crackers in her purse to stave off the distraction of hunger pangs. She offers this advice for success in high-stakes testing: "Prepare beforehand; but on testing day realize that what happens, happens; go into the room with confidence and a positive attitude." She adds, "Whatever you do, don't think your life hinges on [the SAT]. That will just stress you out."

(Foster, 2008)

on the Graduate Record Exam (GRE), which measures achievement in math, verbal, and analytic skills, as well as specialized knowledge in the discipline you hope to enter. Another general high-stakes exam is the Miller Analogies Test, which gauges how well you can do critical and analytic thinking.

If med school or law school looms in your professional plans, then you'll have some other tests to complete to show your readiness. The Medical College Admission Test (MCAT) and the Law School Admission Test (LSAT) provide results that help admissions committees determine the most competitive applicants.

Even if graduate school is not in your plans, you still may face high-stakes testing, such as examinations, in order to enter the career of your choice. For example, the National Council Licensure Exam (NCLEX) determines your readiness for a nursing career. Future educators may have to face the Praxis Series, which tests reading, writing, and math skills in Praxis I and specific disciplinary knowledge in Praxis II, to gain entrance to a teaching career. If you decide on a business career, many businesses may require that you take a test "battery," a set of tests, to qualify for employment. The purpose of such testing is to facilitate the best match between employer and employee.

Once you are successfully engaged in your career, you may be surprised to learn that high-stakes testing may not be over. Many professions emphasize regular evaluation opportunities to determine fitness for promotion or merit.

You may not relish the prospect of having to take tests for gatekeeping purposes, but it is clearly part of the professional landscape. If you have a career objective in mind, it may be useful to go to your campus career center and examine what kinds of testing may be part of your future. You may also benefit from practice exam booklets that you can check out from the library or peruse on the reference shelf at your local bookstore. It's never too early to see what is in store.

Clarify Expectations

- Accept that tests are a fact of life in college and that testing challenges will be harder than they were in high school.
- Use short-term strategies: knowing what to expect, sizing up the teacher, and designing study strategies that suit your learning style.
- Help family members and friends understand the time you must invest to succeed.

Develop Competence

- Adapt your style of study to address how you will be tested on the material.
- Engage in comfort rituals to provide the best foundation for test performance.
- Plan how to use your time in each testing challenge.
- Use general strategies (e.g., proofreading, relaxing) as well as tailored strategies specific to different kinds of tests (e.g., objective, essay, performance).
- Use smart cramming strategies if you haven't had time to prepare.
- Review your results to consolidate your learning and to plan better study strategies.

Manage Life

- Use effective long-term strategies: pacing yourself, protecting your health, and getting in the right frame of mind.
- Reduce your test anxiety through positive self-talk, appropriate preparation, and relaxation strategies.
- Handle emergencies immediately and honestly.

Connect and Communicate

- Don't waste a semester. A bad semester will have a whopping impact on your cumulative GPA.
- Use good judgment when you challenge your instructor's judgment about the fairness of a grade.
- Avoid the ugly personal outcomes of cheating, including possible expulsion from school if you are caught.

Build a Bright Future

- Work on the best grade-point average you can from the start and set a high personal standard to build your character.
- Pursue your unique path for distinction.
- Ready yourself for a future that involves high-stakes testing in professional life.

 Visit the College Success CourseMate for *Your Guide to College Success* for interactive resources at login.cengagebrain.com

Review Questions

1. How is testing different in college compared to high school?

   _____

   _____

   _____

2. Describe three cues an instructor might provide to signal when some content may be placed on an exam.

   1. _____

   2. _____

   3. _____

3. What is an effective strategy for securing the privacy and quiet you need to prepare properly, whether you are dealing with roommates or family members?

   _____

   _____

   _____

4. List a few specific types of tests, followed by a description of an appropriate study strategy.

   Test: _____   Study Strategy: _____

   Test: _____   Study Strategy: _____

   Test: _____   Study Strategy: _____

5. Why should you take time to plan your "attack" on a test?

   _____

   _____

   _____

6. Describe a few specific ways to overcome test anxiety. What method would serve you best?

   _____

   _____

   _____

7. Why should you review your test results carefully when the instructor returns your work?

   _____

   _____

   _____

8. Describe the best approach a student can take to ask a faculty member to reevaluate a test grade.

_____

_____

_____

9. What advantages follow when you avoid the temptation to cheat on tests? List three disadvantages that can result from cheating.

1. _____

2. _____

3. _____

10. What are some examples of high-stakes testing that can influence your options after graduation?

_____

_____

_____

SELF-ASSESSMENT 9.1

How Well Do I Test?

Rate how often you use these skills.

	Always	Usually	Sometimes	Never
As part of my general test-taking strategy				
I stay relaxed during the exam.	_____	_____	_____	_____
I look at the entire test before I start.	_____	_____	_____	_____
I read the instructions carefully.	_____	_____	_____	_____
I concentrate even when distracted.	_____	_____	_____	_____
I ask the instructor for help when I'm confused.	_____	_____	_____	_____
I move on when I get stuck.	_____	_____	_____	_____
I look for cues in other parts of the test.	_____	_____	_____	_____
I proofread my work.	_____	_____	_____	_____
In multiple-choice questions				
I read the test items carefully and completely.	_____	_____	_____	_____
When I'm uncertain which answer is right, I take steps to rule out the alternatives that are wrong.	_____	_____	_____	_____
I mark the correct answer clearly and consistently.	_____	_____	_____	_____
I change my answers only when I'm certain I should do so.	_____	_____	_____	_____
When I don't know an answer, I guess.	_____	_____	_____	_____
When stumped, I look for clues in the question's structure.	_____	_____	_____	_____
On true/false items				
I go with my hunches.	_____	_____	_____	_____
I avoid looking for patterns on the answer sheet.	_____	_____	_____	_____
I analyze qualifying terms (such as *always*, *never*).	_____	_____	_____	_____
I try to find exceptions to the rule.	_____	_____	_____	_____
On fill-in-the-blank questions				
I don't loiter when stumped.	_____	_____	_____	_____
In short-answer questions				
I write brief, logical answers.	_____	_____	_____	_____
In essay questions				
I underline the verbs in the question to help figure out what kind of thinking I need to do.	_____	_____	_____	_____
I think and outline before I write.	_____	_____	_____	_____
I reflect the question in my opening sentence.	_____	_____	_____	_____
I write main ideas first and fill in details and examples later.	_____	_____	_____	_____
I don't bluff when I don't know.	_____	_____	_____	_____
I write for readability.	_____	_____	_____	_____
I'm careful about using humor.	_____	_____	_____	_____

Now go back over the list and circle the test-management skills that you marked "rarely" or "never." Check your calendar for the date of your next exam. Use your goal-setting skills to make improvements for that exam.

Know Yourself

Minimizing Regret

Check the category that applies to you:

Maximum Regret: I feel distress following the majority of exam performances due to improper planning.
Moderate Regret: I feel distress following about half of my exam performances due to improper planning.
Minor Regret: I rarely feel distress following my exam performances due to effective planning.
No Regrets: I never feel distress following my exam performance due to effective planning.

What can you do to minimize regrets about inadequate preparation for testing? What specific steps should you take in the next week or so to avoid regret?

© Cengage Learning 2013

SELF-ASSESSMENT 9.3

How Serious Is My Test Anxiety?

Check the category that best describes the way you feel when you take tests:

	Never	Occasionally	Regularly
I feel physically ill just before a test.			
I have trouble completing tests, because I fret about what will happen when I fail.			
I can't seem to organize my time to prepare well for exams.			
I know I could do better if I could ignore how nervous I feel during tests.			
I struggle with stomach pain and bathroom urges just before a test.			
My mind has gone completely blank during the middle of an exam.			
I fear that on a test I'll end up turning in the worst performance of the entire class.			
I have difficulty getting a good night's sleep before a test.			
I'm very concerned about what my instructor will think of me if I don't do well on a test.			
I get more distracted during the test than other students seem to.			
I start to panic when other students finish their exams while I'm still working.			
I know the material better than my exam score indicates.			
I know I won't be able to have the kind of future I want unless I can get a better grip on my testing fears.			

These items give you a general idea about how seriously test anxiety may be interfering with your test performance. If you marked any items "regularly" or marked several "occasionally," you might benefit from a more in-depth assessment of your test anxiety. Contact the study skills center on your campus.

After evaluating the nature of your difficulty, the study skills specialists can make specific recommendations to help you master your anxiety. If you're seriously troubled by test anxiety, seek counseling.

SELF-ASSESSMENT 9.4

Your Personal Honor Code

Check the items with which you agree.

Under what circumstances do you think most students might be inclined to cheat?

When it's unlikely that they would be caught	_____
When they feel desperate to get a better grade	_____
When a great deal is riding on a particular grade	_____
If they haven't managed their time well enough to study effectively	_____
When they might be teased by their peers if they refused to cheat	_____

Other: _____

If someone is caught cheating, which consequence do you think is the most appropriate?

Expulsion from school	_____
Failure in the course where the cheating occurred	_____
Failure of the assignment on which the cheating occurred	_____
Review by the school's honor board	_____
Public censure	_____
Repeating the assignment without cheating	_____
Depends on the cheater's history	_____

Other: _____

Check off the things that discourage you from cheating:

I would lose my self-respect.	_____
I would be frightened of getting caught.	_____
I want my test results to accurately reflect my learning.	_____
I consider it my honor to uphold academic integrity.	_____
I don't want to give in to group pressure to do things that I don't believe in.	_____

Other: _____

Will you be able to withstand the temptation to take the easy (but risky) way out of making the grade?

Clarify Expectations

1. Then and Now

Think about the grades you made in high school. How much time did you put into studies then compared with now?

- Are you managing the same levels of achievement? _____

_____

- Have you had to increase your effort just to hold your ground? _____

_____

- Are you now studying harder than you ever have? _____

_____

- Is that effort resulting in the achievement you're aiming for? If not, what steps should you take to feel more satisfied?

_____

_____

2. "Psych-Out" Practice

Focus on the course that seems to be giving you the greatest challenge. As you listen to your instructor in class, take the extra step of adding a highlight to those portions of your notes that fit with the strategies described in "psyching out" your instructor. Will identifying higher priorities from the instructor help you at exam time?

_____

_____

_____

_____

Develop Competence

3. Format Fever

Students differ in the preferences they have for the formats in which they are tested. Some students love the challenge of crafting a solid essay response to a well-framed question. They may dislike the precision required in multiple-choice questions. Other students live in stark fear of having to write what they know. Instead they thrive on the opportunity to hammer a set of multiple-choice questions. Rank the following test formats in the order of your preference:

_____ fill-in-the-blank

_____ multiple-choice

_____ true/false

_____ essay

In your journal, speculate about why you ordered the formats as you did. How does your achievement history influence your choice? Does your learning style dictate which formats are more appealing?

_____

_____

_____

4. Decode Essay Instructions

Find some examples of essay questions, preferably ones from tests you took this term. Circle the verbs that represent the kind of thinking the instructor has asked you to do in completing the essay. Think about what kind of question is being asked. How will this decoding exercise influence your study strategy for the exams you will face in the future?

_____

_____

_____

_____

Manage Life

5. Promote Better Test Preparation

Create a Website for one of your courses in which you explore the hazards of cramming or offer six bits of good advice about how to succeed on tests in that class. Make an appointment with the instructor for feedback. If the feedback is positive, perhaps your Website can be incorporated in the planning the next time the course is taught.

_____

_____

_____

6. On the Rebound

Imagine that you get back your first dismal grade despite making a serious effort at mastering the content of the exam. Which of the following steps are you likely to engage in as part of your recovery?

_____ Cry like a baby

_____ Review exam to see where you fell apart

_____ Review your notes to see what elements might be missing

_____ Review the exam to determine if the instructor made grading errors

_____ Compare your test results to your peers'

_____ Make an appointment with the professor to get feedback on preparation

Connect and Communicate

7. Grades: Carrots or Sticks?

Many students thrive in graded systems. They like the clear-cut messages they get when their efforts are rewarded by good grades. However, other students find grades less rewarding. They think competition for grades undercuts meaningful learning and feel stressed out by the process. With a group of students, discuss the advantages and disadvantages of using grades to evaluate learning. Which system would most effectively motivate your learning?

_____

_____

_____

8. What's the Risk?

Locate a copy of your school's honor code or procedures that govern academic integrity. Review it to determine the risks involved in cheating. In most cases, the outcomes of being caught and punished for cheating are fairly severe. How can you reconcile these outcomes with the fact that 75 percent of college students report cheating at some point in high school or college or both? Consider how learning styles and personality factors might influence the decision to cheat.

_____

_____

_____

🎓 Build a Bright Future

9. Predict a Stellar First Semester

You may be halfway through the semester. Ask your professors to provide a midterm estimate of your grades based on your performance to date. If they are unwilling or unable to do so, substitute your own estimate based on the grades you have received to date. Calculate what you anticipate your grade-point average to be. If you are accurate, identify what the implications of your GPA would be. Are you safe? Headed to probation? Destined for the Dean's List?

_____

_____

_____

_____

10. What Lies Ahead

Based on your best guess of where you hope to head for a career, identify the likely high-stakes tests that may loom in your future. Identify the cost of taking the exam and any other details about its administration (e.g., cost, location, timing) that could be useful to you in the future. Then see if you can find an individual who took the exam and talk to him or her about the experience.

_____

_____

_____

_____

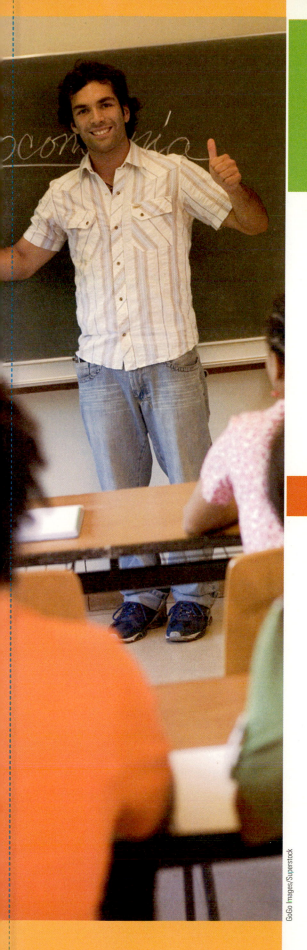

Express Yourself

Chapter 10

KNOW YOURSELF

ONE EXCITING ASPECT OF COLLEGE is the opportunity to develop confidence in your self-expression, whether you are debating, persuading, crusading, or editorializing. In this chapter, you'll explore ways to improve your writing and speaking skills. You'll also learn strategies for overcoming common problems involving communication. To evaluate where you stand right now, place a check mark in the category that most applies to you.

Am I an Effective Communicator?

	Very Much Like Me	Somewhere In Between	Not at All Like Me
I pursue opportunities to practice effective communication skills.			
I can design and execute projects involving research.			
I pay attention to audience characteristics to maximize my communication success.			
I avoid completing communication projects at the last minute.			
I polish writing projects to showcase my ideas properly.			
I know how to avoid problems with plagiarism.			
I seek criticism from other people to improve the quality of my work.			
I use strategies to engage the audience during speeches.			
I know how to control jitters when communicating.			
I coordinate my projects to enhance my future job possibilities.			

GoGo Images/Superstock

327

Rhiana Gunn-Wright
Putting Words to Work

Rhiana Gunn-Wright's passion for words and language began from the moment she could hold a book. Her interest in writing took off when she began publishing in her high school newspaper and then participated in a summer journalism camp. Her excellence as a high school student landed her a prestigious Jack Kent Cooke scholarship to Yale, where her love affair with words flourishes. She describes the process of coming up with something beautiful out of nearly nothing as "incredible."

Despite her awe of great writing, Rhiana states that all writing is hard. Trying to reflect the energy and emotions behind her thinking in a clear and organized manner takes substantial work. Although her least favorite form of writing is the academic essay, she recognizes that each essay gives her an opportunity to improve her critical thinking and become a better writer. She also makes sure that when she receives any developmental feedback from teachers that her rewriting must demonstrate that she improved the piece and also developed herself as a writer.

Although she gets feedback that she is a "natural" when it comes to speaking, Rhiana claims she became more comfortable with herself as a speaker when she moved into adulthood. "I have always worried that I spoke too differently from people around me, but over time, I have just accepted my voice." She strives to be clear, thoughtful, and tactful to maximize her impact.

If Rhiana Gunn-Wright has her way, 10 years after graduation she'll be working as the editor-in-chief of *Vibe Magazine*, a publication for hip-hop musicians that was founded by jazz musician Quincy Jones. In the meantime, she makes a point to invest serious time in her community. She tutors refugees in reading and advocates for the rights of women and minorities. She honed her expression skills by helping to organize a Black Solidarity conference at Yale. "My mother always taught me that responsibility and opportunity come in a package. With my opportunities, I must give back to the community."

College offers unique opportunities to refine your speaking and writing skills. As shown by Rhiana Gunn-Wright's story, effective self-expression can help open doors. Examine the chapter outline to see which aspects of the chapter will be most helpful to you.

(Source: Jack Kent Cooke Foundation, 2011)

BUILD A BRIGHT **FUTURE**

CLARIFY EXPECTATIONS

CONNECT COMMUNICATE+

KNOW YOURSELF

DEVELOP COMPETENCE

MANAGE LIFE

Clarify Expectations

If you connect well with others and can usually think of the right thing to say at the right time, you may be a natural communicator. Even if you don't think that you are a good writer or speaker, you can improve your writing and speaking skills a great deal (Hybels & Weaver, 2012). Most of us need practice and hard work to get there. Becoming a better writer and speaker during college increases your ability to tackle the communication challenges you'll face after graduation.

If you do not have plans that include writing the world's next great novel or becoming a world-class politician, you may wonder why you have to spend so much time in college refining your writing skills and giving speeches. The reason is that in most professional worlds, skilled writing and public speaking can be critical to your success. If you choose your college opportunities carefully, you'll learn to express yourself in writing and speaking with precision, poise, and polish (Floyd, 2011).

Beginning communication assignments usually concentrate on writing and speaking about personal experiences. As you progress further into your major, communication performances, tailored to your chosen discipline, will become more challenging. With some practice, you can significantly improve your skills by graduation to be ready for the professional demands that follow college. How much better you become will depend on how you clarify expectations and make the most of your communication opportunities.

Examine the Goal

Make sure you understand the goal of the assignment from the instructor's point of view. Look at the syllabus and try to link the specific assignment to the overall goals of the course. Ask questions to clarify anything that is unclear. Compare your ideas with your classmates' perceptions. Actively evaluate how the goal of the assignment can help you achieve your personal writing goals. For example, if your assignment is to write a three- to five-page essay, you might opt for the shorter three-page goal to help you work on developing short, coherent arguments. Tailor assignments to your career goals. For example, if you are interested in advertising, you might choose to write a persuasive essay.

Identify the Purpose

If you're fortunate, you'll have an opportunity to write in a variety of formats in multiple college courses that will prepare you for the diverse writing demands in professional life. Before you begin writing, review the directions and make sure you understand the purpose of the assignment. There are five basic purposes for writing in college:

1. *To explain an idea or provide information*. The name for this kind of writing is *expository*. Research papers and essays often have an expository purpose. Instructors often assign research papers to develop your research skills as well as your writing skills. Essays develop your writing and reasoning skills and demonstrate your ability to think analytically about the subject you're learning.

2. *To persuade or argue a point*. This type of assignment often combines writing and problem-solving skills and can benefit from the following organizational strategy:
   - Define the problem and its impact clearly.
   - Describe the origin of the problem.
   - Identify any other relevant factors.
   - Propose a solution.
   - Predict the impact of the solution, including negative outcomes.
   - Develop a follow-up strategy.

3. *To describe an experiment or process, or to report on lab results*. In science classes, you may work independently or collaborate on a lab report that describes a specific scientific procedure. Lab reports are usually highly structured, with the format based on a set of conventional headings. For example, a botany instructor might ask you to experiment with how different nutrient levels affect plant growth. The lab report will contain the following sections:
   - Introduction: the nature of the problem, including relevant research
   - Methods: the procedure used to investigate the problem
   - Results: the findings
   - Discussion: the significance of the results; improvements to the procedure

4. *To reflect on your own experience*. Journal writing lets you explore the personal significance of what you are studying. Instructors usually don't grade journals in a traditional way. They will give you feedback about your insights or the seriousness of your effort. Although research may not be required in such projects, it's a good idea to connect with course concepts to show what you have learned.

5. **To create an original piece of writing.** Literature instructors may assign creative writing projects, such as poetry and short stories, to foster an appreciation of these genres. Don't rule out doing research in reflective assignments. Locate authors whose style you admire. Do some background reading on a topic that might focus your work.

One writing format you will have to master involves writing up the results of experiments in a lab report.

Know Your Audience

One crucial detail you need to pay attention to in any communication project is the intended audience (Pearson et al., 2011). Are you writing solely for your instructor? Should you be preparing a speech for your fellow students or pretending that they are a professional group? The nature of the audience can dictate how complex your communication should be. Some audiences may be forgiving about ignoring rules of proper grammar; for other audiences, you may need to avoid using too much professional jargon. If an assignment doesn't specify the audience, be sure to ask your instructor so you know how to develop the right tone and level of complexity.

Get Organized

For some people, coming up with ideas isn't the hard part. Rather, developing the organization and having the discipline to bring good ideas under control can be the most difficult aspects of communication projects (Maxwell, Meiser, & McKnight, 2011). It is easier to live up to your instructor's expectations if you get prepared for your project.

Stock Your Reference Shelf Good communicators rely on expert help. Many resources may be embedded in the word processing program in your computer, and a wide variety of references are available online. Still, it may be worth the investment to obtain easily accessible print references that will help you develop and express your ideas. For example:

- A *dictionary* can help you with definitions, pronunciation, and spelling.
- A *thesaurus* provides synonyms and can help you expand your vocabulary.
- An *atlas* provides geographic facts and figures.
- A *style manual* details grammar and writing conventions such as the American Psychological Association's and the Modern Language Association's procedures.
- A *book of quotations* features proverbs and memorable quotations organized by topic, author, or key phrases.

Find a Place to Write Most writers say that they need uninterrupted time to think about their writing. Find a quiet place where you won't be interrupted. Hang a "Do Not Disturb" sign on your door to reduce distraction. Don't answer the phone or respond to text messages.

Adopt Comforting Rituals Many writers exercise superstitions about the conditions in which they write the best. It may be the use of a special pen, a cup of earl grey tea, or the quiet presence of the family cat. Rhiana Gunn-Wright, the student you read about at the beginning of this chapter, makes a point to wear her glasses when writing because it makes her "feel smarter." However, many students feel like they can't quite settle down until those preconditions are in place. As long as the ritual is not too time-consuming, it may serve as good signal to help you get down to business and avoid wasting both time and energy.

Do Solid Research

Many writing and speaking assignments require research to flesh out facts, figures, and background information about your topic (Gamble & Gamble, 2010). Good research involves gathering reliable sources of information from a variety of resources such as books, journals, and Internet sites. Good research is important for many types of writing and speaking assignments, providing the basic information you then craft into your final presentation (Maxwell et al., 2011).

Gather Sources How many research sources should you include in your project? Sometimes instructors will specify a minimum number; sometimes they won't. You may not have a clear idea about what will work best until you have done some research. Think responsibly about how many sources you will actually need to develop the most effective argument, but plan to look at more materials than you ultimately will refer to in your work. Not every resource you read will be relevant in the end. Choose those that help you develop a sound argument. Quality of evidence, not quantity, will impress your instructor.

Good researchers find, and carefully build, appropriate and persuasive evidence (Tubbs, 2010). For example, you can include statistics in a political science essay because numerical evidence communicates information about such matters as voting trends and government spending. However, citing statistical evidence in an expressive essay or a piece of literary criticism assigned in a humanities class probably won't work. The point of any formal expressive assignment is to demonstrate your knowledge of course-related ideas and accepted conventions.

As you do your research, also find sources that argue *against* your assertions. Although this suggestion may surprise you, anticipating potential reader criticisms and defending against them in your writing strengthens your overall argument.

Make sure you have recorded the complete reference for each source *as you go.* It's frustrating to assemble a reference list at the end of your work only to discover that the publication date, an important page number, or an Internet address is missing.

Master the Library Get to know your library's resources so you can locate information quickly. Take a tour if you haven't already done so. If you have trouble locating what you need, ask! Most librarians enjoy helping students. Approach the librarians who appear friendliest, or pursue those with the most specialized knowledge on your topic.

Although libraries maintain many print resources in a reference room and elsewhere throughout the library,

Knowing the significance and location of different kinds of resources can save you valuable time in the library.

most have converted substantial resources into electronic formats, including electronic databases. These will direct you to original or *primary* sources (for example, books and journal articles), *secondary* sources (for example, textbooks and other sources that review primary works), or popular press items. References to research or expert opinions that you use in your research are called *citations*.

On most campuses, the library can be accessed electronically with a student number and pass code. Once you gain access, you will be able to download a full range of electronic resources. However, a personal visit to the library, where you can obtain materials not available online, may be a more strategic way to go, since not all pertinent resources are available digitally.

Your research assignment may specify which types of sources you can use. Most instructors prefer original (primary) sources. They also are more impressed by journal articles that are "peer reviewed." This means that the article was critically analyzed and then approved by other experts in the field. Check with your instructor whether some sources, such as popular magazines, are off-limits.

Once you've collected several sources, discard the unhelpful ones. Really. Read the ones with potential carefully, taking notes that will help you represent the author's ideas. Some successful writers like to collect pertinent information on 3- by 5-inch note cards or use electronic note-taking systems that may be available through the library so they can easily reorganize during the writing process.

Use the Internet Whether you use the library, the Internet, or both, your search will begin with a key word or two that you'll enter into an appropriate database. When using the Internet, do key word searches on several search engines to see what the nature of the discussion might be on the topic you have in mind. For example, if your American history class requires a paper on World War II, start with a basic concept, such as "VE Day." Using that key word, though, may produce so many "hits" that you could be overwhelmed. If this is the case, narrow your search to something more specific, such as the economic impact of VE Day, to find more targeted information. If, conversely, your search produces too few hits, broaden the concept until you find some resources that will help you.

Realize that relying on the Internet can be risky. The information on the Internet isn't always reliable (Blumenstock, 2008). Because anyone can post anything, it's hard to sift out the gold. Don't assume that an Internet source will be acceptable.

However, instructors are likely to accept Internet citations that are:

- written by a recognized authority in the field.
- supported by a reputable host group.
- peer reviewed.
- credible and unbiased.

Develop Competence

Whether your project involves writing or speaking, the process you will use concentrates on some predictable stages. In this section you will learn about how to develop a writing project. You will learn about specific strategies for improving your speaking skills in a later section, "Connect and Communicate."

Build a Thesis

Many instructors will select your topic, at least in a broad, general way. However, you still may have to narrow it down and focus it to create a working thesis (Tompkins, 2012). The *thesis* is a statement that simultaneously summarizes your writing intentions and engages prospective readers.

Find a Fertile Topic Choosing well can help you take responsibility and embrace the work that lies ahead. What strategies can help?

1. Look through your notes. What concepts stand out as the most interesting to you?
2. Examine your textbook and course readings, look through an encyclopedia, or cruise the Internet to spark your imagination.
3. Explore your personal experience. Think about aspects of the assignment that naturally connect to your own life. For example, novelist Patricia Cornwell achieves significant success in writing mystery novels based on her life in the coroner's office.
4. Consider what topic would be the most fun or would have the most future value for you. Are there topics that will connect in a meaningful way to your future career plans? Give those ideas top consideration.
5. Carry a small notebook or maintain a separate file in which you can capture ideas that come to you. Think often about your topic to sensitize yourself to ideas that might strengthen the development of your argument. Although popular media resources such as magazines and television programs may not be acceptable resources for a formal research paper, they can suggest interesting directions for more formal research.
6. If the assignment is relatively focused to begin with, you may able to jump right in and read about it. Additional reading will spark ideas and interest.
7. Consider developing a "research stream." When you choose topics for projects, keep your long-term career goals in mind. Good students see the value of an ongoing focus for their college papers (Hansen & Hansen, 1997). They develop a research stream that begins with the first paper they write and builds with each new project. This way they don't have to start from scratch with each assignment, and they can manage greater depth each time. But make sure you don't use the same paper for multiple assignments. Most instructors consider this a violation of academic integrity.

Narrow the Topic As you explore possible topics, avoid those that are too large, too obscure, too emotional, or too complicated for you to cover within the allotted time (Tompkins, 2012). Do not write or speak about areas where you have little knowledge, because it's easier to stay engaged with a project when you have personal interest. Conduct research until you have the knowledge you need to succeed. You may need to redefine the project several times before settling on a topic that speaks to you. Once you have a general notion of what you want to write about, play around with the ideas to begin to make them your own. Here are some ideas on how to redefine and narrow your thesis:

Freewrite Freewriting involves writing without stopping for a set period of time, usually 5 to 10 minutes, to help get your thoughts on paper. After freewriting, review your work to see if any key ideas stand out. When you have identified key concepts in your writing, do another freewrite on these topics until you have a more specific concept for your paper. Spontaneous writing may help you uncover new ideas, questions, and connections. Simply write whatever you think about the topic and save the parts that have potential.

Brainstorm Concentrate on the assignment and write down all of the concepts or ideas that occur to you. Don't worry about the order, clarity, or meaning of the ideas. Just write down everything that comes to mind. Following your brainstorming session, impose some order on what you have produced. Draw connecting lines. Strike out distracters. Make new concept maps that display the most meaningful connections as the basis for your writing.

Pausing during group process to freewrite may produce new insights.

Talk It Out You may find it easier to narrow your topic by pretending that you're talking to a friend. Once you have some ideas to work with, jot down the parts of the conversation you liked and proceed to the formal aspects of writing. Or talk to real friends and colleagues. Use the most interesting parts of that conversation to launch your own perspective.

Ask Questions Journalists follow a specific protocol that can lead to good writing. Using their strategy, tackle your writing task by asking *who?*, *what?*, *when?*, *where?*, and *why?* Answers to those questions can often provide new direction to your work.

Create a Working Thesis After you have narrowed your topic to an area of specific interest, refine it even further by developing a thesis. Your *thesis statement* conveys your general position on the topic and guides the direction of the writing that will support your thesis. The thesis is essential because it focuses your topic and provides a clear direction for your thinking, research, and writing.

A good working thesis:

- reduces the topic to a single controlling idea, unifying opinion, or key message.
- presents your position clearly and concisely, in one sentence.
- makes a statement that can be supported by statistics, examples, quotes, and references to other sources within the time and space constraints of the assignment.
- creates interest in the topic.
- establishes the purpose of the paper.
- outlines the approach or pattern of organization.

Each paragraph should develop a separate but connected point that supports your thesis. For example, your art history instructor might ask you to contrast the work of two Impressionist painters. Your thesis statement might read as follows: "Both Manet and Monet are important Impressionist artists, but Monet's work has achieved wider popularity." Subsequent paragraphs could address the following elements of the thesis statement:

- What is Impressionism?
- Why do critics consider the two artists important?
- What distinguishes the work of each?
- What evidence suggests that one artist is more highly regarded than the other?

To answer each of these questions, include expert opinions found in your research. Don't be afraid to modify your thesis. If your research is not supporting it, restate your thesis to reflect the supporting evidence. Sometimes you will need to do some preliminary research before you can even write your thesis statement.

Design a Writing Plan

Many students overconfidently sit down the night before a paper is due and dash off a first draft to submit the next day. In most cases, that plan will guarantee unhappy feedback. Good writing requires time and a plan for how to use that time most effectively (Tompkins, 2012).

Examine the due date for the assignment and work backward to allow the right amount of time to get the job done. Make sure that you factor in how assignments in other classes must be addressed in your overall timetable. Chapter 3 offers helpful hints about time management for writing projects. Figure 10.1, "A Sample Timetable for a Writing Deadline," provides additional guidance.

Prepare an Outline You may be able to write a paper start to finish without a roadmap, but most of us need the warmup—an outline. An outline can help you represent the scope of your thoughts, incorporate your research, and make your best argument.

The Informal Outline An informal outline lists the points you will cover in your paper. Putting them down allows you to begin to organize and group them into related clusters. As you find connections and consolidate points, you should revisit your thesis. Does the evidence still support it? Do you need to restate it? If you haven't already written a working thesis, this consolidation of ideas should lead to one. Outlining often reveals areas that require further research.

One to two months before the deadline	Select your topic. Map your ideas. Develop your writing plan. Begin to develop a thesis statement. Start your research.
Two weeks before the deadline	Develop individual sections of your paper. Revise with vigor. Complete your research. Finalize your thesis statement.
The week before the deadline	Polish the individual sections of the paper. Create an interesting title. Check your references for accuracy. Obtain some feedback from a friend.
The night before the deadline	Combine the parts of the paper. Print the final draft. Proofread your paper. Assemble the paper.
The morning of the deadline	Proofread your paper one more time.

© Cengage Learning 2013

FIGURE 10.1 A Sample Timetable for a Writing Deadline

The Formal Outline A formal outline provides a more structured order to your points, identifying which are the key ideas and which are subordinate. The key ideas become paragraphs, with the subordinate ideas providing supportive evidence.

Write with Impact

Over time, writing projects improve your writing skills, develop your confidence as a writer, and build your self-esteem. What steps produce the best success?

Prepare Your First Draft The draft stage is an important first step in the process of actually writing your paper or speech. However, don't confuse a first draft with a final presentation. Following are some important things to keep in mind when first drafting your assignment.

Know Your Objective and Strike the Right Tone Keeping your objective in clear view can help you make the right decisions. For example, some writing assignments require an objective and precise presentation of the facts. In other projects you must be exploratory and imaginative. Some projects work best with a casual tone; others may require a polished, professional presentation.

Keep It Casual and Keep It Moving In your first draft, don't get bogged down. Write quickly. If you've done your research and have given yourself enough time to think about the project, you'll be surprised at how much you know without referring to your note cards.

You don't have to write in a particular order. Develop the points that you know best first and end with those that require more thinking or references to research. Consider writing your introduction last and your conclusion first. This way you will know where you're going, and all paragraphs must lead to that ending. Set subgoals for how much writing you want to accomplish in any given sitting. For example, it may help to draft the conclusion one day and key paragraphs on other days.

Organize Your Argument Formal papers usually have three parts: an introduction, a body, and a conclusion:

- *The introduction.* The introduction, which contains the thesis statement, lays a foundation for the rest of the piece. Good writers establish the context or the purpose for writing, even when the instructor is the audience. They state their intentions early and anticipate the kinds of information readers might want to know to help them understand the motive in writing. Throughout the paper, keep in mind what your audience already knows and what they need to know.
- *The body.* The body of the paper should include your opinions and the evidence that supports your argument. Each paragraph in the body should

introduce a separate idea and support it with details such as quotes, examples, statistics, and references to other sources. Each paragraph should follow logically from the one before, and all paragraphs must relate to the thesis of the paper.

- *The conclusion.* In a long paper, your conclusion should summarize your argument or review your main points. Make sure that your conclusion fits with the thesis statement you established at the beginning.

Revise and Revise Again Always leave plenty of time for revision (Cunningham & Cunningham, 2010). It is the single most important part of the writing process. In fact, you should plan to spend at least 50 percent of your time on this part of the writing process. For most papers, you likely will have at least several working drafts before you write the final draft.

Assess It After you have finished the first draft, put it aside for a couple of days. Each draft should be separated by at least a day of time away from the paper. This "away time" gives your brain a chance to process the material at a subconscious level, allowing you to come back to it with a fresh perspective.

Reread It Before you begin your revision, read it aloud to yourself or someone else. How does it sound? Does it flow? Does it make sense? Is it too long or too short? You may find you need to do more research to expand on certain points that don't seem adequately supported. You should go through and put a check mark next to the passages that are fine and a question mark next to any areas that require work.

Seek Feedback Most writers benefit from reviews by others. When your draft is almost finished, get feedback from others who write well. Ask them to point out places where you're not clear and to identify points that need further development. Avoid getting feedback from friends who may be struggling with their own writing, or you could pick up their bad habits. Your campus likely has a writing center where experts can help you improve your writing or recommend a writing tutor. Your instructor also may be willing to read an early draft of a paper.

Write the Appropriate Length Beginning writers sometimes struggle with knowing how much to write. Typically, they write too little rather than too much. Check your writing to see that you have explained your intentions to the reader. Provide forceful examples. Make sure that the parts connect to each other with good transitional sentences. All writing elements should follow logically from your original thesis statement.

Some writers have the opposite problem. Their long-winded sentences contain nonessential elements. For example, phrases such as "It is well known that" or "There are many things that" are usually unnecessary; they flatten good writing. Using too many adjectives and adverbs also slows down the reader and reduces your writing's impact. In good writing, "less is more" once you have explained your ideas adequately.

Here is a predictable academic ritual:

You: "How long should this paper be?"
Instructor: "As long as it takes."

You feel exasperated by the instructor's answer, and she feels discouraged by your question.

You want a straightforward answer, such as "five pages," so that you can plan how to go after the right number of resources to fit the assignment length. As you see it, the desired length of the assignment will dictate the intensity of the effort that will go into your final product.

The instructor's response comes from another perspective. The instructor developed the assignment to encourage you to explore an interesting idea. Typically, he would much rather give free rein to your exploration than constrain the process with an artificial boundary.

What strategy would work better to get you the input that you need? Communicate your interest in the topic you have chosen and express the concern that you may be tempted to write too much. Ask if there are upper limits that will stress the instructor's patience. Ask to see some successful past models on similar assignments once you establish your intention to invest yourself in the assignment's central ideas, rather than unintentionally communicating that you will be striving to meet the instructor's minimum expectations.

"This has merit, but could you go back through and add more *likes* and *you knows*?"

Edit Editing involves making stylistic changes, as well as modifying sentence structure and correcting spelling, punctuation, and grammatical errors.

Refine Your Style Your communication should provide a showcase for your distinctive point of view. When it captures exactly what you think and feel, the thrill can be comparable to getting a hole-in-one or taking a first prize. What are some strategies to achieve a memorable style in your writing and speaking? McKowen (1996) offers the following suggestions:

- Add more words only when it will enhance your impact.
- Remove words, brutally if necessary, to clarify your meaning.
- Replace words when you know there's something not quite right about your choice.
- Shorten sentences to make your writing crisper.
- Rearrange sentences until you find what works best.

Write with an active voice, using action verbs. Be specific, using descriptive language that draws on the senses; uses specific, concrete nouns; and avoid using too many adverbs and adjectives.

Resist the urge to use overblown language just because you are in college. Journalist Edwin Newman (1976), in *A Civil Tongue*, suggested that we embellish language to appear smarter than we really are. He cites as examples these gems from his personal experience:

- "In order to improve security, it is requested that, effective immediately, no employees use the above subject doors for ingress or egress to the building." (Don't use these doors.)
- "I don't wish to defray, but I'll particularize that with more specificity at a later date." (I'll give you more details later.)

You don't want your readers to scratch their heads in wonder because they can't decode your message. Strive to use precise, clear language to the best effect. Limit your use of superlatives. Think of how often we hear "amazing," "fantastic," "incredible," "awesome," and so on. Overuse of such words can have adverse long-term effects on how people interpret your experience. For example, if you

Top Ten Grammar Violations in College

What are some of the most frequent grammar violations that trigger a negative mindset in your instructors when they grade your writing? Instructors tend to recoil when they see grammatical errors such as these:

- *"Me and Todd* went to the store."
  → *"Todd and I* went to the store." (proper pronoun use)
- "A *person* should follow *their* own dream."
  → *"People* should follow *their* own dreams." (noun–pronoun agreement)
- "The football *was thrown* by the quarterback."
  → "The quarterback *threw* the football." (active voice)
- "Do you know where you're going *to?"*
  → "Do you know where you're going?" (unnecessary preposition; avoid using *where at* and *where to*)
- "I like Lady Gaga's music a lot."
  → "I really like Lady Gaga's music.*"* (You don't need *a lot* or, worse, *alot.*)
- "I *except* your apology."
  → "I *accept* your apology." (if I want to make up)
  → "I *except* you from my apology." (if I'm still angry)

(The two preceding examples respectively show the proper use of *accept,* meaning to go along with, and *except,* meaning to set aside.)

- "My homework *effects* my mood."
  → "My homework *affects* my mood." (As a verb, *affect* means to influence; *effect* means to create but is used more rarely.)
- "I plan to win *irregardless* of what you do."
  → "I plan to win *regardless* of what you do." (*Irregardless* is not a proper word.)
- "I *could* care less."
  → "I *couldn't* care less." (If you could care less, it implies you are still bothered.)
  - "I *can't hardly* finish my work."
    → "I *can hardly* finish my work." (*Can't hardly* is a double negative.)

---

are "desolate" at missing a dinner date, how would you describe your feelings when someone close to you dies? If your new computer game is "awesome," how would you describe the Grand Canyon? Invest some time in selecting just the right word to get your point across.

Will the time you spend on refining your style pay off? A sign posted by a writing teacher on her door nicely illustrates this principle:

First draft:
"I think about you all the time and admire you for all your many qualities.
I probably even love you.
I could go on and on. . . . "

Final draft:
"How do I love thee? Let me count the ways."
—*Elizabeth Barrett Browning, 19th-century poet*

Follow the Rules Effective writers follow the rules or conventions (for example, grammar and spelling) of good writing (Crow, 2010). As you get closer to your final draft, make sure that your writing has followed these rules. Specific style manuals will also help you adjust to different disciplinary conventions.

The American Psychological Association (APA) offers the standard for writing in the natural and social science disciplines; you can find tips for using APA style at http://www.apastyle.org. The Modern Language Association (MLA) publishes another common set of guidelines, and you can read helpful pointers for this approach online at http://webster.commnet.edu/mla/index.shtml. Ask your instructor which style manual is best for your purpose.

Instructors vary in how much they care about such conventions. Some simply reject papers that include substantial problems with spelling, grammar, and sentence structure. Others overlook these matters if the ideas expressed in the paper are good. Some instructors are sticklers about learning and implementing a specific format. They may provide a style sheet that states how you must write the paper. Others may not specify guidelines but expect you to observe general principles of good writing that you've learned in composition class.

Use Proper Grammar Even seasoned writers have questions about grammar in their writing. Have a reference manual handy during polishing and proofreading. Consult Danger Zone: "Top Ten Grammar Violations in College" to help your papers get the most enthusiastic reception.

Punctuate Precisely Punctuation marks pace how the audience reads your writing. Here are general rules for the most challenging punctuation uses:

- *Semicolons*. Use to connect thoughts that are closely related; use these sparingly. Semicolons go well before *however, therefore, for instance*, and so on. Also use them to separate items in a series that contain commas—for example, "The scores were Sean, 12; Juan, 8; and Dawn, 7."

- **Dashes and exclamation marks**. These marks—favorites of the tabloid press—add drama. Use them in informal projects, but in limited ways in formal work.
- **Quotation marks**. Quotes longer than three lines require special indentation and marking. In shorter uses, most punctuation marks belong inside quotation marks.
- **Apostrophes**. Use apostrophes for contractions (for example, *can't, don't, wouldn't*) and possessive indicators (*Ted's, the child's, the women's*). Good writers generally avoid using contractions in formal work. Take note that *its* and *it's* are not the same. *Its* is the possessive form of the pronoun *it*. *It's* is a contraction of *it is* and does not indicate possession. (Example: *It's* a good thing that working hard is *its* own reward.)

Spell Accurately Some lucky people are naturally good spellers. They imagine how each word looks, sound words out, and memorize spelling conventions (for example, "*i* before *e* except after *c*"). However, even good spellers use the dictionary or the computer's spell-checker to help polish their papers.

A spell-checker won't catch all errors. Be vigilant about the challenges of homonyms, words that sound alike but mean something different. They can easily slip into writing and elude even careful proofreaders. For example:

- *two* versus *too* versus *to*
- *their* versus *there*
- *hear* versus *here*
- *weather* versus *whether*

Finish in Style Before you submit your final paper, take a few additional step to make your work stand out in the pile your instructor will be evaluating.

Choose the Right Ending You've spent a great deal of time developing just the right approach in your essay, but some closing strategies can weaken the impact of your work. Monitor how you conclude your work to maximize your writing success (Raimes, 2002):

- **Don't apologize**. If you find yourself apologizing for either the inadequacy of your argument or the substandard quality of your writing, you need to keep refining your work.
- **Don't bore your reader**. Although you may be communicating many of the same ideas that you did in the introduction, be sure to vary how you express them.
- **Don't introduce new ideas**. If you open up new questions, you owe the reader a longer paper and a later conclusion.
- **Don't contradict yourself**. Your point of view throughout the paper should be consistent or your reader will be confused about your purpose.

Pick a Compelling Title Many assignments require a title. Some writers wait until the project is almost completed before creating a title that captures the appeal of the work. Which paper would you rather read?

An Analysis of the Poetry of the Beat Generation

OR

The Poet's Place in the Beat Generation

OR

Where Has All the Rhyming Gone? Poetry from the Beat Generation

Both the second and third options are likely to engage the reader more successfully than the dull approach in the first title.

Produce a Professional Product Your writing is an extension of yourself. Your final product not only reveals your ability to construct an argument but also communicates your pride about your own work. Smudge-free, easy-to-read writing says a great deal about your high standards and professionalism. Most instructors expect you to use a computer with word-processing software to produce your paper. That way you can revise easily.

Although word processors can save time, they can also frustrate you if you overlook some simple precautions. Nothing is more frustrating than having the power go down after you've been working on your computer for hours. In this situation you could lose everything that has not been saved unless your computer's battery provides a safety net. Save frequently as you write. Or turn on the automatic save function so you won't have to think about doing it manually. Make a backup copy—just in case. Label your files so you don't have to waste time searching multiple files to find your paper.

Have a backup plan. Even the most reliable computer can fail when you need it most. If you've duplicated your work on a portable medium, make sure you know where you can find a compatible system to use in a pinch. Your campus computer center will provide some backup machines.

Include a cover page with the title of the paper, your name, your instructor's name, the course, and the date, unless your instructor requires a different format. Be sure to number the pages. Ask each of your instructors for other format preferences, including whether they prefer some sort of binder or folder. Many instructors disdain this approach as a waste of money and resources. By contrast, some think a cover gives a more professional look.

Proofread the Final Draft Proofreading can be tricky. You may be so close to what you've created that you can't spot errors easily. A break can help. For example, by returning to the paper later, you can feel more confident about catching the subtle errors that you might miss when tired. Proofreading your paper aloud may help you catch more errors.

Altering your usual method of reading may help you see weak sentence structure. When you think that you've caught all errors, proofread one more time. If the errors are minor, you won't need to print another copy. Making last-minute proof marks on your paper signals to your instructor that you made a final pass to ensure that the work represents your best effort.

Evaluate Your Work Upon finishing a paper, good writers assess the quality of their work. In general, good writing should achieve three important outcomes (Simon, 2006):

- Conciseness: saying what you mean in the fewest words possible
- Clarity: communicating carefully what you mean
- Coherence: organizing your work so that it hangs together well

For a detailed evaluation on your writing effectiveness, complete Know Yourself: Self-Assessment 10.1, "What Are My Writing Strengths and Weaknesses?," toward the end of the chapter on page 358 to explore the reviewing skills that will lead to better papers. If you formally evaluate the quality of your work early enough, you still may have time to revise it and earn a better grade.

Meet Deadlines Turn projects in on time or negotiate an exception with an instructor before the deadline. Although you may have written the best paper in the history of the class, many instructors penalize late submissions. Some even refuse to accept them.

Solve Writing Problems

Even the best writers sometimes run into problems that can keep them from achieving their goals. The first problem may be that they look only at the grade that comes back on a paper, never taking the time to read and carefully consider the instructor's comments. Other common problems include difficulty developing a distinctive voice.

Learn from Feedback Instructors vary in the methods they use to evaluate papers. Some simply assign a grade that captures the overall quality of your work—an approach sometimes referred to as *holistic grading*. Others provide detailed feedback, often relying on a *rubric*, or formal set of criteria, to detail your strengths and weaknesses. When you receive detailed feedback on an assignment, read it carefully. You may learn something that will help you with future assignments.

A river of red ink can be hard to take. Read extensive criticisms quickly and then take some time to recover before you try to learn from the feedback. Let yourself be disappointed. Maybe even mope a little. Then return with the intention of learning what to do to improve your writing. Remember, we all often learn more from mistakes than from successes.

Ask for feedback if you don't understand your grade. Many instructors believe that students are willing to settle for a summary judgment—a grade—with little or no justification. However, when you don't understand how your instructor derived your grade, ask. Specific feedback on your strengths and weaknesses is essential to becoming a good writer and may provide the guidance you need to do better in the course if there is time to recover.

Monitor your growth as a writer by keeping track of how your papers are improving. Review your collection of papers now and then, especially when you're disappointed by an evaluation. Some college programs may require you to construct a portfolio of your work to track your progress. Establishing a *portfolio* (print or digital folder of past papers, organized chronologically) will also help you establish a research stream, as discussed earlier in this chapter.

Find Your Unique Voice Some college students struggle with self-esteem issues, and expressive projects that involve writing and/or speaking may expose their personal uncertainty. From past experience, some worry that their ideas will be poorly received. Communication projects provide a way to discover, express, and polish your thoughts. Your instructors don't expect perfection. In fact, projects that are too well crafted can generate concern and suspicion. Most instructors enjoy working with you to find your voice. Your self-esteem as a communicator will grow if you work hard at producing effective writing and communication projects.

Although most instructors favor logical and uncluttered writing, many respond enthusiastically to work that has a creative flair. Consider what it must be like for the instructor to grade one essay after another that strives merely to meet a narrow set of criteria.

Seeking feedback from your instructor will make you a stronger writer.

Rajiv Srinivasan

A Humanitarian in Uniform

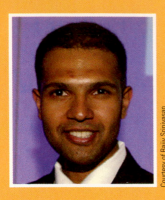

Courtesy of Rajiv Srinivasan

His expertise with website communication led Rajiv Srinivasan to facilitate humanitarian efforts during his service in Iraq.

Rajiv Srinivasan, a comparative politics and Arabic major at the U.S. Military Academy at West Point, demonstrated his expert communication skills in establishing a nonprofit enterprise, Beyond Orders, to provide support to the people of Iraq (Marklein, 2008).

Rav was inspired by how much humanitarian work the troops were trying to do in Iraq, and he coordinated the website at www.beyondorders.com to identify specific needs and match them to potential donors. According to Rav's website, "Every day, countless U.S. troops in Iraq freely spend their own time and money to make life better for the Iraqi people. They actively send letters home to scrounge up money for school supplies, form soccer leagues for teens traumatized by war, and even fix broken tires for local children." Rav's efforts have produced more than 100 deliveries of badly needed supplies. *USA Today* acknowledged his efforts by naming him to the 2008 All America Scholar team.

(Marklein, 2008)

Like most other people, instructors generally appreciate variety, unusual insights, and even some humor in their students' assignments. You can build a distinctive approach in various ways. Find out what other students typically do and then do something different. Consider a unique slant for the project. Create an engaging title. Use a thesaurus to expand your word choice. Add interesting quotations.

Manage Life

Becoming an effective communicator involves some important skills, including strategies to increase confidence in your abilities, decrease procrastination, and overcome writer's block.

Build Your Confidence

The following strategies can help you develop confidence in your ability to get your message across in any medium:

- *Seek opportunities*. When something is unsettling, such as the prospect of giving a speech or subjecting your writing to a critical review, it is natural to want to retreat from the situation. However, the only way you can improve your communication skills is to practice, practice, practice. When you are given an opportunity to write or speak in a class, take it!
- *Build from strength*. Take stock of what you do well in communication assignments and concentrate on adding one more area of strength with each new assignment. For example, suppose that you can write a good sentence but have trouble stringing sentences together in paragraphs that have impact. Concentrate on coherent paragraph development as the next area to master.
- *Develop an overarching plan*. Feedback on your communication skills is generally helpful, regardless of the class in which it originates. Consolidate such feedback from multiple sources. Then set some overall goals for improving those skills in all of your assignments.
- *Pursue feedback vigorously*. Your skills will grow best when critics reinforce your strengths as well as point out your deficits. To build your confidence, make certain that you get confirmation on what you did well. Seek out additional points of view if you can't get positive feedback from your instructor.
- *Don't crumble if you misfire*. Even expert communicators foul up from time to time. A shaky speech or a less-than-ideal paper should encourage you to prepare better or rehearse better so that your next effort will be stronger.

Stop Procrastinating

Like many writers, you also may struggle with getting down to business. Sometimes other more pressing projects intrude or distract. Or the project may be one in which you have little interest. In any case, you may suddenly find yourself with a deadline looming before you and end up submitting an assignment that you dashed off at the last minute. Submitting a rough draft may make your instructor think that you weren't taking the task seriously. To combat procrastination, plan a reasonable schedule that breaks your research and writing into manageable parts, like the one outlined in Figure 10.1. Then stick to it. Reward yourself for completing each phase.

Also avoid getting caught up in procrastinating activities, such as cleaning the silverware drawer, that turn into major time sinks.

Unlock Writer's Block

It's normal to worry about how well you will do in the writing and speaking challenges that lie ahead for you. There may be times when you have nothing to say. Don't panic. All writers face times when inspiration fails and words don't come easily. Interestingly, one good response is to write about your writer's block. Write about how it feels to be empty or stuck. Describe the nature of your blocks. You may gain insight into your resistance and find ideas that will get you moving. Another good step is asking for a conference with your instructor.

By talking about the assignment, your instructor can offer tips or hints that can unleash your creativity. Ask whether your instructor has any model student papers. By observing how others tackled related problems, you may be able to spark some ideas of your own.

Practice Integrity

Communication projects can be both exciting and challenging. Sometimes this challenge encourages students to cut corners, presenting others' work as their own. Make a communication project an opportunity to practice honest, appropriate behavior and build your integrity.

Get Past Perfection For high-achieving students, both writing and speaking performances can be daunting because both represent a threat to being perfect. Although striving to do things well will usually produce positive outcomes, perfectionism can be maladaptive in college because it intensifies the stress that college already produces.

Every paper or speech provides lots of opportunities to slip up. For example, no matter how much you rehearse, you can skip over something important that you planned to say. Nerves can make you choke or go into overdrive so that you may not be easy to understand. Technology failures can turn the whole episode into a time-wasting yawn for the audience. You can even drop your note cards.

What strategies can you use to put your performance in perspective?

1. Remember that this one performance is not your only shot at getting your desired grade.
2. Recognize that humans are simply prone to error. Making mistakes is normal.
3. Compare the threat of the present challenge to something truly significant. For example, how does a blown speech compare to world hunger?

Spotlight On... Courtney Martin

Overcoming Perfection

Courtney Martin understands well the challenge of striving for perfectionism. During her undergraduate years at Barnard College, she became fascinated with how many female students seemed to be caught up in a quest for perfection. As a consequence, she began to focus on the way perfectionism interferes with quality of life. She achieved a master's degree in writing from the Gallatin School and ultimately developed her unique voice in a book entitled *Perfect Girls, Starving Daughters: The Frightening New Normalcy of Hating Your Body.* Her contribution has spoken to contemporary feminists and led her to tour campuses to help put an end to the tyranny of perfectionism. Her work was recognized with the Elie Wiesel Prize in Ethics. In her spare time, Courtney likes to hang out with her writing friends and conspires to get a fad of unselfconscious dancing to catch on.

Courtney Martin turned her interest into expertise in understanding how perfectionism interferes with great expression.

Ronald Martin

4. Laugh. Own up to the fact that having such sky-high expectations, considering the range of things that can go wrong, is a little goofy.

Types of Plagiarism *Plagiarism* means presenting someone else's words or ideas as your own. This is a serious academic offense. Most campuses specify harsh outcomes for those found guilty. Plagiarism can shortchange your learning, severely risk your academic health, and ruin your reputation.

Experts suggest that students who plagiarize generally fall into one of two categories: those who accidentally plagiarize and those who do it on purpose (Harris, 2001). The penalties for inadvertent plagiarism can be just as severe as for intentionally misrepresenting your work, so make sure you understand the rules.

Accidental Plagiarism Inadvertent plagiarizers can fall into the trap by not knowing the rules that govern appropriate citation. For example, some students erroneously think that they can lift words from a source if they simply cite it. Wrong! Importing an author's words directly into your own work requires quotation marks and proper citation. Some students believe that if you change a word or two in a sentence, that's good enough. It's not. Both strategies can make you vulnerable to charges of plagiarism by alert instructors. Check out your understanding of the rules by taking Know Yourself: Self-Assessment 10.2, "Are You at Risk for Plagiarism?," on page 359 at the end of the chapter.

Plagiarism represents a particular threat to international students for whom English is a second language (Carroll & Rayn, 2005). Their inclination to rely too heavily on a written source may have a lot to do with their larger struggle in understanding abstract ideas. In cultures where there is less emphasis on the individual, collaboration to achieve an outcome is not only acceptable, but praiseworthy. It makes American boundaries about individual effort harder to figure out.

Purposeful Plagiarism Why would anyone plagiarize on purpose? Some students may have been trained in a different tradition. For example, some foreign students have learned to cite a source word for word to "honor the writer" (Harris, 2001). However, others may be looking for a shortcut to produce a project that they can submit for a grade. They may feel swamped by too many deadlines or insecure in their own writing skills. They may think that their instructors don't really read the papers and use that assumption to justify not going to the trouble of writing an original one. Unfortunately, some students also enjoy defying authority. They relish the opportunity to outsmart the instructor by not getting caught when submitting the work of others as their

Suppose you are writing a paper for psychology class about the meaning of body piercing in contemporary culture.

From your literature review, imagine that you have found a great resource in a recent article published in a peer-reviewed journal by Lydia Gray.

How do you incorporate Gray's ideas to support your argument? You have two options:

Appropriate Citation with Quote:

Gray (2001, p. 55) stated, "Body piercing represents a teenager's attempt to shock her parents and distance herself from their values."

> *Your citation gives full credit to the person who originated the idea. The quote marks tell the reader that the author stated the argument in these words on a specific page in the original resource. Use quotations sparingly, but do so when the author has used especially vivid words or examples and their impact would be lost by paraphrasing.*

Appropriate Citation with Paraphrase:

Gray (2001) speculated that adolescents may alienate their parents on purpose by certain behaviors, such as body piercing, that don't fit with their parents' value system.

> This approach is the preferred way to cite evidence in most cases. It honors the author and the idea but relies on your ability to translate the idea into your own words.

When do you run the risk of being accused of plagiarism?

Overt Plagiarism: Direct Use of Author's Words, No Paraphrase, No Citation

Gray originally stated,

"Body piercing represents a teenager's attempt to shock her parents and distance herself from their values."

You write in your paper:

Body piercing represents a teenager's attempt to shock her parents.

> *Using this line, word-for-word, in your paper misrepresents the idea as your own. Merely leaving off the last half of the sentence does not protect you from the accusation of stealing the author's words.*

Overt Plagiarism: Direct Use of Author's Ideas, Insufficient Paraphrase, No Citation

Gray originally stated,

"Body piercing represents a teenager's attempt to shock her parents and distance herself from their values."

You write in your paper:

Body piercing can be a girl's attempt to upset her parents and distance herself from their values.

> *Substituting a few words in the author's original sentence and not giving credit to the author for the original idea counts as plagiarism.*

FIGURE 10.2 **From Original Source to Proper Citation**

own. See Figure 10.2, "From Original Source to Proper Citation," to help you avoid suspicions of academic misbehavior.

Consider examples you have seen of students who plagiarize to meet their course requirements. How do they do it? They may borrow a paper from a friend, download a paper from the Internet, build a paper from multiple cut-and-pasted resources, "recycle" a paper from a prior class, or even buy a term paper on the Internet.

How do they get caught? Not all faculty members pay careful attention, but the ones who do pay attention use well-developed strategies to identify plagiarism. Among obvious factors, instructors look for (Harris, 2001):

- inconsistent "voice" throughout the paper.
- vocabulary that doesn't fit with what the student should know.
- sentence structure that is too complex for the student's level.
- content that doesn't quite fit with the topic.
- parts of the paper that don't fit together well.
- missing important recent references.
- inconsistent format throughout the paper.

In addition, some students plagiarize sloppily. They leave clues for a careful reader that will lead to their downfall, such as the date when the paper was written for another class. Instructors can also test-drive portions of papers through electronic databases or can even Google passages to narrow down whether a project is original.

Protect Yourself Being accused of plagiarism can be extremely stressful, both for you and for your instructor. How can you avoid the complications of being involved with a plagiarism accusation?

If you end up getting drawn into a plagiarism inquiry, cooperate with your instructor. You have the right to due process. Be prepared to bring your resources, to share what you know about the information in the project, and describe how you completed your work. You may be able to resolve the problem with a sound explanation. If that approach is unsuccessful, familiarize yourself with your campus procedures and batten down the hatches. It's going to be a stormy sea ahead.

Prevent Plagiarism Commit to expressing only your own ideas, not solely to avoid the punishing consequences of plagiarism suspicion but also to take advantage of showcasing your best thinking. The following are some strategies to help you avoid being accused of plagiarism during your college career.

- *Paraphrase when you do research.* As you take notes from various resources, translate the ideas of others into your own words. Compare what you have written with the original source to make sure that your paraphrase captures the spirit of the ideas written, not the actual words and phrases.
- *Give proper credit.* When you directly quote or refer to the ideas of another writer, provide source information in the format your instructor requires.
- *Make your own observations stand out in your notes.* Put your own ideas in the margin or print them so that they look physically different from the ideas you received from others. Later you can use your own observations without fear of committing plagiarism.
- *Use quotations sparingly.* Rely on the words of experts only when their writing is so elegant that your paraphrase will not do it justice. Using many or long quotations is a sign that you're uncomfortable expressing your own ideas.
- *Develop a protective attitude about your intellectual property* (Lathrop & Foss, 2007). Avoid loaning or selling your paper. Don't store any papers on a shared computer. Make copies of your work references. Maintain an active portfolio to help you document your ownership. Talk with your instructor about how the work is going. If your paper goes missing, report it immediately to your instructor.

Connect and Communicate

Although both speaking and writing provide an opportunity to express yourself, speaking differs from writing in significant ways. When you write, you can refine your work until it says exactly what you want. However, when you speak, even though you can practice to a fine point, the reality of live performance adds a whole new communication challenge. Whether exhilarating or deflating, you experience the direct reaction of the audience when you speak.

Pursue the Spotlight

Your college experience will likely include opportunities to improve your speaking skills by working individually and collaborating with others (Adams & Galanes, 2012). For instance, you may be asked to address the class formally by delivering a carefully researched position or to give an extemporaneous speech on a topic given just moments beforehand. Some courses promote expressive reading of dramatic works. These opportunities will refine your public-speaking skills, including pacing, voice quality, and connecting to the audience.

Group speaking projects include case presentations, panel discussions, and debates. These projects are most successful when group members can coordinate their individual pieces and practice together (Gregory, 2010). However, having to work in a group can sometimes make these assignments even more challenging, especially if you end up with a team member who fails to meet the group's expectations.

You also can learn about speaking by observing good speakers. College campuses often host dynamic speakers who can show you how it's done. In addition, you can get experience in the spotlight by asking questions at the end of the speech. If that option feels overwhelming at first, approach the speaker with your questions or comments when the speech is over. Most speakers want your feedback. By being an active audience member, you can learn a great deal about good speaking skills.

Video recorders have captured a variety of brilliant speeches that showcase masterful communication. Some of these may be available on DVD or over the Internet. Take advantage of lessons from speakers at the height of their persuasive skills to inspire you to do your best.

Rehearse using available technology to ensure a smooth, effective presentation.

Write a Good Speech

All famous speeches were written before they were delivered and became memorable. Keep in mind that the skills involved in preparing good papers also apply to good speeches. For example, you will want to develop a thesis statement, research your topic, create an outline, and organize your points into an introduction, main body, and conclusion. What additional strategies can you apply?

Define Your Purpose Know your goal. Are you supposed to persuade? Inform? Entertain? Debate? Your purpose will determine how to use resources and structure your speech so that you can achieve success. It also will help you avoid running too short or too long. Talk with your instructor about your intentions. Submit a thesis statement, outline, or concept map before your scheduled presentation time, if the instructor is willing to review your ideas. Ask for comments to help you stay close to the goal of the assignment.

Engage Your Audience A college audience usually provides a uniquely supportive learning environment in which to give a speech. After all, your peers will be in your shoes before the term is over. If you assume that your audience is supportive, you may feel less apprehensive about giving the speech. Identify your purpose early in your speech. Keep in mind what your audience knows already and what it needs to know. However, never omit your purpose, even if the audience already knows it. It's best to be brief but clear.

Effective speakers address the audience on its level (Hasling, 2010). For example, if your college recruits you to talk to high school students about college life, your vocabulary and examples might be different from those in the same kind of speech given to the students' parents. Good speakers also try to understand the values of their audience so that they appeal to their listeners most effectively.

Build Your Message An anonymous speech instructor once recommended the perfect structure for public presentations: "Tell 'em what you are going to tell 'em, tell 'em, then tell 'em what you told 'em." Although this approach might sound boring, repeating the key ideas of a speech really helps. As in good writing, the main point of the speech serves as the backbone, and each portion of the speech must support it.

Many speakers hand out a printed outline of a speech or rely on PowerPoint slides to help the audience follow the speech. As you construct the body of your talk, pay attention to the kinds of support that appeal most to the audience. You don't have to overwhelm your audience with statistics and stories to make your point. Choose your evidence carefully to create both emotional and logical appeal. Class speeches should reflect what you've learned from the course. You can draw ideas from the textbook, class notes, or other readings that relate to what you're studying. However, if you give a speech that shows no evidence of what you've learned from the course, your grade will probably suffer as much as your audience.

Deliver a Good Speech

If you have invested time wisely in getting your ideas together, a speech gives you the opportunity to shine. How can you get the most out of these opportunities?

Rehearse The time put into rehearsal often makes or breaks a speech (Nelson, Titsworth, & Nelson, 2012). If you know your speech well enough, you should need your note cards or PowerPoint slides only for cues about what you intend to say. Otherwise, you may be tempted to read what you've written, and this practice disconnects you from the audience. Because effective speakers know their own intentions and order of ideas, they don't need to rely heavily on their notes or a memorized script. They give the impression of connecting with the audience by talking with them rather than reciting from memory or reading directly from a prepared text.

Look the Part How you look will influence your speaking success. Dress to meet the expectations of the audience. For example, some formal speeches may work better if you dress less casually. How you dress should not distract from your message. Your clothes should be comfortable without being distracting. Make sure that your shoes match. Avoid playing with your hair and jewelry. You will want the audience to pay attention to your message, not your fashion sense.

Start your speech with a personal experience or humor. Introduce an interesting news item, quotation, or event that the audience will remember. In all cases, conclude your opening with a statement of your objective and a description of where you intended to go.

Polish Your Delivery Stand straight and breathe in a controlled manner. Speak clearly and confidently. Make gestures that are purposeful, directing attention to underscore what you are saying. Look your audience in the eye. And don't forget to smile or frown appropriately to express the emotion you feel about your topic. Even casual speeches benefit from the polish that comes from practice. Minimize the number of pauses, "ums," "ahs," and other interruptions that invite your audience to stop listening.

Effective speakers also project their voices to reach people at the back of the room and put life into their voices to keep listeners' attention (Brydon & Scott, 2011). A monotone delivery, bad grammar, and sloppy sentence structure can be lethal. When you practice giving your speech to a friend, ask for specific feedback on grammar and language.

Use Media Effectively Good speakers use a variety of means to make their ideas believable, including stories, video clips, quotations, statistics, charts, and graphs. Every element should play a meaningful role in the development of the speaker's position. Demonstrate expert technological skills by applying these tips:

- *Choose the right technology for the right purpose and setting.* Using PowerPoint in a room with too much light for clear viewing is worse than not using technology at all. Sometimes chalk and a blackboard may be more engaging for (and more visible to) your audience.
- *Use bullets rather than full text when creating slides.* The level of detail should be enough to help the audience follow along rather than read along with you.
- *Make the font large enough on slides to be legible.* Consider an 18-point font for PowerPoint slides. Don't apologize to the audience if they cannot read what you are presenting; build the slides so that they can.
- *Don't turn your back on the audience.* You are the most important element of your presentation, not your slides.
- *Avoid excessive PowerPoint animations and effects.* You don't want people focusing on your effects rather than your message.
- *Be sure to set audio and video devices to play at exactly the portion you wish to use.* Nothing loses your audience faster than watching a speaker bumble through a search for a short clip.
- *Practice with whatever technology you use so that your delivery is smooth.* Wasting your allocated time bumbling through support technology quickly dampens your listeners' interest.

Finish Gracefully When you conclude your speech, return to your key themes. Summarize what you've covered, and emphasize any actions the audience should take as a result of your speech.

If you've given a long speech, repeat your objectives. Then smile and prepare to receive your applause. Many instructors include a question-and-answer period following a student's speech. Such activity encourages you to think on your feet and to learn how to manage unexpected events. See Highlight: "Winning in the Home Stretch" for strategies on managing questions at the end of your talk.

Improve Your Speaking Skills

Good speaking skills don't develop overnight. By revisiting your performances after the fact, you can improve your technique for the future.

Evaluate Your Work Good speakers check the quality of their speaking as they rehearse, as well as during and after the actual performance. Complete Know Yourself: Self-Assessment 10.3, "What Are My Speaking Strengths and Weaknesses?," at the back of the chapter on page 360 to examine your speaking skills in detail.

Solve Delivery Problems You will likely experience a variety of speeches during your college career. Some will dazzle you. Others will be painful to listen to. When speaking to a group, many students choke up, tear up, or show other obvious signs of nervousness.

OVERCOMING PUBLIC SPEAKING ANXIETY

A.BACALL

Although you just delivered a fine speech, your challenge is not over yet. Now it is time for the question and answer (Q&A) segment that often follows the delivery of your speech. When your classmates ask questions that stump you, consider these strategies for coping with the strain:

- *Ask for a restatement of the question.* This technique can give you clues to help you answer the question or provide extra time to think through your response.
- *Say "I don't know."* Sometimes it's best to admit that the questioner poses a new topic for you, and then move on. No one expects a speaker to have all the answers. You can also speculate about an answer, but identify your answer as speculative.
- *Ask the questioner for an opinion.* Many people who ask questions have their own ideas about what constitutes a satisfying answer. Your audience will view your willingness to share the stage as gracious, and the gesture gives you additional time to respond.
- *Acknowledge great questions.* Your classmates may be trying to help you strut your stuff rather than catch you off guard.

Delivery problems can undermine your effectiveness. However, you can draw from several strategies to put yourself at ease.

- *Diagnose your problem carefully.* If you routinely choke up during oral presentations, identify when the problem occurs and whether there are any consistent causes. Contrast those situations with other performances that have been more satisfying. This analysis will help you find ways to improve your delivery.
- *Anticipate what your body will need.* Breathe deeply and stretch your muscles beforehand to give your body signals about your intention to control your nervousness. Take a bathroom break before your talk begins. Have a glass of water handy to relieve parched lips and to give yourself time to regain your composure.
- *Organize yourself to maintain control.* Prevent losing your place by using well-organized, easy-to-read note cards. Number the cards so that you can restore their order quickly if you drop the stack. It happens!
- *Use technology strategically.* A tape or video recorder during rehearsal can provide clues about where your delivery suffers. If you use technology during your presentation, rehearse blending these elements with your talk. A graceful pause to review a slide can focus audience attention on your content and away from your own anxiety.
- *Reduce distracting mannerisms or gestures.* Practice avoiding these problems until you're satisfied that you can perform smoothly.
- *Enlist audience support.* If you announce that your hands are shaking or your knees are knocking, your audience will think about your hands or knees and not your ideas. If you lose your place, however, admit the problem to the audience and then stop and regain your control. If you feel overwhelmed, tell the audience that this topic is hard for you. They'll appreciate your candor and support you.

Seek a Second Chance All great speakers suffer an occasional bad performance. Recognize your potential to learn from experiences that don't go well. Commit yourself to better preparation, goal setting, and improved performances in the future. See if you can work out a second chance with your instructor. Sometimes your speech can be video-recorded in the college media facilities so that the instructor can review it at a convenient time. Whether this second chance improves your grade or not, your positive practice will help you turn in a performance in which you have greater pride.

Build a Bright Future

Succeeding in college can sometimes make all the difference in whether you earn your living mainly by using communication and thinking skills or primarily using your hands. Even if you don't like a particular assignment, you can make it more palatable if you think about it as a way to refine your skills to help you secure the job of your dreams.

See the Career Connection

How will your writing assignments help you build professional-level skills? Writing essays, lab reports, and papers in college prepares you to write effective memos, proposals, and reports in the work world. Practice in editing and proofreading will improve your attention to detail. Writing projects also encourage the kind of creativity that fields such as advertising, publishing, and marketing value highly.

Successful speaking assignments build self-confidence that can translate into successful job interviews. Classroom speaking also provides practice for supervising, persuading, negotiating, selling, and other aspects of working with the public.

Build a Professional Portfolio

Building a strong portfolio of your work will produce multiple good outcomes for your future. It will:

- make your projects easier to showcase.
- allow you to build a concentration of expertise that can help you to be more competitive in the job market you aspire to conquer.
- facilitate the practice of collecting your best work so that you will have examples of your expertise when you are ready to compete.

Capture your best performances. Increasingly, successful job candidates can direct employers to a website that can include samples of both written and oral presentations that may prove you worthy of the job you want.

However, if you collect a wide range of materials, select from the materials you have gathered specifically to make the most persuasive case. If you insist on showcasing everything you have ever done, future employers will worry that you need too much attention.

Avoid Internet Sabotage

Recognize that images and written communications that you place on the Internet can take on a life of their own. If you had a particularly "jubilant" spring break, you may have been tempted to share your revelry in a public forum. Once published digitally, you can't exercise much control over undoing the potential damage.

Employers have learned to do their homework on potential new employees. Whether you think it is fair or not, they may "Google" you to see if there is any evidence to suggest that your character may be less than stellar. You don't want to sabotage your long-term success by inappropriate postings or photos.

Similarly, you can protect your immediate future by watching what you post on the college server. For example, underage students who posted photos on a social network of drinking on college grounds before a theater performance were surprised the following Monday to learn that they would be facing disciplinary action. An alumna who had been interested in the latest production informed the dean, who had to take action based on the obvious evidence that the students had violated the student code of behavior. Making choices that reflect positive values reduces your risk that your behavior can come back to haunt you.

Summary Strategies for Mastering College Success

Clarify Expectations

- Clarify your goals for improving your writing.
- Identify the purpose for your writing.
- Know your audience and write with a specific purpose in mind.
- Get organized and do solid research by using reference books, a timetable, and an outline to aid your writing. Develop your writing strategy and stick to the plan.

Develop Competence

- Build a thesis for what you are writing. Use strategies to generate ideas and refine your topic.
- Design a writing plan. Start early, revise regularly, and meet deadlines.
- Write with impact. Organize your argument with an introduction, a main body, and a conclusion. Learn from your instructor's feedback. Develop your distinctive voice and writing flair.

Manage Life

- Build confidence by seeking opportunities to express yourself. Overcome common problems that block expression.
- Stop procrastination.
- Unlock writer's block through careful planning.
- Avoid plagiarism through careful note taking and proper citation practices.

Connect and Communicate

- Pursue the spotlight by pursuing opportunities to speak in different contexts that will help you polish your speaking skills. Learn to relax to overcome speech jitters.
- Write a good speech by following instructions carefully to achieve the best outcomes.
- Rehearse until you aren't dependent on notes, which will help you deliver a good speech.
- Improve your speaking skills by using technology wisely to support your ideas, not distract from them.

Build a Bright Future

- Recognize why future employers place high value on communication skills.
- Consider developing a portfolio to showcase your work.
- Avoid taking risks in what you post on the Internet.

 Visit the College Success CourseMate for *Your Guide to College Success* for interactive resources at login.cengagebrain.com

Review Questions

1. What are the five purposes of college writing assignments?

_____

_____

_____

_____

_____

2. What are some specific steps you should take to get organized for a communications project?

_____

_____

_____

_____

_____

3. What is a thesis statement? Why is it important?

_____

_____

_____

_____

_____

4. What tips should you follow to make your writing and speaking more engaging for the audience?

_____

_____

_____

_____

_____

5. Describe some strategies you can use to build your confidence as a communicator.

_____

_____

_____

_____

_____

6. Why should students avoid plagiarism? List a few strategies for making sure you don't plagiarize.

_____

_____

_____

_____

_____

7. What are some typical problems you might face in giving formal speeches, and how can you overcome them?

_____

_____

_____

_____

_____

8. What are some ways to recover from disappointing performances in communication?

_____

_____

_____

_____

_____

9. List a few ways that good writing and speaking skills can improve your job performance.

1. _____

2. _____

3. _____

10. Why should you exercise caution about the kinds of communication you post on the Internet? What are the short-term and long-term dangers?

_____

_____

_____

_____

_____

What Are My Writing Strengths and Weaknesses?

Once you've completed at least one formal college writing assignment, examine your work using the guidelines here (based on Alverno College, 1995). The feedback or grade you received from your instructor may provide some clues about areas that you need to improve. Keep the writing criteria handy to help guide your future writing projects.

Writing Criteria	Completely	Partially	Barely or Not at All
I followed the instructions.			
I established appropriate context and kept this focus throughout.			
I crafted the style of the paper and selected words carefully to suit the purpose.			
I showed conscientious use of appropriate conventions, including spelling and grammar.			
I structured the paper, including an introduction, main body, and conclusion.			
I included evidence to support my thesis.			
I added content that reflected learning that was specific to the course.			

Now review your responses to these criteria and answer the following:

- What are your writing strengths?
- What do you need to improve?
- Is this pattern typical of your writing projects?
- What strategies will help you improve?
- Would it be useful to consult with the campus writing center?

Source: "What Are My Writing Strengths and Weaknesses?" Adapted from *Criteria for Effective Writing*. Copyright © 1995 Alverno College. Reprinted by permission of Alverno College Productions.

 **Know Yourself**

Are You at Risk for Plagiarism?

Which of the following are acceptable ways to acknowledge the ideas of others in your own writing?

_____ Reproducing the writer's original words—with quotation marks

_____ Reproducing the writer's original words—without quotation marks

_____ Leaving out a portion of the writer's original sentence

_____ Rearranging the words in the writer's original sentence

_____ Substituting a few words in the writer's original sentence

_____ Identifying the writer, but putting the original sentence in your own words

_____ Without identifying the writer, putting the original sentence in your own words

There are only a few appropriate strategies you can use to acknowledge the work of others. These include:

- Reproducing the writer's original words—with quotation marks
- Identifying the writer, but putting the original sentence in your own words

Keep this information in mind when preparing all of your writing assignments, regardless of the discipline.

What Are My Speaking Strengths and Weaknesses?

Even if you haven't already had a speaking assignment in college, you've probably developed a sense of your strengths and weaknesses in giving presentations. Review the following, based on Alverno College's *Writing and Speaking Criteria* (1995), to determine how effective you are as a public speaker. Keep these speaking criteria available to help you in future speaking assignments.

Speaking Criteria	Routinely	Often	Rarely
I connect with the audience by talking directly to them rather than reading my notes or delivering a memorized script.			
I state my purpose and keep this focus throughout.			
I craft the style of the speech and select words carefully to suit the purpose.			
I effectively deliver the speech, using eye contact, supportive gestures, and effective voice control.			
I follow appropriate conventions, including grammar.			
I organize the speech well, including the introduction, main body, and conclusions.			
I include evidence that supports and develops my ideas.			
I use media effectively to help the audience grasp key ideas.			
I include content that reflects my learning from the course.			

Now review your accomplishments in speaking:

- What are your strengths?
- What criteria show that you need to improve?
- Is this pattern typical of your speaking projects?
- What strategies should you pursue?

Clarify Expectations

1. Librarians to the Rescue

Make an appointment with a librarian and explain that you want some guidance in using digital strategies to conduct research. Since changes happen regularly in what the library can offer, this appointment ensures that you are current in your knowledge. What turned out to be new and different that you didn't expect?

_____

_____

_____

_____

2. Your Lucky Charm

Reflect on whether you have adopted any good luck rituals to support your writing. If this is an alien concept for you, talk to three friends and see what comfort strategies they use to help them produce good writing. Write a short paragraph in which you discuss whether such practices are helpful or simply superstitious.

_____

_____

_____

_____

Develop Competence

3. Exploiting Your Life

Novelist Patricia Cornwell exploited many elements of her own personal life when she constructed her series about coroner Kay Scarpetta. Make a list of important events in your own life that might become a resource for future expressive writing projects. Keep the list in your day planner or somewhere else that you can refer to easily throughout your college career.

_____

_____

_____

_____

4. The Liberal Arts Flair

Many expert communicators find that the well-placed quotation can be an effective way to craft elegant writing. Quotations can be used to open or close a speech or paper with some drama. Examine your upcoming work assignments to identify some possibilities for using quotes to elevate the stature of your writing. Either use print quotation sources or go online to exploit any of the excellent quotation sites that will help you find just the right embellishment. Find at least five quotes that would produce your intended effect.

_____

_____

_____

_____

Manage Life

5. The Cost of Plagiarism

List some reasons why a student might resort to plagiarism to satisfy a course requirement. After each reason, list a potential justification for this act. Finally, list all of the consequences of plagiarism, whether the student is caught or not.

1. Reason: _____ Justification: _____

2. Reason: _____ Justification: _____

3. Reason: _____ Justification: _____

4. Consequences: _____

How does this exercise influence your own ability to resist taking the easy way out on writing assignments?

_____

6. One More Go-Around

Commit yourself before the next writing assignment to leaving extra time at the end of the process. Finish your work 1 week ahead of the deadline. Try several different revision strategies:

- Sleep on it.
- Read it aloud to friends.
- Work your way backward through the paper paragraph by paragraph.
- Scrutinize word choice to see if you have chosen the right word for the right effect.
- Use computer functions to check spelling and grammar.
- Proofread 2 hours before the deadline to catch any final errors.

Which of these strategies seem to work best to help you produce your most effective writing?

_____

_____

_____

Connect and Communicate

7. The View from the Audience

Recall a time when you observed someone making a bad speech.

- At what point did you recognize that the speech would be unsatisfying?

  _____

- Did the speaker make any attempts to correct the failing outcome during the speech?

  _____

- How did you feel as you watched the speech flop?

  _____

- What advice could you have offered the speaker to turn the speech around?

  _____

- How should these observations influence your preparation for future speaking challenges?

  _____

8. PowerPointers

You have probably already been exposed to many PowerPoint lectures that vary in their quality. Select one of them and think about ways that the speaker could have improved the delivery of information. Make some notes about what worked and what didn't work. How might your critique influence your own strategies when it is your turn?

_____

_____

_____

_____

_____

_____

Build a Bright Future

9. What Are Your Writing Trends?

Begin a collection of papers from your courses to establish your writing portfolio. Arrange them in chronological order in a file folder or binder. What trends are apparent in the feedback that you are receiving?

Is the positive feedback you are getting consistent with your own self-image as a writer?

_____

Does the negative feedback you are getting provide clues about where you should concentrate your efforts to improve?

_____

Do you see a potential "research stream" that you can capitalize on in future writing projects?

_____

10. Google Yourself

Conduct a Google search by putting your name in quotations. If you have a common name, you may need to add some other identifiers such as your city or state. Carefully examine what the Internet has already collected about you. Have you discovered anything that you wish was not out there for digital explorers to view? If so, are there any strategies you can take to limit the damage? If not, what strategies can you put in place to avoid future postings that promote invasion of your privacy?

_____

_____

_____

_____

_____

_____

Take Charge of Your Physical and Mental Health

KNOW YOURSELF

THERE IS NO GETTING AROUND IT. College has many stressful moments, and stress has an impact on health. As a student and beyond, value and protect your physical and mental health. Motivating yourself to be physically and mentally healthy will help you to balance your life and to stay on track as you pursue your academic goals. For each item below, place a check mark in the box that best captures how effectively you are currently taking care of your physical and mental health.

Am I Taking Care of Myself Physically and Mentally?

	Very Much Like Me	Somewhere In Between	Not at All Like Me
I live a healthy lifestyle.			
I strive to eat nutritiously.			
I am satisfied with my level of exercise.			
I am usually alert and attentive due to sufficient sleep.			
I don't smoke or use tobacco.			
I don't take harmful drugs or drink to excess.			
I show resilience under stress.			
I know how to find professional help.			
I make wise sexual decisions.			
I know why employers value healthy employees.			

Andresr/Shutterstock.com

Blake Geoffrion
Magic on Ice

REBECCA COOK/Reuters/Landov

Blake Geoffrion's decision to complete his degree at University of Wisconsin helped him capture the 2010 Hobey Blake Award for best collegiate hockey player.

When Blake Geoffrion picked up a hockey stick and developed into a kind of phenomenon on the ice, he joined a tradition for which his family is well known. His father, grandfather, and great-grandfather were formerly members of the Montreal Canadiens. Getting elected to the Hockey Hall of Fame is a way of life in his family, and Blake appears to be on his way to the same kind of acclaim. He received the 2010 Hobey Baker Award for the collegiate hockey player of the year due to his stellar performance as a forward at the University of Wisconsin (Lerch, 2010).

Because of his outstanding promise as a hockey star, Blake was drafted to join the Nashville Predators. However, rather than turning professional and abandoning his degree pursuits, Blake decided that he really wanted to play out his senior year at Wisconsin. He explained his choice as "I wanted to get my degree. I wanted to come back and win a national championship. I knew we had a good team, a national-champion caliber type team."

His loyalty paid off. At 28 points, he was the top scorer in the Western Collegiate Hockey Association and was the second-ranked scorer in the nation. Although his team just missed winning the national championship, the accolades poured in. In addition to the Hobey Baker Award, Blake was named to the WCHA all-star team and nominated for the 2010 ESPY Award for Best Male College Athlete.

Badger coach Mike Eaves commented that Blake's upbeat attitude was an even more important factor in his public acclaim than his scoring ability. The coach commented, "Blake was out for a couple of games and a couple of guys came up and they said, 'You know, we're a really different team without Blake.'" Blake's leadership, drive, and commitment to his team *and* his education made him a standout, on and off the ice.

Although not everyone can shine in the national spotlight like Blake Geoffrion, everyone can benefit from a healthy lifestyle and an upbeat approach to life. Look at the nearby chapter outline to see where you might concentrate your efforts on building a healthy lifestyle.

 ## Clarify Expectations

Your health is influenced by many factors—heredity, the environment, health education, the availability of healthcare, and lifestyle. Some of these factors, like heredity, are out of your personal control, but the factor that is probably the most important, and entirely in your control, is lifestyle. *Lifestyle* is your way of living—your attitudes, habits, choices, and behavior. To evaluate your lifestyle now, complete Know Yourself: Self-Assessment 11.1, "Is Your Lifestyle Good for Your Health?," at the back of the chapter on page 391.

Develop Healthy Expectations

How much do you value your physical and mental health? Having healthy expectations for strong physical and mental health leads to setting goals, planning how to achieve them, and monitoring progress (Aspinwall, 2011). Like everything worthwhile, your vigor and health depend on your motivation to follow through.

Self-esteem is also a factor in living a healthy lifestyle. It is a circular argument. If you have high self-esteem, you're more likely to embark on and adhere to a program of improvement than if you have low self-esteem. If you are fit, you'll tend to have higher self-esteem. In contrast, low self-esteem may drive you into bad habits to give you a short-term, but transient, solution from feeling bad. Low self-esteem makes it harder to take on the fitness challenge.

Consider having a healthy body weight. Individuals who have high expectations for being able to control their health behavior are more likely to be motivated to take care of themselves. If they start to become overweight, they set goals, plan weight loss strategies, and monitor their progress toward the goal of returning to a healthy weight. Further, reaching and maintaining weight goals tends to boost self-esteem.

Many college students, especially males, don't adequately use health services that are available to them.

Good health requires healthy habits. By making some lifestyle changes, you may be able to live a much longer, healthier, happier life. In fact, lifestyle changes can reduce the risk for as many as 7 of the 10 leading causes of death (such as heart disease, stroke, and cancer). Yet most of us tend to deny that the changes we think other people need to make also apply to us.

Understand Risks to Good Health

If you are like many college students, you're not nearly as healthy as you could be. Time pressures, easy access to alcohol, shared living conditions, and a host of other threats contribute to decisions that may not always be the healthiest.

Emerging adults have some hidden health risks. Ironically, one risk stems from the fact that they often bounce back quickly from physical stress and abuse. This resilience can lead them to abuse their bodies and neglect their health. The negative effects of abusing one's body do not always show up immediately, but at some point later, you may pay a stiff price.

In general, male college students engage in riskier health habits than females do. For example, they are less likely to consult a physician or health care provider when they have unfamiliar physical symptoms and less likely to go to scheduled health checkups. They are more likely to be substance abusers.

The following lifestyle patterns have been linked with poor health in college students: skipping breakfast or regular meals, relying on snacks as a main food source, overeating, smoking, abusing alcohol and drugs, avoiding exercise, not getting enough sleep, and making unwise sexual decisions. Do any of these habits apply to you?

Act on Warning Signs

Some unhealthy conditions produce symptoms that shouldn't be ignored or else you place your health at serious risk. Seek medical attention without delay if you experience any of the following (Hahn, Payne, & Lucas, 2011):

- A lump in your breast
- Unexplained weight loss
- A fever for more than a week
- Coughing up blood
- Persistent or severe headaches
- Fainting spells
- Unexplained shortness of breath

If you are inclined to think about worst-case scenarios, a warning sign can be pretty scary. In some circumstances, these symptoms can signal a cancer or other serious problems. In many cases, though, a thorough medical exam will confirm that nothing serious is wrong and reduce your expectations that the worst will happen. Either way, it is always best to be well informed about your health.

Develop Competence

In this section, you will get down to the basics of staying physically healthy. Becoming ill is hazardous to college success. Chances are, you are probably not doing all you can to be healthy. Let's look at the six important areas for managing your physical health: exercise, nutrition, eating, substance use, germ avoidance, and safe driving tactics.

Exercise Regularly

Exercise alone is not going to ensure that you reach your academic goals. However, the fact that it can help you process information more effectively and generate new brain cells is clearly linked with thinking, learning, and academic success (Greenwood & Parasuraman, 2010). Exercise has also been shown to:

- increase cardiovascular fitness.
- create lean body mass and reduce body fat.
- increase strength and muscular endurance.
- improve flexibility.
- produce a greater life expectancy.
- reduce stress symptoms.
- improve mood and lessen depression.
- raise self-esteem.

If you don't exercise now, how can you motivate yourself to get going? Following are some effective strategies that can help you to think critically and make good decisions about improving your health:

- *Confer with a trainer.* Many colleges will give you access to professional staff—or exercise majors aspiring to be personal trainers—who can assess where you are and help you plan how to get to a healthier profile.
- *Visualize no change.* Ponder for a moment what the outcome will be of making no change in your health practices. Weight problems, physical inflexibility, and chronic health issues will drain away your quality of life.
- *Make time for exercise.* It's easy to sabotage your own commitment to exercise with excuses. If your excuse is "I don't have time," find it. Ask yourself, "Am I too busy to take care of my health? What do I lose if I lose my health?"
- *Schedule exercise.* Make exercise a high priority in your regular commitments. Don't let unimportant things interfere with your exercise routine. Don't make excuses. Commit to a pattern that you can reasonably adhere to despite your busy schedule.
- *Find a serious partner.* If you have a commitment to exercise with someone who is serious, it will be a lot harder to blow off your exercise in favor of a less healthful activity. Play tennis, do yoga, zumba dance, or learn tai chi. You may have to try out a few activities before you find the activity that can sustain your interest.
- *Chart your progress.* Record each of your exercise sessions in a systematic way. Use a notebook or a calendar, for example. This practice can help you to maintain the momentum you need to work out regularly.

Get Enough Sleep

Most of us have occasional sleepless nights, but college students have twice as many sleep problems as the general population (Brown, Buboltz, & Soper, 2001). Sometimes you can't sleep soundly because stress makes it hard to "turn off." In this case, you don't deliberately lose sleep. However, you can intentionally lose sleep repeatedly for nonacademic reasons, such as partying and talking late with friends (Galambos, Howard, & Maggs, 2011), tending to sick family members, or not being able to disengage from a video game. Of course, many college students deliberately pull all-nighters now and then to study and especially to cram for a test.

Living in a residence hall makes sleeping well a little more complicated. The residence hall might be noisy, or your roommate might not have a class until noon and stays up late while you have a class at 8 A.M. Earplugs and an eye mask might be just the solution you need to overcome the extra sleep challenges "dorm" life provides.

Recent research suggests that more than 60 percent of college students can be categorized as poor-quality sleepers (Lund et al., 2010). In this study, poor-quality sleep was linked to worse physical and mental health, and the students reported that their sleep suffered because of emotional and academic stress. Many students think that sleeping late on weekends makes up for lost sleep, but this is not the case.

How Much Sleep Do You Need? Most students need at least 8 hours of sleep to function competently the next day. But many college students do not get this much sleep and therefore don't function at optimal levels the following day (Insel & Roth, 2012). Some experts argue that a more realistic total for traditional-aged students—who are at the end of the substantial physical changes that take place during adolescence—is 9 to 10 hours a night (Crowley, Acebo, & Carskadon, 2007). Yet college students average only about 6.5 hours of sleep per night. Many are unaware that their academic difficulties can be related to their sleep habits (Brown & Buboltz, 2002).

How Can You Capture More Sleep? Sleep experts suggest that there are many strategies that can help you catch the "z's" you need, including:

- *Get into a regular daily routine*. Try to go to sleep and wake up at approximately the same time each day. Avoid turning on the television so you don't get hooked on a program that will rob you of what you need.
  - *Make sure your sleeping area is conducive to sleeping*. Your bedroom should have minimum light, minimum sound, a comfortable temperature, and good ventilation.
  - *Do something calming before you go to bed*. Soft music can help you unwind at the end of the day, but don't do homework right up to the moment before you want to drop off. Avoid discussing stressful problems before you go to bed. Don't bring up money or relationship problems if you hope to fall asleep quickly.
  - *Cut out naps*. It's okay to take a brief nap after lunch, but do not take naps that last more than an hour, and make sure to take them no later than 3 P.M. Napping during the day can interfere with night sleeping.
  - *Exercise regularly during the day*. Don't exercise just before going to bed, because exercise increases your energy and alertness.
  - *Manage your time effectively*. If you've been managing your time well, you don't have to worry about getting things done, which can often stave off the onset of sleep.
  - *Contact your college health center or physician*. If the above strategies don't work, get some help from health professionals. Although they may prescribe some short-term sleep aids to get you back into a regular cycle, avoid becoming dependent on substances to get your 8 hours. Protracted use can sometimes produce the paradox of rebound insomnia (sleeplessness).

© moodboard/Corbis

What are some concerns about the sleep patterns of many college students?

Eat Nutritiously

Many college students have poor eating habits. One study of college students found that 60 percent ate too much artery-clogging saturated fat and 50 percent didn't get enough fiber in their diets (Economos, 2001). Almost 60 percent said that they knew their diets had gone downhill since entering college.

Being Overweight Obesity has become a major health risk in the United States and in many countries around the world. Strong evidence of the environment's influence on weight is the doubling of the rate of obesity in the United States since 1900. A whopping 60 percent of Americans currently are overweight or obese. A recent analysis indicated that 80 percent of American adults will be overweight or obese by 2030 if current weight trends increase (Beydoun & Wang, 2009).

This dramatic increase likely stems from the greater availability of food (especially food high in fat), the use of energy-saving devices in daily life, and declining physical activity. Obesity is linked to increased risk of hypertension, diabetes, cardiovascular disease, and early death (Schiff, 2011).

The "freshman 15" refers to the approximately 15 pounds that many first-year students gain. The weight often shows up in the hips, thighs, and midsection. Why do first-year students pack on the pounds? During high school, many students' eating habits are monitored by their parents, so they tend to eat more balanced meals. Once in college, students select their own diets, which often feature chips, chips, and more chips, plus fast food, ice cream, late-night pizza, and beer. Once the extra 15 pounds arrive, what do first-year students do? They diet.

Dieting has become a way of life for many individuals, including college students. Be wary of diets that promise quick fixes or that sound too good to be true. Aim for a long-term plan that involves eating a variety of vegetables, fruits, and grains and that also includes being physically active on a daily basis. This plan may produce slower results, but it works far better over the long term and is much healthier for you.

One of the best sources of nutritional advice is the *Dietary Guidelines for Americans*, issued by the U.S. Department of Health and Human Services. These guidelines are revised every 5 years. The most recent ones support seven healthy principles, which are presented in Know Yourself: Self-Assessment 11.2, "How Healthy Are My Eating Habits?," at the end of the chapter on page 392.

GLASBERGEN · Copyright 2008 by Randy Glasbergen.

© Randy Glasbergen www.glasbergen.com

"Just a salad for me. A vanilla ice cream salad with hot fudge dressing and marshmallow croutons."

Monitor Substance Use

Irish poet Oscar Wilde once stated, "I can resist everything except temptation." Smoking, alcohol use, and illicit drugs represent temptations that can have far-reaching consequences for completing college successfully.

Resist Smoking Some stark figures reveal why smoking is called suicide in slow motion:

- Smoking accounts for more than one-fifth of all deaths in the United States.
- It causes 32 percent of coronary heart disease cases in the United States.

"There's no shooting—we just make you keep smoking."

- It causes 30 percent of all cancer deaths in the United States.
- It causes 82 percent of all lung cancer deaths in the United States.
- Passive smoke causes as many as 8,000 lung cancer deaths a year in the United States.

Most smokers want to quit. Unfortunately, the same survey offers some more bad news. About half of the smokers had seriously tried to quit smoking but had lost the battle. The immediate addictive, pleasurable effects of smoking are extremely difficult to overcome. There was some good news, though. About half of the people in the United States who ever smoked have quit.

If you're a smoker, how can you quit? Many different strategies have been tried to help people quit smoking. They include drug treatments, hypnosis, and behavior modification. Drug treatments include *nicotine gum*, a prescription drug that smokers chew when they get the urge for a cigarette. Another drug treatment is the *nicotine patch*, a nonprescription adhesive pad that delivers nicotine through the skin. The dosage is gradually reduced over 8 to 12 weeks. Some smokers, usually light smokers, can quit cold turkey.

Avoid Substance Abuse Many college students take drugs (including alcohol) more than they did in high school (Johnston et al., 2010, 2011). Among the reasons for the increased use of drugs among first-year college students are:

- greater freedom from parental supervision.
- high levels of stress and anxiety associated with academic and financial concerns.
- peer use of drugs for recreational purposes.

A summary of the medical uses, short-term effects, and health risks of depressants, stimulants, and hallucinogens is presented in Table 11.1, as is information on overdoses and the risk of physical or psychological dependence on these drugs.

Do You Binge Drink? In a national survey, almost half of U.S. college students said they drink heavily or engage in "binge" drinking (Wechsler et al., 2002). Almost half the binge drinkers reported problems that included missed classes, injuries, troubles with police, and unprotected sex (see Figure 11.1, "The Hazardous Consequences of Binge Drinking"). Binge-drinking college students were 11 times more likely to fall behind in school, 10 times more likely to drive after drinking, and twice as likely to have unprotected sex as were college students who did not binge drink. Date rape also is far more likely to occur when one or both individuals have been drinking heavily.

What are some of the problems college students are likely to encounter when they drink heavily?

Do You Abuse Drugs? The use of drugs for personal pleasure and temporary adaptation can be dangerous (Hart, Ksir, & Ray, 2011). Drug use can lead to drug dependence, personal

TABLE 11.1 Psychoactive Drugs: Depressants, Stimulants, and Hallucinogens

DRUG CLASSIFICATION	MEDICAL USES	SHORT-TERM EFFECTS	OVERDOSE	HEALTH RISKS	RISK OF PHYSICAL / PSYCHOLOGICAL DEPENDENCE
Depressants					
Alcohol	Pain relief	Relaxation, depressed brain activity, slowed behavior, reduced inhibitions	Disorientation, loss of consciousness, even death at high blood-alcohol levels	Accidents, brain damage, liver disease, heart disease, ulcers, birth defects	Physical: moderate; psychological: moderate
Barbiturates	Sleeping pill	Relaxation, sleep	Breathing difficulty, coma, possible death	Accidents, coma, possible death	Physical and psychological: moderate to high
Tranquilizers	Anxiety reduction	Relaxation, slowed behavior	Breathing difficulty, coma, possible death	Accidents, coma, possible death	Physical: low to moderate; psychological: moderate to high
Opiates (narcotics)	Pain relief	Euphoric feelings, drowsiness, nausea	Convulsions, coma, possible death	Accidents, infectious diseases such as HIV (when the drug is injected)	Physical: high; psychological: moderate to high
Stimulants					
Amphetamines	Weight control	Increased alertness, excitability, decreased fatigue, irritability	Extreme irritability, feelings of persecution, convulsions	Insomnia, hypertension, malnutrition, possible death	Physical: possible; psychological: moderate to high
Cocaine	Local anesthetic	Increased alertness, excitability, euphoric feelings, decreased fatigue, irritability	Extreme irritability, feelings of persecution, convulsions, cardiac arrest, possible death	Insomnia, hypertension, malnutrition, possible death	Physical: possible; psychological: moderate (oral) to very high (injected or smoked)
Hallucinogens					
LSD	None	Strong hallucinations, distorted time perception	Severe mental disturbance, loss of contact with reality	Accidents	Physical: none; psychological: low
Marijuana	Treatment of the eye disorder glaucoma	Euphoric feelings, relaxation, mild hallucinations, time distortion, attention and memory impairment	Fatigue, disoriented behavior	Accidents, respiratory disease	Physical: very low; psychological: moderate

From *Adolescence*, Ninth Edition by John Santrock. Copyright © 2003 McGraw-Hill Companies, Inc. Reprinted by permission of the publisher.

THE TROUBLES FREQUENT BINGE DRINKERS CREATE FOR . . .

Themselves[1] (% of those surveyed who admitted having had the problem)		and Others[2] (% of those surveyed who had been affected)	
Missed a class	61	Had study or sleep interrupted	68
Forgot where they were or what they did	54	Had to care for drunken student	54
Engaged in unplanned sex	41	Were insulted or humiliated	34
Got hurt	23	Experienced unwanted sexual advances	26
Had unprotected sex	22	Had a serious argument	20
Damaged property	22	Had property damaged	15
Got into trouble with campus or local police	11	Were pushed or assaulted	13
Had five or more alcohol-related problems in a school year	47	Had at least one of the above problems	87

[1]Frequent binge drinkers were defined as those who had had at least four or five drinks at one time on at least three occasions in the previous two weeks.

[2]These figures are from colleges where at least 50% of students are binge drinkers.

From H. Wechsler, A. Davenport, G. Dowdall, B. Moeykens, and S. Castillo, "Heath and Behavioral Consequences of Binge Drinking in College" from *Journal of the American Medical Association*, Vol. 272, No. 21, December 7, 1994. Copyright © 1994 by the American Medical Association. All rights reserved.

FIGURE 11.1 The Hazardous Consequences of Binge Drinking in College

distress, and, in some cases, fatal diseases. What initially was intended for pleasure and stress reduction can turn into pain and problems. See Danger Zone: "Let's Get Hammered" to explore the long term consequences of drug abuse.

Know Yourself: Self-Assessment 11.3, "Do I Abuse Drugs?," at the back of the chapter on page 393, can help you judge whether you are a substance abuser. If you have a substance abuse problem, what can you do about it? You can:

- *Admit that you have a problem*. This is tough. Many students who have a substance abuse problem won't admit it. Acknowledging that you have a problem is the first major step in helping yourself (Kenney, 2012).
- *Listen to what others are saying to you.* Chances are that your roommate, a friend, or someone you've dated has told you that you have a substance abuse problem. You probably have denied it. They are trying to help you. Listen to them.
- *Seek help for your problem*. There are numerous resources for students who have a substance abuse problem. These include Alcoholics Anonymous, Cocaine Anonymous (CA), Al-Anon, and Rational Recovery Systems. Most towns have one or more of these organizations, which are confidential and are led by people who have successfully combated their substance abuse problems. They can help you a great deal. Also, the health center at your college can provide help.

Avoid Contamination

It starts with a little tickle. Then a scratch. Then your nose begins to plug up. Soon you feel like you're under water. Although you might think getting sick will provide you some extra time in bed

DANGER ZONE

Let's Get Hammered

Art tells his friend, "It's been a bummer of a week. I blew two tests. I'm depressed. Let's get hammered." And they do. They drink a fifth of gin and pass out. Sound common? Harmless?

It's common, but definitely not harmless.

When students get wasted, they can get arrested and go to jail, have car wrecks, get monster hangovers, accidentally set dorm rooms on fire, flunk out of school, damage property, and make bad, life-altering sexual decisions. Getting drunk as a chronic condition gives evidence that you place great value on short-term pleasure seeking, even at the sacrifice of important, long-term, life goals.

Limit your time with someone who likes to get drunk. Don't go to or linger at parties where getting hammered is the main objective. When tempted, keep in mind all the things that can go wrong when you lose control and consciousness. Also, keep thinking about how you'll feel the next day.

to catch up on your studies, the truth is you will usually feel too lousy to make good academic use of the time.

College environments will give you plenty of exposure to viruses, bacteria, and infections. What are some steps you can take to protect your health or the health of others?

- *Wash your hands frequently.* A good hand-washing technique involves soap, vigorous rubbing of the hands, and time. About 20 seconds—or the amount of time it takes to sing "Old McDonald"—will make your germ prevention effective. Pack an antiseptic gel for emergencies. Some people have turned to minimizing shaking hands to avoid unnecessary exposure and frequent hand washing.
- *Prevent the spread.* Cover when you cough. If you are likely to contaminate others, you should just stay home.
- *Consider flu shots.* Increasingly, health officials believe that flu shots may reduce both the likelihood and duration of influenza for everyone, not just those who have vulnerable health problems. You may be able to get a shot from the student health center.
- *Get some flip-flops.* If part of college life entails sharing a communal bathroom with multiple users, get and regularly use flip-flops in the bathroom shower to reduce the likelihood of an outbreak of athlete's foot.

Reduce High-Risk Driving Practices

A growing area of concern for college students is the risk of distracted driving. It seems simple enough. You are driving along and hear your cell phone ring. You distract yourself to locate the phone and initiate the call. You drive one-handed and manage well most of the time. The problem is that it only takes diverted attention for a split-second to end up with a rear-end collision or worse. In addition, many college students are overconfident about their ability to multitask. They try to text message at intersections or while driving on long stretches of road with little traffic. It is too easy to have your attention become dominated by messaging so your capacity to respond to emerging conditions is seriously impaired.

Manage Life

Emotional challenges abound in college. Some threats diminish the quality of your college experience. Other threats are far more serious. In this section, we will explore serious threats to mental health, including eating disorders, depression, and suicide. We also examine strategies for safeguarding your mental health and finding appropriate assistance when necessary.

Put an End to Eating Disorders

Poor self-esteem, chronic dieting, and other symptoms related to eating disorders appear to be common, especially among

By permission of Mike Luckovich and Creators Syndicate, Inc.

young women before and during college (Vohs et al., 2001). Eating disorders are intrusive, attention-getting, and sometimes fatal.

Anorexia Nervosa An eating disorder that involves the relentless pursuit of thinness through starvation, *anorexia nervosa* can eventually lead to death. Most anorexics are Caucasian female adolescents or young adults from well-educated middle- and upper-income families. They have a distorted body image, perceiving themselves as overweight even when they become skeletal.

Experts have proposed numerous causes of anorexia nervosa. One is the cultural obsession with thinness. Another explanation is that anorexics grow up in families with high demands for academic achievement. Consequently, people with anorexia feel ensnared by perfectionism. Unable to meet these high expectations and control their grades, they turn to something they can control: their weight.

Bulimia Nervosa *Bulimia nervosa* is a disorder that involves binging and purging. Whereas anorexics can control their eating, bulimics cannot. Purging may start out as a simple strategy to keep ingested food from turning into fat. However, the act of purging can quickly become an out-of-control ritual of gagging and vomiting, hardly a healthy way to maintain a reasonable weight. Bulimia can produce gastric and chemical imbalances in the body as well as long-term dental damage. In addition, depression is common in bulimics.

Normalizing Eating Individuals who suffer from eating disorders truly do suffer. Their overwhelming need to appear perfect drives them into secret activities, whether it is late-night refrigerator raiding or surreptitious bathroom visits to purge. They are driven to coordinate their activities carefully to avoid being caught in the act.

To shake the belief system justifying such harmful behavior and the practices that could potentially turn fatal, professional intervention is usually required. If you have anorexic or bulimic tendencies or characteristics, go to your college health center as a first step. Since the problem is such a common one on campus, they will have some good ideas for how to get your eating practices back to normal.

Tackle Depression and Prevent Suicide

The rate of suicide in the United States has tripled since the 1950s. An estimated 1,100 college students will commit suicide during the next academic year, making suicide the second leading cause of death among college students (Martindale, 2011). Since 1960, the suicide rate for young adults (aged 15–24) has skyrocketed at a rate of 200 percent. Why are college students so vulnerable?

A national survey conducted by the American College Health Association (2007) of more than 90,000 students on 177 campuses revealed that feeling hopeless, overwhelmed, mentally exhausted, sad, and depressed is not uncommon in college students. Figure 11.2, "College Students' Mental Health Difficulties in the Past Year," indicates the percentage of students who had these feelings and the number of times a year they experienced them.

Who Is at Risk? Each of us feels blue or "down in the dumps" some of the time. Brief bouts of sad feelings and episodes of discontent with the way our lives unfold are normal. If sad feelings last for only a few hours, a few days, or a few weeks, you won't be classified as depressed. But if the sadness lingers for a month or more and you feel deeply unhappy and demoralized, you probably are in a state of depression.

Depression is so widespread that it's called the "common cold" of mental disorders (Nolen-Hoeksema, 2011). A man's lifetime risk of having depression is 10 percent. A woman's lifetime risk is much greater—almost 25 percent.

Depression left unchecked can make suicide an attractive option. The decision to commit suicide is influenced by a number of factors. Social elements, such as peer group pressures, social isolation, or absence of family support, may be influential. Psychological factors, such as impulsiveness or drug abuse, can contribute. Significant losses, either through broken relationships, financial downturns, or humiliating experiences, can sometimes provide a trigger. Another crucial ingredient in a successful suicidal plan is the ease of access to guns or drugs.

MENTAL HEALTH DIFFICULTY	1–4 TIMES %	5–8 TIMES %	9 OR MORE TIMES%
Felt things were hopeless	38	11	13
Felt overwhelmed with all I had to do	32	25	37
Felt mentally exhausted	32	24	36
Felt very sad	45	16	18
Felt so depressed it was difficult to function	27	7	9
Seriously contemplated suicide	7	1	1
Attempted suicide	1	.1	.1

College Students' Mental Health Difficulties in the Past Year from The American College Health Association (2007). American College Health Association National College report (abridged). *Journal of American College Health*, 55, Table 17, p. 205. Used with permission.

FIGURE 11.2 College Students' Mental Health Difficulties in the Past Year

What Are the Warning Signs? Severely depressed individuals often show disturbance in basic functions: inability to sleep, loss of appetite, loss of energy, social withdrawal, concentration difficulties, and diminished interest in prior passions. Individuals contemplating suicide may discuss their feelings of hopelessness and express a preoccupation with death. They sometimes give away their most prized possessions as a means of getting closure and saying goodbye.

What Can Be Done? Increasing numbers of college students are taking antidepressants, drugs that are designed to reduce depression. Researchers have found that antidepressant drugs work best when combined with psychotherapy, a nonmedical process used by mental health professionals to help individuals overcome their problems (Barlow & Durand, 2012). Nondrug treatments such as regular exercise also have shown positive benefits in reducing depression. A very good book to read if you are experiencing depressive symptoms is *The Feeling Good Workbook* by David Burns (1999), which has a number of valuable exercises to help individuals cope more effectively with depression.

Serious depression may need expert intervention. However, getting someone who has lost all hope to explore that option is never easy. If someone you know seems in trouble, contact campus officials in Student Affairs. They are obligated to intervene and can take drastic measures to keep the individual safe until the crisis passes.

On the other hand, if the individual is open to talking about how he or she feels, the following are some strategies you can use:

- *Stay calm.* In most cases, there is no rush. Sit and listen—really listen—to what he or she is saying. Be understanding and emotionally support his or her feelings.

- *Deal directly with the topic of suicide.* Even seriously depressed people have mixed feelings about death and may be open to help. Don't be afraid to talk directly about suicide. Ask, "Have you been thinking about hurting yourself?" You won't be "planting" the idea but merely creating a pathway for sharing the pain.
- *Encourage problem solving and positive actions.* Remember that the person in the crisis is not thinking clearly. Encourage him or her to avoid making any serious, irreversible decisions while in the crisis. Ask for a "no harm" pledge until you can get professional intervention. Talk about the alternatives that might create hope for the future.

Safeguard Your Mental Health

Effectively managing your mental health is as important for college success as managing academic challenges (Kearney & Trull, 2012). In this section, we describe strategies that can help you effectively cope with such problems.

Identify Typical Stressors According to the American Academy of Family Physicians, two-thirds of all medical office visits are for stress-related symptoms. Stress is also a major contributor to heart disease, accidental injuries, and suicide. A number of life events have been identified as stressful enough to affect students' physical and mental health significantly, including dealing with academic performance (Folkman, 2011). The first year of college may be by far the most stressful for students (Sher, Wood, & Gotham, 1996).

What are the most common stressors for college students? In one study, the academic circumstances creating the most stress for students were tests and finals, grades and competition, professors and class environment, too many demands, papers and essay exams, career and future success, and studying (Murphy, 1996). In this same study, the personal circumstances that created the most stress for students were intimate relationships, finances, parental conflicts and expectations, and roommate conflicts.

Ineffective Coping Strategies Not everyone responds the same way to stress; some of us have better strategies than others. For example, a survey of students at the beginning and end of their first year of college found that negative coping strategies, such as using alcohol to feel better and indulging in excessive self-criticism, predicted worse physical and mental health at the end of year (Pritchard, Wilson, & Yamnitz, 2007).

You may be using unsuccessful strategies in coping with stress. Avoidance strategies may make you feel better, but only temporarily. Among the ineffective strategies for managing stress are the following:

- Repressing it so you don't have to think about it
- Displacing it by taking it out on other people
- Suppressing it so you keep your feelings to yourself
- Denying it by refusing to believe what is happening
- Diverting from it through uncontrolled eating
- Drowning it through uncontrolled drinking

Effective Coping Strategies In contrast to ineffective approaches, being optimistic and having high self-esteem predict better physical and mental health. Coping means managing difficult circumstances, solving personal problems, and reducing stress and conflict. Coping effectively with stress is essential to making your life more productive and enjoyable (Greenberg, 2011). What are some strategies that pay off?

Reappraise Stress To cope successfully, it helps to see the circumstances as a challenge to overcome rather than an overwhelming, threatening stress. Besides obtaining your college degree, your mental health goal in college should be building your resilience so that you can overcome stressors in the future.

Think Positively *Optimism* involves the expectation that good things are likely to happen in the future (Aspinwall & Tedeschi, 2010). In one study, college students were initially identified as optimists or pessimists (Peterson & Stunkard, 1986). Then their health was monitored over the next year. The pessimists had twice as many infections and doctors' visits as the optimists did. In another study, being optimistic predicted positive physical and mental health outcomes for first-year students (Pritchard, Wilson, & Yamnitz, 2007). Thinking positively helps to put you in a good mood and improves your self-esteem. It also gives you the sense that you're controlling your environment rather than letting it control you (Aspinwall, 2011).

How can you develop a more optimistic outlook? One way is to use positive thinking to challenge self-defeating thoughts (Greenberg, 2011). This strategy helps you to avoid ruminating and wallowing in self-pity when bad things happen. Pessimists tend to use absolute, all-encompassing terms to describe their defeats. They often use words like *never* and *always*. If this sounds like you, dispute these negative thoughts in a self-confident, positive way to reduce self-blame and negative feelings.

Unchallenged negative thinking has a way of becoming a self-fulfilling prophecy. That is, if you tell yourself you can't do something well, you won't. How can you monitor your self-talk? At random times during the day, ask yourself, "What am I saying to myself right now?" Potentially stressful moments are excellent times to examine your self-talk. You also can ask friends to give you feedback on your negative or positive attitudes.

Relax When you think of relaxation, activities such as unwinding in front of the TV, listening to music, and taking a walk probably come to mind. However, a different form of relaxation can help you cope with anxiety and stress. It's called *deep relaxation.*

Try the following to attain a deeply relaxed state (Davis et al., 2008):

1. In a quiet place, either lie down on a couch or bed or sit in a comfortable chair with your head supported.
2. Get into a comfortable position and relax. Clench your right fist tighter and tighter for about 5 seconds. Now relax it. Feel the

looseness in your right hand. Repeat the procedure with your left hand. Then do it with both hands. When you release the tension, let it go instantly. Allow your muscles to become limp.

3. Bend your elbows and tense your biceps as hard as you can. After a few seconds, relax and straighten out your arms. Go through the procedure again. Tighten your biceps as hard as you can for a few seconds and then relax them. As with your biceps, do each of the following procedures twice.

4. Turn your attention to your head. Wrinkle your forehead as tightly as you can, then relax it. Next, frown and notice the strain it produces. Allow your mouth to relax. Close your eyes now. Squint them as hard as you can. Notice the tension. Now relax your eyes. Let them stay closed gently and comfortably. Now clench your jaw and bite hard. Notice the tension throughout your jaw. Relax your jaw.

5. Shrug your shoulders. Keep the tension as you hunch your head down between your shoulders. Then relax your shoulders.

6. Breathe in and fill your lungs completely. Hold your breath for a few seconds. Now exhale and let your chest become loose. Repeat this procedure four or five times. Tighten your stomach for several seconds. Now relax it.

7. Tighten your buttocks and thighs. Flex your thighs by pressing your heels down as hard as you can. Relax and feel the difference. Next, curl your toes downward, making your calf muscles tight. Then relax. Now bend your toes toward your face, creating tension in your shins. Relax again. To avoid muscle cramping, don't overtighten your toes.

Initially you may need 20 to 30 minutes to reach a deeply relaxed state, but with practice, many students can become deeply relaxed in 2 to 3 minutes.

Write about Stress Writing about stress can help to reduce your stress. Here are some recommended strategies for writing about stress (Pennebaker, 1997):

- *What to write.* You don't need to write about the biggest trauma in your life. Write about issues that currently bother you and preoccupy your thinking. Write as objectively as you can about an experience that troubled you. Express your emotions and write as deeply as you can about your feelings.
- *How to write.* Just start and keep writing. If you get stuck, go back and repeat what you were writing before you got stuck.
- *What to expect.* Writing about your stress is not a cure-all. It is not a substitute for tackling problems that may keep you sad, angry, or frustrated. However, writing about stress can help you see things from a better perspective. You may feel sad or depressed for several hours after writing about your stress, but most people report that they feel relieved, happier, and more content over time when they write about their stress.

In sum, writing about your stress not only provides a release of pent-up tension but also can stimulate you to think about ways to cope more effectively with the stress (Pennebaker, 2001).

Modify Bad Habits To manage physical and mental health challenges, take charge of your life by changing bad habits. One very effective way of managing virtually any aspect of your physical or mental health is to develop a self-control program (Miltenberger, 2012). See Highlight: "Designing a Self-Control Program" for some pointers on reducing bad habits.

Designing a Self-Control Program

Here are the five steps you can follow in developing a self-control program to improve your physical and mental health (Martin & Pear, 2011):

1. **Define the problem.** Which aspect of your health would you like to control more effectively? For one person, the change objective might be "lose 30 pounds," for another it might be "quit smoking," and for yet another person it might be "engage in aerobic exercise for 30 minutes, 4 days a week." What aspect of your health do you want to change? Be specific to come up with a measurable goal.

2. **Commit to change.** Some good strategies for committing to change include the following:
   - Tell others about your commitment to change. Going "public" can make you more mindful about your intentions.
   - Rearrange your environment to provide frequent reminders of your goal. Make sure the reminders are associated with positive benefits of reaching your goal rather than threats about failure that reinforce low self-esteem.
   - Plan ahead for ways that you can deal with temptation, tailoring these plans to your program. If you can't resist your impulse, don't punish yourself. Recommit to your plan.

3. **Collect data about yourself.** This step is especially important in decreasing excessive behaviors such as overeating and frequent smoking. Make up a chart and monitor what you do every day in regard to what you want to change.

4. **Design a self-control program.** A good self-control program usually includes both long-term and short-term goals, as well as a plan for reaching those goals.

5. **Make the program last.** Establish specific dates for post-checks. Establish a buddy system by finding a friend with a similar problem. The two of you can set maintenance goals and once a month check each other's progress.

Reach Out to Others

Especially when it comes to managing mental health, you are not alone. You have both professional helpers and others in your life (e.g., friends, religious support people, and relatives) who can help you to stay the course or regain your balance.

Seek Professional Help When should you seek professional help? There is no easy answer to this question. However, as a rule, seek psychological help when:

- you feel psychological distressed, helpless, or overwhelmed.
- your life is seriously disrupted by your problems.
- people you care about express concern for your well-being.

Some students may not admit their problems or seek help for them because they fear others will think they are weak. It takes courage to face your problems. Instead of a weakness, consider it a strength to admit that you have a problem and are willing to seek help for it. You'll be doing something about a problem that stands between you and your goals. Figure 11.3, "College Students' Main Reasons for Seeking Counseling," shows some reasons why college students have sought counseling.

The counseling or health center at your college is a good place to go if you think that you have a mental health problem. The center will probably have staff to help you or will refer you to a mental health professional in the community. Clinical psychologists, counselors, and social workers use psychotherapeutic strategies, and psychiatrists perform therapy and also can prescribe drugs to alleviate symptoms.

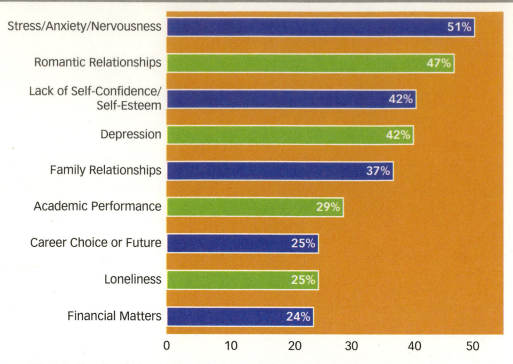

From "Clients Problem Checklist," Student Counseling Center, Illinois State University. Reprinted by permission.

FIGURE 11.3 College Students' Main Reasons for Seeking Counseling

Making changes can be hard. Be patient and allow time for professional help to work. Part of the success of therapy involves developing a positive relationship with the therapist, so it may take several sessions for you to notice a change. Also, if you do seek professional help, continue to evaluate how much it is benefiting you. Not all therapists and therapies are alike. If you become dissatisfied, ask to be referred to someone else. More information about mental health professionals is provided in the resource section on the website for this book.

Secure Personal Support In stressful times, family members, friends, classmates, coworkers, a mentor, and others can help by reassuring you that you're a valuable person who is loved. Knowing that others care about you can give you the confidence to tackle stressful circumstances.

Recognize and enhance positive influences in your own life (Taylor, 2011). Following are some effective ways to build your resources for improving your physical and mental health.

- *Hang out with friends who adopt healthy behaviors.* The types of friends you connect with often have a powerful influence on your health. Communicating with friends who engage in positive health-enhancing behaviors will help you practice such positive behaviors. For example, if most of your friends are couch potatoes, think about expanding your friend base to include several college students who work out at the gym on a regular basis.

- *Connect with a support group.* Support groups for a wide range of physical and mental health problems are plentiful. The *Authoritative Guide to Self-Help Resources in Mental Health* (Norcross et al., 2003) provides the names and contact information for national support groups in a number of physical and mental health areas.

- *Take a class on personal health and/or health and well-being.* Most colleges have courses on personal health or health and well-being that can provide you with valuable knowledge and strategies for being physically and mentally healthy.
- *Read a good book or explore Web resources.* A very good resource for finding self-help books and Internet sites on aspects of mental health, such as eating disorders, addiction, anxiety, depression, and stress management, is the previously mentioned *Authoritative Guide to Self-Help Resources in Mental Health* (Norcross et al., 2003).

To evaluate the support you have for any physical or mental health problem(s) you have or might develop in the future, place a check mark in the appropriate space next to each item in Know Yourself: Self-Assessment 11.4, "My Health Resources," at the end of the chapter on page 394.

Connect and Communicate

An important aspect of physical and mental health functioning for most people involves establishing and maintaining a satisfying social and sexual life. A major portion of emerging adulthood—from 18 to 23 years of age—has recently been called the most sexualized period in life (Regnerus & Uecker, 2011).

At the beginning of emerging adulthood, surveys indicate that slightly more than half of individuals have engaged in sexual intercourse, but by the end of emerging adulthood (age 25), most have had sexual intercourse (Lefkowitz & Gillen, 2006). Thus, emerging adulthood is a time when most individuals are both sexually active and unmarried. One study found that 30 percent of emerging adults reported they had "hooked up" (had sex without romance; a one-night stand) with someone and had sexual intercourse during college (Paul, McManus, & Hayes, 2000).

Make Smart Sexual Decisions

Emerging adulthood has potential sexual risks. Making smart sexual decisions has never been more important than today because AIDS, other sexually transmitted infections, and unwanted pregnancy pose life-altering challenges (Crooks & Baur, 2011). In this section of the chapter, you will come to grips with

Jennifer Burdette | Spotlight On...

Reaching Out

Communication arts major Jennifer Burdette learned that the first year in college can throw some unexpected obstacles your way that can compromise success. With very little notice, she was notified that her healthcare coverage had been compromised and had to move quickly to make alternate arrangements to address her seizure disorder, a serious, chronic healthcare need. The health support system at University of Louisiana at Lafayette helped her navigate some new strategies for managing her healthcare concerns. When she took pains to help her faculty understand the implications of trying to manage her health concerns, she found them to be sympathetic and supportive.

Jennifer also endured some serious emotional losses. She not only lost a longtime romantic partner due to the stresses of being apart but also lost a friend who passed away.

Jennifer reached out to a particularly approachable faculty member who was instrumental in helping her develop the resilience she needed. Despite the challenges, at the end of the first semester, Jennifer managed an impressive 3.5 average.

Jennifer endorses the importance of asking for the help you need to accomplish your goals. "In fact, it is great to have someone to talk to for every different dimension of your life—professional, academic, and personal relationships." Her success illustrates how to expand your problem-solving resources by identifying and forging bonds with those who can help you achieve your dreams.

Courtesy of Jennifer Burdette

the ways in which bad sexual decisions can disrupt your plans for college success and alter your life.

Individuals have varying attitudes about sex. To evaluate your sexual attitudes, complete Know Yourself: Self-Assessment 11.5, "My Sexual Attitudes," at the end of the chapter on page 395.

Avoid Sexually Transmitted Infections

Sexually transmitted infections (*STIs*) are infections contracted primarily through sex. This includes intercourse as well as oral–genital and anal–genital sex. STIs affect about one of every six adults.

No single STI has had a greater impact on sexual behavior or created more fear in the last several decades than HIV/AIDS. Experts say that HIV can be transmitted by sexual contact, sharing of hypodermic needles, blood transfusion, or other direct contact of cuts or mucous membranes with blood or sexual fluids (Hyde & DeLamater, 2011). It's not who you are but what you do that puts you at risk for getting HIV. Anyone who is sexually active or uses intravenous drugs is at risk. No one is immune.

What can you do to reduce the likelihood of contracting an STI? First, recognize that the only completely effective strategy is abstinence. But if you do choose to have sex, here are some ways to reduce your chances of being infected (Crooks & Baur, 2011):

1. *Get to know your partner well before you leap*. Spend time getting to know a prospective sexual partner before you have sex with him or her.

Use this time to convey your STI status and inquire about your partner's. Keep in mind that people are not always honest about their sexual history. It is dangerous to presume good will and good health from unfamiliar sexual partners, and the consequences of risk taking could be lethal.

2. *Assess risk status*. If you've had previous sexual activity with others, you may have contracted an STI without knowing it. Many STIs don't produce detectable symptoms. If you care enough to be sexually intimate with a new partner, you should be willing to be open with him or her about your own physical sexual health.

3. *Get a sexual screening.* Many experts on sexuality now recommend that couples who want to begin a sexual relationship abstain from sexual activity until both undergo medical and laboratory testing to rule out the presence of STIs. If cost is an issue, contact your campus health service or a public health clinic in your area.

4. *Use condoms.* When correctly used, condoms help to prevent the transmission of many STIs. Condoms are most effective in preventing chlamydia, gonorrhea, syphilis, and HIV. They are less effective against the spread of genital herpes and genital warts.

5. *Avoid having sex with multiple partners.* One of the strongest predictors of getting HIV, chlamydia, genital herpes, genital warts, and other STIs is having sex with multiple partners.

If you have sex, be proactive rather than reactive. Use effective contraception and protect yourself against STIs. Promiscuity greatly increases your chances of contracting HIV and other STIs. Think before you act.

auremar/Shutterstock.com

Protect against Unwanted Pregnancy

Most college students want to control whether and when they have children. That means either abstaining from sex or using effective contraception. Unfortunately, students who feel guilty and have negative attitudes about sexuality are less likely to use contraception than are students who have positive attitudes about sexuality. As a consequence, they are more vulnerable to unwanted pregnancy and its life-disrupting effects.

Following are the main contraceptive choices that can promote conception when the time is right and the partners are ready to deal with the consequences (American Pregnancy Association, 2011):

- *Abstinence.* This is the only strategy that is 100 percent effective in preventing unwanted pregnancy. You may find some support groups on campus to reinforce this lifestyle.
- *Oral contraceptive.* Advantages of birth control pills are a low failure rate (e.g., less than 1 percent when taken properly) and low interference with sexual activity. However, the pill can have adverse side effects for some women, such as blood clots, nausea, weight gain, and moodiness, and it does not protect against STIs. An extended-cycle birth control pill, Seasonale, causes women to have only four periods per year.
- *Male condom.* A main advantage is protection against STIs. However, a small proportion of condoms break. The failure rate for male condoms is about 14 percent. Improve protection by using a spermicide with condoms.
- *Female condom.* A female condom is a sheath, usually made of latex rubber, that is inserted into the vagina. The failure rate for the female condom is about 21 percent.
- *Emergency contraception.* Emergency contraception, also called the "morning-after pill," can prevent pregnancy when taken within 72 hours after unprotected intercourse. Although the hormone-based pills have no long-term, serious side effects, transient side effects can include nausea, fatigue, headache, breast tenderness, and unexpected bleeding.
- *Ortho Evra patch.* An alternative to the pill, the hormonal patch is placed on the body once a week for 3 weeks and then removed to allow for a menstrual period. If used as directed, the patch has a very effective rate of preventing pregnancy. One concern about the patch is that it can produce blood clots.
- *Diaphragm.* This consists of a latex dome on a flexible spring rim that is inserted into the vagina with contraceptive cream or jelly. The diaphragm must be fitted by a skilled medical practitioner. The failure rate for the diaphragm is approximately 20 percent.
- *Spermicides.* These include foam, suppositories, creams, and jellies that contain a chemical that kills sperm. According to the American Pregnancy Association, using only spermicide for contraception fails 26 percent of the time. Spermicides should be used with other barrier methods, such as condoms or diaphragms, to reduce risk of pregnancy.
- *Intrauterine device (IUD).* The IUD, a small plastic device that is inserted into the vagina, requires insertion by a physician. The IUD's advantages include uninterrupted sexual activity and simplicity of use with a low failure rate (1–2 percent). Possible disadvantages include pelvic inflammation and pregnancy complications.
- *Norplant.* Norplant consists of six thin capsules filled with a synthetic hormone that are implanted under the skin of a woman's upper arm. Its

negatives include potential bleeding and hormone-related side effects; however, Norplant has among the lowest failure rates (e.g., less than 1 percent) of any form of contraception.

- *Depo-Provera*. Depo-Provera is an injectable contraceptive that lasts 3 months. Users have to get a shot every 12 weeks but experience a failure rate of less than 1 percent. Depo-Provera can cause menstrual irregularities.
- *Vaginal ring*. Called the Nuva Ring, this device is placed in the vagina and releases synthetic hormones. It is worn for 3 weeks and then removed for 1 week to allow for a menstrual period. The failure rate of the vaginal ring is less than 2 percent when correctly used.
- *Sterilization*. Tubal ligation is the most common sterilization procedure done for women. It involves severing or tying the fallopian tubes. The male sterilization procedure, vasectomy, involves cutting the sperm-carrying ducts.

Using no contraceptive method, trying to withdraw the penis just before ejaculation, and practicing periodic abstinence are not wise strategies for pregnancy prevention. If you are sexually active, compare the various contraceptive methods and choose the one that is the safest and most effective for you.

# Build a Bright Future

You might not often think about the topics of this chapter as being important for your work after college and advancement in your career. However, engaging in behaviors that enhance your physical and mental health, rather than health-compromising actions, will benefit not only your college success but also your ability to secure a good job after college, your work life in the job, and your career success.

Turn Problems into Careers

It is not unusual for students who have experience with life-threatening illnesses to aspire to a career in healthcare. Athletes regularly consider majors in exercise science to help promote healthy practices through satisfying careers in the wellness industry. Consider whether your own challenges in maintaining good physical and mental well-being can offer some career direction.

Enhance Your Job Prospects

Being physically healthy will improve your chances of landing a good job after you complete college and advancing your career. A healthy appearance can inspire confidence from your future employer. If you eat nutritiously and exercise regularly, chances are you will present a more positive image when you interview for jobs.

Not smoking and avoiding drugs are other health-enhancing behaviors that are likely to help you advance in your career. Workplaces are increasingly smoke-free, and employers know that employees who smoke and drink heavily have more health problems and are more likely to develop diseases that will increase the healthcare costs of their business. It is no coincidence that businesses are increasingly providing on-site locations for employees to exercise regularly or are willing to pay for memberships to workout facilities. They realize that such health practices will decrease the number of days their employees work and reduce the businesses' escalating healthcare costs.

Developing and sustaining good health habits in college can help you perform optimally in your work and career after college. For example, not overcoming habits that deprive you of sleep reinforces inadequate project-management strategies at work. You will make more mistakes and process information less efficiently in your work after college if you can't develop better strategies to secure restorative sleep.

Manage Job Stress

Being mentally healthy also will enhance your opportunity for making a good impression in job interviews and benefit your career advancement. Job interviews can be very stressful. The strategies you read about in this chapter about coping with stress, such as learning to relax and disputing negative self-talk, can benefit you on job interviews as well in your career after college.

Summary Strategies for Mastering College Success

Clarify Expectations

- Develop high expectations for being a healthy person and work toward a healthy lifestyle.
- Avoid common risks to college students.

Develop Competence

- Exercise regularly to keep a clear head and a vigorous energy level.
- Eat a variety of healthy foods to achieve a healthy weight, and avoid going on extreme, unhealthy diets.
- Get enough sleep, which for most college students means 8 hours each night to maximize alertness and productivity.
- Avoid relying on drug substances to stay involved, alert, and attentive.
- Wash your hands regularly to reduce exposure to flu and colds.

Manage Life

- Monitor negative thoughts and feelings to know when to intervene.
- Engage in targeted stress-management practices to improve your resilience.
- Design a self-control program to rid yourself of bad habits.

Connect and Communicate

- Make the right sexual decisions to avoid sabotaging your plans for college success.
- Increase your understanding of sexually transmitted infections.
- Choose the most appropriate method to protect yourself against unwanted pregnancy.

Build a Bright Future

- Turn problems and interests into potential careers.
- Present a healthy image on job interviews to improve your chances of advancing in a career.
- Improve your mental health on the job by practicing stress-management techniques that you learn in college.

 Visit the College Success CourseMate for *Your Guide to College Success* **for interactive resources at login.cengagebrain.com**

Review Questions

1. What's the relationship between self-esteem and fitness?

   _____

   _____

   _____

2. What are some risks to college students if they don't engage in positive health habits?

   _____

   _____

   _____

3. List three strategies you can implement to exercise more often, eat more appropriately, and sleep more effectively.

   Exercise strategies:

   1. _____
   2. _____
   3. _____

   Nutrition strategies:

   1. _____
   2. _____
   3. _____

   Sleep strategies:

   1. _____
   2. _____
   3. _____

4. What are some practices people use to reduce stress through substance use or abuse?

   _____

   _____

   _____

5. Describe three strategies that you can use to reduce your exposure to germs.

   _____

   _____

   _____

6. List four effective ways of coping with stress.

1. _____

2. _____

3. _____

4. _____

7. How can you tell if you have a mental health problem? If you think you have one, what should you do?

_____

_____

8. What are some important resources you can connect with to protect yourself from developing health problems and to reduce health problems if you develop them?

_____

_____

9. What can you do to protect yourself from sexually transmitted infections and unwanted pregnancy?

_____

_____

10. How might your physical and mental health in college be linked to your work and career success after college?

_____

_____

Is Your Lifestyle Good for Your Health?

Your lifestyle includes many components: the ways you work, relax, communicate, and perform other activities. The following assessment is designed to help you explore your lifestyle choices and determine whether they are affecting you positively or negatively. Your responses will help you understand the impact of your lifestyle on your health.

Directions: Respond to each of the statements with one of the following designations: 5—definitely true; 4—mostly true; 3—not sure; 2—mostly false; 1—definitely false.

Write the number that corresponds to your answer in the blank at the left.

_____ I am doing well in school.

_____ I am enjoying myself, not feeling bored or angry.

_____ I have satisfying relationships with other people.

_____ I express my emotions when I want to.

_____ I use my leisure time well and enjoy it.

_____ I am satisfied with my sexual relationships.

_____ I am satisfied with what I accomplish during the day.

_____ I am having fun.

_____ I am making use of the talents I have.

_____ I feel physically well and full of vitality.

_____ I am developing my skills and abilities.

_____ I am contributing to society.

_____ I am helpful to other people.

_____ I have a sense of freedom and adventure in my life.

_____ I feel joy or pleasure on most days.

_____ I feel that my body is fit enough to meet the demands made upon it.

_____ I feel rested and full of energy.

_____ I am able to relax most of the day.

_____ I enjoy a good night's sleep most nights.

_____ I usually go to bed feeling happy and satisfied about the day.

Scoring: Add up the numbers in your answers.

If your score was 90 to 100, you are making lifestyle choices that promote good health. Your lifestyle is making a very positive contribution to your health.

If your score was 80 to 89, you are doing well in many areas. Many of your lifestyle choices are healthful ones. Look at the statements that you marked with a 1, 2, or 3 for areas that need improvement.

If your score was 61 to 79, several aspects of your lifestyle could use improvement. Statements to which you responded 1, 2, or 3 indicate areas where you could do better. Your lifestyle choices may be negatively affecting your physical, emotional, intellectual, social, or spiritual health.

If your score was 60 or below, your lifestyle puts your health at high risk. Carefully review your responses, focusing on statements that you marked with a 1 or 2, and decide what you can do now to make better lifestyle choices. Altering your lifestyle will help you preserve your health.

Source: Is Your Lifestyle Good for Your Health? From R. Allen and S. Linde, *Lifeagain*, pp. 25–26. 1981. Human Resources Institute, LLC. www.healthyculture.com.

SELF-ASSESSMENT 11.2

How Healthy Are My Eating Habits?

After you have read about each principle, place a check mark next to the category that best reflects your eating habits.

_____ **Very Much Like Me**   _____ **Somewhere In Between**   _____ **Not at All Like Me**

1. *Eat a variety of foods.* Healthy adults need to eat at least three servings of vegetables, two of fruit, and six of grain products every day. Megadoses of supplementary vitamins are no substitute for a healthy diet, and they can be harmful. Avoid them. Use the four basic food groups to evaluate your diet:

   - The milk group (cheese, yogurt, milk)
   - The fruit and vegetable group
   - The grain group (cereals, bread, pasta)
   - The meat group (poultry, fish, red meat, and nuts)

2. *Maintain a healthy weight.* Some college students are overweight; others, underweight. Preoccupation with dieting can lead to dangerous loss/gain cycles that put stress on your body. Strive to maintain a reasonable, manageable weight.

3. *Avoid fatty foods.* Unfortunately, many of the best-tasting foods are the worst for you. Fat is found in large quantities in fried foods (fried chicken, doughnuts), rich foods (ice cream, pastries, cookies), greasy foods (spare ribs, bacon), and many spreads (butter, mayonnaise). Cholesterol, a chemical compound that is a key contributor to heart disease, is found only in animal products. In contrast, yogurt is low in saturated fat.

   Fitness expert Covert Bailey (1991) says that if you throw a pound of butter in a swimming pool, it will float just like a cork. The fat in your body will float in the same way, so the fatter you are, the more you'll float. Bailey says that he once had a friend who floated so well he could read a book while coasting along on top of the water in a swimming pool. If you have more than 25 percent body fat, you'll float easily. At 13 percent or lower, you'll sink quickly. Healthy body fat percentages vary for women and men. The highest healthy body fat content is 22 percent for women, 15 percent for men. Unfortunately, the average woman has 32 percent body fat; the average man, 23 percent.

4. *Substitute plenty of vegetables, fruits, and grain products.* Replace fatty foods with more healthful sources of starch and fiber. Eat grain products, legumes (dried beans, peas), fruits, and vegetables not cooked in fat. Increased fiber intake can contribute to regularity in the short term and reduce gastrointestinal problems, such as colon cancer, in the long term.

5. *Use sugar in moderation.* In addition to table sugar, other common sugar products include brown sugar, syrups, honey, jams, jellies, ice cream, cookies, cakes, and most other desserts. If you can't resist dessert, try eating fresh fruit instead of foods with added sugar.

6. *Increase fluid intake.* Strive to have water close by to improve your hydration. Replace soft drinks with water to reduce calorie intake and avoid negative dental consequences.

7. *Use sodium in moderation.* Some people are sensitive to sodium and are at risk for hypertension (persistent high blood pressure). To reduce the sodium in your diet, eat less salt. Be aware that there is a surprisingly high level of salt in many prepared foods—from canned soups to soy sauce, and of course, many restaurants serve food with high salt content. Get in the habit of flavoring your food with lemon, spices, herbs, or pepper rather than salt.

Look back at the seven areas in which you placed check marks. Make a decision now to place higher priority on healthy eating as part of your identity as a healthy person, not an unhealthy one.

Source: U.S. Health and Human Services, U.S. Government material.

SELF-ASSESSMENT 11.3

Do I Abuse Drugs?

Check Yes or No to the right of each question below.

	Yes	No
I have gotten into financial problems because of using drugs.		
Using alcohol or other drugs has made my college life unhappy at times.		
Drinking alcohol or taking other drugs has been a factor in my losing a job.		
Drinking alcohol or taking other drugs has interfered with my preparation for exams.		
Drinking alcohol or taking drugs is jeopardizing my academic performance.		
My ambition is not as strong since I started drinking a lot or taking drugs.		
Drinking or taking other drugs has caused me to have difficulty sleeping.		
I have felt remorse after drinking or using other drugs.		
I crave a drink or other drugs at a definite time of the day.		
I want a drink or another drug the next morning.		
I have had a complete or partial loss of memory as a result of drinking or using other drugs.		
Drinking or using other drugs is affecting my reputation.		
I have been in a hospital or institution because of drinking or taking other drugs.		

College students who responded Yes to these items from the Rutgers Collegiate Substance Abuse Screening Test were more likely to be substance abusers than those who answered No. If you responded Yes even to just one of the thirteen items on this drug-abuse screening test, you're probably a substance abuser. If you responded Yes to any items, go to your college health or counseling center for help with your problem.

Source: Reprinted with permission from Research Documentation, Inc., publisher of the Journal of Studies on Alcohol, now the Journal of Studies on Alcohol and Drugs (www.jsad.com).

Know Yourself

SELF-ASSESSMENT 11.4

My Health Resources

If I have physical or mental health problem(s), how likely is it that I can connect with the following support system(s) to help with the problem(s)?

	Likely	Maybe	Unlikely
1. Family members	_____	_____	_____
2. Family healthcare providers	_____	_____	_____
3. Friends	_____	_____	_____
4. Support groups	_____	_____	_____
5. Classmates	_____	_____	_____
6. College health service	_____	_____	_____
7. Mentor	_____	_____	_____
8. Coworkers	_____	_____	_____
9. Quality books	_____	_____	_____
10. Quality Internet sites	_____	_____	_____
11. Other	_____	_____	_____

How good is the health support system you can connect with if you have health problem(s)? Did you identify health resources and support in this exercise that you currently don't have and that might help you? If so, begin to explore and contact these resources and support systems.

_____

_____

_____

© Cengage Learning 2013

394 **CHAPTER 11** Take Charge of Your Physical and Mental Health

My Sexual Attitudes

Indicate your reaction to each statement below by choosing a number from 1 to 5 according to the following scale. (The letters to the left of each question will help you interpret your responses.)

Agree Strongly	Agree Somewhat	Cannot Decide	Disagree Somewhat	Disagree Strongly
5	4	3	2	1

(P) _____ Premarital intercourse between consenting adults is acceptable.

(C) _____ Sexual intercourse is a kind of communication.

(O) _____ Oral sex can provide more effective sexual stimulation than does intercourse.

(LGB) _____ Lesbians, gay males, and bisexuals should be eligible for jobs where they may serve as role models for children.

(M) _____ Masturbation is acceptable when the objective is simply to attain sensory enjoyment.

(O) _____ Oral sex should be viewed as an acceptable form of sex play.

(C) _____ Communication barriers are the key factors in sexual problems.

(LGB) _____ Being a lesbian, gay male, or bisexual should be regarded as a personal inclination or choice.

(M) _____ Relieving tension by masturbating is healthy.

(O) _____ Women should be as willing as men to participate in oral sex.

(P) _____ Women should experience sexual intercourse before marriage.

(P) _____ Many couples live together because the partners have a strong sexual need for each other.

(C) _____ The basis of sexual communication is touching.

(P) _____ Men should experience sexual intercourse before marriage.

(M) _____ Masturbation should be encouraged in certain circumstances.

(LGB) _____ Having sex with a same-sex partner, or with a same-sex and opposite sex partner, is an acceptable practice.

Now total your responses for each letter category listed to the left of each question and find your grand total.

	Total	Category	Liberal	Undecided	Traditional
(C)	_____	Sexual communication	15–12	11–7	6–3
(LGB)	_____	Gay male, lesbian, and bisexual	15–12	11–7	6–3
(M)	_____	Masturbation	15–12	11–7	6–3
(O)	_____	Oral sex	15–12	11–7	6–3
(P)	_____	Premarital intercourse	20–12	15–9	6–4
	_____	Grand total	80–60	59–37	36–16

Questions:
In which categories do you have the most extreme opinions, positive or negative?
Do any of your scores reveal an attitude that you might not have expected in yourself?
Would you be able to cope with sexual matters better if any of your expressed attitudes changed? Which ones?

Think about your sexual behaviors and sexual attitudes:
Do you consciously make decisions about your sexual behaviors?
Would it be better if you did?
Are your decisions about sexual behaviors ever inconsistent with your attitudes?

Source: "My Sexual Attitudes," adapted from, Robert F. Valois, "The Valois Sexual Attitude Questionnaire," pages 52–54, *Wellness R.S.V.P.*, First Edition, 1981, Benjamin/Cummings Publishing Company, Inc., Menlo Park, CA, copyright © 1992 by Valois, Kammermann & Associates and the authors. Used with permission of Valois, Kammermann & Associates and the authors.

Clarify Expectations

1. Develop Great Expectations

Chances are that you can improve one or more areas of your health behavior. In which area(s) do you want to improve your health? How confident are you that you can make these changes? Write about three expectations you have for improving your health and what you plan to do about the problem(s).

1. _____

2. _____

3. _____

2. Better Forewarned

Think about a time when you or a loved one had a scary encounter with a warning sign. How did it turn out? Did you take appropriate actions to get the problem identified and treated? Based on this experience, what kinds of arguments would you make regarding paying attention to health warning signs?

_____

_____

_____

Develop Competence

3. Keeping Tabs and Making Changes in Diet

Do you think you have a healthy diet? Let's find out. For 1 week, keep track of everything you eat and the times you eat meals and snack. Record this information in a food journal. At the end of the week, review your data. How healthy was your diet? Were there particular days or times when you tended to eat more sweets? List your healthy eating habits and your unhealthy habits below. Then think of ways you can replace unhealthy habits with healthy ones.

Healthy habits: _____

Unhealthy habits: _____

Replacement strategies: _____

- Did you refuse to believe what was happening or accept the circumstances?

_____

- Did you try to reduce the stress by eating and drinking more?

_____

4. Logging On to Sleep like a Log

Critically evaluate your sleep habits. Do you have trouble falling asleep or remaining asleep for the entire night? How often do you feel well rested when you wake up? Keep a sleep journal for 1 week. Record your eating and drinking habits each evening, the time you go to bed, any difficulties sleeping throughout the night, and the time you wake. Do you see any patterns that might be impacting your ability to get a good night's sleep?

_____

_____

_____

📁 Manage Life

5. Examine Your Coping Style

This is a good time to take stock of your coping style. Think about how you tend to cope with stress. Examine your life in the last few months. Pick one especially stressful circumstance and think about how you appraised the stress:

Was it threatening or harmful? _____

Was it challenging? _____

Describe three strategies you could have used that might have produced short-term stress reduction but long-term dysfunction:

1. _____

2. _____

3. _____

In retrospect, what would have been the most effective strategy to manage the stress? If you performed optimally, congratulations! If there is room for improvement, how can you benefit from this learning experience to improve your response quality in the future?

_____

_____

_____

6. Write about Your Stress

Follow the advice given earlier in the chapter section "Write about Stress," and over the next 4 days, write about your deepest emotions and thoughts pertaining to the most upsetting experience in your life. Did this writing exercise make you feel better or worse about this experience? Why?

_____

_____

_____

Connect and Communicate

7. Rank Your Risk

Suppose you are interested in helping a friend avoid pregnancy. Based on what you learned about contraception in this chapter, rank-order the various methods of birth control in terms of their failure rates.

_____

_____

_____

What do you conclude would be the safest method to pursue?

_____

_____

8. Hooking Up or Getting Hooked?

Make up a short story about the worst possible outcome from a casual hookup. Which ugly consequence of poor sexual judgment will serve as the co-star? What can you predict about the long-term consequences of your misjudgment?

_____

_____

_____

 **Build a Bright Future**

9. A Healthful Foundation for a Future Career

The career I most want to pursue:

_____

_____

My current physical health habits that might help me to succeed in this career:

_____

_____

My current physical health habits that might harm my ability to succeed in this career:

_____

_____

My plan to reduce these negative physical health habits:

_____

_____

10. The Healthy (and Happy) Job Interview

What five health-related tips can you offer a friend who is getting ready to audition for her ideal job?

1. _____

2. _____

3. _____

4. _____

5. _____

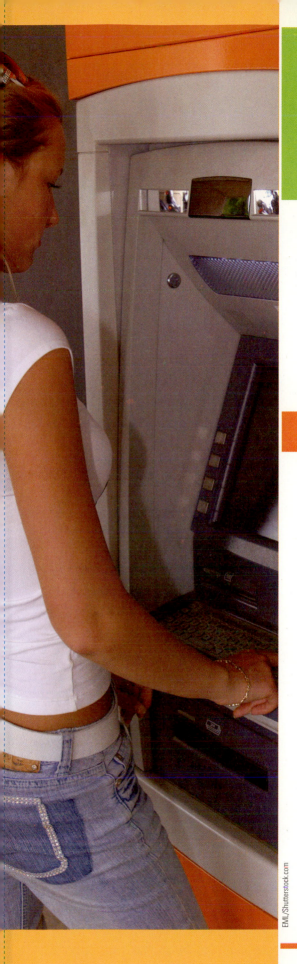

Manage Money Intelligently

Chapter 12

KNOW YOURSELF

MONEY PLAYS A VERY IMPORTANT ROLE in college success. Without proper financial support, college will be rough going. Knowing how to manage your finances appropriately is key to achieving many of your current and future goals. To get an idea of your financial know-how, read the following list below and place a check mark next to the item in the box that best applies to you.

Am I a Good Financial Manager?

	Very Much Like Me	Somewhere In Between	Not at All Like Me
When I spend money, I consider whether it's a wise purchase.			
I know what financial success means to me.			
I can accurately describe my regular monthly expenses.			
I know where I would get money in the event of an emergency.			
I organize my spending effectively by using a budget.			
I am aware of how to establish good credit and avoid unwise use of credit cards.			
I have a plan in case I get into debt.			
I resist short-term feel-good strategies that strain my budget.			
I can describe various financial aid resources at my disposal.			
I recognize the demands of succeeding in college and have planned my work schedule accordingly.			

EML/Shutterstock.com

401

Robbie Brown
Managing Money Wisely—and Making a Difference

Robbie Brown worked hard to earn scholarships to Emory University that paid for some of his tuition and his living expenses. Through careful money management, he was able to cover his needs during college. As a senior, he was awarded a top honor: the Lucius Lamar McMullan Award. This prize is given to an Emory graduate who shows promise of becoming an outstanding future leader, not just in the United States, but globally. Robbie now lives in Scotland and is pursuing further education at the University of St. Andrews.

The McMullan Award comes with a generous $20,000 prize for the recipient to use for any purpose. Because Robbie had managed his finances smartly and needed little, he was able to do something that illustrated the type of leader others already knew he was. He gave the award money away.

Photo Courtesy of Robbie Brown

Through savvy money management, Robbie Brown not only achieved his personal goals but also helped others achieve theirs.

At Emory, Robbie had met a woman named Elizabeth Sholtys who had founded an orphanage in India for street children—remarkably, during her first year of college—while getting part of her education there (Tomb, 2010). Robbie and Elizabeth had spoken a few times about India and about Elizabeth's home for street children, and he had mentioned perhaps wanting to visit the orphanage. Then, when the money came his way, he realized that he could do much more. While Elizabeth was in transit to India, Robbie sent her a text message and a voicemail offering the donation of his full award. She later reported that she had been "blown away" upon first hearing of his intentions. Elizabeth's Ashraya Initiative for Children expanded to involve health clinics, education programs, and community outreach services that serve thousands.

When Robbie talks about Elizabeth, he says she's the most incredible and inspiring student he has ever met. But most of us would say that he is pretty inspirational himself.

Because of his sound financial management and keen sense of global responsibility, Robbie was able to make a difference to people who really needed him. Examine the nearby chapter outline to anticipate where within the chapter you are likely to learn the most about effective money management.

 Clarify Expectations

For many students, college marks the start of financial independence and the first time they are faced with their own decisions regarding money. For students starting college later in life, college expenses compete with existing financial burdens. Maybe you are taking care of a family at this point in your life but also place great value on a college education. Whatever your circumstances, this chapter is designed to help you manage money during college so that you can concentrate on learning and graduating.

If you have come directly from your parents' home, you may have become used to having someone take care of your financial needs. In college, you are beginning your independence and should start living within your own financial limits. Even if you still get money from your parents, lead a responsible lifestyle and let them know how much you appreciate their sacrifices.

Evaluate the Importance of Money

People differ in how much importance they place on their money. For some, making lots of money is central to their happiness. For others, money is a lesser priority. Determining the relative importance of money will guide you in your planning. See Know Yourself: Self-Assessment 12.1, "Where Does Money Rank?," on page 428 at the end of the chapter to help you identify and prioritize these values.

Look to the Future

Although your fundamental values are likely to remain the same, your financial circumstances will change. You've probably already thought about your earning potential after graduation. Having your degree will give you the opportunity to

get a good-paying job or, if you are currently working, a better-paying job than you now have.

The sacrifices you may be required to make when you are in college will be difficult. But if you talk with people who have graduated and landed a professional job, they will tell you that all the sacrifices were worth it. Careful budgeting and money management may seem burdensome and unnecessary, but they will ensure that you meet your education objectives. They also will guarantee increased earning power after college.

In 2009, the median salary in the United States for a person with a 4-year college degree was $56,072 ($1,025 per week) compared with $32,552 ($626 per week) for an individual with only a high school diploma (see Figure 12.1, "Median Earnings and Tax Payments by Education Level"). As an added bonus, college graduates report that they are healthier than high school graduates.

What will a higher income mean for you? It could mean that you will be better able to care for yourself or your family, to leave a legacy for your children, or to make your local community a better place. In fact, research indicates that more education is associated with more volunteering to help others. In 2009, 43 percent of adults who were college graduates

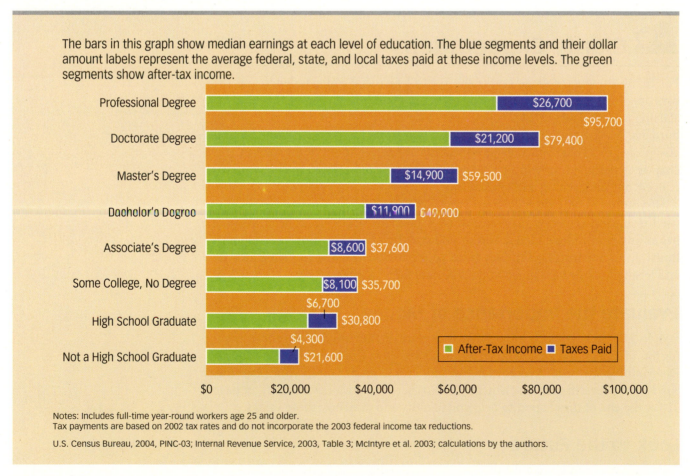

The bars in this graph show median earnings at each level of education. The blue segments and their dollar amount labels represent the average federal, state, and local taxes paid at these income levels. The green segments show after-tax income.

Level of Education	Taxes Paid	Total
Professional Degree	$26,700	$95,700
Doctorate Degree	$21,200	$79,400
Master's Degree	$14,900	$59,500
Bachelor's Degree	$11,900	$49,000
Associate's Degree	$8,600	$37,600
Some College, No Degree	$8,100	$35,700
High School Graduate	$6,700	$30,800
Not a High School Graduate	$4,300	$21,600

Legend: ■ After-Tax Income ■ Taxes Paid

Notes: Includes full-time year-round workers age 25 and older.
Tax payments are based on 2002 tax rates and do not incorporate the 2003 federal income tax reductions.

U.S. Census Bureau, 2004, PINC-03; Internal Revenue Service, 2003, Table 3; McIntyre et al. 2003; calculations by the authors.

FIGURE 12.1 Median Earnings and Tax Payments by Level of Education

engaged in volunteer work, compared to only 20 percent of high school graduates (U.S. Bureau of Labor Statistics, 2009b). Or perhaps you will use some of your money to make a difference outside your own community, as Robbie Brown did as described in the Spotlight On feature at the beginning of the chapter.

Build a Budget

Most people produce a budget as the foundation of their financial planning. A *budget* balances income and expenses to determine where your money should go. Why have a budget? It will help you

- avoid the strains that come with out-of-control finances.
- recognize where you need to make changes to meet your monetary goals (Anderson, 2011).
- lower your stress because you will be able to get more of what you want (Fife, 2011).

Use the following steps to determine the best way to allocate your funds.

Identify Assets Most of your income, such as work paychecks and family financial support, is obvious. But be sure not to overlook additional resources such as predictable special-occasion checks, cash from selling textbooks back at the end of the semester, and earnings from summer jobs. Accurately predicting your annual income stream is a very important aspect of financial planning.

Specify Expenses Some expenses are easy to anticipate and track. Regular payments for goods and services such as rent, payments on car loans, and your phone bill generally have concrete records for easy reference and tallying. These are considered fixed expenses because the amount is fairly predictable or *fixed* each month.

It is more difficult to anticipate and track variable expenses (Langer, 2010). For example, what you do with friends will vary from month to month. You may experience a month or two in which you do a lot of socializing and go out to dinner, shows, and sports events quite a bit. But when the financial demands of college increase, you may need to find other diversions rather than going out and spending. Be sure to acknowledge all the ways that you spend money. Not owning up to your bad money habits will result in nagging feelings of guilt, frustration, and the sense that you are doing less than your best.

Choose a Budget Timeframe Do you want to manage your money on a monthly basis, look ahead 6 months, or plan for an entire year? When you first begin to make a budget, or when you have a major financial change in your life, you may want to work from month to month. This strategy lets you focus

Jenn Belding

Spotlight On…

Adjusting Expectations

Jenn Belding exudes energy. When she was a psychology major at Georgia Southern University, she conducted research with several professors, served as a peer mentor to other psychology majors, and still managed to bake cookies for her classmates at least once a week. Because of her level-headedness, she was elected to serve on a university advisory board. This same positive quality served Jenn well when it came to dealing with college finances. She says, "The long and short of financial issues is that it all comes down to balance. People will tell you that they have plenty of money or no money, when in reality neither of these descriptions is true. We all have at least some money, but how much we have is relative. You have to adjust your expectations for what you can afford and what you need to save for."

Janie H. Wilson

Manage Money Intelligently **CHAPTER 12** 405

more closely on the short-term flow of your money and to make adjustments when needed. After you've established a routine income and expense cycle, you can plan for longer periods of time.

Look Forward and Backward You also can choose to approach budgeting proactively or reactively. *Proactive budgeting* involves anticipating your upcoming expenses and making sure they do not exceed your projected income. In this case, you set limits on what you will spend in each expense category to stay within your budget. *Reactive budgeting* involves looking back at what you have earned and what you have spent over a period of time. After you see where the money is going, you can itemize miscellaneous purchases into meaningful budget items and plan for them in the future. As you can see, effective budgeting involves a combination of planning ahead and looking back. Figure 12.2, "My Monthly Budget," is an example of an actual budget you can use to practice what you have learned in this section of the chapter.

Plan to Save In addition to your monthly expenses, you should budget to save at least a little money each month. When you commit to saving money regularly, you will be better equipped to deal with unforeseen circumstances. In addition, practicing good savings habits now will produce satisfying long-term gains because your savings will have a longer timeframe to accrue interest. One caution is to pay off high-interest credit card debt before trying to build up savings. It won't help you to save money at 3 percent interest while owing 20 percent on credit card debt.

Expect Emergencies Everyone encounters unexpected events that involve unanticipated expenditures. Given the inevitability of such emergencies, figure out in advance how you plan to deal with them. Keep in mind that the farewell concert tour of your favorite recording artist may feel like an unexpected must, but you may be the only one who considers it an emergency. Establish a savings plan, but don't plan to use "emergency" funds.

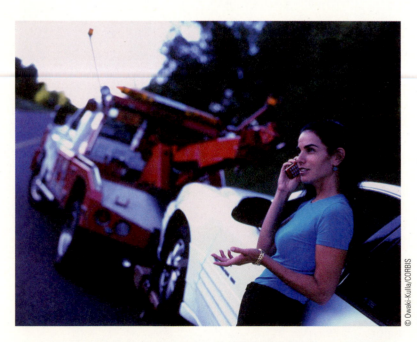

If an emergency occurs, are you financially prepared for it? Plan ahead so that you will be able to cover unanticipated expenses.

Develop Competence

Smart money managers go beyond basic budgeting to maximize their assets and get the most use from them. They know how to get the best service from banks. And they know how to minimize debt.

Learn to Save

Saving money is all about making choices. One wise move toward becoming a great money manager is identifying something you want in the future and taking steps to afford it. Whether you want to take your date to the hottest new restaurant in town, sign up to study abroad, or own a new car, putting money away to accomplish personal goals

Fill in your budget plan for the next month in the **Planned** column. Then monitor your income and expenses in the next month. A good monitoring strategy is to keep track of all your expenses in a small notebook each day. Keep a running tab of all your expenses for the next month. At the end of the month, write down your actual income and expenses in the **Actual** column.

	Planned	Actual
Income for the month		
Family	$ _____	$ _____
Financial aid	$ _____	$ _____
Work (after taxes)	$ _____	$ _____
Miscellaneous income (gifts, etc.)	$ _____	$ _____
Total income for the month:	$ _____	$ _____

Fixed expenses for the month

Fixed expenses are those expenses that will remain fairly consistent from month to month. For example, you can expect to pay the same rent from one month to the next.

	Planned	Actual
Housing/rent	$ _____	$ _____
Car payment	$ _____	$ _____
Child care	$ _____	$ _____
Telephone	$ _____	$ _____
Tuition and fees	$ _____	$ _____
Books	$ _____	$ _____
Insurance – car	$ _____	$ _____
Insurance – health/dental	$ _____	$ _____
Savings	$ _____	$ _____
Total fixed expenses for the next month:	$ _____	$ _____

Variable expenses for the month

Variable expenses are expenses that will differ from month to month.

	Planned	Actual
Food	$ _____	$ _____
Gas/oil changes; car maintenance	$ _____	$ _____
Transportation (bus fees, taxi cab expenses)	$ _____	$ _____
Utilities	$ _____	$ _____
Laundry/dry cleaning	$ _____	$ _____
Office supplies	$ _____	$ _____
Medical expenses/prescriptions	$ _____	$ _____
Toiletries/health and hygiene Items	$ _____	$ _____
Hair care/beauty treatments	$ _____	$ _____
Entertainment	$ _____	$ _____
Clothing	$ _____	$ _____
Gifts for friends/relatives or donations	$ _____	$ _____
Gym or health club fees	$ _____	$ _____
Total variable expenses for the next month:	$ _____	$ _____

Add up your total fixed and variable monthly expenses and then subtract this total from your total monthly income. This determines whether your balance at the end of the next month will be positive or negative.

FIGURE 12.2 My Monthly Budget

© Cengage Learning 2013

shows signs of a mature financial thinker. It also puts a positive spin on saving. When you focus on the future, it is much easier to put money into savings.

Of course, don't plan on using all your savings at once—you still need to have an emergency reserve. However, if you can anticipate the cost of your future goals, you can determine how long it will take to reach them based on how much you budget for savings each month. You may even be surprised at what you are willing to cut back on in order to reach your goal sooner.

Pursue Big Savings You can do many things on a larger scale to save money, such as having additional roommates to share the rent, forgoing cable television, and using public transportation or a bike instead of owning a car. Daily sacrifices will lead to a huge payoff in the future.

Many schools on a semester system require you to pay for each credit hour up to 12 but allow you to take anything over 12 credit hours for free. This strategy is particularly useful if you don't have to work and can concentrate on studying. If you do have to work part-time, weigh the possibility of adding an extra class that won't be too challenging.

Think creatively about opportunities, on and off campus, for expanding your available funds. For example, faculty may recruit house sitters for specific blocks of time or look for competent students to provide regular childcare.

Look for Deals Clipping coupons is a great way to save money on necessary expenses. Clip only coupons that you realistically need, to avoid wasting time and money. Design a savings system that you can manage easily, such as an accordion file with marked categories. Keep the file highly visible and easily accessible, because coupons and fliers are useless if you forget about them. Discard expired coupons and offers so that your file doesn't overflow and become neglected.

As a student, you may have many other opportunities to save. For example, you can do the following:

- Seek out on-campus events offering free food and entertainment.
- Look for local "two-for-one" or student discounts in restaurants and movies.
- Avoid paying for tutoring help if you can get it for free on campus.
- Read books, magazines, and newspapers from the library instead of buying them.
- Check the Web for discount travel options for students.
- Use the college gym rather than joining a health club.
- Make meals in batches and freeze serving-sized portions to reduce pizza costs.
- Consider a food co-op to make and share meals with others.
- Control your cash to avoid user fees at ATMs.
- Purchase a "cloud" of Internet service with people in neighboring apartments who can share the cost.
- Consider buying prepaid minutes that put you on a budget, because once you've used your minutes for the month, they're gone!

Establish Bank Accounts

Chances are good that you already have experience with managing a bank account. What you may not know is how widely services can vary among banks. Most banks have a website where you can gather the information. Some even allow you to apply for an account online, without having to visit the actual bank.

Specifically check for student banking services. There are often reduced and waived fees for student accounts, and the minimum amount required to open the account, as well as the minimum daily balance, may be significantly lower for students than for others. The two primary types of bank accounts are checking and savings accounts.

Checking Checking accounts allow you to draw money regularly through the use of checks or a debit card. One of the primary considerations you need to research prior to choosing a bank and opening a checking account is the fees. There can be monthly maintenance fees, a charge for your checks, fees for processing each check you write, and even service charges for speaking with bank tellers instead of using the automated teller machine (ATM) for your banking needs. Some banks do waive some or all of these fees if you open a savings account in addition to your checking account or if you are a student.

A second consideration when selecting a bank is the availability of free online banking. Online banking (including paying your bills online) is so convenient and useful that you should consider opening a checking account only with a bank that has joined the digital age. Another advantage of online banking is the constant access to monthly statements.

When opening a checking account, inquire about the following:

- Is a minimum amount required to open the account?
- Must you keep a minimum balance in the account? If so, what are the penalties for going below the minimum?
- What does the bank charge for a box of checks? (You probably won't need checks often, but they are one more expense.)
- What happens if you bounce a check? Does the bank cover it and charge you a fee, or instead return it to the person to whom it was written?
- Does the bank offer an ATM card? What are the fees for using it at your bank and its branches? What is your bank's fee for using it at other banks' ATMs?
- Does the bank offer a debit card? What fees and conditions apply?
- Does the bank offer online services? Can you conduct transactions or just check your balance? If the bank does not offer online banking, consider choosing a different bank.

Savings A savings account is a safe place to put away money where you won't be tempted to touch it. It can also earn a small amount of interest and grow over time. Opt for a bank that offers online access to savings accounts so that you can watch your balance grow.

Money market accounts are a more sophisticated type of savings account. You will have to keep a higher balance, but some of these accounts offer the benefit of overdraft protection. If you write more checks than you have money for in your checking account, the bank will cover them without charging you a fee or returning the checks to the recipient.

Whichever type of account you choose to open, there is likely to be a minimum initial amount required for deposit. This is typically lower for checking accounts, with some student accounts requiring a deposit as small as $10 to $25. Savings accounts tend to require at least a $100 initial deposit, and money market accounts usually require around $1,000. Bring cash, a check, or a money order with you when you go to open your accounts.

Take Advantage of Additional Services Most accounts entitle you to an ATM card, which enables you to withdraw cash at numerous locations. Any branch of your bank will have an ATM, as will branches of other banks and other business locations. Before you open an account, make sure that ATM use within your own bank network will be free, and when any ATM warns you about a charge, stop the transaction unless it is an emergency.

Debit cards, sometimes called check cards, look like credit cards but function like checks. When you make a purchase, the amount is automatically deducted from your checking account. Some check cards double as an ATM card. Debit or check cards offer a safer means to make purchases than carrying around a lot of cash. They also may be used for automatic bill payment, which allows you to have your monthly bills deducted from your checking account automatically. The downside of check cards is that they are easy to pull out and use without much thought.

But the good news is that online banking allows you to see your purchases almost immediately, making it very easy to keep track of what you buy. If you use checks instead, you'll have to wait days or weeks for the check finally to show up online, and you're more likely to think you have more money in the bank than you actually have.

Manage Your Accounts Once you've put your money in the bank, it is important that you keep organized records and stay on top of managing where the money goes.

Keep Track of Your Checks A major benefit of having a checking account is that it makes keeping track of your money quite easy. Get into the habit of checking your online account every day or two to verify that deposits and purchases show up accurately. Remember, banks can make mistakes. If you can't figure out your account after a couple of tries, call to speak with someone at your bank as soon as possible. Finally, if you are a good customer and you eventually make a mistake, such as overdrawing your account, ask to have the penalty fees waived; sometimes the bank will give you a break. It doesn't hurt to ask politely.

Monitor Savings The best plan for managing savings is to commit to regular monitoring. Some banks even offer the option of having a certain dollar amount automatically transferred from your checking account to your savings account each month. As it is deducted monthly from checking, you simply note it in your budget and it becomes part of your financial plan. And, because you don't have to make the effort to deposit it each month, you are more likely to see your savings grow.

Just like your checking account, you will note transactions in your savings account—either on paper or online. (Your withdrawals should be few and far between.) Your savings account statements will list both deposits and withdrawals along with any interest you have earned. Most savings accounts accrue interest. The rate is generally low, but the income is there nevertheless.

Invest for the Future

If you have some substantial savings and want your money to grow beyond your monthly deposits, consider investing it. With certain investments, such as mutual funds, which place your assets with professional managers to oversee a diverse portfolio, a small regular investment in savings can yield dramatic results over a long period of time. For example, if you invested only $100 in an opportunity that yielded 4 percent return, after 20 years the value of the investment would be $220.50. On the other hand, if you consistently deposited $100 per month to build your nest egg at the same rate of return, the long-term value would be dramatic. In 20 years, your long-term investment would grow to approximately $36,500. Over a 40-year period, your investment would exceed $118,000. That means you would have put in $48,000 over 40 years, and the other $70,000 is pure interest! However, keep in mind that interest earned on such investments varies depending on such factors as how strong a nation's economy is. Consider contacting a financial planner to find out some good investment strategies.

Understand Credit

Our society provides many alluring opportunities for spending money that we don't have. With a student loan, we can get a much-needed education. We can also use our promise to pay (our credit) to buy a car, home, or new clothes. Credit can be a wonderful option when we use it correctly. But it can cause serious, long-lasting problems if we misunderstand and abuse it (Maeda, 2011). When weighing your financial decisions, you need to understand credit and think things through carefully before using it.

Know the Basics Before you can determine whether credit is the right choice for you, and to implement it correctly, you need to be familiar with some basic terms and concepts. Figure 12.3, "Common Credit Terms," provides a handy list of key definitions.

Before you start signing any agreements, you need to recognize what your liability will be in the credit world. See Highlight: "Credit Comes with Responsiblity" to make sure you know what you will be getting into.

Know the Myths In addition to knowing the basics about credit, you also need to know the myths that surround credit. These myths include the following:

1. If you check your credit report, it will drop your score. Wrong!
   Actually, your informal inquiry should not influence your number.

Character = The willingness of a potential borrower to repay the debt as determined by his credit history.

Cosigner = A person who, by his signature on a contract, guarantees payment of a debt and is liable for the debt if the original signer defaults.

Credit = A trust that goods and services received now will be paid for in the future.

Credit History = A continuing record of a borrower's debt commitments and how well these have been honored.

Credit Rating = A record of an individual's past credit behavior; rating system assigned by the credit grantor to reflect past credit behavior. Each credit grantor establishes its own criteria for extending credit.

Debtor = A person who receives credit and promises to repay.

Default = Failure to meet payment or to fulfill an obligation.

Finance Charge = The amount charged for the use of the credit services.

Interest = Amount paid for the use of credit over a period of time, expressed as a percentage.

Line of Credit = The dollar amount a lender is making available to a borrower, which may or may not be borrowed.

Overdraft = A check written for an amount exceeding the balance in the signer's account.

Principal = The amount to be paid on the original amount borrowed, not on the interest amount added to the loan.

Repossession = Act of reclaiming property pledged as collateral purchased on credit; for payment that is past due.

FIGURE 12.3 Common Credit Terms

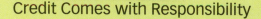

Credit Comes with Responsibility

Establishing a good credit history is important for you as a college student, because many of the things you rely on in daily living depend on it. For example, many utility companies require a credit check before they will open an account for you. Looking into the future, you might need to lease a car or get a mortgage for a home.

There are several things you should know about establishing credit:

1. Successfully managing a checking or savings account at a bank or credit union is a good means of establishing credit.
2. Creditors look for stability. If possible, remain with the same employer and maintain your place of residence for at least a year prior to applying for any major form of credit.
3. Utilities such as electricity and cable and phone service are considered part of your credit history, particularly when you are just beginning to establish credit. Pay your bills for these services on time!

4. Having someone cosign on a loan may help you to secure it, but be sure that person has a good credit history. If your partner defaults on payments, you will be responsible for the remaining balance.
5. If you do take out a small loan, be sure to make regular, timely payments. Don't use the "grace period" during which time expectations for repayment are suspended. Pay before the first due date to avoid marks against your credit.
6. Application for credit of any kind will be noted on your credit report as an inquiry. Numerous inquiries may cause denial of future credit.
7. If you do use a credit card, pay all your bills on time and in full, if possible.
8. Some current and prospective employers may ask to look at your credit report. Consider what it might tell them if it is problematic.

Remember that using credit comes with a great deal of responsibility. Before you take on any major financial obligation, know the terms and conditions of the agreement.

Log on to www.AnnualCreditReport.com, where you can get a free credit report every year. Be sure to ask only for the *free* report and not for anything with a fee. Also, the report will not include your credit score or rating, but you really don't need to know the score. Instead, review the details of the report to see if there are any problems with your credit.

2. If you close an old account or pay off a past negative balance, it will automatically improve your credit. Wrong! Credit standing reflects past action, so the effects of bad credit strategies will linger even if you change your ways.
3. If you cosign for a loan, you aren't responsible for it. Wrong! This strategy can leave you holding the bag.

Avoid Problems with Credit Cards College students are a major draw for credit card companies. In fact, you may find that you have already been preapproved for several credit cards and can begin charging purchases at any time. Although you shouldn't be discouraged from having a credit card, using it requires caution. In 2008, the average U.S. undergraduate college student had a credit card debt of $3,173, an increase from $2,169 in 2004 (Chu, 2009).

One thing to know is that the average credit card debt for first-year students is $1,585 and that final-year students average a balance of $2,864 (Nellie Mae, 2005). Another fact—and one that may surprise you—is that approximately 56 percent of college seniors carry four or more credit cards! Accumulating more debt and possessing more credit cards across the college years indicate poor financial planning.

Calculate the Costs of Credit Credit card companies often offer cards to students along with several "perks." These goodies can include everything from free hats and T-shirts to very low interest rates and deferred annual fees. But what may look enticing in the beginning can catch up with you very quickly.

If you decide that you need a credit card, don't be drawn in by the temptations of "free" stuff. Instead, make sure that you shop around. Interest rates, or annual percentage rates (APRs), can range from as little as 8.99 percent to more than 20 percent! And even if the company offers a low introductory rate, it usually only lasts 6 months, at which point the interest rate can skyrocket. In addition to interest, check whether the credit card company charges an annual fee.

Many companies have credit cards designed specifically for students. They often have no annual fee but tend to have higher interest rates (15–20.9 percent). Some cards offer additional benefits, such as frequent flyer miles, systems for earning points toward free merchandise and dining, annual rebates of 1–2 percent of your total yearly expenditures, access to low-interest student loans, and consumer protection so that you won't be responsible for unauthorized purchases.

No matter what "good deal" you may find on a credit card, don't assume that it will keep you out of trouble. You are still responsible for charging only what you can afford and making timely payments.

"I intentionally maintain a bad credit rating so no one will be tempted to steal my identity."

Pay the Balance Every Month Although most credit cards allow you to keep a balance on your card (called *revolving credit*) and require that you pay only a minimum balance each month, the best and safest way to use a credit card is to charge only what you know you can completely pay off when the bill arrives. Unfortunately, only 21 percent of undergraduates with credit cards reported that they pay off all their cards each month (Nellie Mae, 2005).

What happens if you pay only the minimum? Let's look at a concrete example (Barrett, 2003). Suppose you take a spring break vacation and charge your $1,000 trip. When you return, you can manage to make only the minimum payment. At prevailing interest rates, it could take more than 15 years to pay off your 1 week of fun if you continually pay only the minimum. Furthermore, the original $1,000 expense will cost closer to $2,400 when your account is finally settled (Tyler, 2001). Continually paying only the minimum will mean taking years to clear your debt. In contrast, when you pay your bill in its entirety, you do not incur any debt with your card.

Pay less than the entire balance only if you know that you'll be able to cover your current expense *and* the remaining balance next month (Paretta, 2011). Alternatively, avoid using the card at all for the next month so that you have only the remaining balance to pay. However, don't forget to calculate the interest that will accrue on the amount that's not yet paid off—you'll owe that, too. For a look at the effects of compounded interest, see Figure 12.4, "Be Cautious about Compounding."

Having a credit card is a fundamental means of establishing credit, so use it in such a way as to ensure you are establishing good credit. For example, be

Before you take on the responsibilities of choosing and using a credit card, it is important for you to be aware of the significant impact the interest will have on the price you ultimately pay for things. Investigate the rate at which your interest *compounds*— monthly, weekly, or daily. There is a big difference between interest added to your existing balance once at the end of the year, and interest that is calculated monthly based on your remaining balance, and *added to that balance* each month.

Take a look at the following scenario in which the individual charged $500 and is only paying the minimum requirement of $10 a month. If the individual never charges another thing for the rest of the year, despite putting $120 toward paying off the principal balance, hardly a dent was made. The calculations are based on a 17 percent APR—a very common interest rate for student credit cards—which has a monthly rate of 1.42 percent.

	Month 1	Month 2	Month 3	Month 4	Month 5	Month 6	Month 7	Month 8	Month 9	Month 10	Month 11	Month 12
Unpaid Balance	$500.00	$497.10	$494.16	$491.18	$488.15	$485.08	$481.97	$478.81	$475.61	$472.36	$469.07	$465.73
Interest	$7.10	$7.06	$7.02	$6.97	$6.93	$6.89	$6.84	$6.80	$6.75	$6.71	$6.66	$6.61
Minimum Monthly Payment	$10.00	$10.00	$10.00	$10.00	$10.00	$10.00	$10.00	$10.00	$10.00	$10.00	$10.00	$10.00
Balance Due	$497.10	$494.16	$491.18	$488.15	$485.08	$481.97	$478.81	$475.61	$472.36	$469.07	$465.73	$462.34

After an entire year, $462.34 is still owed on the initial $500 charge! Out of the $120 paid, only $37.66 went toward paying the principal, while $82.34 was spent on the interest alone.

Imagine if you had charged that money for a spring break trip—the memories might be fading, but you can't afford to go this year, since you're still paying for last year. Maybe you purchased new clothes, but they don't fit anymore. You'll still be paying for them whether or not you're still wearing them.

You can continue to calculate this scenario and others at http://www.bankrate.com.

FIGURE 12.4 Be Cautious about Compounding

sure to make your payments on time. Mail your payments early enough to allow sufficient time for them to reach their destination by the due date, or pay them online far in advance. Late payments are one more way of spending more money than is necessary, and in some cases they are noted on your credit report.

Just as with your checking account, if you're a good customer and make one mistake (such as missing a payment due date), call to apologize and ask for the fee to be waived. Another benefit of being a good customer is that it might make you a candidate for a lower interest rate. If you have established good credit but know that your rate is high, call the credit card firm and ask for a lower rate. If the company refuses, consider looking for a better rate with a different card company. Then, if you succeed in getting a better rate, close the old account. Credit card companies generally do not like to lose a good customer, so they'll try to give you what you want.

One benefit of using a credit card is that it provides itemized records of your purchases. Online statements can give you the most up-to-date information on your account. In addition, your monthly statements will be very useful for assessing your budget, categorizing your expenditures, and even preparing your taxes.

Use Credit Only for Emergencies If you decide that you need a credit card only for emergency situations, remember that all of the above information still applies. First, be sure to define what a true emergency is. If you begin to define "emergency" as any situation in which you are without cash, your debit card, or checkbook, be careful. All that using the card does is relieve you of having to pay the full cash amount at the time of the "emergency." You will still receive a bill within a month for anything charged on your card, and you will be responsible for making the payments. Of course, you can pay off the bill in monthly increments if you need to, but you will be charged interest. Further, if you have other purchases on the card, you will have a larger balance on which the finance charges will be based.

For financial safety's sake, think of an emergency only as a circumstance in which you do not have the money for something you absolutely cannot do without. Included would be such necessities as medical assistance; safe, reliable transportation; food; and required school supplies. In a true emergency, you will have no other means for obtaining what you need. And always consider your options in situations that involve decisions about using credit. For example, can you go to the campus health center instead of a private doctor?

Say Goodbye to Debt

Sometimes debt is unavoidable. What's important to understand is how to get out of debt as quickly as possible. When you recover from a negative balance, you can get your budget back on track and begin repairing your credit history. In some cases, creditors actually applaud your documented recuperation from being in debt.

Reduce Your Expenses Today, most of us live fairly luxurious lives—even in college. It is the norm for a college student to have his or her own personal computer, an elaborate entertainment system, a car, and cash for first-rate entertainment, such as sporting events and concerts. If you have overextended yourself and find yourself in debt, the first thing to do is to reduce your expenses.

Spending less can take many forms. Certainly, eliminating true luxuries such as expensive concert tickets and frequent dining out is one way to save money. But to get serious about cutting costs, you need to review your basic living expenses:

- *Where you live.* Could you move to a cheaper place? Get an additional roommate (or two)? Move home?
- *Utilities.* Pay attention to your utility use. Shower quickly, turn off all the lights, and keep the air conditioner at a reasonable level.
- *Transportation.* Take public transportation and eliminate your insurance and gas bills.
- *Food.* Fast food costs add up. Start grocery shopping and find quick and easy recipes in the library or online. Become a coupon clipper.
- *Television.* Opt for the basic cable or rent an occasional movie.
- *Telephone.* Monthly landlines can be expensive due to multiple surcharges and taxes. Consider looking for a good cell phone deal and only using that.
- *Computer.* If your school has computer labs, you can probably get by without your own. Sell yours and cancel your account with your Internet service provider.
- *Entertainment.* Redefine what you do for fun. Go to the park for a picnic. Hike. Ride a bike. Play board games with friends. Go to free campus events.

Escape Debt Sooner Getting out of debt requires sacrifice. But you may be surprised to discover that you actually enjoy your new, simplified lifestyle. If you find yourself in debt, there are several options to consider. First, investigate the possibility of financial aid. If you can secure a student loan or even qualify for some scholarships or grants, the aid will free up money that you would have used for tuition and books; you can apply that money to paying off your debts. If your debts are substantial, you may want to investigate consolidating all of your loans to make your management task easier (Gobel, 2010). Remember, student loans won't have to be paid off until you graduate, and they typically have very low interest rates.

To get a handle on outstanding accounts, even making slightly larger payments on your smallest bills is helpful (Princeton Review & Chany, 2011). This way, you pay them off at a faster rate, at which point you can then do the same thing with your larger debts. When you make a larger than required payment, the extra money is applied to the principal balance rather than the interest. Once your principal sum is paid, your balance is zero.

Begin making purchases with cash only. This practice will force you to reduce your buying to things you really need and to avoid unnecessary luxuries. You also can keep immediate track of where your money is going and see clearly that when it's gone, it's gone.

Consider Friends and Family Although you may want to be independent and make it on your own, it's wiser to ask for help than to accumulate too much debt. Ask your parents or a close relative to loan you some money so that you can get your finances under control. Have a good reason to ask for help. Develop a well-thought-out plan, and take a respectful, adult ("can we talk?") approach. You may even want to make the agreement official by drawing up a contract for repayment terms and conditions. Family and friends want to see you reach your goals, and thus they are likely to be supportive and understanding.

Manage Life

In college, financial success should be marked by your ability to take the course load you want and have enough time to study and do well in your classes, while having as little stress stemming from money worries as possible. In Know Yourself: Self-Assessment 12.2, "Your Money and You," at the end of the chapter on page 429, you can assess your current financial functioning and gauge whether you should be concerned.

Recognize the Threat of Debt

Money is a concern for many college students. In a recent national survey of first-year college students, 55 percent reported some concern about finances and 11 percent said they had major concerns (Pryor et al., 2009). In this survey, more than half were worried about financing college and one in five students had major college financing concerns. Nothing will disconnect you from college faster than running out of money. If you can't manage your money now, it is not likely you'll do any better when you have more to spend.

College students can quickly get into debt by simply spending more money than they have. Credit cards and student loans can pile on responsibilities that have long-lasting effects. The average debt for graduating college seniors in 2008 was $24,000, an increase from $18,650 in 2004 (Reed & Chang, 2010). In fact, in 2004 two-thirds of all 4-year college graduates left school with student debt (www.uspirg.org).

Guard against Money-Related Compulsions

Sometimes leisure activities can leave you penniless. Both gambling and shopping can turn problematic when you can no longer control when to stop.

Engaging in gambling online and playing the lottery are very risky choices for your financial well-being.

Avoid Gambling You might find yourself drawn to card games or Internet betting, two common gambling temptations for college students and others. One study indicated that more than 50 percent of college males gamble on a monthly basis (Annenberg Public Policy Center National Risks Survey, 2005). The percentage of college females who gamble is consistently smaller but still a potential problem. Oddly enough, college students report that they gamble not just for entertainment but also to supplement their income. Over 40 percent of respondents in a sample of college students said that winning money was their primary reason for gambling (Neighbors et al., 2002). Clearly, winning isn't something you can count on—and losing at some point is guaranteed!

Oddly enough, winning the lottery is no guarantee of happiness (Granato, 2006). If you manage to prevail over the astronomical odds of winning, it doesn't change your fundamental satisfaction with life. If you were happy before the big win, you will remain so. If you were unhappy, the lottery win will not cure your ills. Nearly one-third of lottery winners become bankrupt within a few years due to their improper fiscal management.

Limit Excessive Shopping Although some shopping is a virtual necessity, some individuals pursue shopping with a vengeance. If shopping seriously outstrips your available financial resources, you may be a victim of compulsive shopping (Lee, 2003). These unfortunate individuals lose control and amass more shoes or other clothing items that can reasonably fit in a standard closet.

Experts suggest that somewhere between 2 and 8 percent of American adults, mostly women, suffer from shopping addiction. If you experience the pull toward the siren call of clearance sale, you are in good company. Princess Diana, Jackie Onassis, and even Mary Todd Lincoln complained of struggling with shopping compulsions (Wesson, 1990).

The act of purchasing a new item produces a sense of euphoria, pride, and self-confidence. But the high is a fleeting one. When the euphoria subsides, you are left with lots of goods you don't really need, credit card bills that will knock your new socks off, and a good mix of guilt and depression. To relieve the bad feelings, compulsive shoppers go buy more goods, initiating the cycle all over again.

Complete Know Yourself: Self-Assessment 12.3, "Are You a Compulsive Spender?," at the end of the chapter on page 430 to see whether you show signs of problematic spending.

Overcoming a compelling urge to shop is not easy, but it can be done (Wesson, 1990). Your goal is to become a "balanced" shopper, and that requires developing some insight into the needs that drive the frenzied activity. You need

"I think what we really need is a *splurge* protector."

to focus on making sure that you take on no new debt and challenge some of the bad habits that drive your spending. Other suggestions include:

- **Shop alone.** Don't be influenced by people who undermine your willpower.
- **Avoid "slippery" places.** If flea markets are your failing, steer clear. Stay away from places where you have demonstrated that it is hard for you to control spending.
- **Shop from a list.** Don't let yourself yield to something that appeals unless you have established a prior need.
- **Trash catalogs.** Don't have money-losing options so easily available.
- **Don't buy "just in case" presents.** Shop only in response to a specific need.
- **Use a calculator.** Add up your purchases as you go.
- **Adopt a "cash only" policy.** Take only what you can afford to spend.
- **Reward yourself with nonmonetary pleasures.** Treat yourself to a drive, a walk around the lake, a good book from the library, or any other "free" reward.

If these measures don't work to reduce the problem, seek professional assistance to gain more insight into your motivation. Consider joining a local chapter of Debtors Anonymous, if one is available to you.

DANGER ZONE

When Disaster Strikes

If at any point you realize that your financial problems have reached a serious level, thoroughly review all your options before you consider leaving school. Following are some helpful strategies.

- **Specify your problems.** Begin by mapping out all of your debts and to whom they're owed. By visualizing your financial demands, you can create a plan to begin eliminating them.
- **Tally your resources.** Now make a list of your income possibilities that you can put toward your debts. Also note any ideas for increasing your income, such as financial aid options and working extra hours.
- **Identify strategies for cutting back.** List all the ways that you could reduce the expenses in your life. Don't hold back. Consider all the things that contribute to your living and entertainment expenses. Add up the money you will save if you

Don't Drop Out

The majority of students who drop out of college have a GPA of 2.8 or above (National Center for Public Policy in Higher Education, 2004). Obviously, then, they aren't leaving because they can't do the work. Instead, money problems often are to blame. When you become a good money manager, you free yourself to focus on your education. See Danger Zone: "When Disaster Strikes" to review some tips on how to "stay the course" despite financial pressures.

Connect and Communicate

Connecting and communicating effectively can often come in handy in financial matters. Extend your capacity to solve financial problems by exploring financial aid opportunities on campus. Also, roam the financial expertise available in the digital world.

Pursue Financial Aid

Whatever your situation, it makes good financial sense to research your financial aid opportunities. The best place to start is at your campus's financial aid office. Before you go, make an appointment to meet with one of the staff financial aid advisers. Don't consider it a one-time visit. Map out a plan for funding your education in its entirety, and expect to meet with your financial aid adviser prior to each semester. If you develop this relationship, your adviser will be more likely to keep abreast of your situation and alert you to any new options that arise, and you can feel good knowing that someone is always working on your behalf.

Skilled counselors can instruct you regarding the vast array of financial aid that exists for students of all nationalities, religions, majors, ages, and talents. There is aid money specifically designated for women; disabled students; international students; students planning to attend law school, business school, and graduate school; and gay and lesbian students.

Scholarships Scholarships are a form of gift aid—monetary awards that the student does not need to pay back. Money for scholarships can be provided by any number of groups, organizations, or schools. They are usually awarded on the basis of academic merit or a particular talent or skill, such as athletics or music, but not always. Some take into account financial need; others do not (The College Board, 2010). Many are awarded to the most qualified students meeting certain eligibility requirements, such as membership in a particular organization (e.g., Girl Scouts/Boy Scouts), participation in a group (church, band, thespians), or children of parents who work for a certain business or are members of a civic group (Kiwanis, Shriners, and so on).

Scholarships may be awarded on a one-time basis or may be available for renewal each semester based on performance in school and continued participation in a designated group or major. The application process may be highly involved, with many applications requiring students to write an essay about themselves, to obtain letters of recommendation, and even to go through a personal interview. Although somewhat time-consuming, putting together scholarship applications can be very rewarding. Keep in mind that even if you don't receive a scholarship the first time you apply, you may be chosen the next time around. Be persistent.

Grants Another form of gift aid is grants. Unlike many scholarships, grants are awarded on the basis of financial need. The most common grant is the federal Pell Grant, and the amount available to students each year is based on the funding allotted by Congress. For example, the awards for 2007–2008 ranged from $400 to a little over $4,300.

A combination of factors determines the amount each student receives. These include whether the student is full-time or part-time (both are eligible for aid), what the cost of attending school is, and how much money the student's family is able to contribute to the student's education. The government uses a specific formula to calculate this figure based on information the student provides in the Free Application for Federal Student Aid (FAFSA). There are no academic requirements or GPA minimums necessary to receive a Pell Grant; however, certain schools are not considered eligible.

DANGER ZONE (Cont.)

cut out cable TV, stop eating out, and get a roommate. Now act on your options.

- **Talk to a friendly instructor.** He or she might have ideas about where to go on campus for financial advice or help.

- **Approach your creditors.** Go down your list of those to whom you owe money and speak with each. Be honest in telling your creditors about your circumstances, and see whether they are willing to work with you to defer your payments over a longer period of time. Go to them with a specific plan that details the amount of money you are certain you can pay on a weekly or monthly basis. An earnest approach and sincerity about wanting to remain in school will help.

- **Seek credit counseling.** Credit counseling services can be found in most major cities, but your school's financial aid office also may provide this service. People there can help you put together a workable plan for paying off your debts and may serve as liaisons between you and your creditors.

- **Talk to your family.** It is likely that your family members want to see you succeed and graduate. You may want to be independent, and your parents may have told you that you're on your own, but in times of crisis they may be the key to your staying in school. They may simply give you money to help out, or they may offer you a no-interest or low-interest loan. It doesn't hurt to ask. That's what families are for.

- **Reduce your course load.** If your situation requires that you either spend less money on school or work significantly more hours in order to catch up financially, consider dropping at least some classes.

- **Commit to recovery.** Once you have devised your plan and put it in motion, see it through. Know that it is possible to get yourself out of debt, even if it takes a while.

- **Keep your goals in sight.** Nothing should motivate you more than realizing you are making progress toward your future. As long as you remain in school, you are getting closer to graduation with every semester.

Spotlight On... Reshma Tharani

Making College Low Cost

Although she got her baccalaureate degree from one of the country's most expensive colleges, Reshma Tharani paid only a fraction of the typical $50,000 cost of a New York University degree. Reshma was a "first-generation" college student who wisely decided to invest her first 2 years at Nassau Community College for less than $2,000 a semester. Besides turning in a stellar academic performance, she made a point to regularly see an academic counselor, who helped her assemble an impressive financial aid package so that she could attend NYU. She also received a Jack Kent Cooke Foundation scholarship that targets high-performing transfer students. Reshma concluded, "I had great professors at both places, but at Nassau I never had any huge classes, where no one knows your name. And when I hear friends talking about all the loans they have to pay back, it makes me feel better about my decision." Following graduation, Reshma was able to start her professional career as a third-grade teacher in Valley Stream, New York, without the massive debt burden that so many less financially savvy students face.

(Source: Merrow, 2007)

For students with exceptional financial need (as determined by the federal government's lowest expected-family-contribution calculation), there is the Federal Supplemental Education Opportunity Grant (FSEOG). Students awarded a Pell Grant have priority to receive an FSEOG but are not guaranteed the aid. Contributing factors in determining funding from this grant are the level of need, the funding and financial aid policies of the school the student attends, and the date the student applies for the grant. Your institution's financial aid office provides applications and information regarding both grants.

Loans In addition to gift aid, loans are available to help pay for your college education. The largest source of loan money comes from the federal government (Maeda, 2010). Government loans are very appealing because they offer many ideal conditions for borrowing money. The interest rates are low, there are less stringent credit requirements, and repayment may be postponed until after graduation and/or spread over a longer period of time than is the case for traditional loans.

The first step in acquiring a federal loan is to fill out a FAFSA form, mentioned in the previous section. As the name *Free* Application for Federal Student Aid indicates, it costs nothing to obtain and submit the form; and you can even complete and submit it via the Internet. States and schools also may use the information on your FAFSA form to determine eligibility for other aid programs such as grants and scholarships. The FAFSA requires that students and their parents provide extensive information on family occupations and income, as well as tax return materials. An online copy of the FAFSA is available at www.fafsa.ed.gov, and assistance for filling out the form, along with frequently asked questions, can be found at studentaid.ed.gov.

The Stafford Loan is the name of a common federal loan for students. The Stafford Loan program has two forms, depending on the source of the funds:

- In the Federal Family Education Loan Program (FFELP), the loan is obtained through private lenders but with a guarantee against default by the federal government. See whether your school offers this option if you are interested in it.
- In the Federal Direct Student Loan Program (FDSLP), the loan is provided directly by the government but is administered by "direct lending schools" that give the money directly to students and their parents.

A Stafford Loan may be either subsidized or unsubsidized. A subsidized Stafford Loan involves the government's paying the interest for the duration of your time in school and requires demonstration of financial need. An unsubsidized Stafford Loan requires you to pay the interest; however, the terms allow you to defer payments until after graduation. Financial need is not a qualifying factor in obtaining an unsubsidized loan, but the amount you may borrow will vary depending on whether you are still a dependent of your parents or are financially independent.

Another federal loan program, the Perkins Loan, is designed for students with exceptional financial need. The Perkins program is campus-based; thus, your school's financial aid office determines the amount awarded. A Perkins Loan has extremely favorable terms if you qualify. The federal government subsidizes this kind of loan while you are in school, as well as during a 9-month grace period; the interest rate is then 5 percent, and you have 10 years to repay your debt. A Perkins Loan also may be used to supplement other loan-based income that does not completely meet your financial needs.

A different option is the federally sponsored PLUS program (Parental Loans for Undergraduate Students). The PLUS system allows parents to borrow up to the full cost of their child's education (less the amount of other aid received). Still another choice is a private loan, available through banks, credit unions, and savings and loan institutions. The conditions of eligibility, interest, and repayment for private loans vary by institution, so you need to research these carefully before pursuing any particular one.

Under certain circumstances, through so-called loan forgiveness programs, the federal government may cancel all or part of your federal loan repayment. For example, participation in AmeriCorps, the Peace Corps, VISTA (Volunteers in Service to America), the National Defense Education Act, and other service programs will qualify you for partial or complete loan forgiveness. To find out more about these service programs and the financial advantages they offer, talk with a financial aid adviser or contact each organization directly.

Get Digital Help

A wide range of helpful resources for effectively managing your money is available on the Internet. One in particular will help you manage many aspects of your finances: www.mint.com. This award-winning site is free, and it categorizes your financial transactions to see where you are spending money, guides you in setting budgets, and helps you to save money. At www.mint.com, you also can connect with agencies where you can obtain your all-important credit score. You will be able to compare the pluses and minuses of a number of major credit cards at this site.

Another good digital resource for managing your money more competently is www.youngmoney.com/credit-debt/. Among the topics you can read about there are credit basics, credit reports, paying for college, and getting out of debt.

Build a Bright Future

As you strive for academic success, you can also put in place a good foundation for the expertise in financial management that will make you a valuable professional. In this section, learn about the contributions of working during college and how those experiences can enhance your career options after graduation.

Get a Job

The American Council of Education (2006) reported that a robust 78% of undergraduates claimed being employed while they pursued a degree. On average, employed students worked approximately 30 hours per week. This pattern has been stable for over a decade. Another study found that students who worked more than 25 hours a week said that working interfered with their academic achievement (King & Bannon, 2002). Sixty-three percent of those students, however, reported having no choice but to work that much to pay for their education.

It's true that it takes a lot of money to get a college education, but it also takes a lot of studying and hard work. Although many students find it necessary to work to pay for college, that same effort to earn the required fees may hinder one's progress toward actually earning the degree itself.

This situation can lead to very difficult and frustrating outcomes. Students who work long hours are more at risk for failing and dropping courses, at which point it is too late to get their money back. In addition to having lost those fees, they will most likely have to register—and pay for—those courses again to graduate. Thus, although working more hours earns you more money, you actually end up losing both money and time when work interferes with your success in school.

It makes much more sense to work less and pass your courses the first time around. However, if working means the difference between staying in school and dropping out completely, by all means, get a job. There are many options available for you to pursue, so take the time to investigate what will work best with your needs and goals.

Look for Jobs with Light Workloads Some jobs require that you be physically present but don't necessarily involve constant effort. These kinds of jobs may allow time for you to do some coursework.

If you enjoy children, you might consider offering your services as a babysitter or part-time nanny. Although childcare involves a high degree of responsibility and attentiveness, the children may nap or play in their rooms by themselves, giving you the chance to read, review, or outline ideas for a paper. Working as a student tour guide or a helper in the library reference room may provide the same study opportunities. Whereas your focus on the responsibilities of your work must be first and foremost, some jobs offer limited "breaks" from the flow of demands, freeing you to spend some time on school tasks.

Be Your Own Boss If you have a talent to share with others, use it to your advantage to make money. If you play a musical instrument or competitive tennis, or if you have an artistic flair, consider giving private lessons. Or you may be an excellent typist or a software expert. These skills also are in high demand.

© Kevin Radford/Superstock

Use your special talents to make some extra money.

If you wish to pursue your own "business," make sure you research competitive fees for your time and expertise (for example, are music lessons going for $10 or $20 an hour? Do typists charge by the page or the hour?). You will also need to advertise. Advertising doesn't require a great deal of money, and, in many cases, you can do it for free. Check out the local bargain newspaper, campus newspaper, or campus bulletin boards to find out what it takes to present your service. You may even consider creating a website highlighting your skills, experience, work availability, and fees. Not only can you make good money from your own knowledge and skills, but when you are your own boss, you can pick and choose when and how much you work.

Be Assertive in Your Job Hunt Jobs will not just come to you; you must seek them out, especially if you are looking for something different from traditional food service or retail store employment. Those jobs are popular but may not allow you the freedom and time to succeed in school.

If you have other ideas of where you might like to work, pick up the phone and call or visit the location in person. You will learn more about the power of networking in Chapter 13. Regardless of the job you choose, demonstrate a strong work ethic. Always work when you are scheduled to work, be on time, do a good job, and avoid gossip. If you have a strong work ethic, your employer will be much more likely to support you when you need extra time to study for tests or to work on a paper.

Investigate Work-Study Programs and Internships

Work-study programs offer opportunities to work either on campus or in the community, earning at least minimum wage or more, depending on the kind of work and required skills for the job. These programs are funded by the federal government or your academic institution or both and are based on financial need. Your income is monthly and paid after work is completed, and the number of hours you work each week is limited, in recognition of the fact that substantial time is required for schoolwork for you to be successful.

Work-study programs focus on employing students either in community service positions or on campus, often in areas related to their course of study. Students who work on campus have the opportunity to become more connected with school, as they frequently see and interact with faculty and staff, meet more peers, and sometimes have additional access to campus resources. They also benefit from having no commute time between going to class and going to work.

You can find out about work-study positions through your campus financial aid office or career services center. If you do not qualify for work study, there still may be part-time employment opportunities on campus. Check career services, the campus newspaper, or your institution's website for listings.

If you have declared a major, you may want to find out if there are any paying internships or co-ops available in your related field. Often local companies will hire students on a part-time basis to help them learn about possible future careers and to connect the company with potential future employees. An internship can be a great job option, not only because of the valuable experience you will gain by working in your chosen field but also because company employers are often sensitive to the needs of students. Because they want you to do well in school, they are likely to work around paper due dates, midterms, and finals. Summer internships are also an option and afford a rich opportunity to work more hours, gain experience, and make additional money to put away for the upcoming semester.

Many jobs, and particularly internships, are not advertised publicly. You can often secure an internship by speaking with instructors in your major and declaring your need and interest. News about job availability around campus may simply travel by word of mouth, so if you are interested, talk to people in different positions in various departments. You will learn more about internships and co-op opportunities in the next chapter.

Anticipate Your Future Career

Just as you should strive to get As in your classes, you will benefit from attaining an A in how effectively you manage your money. Postgraduation debt may be a factor. If you take advantage of any loans during your college years, you will be expected to begin paying them back after graduation. Being aware that you have to incorporate this burden into your financial planning can help direct your budgeting efforts now.

Not being able to manage money effectively in college may affect your ability to get a job after college. Negative credit information can stay on your credit report for several years, so big mistakes in managing money during college can have negative consequences down the road. Employers know that financial problems create major stress in people's lives, not just during college but also in work and careers after college. Thus, employers may check your credit score before they hire you. If the score is low, they may see it as a red flag regarding your character and will be less likely to hire you. Insurance companies, banks, mortgage loan companies, and other businesses may use your credit background in college to help them determine whether to give you a loan for a car, a house, and so on after college.

Clarify Expectations

- Evaluate how important making money will be for achieving happiness.
- Recognize the positive financial effects of completing college.
- Create and use a budget to manage your money.
- Recognize the incredible value of a college education.

Develop Competence

- Figure out a way to start or maintain a savings plan.
- Open a bank account for checking, savings, or both.
- Consider investments if you have the resources and stamina.
- Understand credit basics and avoid problems with credit cards.

Manage Life

- Avoid problems with credit cards by knowing how credit cards work and what your financial responsibilities are when you charge.
- Don't be fooled by the myths that can harm your credit.
- Monitor excess spending for signs that your behavior could be out of your control.
- Take steps to reduce the threat of dropping out due to financial strain.

Connect and Communicate

- Explore financial resources, including scholarships, grants, and loans.
- Make an alliance with a financial aid adviser on campus.
- Manage your finances with digital resources.

Build a Bright Future

- Get a job, but be careful not to compromise your efforts toward your school success.
- Learn to manage your financial resources successfully during college to help ensure that you reach your future potential.
- Not managing your money effectively during college may affect your ability to get a job after college.

 Visit the College Success CourseMate for *Your Guide to College Success* for interactive resources at login.cengagebrain.com

1. Why is it important to look to the future for motivation to become a good money manager now? List three actions you can take now to improve your financial future.

   1. _____
   2. _____
   3. _____

2. Why is a college education such an incredible value?

   _____

   _____

   _____

3. Describe four factors to consider when creating a budget, and explain how a budget can be considered a tool for assessing your finances.

   1. _____
   2. _____
   3. _____
   4. _____

4. What are some advantages of checking and savings accounts? Can you think of any disadvantages?

   _____

   _____

   _____

5. Describe five strategies you can use to increase your assets.

   1. _____
   2. _____
   3. _____
   4. _____
   5. _____

6. Describe three important things to know in order to establish good credit.

   1. _____
   2. _____
   3. _____

Review Questions

7. What are three strategies to eliminate or reduce debt?

1._____

2._____

3._____

8. What is the relationship between financial woes and dropping out?

_____

_____

_____

9. Name three specific opportunities that an on-campus financial aid specialist might be able to offer to a deserving student.

_____

_____

_____

10. What are some strategies to consider when thinking about getting a job during college?

_____

_____

_____

11. Describe some strategies you can use to land a valuable internship in your preferred field.

_____

_____

_____

SELF-ASSESSMENT 12.1

Where Does Money Rank?

Rank the following life values in order of importance to you.

____ comfortable life

____ downtime

____ job success

____ community service/volunteer activities

____ large investment portfolio

____ culture (movies, theater, and so on)

____ new home or condo

____ earning a lot of money

____ prestige/social recognition

____ education/knowledge

____ recreation

____ excitement/stimulation

____ reducing or eliminating debt

____ family activities

____ religion

____ family vacation

____ security

____ friends

____ sense of accomplishment

____ happiness/contentment

____ shopping/spending money

____ health

____ starting/maintaining own business

____ image/personal appearance

____ top-of-the-line products and services

____ independence/autonomy

Evaluate your priorities. How might you manage your money to live your life according to what you value the most?

SELF-ASSESSMENT 12.2

Your Money and You

	Very Much Like Me	Somewhere In Between	Very Much Unlike Me
I usually don't know how much money I have in my wallet at any time.			
I have tried but abandoned following a formal budget.			
I don't really understand investing as a way of increasing my financial resources.			
I have more credit cards than I really need.			
I regularly pay just the minimum amount on my credit cards.			
I haven't thoroughly explored financial support options for students.			
I have had to borrow cash from friends or relatives to make ends meet.			
I have had strain in my relationships due to money management.			
I make purchases without determining if I have found the best deal.			
I don't like talking about my financial circumstances.			
I am drawn to "get rich quick" strategies, such as the lottery.			
My lifestyle goals exceed my financial resources.			

If the majority of your answers fall in the "Very Much Unlike Me" column, chances are that you have made good decisions about your financial management. Your self-discipline will pay off. In all likelihood, your college education will build your income and you will be well-positioned to know what to do with new resources.

If the majority of your answers fall in the "Very Much Like Me" column, it may be time to consider a visit with a financial consultant to help you get your money management under control. You run a high risk derailing your success in college due to financial challenges.

If the majority of your answers fall in the middle, there are some clear areas of improvement you can pursue to make your financial outlook rosier. First, congratulate yourself for any check marks you registered in the right column because these are indicators of financial health. Then pick one or two of the items you checked in the left hand column and start to focus on making some changes that will help you both in the short-term and long-term.

© Cengage Learning 2013

 **Know Yourself**

Are You a Compulsive Spender?

Do any of the following 20 behaviors apply to your relationship with the retail world? Place a check mark next to each behavior that characterizes your spending approach.

_____ Shopping makes me feel almost euphoric.

_____ I buy things to help me escape feeling down.

_____ I stockpile supplies and materials, some of which I don't really need.

_____ I use credit cards much more than I should.

_____ I have felt guilty about my purchasing pattern.

_____ I have bought items from which I've never removed the tags.

_____ I often pick up the tab for my friends.

_____ I regularly fail to balance my checkbook.

_____ I have switched price tags on items in the store.

_____ I can't account for where my money goes.

_____ I am vigilant about exploiting opportunities to buy at sales.

_____ I am often cash poor.

_____ I can be preoccupied with fantasies about winning the lottery.

_____ I sneak purchases into the house so I don't have to defend them.

_____ I avoid opening my mail or answering the phone because of the aftermath of my purchasing pattern.

_____ I lie to others about how much money I spend.

_____ I have purchased luxuries over necessities.

_____ I worry about how to meet my financial obligations.

_____ I always have to use credit cards for unexpected emergencies (e.g., car repairs, vet bills).

_____ Shopping can make me feel irrational and out-of-control.

Not all these behaviors are equally serious, but all of them represent characteristics of individuals who are compulsive spenders. The larger number of behaviors that you checked, the greater your risk of bottoming out from being financially out-of-control. Check with your student support services on campus to see what opportunities might exist to get the intervention you need.

Source: © 2002 Baptist Memorial Health Care Corporation. Adapted from http://www.baptistonline.org/services/community/concern/selfassess.asp.

Clarify Expectations

1. The Money in My Past

Think about your experiences with money in the past—earning it, spending it, getting an allowance.

- What lessons did you learn from your family about money? What did you learn from observing their financial management?

_____

_____

- What lessons from your past do you think will be helpful as you become increasingly financially independent?

_____

_____

2. Imagine That!

Suppose you are one of those very rare individuals who manage to win the lottery. (The odds are not very favorable. Some estimate that it is more likely you will be struck by lightning twice when on horseback!) However, if you inherited sudden wealth, what would you do with that resource? Describe five actions you would take if you didn't have to worry about money. Then examine what those actions communicate about your values. How does your imaginary wealthy existence compare to the real values you express in your routine financial decisions?

_____

_____

_____

_____

 Develop Competence

3. Simplify Life

List some examples of things you have become accustomed to having that you really don't need, but simply enjoy having as a convenience or a little "extra." How much could you save if you didn't have them?

_____

_____

4. In Case of Emergency

Brainstorm about emergency situations you might encounter in the coming year, such as car problems, doctor visits during flu season, or a family crisis requiring a trip home. List these situations below. Then talk with family members or friends to find out to what extent they are willing to help you out in an emergency situation.

_____

_____

 Manage Life

5. What Would I Do Differently?

Write about your experiences so far in managing your finances, including keeping track of any checking and savings accounts you've had. What have you learned in this chapter that you would do differently than you have in the past?

_____

_____

6. A Question of Credit

You've heard many warnings about credit cards for college students, but credit cards also can offer several benefits. Using them appropriately and responsibly is truly a matter of awareness and self-control. What do you find challenging or tempting about having credit cards? What have you done to overcome these challenges and temptations?

_____

_____

 Connect and Communicate

7. It Can't Hurt

With all of the different kinds of financial aid available to students, you may be surprised to find some options that might appeal to you and that would alleviate some of your money concerns. Visit your school's financial aid office and speak with a financial aid adviser to investigate. What are some questions you should prepare?

_____

_____

_____

8. Web to the Rescue

Conduct a Web search for financial planning tips. What concepts will you use to start the search? What are the key pointers you learned? How do you know that the websites from which you harvested ideas were trustworthy?

_____

_____

Build a Bright Future

9. The Ideal College Job

Describe the ideal college job that you think would work best for you. Why do you think it would be such a great job?

_____

_____

10. Define Financial Success

Financial success means something different to everyone. By examining your values, you will be able to define financial success for yourself. Begin with your dreams (and dream big!). What is your financial ideal for the future? Don't feel that you have to use a dollar amount; however, identify what you would like to be able to do and use your money for. Do you see those dreams as a reality based on your career path? If not, what might you more realistically be able to expect in terms of "financial success"?

_____

_____

_____

_____

© Amy Etra/Photo Edit

Explore Careers

Chapter 13

KNOW YOURSELF

THE TIME YOU SPEND EXPLORING CAREERS will help anchor your college work and your success after college. Concentrate on identifying careers that fit with your values and interests. Take advantage of the rich opportunities that help you refine your skills and build your professional network. To evaluate the status of your career exploration, place a check mark in one of the three boxes below next to the item that best characterizes you.

Do I Know Where I'm Headed Professionally?

	Very Much Like Me	Somewhere In Between	Not at All Like Me
I have begun to explore career options and know of at least one that matches with my values.			
I have set career goals and planned how to reach them.			
I know what my skills are and how they will help me in a career.			
I know how my personality might connect with careers.			
I know how to land a great job after college.			
I can capture my work experiences effectively in a resume.			
I have ideas about work experiences during college that might help me with my long-term goals.			
I have networked about careers and job possibilities.			
I have considered the flexibility I will need to cope with professional change in the future.			

© Cengage Learning. All rights reserved. No distribution allowed without express authorization.

Spotlight On...

Darius Graham
Taking Remarkable Initiatives

Darius Graham charted a political future based on his college experience.

Darius Graham had shown remarkable initiative as an undergraduate student at Florida A&M University (FAMU). Graduating in 2006 with a 3.9 GPA as a political science major, Darius had committed himself to many causes that went beyond the classroom walls. His diverse activities as an undergraduate are increasing the likelihood that he will reach his career and life goals of practicing public interest law and making positive changes in the community.

Among the leadership positions that he achieved was his election as attorney general of FAMU's Student Government Association. In that role, Darius wrote the ethics code for the association. He also founded and served as the first president of the Honor Student Association. Under Darius's direction, the association created biweekly lunches that feature different speakers, including community leaders, and launched a tutoring service for FAMU students.

After learning about his accomplishments and community interest, the mayor of Tallahassee appointed Darius to the city's Community Improvement Advisory Council, which provides input to the city about housing, economic matters, and other issues. Darius also was recognized by the Institute of Responsible Citizenship as one of the most outstanding minority students in the United States. As part of this recognition, he was given a summer internship with the U.S. Department of State to work on humanitarian issues in Southeast Asia. During summers, Darius also has participated as an adviser to the Anytown program of the National Conference for Community and Justice, a weeklong camp that brings together students from different ethnic and cultural backgrounds in an effort to reduce stereotyping and improve interethnic relationships.

Keeping his career goals in mind, Darius became an enthusiastic participant in pre-law activities on campus. He managed his time so effectively that he even had some left to found Books All Around (www.booksallaround.org), a literacy initiative that provides books to children from low-income backgrounds.

Regarding his career interests, Darius recalled (*Florida Leader*, 2005), "My freshman year, I drew this web of different careers that I could have and linked them up. . . . Out of every scenario, the outcome was that I would have a humanitarian organization or a charitable organization. So that's really something I want to do, whether I'm politically involved or not."

Darius continued to gain educational and community experiences on his career path to practicing public interest law. In law school, he was editor-in-chief of the *Berkeley Journal of African-American Law and Policy*. In 2008, he published a book, *Being the Difference: True Stories of Ordinary People Doing Extraordinary Things to Change the World*.

Darius graduated from law school at UC-Berkeley in 2009 and joined the law firm of Aiken Gump Strauss Hauer and Field in Washington, DC. Currently, in addition to working at the law firm, he is a commissioner at Serve DC, The Commission on National & Community Service, and a trustee and co-chair of the Young Benefactors Group at the Institute for Responsible Citizenship (Graham, 2011).

Darius Graham's campus activities, leadership roles, work outside the classroom, and summer internship during college provided him with relevant experiences and accomplishments that are placing him on a path to achieve his career goals. Examine the chapter outline and think about the chapter topics that are most likely to place you on a positive work and career path after college.

(Sources: *Florida Leader* [2005], PRWeb [2008], *USA Today* staff [2006], and Graham [2011])

Clarify Expectations

Although the need to identify and seek your perfect job following graduation may feel like it is a long way off, it is never too soon to start thinking seriously about what lies ahead. In this section, you will explore the economic backdrop against which your job-seeking activities will unfold. You will also begin the process of thinking about how your values and needs may determine what jobs you should pursue and which ones you should rule out.

Examine the Employment Landscape

The past few years have seen some wild fluctuations in the economy. Most experts agree that the United States is currently working its way through a deep recession, a period in which economic indicators show reduced activity as reflected by losses in the gross domestic product (GDP). Unfortunately, unemployment figures also verify the economic hard times.

For the first time in several decades, college graduates have also faced increasing unemployment. In 2009, college graduate unemployment crept over the 4 percent mark. However, when compared with unemployment rates of individuals who failed to finish high school (approaching 17 percent), investing in college still appears to be the best strategy on which to build your future. See Figure 13.1, "Unemployment Rates by Level of Education 1992–2009," to see the impact on both levels of education.

Not all graduates are waiting patiently for the job market to reenergize. Trina Thompson made history with her controversial solution to unemployment after college. When she graduated from Monroe College in the Bronx with a major in information technology, Trina had great hopes for a new job and the start of a new career. However, after an unsuccessful 3-month search, Trina decided to sue her college because it failed to live up to its promises about helping her get placed after graduation. She filed a lawsuit in 2009 for $72,000, representing both lost tuition and compensation for stress related to the unsuccessful search. Although she believed her 2.7 grade-point average and regular attendance would impress prospective employers, no one seemed interested in what she had to offer. She concluded that the officials of Monroe College "did not try hard enough to help." But Monroe representatives describe the lawsuit, which is still pending, as "without merit." Without prospects of a high-paying job, Trina is facing enormous pressures in having to pay back her student loans, but was her legal solution realistic?

A recent survey of job-seekers (National Association of College Employers, 2011; [NACE]) identified an average job search duration of 5 months. This timeframe is 2 months longer than just 2 years ago, reflecting the challenges of a sluggish economy. However, the growth in time suggests that those new to the job market must be patient and continue to work on their job skills to be at their competitive best.

Target Growth Areas

As you explore the type of work you are likely to enjoy and in which you can succeed, it is important to be knowledgeable about different fields, industries, and companies. Occupations may have many job openings one year but few another year as economic conditions change. Thus, it is critical to keep up with the occupational outlook in various fields. An excellent resource is the *Occupational Outlook Handbook*, which is revised every 2 years. You can access

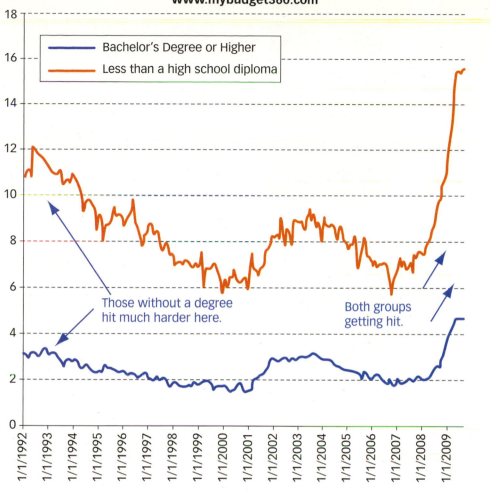

Unemployment Rate: Education Level
www.mybudget360.com

Those without a degree hit much harder here.

Both groups getting hit.

Bachelor's Degree or Higher
Less than a high school diploma

© Cengage Learning 2013

FIGURE 13.1 Unemployment Rates by Level of Education (1992–2009)

the handbook at www.bls.gov/oco/. Based on the 2010–2011 edition, service-providing industries are expected to generate the most new jobs through 2018.

Although no occupation is recession-proof, some areas appear to show more promise than others (Ryan, 2011). Specific career areas that continue to be the least vulnerable to recession include nursing, engineering, finance, and accounting. In addition, the following areas seem to show opportunity for growth and job satisfaction in the coming decade:

- *Health care*, including physical and massage therapy, athletic training, dental hygiene, optometry, lab science, and physician assistance
- *Social services*, including educational administration, sales management, meteorology, firefighting, and court reporting
- *Technology*, including computer support, computer programming, security specialists, software engineering, and information technology
- *Creative and social services*, including foreign language translation, special education, mediation, urban planning, film and video editing, multimedia art, and technical writing
- *Business careers*, including meeting planners, public relations specialists, trainers, logisticians, and financial advisers

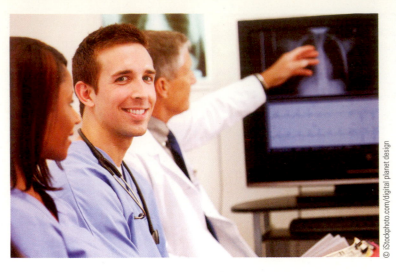

Nursing and other careers in health care provide more job openings in challenging economic times than many other careers.

- *Environmental concerns*, including environmental engineering technology and hydrology

Projected job growth varies widely by educational requirements. Jobs that require a college degree are expected to grow the fastest. Education is essential to getting a high-paying job (*Occupational Outlook Handbook*, 2010–2011). Of jobs requiring a college degree, those involving technology and computers are expected to have the greatest percentage increase through 2018.

The *Occupational Outlook Handbook* provides excellent information about what workers do on the job, working conditions, training and education needed for various jobs, and expected job prospects in a wide range of occupations. Libraries are also good sources for finding out more about careers. A good strategy is to ask a librarian at your college or university to help you with your career information search.

Recognize Values and Boundaries

Making the right career choice is a critical step in the journey of life. This is a good time to get motivated to consider several different career paths and evaluate how your values, interests, abilities, and skills fit with the careers you have in mind. You also must consider any relevant constraints.

Match Your Values An important first step in choosing career options is to know your values. Knowing what you value most—what is important to you in life—will help you refine your career search and choice.

Some people want to pursue a career in which they help others. Some desire a career that is prestigious. Others seek one in which they will make a lot of money. Yet others want one that will give them plenty of time for leisure and family interests. Complete Know Yourself: Self-Assessment 13.1, "My Values and Career Pursuits," at the back of the chapter on page 461 to examine your values in relation to your career pursuits.

Clarifying your values helps you zero in on the careers that will likely be the most meaningful and rewarding to you. When you clearly establish, and then align, your values, career choice, and career goals, your internal motivation to think and learn will be strengthened.

Know Your Constraints Although your values can typically provide some momentum toward getting what you want out of professional life, recognize

Spotlight On...

Paul Haas

A Returning Student Who Loves His Work

Returning student Paul Haas's work reflects his values, especially values that involve working with people and caring about others. He graduated with a nursing degree from a community college, the College of San Mateo, in California and is currently employed at a hospital in San Mateo with a well-paying job that he loves. During community college, he worked as a camp counselor, became an administrative assistant in a drug treatment program, and worked as a medical technician. In Paul's words, "The one job I had that didn't involve working with people made me miserable."

that there may be forces in play that make it harder for you to pursue what you want to do. For example, consider the following questions:

- Are you willing to relocate? Or do you wish not to stray too far from your hometown?
- Can you tolerate work that is heavily mediated by computer? Or is the prospect of facing the computer screen one that fills you with dread?
- Are you willing to travel? Or do you dislike spending time in airports and traffic jams?
- Do you have massive loans that will need to be repaid? Or are you free to take a position at any income?

Knowing what you don't want can also help clarify your expectations about what positions will help you achieve your version of the good life.

 # Develop Competence

Before you know it, you will be graduating and then moving on, either for further education or into a career or job. What you do now and through the remainder of your college years builds the foundation for getting into the graduate program or professional school of your choice or for creating an awesome resume. Let's take a look at the specific skills you need to concentrate on to be at your most competitive for landing a job both during and after college.

Refine Career Goals

From your self-evaluation and increased knowledge of careers, a picture should begin to emerge about what kind of work you would like to do and where you want to do it. Once you have decided on one or more careers that you would like to pursue, it is useful to think about some long-term and short-term goals. It is important that you be able to articulate these goals to employers and interviewers. The kind of information you should think about incorporating in your career goal setting includes the following (OCS Basics, 2004):

- Major career field target
- Preferred type of work, including the ideas or issues you would like to pursue
- Income requirements
- Geographical requirements (urban/rural location, mobility, nearness to home, climate, and so on)
- Special needs (training, management development, advancement opportunities, career flexibility, entrepreneurial opportunity, and so on)
- Industry preferences (manufacturing, government, communications, nonprofit, high tech, products, services, and so on)

When you begin considering what career is right for you, it's wise to have several careers in mind rather than just one. In a recent national survey of first-year college students, only 13.5 percent believed that there is a very good chance that they will change their college major, and only 12.8 reported that there is a very good chance that they will change their career choice (Pryor et al., 2009). In reality, though, far more students will change both of these choices. As a first-year student, it pays to be knowledgeable about more than just one major or career field. It also pays to develop a wide variety of general abilities, such as speaking and writing skills, that will serve you well in various fields.

Assess Career Skills

Career skills include both your academic and personal strengths. Some skills come easily, while others are more difficult to learn. Honestly evaluating your areas of strength and weakness will help you a great deal in realistically appraising majors and careers.

SCANS Skills The U.S. Department of Labor issues reports created by the Secretary's Commission on Achieving Necessary Skills (SCANS). The SCANS reports describe skills and personal qualities that will benefit individuals as they enter the workforce. It focuses on four types of skills and personal qualities: basic, thinking, personal, and people. You have already studied about and completed exercises related to many of these skills and personal qualities in this book. As you read, consider which skills represent areas of strength or weakness for you.

Basic Skills Basic skills include the following:

- *Reading*
  Identify basic facts.
  Locate information in books and manuals.
  Find meanings of unknown words.
  Judge accuracy of reports.
  Use computers to find information.
- *Writing*
  Write ideas completely and accurately in letters and reports, with proper grammar, spelling, and punctuation.
  Use computers to communicate information.
- *Mathematics*
  Use numbers, fractions, and percentages to solve problems.
  Use tables, graphs, and charts.
  Use computers to enter, retrieve, change, and compute numerical information.
- *Speaking*
  Speak clearly.
  Select language, tone of voice, and gestures appropriate to an audience.
- *Listening*
  Listen carefully to what a person says, noting tone of voice and body language.
  Respond in a way that indicates an understanding of what is said.

Thinking Skills Thinking skills include the following:

- *Creative thinking*
  Use imagination freely, combining information in innovative ways.
  Make connections between ideas that seem unrelated.
- *Problem solving*
  Recognize problems.
  Identify why a problem is a problem.
  Create and implement solutions to problems.
  Observe to see how effective a solution is.
  Revise as necessary.
- *Decision making*
  Identify goals.
  Generate alternatives and gather information about them.
  Weigh pros and cons.
  Choose the best alternative.
  Plan how to carry out your choice.

- *Visualization*
  Imagine building an object or system by studying a blueprint or drawing.

Personal Qualities Personal qualities include the following:

- *Self-Esteem*
  Understand how beliefs affect how a person feels and acts.
  Listen and identify irrational or harmful beliefs that you may have.
  Know how to change these negative beliefs when they occur.
- *Self-Management*
  Assess one's own knowledge and skills accurately.
  Set specific and realistic personal goals.
  Monitor progress toward goals.
- *Responsibility*
  Work hard to reach goals, even if a task is unpleasant.
  Do quality work.
  Have a high standard of attendance, honesty, energy, and optimism.

People Skills People skills include the following:

- *Social*
  Show understanding, friendliness, and respect for others' feelings.
  Be assertive when appropriate.
  Take an interest in what people say and why they think and behave the way they do.
- *Negotiation*
  Identify common goals among different people.
  Clearly present your position.
  Understand your group's position and the other group's position.
  Examine possible options.
  Make reasonable compromises.
- *Leadership*
  Communicate thoughts and feelings to justify a position.
  Encourage or convince.
  Make positive use of rules or values.
  Demonstrate the ability to get others to believe in and trust you because of your competence and honesty.
- *Teamwork*
  Contribute your ideas to the group in a positive manner.
  Do your own share of the work.
  Encourage team members.
  Resolve differences for the benefit of the team.
  Responsibly challenge existing procedures, policies, or authorities.

Additional Skills The National Association of College Employers conducted a survey of its members. The employers ranked oral communication, interpersonal relations, and teamwork as the three most important skills of a prospective job candidate (Collins, 1996). All of these skills involve communicating effectively. Employers also value candidates with the following abilities:

- speaking skills
- leadership skills
- interpersonal skills
- proficiency in field of study
- analytical skills
- writing skills
- teamwork skills
- computer skills
- flexibility

To get an impression of how effective your communication skills have become, see Know Yourself: Self-Assessment 13.2, "How Good Are Your Communication Skills?," at the end of the chapter on page 462.

Self-Management Skills When people think of work-related skills, technical skills, such as writing, speaking, and computer proficiency, tend to come to mind. Although these skills are important, self-management skills, sometimes referred to as *self-regulation*, are essential for career success. Complete Know Yourself: Self-Assessment 13.3, "My Self-Management Skills," at the back of the chapter on page 463 to get a good idea about how self-sufficient you can be in work settings.

The skills and qualities you checked off in Know Yourself: Self-Assessment 13.3 are among the most important things a prospective employer should learn about you. They have to do with your ability to be a competent worker in many different situations and to adapt to challenging tasks. Even so, most job-seekers don't understand how crucial these skills are and don't mention them during interviews. Don't make this mistake.

Pass the Test

You may remember two personality scales introduced in Chapter 5, the Myers-Briggs Type Inventory (MBTI) and the Five Factor Personality Model. These two approaches to evaluating personality styles are especially relevant to learning styles. The MBTI was not designed as a career assessment tool, but it is often used alongside interest and aptitude assessments to provide career direction. The career counseling center on campus uses the MBTI or other career-related inventories to help you develop a match between your interests and your career direction.

The "Big Five" personality traits (openness, conscientiousness, extraversion, agreeableness, and neuroticism/emotional instability) have not been widely used to direct career choice. However, this typology has been used to assess work and nonwork environments that affect career change, work performance, and job satisfaction (Day & Schleicher, 2006).

The Holland Self-Assessment Interest Inventory One of the most commonly used systems for examining the link between personality style and career choice was developed by John Holland (1997). Holland believes that there are six basic personality types: realistic, investigative, artistic, social, enterprising, and conventional (see Figure 13.2, "Holland's Model of Personality Types and Career Choices"). Following is a description of each, linked with some appropriate careers.

- *Realistic.* People who have athletic or mechanical ability; prefer to work with objects, machines, tools, plants, or animals; or to be outdoors. They often are less social, have difficulty in demanding situations, and prefer to work alone. This personality type matches up best with jobs in labor, farming, truck driving, construction, engineering, and flying.
- *Investigative.* People who like to observe, learn, investigate, analyze, evaluate, or solve problems. They are interested in ideas more than people, are rather indifferent to social relationships, are troubled by emotional situations, and are often aloof and intelligent. This personality type matches up with scientific, intellectually oriented professions.
- *Artistic.* People who have artistic, innovative, or intuitional abilities and like to work in unstructured situations using their imagination and creativity. They enjoy working with ideas and materials that allow them to express themselves in innovative ways. They value nonconformity, freedom, and ambiguity. Sometimes they have difficulty in social relationships. Not many

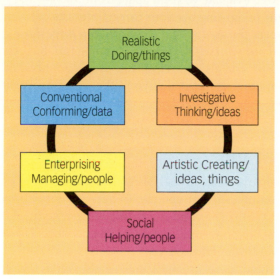

FIGURE 13.2 Holland's Model of Personality Types and Career Choices

jobs match up with the artistic type. Consequently, some artistic individuals work in jobs that are second and third choices and express their artistic interests through hobbies and leisure.

- *Social.* People who like to work with other people to enlighten, inform, help, train, or cure them, or are skilled with words. They tend to have a helping orientation and like doing social things more than engaging in intellectual tasks. This personality type matches up with jobs in teaching, social work, and counseling.
- *Enterprising.* People who like to work with people, influencing, persuading, performing, leading, or managing for organizational goals or economic gain. They may try to dominate others to reach their goals and are often good at persuading others to do tasks. The enterprising type matches up with jobs in sales, management, and politics.
- *Conventional.* People who like to work with data, have clerical or numerical ability, carry out tasks in detail, or follow through on others' instructions. They function best in well-structured situations and are skilled at working with details. The conventional type matches up with jobs in accounting, banking, and secretarial work.

Most people are a combination of two or three types. Holland's system takes this factor into account in matching up a person's type with careers.

Be Test Wise Richard Bolles (2011), author of the popular book *What Color Is Your Parachute?* offered these rules for taking career tests:

1. *There is no one career test that always gives better results than others*. One career test may work well for you; another one, for your best friend.
2. *You should take several tests, not just one.* You likely will obtain a better picture of your career interests from as many as three or more tests rather than just one.
3. *Consult your intuition.* You likely know more about yourself than a test does. Treat no test outcome as "gospel." If the test results seem just dead

wrong to you, evaluate yourself apart from the test and use your intuition as part of figuring out your career interests.

4. ***You are never finished with a test until you have done some good, hard thinking about yourself.*** Career tests can be fun, but reading the results is not enough. You also need to think deeply about what makes you different from others, what makes you (like your fingerprints and the irises of your eyes) unique. This deeper inquiry about yourself can help you find the careers that are likely best for you.

Land a Great Job

Career exploration involves investigating the world of work and becoming knowledgeable about different careers. When you are thinking about what type of work you are likely to find rewarding and satisfying, you will benefit by exploring different job opportunities while still in college. Do some research and gather information from many sources.

A career-oriented position may not be the only job you are thinking about for the future. You also might be looking for a part-time campus job, a job between terms, or one for next summer. As with exploring potential careers, finding the right job involves doing your homework and becoming as knowledgeable as you can about jobs in which you have an interest. Keep in mind that a part-time campus job may help you gain an interesting full-time job after you graduate. Among the most important things for you to do in your job search are to:

1. know what employers generally want.
2. research the job details.
3. create a resume and write various letters.
4. prepare for a job interview.

Know What Employers Generally Want In the national survey of employers of college students mentioned earlier in the chapter, employers said that first-year students need to be already thinking about the career they want to pursue (Collins, 1996). Graduation and job hunting are only a few years away. Much of what employers look for in top job candidates (such as relevant experience) takes time to acquire. The employers especially recommend that first-year students focus on obtaining:

- work-related experience.
- good grades.
- computer skills.
- leadership positions.
- participation in campus or extracurricular activities.

Research the Job Details Research the type of job that you want, identifying the skills and experience needed to perform it. Determine both the general requirements of the job and the day-to-day tasks and responsibilities. Brainstorm about a potential employer's needs, attitudes, and goals. Also research the company or employer in general. If you can determine the company's philosophy, you will be able to determine more accurately how you might contribute to the company and whether it is a good match for you.

"Your resume is excellent, but your Facebook page lacks the imagination we want in a new employee."

The more you know about the job, the stronger a candidate you will become. Check out ads in newspapers and use Web resources related to your interests and skills. If you are looking outside your geographic area, read local newspapers via the Web. Two other websites stand out for their benefits in a job search. *The Riley Guide* (www.rileyguide.com) has an online tutorial that takes you through a series of steps on how to use the Internet in a job search. *The Job Hunter's Bible* (www.jobhuntersbible.com) is also a valuable job-hunting resource.

Create Winning Materials To land a great job, you are going to need a good resume. You also need to know how to write a variety of letters and possibly branch into other kinds of media to make your most persuasive case.

Resume A resume is a clear and concise description of your interests, skills, experiences, and responsibilities in work, service, extracurricular, and academic settings. There are a number of different styles for resumes, and no particular one is considered universally the best. Use white paper, a font size of 10 to 12 points, and black type. There should be no errors whatsoever—misspelled words, grammatical errors, typos—in your resume. Also, it must be an accurate reflection of your job history and accomplishments. Lies on your resume will catch up with you.

Three types of resumes are most commonly used (OCS Basics, 2004):

1. *Chronological.* This is the most common format, which describes your experiences in reverse chronological order, beginning with your most recent experiences.
2. *Functional.* This highlights your marketable skills by organizing your accomplishments by skill or career area. This format may be the best choice if you have limited work experience related to the job for which you are applying.
3. *Achievement.* This format highlights prior work or academic accomplishments. Use it as an alternative to the first two formats when your accomplishments are centered on a particular skill or experience category.

Most resumes include the following parts (Writers Workshop, 2006):

- NAME: Centered and boldface font.
- ADDRESS: Present and permanent. May include your phone number and/ or e-mail address.
- JOB OBJECTIVE: This likely will be different for each job you apply for. It summarizes your reason for submitting a resume (the position you desire) and your qualifications. The rest of your resume should relate to and support your job objective.
- EDUCATIONAL RECORD: Begin with your most recent education (college you are now attending) and list all schools attended and degrees earned since high school. Indicate your major and areas of specialization. You may want to include your GPA if you have a B average or better. You might list distinctions and honors, such as the dean's list or scholarships, or you can save these for a separate category, "Awards and Honors."
- EMPLOYMENT HISTORY: List the dates, job title, and organization involved in each job you have held. Do not disclose salary information. This section is organized in reverse chronological order; that is, you begin with the most recent job and conclude with your first. Remember that in this section you can include volunteer jobs or working with an instructor on a project if these experiences are relevant. Alternatively, these could be placed under "Educational Record" if they are academic, or under "Special

Skills" or "Activities." Be sure to include a brief description of your work on each job, the tasks you performed, the skills you acquired, any special responsibilities or projects, and promotions or achievements.

- SPECIAL SKILLS: List any skills that are relevant to the job you want but are not mentioned elsewhere on the resume. For example, list expertise with specific software packages or fluency in foreign languages.
- PROFESSIONAL AFFILIATIONS AND ACTIVITIES: List your membership in any professional organizations and any active role or office you have held. Do not include personal interests or leisure activities.
- HONORS AND AWARDS: List any honors you have earned or awards you have received since high school. If you have two honors or less, delete this section and include the information with the "Professional Affiliations" section or under an "Honors and Activities" heading.
- REFERENCES: Don't include references on your resume unless they are specifically requested. State "References available upon request," and take a typed list of two to four references with you to any job interview (list name, title, organization, relationship, address, and phone number).

Some good strategies for writing winning resumes include the following (Writers Workshop, 2006):

- **Do a self-evaluation.** Jot down all your significant experiences, including jobs, course projects, internships, volunteer work, and extracurricular activities. Analyze your experiences in terms of skills that most resemble those needed in your desired career.
- **Write.** After you have determined which experiences are most relevant to the job you want, write short descriptive phrases for each job activity. Use action verbs such as *prepared, monitored, organized, directed,* and *developed.* Emphasize skills by writing phrases such as "designed new techniques for. . . ." Use bullets with short sentences rather than lengthy paragraphs. Whenever possible, give specific evidence to illustrate your skills, such as "Designed new techniques for computer processing, saving the company $50,000 over a one-year period." Decide which of the three resume styles that we have considered best suits your needs; then write a draft of your resume on a word processor.
- **Skip.** Avoid including details that are irrelevant, too personal, or otherwise give the wrong impression of your work ethic or professional capabilities.
- **Revise.** Let your draft sit for a day or two, and then critically reexamine it. Ask other people to look at your resume and to give you their honest reactions. Based on these critical analyses, revise the resume.
- **Print.** When you have written a draft you like, print out an error-free copy on a quality printer and have it photocopied onto good paper. Your final resume should be only one or two pages. If it is longer, be suspicious of irrelevant or unnecessary material. If your resume is two pages, make sure the most important information is on the front page.

Letters Letters provide a great opportunity to communicate in a personal and professional manner. They give you a chance to stand out in a crowd. One important guideline is to never use a form letter. Always tailor each letter individually to the person you are writing to. Address a letter to the individual by name and include the person's title and address. If you don't know this information, call or consult the

"Oops! The padding just fell out of your résumé."

company's website. Among the different types of letters you might need to write are employment inquiry letters, cover letters, and thank-you letters (OCS Basics, 2004):

- *Employment inquiry letter.* You can write an employment inquiry letter if you have identified a specific organization for which you would like to work. You are not asking for a job but for advice and information. Introduce yourself and concisely explain why you are writing. Then, demonstrate that you have researched the company, highlight your relevant experience, and clarify why you think you are well qualified for this type of work. Finally, express your interest in obtaining advice from this person, and state that you will call at a specific time, usually in about 1 week, to arrange a time to meet.

- *Cover letter.* A second type of important job letter is a cover letter that introduces you to a potential employer. Never send a resume to a potential employer without a cover letter. The cover letter briefly describes your qualifications, motivation, and interest in the job. Don't just repeat information in the resume, but come up with fresh phrases and sentences related to your experiences, skills, and the job you want.

- *Thank-you letter.* Get in the habit of writing thank-you letters to the people related to your job search within 24 hours of meeting them. Do so after an informational meeting with someone you met through networking— and always send a thank-you letter following a job interview. It might be tempting to follow up with an e-mail, as it tends to be more efficient. However, a formal letter sent through "snail mail" is much more impressive and memorable. Don't cut corners here.

Digital Materials Technologically sophisticated employers may appreciate your use of electronic media to provide evidence not only of what you have accomplished but also of what you can do using computer skills. Consider assembling a website specific to your job search that includes work samples that might interest employers. The website should provide a good reflection of your work ethic. For example, the content should reflect attention to detail, clarity, and professional standards.

On the other hand, don't be surprised to have your social networking come back to haunt you once the job search is under way. Employers can Google you and check out your status on accessible networks to find out information that may shed some light on your character.

Ace the Interview A key step in getting the job you want is to perform well in an interview. The following are some strategies for success (Yate, 2011):

- *Be prepared.* Interviewers ask for detailed examples of your past experience. They figure you'll do as well on the new job as the old one, so the examples you give can seal your fate.

- *Know your resume.* Resumes are important. Employers use them to decide whether they want to interview you in the first place and will often ask questions about what they contain. Be sure to review what they already know from what you have written about yourself before you begin talking.

- *Prepare some questions.* Employers are impressed by applicants who have taken the time to learn about their organization. This is true whether you are interviewing for a part-time job at your college library or for a full-time job in a large company after you graduate. Review the job's requirements with the interviewer. Demonstrate both curiosity and effective research skills by what you ask.

The Bumbled Interview

What are the most significant errors you can make that will send employers running the other way (Doyle, 2011)?

- **Avoid preparation**. Employers will assume you have done your homework and have some basic understanding of the company, its values, and its track record. If you are obviously winging it, it sends a signal to a potential employer that you might not take the real job very seriously.

- **Violate the dress code**. Especially in the Internet age, when business casual could be deemed too dressy, do some sleuthing to figure out what the appropriate dress code for the company appears to be. Watch people arrive for work and take note of the degree of formality employees strive to achieve.

- **Treat employees differently based on status**. Direct eye contact, a smile, and a firm handshake should characterize your treatment of everyone you meet. Some employers watch to see if you treat lower-status employees with less respect.

- **Stay connected by phone**. Shut your phone off or set it to vibrate. Nothing should take precedence over the face-to-face discussion that could determine your future.

- **Dominate the discussion**. Although the interview is focused on you and your accomplishments, make your answers succinct. Avoid tangents that could give indications that you have trouble staying "on point."

- **Appear uncommunicative**. Just as talking too much can be a problem, so can talking too little. Avoid one- or two-word answers. Try to elaborate in ways that will enhance your employer's interest.

- **Obscure your past.** Be prepared for questions if your resume includes gaps that need explanation. Explain the gaps without adopting a defensive posture.

- *Anticipate what questions you'll be asked.* Do some practice interviews. Typical interview questions include "What is your greatest strength?" "What interests you the most about this job?" "Why should I hire you?" Also be prepared for potential curve balls. For example, how would you respond to "Tell me something you're not very proud of" or "Describe a situation where your idea was criticized"? These are examples of questions some interviewers ask to catch you off guard and to see how you handle the situation.
- *Keep your cool.* Always leave in the same polite, composed way you entered.
- *Decide whether you want the job.* If so, ask for it. Tell the interviewer that you're excited about the job and that you believe you can meet its needs and expectations. If it isn't offered on the spot, ask when the two of you can talk again.
- *Follow up.* Immediately after the interview, send your follow-up letter. Keep it short, less than one page. Mail it within 24 hours of the interview. If the decision is going to be made in the next few days, consider hand-delivering the letter. If you do not hear anything within 5 days, call the organization to ask about the status of the job.

When so much is at stake, it is hard to believe that job applicants would not take special pains to do everything possible to create the right impression. See Danger Zone: "The Bumbled Interview" for some examples of bad interviewing strategies.

Manage Life

As we considered in Chapter 11, students can manage both work and academic life by participating in part-time or summer work, internships, and cooperative education (co-op) programs relevant to their fields of study. The experience you gain can be critical in helping you get the job you want when you graduate. Many of today's employers expect job candidates to have this type of hands-on experience.

Work experience can also influence your starting pay. For example, the NACE survey for 2011 established that individuals who had internships in the employment history were paid on average $7,000 more in their starting salary than those who had no such experience (Ryan, 2011).

Explore Part-Time and Summer Jobs

College students benefit more when their jobs are on campus rather than off. Working on campus keeps students more in touch with the life of the college community—and it takes them less time to commute to their job! Also, on-campus jobs are more likely to be linked with academic pursuits. A good strategy for finding out about on-campus jobs is to go to the financial aid office at your college and ask for a list of available part-time positions. See whether any of them will help you develop skills for a future career.

Most departments on a college campus hire student assistants, usually to perform specialized duties such as website design, data input, or clerical or reception work. If you are interested in a major and career in psychology or biology, you might want to go to these departments and ask if any student assistant jobs are available. If you are hired, be careful to observe regulations about appropriate access to files as well as confidential treatment of what you learn on the job.

With advance planning, summer jobs can provide good opportunities not only to earn money but also to take part in experiences relevant to your major and your career interests. Getting a summer job that is related to a potential future career can give you a glimpse of the day-to-day aspects of the career and provide insight into whether this is the type of life work you want to do. Even if you don't find a part-time or summer position that is relevant to your career interests, most jobs allow you to demonstrate work-related skills and a work ethic that any prospective employer will find attractive.

Do an Internship or a Co-op

Many college students ask questions about the future: How do I figure out what I want to do? How do I get a job if I don't have any experience? How do I get experience without a job? What if I spend 4 years studying in a particular major and it turns out I don't like it? Internships and co-op experiences can help you answer these questions. These are jobs in the real world that are linked to your academic and career interests. Recall from the chapter-opening profile how Darius Graham completed a summer internship to further his career development interests.

Internships Most internships are part-time jobs that last for about 3 to 6 months, although some last longer. The only time that they might be full-time is in the summer and in periods when you aren't taking classes. Some internships pay a little money, but most don't include a salary. Nonetheless, they can significantly help you down the road when you begin looking for full-time employment and a career after college. One study found that students who served in internships during college were 15 percent more likely to find employment after graduation, and 70 percent said that they were better prepared for the workplace because of this internship experience (Knouse, Tanner, & Harris, 1999).

Here are some recommendations for internship opportunities:

- Check with your academic adviser or the campus career center to find out about the internship opportunities that are available.
- Attend job fairs. Employers often use job fairs to identify students for co-op or internship experiences.
- Contact the chamber of commerce in the city where you are attending college or in the city where you will be living next summer.
- Network. Talk with friends, family, instructors, professionals in the field in which you are interested, and others. Let them know that you want to obtain an internship experience.
- If a particular company interests you, contact the company to see if it has internships that are available.
- The Internet has sites that can be helpful. The following site lists many internships: www.internjobs.com.

DANGER ZONE (Cont.)

- *Interrupt the questioner*. Even if you know what direction the question will take, be patient. Interruption demonstrates problematic self-control. You may end up answering the question partially or wrong.
- *Criticize past employers*. If you speak poorly about a prior supervisor, a current supervisor recognizes that you are likely to broadcast similar complaints about new employers. In fact, the employers may know each other, and perhaps even be friends, making your error hard to forgive.
- *Fail to follow up*. In the crush of interview activity, you may be rushed to state everything you need to secure the offer. Use a follow-up letter to express your appreciation of the time invested and share any final, helpful details.

Working during college can help you build career-related skills and demonstrate an impressive work ethic.

© iStockphoto.com/See Hear Media, Inc.

Tanya Gonzales

Exploiting Internship Opportunity

After graduating from the University of Colorado, Denver, Tanya Gonzales was hired by Denver TV station KMGH. She has worked her way up to promotions producer in just a few years with the station. Tanya says, "I wouldn't have my job if I didn't do my internship." She recalls that networking was very important in her internship search, and she recommends these strategies for internship success: "(1) be enthusiastic, (2) absorb as much as you can, and (3) do things you are afraid to do."

(Source: Department of Communications, University of Colorado at Denver, 2008)

- Explore *Internships* (Fishberg et al., 2005), a book that lists more than 40,000 internships. If it is not available on your campus, call 1-800-338-3282 to find out where you can find it.

Co-ops Cooperative education programs (co-ops) pay a salary and typically last more than a year. Many co-op programs offer academic credit, and a typical student makes anywhere from $2,500 per year early in his or her undergraduate study to $14,000 per year toward the end of the undergraduate program (National Commission on Cooperative Education, 2008). In 4-year colleges, you may not be able to pursue a co-op experience until your junior year, whereas in 2-year colleges the co-op experience may be available to both 1st- and 2nd-year students.

In a national survey of employers, almost 60 percent said their entry-level college hires had co-op or internship experience (Collins, 1996). More than a thousand colleges in the United States offer co-op programs.

Co-ops and internships let you test your career objectives and can help you identify your talents and acquire valuable skills that you may need in a future career. Before seeking a particular co-op or internship, ask yourself these questions:

- What type of work do I want to do?
- In what field?
- In what type of organization do I want to work?

Contribute through Service Learning

A wide range of life experiences during college may also help you explore your values related to careers. One example is *service learning,* which involves engaging in activities that promote social responsibility and service to the community (Hart, Atkins, & Donnelly, 2006). In service learning, you might tutor, help older adults, volunteer in a hospital, assist in a daycare center, or clean up a vacant lot to make a play area. As described in the chapter-opening "Spotlight On," Darius Graham participated in a wide range of service-learning activities in his effort to improve the lives and opportunities of students and people in the community. And he is continuing his efforts to improve the community in his work after college.

There are some signs that U.S. college students are shifting toward a stronger interest in the welfare of society. For example, the percentage of college freshmen who said they were strongly interested in participating in community action programs in the coming year increased from 18 percent in 1990 to 31 percent in 2009 (Pryor et al., 2009).

Why should you participate in service learning during your college years? Researchers have found that when students participate in service learning the following things happen (Benson et al., 2006):

- Their grades improve, they become more motivated, and they set more goals.
- Their self-esteem improves and they become less self-centered.
- They increasingly reflect on society's moral order and social concerns.

MATT SMITH/Express-Times/Landov

What are some positive outcomes of participating in service learning?

If you are not currently participating in service learning, make it a priority to get involved in at least one service-learning experience before the end of this term. You and the recipients of your service learning will benefit from your efforts. Your college likely has a service-learning office or organization that can help you get involved in a service-learning activity that interests you. You can learn more about service-learning opportunities at these two websites:

- www.servicelearning.org: Learn and Serve's extensive national clearinghouse for information about service learning, including Youth Service in America
- www.rootsandshoots.org: A worldwide service-learning organization that includes a special section for college students

Avoid Work Addiction

It is not too soon to begin paying attention to your potential to get too committed to work at the expense of other important things in your life. If you are taking a full load of courses and working over 30 hours a week, something has to give. Chances are the quality of your academic work will suffer, but you may develop bad habits that can be costly in professional life.

Unlike other addictions, workaholism tends to garner lots of attention and encouragement (Parker, 2011). People who overwork may capture raises, bonuses, and other "perks" associated with the job, but their inability to shut off their work focus can be costly in their personal lives.

What are the costs associated with being obsessed by work? Personal relationships tend to wither. Work relationships suffer as well since workaholics may insist on doing things in a particular fashion, making it hard to work collegially. They may also be unable to delegate, so the mountain of work grows and gets even more overwhelming. Some work addicts develop an array of health problems, including insomnia, fatigue, headaches, and stomach trouble.

Take steps now to ensure that your work life develops in a healthy fashion. Reserve blocks of time on your calendar to reconnect with loved ones and friends. Take regular breaks. Establish and maintain reasonable exercise and nutrition patterns. Reconnect with resources that provide spiritual renewal.

Connect and Communicate

Connecting and communicating are key aspects of career exploration, work, and advancing in a career. Among the important aspects of connecting and communicating related to work and careers are networking, seeing a career counselor, and scoping out Internet resources.

Network

Networking is making contact and exchanging information with other people. Check with people you know—your family, friends, people in the community, and alumni—about career information.

They might be able to answer your questions themselves or put you in touch with people who can. For example, most college career centers have the names of alumni on file who are willing to talk with students about careers and their work. Networking can lead to meeting someone who can answer your questions about a specific career or company. This is an effective way to learn about what

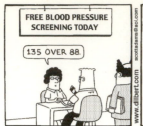

type of training is necessary for a particular position, how to enter the field, and what employees like and don't like about their jobs.

Following are some good strategies for networking effectively (OCS Basics, 2004):

- *Use a wide net.* People you can network with? Everybody! This includes your instructors, guest speakers, people in line at the coffee shop, your parents, their friends, neighbors, high school teachers, tutors, lab supervisors, alumni of your high school and college, and staff members of community organizations. Network wherever you go.
- *Be well prepared.* Be able to spell out clearly as much as you know about what you are looking for in a job.
- *Show professionalism.* Always be courteous, considerate, and gracious. Write a thank-you letter when people take the time to meet with you.
- *Give back.* Know enough about the people you meet in networking to keep their needs in mind. You may be able to pass along ideas, articles, and contacts that will interest them.

Seek Career Counseling

You might want to talk with a career counselor at your college. This professional is trained to help you discover your strengths and weaknesses, evaluate your values and goals, and assist you in figuring out what type of career is best for you. The counselor will not tell you what to do but rather will offer helpful guidance. For example, you might be asked to take an interest inventory, which the counselor can interpret to help you explore various career options. See Highlight: "Chart the Unknown" to develop your long-term career planning.

Scope Out Internet Resources

The dramatic growth of websites has made countless resources for job possibilities and careers instantly available. Most companies, professional societies, academic institutions, and government agencies maintain Internet sites that highlight their latest information and activities.

The range of career information on the Internet tends to overlap with what is available through libraries, career centers, and guidance offices. However, no single network or resource is likely to contain all of the information you're

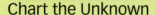

HIGHLIGHT

Chart the Unknown

Only a few years ago, the ideal job was one you landed right after graduation, and, if you were lucky, you stayed with the company for 30 years until you were handed a gold watch with a pat on the back for a job well done. Those days are gone, but that might not be such a bad thing. Challenging economic environments encourage you to think broadly about the kinds of careers that can interest you. Even if you aspire to an ideal job, it is best to have a backup plan. Be knowledgeable about more than just one career field. It also pays to develop a wide range of general abilities, such as speaking and writing to diverse audiences, that will serve you well in different jobs in multiple fields.

searching for, so explore different sources. As in a library search, look through various lists by field or discipline or by using key words.

The Internet also contains some pitfalls. Beware of job-related sites that probe you for too much personal information under the guise of helping you. Never give out your Social Security number, credit cards, or banking information to Internet brokers who promise to find employment for you. Do your homework on the companies so you don't end up worse than unemployed.

 # Build a Bright Future

The finishing touches on preparing for your career involve the effort you will need to plan for the inevitable and unpredictable changes in direction that your career is likely to have, and to gather some perspective as your college success course comes to an end.

Dream Big

Once you have settled into your shiny job, all may be well. Your employers may be responsive and respectful, and you may make a commitment to live out your entire career in one place. However, statistics suggest that that outcome may be unlikely. On average, most people change careers several times before retirement. Under what circumstances are you likely to move on (McKay, 2011)?

- *When your personal circumstances change.* Your goals and values may be changed due to shifts in your life status. As a parent, you will be more inclined to embrace nonrisky ventures. When the children are grown, you may be freer to pick up and start a new adventure.
- *When the nature of your occupation changes.* A generation of secretaries found their jobs dramatically changed with the advent of personal computers. When something changes occupational demand, it can affect your longevity as well as your interest and enthusiasm.
- *When your work is overwhelming.* Some jobs entail so much stress that it is difficult to stay the course. In extreme cases, workers can report burnout, reducing their motivation to work efficiently or effectively.
- *When your work isn't stimulating enough.* Even if it is a high-paying position, if a job doesn't provide enough intellectual stimulation, it is challenging to do your best. Lackluster performance is hardly going to lead to promotions and pay raises or new opportunities in the company.
- *When you get crosswise in workplace politics.* Whether you alienate the boss or experience shunning from fellow employees, sometimes you may wear out your welcome. In those situations, a change of pace and direction may be in order, especially if you are bucking majority opinion.
- *When you spot a better opportunity.* You may want to submit your notice for a bigger position, a better-paying position, or just a new set of challenges.

Recognize that those who are prepared to make changes quickly and move on will be better prepared to embrace the opportunities that the future will bring.

Put It All Together

Throughout this book and especially in this chapter, we have extensively explored many aspects of how important your college experiences are for building a bright future, especially your ability to succeed in work and a career after college. In this final section, we review some of the key aspects discussed throughout the book and how they connect with work and careers.

Chapter 2: Pursue Resources Connecting with resources, including extra-curricular activities and the community, can help you to develop a more balanced, broad appeal to employers when you seek a job after college. Selecting the best major(s) through consultation with your academic adviser can help you connect with careers that best match your interests and values. Becoming competent in technology is a valuable skill for future work and careers after college.

Chapter 3: Manage Time Wisely Good time-management skills are essential for success in any job or career. Learning how to manage your time effectively during college—through planning for the year, term, month, week, and day—and then monitoring your time use will help you to develop excellent time-management skills that will make you a successful worker after college and enhance your chances of advancing in a career.

Chapter 4: Master Communication Skills and Build Relationships Communication skills, such as listening, avoiding barriers to verbal communication, tuning in to nonverbal messages, and using communication to resolve conflict, will benefit you enormously in your work and career after college.

Chapter 5: Navigate Differences Evaluate your learning style and link it to a major(s) and the career(s) you may want to pursue. Target an intelligent career, connecting your natural talents with possible career options. Find the right mix of intellectual strengths, learning preferences, and personality styles to choose the right major for you and prepare you for entering the best work and career choice after college. However, keep a flexible outlook because the career you pursue may not have emerged yet as a viable option. Find a suitable mentor as part of beginning to develop a professional network that will help you to realize your dreams after college.

Chapter 6: Expand Thinking Skills How effective you are as a thinker—your ability to think critically, reason, solve problems, make good decisions, and think creatively—will be more important than the bank of specific facts you have accumulated in college for most work and careers after college.

Chapter 7: Take Winning Notes Any profession you enter will test you on how well you can listen and read. Learning how to listen and read effectively in college will help you to develop good habits that you can carry into your work and career. Taking good notes in lectures and reading will prepare you for effectively engaging in these important skills in work and a career after college as well.

Chapter 8: Enhance Your Study Skills and Memory By developing good study strategies in college, you are forming the foundation for having effective strategies to solve problems and deal with key issues in your work and career following college. Using good memory strategies in college will also improve your chances of retaining important information in your work and career after college.

Chapter 9: Succeed on Tests Doing well on tests is a key factor in achieving a high grade-point average, and a high GPA indicates to future employers that you have the ability to do well in challenging situations, including handling tasks and deadlines by planning and preparing. When you seek a job after college, you likely will need one or more letters from instructors in the courses you have taken. Clearly, instructors are likely to write a better recommendation if you have gotten high grades on their tests and in their course.

Chapter 10: Express Yourself Writing and speaking skills are among the most important skills that employers look for in hiring college graduates. Improving your writing and speaking skills during college will significantly improve your chances of landing a great job after college and help you advance in a career.

Chapter 11: Take Charge of Your Physical and Mental Health Practicing good physical and mental health during college will prepare you for engaging in healthy behaviors on a job and in a career following college. Engaging in such physical health behaviors as eating well and exercising regularly, and in such mental health behaviors as coping effectively with stress, will help you do well not only in college but also in your work and career after college.

Chapter 12: Manage Money Intelligently Taking control of your finances during college prepares you to be a good money manager after college when you start making more money. Recognize the incredible value of doing well in college to increase your income after college.

Manage Life

- Develop work skills through part-time and summer employment.
- Seek work preparedness through internships, co-ops, and service learning.
- Make rich connections through service-learning projects.

Connect and Communicate

- Develop professional networks to expand your job possibilities.
- See a career counselor to explore career options.
- Scope out Internet resources related to job possibilities and careers.

Clarify Expectations

- Recognize that college education produces some buffering over limited education even in deep recessions.
- Identify the occupations that show the greatest sturdiness for job growth.
- Identify positive values that inspire movement toward jobs as well as boundaries that limit some considerations.

Build a Bright Future

- Prepare to be flexible regarding what the future holds.
- Review the broad range of career-related topics to promote your best performance.

Develop Competence

- Set career goals, including long-term and short-term goals related to the college major(s) and career(s) you want to pursue.
- Assess your workplace readiness, including self-management.
- Link your personality and career choice in the context of Holland's system.
- Research your prospects and prepare yourself carefully for job interviews.

 Visit the College Success CourseMate for *Your Guide to College Success* for interactive resources at login.cengagebrain.com

1. How important is it to link your career interests with your personal values? Explain.

_____

_____

_____

2. What impact does a recessionary economy have on job prospects?

_____

_____

_____

3. What general areas show the greatest possibilities for growth?

_____

_____

_____

4 What are the main types of SCANS skills that can benefit workers when they enter the workforce? List these and give an example of each.

Skill	Example
1. _____	_____
2. _____	_____
3. _____	_____
4. _____	_____

5. According to Holland, what are six personality types that can be assessed to link up with various careers?

1. _____

2. _____

3. _____

4. _____

5. _____

6. _____

6. What are some mistakes people make during the job interview?

_____

_____

_____

7. List three strategies for creating a strong resume. Which one do you think will work best for you?

1. _____

2. _____

3. _____

8. Describe three types of letters that are part of the career-exploration process. List a few aspects of each.

1. _____

2. _____

3. _____

9. What are some developments that can prompt you to move on once you have landed a job?

1. _____

2. _____

3. _____

4. _____

10. What are four of the most effective ways to acquire work experience while you are still in college?

1. _____

2. _____

3. _____

4. _____

11. Describe some advantages of networking to explore career opportunities.

_____

_____

_____

_____

_____

_____

12. Discuss some benefits that Internet resources might provide in searching for jobs and exploring careers.

_____

_____

_____

_____

SELF-ASSESSMENT 13.1

My Values and Career Pursuits

Place a check mark next to those values you consider important in a career.

____ work with people I like

____ feel powerful

____ have peace of mind

____ make a lot of money

____ be happy

____ have self-respect

____ contribute to the welfare of others

____ not have to work long hours

____ be challenged mentally

____ be self-fulfilled

____ have opportunities for advancement

____ work in a setting where moral values are emphasized

____ have plenty of time for leisure pursuits

____ have plenty of time to spend with family

____ work in a good geographical location

____ be creative

____ work where physical and mental health are important

____ other: _____

____ other: _____

____ other: _____

As you explore careers, keep the values you checked off in mind. How do those values match the careers you've thought about pursuing? Explain.

_____

_____

_____

_____

_____

_____

SELF-ASSESSMENT 13.2

How Good Are Your Communication Skills?

Among the skills that employers want college graduates to have, communication skills are the most important. Honestly examine your communication skills. Rate yourself from 1 to 5 on the following:

	Weak				Strong
Speaking skills	1	2	3	4	5
Interpersonal skills	1	2	3	4	5
Teamwork skills	1	2	3	4	5
Writing skills	1	2	3	4	5
Listening skills	1	2	3	4	5

Find out how important each of these skills is for the job you want to pursue when you graduate from college. What are your strengths and weaknesses? What can you do now to start improving your areas of weakness?

SELF-ASSESSMENT 13.3

My Self-Management Skills

Calculate your Self-Management score by adding up all of the "agree" checkmarks to the 20 statements below that characterize your ability to regulate your goal accomplishment in the workplace. The higher the score, the greater your workplace self-sufficiency.

Agree   Disagree

_____   _____   I can make myself go to work even when I'm not in the mood.

_____   _____   I typically complete assignments on time.

_____   _____   I can manage working on more than one goal at a time.

_____   _____   I can complete tasks that require a great deal of persistence.

_____   _____   I know how to help a team stay on track.

_____   _____   I can deliver criticism without being offensive.

_____   _____   I look for new and interesting ways of solving problems.

_____   _____   I take care of myself physically so I have the right work energy.

_____   _____   I look forward to feedback as an opportunity to improve.

_____   _____   I usually develop back-up plans in case anything goes wrong.

_____   _____   I keep my work space optimally organized.

_____   _____   I work hard to cultivate my relationships with supervisors.

_____   _____   I know when to reach out to others for help.

_____   _____   I can delay gratification until after a task is complete.

_____   _____   I keep promises to promote the development of trust.

_____   _____   I do what I can to minimize workplace gossip.

_____   _____   I own my part in making errors.

_____   _____   I demonstrate initiative to improve work outcomes.

_____   _____   I can set work aside to facilitate getting my energies recharged.

_____   _____   I try to promote positive workplace morale.

Focus on the "disagree" items. What would be your top two priorities for making some changes in your ability to manage in the workplace?

Source: J. M. Farr, *America's Top Jobs for College Graduates*, 3rd ed. (Indianapolis, IN: JIST Works, 1999): 365–366. Reprinted with permission.

Your Journal

 Clarify Expectations

1. My Ideal Job

If you have not done so yet, complete Know Yourself: Self-Assessment 13.1 before you do this exercise.

- Write down your ideal occupation choice.

_____

_____

- Describe the degree you'll need for your ideal job, such as an AA, BA, MA, or PhD. How many years will this take?

_____

_____

- On a scale of 1 to 10, estimate your chances of obtaining your ideal job.

Poor   1   2   3   4   5   6   7   8   9   10   Excellent

- What can you do now to increase your chances of obtaining this career?

_____

_____

2. Matching Personal Values to Career Options

List three personal values that are important to you.

1. _____

2. _____

3. _____

Write about how well these personal values match up with the career(s) you want to pursue.

_____

_____

_____

Develop Competence

3. Predicting Holland's Inventory

Take a look at the dimensions of the Holland Inventory. Which of the six categories is most like you? Which of the six is least like you?

_____

_____

_____

If you can make arrangements to take the Holland, compare your test results to your prediction. Were you on target or off the mark?

_____

_____

_____

_____

_____

_____

4. The Dreadful Cover Letter

Demonstrate your understanding of what it takes to make a good impression on a prospective employer by writing a profoundly bad cover letter for a job. Identify what errors are present in the letter that would alienate a future boss.

_____

_____

_____

_____

_____

_____

_____

📁 Manage Life

5. My Work Skills

List all of the work experiences you have had so far.

_____

_____

Are any of these related to any careers that might interest you? Why or why not?

_____

_____

What kind of career-related or general work skills have you demonstrated in these jobs that might be attractive to a potential employer?

_____

_____

6. What's the Advantage?

What are the fundamental similarities and differences between internships and co-ops?

_____

_____

💬 Connect and Communicate

7. Visit Your College's Career Center

Visit the career center at your college. Write down the relevant contact information for future reference.

_____

_____

What materials and services are available for your career search?

_____

_____

Consider making an appointment with a career counselor. List a few questions you would like to discuss.

_____

_____

8. Networking

Imagine you have been invited to a local event that features networking. Develop five questions that you could use to meet new people and generate business prospects.

1. _____

2. _____

3. _____

4. _____

5. _____

Build a Bright Future

9. Practice a Job Interview

Get together with someone in your college success class and practice a job interview related to a career. Have your class partner interview you, and then you interview him or her. Before you do the interviews, be sure to review the Danger Zone box in this chapter titled "The Bumbled Interview." Write about your practice job interviews.

_____

_____

_____

10. Current and Future Resume

Based on what you have read in this chapter, begin creating or updating your resume. List your education, work experience, high school or college campus organizations, and extracurricular activities. List any honors or awards you have achieved. Then write down what you would like your resume to look like when you apply for your first job after college. How do the two differ?

_____

_____

_____

_____

References

A

Adair, J. (2010*). Decision and problem solving strategies*. London: Kogan.

Adams, K. L., & Galanes, G. J. (2012). *Communicating in groups* (8th ed.). New York: McGraw-Hill.

Adler, R. B., & Proctor II, R. F. (2011). *Looking out/Looking in* (13th ed.). Boston: Wadsworth.

Alberti, R., & Emmons, M. (1995). *Your perfect right* (7th ed.). San Luis Obispo, CA: Impact.

Alverno College. (1995). *Writing and speaking criteria*. Milwaukee, WI: Alverno Productions.

American College Health Association. (2007). American College Health Association National College Health Assessment spring 2006 reference group data report (abridged). *Journal of American College Health, 55*, 195–206.

American Council of Education. (2006, May). *Issue brief: Working their way through college: Student employment and its impact on the college experience*. Retrieved from http://www.acenet.edu/AM/Template.cfm?template=/CM/ContentDisplay.cfm&ContentFileID=1618

American Pregnancy Association. (2011). *Spermicide*. Retrieved from http://www.americanpregnancy.org/preventingpregnancy/spermicide.html

American Psychological Association. (2002). *Controlling anger—before it controls you*. Retrieved from http://www.apa.org/pubinfo/anger.html

Anderman, E., & Anderman, L. (2010). *Classroom motivation*. Upper Saddle River, NJ: Pearson.

Anderson, L. W., & Krathwohl, D. R. (Eds.). (2001). *A taxonomy for learning, teaching, and assessment: A revision of Bloom's taxonomy of educational objectives*. New York: Longman.

Anderson, R. (2011). *Credit 911*. New York: Wiley.

Annenberg Public Policy Center National Risks Survey. (2005). *Card playing trend in young people continues*. Retrieved from http://www.annenbergpublicpolicycenter.org/Downloads/Adolescent_Risk/Gambling/GamblingRelease20050928.pdf

Appleby, D. (1997, February). *The seven wonders of the advising world*. Invited address at the Southeastern Teachers of Psychology Conference, Kennesaw State University, Marietta, GA.

Arnett, J. J. (2007). Socialization in emerging adulthood. In J. E. Grusec & P. D. Hastings (Eds.), *Handbook of socialization*. New York: Guilford.

Arnett, J. J. (2010). *Adolescence and emerging adulthood* (4th ed.). Upper Saddle River, NJ: Pearson.

Aronson, E., Blaney, N., Stephan, C., Sikes, J., & Snapp, M. (1978). *The jigsaw classroom*. Beverly Hills, CA: Sage.

Aspinwall, L. G. (2011). Future-oriented thinking, proactive coping, and the management of potential threats to health and well-being. In S. Folkman (Ed.), *The Oxford handbook of stress and coping*. New York: Oxford University Press.

Aspinwall, L. G., & Tedeschi, R. G. (2010). The value of positive psychology for health psychology: Progress and pitfalls in examining the relation of positive phenomena and health. *Annals of Behavioral Medicine, 39*, 27–34.

Astin, A. (1993). *What matters in college: Four critical years revisited*. San Francisco: Jossey-Bass.

Athanasou, J. A., & Olasehinde, O. (2002). Male and female differences in self-reported cheating. *Practical Assessment, Research and Evaluation, 8* (5). Retrieved May 21, 2006, from http://PAREonline.net/getvn.asp?v=8&n=5

B

Bailey, C. (1991). *The new fit or fat* (Rev. ed.). Boston: Houghton Mifflin.

Bandura, A. (2006). Going global with social cognitive theory: From prospect to paydirt. In S. I. Donaldson, D. E. Burger, & K. Pezdek (Eds.), *The rise of applied psychology*. Mahwah, NJ: Erlbaum.

Bandura, A. (2010). Self-efficacy. In D. Masamoto (Ed.), *Cambridge dictionary of psychology*. New York: Cambridge University Press.

Banks, J. A. (2008). *An introduction to multicultural education* (4th ed.). Boston: Allyn & Bacon.

Barber, B., Stone, M., & Eccles, J. (2010). Protect, prepare, and engage: The roles of school-based extracurricular activities in students' improvement. In J. Meece & J. Eccles (Eds.), *Handbook of research on schools, schooling, and human development*. New York: Routledge.

Barlow, D. H., & Durand, M. (2012, in press). *Abnormal psychology* (6th ed.). Boston: Cengage.

Barrett, J. (2003). *Excessive credit card use causes student debt woes*. Retrieved from http://www.youngmoney.com/credit_debt/get_out_of_debt/021007_03/

Bauer, L. (2010, May 19). Once-oldest college grad earns her master's at 98. *Columbus Dispatch*. Retrieved from http://www.dispatch.com/live/content/life/stories/2010/05/19/once-oldest-college-grad-earns-her-masters-at-98.html

Baumrind, D. (1991). Parenting styles and adolescent development. In J. Brooks-Gunn, R. Lerner, & A. C. Petersen (Eds.), *The encyclopedia of adolescence*. New York: Garland.

Baxter Magolda, M. B. (1992). *Knowing and reasoning in college*. San Francisco: Jossey-Bass.

Beck, J. (2002). Beck therapy approach. In M. Hersen & W. H. Sledge (Eds.), *Encyclopedia of psychotherapy*. San Diego, CA: Academic Press.

Beghetto, R. A., & Kaufman, J. C. (Eds.). (2011). *Nurturing creativity in the classroom*. New York: Cambridge University Press.

Beglar, D., & Murray, N. (2010). *Contemporary topics 3: Academic and note-taking skills (advanced)* (3rd ed.). Upper Saddle River, NJ: Pearson.

Bell, K. E., & Limber, J. E. (2010). Reading skill, textbook marking, and course performance. *Literacy Research and Instruction, 49*(1), 56–67.

Benson, P. L., Scales, P. C., Hamilton, S. F., & Sesman, A. (2006). Positive youth development: Theory, research, and applications. In W. Damon and R. Lerner (Eds.), *Handbook of child psychology* (6th ed.). New York: Wiley.

Beydoun, M. A., & Wang, Y. (2009). Gender-ethnic disparity in BMI and waist circumference distribution shifts in U.S. adults. *Obesity, 17,* 169–176.

Bitter, G. G., & Legacy, J. M. (2008). *Using technology in the classroom* (7th ed.). Boston: Allyn & Bacon.

Bjork, R. A. (1994). Install impediments to effect training. In D. R. Druckman & R. A. Bjork (Eds.), *Learning, remembering, believing: Enhancing human performance.* Washington, DC: National Academies Press.

Bjork, R. A. (1994). Memory and metamemory considerations in the training of human beings. In J. Metcalfe & A. Shimamura (Eds.), *Metacognition: Knowing about knowing.* Cambridge, MA: The MIT Press.

Bjorklund, D. F. (2012). *Children's thinking* (8th ed.). Boston: Cengage.

Blauwet, C. (2011). *Cheri Blauwet.* Retrieved January 4, 2011, from www.cheriblauwet.com

Blonna, R., & Paterson, W. (2007). *Coping with stress in a changing world* (4th ed.). New York: McGraw-Hill.

Bloom, B. S., Englehart, M. D., Furst, E. J., & Krathwohl, D. R. (1956). *Taxonomy of educational objectives: Cognitive domain.* New York: David McKay.

Blumenstock, J. E. (2008). *Automatically assessing the quality of Wikipedia articles.* Retrieved from http://escholarship.org/uc/item/18s3z11b

Bolles, R. (2011). *What color is your parachute?* (Rev. and updated ed.). Berkeley, CA: Ten Speed Press.

Bonnie, C., & Sternberg, R. J. (2011). Learning to think critically. In P. A. Alexander & R. E. Mayer (Eds.), *Handbook of research on learning and instruction.* New York: Routledge.

Bosch, T. (2010, December 22). Maya Moore: Some quick facts on the UConn basketball superstar. *AOLNews.* Retrieved from http://www.aolnews.com/2010/12/22/uconns-maya-moore-leads-womens-team-to-longest-ever-ncaa-basket/

Bourne, E. J. (1995). *The anxiety and phobia workbook* (2nd ed.). Oakland, CA: New Harbinger Publications.

Brandyon, S. (2011). *Academic writing and research. How to write an e-mail to a professor.* Retrieved January 8, 2011, from http://www4.ncsu.edu/~sgbranyo/WritinganEmailtoYourProfessorInstructor.htm

Brandywine, P., et al. (2011). *Email a professor.* Retrieved January 8, 2011, from http://www.wikihow.com/Email-a-Professor

Bransford, J. D., & Stein, B. S. (1984). *The ideal problem solver.* New York: Freeman.

Brisette, I., Scheier, M. F., & Carver, C. S. (2002). The role of optimism in social network development, coping, and psychological adjustment during a life transition. *Journal of Personality and Social Psychology, 82,* 102–111.

Brown, D. P. (2010). *Time management for college students.* Amazon Digital Services: Learning Life eBooks.

Brown, F. C., & Buboltz, W. C., Jr. (2002). Applying sleep research to university students: Recommendations for developing a student sleep education program. *Journal of College Student Development, 43,* 411–416.

Brown, F. C., Buboltz, W. C., Jr., & Soper, B. (2001). Prevalence of delayed sleep phase syndrome in university students. *College Student Journal, 35,* 472–476.

Browne, M. N., & Keeley, S. M. (1990). *Asking the right questions: A guide to critical thinking* (3rd ed.). Englewood Cliffs, NJ: Prentice Hall.

Brydon, S. R., & Scott, M. D. (2011). *Between one and many: The art and science of public speaking* (7th ed.). New York: McGraw-Hill.

Burns, D. (1999). *The Feeling Good Workbook.* New York: Avon.

Butin, D. W. (2005). *Service-learning in higher education: Critical issues and directions.* New York: Palgrave Macmillan.

C

Cacioppo, J. T. (2002). Emotion and health. In R. J. Davidson, K. R. Sherer, & H. H. Goldsmith (Eds.), *Handbook of affective sciences.* New York: Oxford University Press.

Callahan, D. (2004). *The cheating culture. Why more Americans are doing wrong to get ahead.* New York: Harcourt Brace.

Cameron, J. M., et al. (2010). Drinking game participation among undergraduate students attending a national Alcohol Screening Day. *Journal of American College Health, 58,* 499–506.

Canfield, J., & Hansen, N. V. (1995). *The Aladdin factor.* New York: Berkeley.

Carnett, J. (2007). Invention awards: The glove that saves lives. *Popular Science.* Retrieved from http://www.popsci.com/scitech/article/2007-05/invention-awards-glove-saves-lives

Carpenter, S. (2001, October). Sleep deprivation may be undermining teen health. *The Monitor, 32,* 42. Retrieved January 13, 2011, from http://www.apa.org/monitor/oct01/sleepteen.aspx

Carroll, J., & Rayn, J. (2005). *Teaching international students: Improving learning for all.* London: Routledge.

Carroll, J. L. (2007). *Human sexuality* (2nd ed.). Belmont, CA: Wadsworth.

Carsakdon, M. A. (1999). Consequences of insufficient sleep for adolescents: Links between sleep and emotional regulation. In K. L. Wahlstrom (Ed.), *Adolescent sleep needs and school starting times.* Bloomington, IN: Phi Delta Kappa Educational Foundation.

Carskadon, M. A. (2006, April). *Adolescent sleep: The perfect storm.* Paper presented at the meeting of the Society for Research on Adolescence, San Francisco.

Chang, E. C., Watkins, A., & Banks, K. H. (2004). How adaptive and maladaptive perfectionism relate to positive and negative psychological functioning: Testing a stress-mediation model in black and white female college students. *Journal of Counseling Psychology, 51,* 93–102.

Christy, A. (2005, May 4). Paralyzed, but not in her spirit: Spinal cord injury leads to a proactive outlook on life. *The Daily Aztec,* San Diego State University. Retrieved from http://media.www.thedailyaztec.com/media/storage/paper741/news/2005/05/04/City/Paralyzed.But.Not.In.Her.Spirit-947380-page2.shtml and http://www.fight2walk.org/about/team_rachelle_taylor.htm

Chu, K. (2009, April 12). Average college credit card debt rises with fees and tuition. *USA Today.* Retrieved January 8, 2011, from www.usatoday.com/money/perfi/credit/2009-04-12

Cizek, G. J. (1999). *Cheating on tests: How to do it, detect it, and prevent it.* Mahwah, NJ: Erlbaum.

Cizek, G. J., & Burg, S. S. (2006). *Addressing test anxiety in a high-stakes environment: Strategies for classrooms and schools.* Thousand Oaks, CA: Sage.

Clark, M. R. (2005). Negotiating the freshman year: Challenges and strategies among first-year college students. *Journal of College Student Development, 46,* 296–316.

Clarkson University Magazine. (2006, Fall). *Clarkson's REU in China program.* Retrieved February 1, 2008, from http://www.clarksonalumni.com/stay_connected/magazine/fall_06/china.html

CNET Tech. (2002). *When games stop being fun.* Retrieved from http://news.net.com/2100-1040-881673.html

Colby magazine. (1999, Summer). *Sharing the spotlight* (about Walter Wang). Retrieved from http://www.colby.edu/colby.mag/issues/sum99/life/4.html

College Board. (2004). *Education pays 2004: Trends in higher education series.* Retrieved March 10, 2008, from http://www.eaop.org/documents/college_board_edu_pays_2004.pdf

College Board. (2010). *Scholarship handbook 2010.* Princeton, NJ: College Board.

College of San Mateo. (2008). *CSM student success story: Karina Orocio.* Retrieved January 19, 2008, from http://www.collegeofsanmateo.edu/webpages/Karina_Orocio.pdf

College of San Mateo. (2008). *CSM student success story.* Retrieved February 1, 2008, from http://www.collegeofsanmateo.edu/webpages/studentsuccess.asp

College Success Planner. (2000). Belmont, CA: Wadsworth.

Collins, M. (1996, Winter). The job outlook for '96 grads. *Journal of Career Planning, 23,* 51–54.

Conley, M. W. (2012). *Content area literacy: Learners in context* (2nd ed.). Boston: Allyn & Bacon.

Courtenay, W. H., McCreary, D. R., & Merighi, J. R. (2002). Gender and ethnic differences in health beliefs and behaviors. *Journal of Health Psychology, 7,* 219–231.

Covey, S. R. (1989). *The seven habits of highly effective people.* New York: Simon and Schuster.

Covey, S. R., Merrill, A. R., & Merrill, R. R. (1994). *First things first.* New York: Simon and Schuster.

Creating Success website. *Success stories: Brian Long.* North Carolina Community Colleges. Retrieved January 18, 2011, from http://www.nccommunitycolleges.edu/successsstories/story.aspx?story=868

Crooks, R., & Baur, K. (2011). *Our sexuality* (11th ed.). Boston: Cengage.

Crow, J. (2010). *Unleashing your language wizards.* Boston: Allyn & Bacon.

Crowley, S. J., Acebo, C., & Carskadon, M. A. (2007). Sleep, circadian rhythms, and delayed phase in adolescence. *Sleep Medicine, 8,* 602–612.

Csikszentmihalyi, M. (1995). *Creativity.* New York: HarperCollins.

Csikszentmihalyi, M. (1997). *Finding flow.* New York: Basic Books.

Cunningham, C. (2008). *Success stories: Lane opens doors for minority students.* Retrieved January 18, 2008, from http://www.lanecc.edu/mpr/success/story10.htm

Cunningham, P. M., & Cunningham, J. W. (2010). *What really matters in writing: Research-based practices across the curriculum.* Boston: Allyn & Bacon.

Cutrona, C. E. (1982). Transition to college: Loneliness and the process of social adjustment. In L. A. Peplau & D. Perlman (Eds.), *Loneliness: A sourcebook of current theory, research, and therapy.* New York: Wiley.

D

Damon, W. (2008). *The path to purpose.* New York: Free Press.

Davis, M., Eshelman, E. R., McKay, M., & Fanning, M. (2008). *The relaxation and stress reduction workbook* (6th ed.). Oakland, CA: New Harbinger.

Day, D. V., & Schleicher, D. J. (2006). Self-monitoring at work: A motive-based perspective. *Journal of Personality, 74,* 685–713.

DeFleur, M. L., Kearning, P., Plax, T., & DeFleur, M. H. (2005). *Fundamentals of human communication* (3rd ed.). New York: McGraw-Hill.

Dement, W. C., & Vaughn, C. (2000). *The promise of sleep.* New York: Dell.

DeVito, J. (2004). *Interpersonal communication workbook* (10th ed.). Upper Saddle River, NJ: Prentice Hall.

Diamond, L. M., Butterworth, M., & Savin-Williams, R. C. (2011). Clinical issues facing sexual minorities. In D. H. Barlow (Ed.), *Oxford handbook of clinical psychology.* New York: Oxford University Press.

Diener, E., & Seligman, M. E. P. (2002). Very happy people. *Psychological Science, 13,* 81–84.

DiGilio, J. J., & Lynn-Nelson, G. (2008). *The millennial invasion: Are you ready?* Retrieved January 18, 2008, from http://findarticles.com/p/articles/mi_mOFWE/is_11_8/ai_n9543851

Does a college degree protect your career? *Unemployment rate for college graduates highest on record.* Retrieved January 30, 2011, from http://www.mybudget360.com/does-a-college-degree-protect-your-career-unemployment-rate-for-college-graduates-highest-on-record/

Doyle, A. (2011). *Top 10 interview blunders: How not to interview.* Retrieved from http://jobsearch.about.com/od/interviewsnetworking/a/interviewblund.htm

Duvernoy, S. O. (2010, February 2). Code switch 7 takes on race. *Harvard Crimson.* Retrieved from http://www.thecrimson.com/article/2010/2/2/code-7-race/

Dweck, C. (2006). *Mindset. The new psychology success.* New York: Random House.

Dweck, C. (2012, in press). Social development. In P. Zelazo (Ed.), *Oxford handbook of developmental psychology.* New York: Oxford University Press.

E

Economos, C. (2001). *Tufts longitudinal health study.* Unpublished manuscript. Medford, MA: Center on Nutrition Communication.

Edmonds, E. (2010, January 26). *College gender gap appears to be stabilizing with one notable exception.* Press release. American Council on Education. Retrieved from http://www.acenet.edu/AM/Template.cfm?Section=Press_Releases2&TEMPLATE=/CM/ContentDisplay.cfm&CONTENTID=35338

Elliott, M. (1999). *Time, work, and meaning.* Unpublished doctoral dissertation, Pacifica Graduate Institute.

Emerge. Retrieved January 13, 2011, from http://www.emergeglobal.org/

Encyclopedia of psychotherapy. San Diego, CA: Academic Press.

Epstein, R. L. (2000). *The pocket guide to critical thinking.* Belmont, CA: Wadsworth.

Erikson, E. H. (1968). *Identity: Youth and crisis.* New York: Norton.

Evans, M. (2004, June 1). Ten tips and tricks for the online student. *Tech and Learning.* Retrieved January 13, 2011, from http://www.techlearning.com/article/2388

F

Fahey, T. D., Insel, P. M., & Roth, W. T. (2009). *Fit & well, brief* (8th ed.). New York: McGraw-Hill.

Fairweather, E., & Cramond, B. (2011). Infusing creative and critical thinking into the classroom. In R. A. Beghetto & J. C. Kaufman (Eds.), *Nurturing creativity in the classroom.* New York: Cambridge University Press.

Farr, J. M. (1999). *America's top jobs for college graduates.* Indianapolis, IN: JIST Works.

Ferrari, J. R. (2010). *Still procrastinating.* New York: Wiley.

Fife, M. (2011, January 8). Commentary in R. Lieber, "In college, learning about money." *New York Times*, p. B1.

Fishberg, M. T., Lin, A., Skibiki, I., Able, M., Sullivan, A., Oram, F. A., Heinz, C., & Wagner, A. (2005). *Internships.* Princeton, NJ: Petersons.

Fisher, D., & Frey, N. (2012). *Improving adolescent literacy* (3rd ed.). Boston: Allyn & Bacon.

Fleming, G. (2010). *How to form a study group and keep it on track.* Retrieved from http://homeworktips.about.com/od/studymethods/a/studygroup.htm

Florida Leader. (2005). *Finalist Darius Graham.* Retrieved January 31, 2008, from http://www.floridaleader.com/soty/2005_fi n_Graham.htm

Floyd, K. (2011). *Communication matters.* New York: McGraw-Hill.

Folkman, S. (Ed.). (2011). *The Oxford handbook of stress and coping.* New York: Oxford University Press.

Folkman, S., & Moskowitz, J. T. (2004). Coping: Pitfalls and promises. *Annual Review of Psychology,* Vol 55. Palo Alto, CA: Annual Reviews.

Fort Hays State Virtual College. (2008). *Student success stories.* Retrieved January 19, 2008, from http://www.fhsu.edu/virtualcollege/virtual/stories/index.htm

Foster, C. (2008, October 2). Alpharetta HS senior gets perfect SAT score. *Alpharetta and Roswell Revue and News.* Retrieved from http://www.northfulton.com/Articles-i-2008-10-02-175236.112113_Alpharetta_HS_senior_gets_perfect_score_on_SAT.html

Frank, S. (1996). *The everything study book.* Avon, MA: Adams Media.

Freeman, S. G. (2007, June 20). *A graduate of Stanford by way of a transfer.* Retrieved from http://www.jackkentcookefoundation.org/jkcf_web/content.aspx?page=NewsEv

Fulghum, R. (1997). Pay attention. In R. Carlson & B. Shield (Eds.), *Handbook for the soul.* Boston: Little, Brown. *FYE Mentor Experience.* Colorado College. Retrieved from http://www.coloradocollege.edu/academics/fye/peeradvisor/

G

Galambos, N. L., Howard, A. L., & Maggs, J. L. (2011, in press). Rise and fall of sleep quality with student experiences across the first year of the university. *Journal of Research on Adolescence.*

Galinsky, E. (2010). *Mind in the making.* New York: HarperCollins.

Gamble, T., & Gamble, M. (2010). *Communication works* (10th ed.). New York: McGraw-Hill.

Gardner, H. (1989). *Frames of mind.* New York: Basic Books.

Gardner, H. (1999a). *The disciplined mind.* New York: Simon and Schuster.

Gardner, H. (1999b). *Intelligence reframed: Multiple intelligences for the 21st century.* New York: Basic Books.

Garner, P. W., & Estep, K. M. (2001). Empathy and emotional expressivity. In J. Worell (Ed.), *Encyclopedia of women and gender.* San Diego, CA: Academic Press.

Gewertz, K. (2000). Profile in courage (and loyalty). *Harvard University Gazette.* Retrieved from http://www.news.harvard.edu/gazette/2000/06.08/ellison.html

Gewertz, K. (2004, November 12). Six named Rhodes scholars. *Harvard University Gazette.* Retrieved January 18, 2008, from http://www.news.harvard.edu/gazette/daily/2004/11/22-rhodes.html

Gibson, M. (2010, December 17). Moving out of the Heartbreak Hotel: Tips for going through a breakup in college. *USA Today College.* Retrieved from http://www.usatodayeducate.com/staging/index.php/blog/moving-out-of-the-heartbreak-hotel-tips-for-going-through-a-break-up-in-college

Glater, J. (2006, May 18). Colleges chase as cheats shift to higher tech. *New York Times.* Retrieved from http://www.jkcf.org/scholarships/undergraduate-transfer-scholarships/undergraduate-transfer-scholars-in-the-press/a-graduate-of-stanford-by-way-of-a-transfer/

Glier, R. (2006, November 16). All USA Moore is in a class by herself. *USA Today.* Retrieved from http://www.usatoday.com/sports/preps/basketball/2006-11-15-moore_x.htm

Gobel, R. (2010). *Graduation debt.* New York: Cliff Notes.

Goldberg, H. (1980). *The new male.* New York: Signet.

Goldsmith, L., & Hardy, S. (2008, February 24). Thanksgiving for international students. *Student Life.* Retrieved from http://media.www.studlife.com/media/storage/paper337/news/2007/11/19/Scene/Thanksgiving.For.International.Students-3109564.shtml

Goleman, D., Kaufmann, P., & Ray, M. (1992). *The creative spirit.* New York: Plume.

Good News Blog. (2007). *Single mom balances school, family, named USA Today Academic All-Star.* Retrieved January 27, 2008, from http://www.goodnewsblog.com/2007/03/13/single-mom-balances-school-family-named-USA-today-academic-all-star

Gordon, T. (1970). *Parent effectiveness training.* New York: McGraw-Hill.

Gottman, J. M., & Gottman, J. S. (2009). Gottman method of couple therapy. In A. S. Gurman (Ed.), *Clinical handbook of couple therapy* (4th ed.). New York: Guilford.

Gottman, J., & Silver, N. (1999). *The seven principles for making marriages work*. New York: Crown.

Graham, D. (2011). *Darius Graham*. Retrieved January 2, 2011, from www.linkedin.com/in/dariusgraham

Granato, S. (2006). *Winning the lottery, curse or blessing? Facts about winning millions in the lottery*. Retrieved from http://www.associatedcontent.com/article/70165/winning_the_lottery_curse_or_a_blessing.html?cat=7

Grathwohl, C. (2011, January 7). Wikipedia comes of age. *Chronicle of Higher Education*. Retrieved from http://chronicle.com/article/wikipedia-comes-of-age/125899/?sid=cr&utm_source=cr&ut

Gray, J. (1992). *Men are Mars, women are from Venus*. New York: HarperCollins.

Greenberg, J. S. (2011). *Comprehensive stress management* (12th ed.). New York: McGraw-Hill.

Greenwood, P. M., & Parasuraman, R. (2011, in press). Neuronal and cognitive plasticity: A neurocognitive framework for ameliorating cognitive aging. *Frontiers of Aging Neuroscience*.

Gregory, H. (2010). *Public speaking for college and career with Connect Plus Public Speaking* (9th ed.). New York: McGraw-Hill.

Grynbaum, Michael M. (2004, June 10). Mark E. Zuckerberg '06: The whiz behind thefacebook.com. *The Harvard Crimson*.

Guardado, A. (2010, November 7). Bullying on campus. *The Independent*. Retrieved from http://www.clark-independent.com/life/bullying-on-campus-1.1750305

H

Haag, S., & Perry, J. T. (2003). *Internet Explorer 6.0*. New York: McGraw-Hill.

Hahn, D. B., Payne, W. A., & Lucas, E. B. (2011). *Focus on health* (10th ed.). New York: McGraw-Hill.

Haines, M. E., Norris, M. P., & Kashy, D. A. (1996). The effects of depressed mood on academic performance in college students. *Journal of College Student Development, 37*, 519–526.

Halberg, E., Halberg, K., & Sauer, L. (2000). *Success factors index*. Auburn, CA: Ombudsman Press.

Hallahan, D. P., Kauffman, J. M., & Pullen, P. C. (2012). *Exceptional learners* (12th ed.). Upper Saddle River, NJ: Pearson.

Halonen, J. (2002). Classroom presence. In S. F. Davis & W. Buskist (Eds.), *The teaching of psychology: Essays in honor of Wilbert J. McKeachie and Charles L. Brewer*. Mahwah, NJ: Erlbaum.

Halonen, J. S., & Gray, C. (2001). *The critical thinking companion for introductory psychology*. New York: Worth Publishers.

Halpern, D. F. (1997). *Critical thinking across the curriculum*. Mahwah, NJ: Erlbaum.

Hamm, M. (2004). *Winners never quit!* New York: HarperCollins.

Hansen, R. S., & Hansen, K. (1997). *Write your way to a higher GPA*. Berkeley, CA: Ten Speed Press.

Hansen, R. S., & Hansen, K. (2011). *What do employers really want? Top skills and values employers seek from job seekers*. Retrieved from http://www.quintcareers.com/job_skills_values.html

Harbin, C. E. (1995). *Your transfer planner*. Belmont, CA: Wadsworth.

Harris, R. A. (2001). *The plagiarism handbook: Strategies for preventing, detecting, and dealing with plagiarism*. Los Angeles: Pyrczak Publishing.

Hart, C. L., Ksir, C. J., & Ray, O. S. (2011). *Drugs, society, and human behavior* (14th ed.). New York: McGraw-Hill.

Hart, D., Atkins, R., & Donnelly, T. M. (2006). Community service and moral development. In M. Killen & J. Smetana (Eds.), *Handbook of moral development*. Mahwah, NJ: Erlbaum.

Hasher, L., Chung, C., May, C. P., & Foong, N. (2001). Age, time of testing, and proactive interference. *Canadian Journal of Experimental Psychology, 56*, 200–207.

Hasling, J. (2010). *The audience, the message, and the speaker* (8th ed.). New York: McGraw-Hill.

Hastie, R., & Dawes, R. M. (2001). *Rational choice in an uncertain world: The psychology of judgment and decision making*. Thousand Oaks, CA: Sage Publications.

Hazen, C., & Shaver, P. R. (1987). Romantic love conceptualized as an attachment process. *Journal of Personality and Social Psychology, 52*, 522–524.

Heilman, D. (2007). *Featured alumni: Kristin Beniek*. Retrieved from http://www.saintpaul.edu/alumni/Featured/KristinBeniek.aspx

Hennesey, B. A. (2011). Intrinsic motivation and creativity: Have we come full circle? In R. A. Beghetto & J. C. Kaufman (Eds.), *Nurturing creativity in the classroom*. New York: Cambridge University Press.

Higbee, K. L. (2001). *Your memory: How it works and how to improve it* (2nd ed.). New York: Marlowe and Company.

Higher Education Research Institute. (2007, September). *College freshmen and online social networking sites*. Los Angeles: Los Angeles Higher Education Research Institute, UCLA.

Highline Honors Scholar Program. (2008). *Student success stories: Grace*. Retrieved January 26, 2008, from http://flightline.highline.edu/honors/success/Grace.htm

Hillman, R. (1999). *Delivering dynamic presentations: Using your voice and body for impact*. Needham Heights, NJ: Allyn & Bacon.

Hippie, D. (2010). *Note taking made easy!* New York: Scholastic.com.

Hofstetter, F. T. (2003). *Internet literacy*. New York: McGraw-Hill.

Holland, J. (1997). *Making vocational choices*. Lutz, FL: Psychological Assessment Resources.

Hopkins, J. (2004, April 23). Retrieved from http://www.usatoday.com/tech/products/services/2006-04-23-netflix-ceo_x.htm?POE=TECISVA

Horvitz, L. A. (2006). *Meg Whitman*. New York: Ferguson.

Howatt, W. A. (1999). Journaling to self-evaluation: A tool for adult learners. *International Journal of Reality Therapy, 18*, 32–34.

Howe, N., Strauss, W., & Matson, R. J. (2000). *Millennials rising: The next great generation*. New York: Knopf.

Howland, J. L., et al. (2012). *Meaningful learning with technology* (4th ed.). Boston: Allyn & Bacon.

Howstuffworks. (2007). *2007 BRICK Award Winner: William Hwang*. Retrieved February 3, 2008, from http://people.howstuffworks.com/do-something-brick-awards-winnerwilliam-hwang.htm

Hurtado, S., Dey, E. L., & Trevino, J. G. (1994). *Exclusion or self-segregation? Interaction across racial/ethnic groups on college campuses.* Paper presented at the meeting of the American Educational Research Association, New York.

Hybels, S., & Weaver, R. L. (2012, in press). *Communicating effectively* (10th ed.). New York: McGraw-Hill.

Hyde, J. S., & DeLamater, J. D. (2011). *Understanding human sexuality* (11th ed.). New York: McGraw-Hill.

I

Insel, P. N., & Roth, W. T. (2012, in press). *Connect core concepts in health* (12th ed.). New York: McGraw-Hill.

International Reading Association, Inc. (1994). Reading strategies. *Journal of Reading, 38.*

J

Jack Kent Cook Foundation. (2011). Retrieved January 9, 2011, from www.jkcf.org/our-scholars/current/476-Rhiana-Gunn-Wright

Jandt, F. E. (2004). *An introduction to intercultural communication.* Thousand Oaks, CA: Sage.

Jendrick, M. P. (1992). Students' reactions to academic dishonesty. *Journal of College Student Development, 33,* 260–273.

Jensen, D. R. (2003). Understanding sleep disorder in a college student population. *Journal of College Counseling, 6,* 25–35.

Johns Hopkins University. (2006). *Research: Tribal connections.* Retrieved January 31, 2008, from http://www.krieger.jhu.edu/research/spotlight/prabhakar.html

Johnston, L. D., O'Malley, P. M., Bachman, J. G., & Schulenberg, J. E. (2010). *Monitoring the Future national survey results on drug use, 1975–2009. Volume II: College students and adults aged 19–50.* Bethesda, MD: National Institute on Drug Abuse.

Johnston, L. D., O'Malley, P. M., Bachman, J. G., & Schulenberg, J. E. (2011). *Monitoring the Future national results on adolescent drug use: Overview of key findings, 2010.* Ann Arbor, MI: Institute for Social Research, University of Michigan.

Jonassen, D. H., & Grabowski, B. L. (1993). *Handbook of individual differences, learning, and instruction.* Mahwah, NJ: Erlbaum.

K

Kagan, J. (1965). Reflection-impulsivity and reading development in primary grade children. *Child Development, 36,* 609–628.

Kaplan, R. M., & Saccuzzo, D. P. (1993). *Psychological testing: Principles, applications, and issues* (3rd ed.). Pacific Grove, CA: Brooks/Cole.

Kappes, S. (2001). *The truth about Janeane Garofalo.* Retrieved from http://people.aol.com/people/features/celebrityspotlight/0,10950,169561,00.html

Karabanik, S. A., & Newman, R. S. (2006). *Help seeking in academic settings: Goals, groups, and contexts.* Mahwah, NJ: Erlbaum.

Karlin, S. (2006, May 3). *Young inventors of the world unite.* Retrieved from http://www.spectrum.ieee.org/careers/careerstemplate.jsp?Articleid=i030104

Kearney, C., & Trull, T. (2012, in press). *Abnormal psychology and life.* Boston: Cengage.

Kieffer, K. M., Cronin, C., & Gawet, D. L. (2006). Test and study worry and emotionality in the prediction of college students' reasons for drinking: an exploratory investigation. *Journal of Alcohol & Drug Education.* Retrieved from http://findarticles.com/p/articles/mi_go2545/is_1_50/ai_n29257290/

Keith-Spiegel, P. (1992, October). *Ethics in shades of pale gray.* Paper presented at the Mid-America Conference for Teachers of Psychology, Evansville, IN.

Keller, P. A., & Heyman, S. R. (1987). *Innovations in clinical practice.* Sarasota, FL: Professional Resource Exchange.

Kelly, G. F. (2011). *Sexuality today* (10th ed.). New York: McGraw-Hill.

Kenney, J. (2012, in press). *Loosening the grip: A handbook of alcohol information* (12th ed.). New York: McGraw-Hill.

Kierwa, K. A. (1987). Note-taking and review: The research and its implications. *Instructional Science, 19,* 394–397.

King, T., & Bannon, E. (2002, April). *At what cost? The price that working students pay for a college education.* Washington, DC: U.S. Department of Education, State Public Interest Research Groups' Higher Education Project.

Kinney, J. (2009). *Loosening the grip: A handbook of alcohol information* (9th ed.). New York: McGraw-Hill.

Kisslinger, L. S. (2011). *Contemporary topics 2: Academic listening and note-taking skills* (3rd ed.). Upper Saddle River, NJ: Pearson.

Knapp, M. L., & Hall, J. A. (2010). *Nonverbal communication in human interaction* (7th ed.). Boston: Cengage.

Knaus, W. (2010). *End procrastination now!* New York: McGraw-Hill.

Knouse, S., Tanner, J., & Harris, E. (1999). The relation of college internships, college performance, and subsequent job opportunity. *Journal of Employment Counseling, 36,* 35–43.

Kort-Butler, L. A., & Hagewen, K. J. (2011, in press). School-based extracurricular activity involvement and adolescent self-esteem: A growth-curve analysis. *Journal of Youth and Adolescence.*

Kroger, J. (2006). *Identity development: Adolescence through adulthood.* Thousand Oaks, CA: Sage.

Kroger, J. (2007). *Identity development. Adolescence through adulthood.* Thousand Oaks, CA: Sage.

Ksir, C. J., Hart, C. L., & Ray, O. S. (2008). *Drugs, society, and human behavior* (12th ed.). New York: McGraw-Hill.

L

Lakein, A. (1973). *How to get control of your time and your life.* New York: Signet.

Lane, A. M., Crone-Grant, D., & Lane, H. (2002). Mood changes following exercise. *Perceptual and Motor Skills, 94,* 732–734.

Langer, E. (1997). *The power of mindful learning.* Reading, MA: Addison-Wesley.

Langer, M. (2010). *Quicken 2010.* New York: McGraw-Hill Osborne Media.

Larson, R. B. (2009, December). Enhancing the recall of presented material. *Computers and Education, 53*(4), 1278–1284.

Lathrop, A., & Foss, K. (2007). *Guiding students from cheating and plagiarism to honesty and integrity: Strategies for change.* Westport, CT: Libraries Unlimited.

Lebauer, R. S. (2011). *Learn to listen, listen to learn 1: Academic listening and note-taking* (3rd ed.). Upper Saddle River, NJ: Pearson.

Lee, M. (2003). *Our love hate relationship with dressing, shopping, and the cost of style.* New York: Broadway Books.

Lefkowitz, E. S., & Gillen, M. M. (2006). "Sex is just a normal part of life": Sexuality in emerging adulthood. In J. J. Arnett & J. L. Tanner (Eds.), *Emerging adults in America.* Washington, DC: American Psychological Association.

Lerch, C. (2010, April 9). Geoffrion first Wisconsin player to win Hobey Baker Award. *USCHO News.* Retrieved from http://www.uscho.com/2010/04/09/geoffrion-first-wisconsin-player-to-win-hobey-baker-award/

Lerner, J. W. (2006). *Learning disabilities and related disorders: Characteristics and teaching strategies.* Boston: Houghton Mifflin.

Lever-Duffy, J., & McDonald, J. (2011). *Teaching and learning with technology* (4th ed.). Boston: Allyn & Bacon.

Levine, M. (2003). *The myth of laziness.* New York: Simon and Schuster.

Levinger, E. E. (1949). *Albert Einstein.* New York: Julian Messner.

Lillienfeld, S. O., Lynn, S. J., Namy, L. L., & Woolf, N. J. (2009). *Psychology: From inquiry to understanding.* Boston: Pearson.

Lillienfeld, S. O., Lynn, S. J., Ruscio, J., & Beyerstein, B. L. (2010). *50 great myths of popular psychology: Shattering widespread misconceptions about human behavior.* New York: Wiley-Blackwell.

Loftus, E. F. (1980). *Memory.* Reading, MA: Addison-Wesley.

Loftus, E. F. (1993). The reality of repressed memories. *American Psychologist, 48,* 518–537.

Loftus, E. F. (2003, March). Our changeable memories: Legal and practical implications. *Nature Review Neuroscience, 4,* 231–234.

Lorayne, H., & Lucas, J. (1996). *The memory book.* New York: Ballantine.

Lund, H. G., Reider, B. D., Whiting, A. B., & Prichard, J. R. (2010). Sleep patterns and predictors of disturbed sleep in a large population of college students. *Journal of Adolescent Health, 46,* 124–132.

Lunday, A. (2006). *Two Homewood seniors collect Marshall, Mitchell scholarships.* Retrieved January 31, 2008, from http://www.jhu.edu/~gazette/2006/04dec06/04schol.html

M

Maas, J. (1999). *Power sleep: The revolutionary program that prepares your mind for peak performance.* New York: HarperPerennial.

MacKenzie, A. (1997). *The time trap* (3rd ed.). New York: American Management Association.

MacKenzie, A., & Nickerson, P. (2009). *The time trap* (4th ed.). New York: AMACOM.

Macrae, C. N., & Bodenhausen, G. V. (2000). Social cognition: Thinking categorically about others. *Annual Review of Psychology, 51,* 93–120.

Maeda, M. (2010). *How to wipe out your student loans and be debt free fast.* Ocala, FL: Atlantic Publishing.

Maeda, M. (2011). *How to legally settle your personal and credit card debt for pennies on the dollar.* Ocala, FL: Atlantic Publishing.

Magno, C. (2010). The role of metacognitive skills in developing critical thinking. *Metacognition and Learning, 5,* 137–156.

Mandel Center for Non Profit Organizations. (2010). *Bryan Mauk, MNO '10.* Retrieved January, 2011, from www.case.edu/mandelcenter/grad/testimonials/BryanMauk.html

Marcia, J. E. (1994). The empirical study of ego development. In H. A. Bosnia, T. L. G. Graafsma, H. D. Grotevant, & D. J. de Levita (Eds.), *Identity and development.* Thousand Oaks, CA: Sage.

Marcus, A., Mullins, L. C., Brackett, K. P., Tang, Z., Allen, A. M., & Pruett, D. W. (2003). Perceptions of racism on campus. *College Student Journal, 37,* 611–617.

Marklein, M. B. (2008, February 14). *USA Today,* pp. 1, 2.

Marr, C. (2011). *Kindle note taking with Cynthia.* [Kindle version] Retrieved from Amazon.com.

Marshall Scholarships. (2007). *Scholar profiles: 2007.* Retrieved January 31, 2008, from http://www.marshallscholarship.org/profiles2007.html

Martin, C. Retrieved March 11, 2008, from http://www.courtneyemartin.com/biography.php

Martin, G. L., & Pear, J. (2011). *Behavior modification* (9th ed.). Upper Saddle River, NJ: Prentice Hall.

Martin, J. N., & Nakayama, T. K. (2011). *Experiencing intercultural communication* (4th ed.). New York: McGraw-Hill.

Martindale, G. (2011, January 24). *Suicide and suicidal behavior among college students.* Retrieved from http://www.stateuniversity.com/blog/permalink/Suicide-and-Suicidal-Behaviors-Among-College-Students.html

Martinez, V. (2007). *Pioneer profile: Vanessa Martinez.* Admission and Enrollment Services, University of Wisconsin, Platteville. Retrieved February 3, 2008, from http://www.uwplatt.edu/admission/profile/martinez.html

Massachusetts Institute of Technology. (2011). Student profile: Alia Whitney-Johnson. Retrieved January 13, 2011, from http://cee.mit.edu/node/2666

Matlin, M. (1998). *Cognitive psychology* (3rd ed.). New York: Harcourt Brace.

Matlin, M. W. (2012). *Psychology of women* (7th ed.). Boston: Cengage.

Matsumoto, D., Yoo, S. H., & Fontaine, J. (2008). Mapping expressive differences around the world. *Journal of Cross-Cultural Psychology, 39,* 55–74.

Mauk, B. (2010). Commentary in *Student Spotlight Brian Mauk, MNO Candidate.* Cleveland: Mandel Center for Nonprofit Organizations, Case Western University.

Maxwell, R., Meiser, M., & McKnight, K. S. (2011). *Teaching English in middle and secondary schools* (5th ed.). Boston: Allyn & Bacon.

McCabe, D. L., Trevino, L. K., & Butterfield, K. D. (2002). Cheating in academic institutions: A decade of research. *Ethics and Behavior, 11,* 219–232.

McGivern, G. (2002). *Football's Andrew Hilliard lands elite scholarship award.* Retrieved January 28, 2008, from http://www.stthomas.edu/bulletin/news/200243/Friday/Hilliard10_25_02.cfm

McKay, D. R. (2011). *6 Reasons to make a career change. Could a career change be in your future?* Retrieved from http://careerplanning.about.com/od/careerchoicechan/a/why_change.htm

McKowen, C. (1996). *Get your A out of college: Mastering the hidden rules of the game.* Los Altos, CA: Crisp Publications.

McNally, D. (1990). *Even eagles need a push.* New York: Dell.

McWhorter, K. T. (2000). *Study and critical thinking skills in college* (4th ed.). New York: Longman.

Mercer, C. D., & Mercer, A. R. (2004). *Teaching students with learning problems* (7th ed.). Upper Saddle River, NJ: Pearson.

Merrow, J. (2007, April 22). *The smart transfer.* Retrieved from http://www.jkcf.org/grants/community-college-transfer/ccti-news-publications/the-smart-transfer/

Michael, R. T., Gagnon, J. H., Laumann, E. O., & Kolata, G. (1994). *Sex in America.* Boston: Little, Brown.

Michigan Community College Virtual Learning Collaborative. (2004). *Tips for success.* Retrieved February 11, 2008, from http://vcampus.mccvlc.org/index.asp?dir='welcome'&content='TipsSucc.asp'

Miller, G. A. (1956). The magical number seven, plus or minus two: Some limits on our capacity for information processing. *Psychological Review, 48,* 337–442.

Miller, J. B. (1986). *Toward a new psychology of women* (2nd ed.). Boston: Beacon Press.

Miltenberger, R. G. (2012, in press). *Behavior modification and principles* (5th ed.). Boston: Cengage.

Missimer, C. (2005). *Good arguments: An introduction to critical thinking* (4th ed.). Upper Saddle River, NJ: Pearson Prentice Hall.

Morning Edition. (2005, August 2). *Supplements popular despite scientific evidence.* Retrieved from http://www.npr.org/templates/story/story.php?storyId=4781471

Mount Carmel Health. *Sleep Disorders Test.* Retrieved from http://www.mountcarmelhealth.com/114.cfm

Mrosko, T. (2002). *Keys to successful networking.* Retrieved from http://www.iwritesite.com/keys.html

Murphy, M. A. (2010). *Hard goals!* New York: McGraw-Hill.

Murphy, M. C. (1996). Stressors on the college campus: A comparison of 1985 and 1993. *Journal of College Student Development, 37,* 20–28.

N

Narvaez, D. (2006). Integrative ethical education. In M. Killen & J. Smetana (Eds.), *Handbook of moral development.* Mahwah, NJ: Erlbaum.

National Association of College Employers. (2011). *Job outlook 2011.* Retrieved from http://www.naceweb.org/Research/Job_Outlook/Job_Outlook.aspx?referal=research&menuID=69

National Center for Health Statistics. (2006). *Obesity.* Atlanta: Centers for Disease Control and Prevention.

National Center for Public Policy in Higher Education. (2004). Retrieved March 10, 2008, from http://www.highereducation.org/crosstalk/ct0204/news0204-dropouts.shtml

National Commission on Cooperative Education. (2008). *Frequently asked questions.* Retrieved February 11, 2008, from http://www.co-op.edu/faq.htm

Neighbors, C., Lostutter, T., Cronce, J., & Larimer, M. (2002). Exploring college student gambling motivation. *Journal of Gambling Studies, 18,* 361–370.

Nellie Mae. (2005). *Undergraduate students and credit cards in 2004: An analysis of usage rates and trends.* Retrieved March 10, 2008, from http://www.nelliemae.com/library/research_12.html

Nelson, P. E., Titsworth, S., & Pearson, J. C. (2011). *iSpeak: Public speaking for contemporary life.* New York: McGraw-Hill.

Newby, T., et al. (2011). *Educational technology for teaching and learning* (4th ed.). Boston: Allyn & Bacon.

Newman, E. (1976). *A civil tongue.* Indianapolis: Bobbs-Merrill.

Newman, M. L., Groom, C. J., Handelman, L., & Pennebaker, J. W. (2008). Gender differences in language use: An analysis of 14,000 text samples. *Discourse Processes, 45,* 211–236.

Nichols, R. B. (1961, March). Do we know how to listen? Practical helps in a modern age. *Speech Teacher, 10,* 22.

Nieman, D. C. (2007). *Exercise testing and prescription* (6th ed.). New York: McGraw-Hill.

Nilson, L. B. (2006, July 2). *Getting students to do the reading.* 31st Annual Improving University Teaching Conference, Dunedin, New Zealand.

Noftle, E. E., & Robins, R. W. (2007). Personality predictors of academic outcomes: Big Five correlates of GPA and SAT scores. *Journal of Personality and Social Psychology, 93,* 116–130.

Nola Ochs. (2011). Retrieved January 11, 2011, from http://en.wikipedia.org/wiki/Nola_Ochs

Nolen-Hoeksema, S. (2011). *Abnormal psychology* (5th ed.). New York: McGraw-Hill.

Norcross, J. C., Santrock, J. W., Campbell, L. F., Smith, T. P., Sommer, R., & Zuckerman, E. L. (2003). *Authoritative guide to self-help resources in mental health* (Rev. ed.). New York: Guilford.

Novak, J. D., & Cañas, A. J. (2008). *The theory underlying concept maps and how to construct them.* Technical Report IHMC CmapTools 2006-01 Rev 01-2008. Florida Institute for Human and Machine Cognition. Retrieved from http://cmap.ihmc.us/Publications/ResearchPapers/TheoryUnderlyingConceptMaps.pdf

O

O'Brien, N. P., Goodwin, A. H., & Foss, R. D. (2010). Talking and texting among teenage drivers: A glass half empty or half full? *Traffic Injury Prevention, 11,* 549–554.

Occupational Outlook Handbook. (2010–2011). Washington, DC: U.S. Department of Labor.

OCS Basics. (2002). *Job search basics.* Cambridge, MA: Office of Career Services, Harvard University. Retrieved from http://www.ocs.fas.harvard.edu/basics

OCS Basics. (2004). *Career development.* Cambridge, MA: Office of Career Services, Harvard University.

Oklahoma State University College of Human Environmental Sciences. (2009). *Yolanda Odenyo: Excellence in and out of the classroom.* Retrieved June 4, 2009, from http://www.facebook.com/note.php?note_id=95876411834

Oltmanns, T. F., & Emery, R. E. (2007). *Abnormal psychology* (5th ed.). Upper Saddle River, NJ: Prentice Hall.

P

Packham, G., Jones, P., Miller, C., & Thomas, B. (2004). E-learning and retention: Key factors influencing student withdrawal. *Education and Training, 46,* 335–342.

Paloff, R. M., & Pratt, K. (1999). *Building learning communities in cyberspace: Effective strategies for the online classroom.* San Francisco: Jossey-Bass.

Paretta, J. (2011). *Master the card.* Bloomington, IN: Balboa Press.

Park, C. (2007). *95 year old woman becomes oldest college graduate.* Retrieved from http://www.associatedcontent.com/article/245371/95_yearold_woman_becomes_oldest_college.html?cat=9

Parker, W. (2011). *Reporting from workaholism: Tools for recovery.* Retrieved from http://fatherhood.about.com/od/workingfathers/a/workaholism_3.htm

Parnassus, S. (2009, November 8). Meet AU's busiest student. *The Eagle Online.* Retrieved from http://www.theeagleonline.com/news/story/meet-aus-busiest-student/

Pauk, W. (2000). *Essential study strategies.* Clearwater, FL: H and H Publishing.

Paul, E. L., McManus, B., & Hayes, A. (2000). "Hookups": Characteristics and correlates of college students' spontaneous and anonymous sexual experiences. *Journal of Sexual Research, 37,* 76–88.

Pearson, J. C., Nelson, P. E., Titsworth, S., & Harter, L. (2011). *Human communication* (4th ed.). New York: McGraw-Hill.

Peck, M. S. (1978). *The road less traveled.* New York: Touchstone.

Peck, M. S. (1997). *The road less traveled and beyond: Spiritual growth in an age of anxiety.* New York: Simon and Schuster.

Pennebaker, J. W. (1997). *Opening up* (Rev. ed.). New York: Avon.

Pennebaker, J. W. (2001). Dealing with a traumatic experience immediately after it occurs. *Advances in Mind-Body Medicine, 17,* 160–162.

People in sports: Joe Namath. (2007, December 16). *Seattle Times.* Retrieved from http://seattletimes.nwsource.com/html/othersports/2004075963_peep16.html

Perkins, D. N. (1984, September). Creativity by design. *Educational Leadership,* 18–25.

Peterson, C., & Stunkard, A. J. (1986). *Personal control and health promotion.* Unpublished manuscript, Department of Psychology, University of Michigan, Ann Arbor.

Peverly, S. T., Ramaswamy, V., Brown, C., Sumowski, J., Alidoost, M., & Garner, J. (2007). What predicts skill in lecture note taking? *Journal of Educational Psychology, 99*(1), 167–180.

Pew Research Center. (2010). *Millennials.* Washington, DC: Pew Research Center.

Picciotto, M. (2004). *Critical thinking: A campus life casebook* (2nd ed.). Upper Saddle River, NJ: Prentice Hall.

Porter, B. F. (2002). *The voice of reason: Fundamentals of critical thinking.* New York: Oxford.

Potter, W. J. (2005). *Becoming a strategic thinker: Developing skills for success.* Upper Saddle River, NJ: Pearson Prentice Hall.

Prabhakar, H. (2007). Hopkins Interactive Guest Blog: *The public health experience at Johns Hopkins.* Retrieved January 31, 2008, from http://hopkins.typepad.com/guest/2007/03/the_public_heal.html

Prather, C. W. (2010). *Manager's guide to fostering innovation and creativity in teams.* New York: McGraw-Hill.

Pratt, J. (2008). *Maymangwa Miranda.* Retrieved February 2, 2008, from http://www.lawschool.cornell.edu/successpage.cfm?fMaymangwa&1=Miranda

Prensky, M. (2001). Digital natives, digital immigrants. *New Horizons, 9*(5), 1, 3–6.

Prensky, M. (2010). *Teaching digital natives.* Thousand Oaks, CA: Corwin Press.

Princeton Review & Chany, K. (2011). *Paying for college without going broke, 2011 edition.* Princeton: Princeton Review.

Pritchard, M. E., Wilson, G. S., & Yamnitz, B. (2007). What predicts adjustment among college students? A longitudinal panel study. *Journal of American College Health, 56,* 15–21.

PRWeb. (2008). *New book inspires readers to give back.* Retrieved January 31, 2008, from http://www.prweb.com/releases/2008/1/prweb64875.htm

Pryor, J. H., Hurtado, S., DeAngelo, L., Blake, L. P., & Tran, S. (2009). *The American freshman: National norms fall 2009.* Los Angeles: Higher Education Research Institute, UCLA.

Pryor, J. H., Hurtado, S., Saenz, V. B., Lindholm, J. A., Korn, W. S., & Mahoney, K. M. (2005). *The American freshman: National norms for fall 2005.* Los Angeles: Higher Education Research Institute, UCLA.

PSTCC. (2007, October 17). *Pellissippi State student receives scholarship from death row inmates.* Retrieved January 29, 2008, from http://www.pstcc.edu/community_relations/events/07.html

Pulskamp, A. M. (2007). *Do they belong in college?* Retrieved from http://www.latinocollegemagazine.com:16080/Umagazine/geniuses

R

Raimes, A. (2002). *A brief handbook* (3rd ed.). Boston: Houghton Mifflin.

Ratcliff, J. L., Johnson, D. K., & Gaff, J. G. (2004). *Changing general education curriculum.* San Francisco: Jossey-Bass.

Reed, R., & Chang, D. (2010). *Student debt and and the class of 2009.* Retrieved January 7, 2011, from http://projectonstudentdebt.org/

Regnerus, M., & Uecker, J. (2011). *Premarital sex in America.* New York: Oxford University Press.

Reinders, H., & Youniss, J. (2006). School-based required community service and civic development in adolescence. *Applied Developmental Science, 10,* 2–12.

Ritz, M. (2011). Adjusting to college life. *BraintreePatch.* Retrieved March 12, 2011, from http://braintree.patch.com/articles/adjusting-to-college-life

Robbins, G., Powers, D., & Burgess, S. (2008). *A fit way of life.* New York: McGraw-Hill.

Robins, R. W., Noftle, E. E., & Trzesniewski, K. H. (2005). Do people know how their personality has changed? Correlates of perceived and actual personality change in young adulthood. *Journal of Personality, 73,* 489–521.

Rosen, L. J. (2006). *The academic writer's handbook.* New York: Pearson Longman.

Ryan, J. C. (2011). *Job outlook and prospects for 2011: The usual suspects and some surprises.* Retrieved from http://www.savingtoinvest.com/2011/01/job-outlook-and-prospects-for-2011-the-usual-suspects-and-some-surprises.html

S

Sanio, R. L. 1998. *Working with lesbian, gay, bisexual, and transgender college students: A handbook for faculty and administrators.* Westport, CT: Greenwood.

Sarafino, E. P. (2010). *Self-management.* New York: Wiley.

Savin-Williams, R. (2008). Who's gay? It depends on how you measure it. In D. A. Hope (Ed.), *Nebraska Symposium on Motivation: Contemporary perspectives on lesbian, gay, and bisexual identities.* Lincoln, NE: University of Nebraska Press.

Sax, L. J., Lindholm, J. A., Astin, A. W., Korn, W. S., & Mahoney, K. M. (2001). *The American freshman: National norms for fall 2001.* Los Angeles: Higher Education Research Institute, UCLA.

Schaffzin, N. R. (1998). *The Princeton Review: Reading smart: Advanced techniques for improved reading.* New York: Random House.

Schandillia, A. (2007, June 21). *Spanish visualization tricks.* Retrieved from http://easiestspanish.blogspot.com/2007/06/spanish-visualization-tricks.html

Schiff, W. J. (2011). *Nutrition for healthy living* (2nd ed.). New York: McGraw-Hill.

Schunk, D. H. (2012). *Learning theories* (6th ed.). Upper Saddle River, NJ: Prentice Hall.

Sears, D. O., Peplau, L. A., & Taylor, S. E. (2003). *Social psychology* (11th ed.). Upper Saddle River, NJ: Prentice Hall.

Shapiro, J., & Rich, R. (1999). *Facing learning disabilities in the adult years.* New York: Oxford University Press.

Shaver, P. R., Belsky, J., & Brennan, K. A. (2000). Comparing measures of adult attachment: An examination of interview and self-report methods. *Personal Relationships, 7,* 25–43.

Shaver, P. R., & Mikulincer, M. (2007). Attachment theory and research. In A. W. Kruglanski & E. T. Higgins (Eds.), *Social psychology* (2nd ed.). New York: Guilford.

Shaver, P., & Mikulincer, M. (2012, in press). Recent advances in the study of close relationships. *Annual Review of Psychology, 63.*

Sher, K. J., Wood, P. K., & Gotham, H. J. (1996). The course of psychological distress in college: A prospective high-risk study. *Journal of College Student Development, 37,* 42–51.

Sherman, L., & Ramsey, B. (2006). *Reading glitch: How the culture wars have hijacked reading instruction—and what we can do about it.* Lanham, MD: Rowman & Littlefield.

Simon, L. (2006). *New beginnings. A reference guide for adult learners.* Upper Saddle River, NJ: Pearson Prentice Hall.

Simpson, J. C. (2006, September). Ruminations: Multi-tasking state of mind. *Johns Hopkins Magazine.* Retrieved from http://www.jhu.edu/~jhumag/0906web/ruminate.html

Skinner, K. (1997). *The MSE Oracle System.* Dallas, TX: Southern Methodist University.

Smaldino, S. E., Lowther, D. L., & Russell, J. D. (2012). *Instructional technology for media and learning* (10th ed.). Boston: Allyn & Bacon.

Smith, B. (2007, October 6). *$475,000 set for minority mentoring.* Retrieved January 19, 2008, from http://www.thetimesnews.com/articles/college_6469_html/long_prison.html

Smith, B. L., Macgregor, J., Mathews, R., & Gabelnick, F. (2004). *Learning communities: Reforming undergraduate education.* San Francisco: Jossey-Bass.

Staples, G. B. (2009, September 5). *Four area students score 2400 on SAT—Perfect.* Retrieved from http://www.ajc.com/news/four-area-students-score-131891.html

Steel, P. (2010). *The procrastination equation.* New York: Harper.

Sternberg, R. J. (1988). *The triangle of love.* New York: Basic Books.

Sternberg, R. J. (2011). Individual differences in cognitive development. In U. Goswami (Ed.), *Wiley-Blackwell handbook of childhood cognitive development* (2nd ed.). New York: Wiley.

Sternberg, R. J. (2012). *Cognitive psychology* (7th ed.). Boston: Cengage.

Sternberg, R. J., & Lubart, T. I. (1995). *Defying the crowd: Cultivating creativity in a culture of conformity.* New York: Free Press.

Stewart, J. (2012). *Bridges not walls* (11th ed.). New York: McGraw-Hill.

Strong, B., Yarber, W., Sayad, B., & DeVault, C. (2008). *Human sexuality* (6th ed.). New York: McGraw-Hill.

Strong, R. W., Silver, H. F., Perini, M. J., & Tuculescu, G. M. (2002). *Reading for academic success.* Thousand Oaks, CA: Corwin Press.

Swartz, R. (2001). Thinking about decisions. In A. L. Costa (Ed.), *Developing minds: A resource book for teaching thinking.* Alexandria, VA: Association for Supervision and Curriculum Development.

Swift, A. (2006, May 6). Personal communication.

T

Tamsey, K., & Peale, C. (2010, March 29). *First-generation college students stay the course.* Retrieved from http://www.usatoday.com/news/education/2010-03-30-FirstGenDorm30_ST_N.htm

Tannen, D. (1990). *You just don't understand!* New York: Ballantine.

Tannen, D. (2007). *You just don't understand. Men and women in conversation.* New York: HarperCollins.

Tavris, C. (1989). *Anger: The misunderstood emotion* (2nd ed.). New York: Touchstone.

Tavris, C. (1992). *The mismeasure of woman.* New York: Touchstone.

Taylor, S. E. (2003). *Health psychology* (5th ed.). New York: McGraw-Hill.

Taylor, S. E. (2006). *Health psychology* (6th ed.). New York: McGraw-Hill.

Taylor, S. E. (2011). Affiliation in stress. In S. Folkman (Ed.), *The Oxford handbook of stress and coping.* New York: Oxford University Press.

Teague, M. L., Mackenzie, S. L. C., & Rosenthal, D. M. (2007). *Your health today.* New York: McGraw-Hill.

Terenzini, P. T., Spring, L., Yaeger, P. M., Pascarella, E. T., & Nora, A. (1996). First generation college students: Characteristics, experiences, and cognitive development. *Research in Higher Education, 37*(1), 1–22.

Thompson, W. (2010). *The burden of being Myron Rolle.* Retrieved January 4, 2011, from http://sports.espn.go.com/espn/eticket/story?page=100218/myronrolle

Tomb, D. (2010, August). *Women of the Year: Readers' Choice Award 2010 nominee: Elizabeth Sholtys, 27, Ithaca, New York.* Retrieved from http://www.glamour.com/magazine/2010/08/

women-of-the-year-readers-choice-award-2010-nominee-elizabeth-sholtys

Tompkins, G. E. (2012). *Teaching writing: Balancing process and product* (6th ed.). Boston: Allyn & Bacon.

Tracy, B. (2010). *Goals!* San Francisco: Berrett-Koehler.

Trockel, M. T., Barnes, M. D., & Eggert, D. L. (2000). Health-related variables and academic performance among first year college students: Implications for sleep and other behaviors. *Journal of American College Health, 49*, 125–131.

Trudo, J. *Faces of Gallaudet—Profiles, A diplomat in the making.* Retrieved January 11, 2011 from http://admissions.gallaudet.edu/Academics/FOG/Michelle_morris.html

Tubbs, S. L. (2010). *Human communication* (12th ed.). New York: McGraw-Hill.

Tulving, E. (1972). Episode and semantic memory. In E. Tulving & W. Donaldson (Eds.), *Origins of memory*. San Diego: Academic Press.

Tyler, S. (2001). *Been there, should've done that: More tips for making the most of college* (2nd ed.). Michigan: Front Porch Press.

U

United States Public Interest Research Groups. (2006). *Student debt and consumer costs in the Minneapolis-St. Paul area.* Retrieved March 10, 2008, from http://www.uspirg.org/home/reports/report-archives/affordable-higher-education/affordable-higher-education-reports/student-debt-andconsumer-costs-in-the-minneapolis-st-paul-area2

University of Colorado at Denver, Department of Communications. (2008). *Three communications department alumnae land jobs at Channel 7.* Retrieved February 1, 2008, from http://www.thunder1.cudenver.edu/clas/communication/interships.Alumnae.html

University of Illinois Counseling Center. (1984). *Overcoming procrastination.* Urbana-Champaign: Department of Student Affairs.

University of Illinois Counseling Center. (1994). *Overcoming procrastination.* Urbana-Champaign: Department of Student Affairs.

U.S. Bureau of Labor Statistics. (2003). Washington, DC: U.S. Department of Labor.

U.S. Bureau of Labor Statistics. (2009a). *Education pays.* Retrieved January 8, 2011, from www.bls.gov/emp/ep_chart_001.htm

U.S. Bureau of Labor Statistics. (2009b). *Volunteering in the United States.* Retrieved January 8, 2011, from www.bls.gov/news.release/volun.nr0.htm

V

Vacca, R. T., Vacca, J. A. L., & Mraz, M. (2011). *Content area reading: Literacy and learning across the curriculum* (10th ed.). Boston: Allyn & Bacon.

Vanderbilt University, Academic Support for Student-Athletes. (2005, March). *Student-athletes of the month.* Retrieved February 3, 2008, from http://www.vanderbilt.edu/studentathletes/march05athlete.html

Verderber, R. F., Verderber, K. S., & Sellnow, D. D. (2011). *Communicate* (13th ed.). Boston: Cengage.

Vohs, K. D., Heatherton, T. F., & Herrin, M. (2001). *Disordered eating and the transition to college: A prospective study.* New York: John Wiley.

Von Oech, Roger. (1990). *A whack on the side of the head: How you can be more creative.* New York: Warner.

W

Wales, J. (2011) *Reliability of Wikipedia.* Retrieved January 4, 2011, from http://en.wikipedia.org/wiki/Reliability_of_Wikipedia

Walters, A. (1994). Using visual media to reduce homophobia: A classroom demonstration. *Journal of Sex Education and Therapy, 20*, 92–100.

Watson, D. L., & Tharp, R. G. (2007). *Self-directed behavior* (9th ed.). Belmont, CA: Wadsworth.

Wechsler, H., Lee, J. E., Kuo, M., Seibring, M., Nelson, T. F., & Lee, H. (2002). Trends in college binge drinking during a period of increased prevention efforts: Findings from Harvard School of Public Health College Alcohol Study surveys: 1993–2001. *Journal of American College Health, 50*, 203–217.

Wesson, C. (1990). *Women who shop too much: Overcoming the urge to splurge.* New York: St. Martin's Press.

West, T. (2003). Secret of the super successful . . . They're dyslexic. *Thalamus, 21*, 48–52.

Whimbey, A., & Lochhead, J. (1991). *Problem solving and comprehension.* Mahwah, NJ: Erlbaum.

Whiteside, K. (2003, September 23). *Rejuvenated Hamm still a reluctant star.* Retrieved from http://www.usatoday.com/sports/soccer/national/2003-09-02-ham_x.htm

Whitley, B. E., Jr., & Keith-Spiegel, P. (2002). *Academic dishonesty: An educator's guide.* Mahwah, NJ: Erlbaum.

William Jewell College. (2001). *William Jewell College student Mindy Baccus receives prestigious Marshall scholarship.* Retrieved February 3, 2008, from http://campus.jewell.edu/contacts/headlines/headline_476.html

Williams, R. L., & Eggert, A. C. (2002). Notetaking predictors of test performance. *Teaching of Psychology, 29*, 234–237.

Wilmot, W. W., & Hocker, J. L. (2011). *Interpersonal conflict* (8th ed.). New York: McGraw-Hill.

Wilson, K. (1999). Note-taking in the academic writing process of non-native speaker students: Is it important as a process of product? *Journal of College Reading and Learning, 29*, 166.

Winston, S. (1995). *Stephanie Winston's best organizing tips.* New York: Simon and Schuster.

Wong Briggs, T. (2005, February 16). *College academic all-stars first team.* Retrieved January 18, 2008, from http://www.usatoday.com/news/education/2005-02-16-college-2005-first-team_x.htm

Wong Briggs, T. (2006). *2006 College Academic All-Stars First Team.* Retrieved January 31, 2008, from http://www.usatoday.com/news/education/2006-02-14-college-allstarsfirst-team_x.htm

Wong Briggs, T. (2007, February 14). *Academic skills meet the world.* Retrieved February 1, 2008, from http://www.usatoday.com/news/education/2007-02-14-all-starscover_x.htm

Wong Briggs, T. (2009, June 5). *USA Today.* (2009, June 5). *All-USA College Academic Team.* Retrieved December 22, 2010, from ww.usatoday.com/life/1090429_collegeallstars/flash.htm

Wood, J. T. (2011). *Gendered lives* (8th ed.). Boston: Cengage.

Writers Workshop. (2002). *Writing resumes.* Urbana-Champaign: Center for Writing Studies, University of Illinois. Retrieved from http://www.english.uiuc.edu/

Writers Workshop. (2006). *Writing resumes.* Urbana-Champaign: Center for Writing Studies, University of Illinois. Retrieved July 2, 2006, from www.english.uiuc.edu/

Wuest, D. A., & Bucher, C. A. (2006). *Foundations of physical education, exercise science, and sport* (15th ed.). New York: McGraw-Hill.

Y

Yager, J. (1999). *Creative time management for the new millennium* (2nd ed.). Stamford, CT: Hannacroix Books.

Yate, M. (2011). *Knock 'em dead 2011.* Boston: Adams Media.

Z

Zeidner, M. (1995). Adaptive coping with test situations: A review of the literature. *Educational Psychologist, 30,* 123–133.

Zeurcher-White, E. (1997). *Treating panic disorder and agoraphobia: A step-by-step clinical guide.* Oakland, CA: New Harbinger Publications.

Zucker, R. A., et al. (2006). Predicting risky drinking outcomes longitudinally: What kind of advance notice can we get? *Alcoholism: Clinical and Experimental Research, 30,* 243–252.

Index

A

Abbreviations, usage, 220
ABC method, 75–76
Abilities, overestimation, 79
Abstinence, 385
Academic dishonesty, 310f
Academic integrity, pledge
  (development), 164
Academic lifeline, example, 155
Academic mentor, location, 155
Academic plan, 57
  forging, 33–38
Academic values, creation, 9–10
Accidental plagiarism, 346
Accounts. *See* Checking accounts;
  Savings accounts
  management, 410
Achievement
  identification, 5
  résumés, 447
Acronyms, mnemonic, 261
Action plan, development, 69
Active reading, 223–224
Adulthood, emergence, 5–6
Advice, usage, 104
Adviser, trust, 31–32
Age, influence (recognition), 145–146
Agreeableness. *See* Open to experience,
  Conscientiousness, Extraversion,
  Agreeableness, and Neuroticism
Alternative lifestyles, organizations
  (membership), 148
American Psychological Association
  (APA) writing style, 340
Analytic reading, 224
Anorexia nervosa, 376
Anxious attachment style, 122
Apostrophes, usage, 341
Applications (apps), usage, 191
Arguments
  body, 337–338
  conclusion, 338
  examples, 179f
  formation. *See* Counterarguments;
    Strong arguments
  introduction, 337
  offensive defense, 178
  organization, 337–338
  willingness, 178
Assets, identification, 405
Associate of arts (AA) degree, obtaining,
  37
Associations, expansion, 260
Assumptions, checking, 179–180
Athletes, interaction/priorities, 152

Attachment style
  defining, 122
  recognition, 100–101
Attention, control, 171
Attitudes, assessment, 115
Audience
  knowledge, 331
  support, 352
Auditory learners, 305
Auditory learning, 135
Author, verification, 191
Autonomy, understanding, 151
Avoidance, recognition, 79–80
Avoidant attachment style, 122

B

Baccalaureate degree, 37–38
Bad choices, avoidance, 185–186
Balance, achievement, 14
Bank accounts
  establishment, 408–410
  services, usage, 409–410
Barron's Profiles of American Colleges, 51
Behaviors
  impact, 143
  seductiveness, 147
Bewildering lecturer, 213
Biases. *See* Confirmation bias; Hindsight
    bias
  knowledge, 180
Binge drinking, 372
  consequences, 374f
Biological rhythms, attention, 77–78
Bloom's taxonomy, 256–258
Bodily-kinesthetic awareness, 133
Brainstorming, 189–190, 335. *See also*
    Credentials
Budget
  building, 405–406
  example, 407f
  timeframe, selection, 405–406
Budgeting. *See* Proactive budgeting;
    Reactive budgeting
Bulimia nervosa, 376

C

Calendar, deadlines, 80
Campus
  assistance, 30
  jobs, examination, 62
  knowledge, 29–30
  life, involvement, 7
  part-time work, impact, 84
  success, 15

Campus resources
  knowledge, 27
  usage, 55
    difficulty, 134
Career
  anticipation, 423–424
  boundaries, recognition, 440–441
  choices, 153f
    Holland model, 445f
  college resources, linkage, 50, 62
  communication skills, linkage, 118
  connection, 353
  counseling, 454
  decisions, improvement, 192
  goals, refinement, 441
  investigation, Internet (usage), 165
  options
    discovery, 16–17
    personal values, matching, 464
  pursuits, 461
  selection, skills (relationship), 35f–36f
  skill
    assessment, 442–444
    establishment, 67
  targeting, 153
  time management, 95
Career exploration, 435
  competence, development, 441–450
    journal entry, 465
  connection/communication,
    453–455
    journal entry, 466–467
  example, 436–437
  expectations, clarification, 438–441
    journal entry, 464
  future, building, 455–457
    journal entry, 467
  life management, 450–453
    journal entry, 466
  review questions, 459–460
Cause-and-effect lecture pattern, 213
Central ideas, summarization, 101
Certificate, obtaining, 37
Character development, 17
Cheating
  avoidance, 311
  behaviors, 309
  justification, 310–311
  opportunity, 311
  problem, 309
  reasons, 309–319
  risks, 311
  tolerance, 311
Checking accounts, usage, 409
Checks, tracking, 410

connection/communication,
383–386
journal entry, 398
example, 366
expectations, clarification, 367–368
journal entry, 396
future, building, 386–387
journal entry, 399
life management, 375–383
journal entry, 397–398
professional help, 381–382
review questions, 389–390
Plagiarism. *See* Accidental plagiarism;
Purposeful plagiarism
prevention, 348
protection, 348
risk, 359
types, 346–347
Positive attributes, impact, 174
Positive esteem, nurturing, 112–113
Positive outlook, maintenance, 11
Power (addition), service (usage), 193
PowerPoint, advantages/disadvantages,
48–49
Pregaming, 110
Premise/conclusion, 177
Presentation software, usage, 47–48
Primary accounts, secondary accounts
(contrast), 247
Primary sources, secondary sources
(contrast), 225
Proactive budgeting, 406
Problem
approaches, generation, 183
defining, 182
identification, 182
Problem solver
characteristics, acquisition,
182–183
example, 187
Problem solving, 181–184, 442
lecture pattern, 213
solutions, finding, 181–182
systematic approach, 201
Procedural memory, 257–258
Procedural tests, 295
Process, description, 330
Procrastination
avoidance, 345
elimination, 79–81
evaluation, 92
Productivity, increase, 67
Professional networks, development,
116–117
Professors, reader role, 249
Project management skills, description,
85
Props, mnemonic, 262
Protocol, usage, 180
Psychoactive drugs, list, 373t
Punctuation, precision, 340–341
Purposeful plagiarism, 346–347

Q

Qualifying terms, analysis, 298
Question and answer (Q&A) period,
352
Questions. *See* Essay questions; Fill-
in-the-blank questions; Multiple-
choice questions; Short-answer
questions; True-false questions
asking, 172–174
barriers, 172
formation, 172–174
technique, 217
tool kit, 174
Quiet moments, establishment, 189
Quotation marks, usage, 341
Quotations, usage, 348

R

Rapport, report (contrast), 103
Reactive budgeting, 406
Reader profile, 243
Reading. *See* Active reading; Analytic
reading
acceleration, 229
concentration, 221–222
concept mapping, 229
confusion, impact, 232
Cornell method, 229, 230f
disabilities, special services, 41
effort level, selection, 223f
expertise, usage, 232
goals, 232
ideas
capture, 222–225
connection, 225–227
images, usage, 226
material, previewing, 222
notes, highlighting, 228f
pacing, 292
pattern, 244
primary/secondary sources,
contrast, 225
purpose, recognition, 222
reviewing, 224–225
session, management, 229
skills, 442
skimming, 223
speed, 245
strategies, 222–223, 225f
time/space, planning,
231–232
words/themes/points,
identification, 222
Reason, usage, 175–181
Reasoning
usage. *See* Deductive reasoning;
Inductive reasoning
Reasoning, refinement, 178–181
Records, creation, 236
Reference shelf, stocking, 331
Registration, assistance, 41

Rehabilitation, referrals, 41
Relationships
attachment style, defining, 122
building, 97, 456
communication style, defining, 123
competence, development, 101–107
journal entry, 125–126
connection/communication, 110–116
journal entry, 126–127
control, 97. *See also* Cyberspace
relationships
esteem/confidence, nurturing, 112–
113
example, 98
expectation, clarification, 99–101
journal entry, 125
future, building, 116–118
journal entry, 127
issues, 127
life management, 107–110
journal entry, 126
loneliness, impact, 124
review questions, 120–121
time, maintenance, 81–82
Relaxation, usage, 379–380
Religious beliefs, 149–150
Report, rapport (contrast), 103
Research
databases, 47
execution, 332–333
Internet, usage, 333
paraphrasing, 348
Resilience, demonstration, 17–18
Resources
bookmarking, 236
campus assistance, 235
cut-and-paste shortcuts, avoidance,
235
discovery, 325–236
Internet, usage, 235–236
overestimation, 79
pursuit, 456
quality, monitoring, 235
Resources pursuit, 27
campus resources, usage, 55
competence, development, 31–38
journal entries, 60
connection/communication, 41–50
journal entries, 61
expectations, clarification, 29–31
journal entries, 59–60
future, creation, 50
journal entries, 62
interests, knowledge, 56
life management, 38–41
journal entries, 61
review questions, 53–54
Responsibility, 443
taking, 13
Résumés, 447–448, 467
types, 447
writing strategies, 448

problems/solutions, 274f
skills, building, 276
success, 273
Studying
boundaries, establishment/defense, 255
conditions, 254–255
content, 255–256
digital study buddy, usage, 255
location, knowledge, 254
ratio, 281
space, sharing (strategies), 254–255
strategies, timetable, 294f
time
allotment, 82
protection, 294
timing, knowledge, 255
Study skills enhancement, 251, 456
competence, development, 256–268
journal entry, 285–286
connection/communication, 272–275
journal entry, 287
expectations, clarification, 253–256
journal entry, 285
future, building, 275–277
journal entry, 288
life management, 268–272
journal entry, 286–287
professional skills, usage, 275–276
ratio, 281
review questions, 279–280
Substance use
avoidance, 372, 374
monitoring, 371–374
Suicide
prevention, 376–378
risk, 377
warning signs, 377
Summarization, 227
Summary method, 216
Summary paragraph, usage, 255
Summer jobs, exploration, 450–451
Support system, evaluation, 7
Syllabus
expectation, 163
usage, 142
Systematic decision making, 184–185

T

Tactile learners, 305
Tactile learning (kinesthetic learning), 135–136
Tasks, consolidation, 255
Taxonomy (Bloom), 256
Tax payments, education level (relationship), 404f
Teamwork skills, 276, 443
Technical literacy, 276
Technology
snobbery, 146
tool kit, expansion, 47–48
usage, 44–50, 183, 215–216

Term
plan, creation, 70–72
planner, example, 71
Test anxiety
control, 305
mastery, 305
seriousness, 320
Tests, 445–446. *See also* Essay tests; Objective tests; Procedural tests
academic supplies, usage, 296
approach, 289
balance, 307
emergencies, handling, 306–307
format, study strategies (tailoring), 295
grading systems, understanding, 307–308
hyperventilation, 306
main ideas, skimming, 303
material, guessing, 293
multiple-choice questions, 297–298
multitasking, avoidance, 302
pacing, 302–303
preparation, design, 302
reference aids, usage, 296
resources, organization, 296
sturdiness, 313–314
taking, accommodation, 41
true/false questions, 298–299
work, review, 301
Test-taking strategies, 296–297
deployment, 297–301
Test-taking success, 289, 456–457
assessment, 318
clarification, 297
competence, development, 294–301
journal entry, 323
connection/communication, 307–311
journal entry, 324–325
distractions, 297
example, 314
expectations, clarification, 291–294
journal entry, 322
future, building, 312–314
journal entry, 325
health, protection, 304
life management, 301–307
journal entry, 324
personal honor code, 321
preparation, 295–296
problem, identification, 296
regret, minimization, 319
review questions, 316–317
sabotage, avoidance, 305
weaknesses, 304
work, proofreading, 297
Text
highlighting, 227
personalization, 227
Textbook study aids, usage, 303
Thank-you letter, 449
Themes/patterns, synthesis, 101

Thesis, creation, 334–336
Thinkers, types, 173f
Thinking
clarification. *See* Fuzzy thinking
containment. *See* Sprawling thinking
expansion. *See* Narrow thinking
improvement, 292
opportunities, pursuit, 170
stimulation, criteria, 174
tool, Internet usage, 190–191
Thinking/Feeling (T/F), decision-making emphasis, 139–140
Thinking skills, 442
alternatives, brainstorming, 189–190
competence, development, 170–181
journal entry, 203–204
connection/communication, 189–191
journal entry, 205
differences, 199–200
example, 168–169
expansion, 167, 456
expectations, clarification, 169–170
journal entry, 203
future, building, 191–193
journal entry, 205–206
life management, 181–189
journal entry, 204
review questions, 195–196
variation, 12
Thoughts, interference (reduction), 171
Threats
avoidance. *See* Sexual threats
impact, 104
Time
matrix, 76–77
orientation, 65–66
scheduling, 70–77
wasters, reduction, 78–79
Time management, 1, 63, 370, 456
ABC method, 75–76
avoidance, recognition, 79–80
benefits, 67
commitment, making, 68
commuting time, usage, 82–83
competence, development, 68–77
journal entry, 93–94
connection/communication, 81–83
journal entry, 95
daily plan, execution, 75–77
digital planning, 70
efficiency, 67
80-20 principle, application, 74–75
evaluation, 91
example, 76
expectations, clarifications, 65–67
journal entry, 93
future, creation, 83–86
journal entry, 95–96
Internet, usage, 95
intervention, 81